ANSEL ADAMS

IN THE NATIONAL PARKS

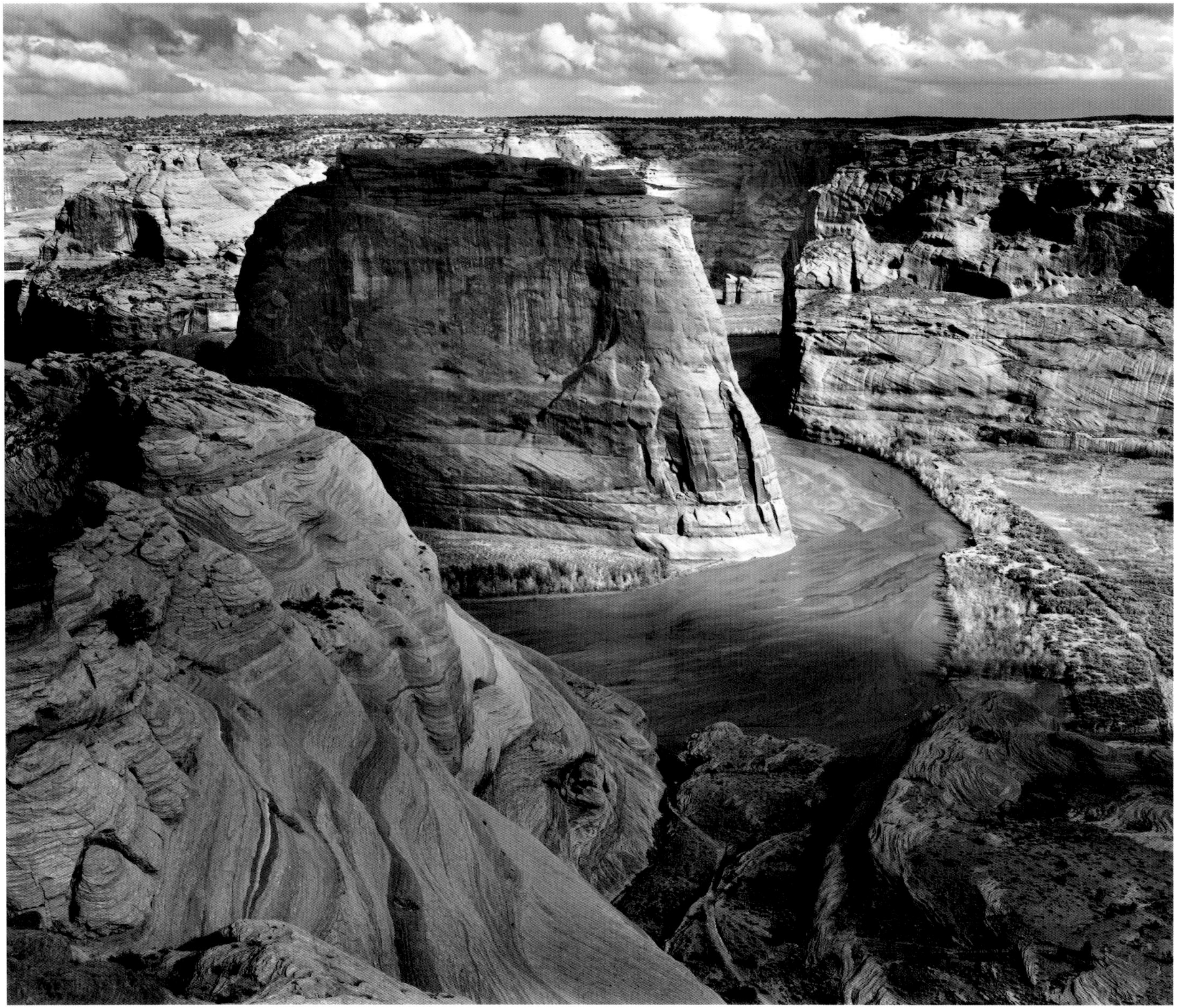

CANYON DE CHELLY FROM WHITE HOUSE OVERLOOK, CANYON DE CHELLY NATIONAL MONUMENT, ARIZONA, 1942

ANSEL ADAMS

IN THE NATIONAL PARKS

PHOTOGRAPHS FROM AMERICA'S WILD PLACES

EDITED BY ANDREA G. STILLMAN

LITTLE, BROWN AND COMPANY · NEW YORK · BOSTON · LONDON

In 1976, Ansel Adams selected Little, Brown and Company as the sole authorized publisher of his books, calendars, and posters. At the same time, he established The Ansel Adams Publishing Rights Trust in order to ensure the continuity and quality of his legacy—both artistic and environmental.

As Ansel Adams himself wrote, "Perhaps the most important characteristic of my work is what may be called print quality. It is very important that the reproductions be as good as you can possibly get them." The authorized books, calendars, and posters published by Little, Brown have been rigorously supervised by The Trust to make certain that Adams' exacting standards of quality are maintained.

Only works published by Little, Brown and Company can be considered authentic representations of the genius of Ansel Adams.

Little, Brown and Company
Hachette Book Group
237 Park Avenue, New York, NY 10017
www.hachettebookgroup.com

First Edition: October 2010

Little, Brown and Company is a division of Hachette Book Group, Inc. The Little, Brown name and logo are trademarks of Hachette Book Group, Inc.

Photography Credits

Photographs on pages 18 and 170 © 1947, Nancy Newhall, © 2010, the Estate of Beaumont and Nancy Newhall. Permission to reproduce courtesy of Scheinbaum and Russek Ltd., Santa Fe, New Mexico.

Photograph on page 24 © Imogen Cunningham Trust.

Photograph on page 27 © Cedric Wright Estate.

Photograph on page 168 © 1947, Beaumont Newhall, the Estate of Beaumont and Nancy Newhall. Permission to reproduce courtesy of Scheinbaum and Russek Ltd., Santa Fe, New Mexico.

Photographs on pages 324, 327, and 329 courtesy Ansel Adams Archive, Center for Creative Photography, University of Arizona.

Library of Congress Cataloging-in-Publication Data

Adams, Ansel.
Ansel Adams in the national parks : photographs from America's wild places / edited by Andrea G. Stillman ; essays by Richard B. Woodward. — 1st ed.
p. cm.
Includes bibliographical references and index.
ISBN 978-0-316-07846-7
1. National parks and reserves—United States—Pictorial works. 2. Wilderness areas—United States—Pictorial works. 3. Landscape photography—United States. 4. Adams, Ansel. I Stillman, Andrea Gray. II. Woodward, Richard. III Title.
E160.A297 2010
973—dc22 2010006981

10 9 8 7 6 5 4 3 2 1

Design by Lance Hidy

Printed in Italy

CONTENTS

EDITOR'S NOTE

ANSEL ADAMS was a "saver." His archive is therefore particularly rich and inclusive, ranging from a letter to Santa Claus he wrote at age five to correspondence from his seventies with President Jimmy Carter. I have been able to draw upon that archive for the quotes included here from Ansel's letters and writings, both published and unpublished, as well as those of his friends. The remarkably extensive correspondence between Ansel and his close friends Beaumont and Nancy Newhall in the 1940s and 1950s amounts to a virtual diary. Beaumont's travel logs are especially valuable, as they give a flavor of what it was like to travel and photograph with Ansel. I worked for Ansel from 1974 to 1980 and could therefore draw upon a wealth of his often-repeated anecdotes and pithy comments as well. I hope that the short texts accompanying the photographs throughout the book capture the infectious humor and zest for life that made Ansel such a remarkable companion and friend.

Additional notes and instructive image comparisons appear at the back of the book.

Andrea G. Stillman

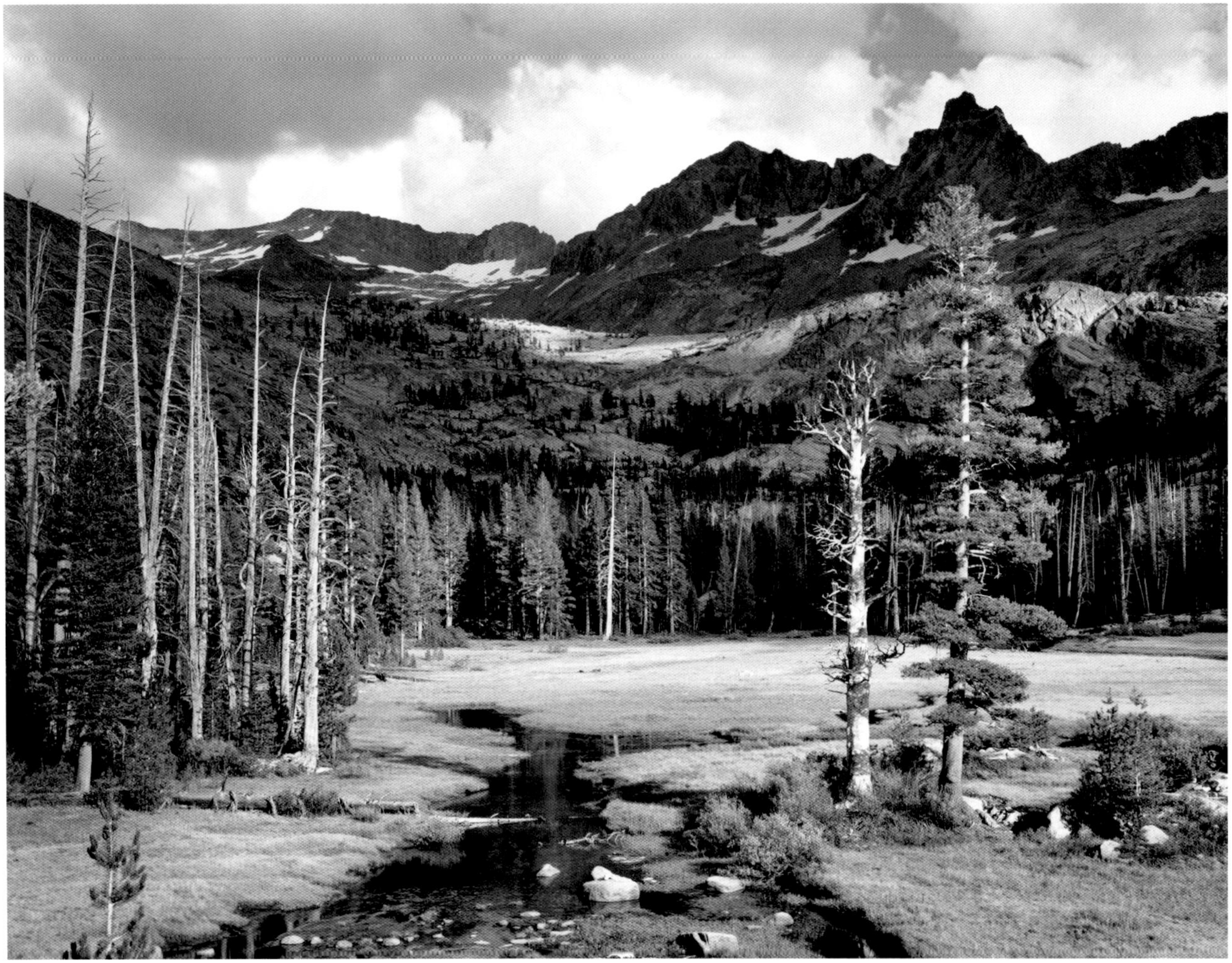

MOUNT ANSEL ADAMS, LYELL FORK OF THE MERCED RIVER, YOSEMITE NATIONAL PARK, CALIFORNIA, C. 1935

A wilderness, in contrast with those areas where man and his works dominate the landscape, is hereby recognized as an area where the earth and its community of life are untrammeled by man, where man himself is a visitor who does not remain.

From the Definition of Wilderness, The Wilderness Act, Public Law 88-577, 88th Congress, Second Session, September 3, 1964

At one with the power of the American landscape, and renowned for the patient skill and timeless beauty of his work, photographer Ansel Adams has been visionary in his efforts to preserve the country's wild and scenic areas, both on film and on Earth. Drawn to the beauty of nature's monuments, he is regarded by environmentalists as a monument himself, and by photographers as a national institution. It is through his foresight and fortitude that so much of America has been saved for future Americans.

Citation from the Presidential Medal of Freedom, conferred on Ansel Adams by President Jimmy Carter, June 9, 1980

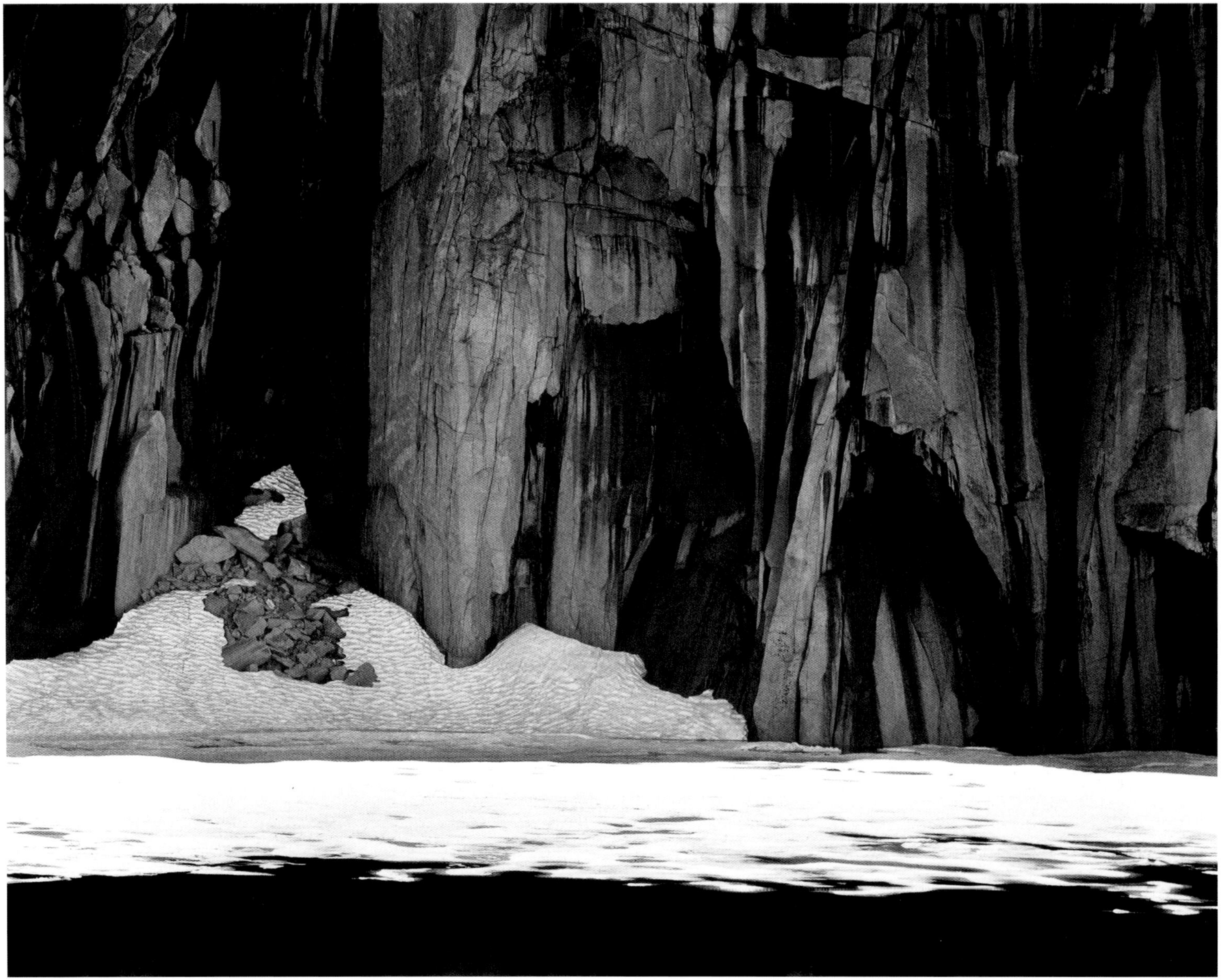

FROZEN LAKE AND CLIFFS, KAWEAH GAP, SIERRA NEVADA, CALIFORNIA, 1932

GIVE NATURE TIME

ANSEL ADAMS

FROM THE COMMENCEMENT ADDRESS • OCCIDENTAL COLLEGE • 1961

I SUPPORT a positive philosophy of life and art. Wherever this leads me, I am sure it is further than were I a practicing pessimist! I frankly profess a somewhat mystical concept of nature; I believe the world is incomprehensibly beautiful—an endless prospect of magic and wonder. Whatever mess we observe is our own responsibility! In general, man has always struggled toward objective excellence and now that some knowledgeable means of achieving it are in his grasp, he may succeed with glory or fail with catastrophe. I remain an optimist and I believe man will, in the end—and on this earth—succeed with glory....

I now venture a few leading statements: one, that there is a profound difference between recreation and *re*-creation and that the experience of nature relates to the latter through what the great National Parks and Wilderness Areas offer us; two, that art is about the only way to bring about an adequate and exciting contact between the realities of society and the implications and potentials of nature; and, three, that man must be guided, not driven, to the appropriate and effective relationship with the world in which he lives....

The appreciation of the natural scene should not be limited only to the grandeurs; the intimate details and qualities of our immediate environment can be revealed and appreciated. To protect these qualities will require a new planning approach of the highest order of sensitivity and effectiveness. We are prone to think of natural beauty—parks, reserves, "dedicated areas," etc.—in terms of locations on maps, restricted by borders and boundaries and viewed "vertically." This pseudo-aerial view can be misleading; our vision is usually projected *horizontally* and the vistas of the world are as important as the actual contact with rock and soil and growing things. Hence, the *prospects,* the glades, the lines of the hills, and the vast expanses of shore and ocean, these too must be preserved....

We must take ALL resources under consideration; *all* resources, because they relate fatefully to our life on earth, reflect certain grandeurs, and deserve not only our attention, but our reverence.

Hence, while it is as essential as ever to protect the National Parks and the Wilderness Areas, it is also essential that we protect the forests, the crops, the minerals and the oceans, and it is essential that we preserve the purity of the air we breathe and the water we drink. Certainly with the technology now available, air and water pollution could be severely reduced if not arrested completely and fully controlled. It is ridiculous to quibble about costs in this regard; the ultimate cost of pollution can be the destruction and death of plants, animals and people....

Clarification, not mere euphoria, is required if we are to succeed. We will have to recognize the oneness of all resources—the economic, the recreational and the spiritual qualities and potentials of the world. The principle of "multiple use"—strongly supported by the United States Forest Service—can, in my opinion, be applied to the first two categories, but not to the third category, represented by the National Parks and the great Wilderness Areas. Unfortunately, recreation and *re*-creation are not sufficiently differentiated to stabilize the policies and decisions of most government and enterprise groups.

There is a constant erosion of the concept and the reality of wilderness. The luxuries of modern life—motorboats, proliferating automobiles, portable radios and television sets—all the comforts of urban shelter transported to the wild places on roads built primarily for this purpose—such as these have served to make mass recreation a very profitable enterprise.

There is certainly nothing amiss with camping, fishing, boating, swimming, skiing and all the other participation and non-participation sports; people do not have enough of these healthful and refreshing experiences. But you do not play ping-pong in a cathedral, rustle popcorn at a string-quartet concert or hang billboards on the face of Half Dome in Yosemite (not all of us would, anyway!).

You must have certain noble areas of the world left in as close-to-primal condition as possible. You must have quietness and a certain amount of solitude. You must be able to touch the living rock, drink the pure waters, scan the great vistas, sleep under the stars and awaken to the cool dawn wind. Such experiences are the heritage of all people.

It is naive to believe that such priceless amenities can be legislated into being and protected for all time. I must remind you that the National Parks exist because of an Act of Congress; this Act could be altered or repealed at any time if the clear majority of our people so desired. In fact, proposals have been made, seriously, to put all Federal Lands under the control of the nearest township, or to sell off all Federal lands to the highest bidder. Surely, this is a most remote possibility; it is not probable, but possible! The continued invasions of roads in the wild areas *are* probable, the gradual destruction of the beauty and intimacy of high-mountain meadows, through over-use, *is* probable. Highly probable also, is the total pollution of our air and water, and the building of extensive urban and suburban "developments"—which can change in time to ghettos or to slums.

To man's technical ingenuity almost everything is possible; to control the probabilities will require another ingenuity, a fresh attitude of respect for, and love of, the land. The reclamationists and the developers speak of the conservationists' "unreality," not realizing there are other realities, other objectives, other accomplishments in the life of man than the poorly modulated technological and economic achievements of our nervous time....

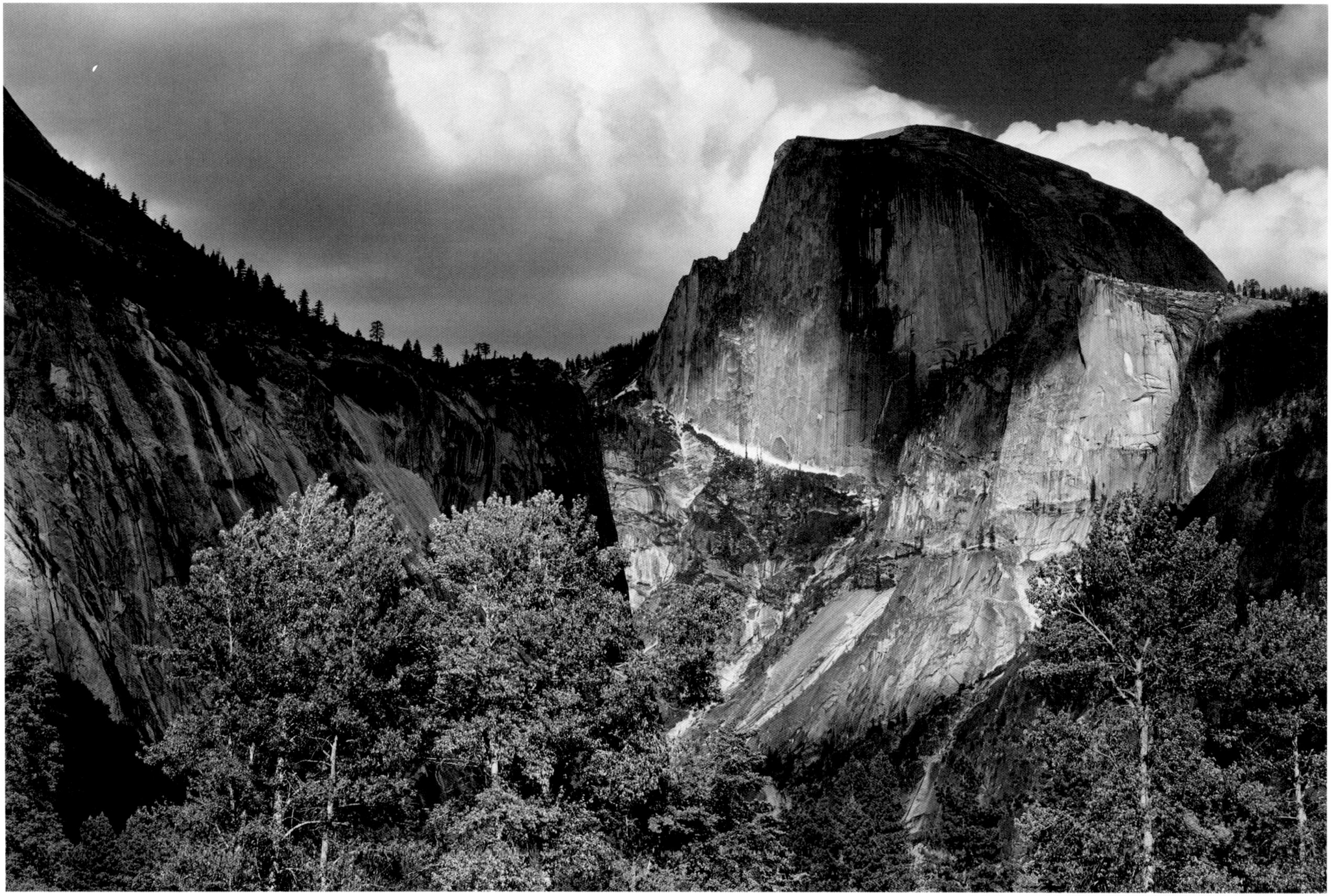

HALF DOME, COTTONWOOD TREES, YOSEMITE NATIONAL PARK, CALIFORNIA, 1932

ANSEL ADAMS, PHOTOGRAPHER

WALLACE STEGNER

FOREWORD TO *IMAGES 1923–1974* • 1974

A PHOTOGRAPH is made, not taken," Ansel Adams says, speaking lightly as is his habit, throwing off wisdoms amid a cloud of jokes, puns, limericks, and laughter. He can be serious, and fundamentally is, but his nature is ebullient and pyrotechnic, and even when he is most serious he is infectious rather than solemn.

A photograph is made, not taken. In that single statement are subsumed his more than fifty years in pursuit of excellence in photography—his exploration of its expressive possibilities; his mastery of its techniques, processes, practical chemistry, and physics; his development of the zone system which has taught tens of thousands to see like a camera and to pre-visualize the finished print before they ever set shutter and lens; and his consistent effort to deal with photography as a fine art.

"The simple statement of the lens" is what he says he is after. But he is the first to insist that the lens can do nothing its operator does not make it do. It is as sensitive as he is, no more. Photography is not button-pushing; the camera does not make its pictures automatically, the way a lighthouse blinks its light. In a gamesome party mood Ansel will sometimes play lighthouse, rotating slowly on his axis, now and then emitting a low, intense, foghorn moan, and at every full rotation gleaming upon the company with teeth and eyeballs that seem to project through the beard a beam visible for miles. That is fun, and also art, for the playfulness of genius is still genius. But it does not convey the essential Adams message. A photograph is made, not taken. A photograph is not an automatic recording, neither is it an accident. It is a concept, a vision of the world translated into shades of gray, communicated "in terms of simple devotion to the medium—a statement of the utmost clarity and perfection possible."

Having gone that far toward solemnity, Ansel is likely to add, with one of those laughs that shake loose everything in the room, "And there's nothing worse than a brilliant image of a fuzzy concept!"

Adams was converted to the brilliant image in 1930, when, in Taos, he looked at some negatives of Paul Strand's and saw in them a luminousness and clarity he had not believed could be captured by a camera. For years he had been in training to be a concert pianist, and was already teaching and performing; but photography had been an increasingly urgent diversion, and his patron Albert Bender of San Francisco had been suggesting it to him as an artistic career. At Bender's instigation he had produced his portfolio "Parmelian Prints of the High Sierras," and in 1930 he was in Taos for the fourth or fifth time, still under Bender's aegis, completing a book of photographs of Taos Pueblo, with text by Mary Austin, which was subsequently printed by the Grabhorn Press. Mrs. Austin evidently thought of the book as essentially hers, with illustrations by Adams. She would be astonished to know what it is valued for—and at—now. Even in his formative years, Adams had a way of making accompanying texts, whether they were by Mary Austin, John Muir, or anyone else, look like mere decoration.

His formative years ended in Taos, which as Nancy Newhall has pointed out was his Paris and his Rome. What Strand showed him hit him like Saul's vision on the road to Damascus. Indecision about his career was ended. He put aside not only the concert career but the soft focus, the atmospheric effects, and the simulation of painting that had marked many of his early photographs, and dedicated himself to "straight" photography, the uncompromising statement of the lens.

By 1932 he had had his first one-man show, and with Edward Weston, Imogen Cunningham, and others had founded Group f/64, whose inaugural exhibition at the De Young Museum in San Francisco was a benchmark in the establishment of photography as a legitimate and distinct art in which the camera is not a substitute brush but a way of seeing. Though f/64 held together only about a year (Adams and Weston both encouraged its breakup because they feared the formation of a coterie), neither Adams nor Weston, nor indeed any of the group, ever abandoned the ideal of precision and sharp focus that had been their reason for coming together, and whose influence persists.

His old Sierra Club friend Francis Farquhar, who as editor of the Sierra Club *Bulletin* published many of his early writings and photographs, has remarked on how swiftly, once he saw his way, Adams achieved a reputation as one of the great photographers of the world. But no one should forget how long the apprenticeship actually was. From the time when he made his first photographs with a box Brownie in

Yosemite in the summer of 1916, when he was fourteen years old, he had been an enthusiastic, precocious, and energetic amateur. In successive years, mostly during the summers when he traded the piano for the mountains, he developed into an increasingly able professional. Nevertheless, he did not make a negative that completely pleased him until he caught Banner Peak and Thousand Island Lake in a clearing storm in 1923—and that was seven years after his beginnings as a photographer. It was three years more before he made another negative that splendid: "Monolith: the Face of Half Dome," so massive, serene, and eternal that it might be the throne of God. Those two still rank among the magnificent statements of his lens, but they were isolated peaks in a range of high competence. After the Taos revelation of 1930 he dedicated himself to the kind of perfection they had half-accidentally achieved.

His training in music guided and greatly subtilized his development as an artist with the camera. It taught him to think of the negative as the score, and the print as the performance, and he transferred from music to photography the effort to achieve the purest clarity of tone. It also taught him that technique is of the essence. If you want to be a pianist, you practice seven or eight hours a day, until your keyboard technique is capable of everything you might demand of it. If you want to be a photographer, you practice until the camera is an extension of eye and hand; you seek the technical means to handle every expressive need. Though in music you deal in sound, in musical tones, and in photography you deal in light, in tones of brightness, perfection is as difficult and as much to be desired in one as in the other.

Perfection, he decided, meant the achievement of the artist's vision, which was not a merely visual perception but a complex act of perception and transference, a conception of the finished print bounded by enclosing lines and translated into values of brightness from almost pure white to almost pure black. In nature, Adams points out, there are colors, brilliant or subtle, that the photographer must see as equivalents on the brightness scale of grays; and in nature there are properly speaking no forms, only shapes. Imagination transmutes shapes into forms, and technique painstakingly realizes the forms in the symbolic system of photographic art, so that a sheet of paper printed in values of gray can actually strike the viewer with more force and suggestiveness than would the natural objects from which it was made. It is Ansel Adams' gift to be able to intensify the emotional effect of visual experience. More than one visitor to the western scenes which Adams has made his own by an act of artistic pre-emption has complained that nothing looks so magnificent as an Adams photograph of it.

Not many photographers had ever taken photography with such seriousness as young Adams, and few if any had ever possessed his double gift of artistic vision and proficiency with all kinds of apparatus and machinery. In only

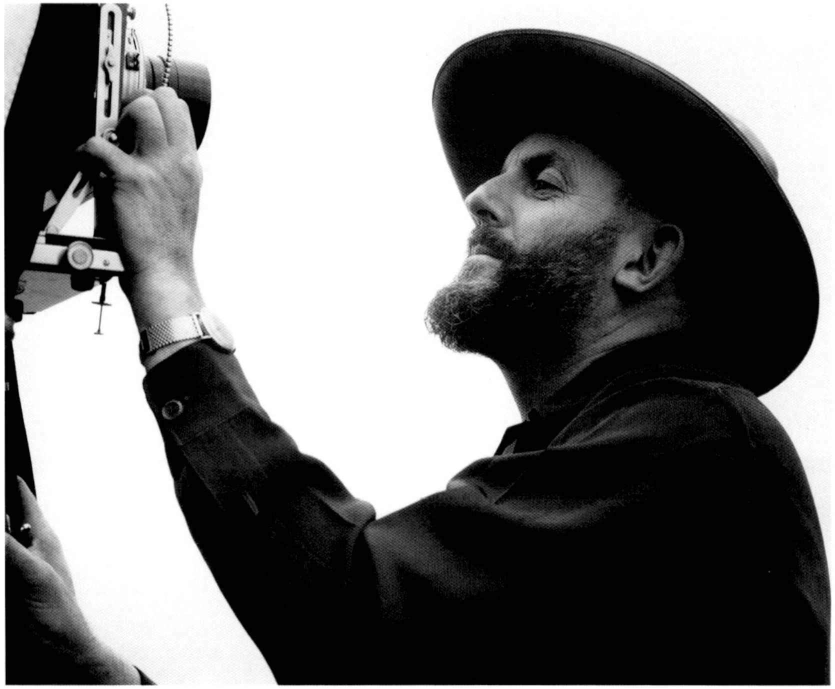

Ansel Adams, c. 1945. By Nancy Newhall

a few years, he was acknowledged to be one of the most gifted technicians in the entire history of photography, and he has maintained his proficiency, constantly testing the art's ultimate possibilities, constantly experimenting, constantly refreshing and enlarging his skill. Even now, when he is past seventy, he experiments all the time, though he has long since determined the capacity and usefulness of every existing sort of lens, filter, light meter, film, exposure technique, paper, developer, and darkroom process. His "zone system" of exposing according to the placement of subject luminances on the exposure scale of the negative has made the principles of sensitometry available to every tyro, and gone a long way toward eliminating the guesswork and "averaging" from exposure. But it is not a rigid system. The vision must always dictate the technique. He denies profanely that he is a Zone Buddhist.

What he has learned he has made available. His five books which together are called *Basic Photo*, as well as his *Polaroid Land Photography Manual* and the series of workshops and seminars that he began for *U.S. Camera* in Yosemite in 1940, renewed at the Museum of Modern Art in 1945, and has conducted annually in Yosemite since 1946, continue to give practical and theoretical instruction to amateurs and professionals alike. In recent years he has added a series of workshops at the University of California, Santa Cruz. He has been artist and technician, teacher and consultant, and always a complete professional.

Yet having become probably the most skilled practitioner of his complex art, he values skill only for what it lets him do. "The excellence of the mechanics is taken for granted," he said in commenting on the great mountain photographs of Vittorio Sella. He is not the sort of purist who will never tamper even slightly with negative or print—as though the camera's wink were the blink of God. He does spot his negatives and prints. But he is no trickster or gadgeteer. Despite his interest in the expansion of photographic possibility, which includes long service as a consultant to the Polaroid Corporation, he dislikes gadgetry and the photographic magazines whose purpose seems to be to persuade people that they can buy their way to artistry by multiplying equipment. Anyone who studies the photographic data Adams provides with his prints and books will discover that he habitually uses only two or three cameras and a few basic lenses and filters, together with the developers and papers he has found best. Limitation, he is convinced, breeds expertise; sometimes he longs for the old wet-plate process that made photographers work harder for their results. "I like to believe that if I found myself restricted to a simple box camera I could create a legitimate and expressive technique around it," he says; for "what the photographer sees, and what he says about what he sees, have far greater importance than the possession of mere mechanical equipment."

The arts have a reassuring way of corroborating one another. Joseph Conrad once similarly disparaged the mere gift of words, remarking that possession of a firearm did not necessarily make a hunter or warrior. And when he came to define the intention of his writing, in the celebrated preface to *The Nigger of the 'Narcissus'*, he might have been speaking of photography, and out of the mouth of Ansel Adams: "My task which I am trying to achieve is... before all, to make you *see*. That—and no more, and it is everything."

It is legitimate to ask of either writer or photographer, "See what?" as well as "See how?" No more than Conrad would Adams interpret the word "see" literally, as referring only to the "recording" of "reality." When Adams asks us to see, he is asking us to see *into*. His mysteries, like his shadows, are never totally black; ghostly textures of meaning lurk in them. His middle tones are rich with detail. His clouds and snow are almost never bleached white, and his skies are rarely bland: almost as much as Paul Strand, he hates photographing on a "bald-headed" day.

There is a sense, he says, in which any picture is only a collection of brightnesses. But his brightnesses, high or low in the scale, are complex—he dislikes the violence of harsh unmodulated contrasts—and they are somehow more than simply the light values that make up rocks, trees, and falling water. They communicate a reverence for the forms of the world. Without yielding a particle of their precision and clarity, they tend always to become hymns to the strength, delicacy, and beauty of the earth. By the time we have examined a characteristic Adams print long enough to say with certainty, "I see," we mean that we not only see, we understand and feel.

Far from using his camera simply to record the external world in the way that is suggested by the cant phrase "photographic realism," Adams believes that as photography "approaches the simulation of reality it withdraws from the aesthetic experience of reality." That is one reason he prefers black and white to color. In black and white there is a cooler distance between the world and its symbolic representation. Black and white demands the act of artistic transformation; it does not allow the easy and vulgar effects suggested by the ironic motto for color photographers: "If you can't make it good, make it red."

He is Whitmanesque in his affection for "the simpler things of the world, humbly or mystically seen." What he focuses on his ground glass is not a reproduction but a vision, an experience, and therefore it is, like all true art that I know anything about, to some extent a self-portrait. "A great photograph is a full expression of what one feels about what is being photographed... and is, thereby, a true expression of what one feels about life in its entirety." At the same time, his kind of photography is an art of "found objects," not of organization and manipulation and self-conscious composition. Composition for Adams, as it was for Edward Weston, is simply the best way of seeing. He will not tinker with a subject beyond removing extraneous objects, he works by natural light, and he rejects the excessive "dodging" and darkroom tricks that attempt to make bad negatives into good ones. The extent of his manipulation is whatever the negative or print demands to become what he pre-visualized. A magician of the darkroom, he will not use his magic to cheat, and by the same token he is unwilling to be at the mercy of someone else's incompetence or dishonesty. By preference he sells his photographs as prints or portfolios. When they are reproduced by printing processes, he stands over the printer—and he long ago learned enough about the printer's trade to instruct most professionals.

Any discussion of Adams' view of art and life comes around eventually to Alfred Stieglitz, whom he first met in 1933 and who in 1936 gave him a one-man show at An American Place—the first one-man show he had given a photographer since he had introduced Paul Strand in 1917. Admiration of the kind that Adams felt for Stieglitz is always to some degree recognition of qualities the admirer already possesses in himself. Stieglitz corroborated Adams' perception of photography as a fine art, and he set him an example of the highest personal and artistic integrity. No one, not even Strand, Georgia O'Keeffe, John Marin, and the people who had made Taos luminous for him at the end of the 1920's, had a stronger influence on him. When in 1948 he published *Portfolio One*, he dedicated it to Stieglitz and took pains to speak of its twelve photographs in Stieglitz's own term: "equivalents." He wanted them understood as what both he and Stieglitz believed art should be, testimonials to "a spiritual identification with the world."

The belief is basic, and has not changed. There are no periods in Ansel Adams' work, though in recent years he has worked more with small cameras and with the Polaroid Land processes. As an artist, he found his way early, and has pursued the way he found. On his seventieth birthday, speaking at the Metropolitan Museum of Art, he re-asserted the Stieglitz position as if forty years of artistic nihilism, experimentation, iconoclasm, cynicism, spiritual muckraking, and the arrogance of fashionable despairs had never intervened. "I believe the artist can accomplish most on the agenda for survival by creating beauty, by setting examples of beauty in order, by emphasizing the concept of the essential dignity of the human mind and spirit . . . I believe, with Alfred Stieglitz, that art is the affirmation of life."

As a professional, Adams has photographed all sorts of things for no reason more artistic than that the interests of his clients demanded their reproduction. He does not apologize for that. When you hang out your shingle, you take what comes. Moreover, "the function of a photograph may be of the simplest practical nature, or it may relate to a most personal and abstract emotion—the sincerity of intention and honesty of spirit of the photographer can make any expression, no matter how 'practical,' valid and beautiful." In fact, every now and then the chance that is an element in all art, and especially in an art concerned principally with found objects, can let a photographer transcend the practical limitations of a job, and bring him face to face with something that he leaps to interpret. Thus "Rails and Jet Trails" came out of an assignment to record the history of Northern California for the American Trust Company, and "Mount Williamson" out of Adams' self-imposed task of rendering justice to the Japanese-American internees at the Manzanar Relocation Camp. Accident favors the prepared. When Hamlet said, "The readiness is all," he might have been voicing a motto for photographers.

Nevertheless, though some of the great images were achieved on journalistic jobs, it is not the professional Ansel Adams, who can produce on order a superb book for American Trust or the Bishop Bank of Hawaii or the University of California, who justifies our profoundest attention. What concerns us is the artist who is unfailingly open to the experience of seeing, and seeing not only the shapes and brightnesses and beauties of the world but "something intrinsic" below the surfaces. This artist feels deeply about what he sees, he has a reverence for the earth in all its variety, delicacy, and strength, but he is the absolute reverse of effusive: he sees with such austerity, even severity, that some have mistakenly called him cold. He has an incomparable technical expertness in communicating what he sees and feels, and for a half-century and more he has gone on making photographs so plainly stamped with his personal artistry that they hardly need his steeple-A signature on them. They have taught thousands how to see; they have become household images; and when much art has been retreating into denial or crying out in pain and anger, they have steadily affirmed life.

That a great Adams photograph literally signs itself is due partly to his qualities as seer and interpreter, but it would be foolish to deny that his most characteristic subject matter has had a good deal to do with it too. He has photographed—greatly—in all sorts of places—Hawaii, New England, the Southwest, California, Alaska, the Canadian

Rockies—and all sorts of subjects—faces, streets, houses, road signs, architectural details, industrial machinery, gravestones, the textures of weathered or charred wood, seascapes, landscapes, peeling bark and growing seaweed and hidden ferns and Gold Rush gingerbread—all sorts of shapes which the eye of the artist and camera transmute into forms of beauty and meaning. Nevertheless, to many people he is the photographer par excellence of grand Nature, especially but not exclusively mountains and especially but not exclusively the Sierra Nevada, that "great Earth gesture" he has been interpreting since the age of fourteen.

The public which celebrates him only as a romantic Nature photographer, a sort of photographic Bierstadt or Moran, does him a disservice. It ignores whole areas of his art, which, as the most casual turning of the pages of this book will show, is of an extraordinary variety. (When the "Eloquent Light" exhibition was shown around the world in 1964, reviewers agreed that not a photographer in the world could have matched it either in sheer bulk or in the quality and variety of the images.) Admirers of Nature photography, too, are not without a certain coterie impulse. They praise Adams for being a champion of conservation, which he is, and a celebrator of unspoiled wilderness, which he also is, but they do not always distinguish clearly between his qualities as environmentalist and his qualities as artist, or between his artistry and his subject matter. Conversely, the limited view of Adams as a Nature photographer has led a few advocates of the faces-in-the-street and industrial-ugliness and human-predicament schools to disparage him as an old man of the mountains, a maker of glorified postcards, a western romantic who goes around re-shooting scenes that W. H. Jackson and Timothy O'Sullivan did better a hundred years ago, and who is, if not indifferent to social injustice and human suffering, at least incapable of photographing humanity as passionately as he photographs cliffs and clouds and snow.

The "glorified postcard" charge needs no comment. Anyone who can call an Ansel Adams photograph a postcard had better find a more plausible life-work than photographic criticism. Neither does the "anti-human" criticism carry any weight, not unless one wants to apply it also to Aeschylus and Bach. But there is a certain validity, at least in my view, to the comments on the photographic portraits, or at least a certain few of them.

Not even Adams' most fervent admirers have been able to make a persuasive case for one kind of portrait, the kind that Adams himself defends on grounds of artistic theory. One critic complains that he photographs rocks as if they were heads, and heads as if they were rocks, and allowing the need of criticism to turn a phrase, there is some truth in the remark. Adams does not believe that "expressiveness," as it is usually conceived, amounts to much. He is not a candid camera man, he does not want to photograph grimaces, and his reasons are not unlike those that Lessing adduced for the blandness of the faces of the snake-strangled Laocoön and his sons. "I photograph heads as I would photograph sculpture," he has written. "The head or figure is clearly presented as an object. The edge, mass, texture of the skin and the general architecture of the face and form are revealed with great intensity. The expression—many possible expressions—are implied." But either because viewers are obtuse or because the implied expressions do not come through, a few of the more formally-posed portraits seem somewhat static and stony, rather like Roman herms, portraits of qualities rather than of people. And the theory, however logical, is not always adhered to. Happily for such viewers as myself, many of the portraits are "expressive" in the best sense, and some of the more candid ones, such as that of Georgia O'Keeffe leering over her shoulder at a New Mexican guide, contradict the theory outright. It is simply too austere a theory for most of us; no purely photographic qualities of intensity, luminosity, purity of line, texture, or range of values are going to compensate for a face in which vivacity has been deliberately erased or muted.

Though some of the portraits do speak to us like church-bells, they are a kind of photography that others have done just as well, and there is a degree of truth in the generalization that Adams is less successful with people than with Nature. With Nature he is not only successful, he is in a class by himself. The observation from which both his few unfavorable critics and his most uncritical admirers take off is that he is, before all else, a poetic and mystical interpreter of Nature, perhaps the greatest who ever cocked a camera. And many of his most impressive images (and not simply because he often enlarges, as Weston, for instance, would not) do reflect Nature in her grandest and most manless aspects.

Nature, one says. Not scenery. Scenery for Adams is a dirty word, an invention of the tourist business, an oversized curio. Nature is something else. Scenery is for profit, Nature is for reverence, and the fewer tracks of man there are in it, the better. "Man, in the contemplation of Nature, need not contemplate his external self," Adams says. With an occasional exception such as "Skiing on Lembert Dome," where the human figure (or figures in some of the versions of the picture) are there simply for the designs they make, I cannot think of a single great Adams landscape in which a human figure appears, even for the usual purpose of scale. Scale, power, size, grandeur, are achieved by other and more difficult means. It is as if man and his petty self-scrutiny had been shrunk back into the camera's eye; as if all subjective emotion were no more than a coating on the lens, a means of purer clarity of vision. Response is *implied,* like expression in the portraits; but what does not seem to me to work consistently in the formal portraits works powerfully in the landscapes.

Nature has been as strong an influence on Ansel Adams as it was on John Muir. He is a Westerner, an outdoorsman,

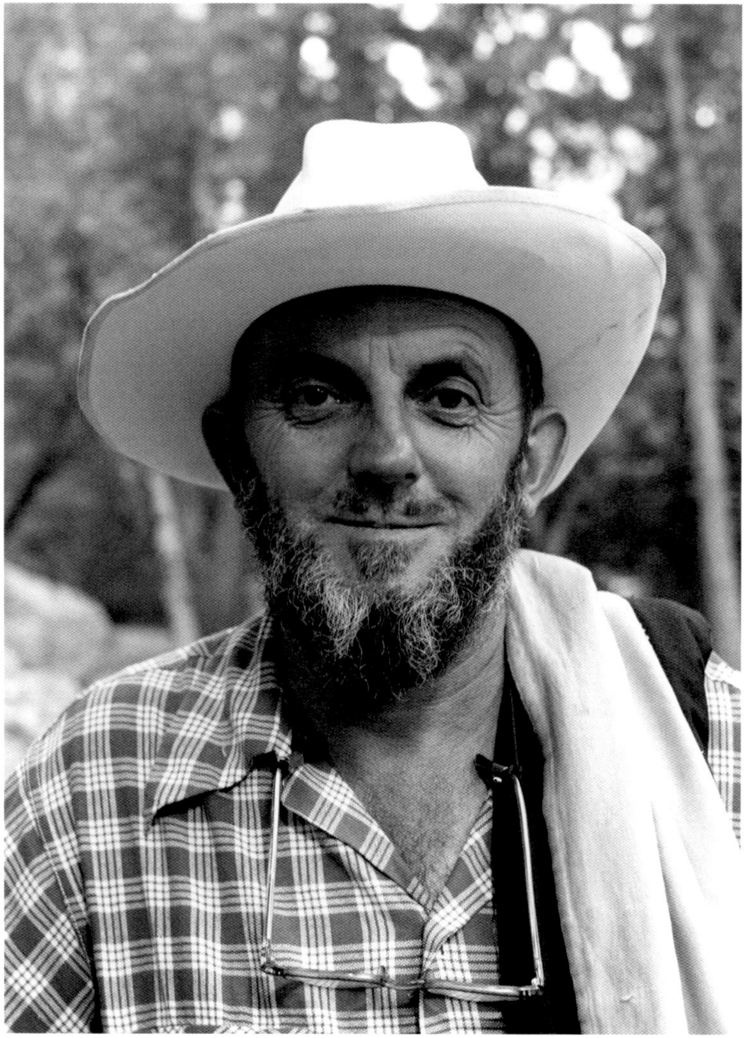

Ansel Adams, 1953. By Imogen Cunningham

a romantic, a mystic, and his art inevitably expresses him. Nature conditioned his boyhood, which he spent in a house overlooking the Golden Gate, exposed to sky and fog and Pacific storms and the dim shine of sea cliffs receding toward Point Reyes. Nature even shaped his face. When he was four, an after-shock of the 1906 San Francisco earthquake threw him down as he ran from the house into the garden, and his sharp, crooked, curious nose has tried to look over his left shoulder ever since.

Yosemite deepened what was already ingrained in him. He never recovered from the love affair that began in the summer of 1916. Four summers of his youth he spent caretaking the Sierra Club's LeConte Memorial Lodge, several others saw him leading club mountaineering expeditions. In 1928 he literally married into Yosemite Valley when he married Virginia Best, daughter of Harry Best, a painter and concessioner of Best's Studio in Yosemite National Park. In 1937 the Adamses moved to the Valley, and have maintained a home there and spent part of every year there for nearly forty years. Even more than Muir, Adams has identified himself with Yosemite and the Sierra, and much of his most magnificent photography derives from there.

One has the impression that, though it was his experience in Santa Fe and Taos that taught him about self-conscious art, it was the Sierra Nevada that taught him to see, and conditioned what he would ever after see most vividly. Growing up in another part of the West, say Arizona or southern Utah, he would have had to come to terms with color, and like his friend Maynard Dixon he might have been influenced by the radically different natural forms of the plateau country. But Yosemite, with its gray granite, cliff shadows, snow, clouds, dark coniferous forests, and light-stung rims, came first. It helped make him the black and white photographer he is. It taught him that even the deepest shadow has half-perceived forms, just as the purest snow or cloud will be pregnant with implicit shadows, and that all the world's wonder lies between nearly-black and nearly-white. Watching Yosemite Valley under sunlight, moonlight, skylight, starlight, stormlight, in greenery and in snow, changing with the passage of every cloud, he had to learn not only to see, but to find the photographic techniques that would capture such changefulness. There is no place in the world that could have shown him more eloquent contrasts: the poetry of ferns under a sheer half-mile cliff, the suddenness of dogwood bursting out from a dark wall of forest.

That was the beginning, and it remained the core, but Adams has added the whole West to it. He has been a migrant, taking off for the Canadian Rockies, Alaska, Hawaii, the Southwest, the desert, and coming in for periods of rest and consolidation to his bases in Yosemite, San Francisco, and in recent years Carmel. At seventy-two he does not make many new negatives. His dehumidified storage vault in Carmel has files of hundreds that have never been printed, some of them perhaps as good as his best, and it will be the work of years to print and study them. But for decades there was hardly a mountain pass, a canyon, a desert sink or gulch or wash, that did not know his old Cadillac with the strong photographing platform on top and its inside full of white-painted equipment cases, tripods, sleeping bag, and camping gear. He still works hours that would destroy many men half his age. In the decades when he was stalking revelation through the stupendous empty places of the West, there were stretches when he hardly seemed to sleep, so open and eager was his eye to catch the miraculous moment or to visualize the combinations of form, scale, and texture that awaited only the transfiguring instant of light.

Photography is the art of miraculous instants—instants of expression, of composition, of gesture, or of light, depending on what kind of photography is going on. It is an art which often has to seize and fix what is already vanishing by the time it is perceived. Of all the varieties of photography, landscape, Adams believes, is the supreme test for the photographer. He has to *catch* the fortunate combination of earth, sky, and cloud—he can't compose or position them, nor does it help him much to move his own point of view. When dealing with near objects, he can achieve great changes by moving his camera a few inches; when photographing landscape he can often move it a hundred yards, or a half mile, and gain little. And there are problems of haze, low color saturation, scale. The camera must, in the small space of the print, convey the very presence of the scene.

And finally there is the need to catch the moment when the light is, in Nancy Newhall's word, most "eloquent," and to expose before that moment is gone. To capture the moments when landscape is revealed under a light supernal in its vividness, the photographer must carry his trained sensibility around with him like a loaded and cocked gun. And also, like any hunter, he must sometimes have the patience to stalk.

Consider two of Adams' best-known images.

One he saw as he was driving back to Santa Fe at dusk and glanced over his shoulder at a village he was passing. The sun was down, but dull light still lay against the church and the adobe houses of the town, and on the faded white crosses of the graveyard. In the east the full moon was well up above the snowy Sangre de Cristo range, and between mountains and moon a lens of stratus cloud floated high in the sunlight that had already left the earth. Sky, cloud, mountains, the long alluvial slope, the broken barranca, the town, the foreground of sagebrush flat, stretched in bands of bright and gray and dark from left to right. And almost dark, going as he looked.

He estimates that he had sixty seconds to stop, leap out, set up tripod and camera, guess the place on the brightness scale for which he wanted to expose (it was no guess, it was like knowing twelve times twelve), set shutter and lens, focus, and expose. Almost before he took the film from the camera, the light faded. But what he caught on that negative, called "Moonrise, Hernandez, New Mexico," is not dark. It glows with a reserved, dusky clarity, it has the "illusion of light" that marks so many of Adams' great photographs. Only the most fantastic purist would complain that the cemetery crosses glow a more ghostly white, almost as if with a light of their own, than they could have had in the light he exposed by. The darkroom magician has interfered there. For this is not a reproduction of Hernandez, New Mexico, at dusky moonrise. It is a vision translated, a concept realized. And done in sixty seconds or less. "Sometimes," Adams says, "I think I do get to places just when God is ready to have somebody click the shutter."

Or take another, made in the same year, 1944. On the west side of the Owens Valley the land rolls once, a rock and sagebrush foothill, and then in one surge goes up ten thousand feet. Seen from the valley in winter, the escarpment is white with snow. The intermediate hill is dun or tan or mottled, depending on the light, and on its flank it wears a whitewashed brand, LP, to indicate that it belongs to Lone Pine High School. The Owens River flows along its foot through a belt of tall leafless cottonwoods. In the foreground is a flat yellow meadow, with horses grazing in it.

Made at any hour, in any light, it is a picture, a splendid snapshot, in spite of the documentary LP. Adams did not grab the image when he came upon it. He studied it, visualizing the finished print. He estimated it as it would appear in various directional lights. Then he went to dinner and to bed. In the chilly pre-dawn blackness of the next morning, he came back. As he waited, clear gray sourceless light grew until it showed him the meadow with its shadowy horses, the mottled foothill, the impressive loom of the Sierra fault-block. He set up the camera and went under the cloth; then he came out and waited. Eventually the sun, breaking over the White Mountains to the eastward, lit and burned like a laser beam on the highest Sierra peak. He watched the pinkish light flood downward until nearly the whole face of the range was blazing with it. He went under the cloth and came out again, and waited.

Then another laser beam slipped past the eastern mountains and tangled itself in the tops of the cottonwoods in the left middle ground. The roll of foothills was still in

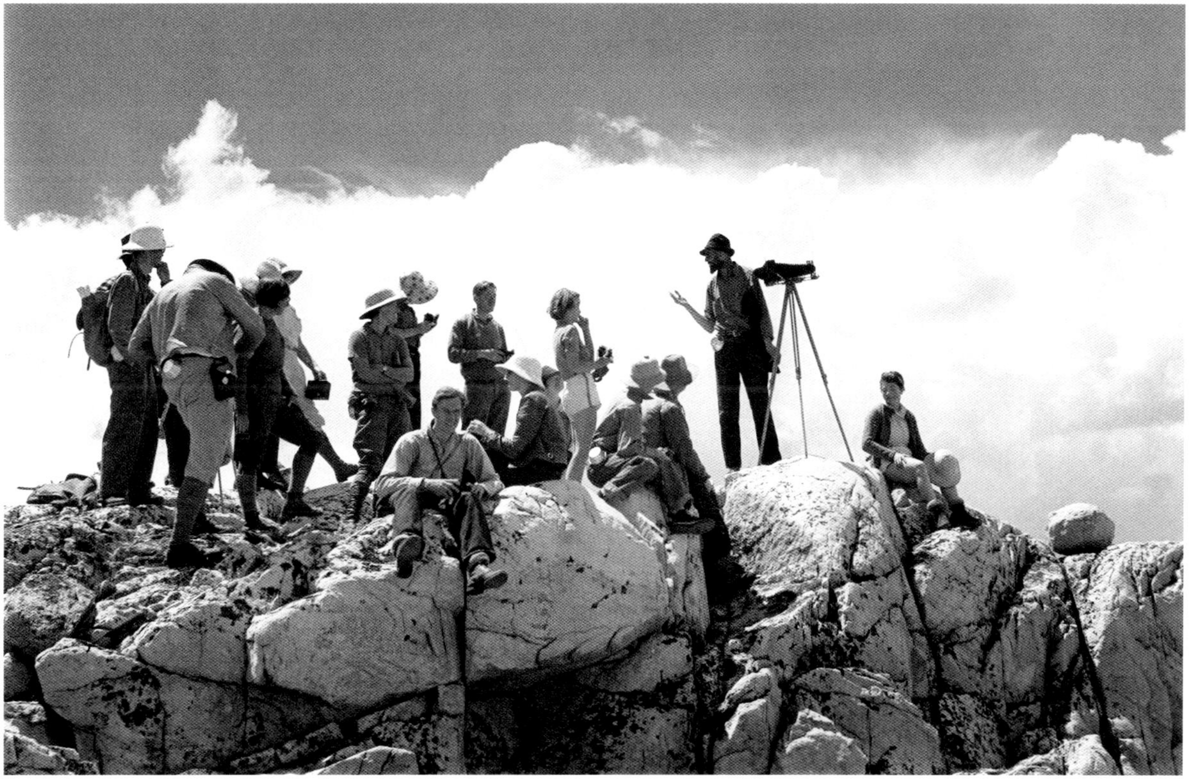

"The Sermon on the Mount," Sierra Club, c. 1935. By Cedric Wright

shadow, the range coldly alight. Nearly at his own level the little smolder of sun grew in the cottonwood branches. He went under the cloth and watched a while, and came out yet again. By then the light had burst past the leftward cottonwoods and was brightening other trees and a patch of meadow along the creek farther to the right. There was a horse grazing there. The light pooled behind him, turning him into a black cutout. Adams went under the cloth again, waited for the precise instant, and clicked the shutter.

The resulting image, called either "Winter Sunrise, Sierra Nevada," or "Sierra Nevada from Lone Pine," represents no seizing of the accidental moment. It was made by patient waiting for the instant that he knew must come, but just as surely as "Moonrise, Hernandez," it is an authentic rendering of miracle. The sky beyond the range is slightly darkened to accentuate the drift of morning clouds. The white magnificence of the Sierra, shadowed with crags and gulches, ripples like a banner across the photograph. Below, as if propping it, the almost-black hill has just enough light on it to show the texture of sage and rock. And it wears no brand. The ugly mantrack has been spotted from the prints. Below the dark hill, almost as if we were watching it grow and brighten, the finger of dawn reaches into the meadow along the creekside. It comes like renewal, rebirth, reassurance. In a moment, as we watch, it will touch and warm the dark silhouette of the grazing horse, as any dawn might touch and warm any life.

I have that print on my wall in an enlargement of about two by three feet, a size that loses some of the brilliance of the image but better suggests the grand scale. I have looked at it, studied it, scores of times, and every time I do so it lifts me. It is like hearing the choral movement of Beethoven's Ninth. Once again darkness has been overtaken by light, as if an earth-promise were being kept.

One returns to Conrad and his definition of the artist's aim: "To arrest, for the space of a breath, the hands busy about the work of the earth, and compel men entranced by the sight of distant goals to glance for a moment at the surrounding vision of form and color, of sunshine and shadows: to make them pause for a look, for a sigh, for a smile—such is the aim, difficult and evanescent, and reserved only for the very few to achieve."

Among the few, Ansel Adams.

ANSEL ADAMS
IN THE NATIONAL PARKS

The dawn wind in the High Sierra is not just a passage of cool air through forest conifers, but within the labyrinth of human consciousness becomes a stirring of some world-magic of most delicate persuasion. The grand lift of the Tetons is more than a mechanistic fold and faulting of the earth's crust; it becomes a primal gesture of the earth beneath a greater sky. And on the ancient Acadian coast an even more ancient Atlantic surge disputes the granite headlands with more than the slow, crumbling erosion of the sea. Here are forces familiar with the aeons of creation, and with the aeons of the ending of the world.

Ansel Adams, from "The Meaning of the National Parks," 1950

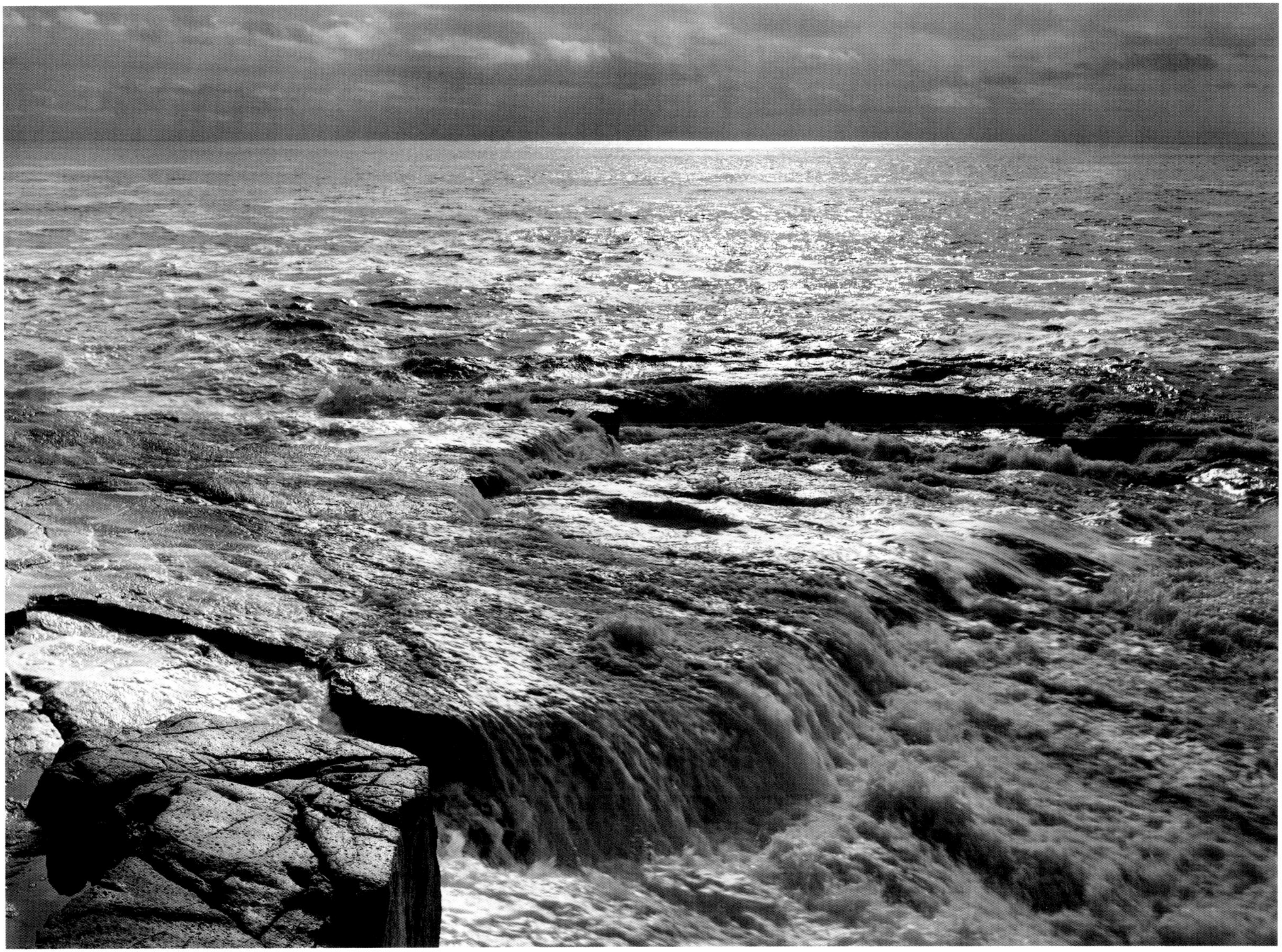

THE ATLANTIC FROM SCHOODIC POINT, ACADIA NATIONAL PARK, MAINE, 1949

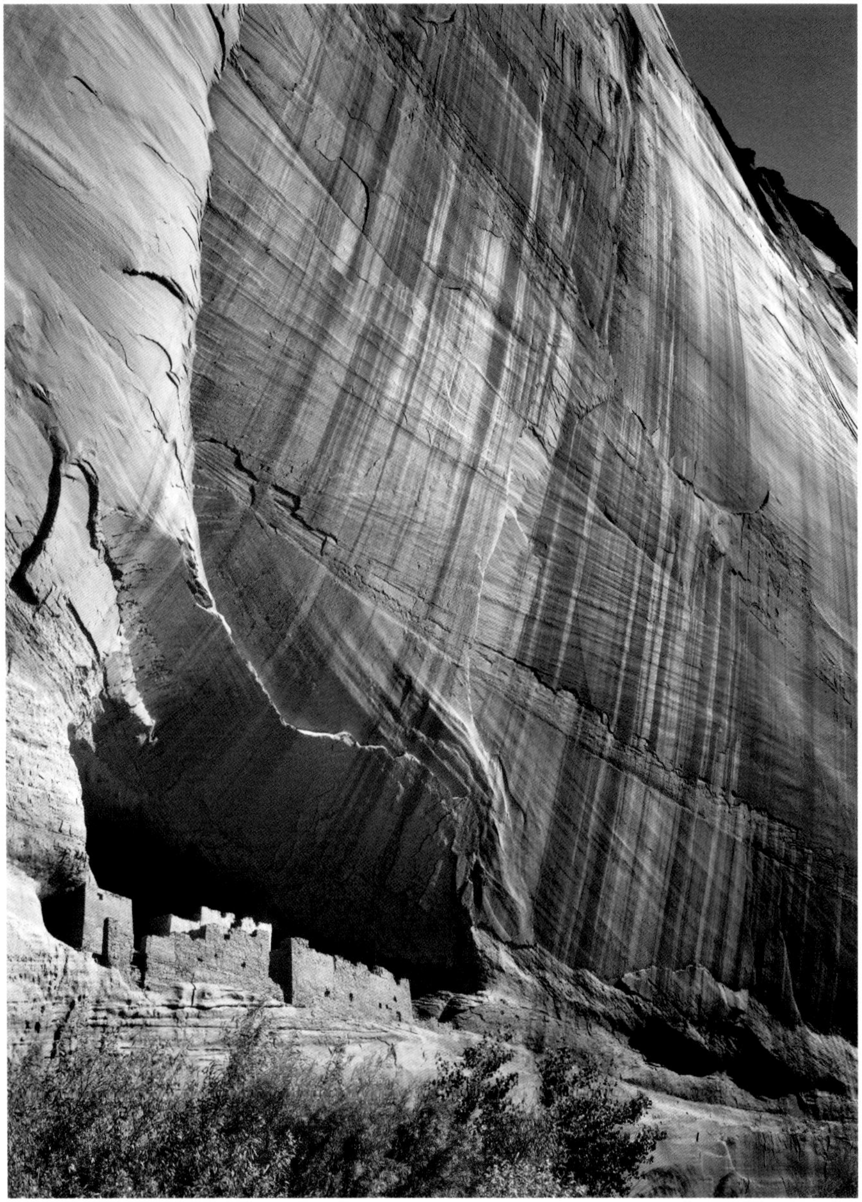

WHITE HOUSE RUIN, CANYON DE CHELLY NATIONAL MONUMENT, ARIZONA, 1942

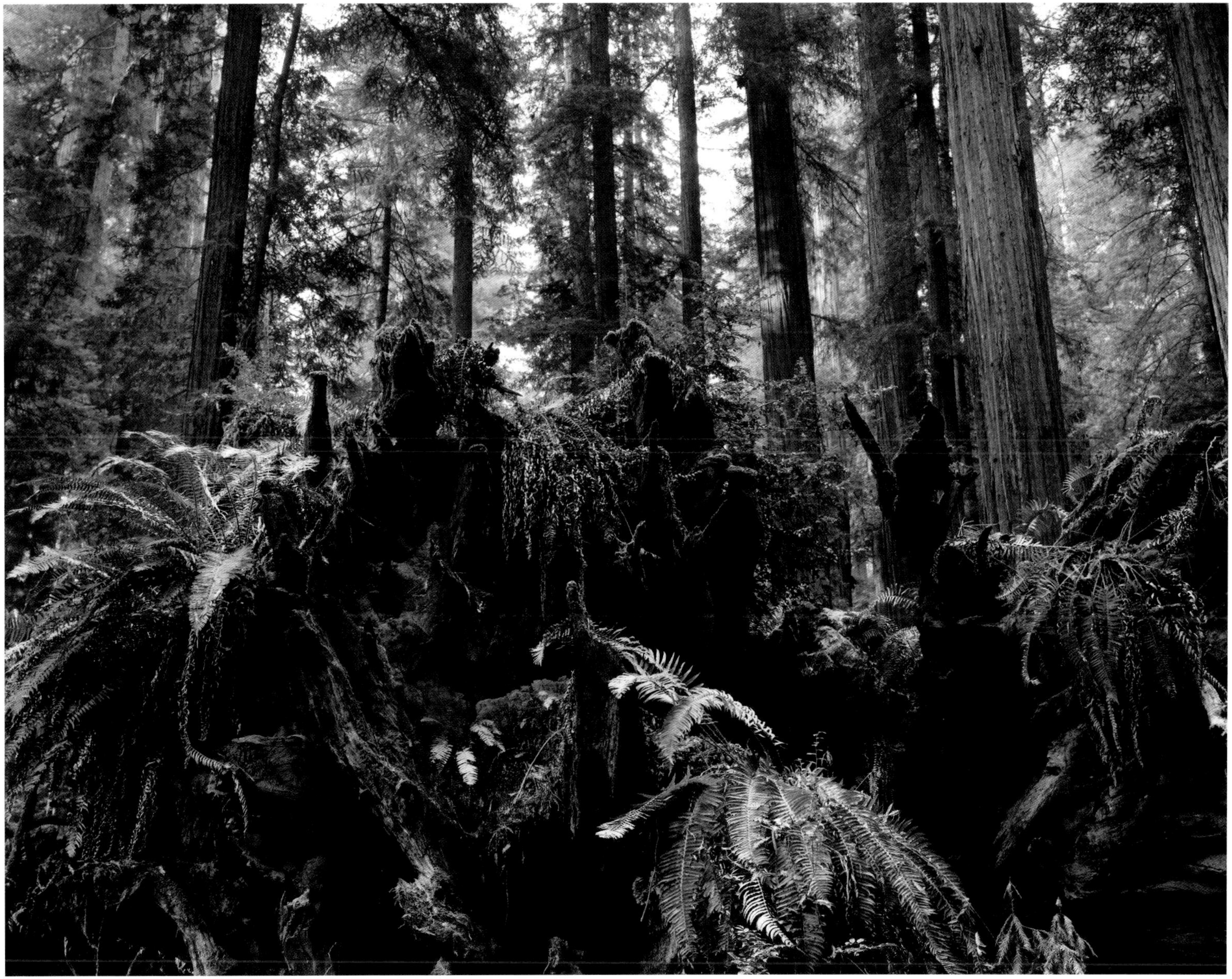

REDWOOD STUMP AND FERNS, ROCKEFELLER GROVE, REDWOOD NATIONAL PARK, CALIFORNIA, 1964

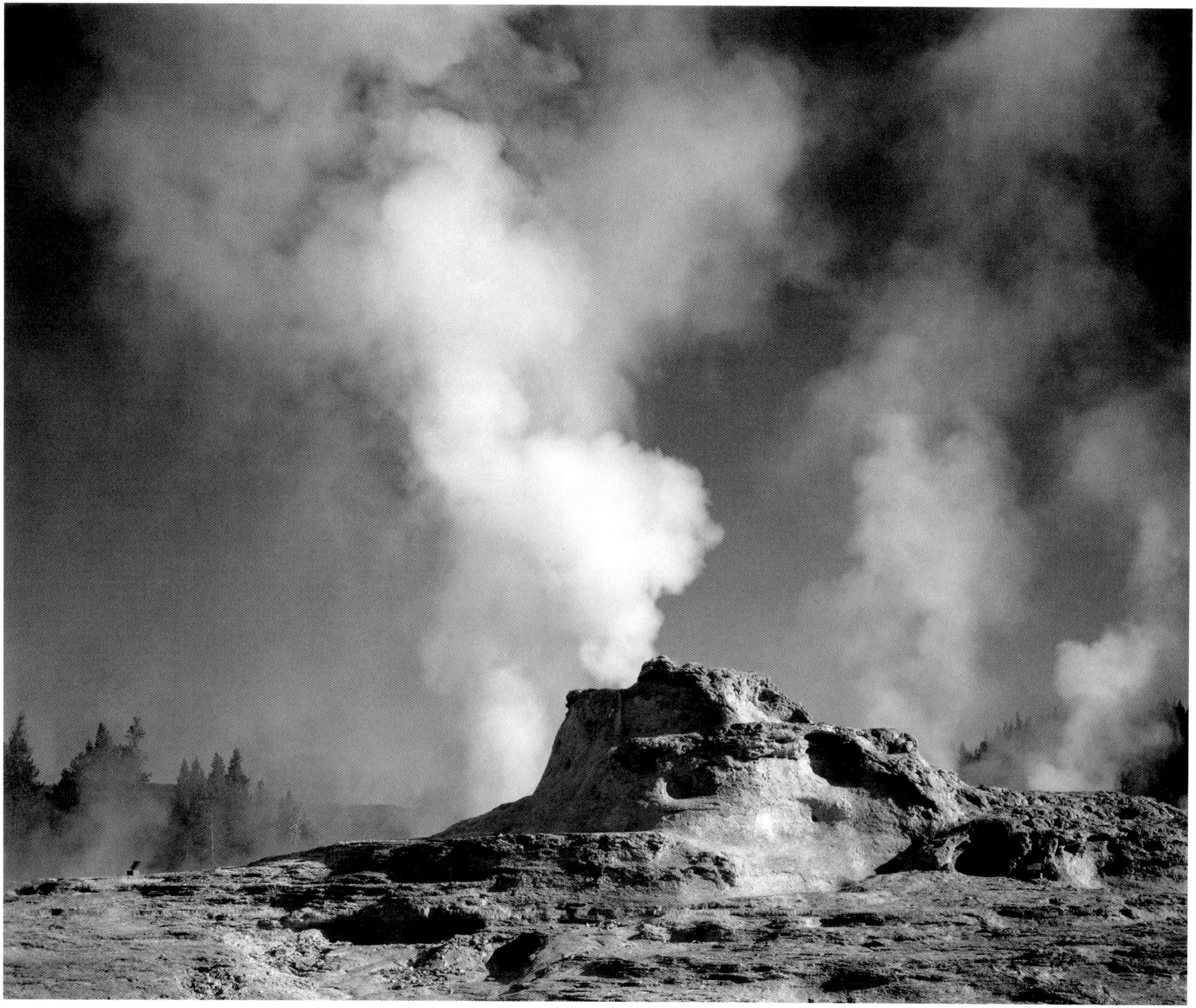

CASTLE GEYSER CONE, YELLOWSTONE NATIONAL PARK, WYOMING, 1942

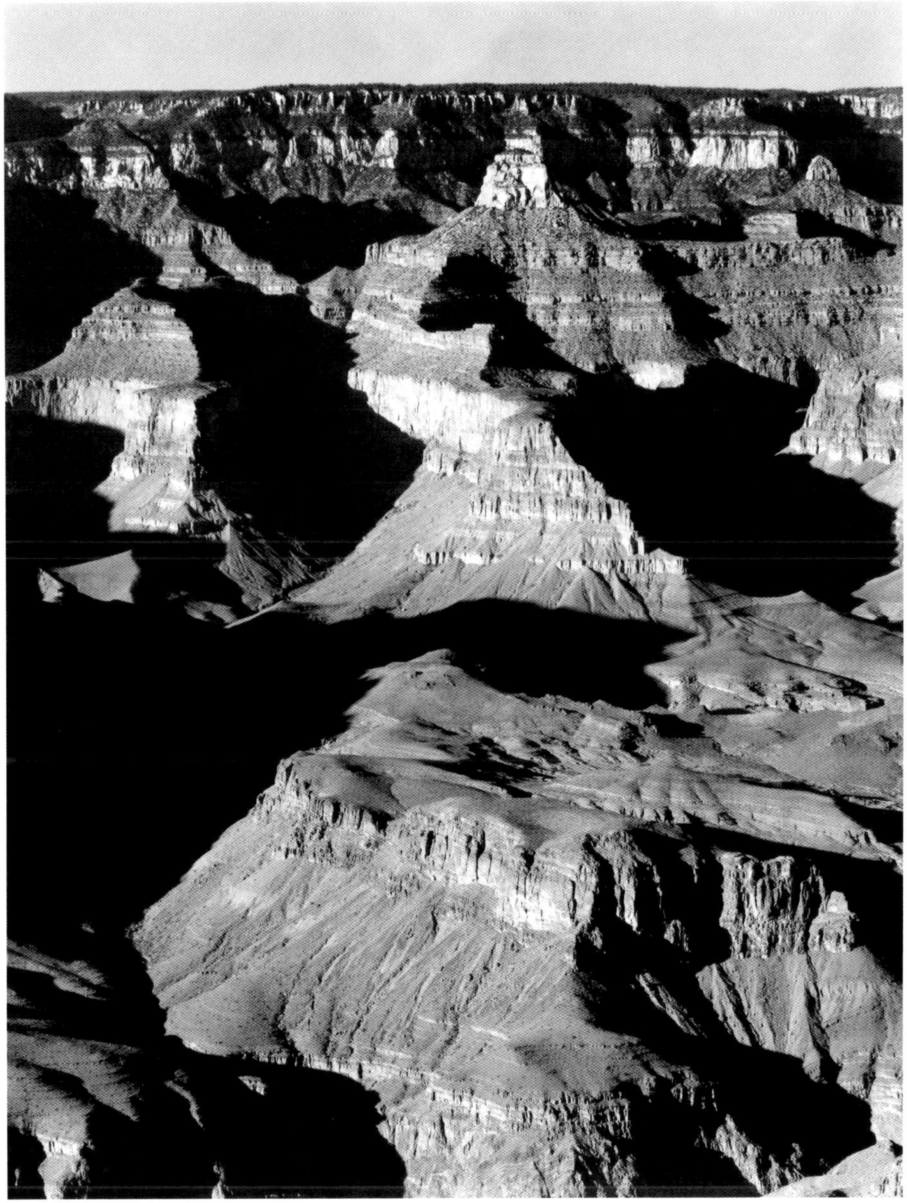

GRAND CANYON NATIONAL PARK, ARIZONA, 1942

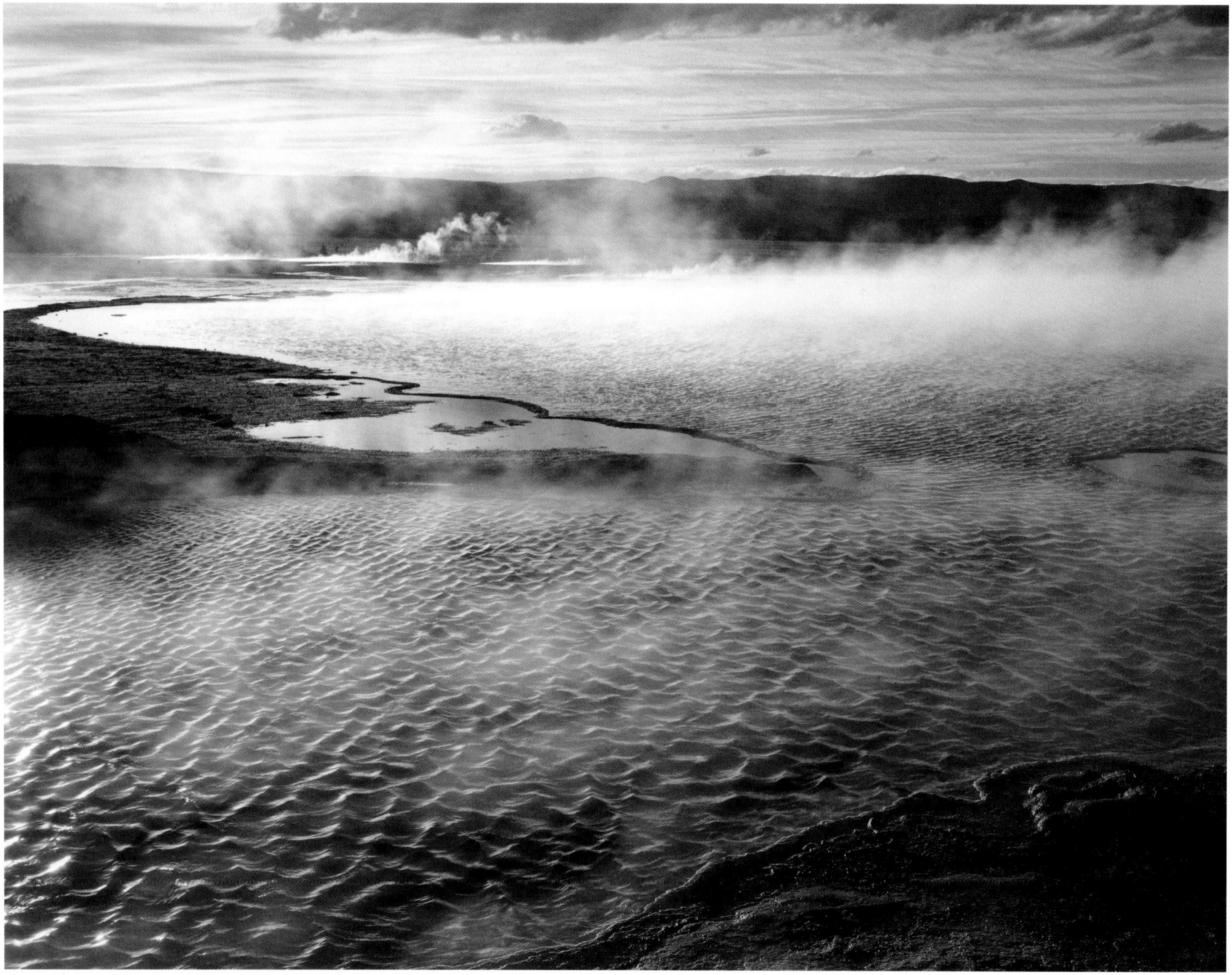

GRAND PRISMATIC SPRING, YELLOWSTONE NATIONAL PARK, WYOMING, 1942

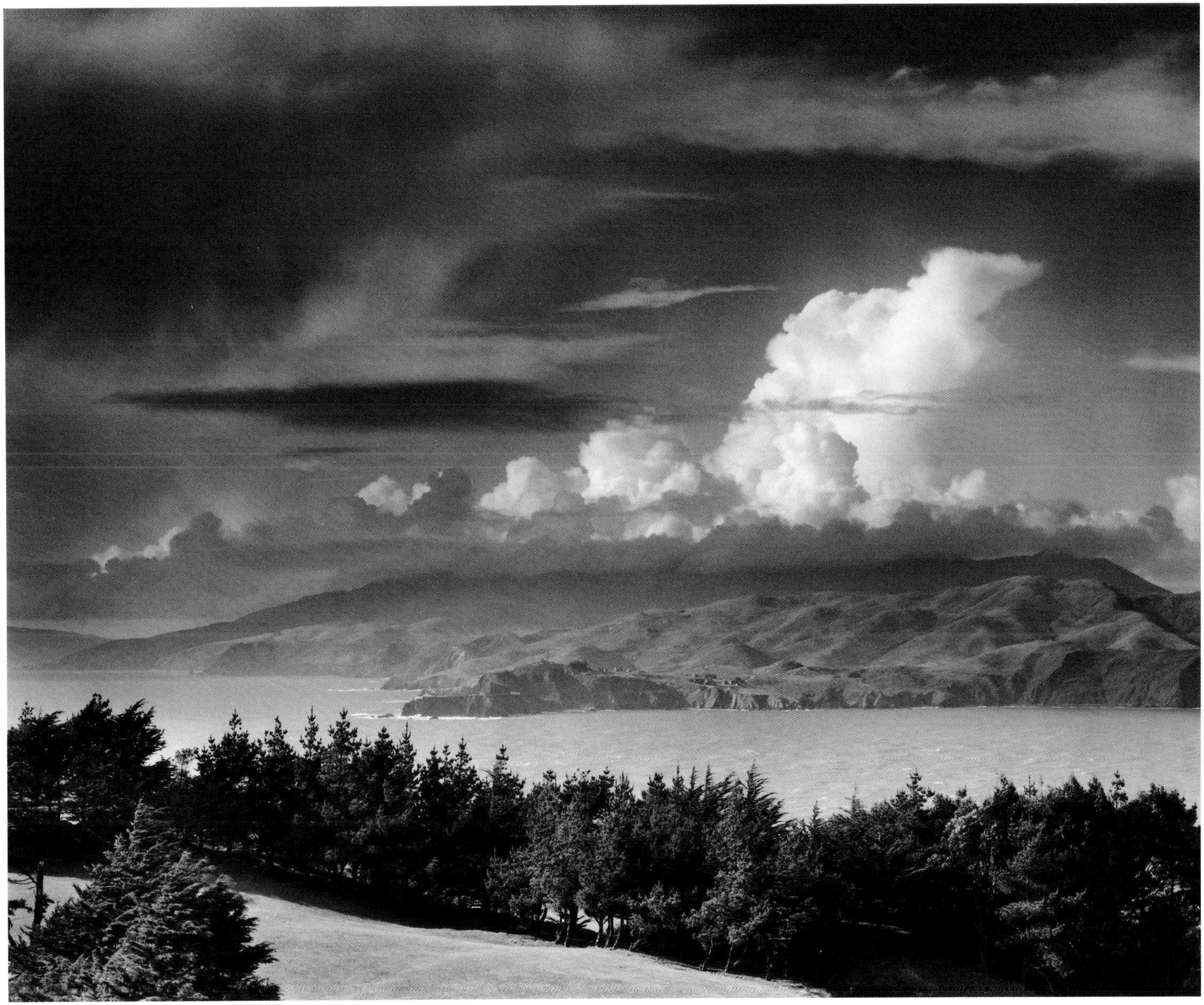

THE GOLDEN GATE HEADLANDS FROM LINCOLN PARK, GOLDEN GATE NATIONAL RECREATION AREA, CALIFORNIA, 1952

When the moon is full, tourists crowd the overlook at Glacier Point to experience this magical view. Flying over this section of the Sierra in the late 1970s en route to the East Coast, Ansel identified every peak: Mount Clark, Gray Peak, Mount Starr King, Triple Divide Peak, and Red Peak. He related that he had climbed each peak at least once and said, "I know the Sierra like the back of my hand."

On his first trip to Yosemite at age fourteen, in 1916, he photographed the High Sierra and Yosemite Valley from this same spot. Over the course of a long career he was to return many times.

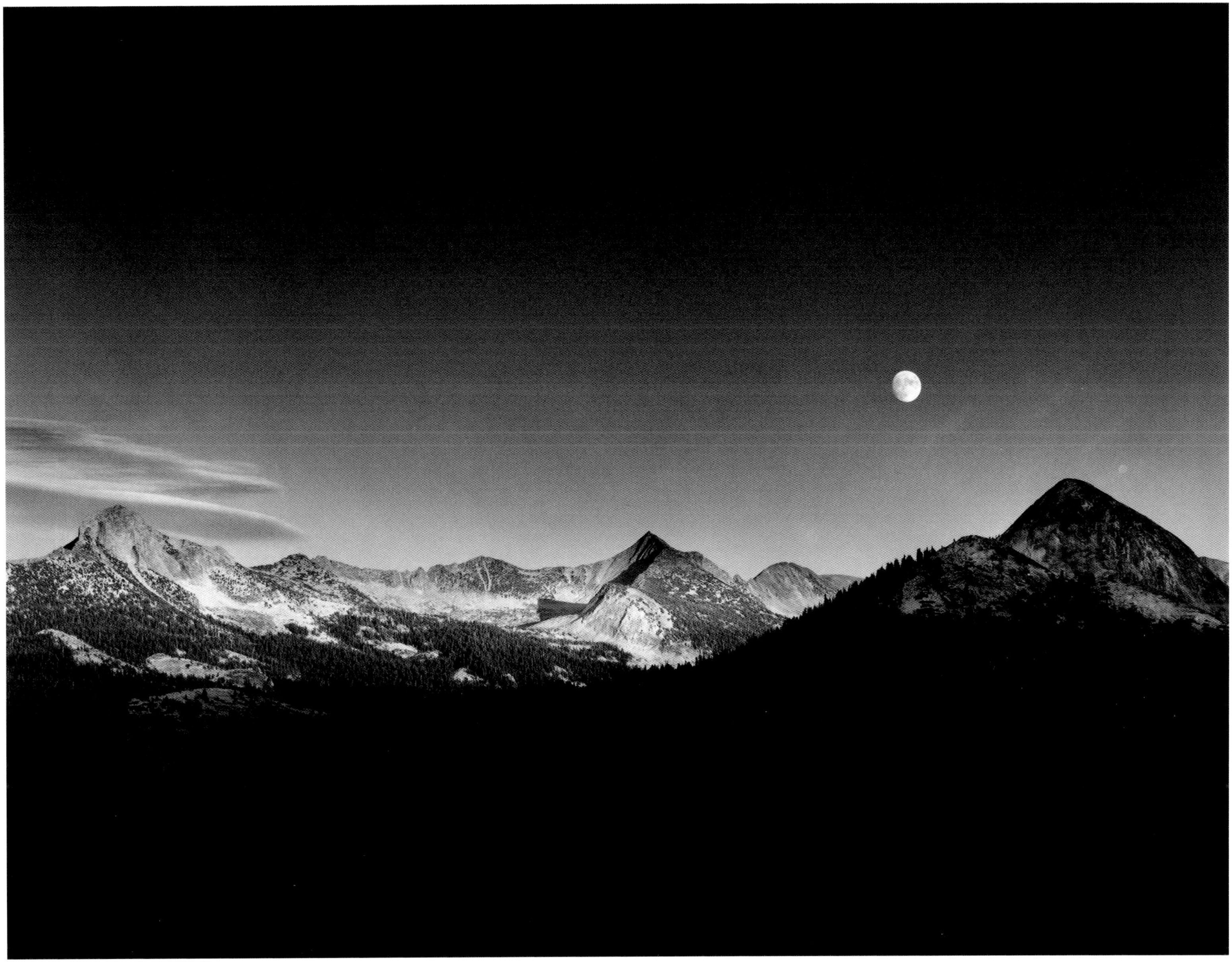

AUTUMN MOON, HIGH SIERRA FROM GLACIER POINT, YOSEMITE NATIONAL PARK, CALIFORNIA, 1948

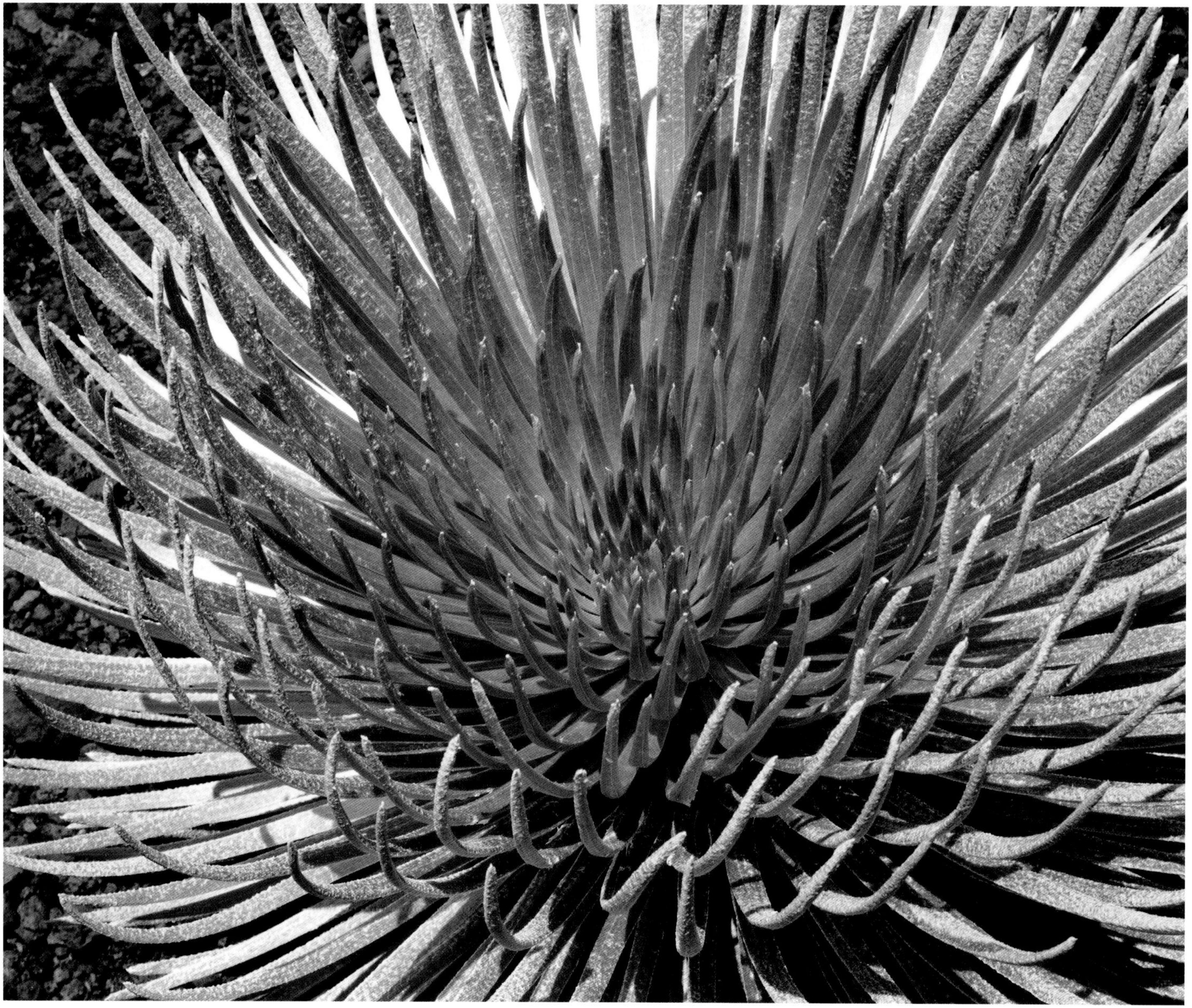

SILVER SWORD PLANT IN THE CRATER OF HALEAKALA, HALEAKALA NATIONAL PARK, HAWAII, 1948

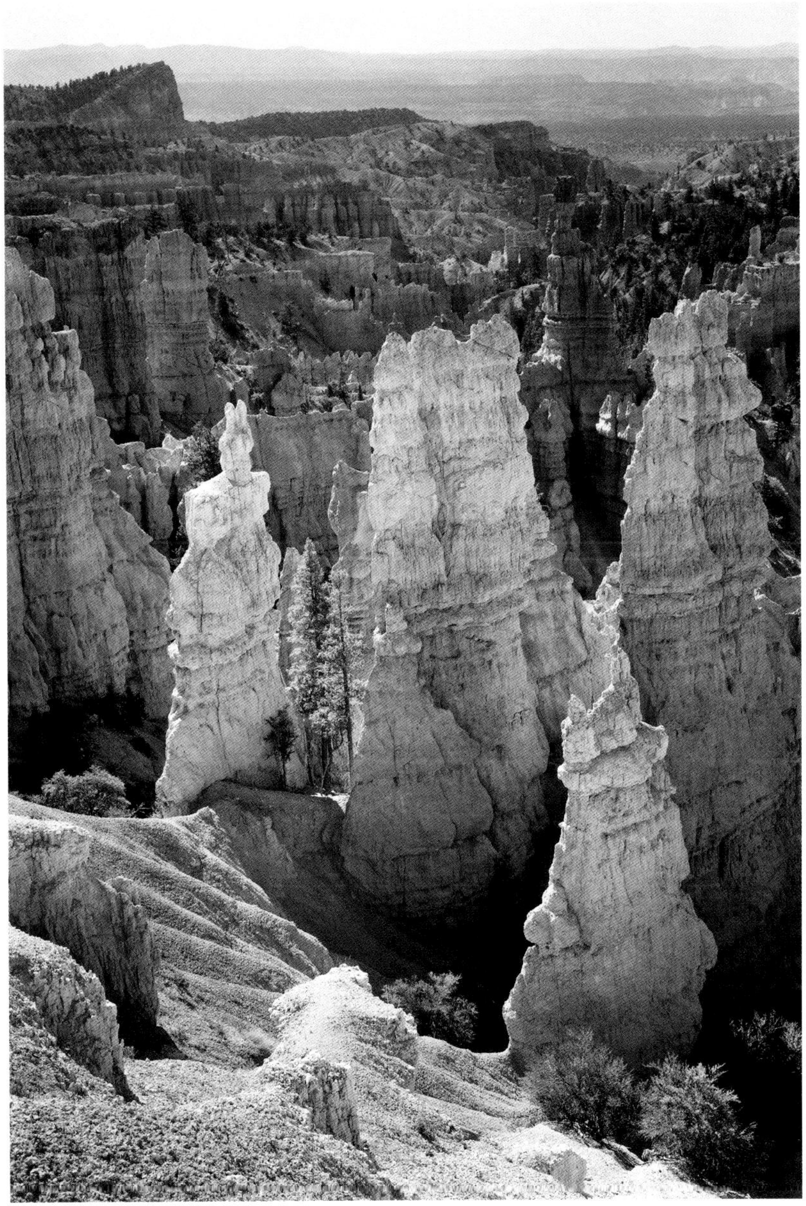

FAIRYLAND, BRYCE CANYON NATIONAL PARK, UTAH, 1947

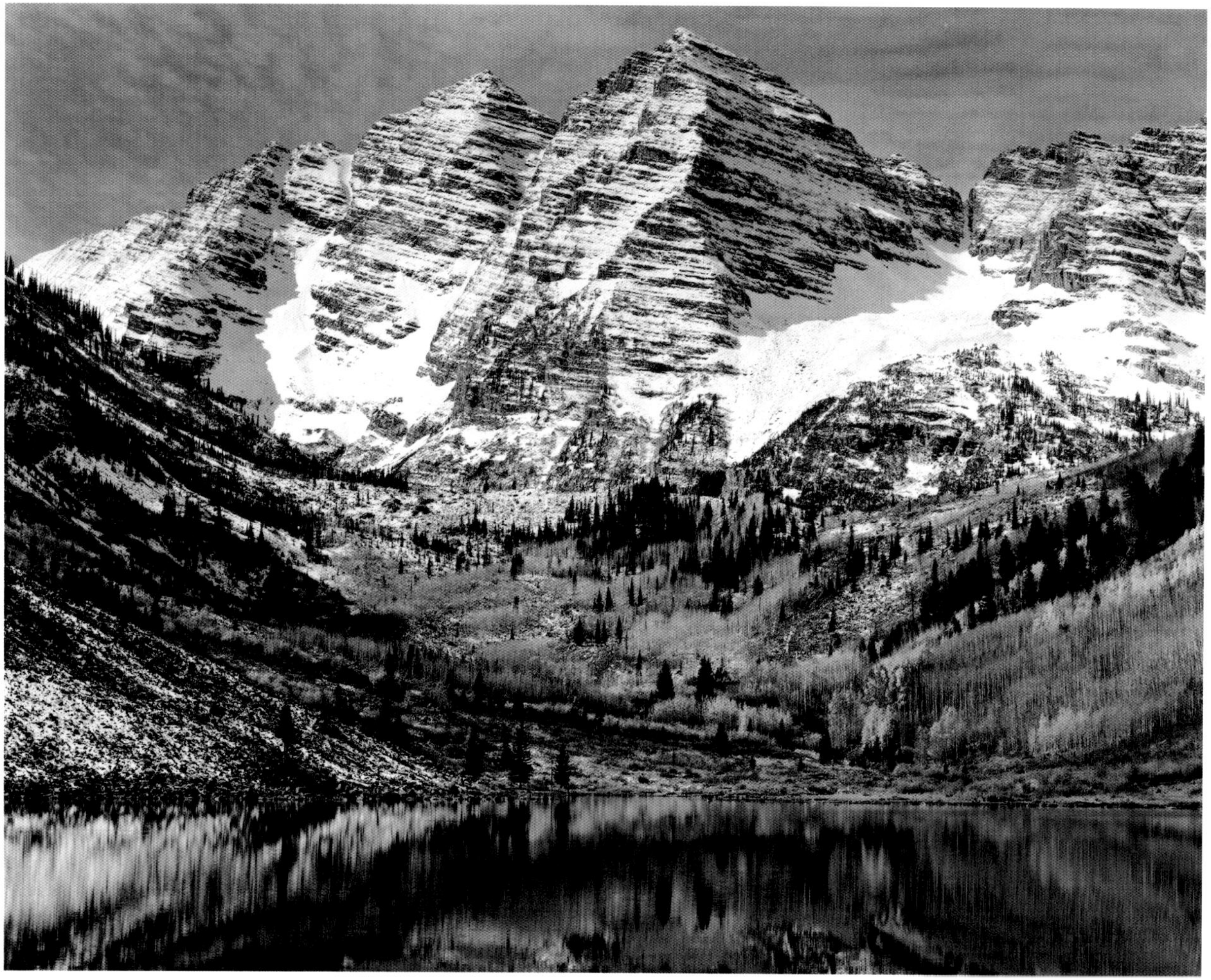

MAROON BELLS, MAROON BELLS-SNOWMASS WILDERNESS, COLORADO, 1951

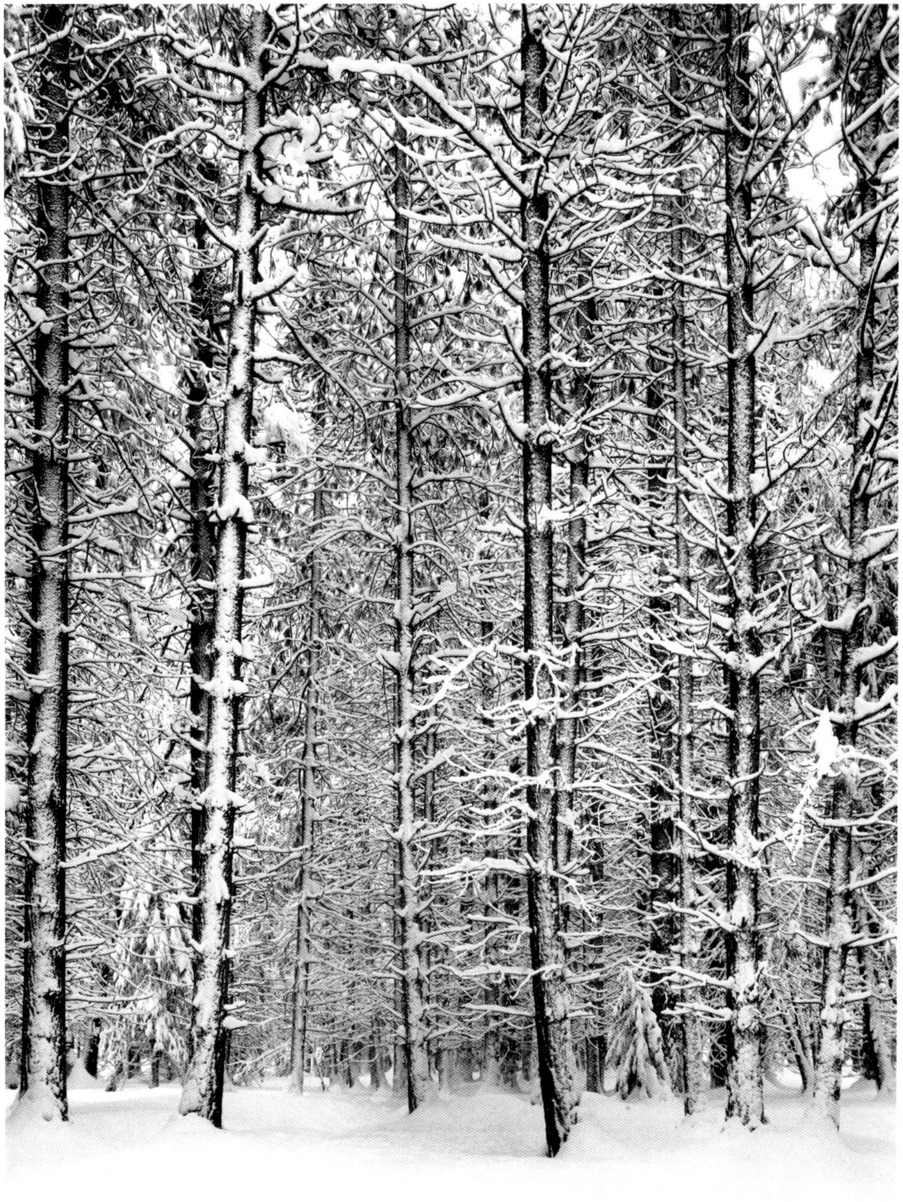

PINE FOREST IN SNOW, YOSEMITE NATIONAL PARK, CALIFORNIA, 1933

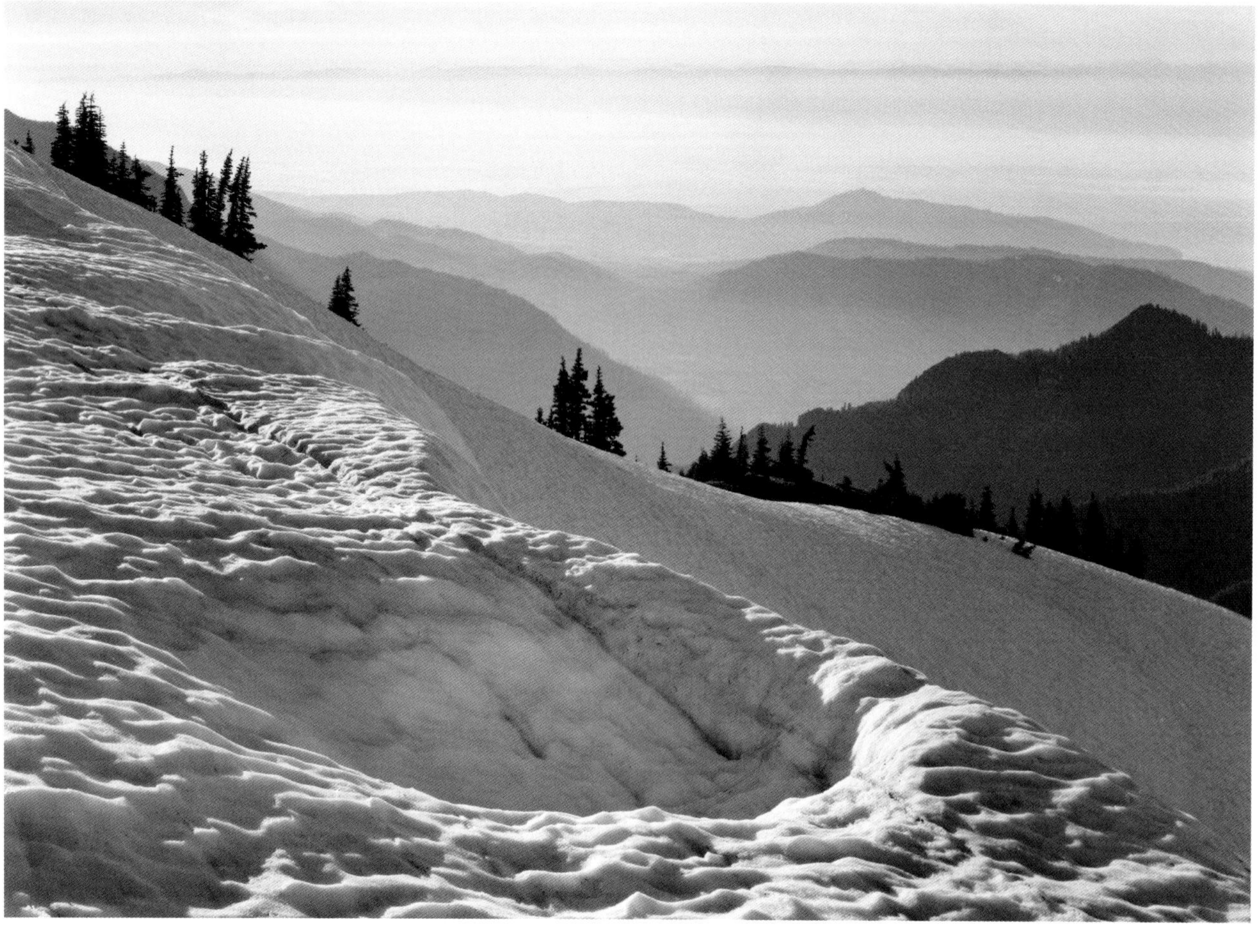

FROM HURRICANE HILL, OLYMPIC NATIONAL PARK, WASHINGTON, 1948

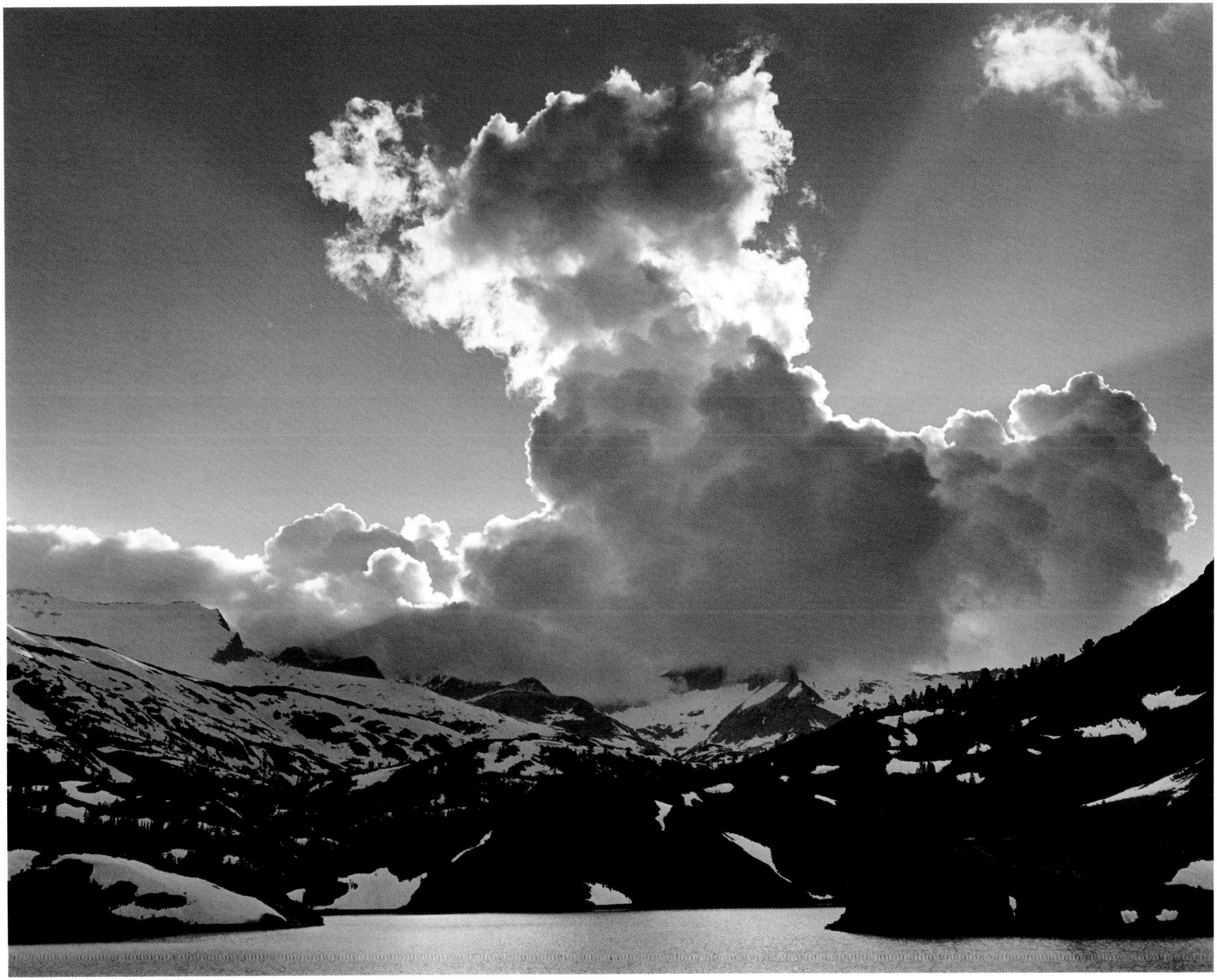

THUNDERCLOUD, ELLERY LAKE, SIERRA NEVADA, CALIFORNIA, 1934

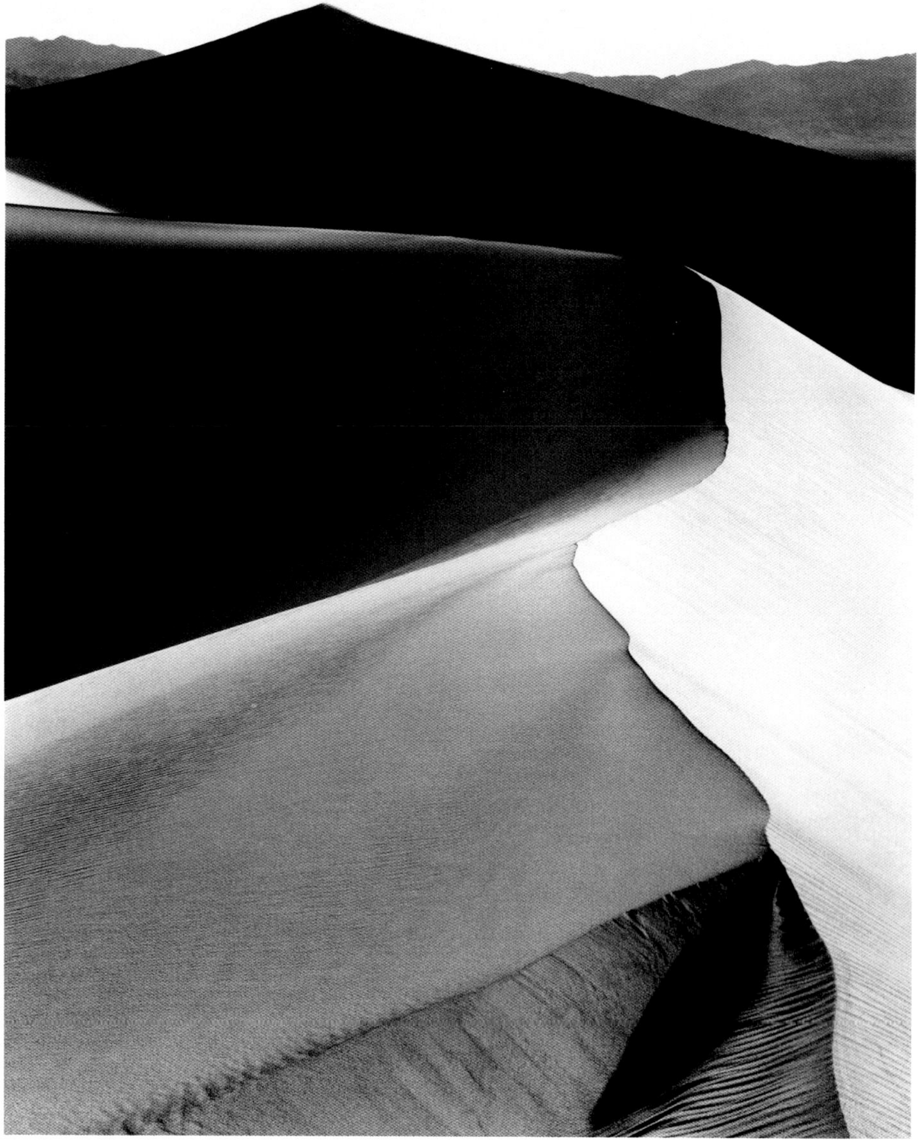

SAND DUNES, SUNRISE, DEATH VALLEY NATIONAL PARK, CALIFORNIA, C. 1948

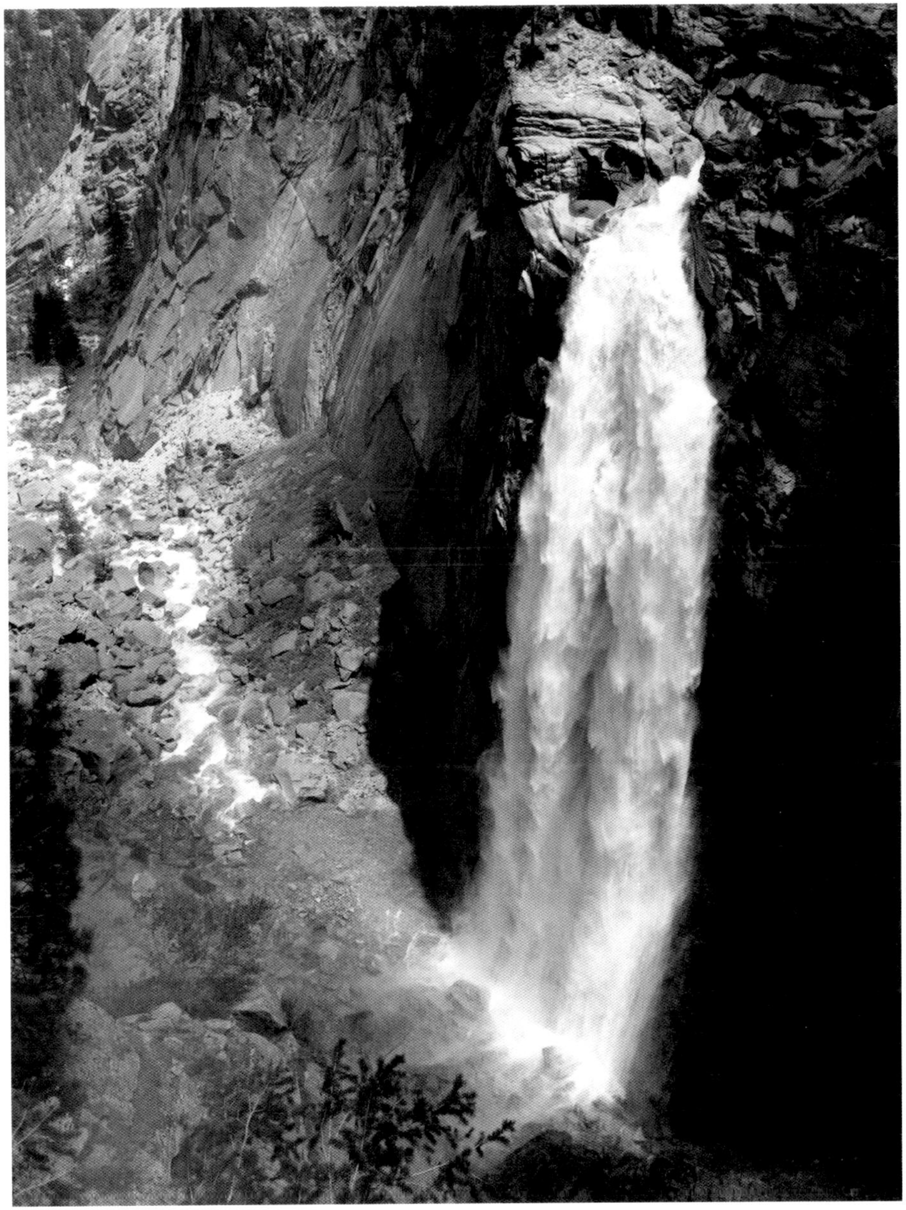

ILLILOUETTE FALL, YOSEMITE NATIONAL PARK, CALIFORNIA, C. 1936

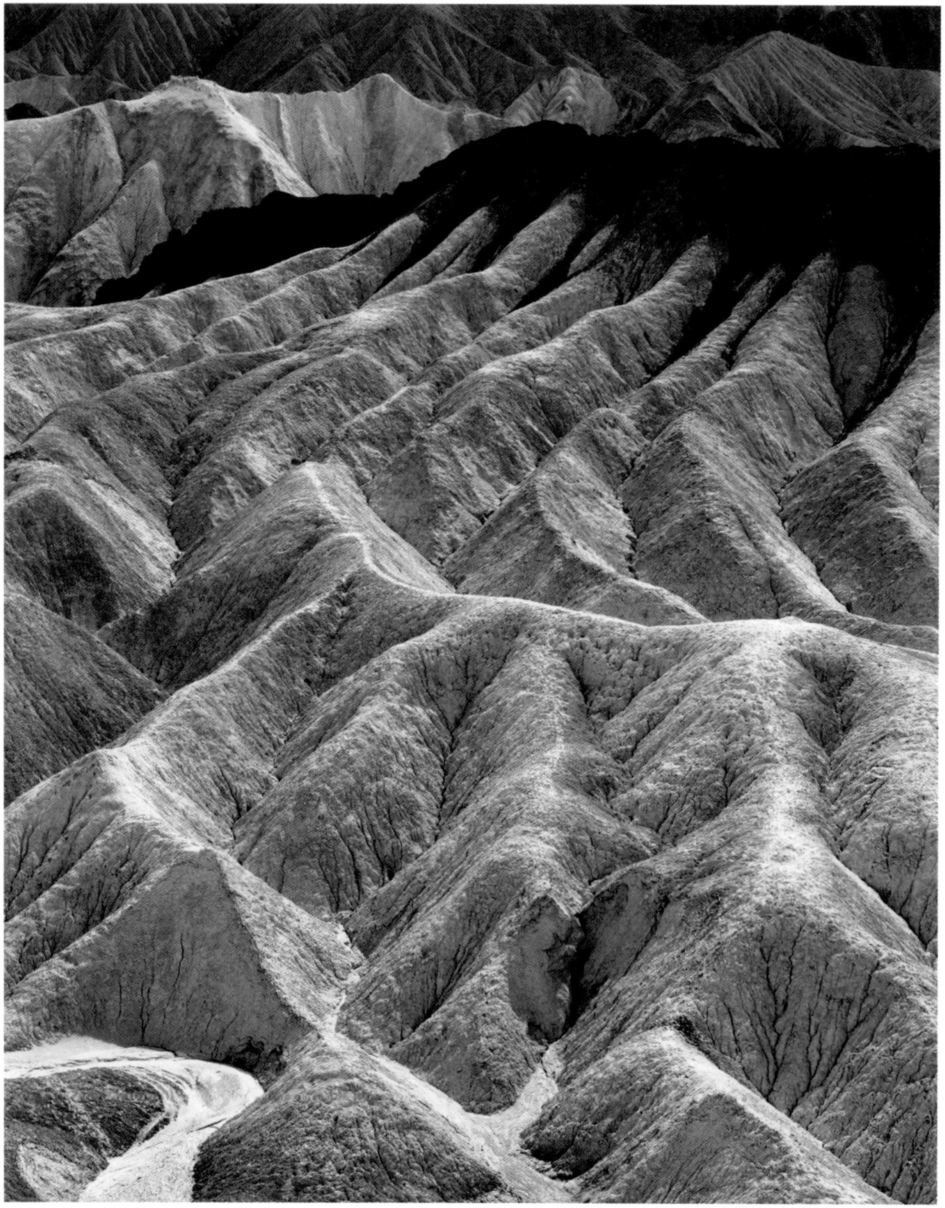

ZABRISKIE POINT, DEATH VALLEY NATIONAL PARK, CALIFORNIA, C. 1942

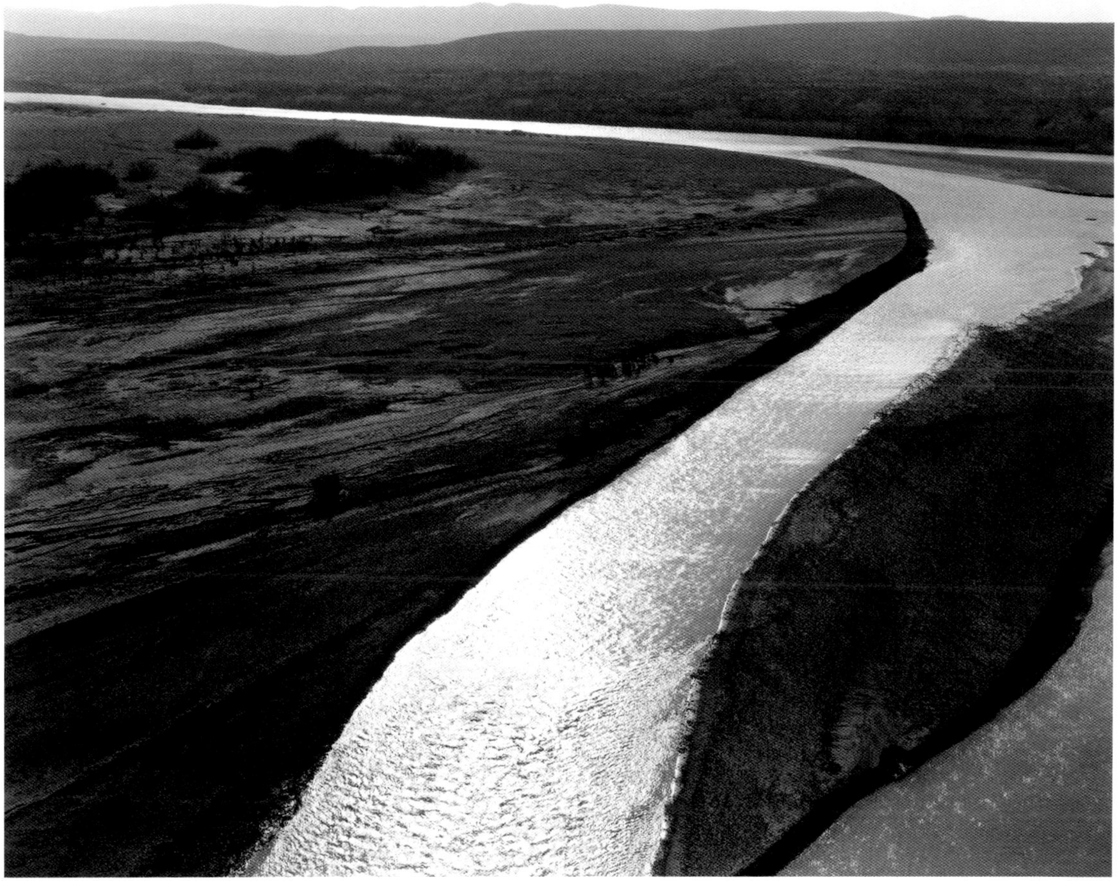

SAND BAR, RIO GRANDE, BIG BEND NATIONAL PARK, TEXAS, 1947

Until 1930, Ansel pursued photography during the summer in Yosemite and the High Sierra; during the winter he studied the piano in San Francisco. He earned a little money giving piano lessons, and one of his students, Isabelle Ellis Greisberg, reminisced in a letter to him in 1981: "My recollection of you goes back to around 1919, when, as a child of ten years of age, I would see you walk by on our block.... Sometimes several of us little girls would call out to you, 'Hello, Daddy Long Legs.' Maybe you never even heard us, for we were somewhat embarrassed by our boldness and would hide."

When Greisberg asked to take piano lessons in her teens, her mother selected the long-legged neighbor as the teacher: "The piano did not come easily for me, but from you I learned to appreciate the finer music and the technique it required.... I recall that on at least one occasion you had prints of Yosemite spread out on the other piano in your living room. That was my first exposure to Yosemite, and then at Christmastime [1924] you stopped by our flat on 21st Avenue to give us a photograph of 'Thousand Island Lake and Banner Peak at Sunset.'"

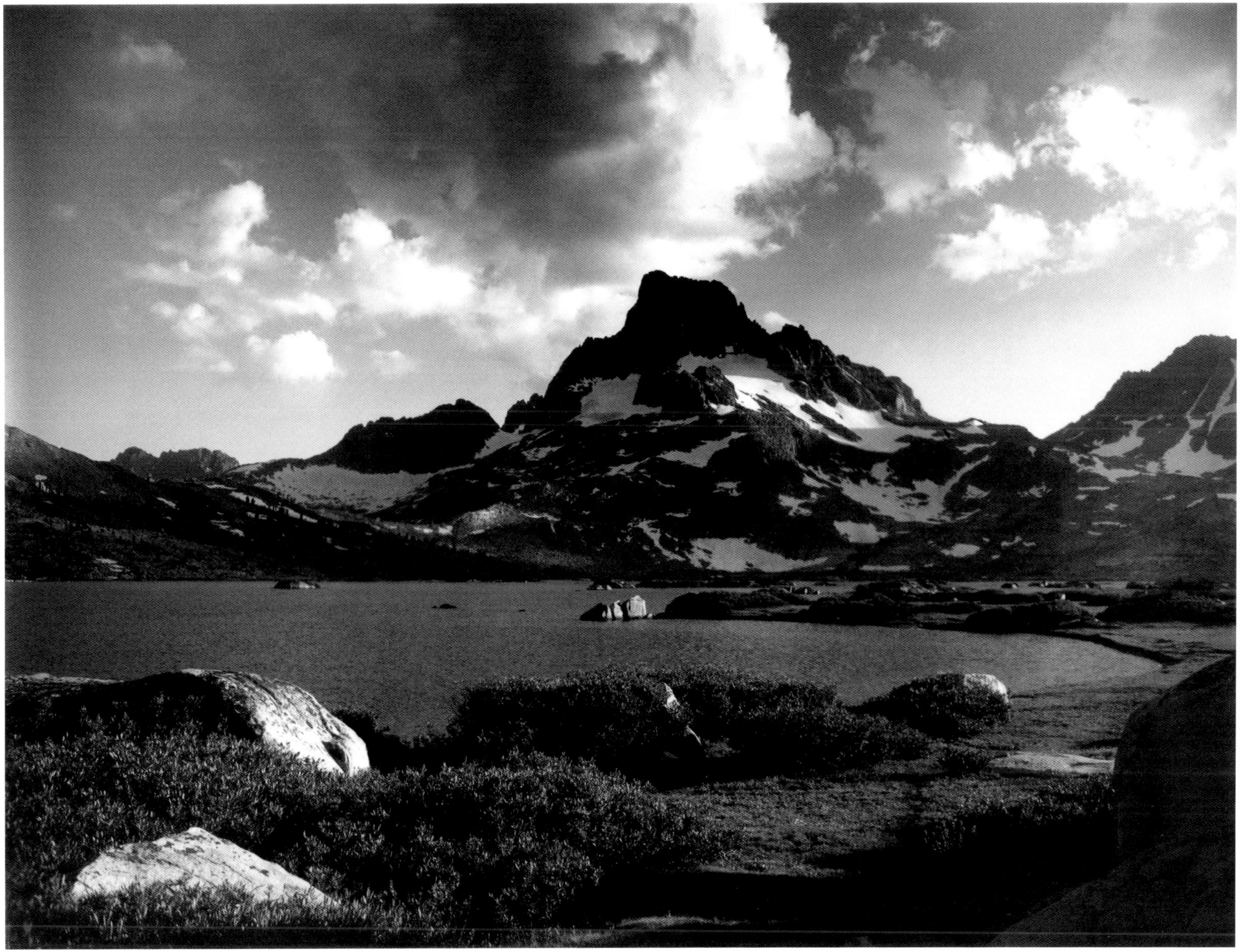

BANNER PEAK AND THOUSAND ISLAND LAKE, SUNSET, SIERRA NEVADA, CALIFORNIA, 1923

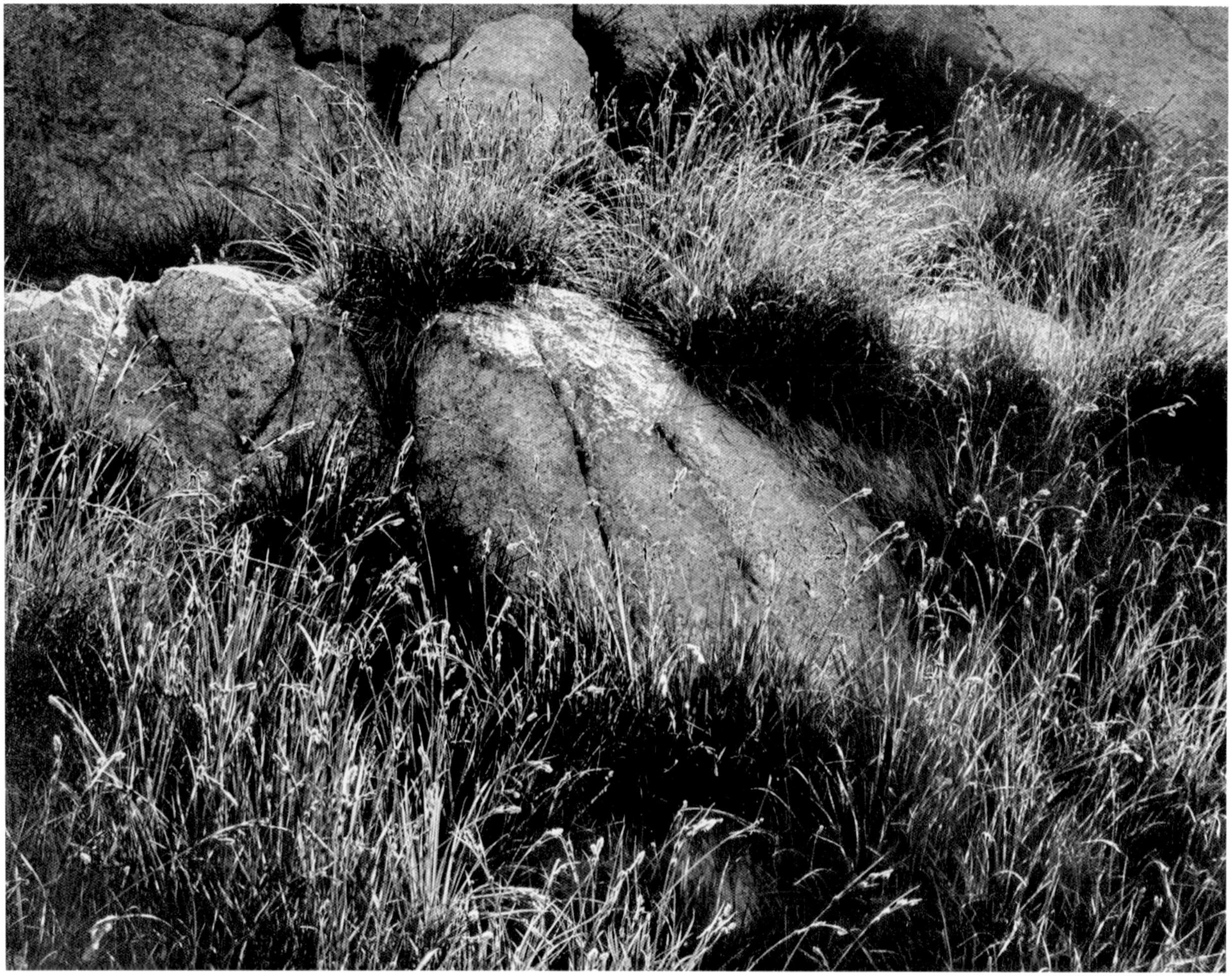

ROCKS AND GRASS, KINGS CANYON NATIONAL PARK, CALIFORNIA, C. 1930

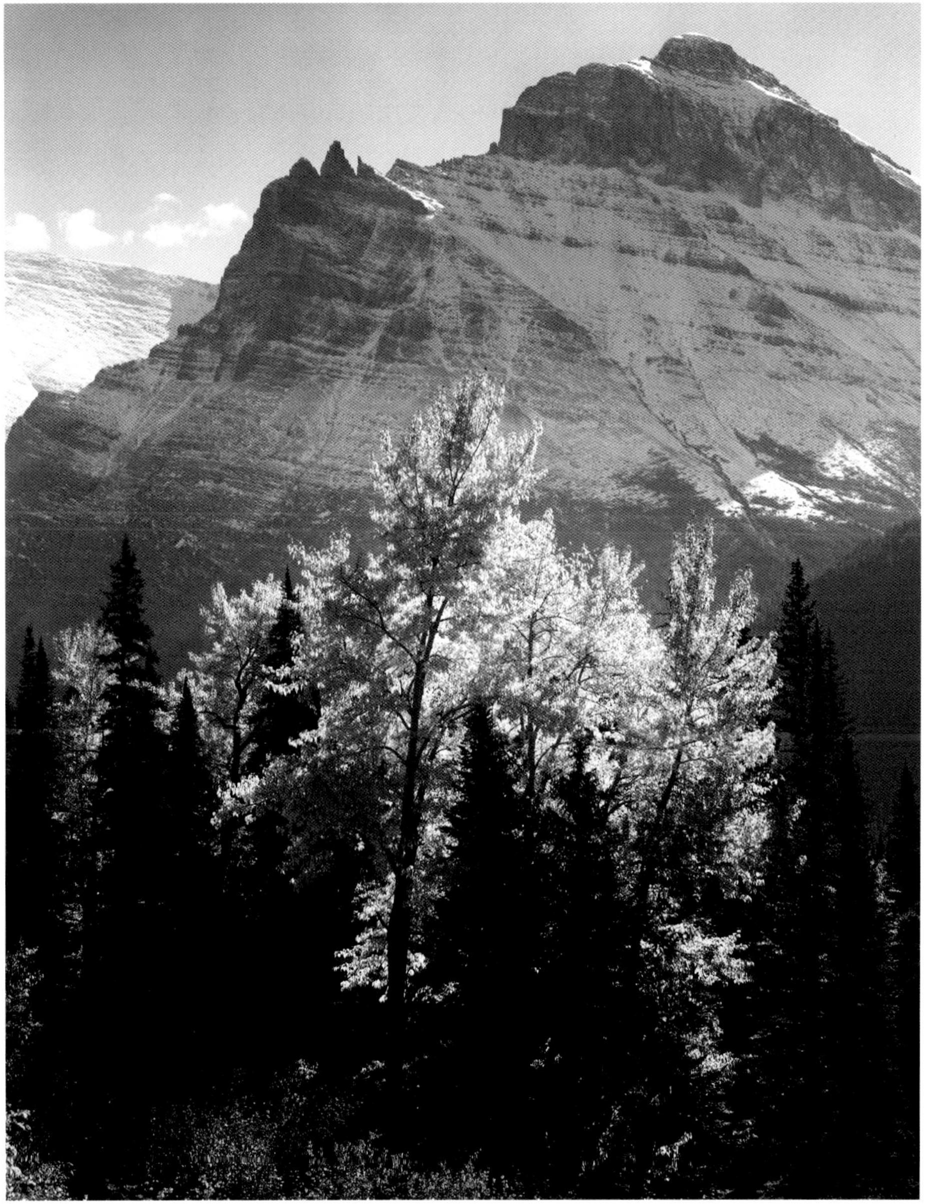

GOING-TO-THE-SUN MOUNTAIN, GLACIER NATIONAL PARK, MONTANA, 1948

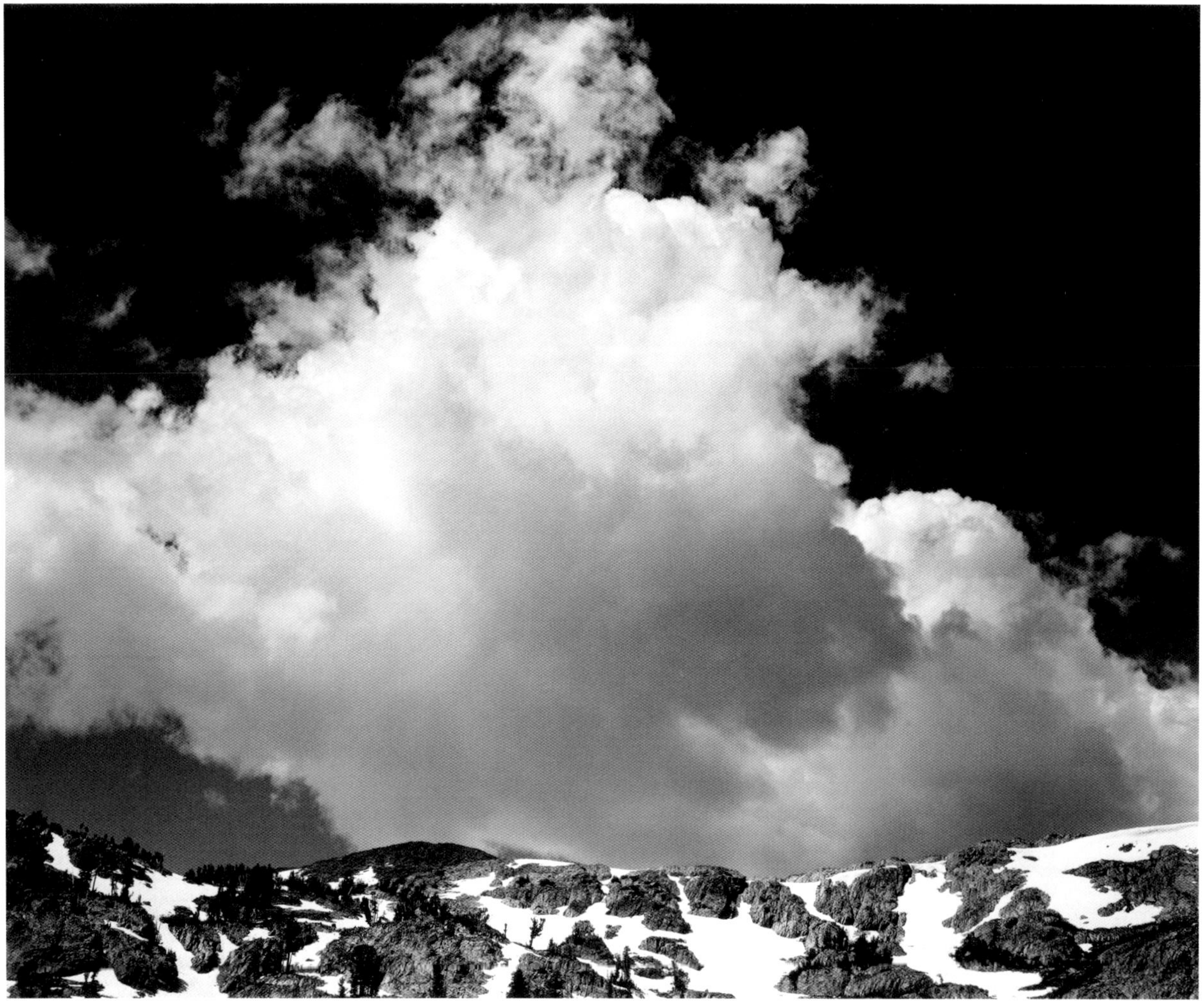

CLOUDS NEAR TIOGA PASS, YOSEMITE NATIONAL PARK, CALIFORNIA, C. 1940

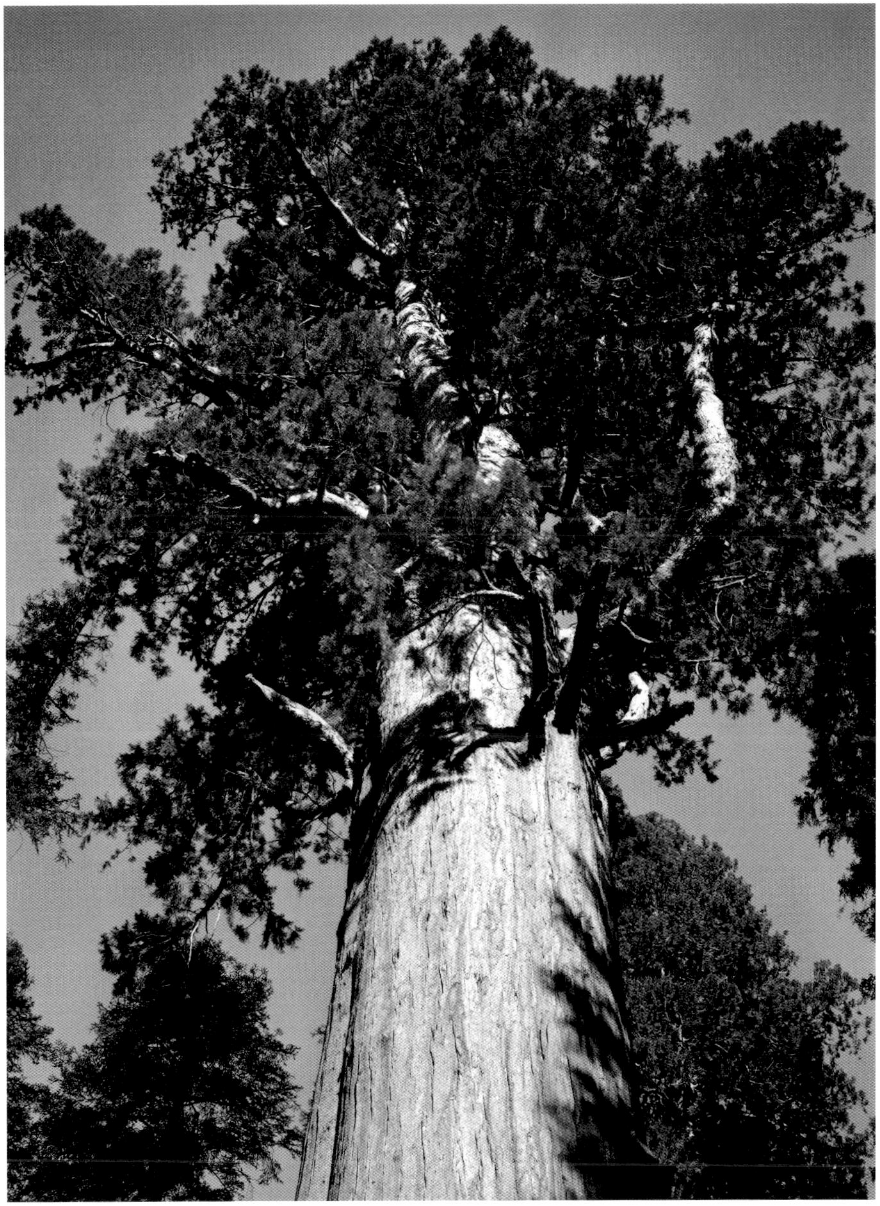

GENERAL SHERMAN TREE, SEQUOIA NATIONAL PARK, CALIFORNIA, 1938

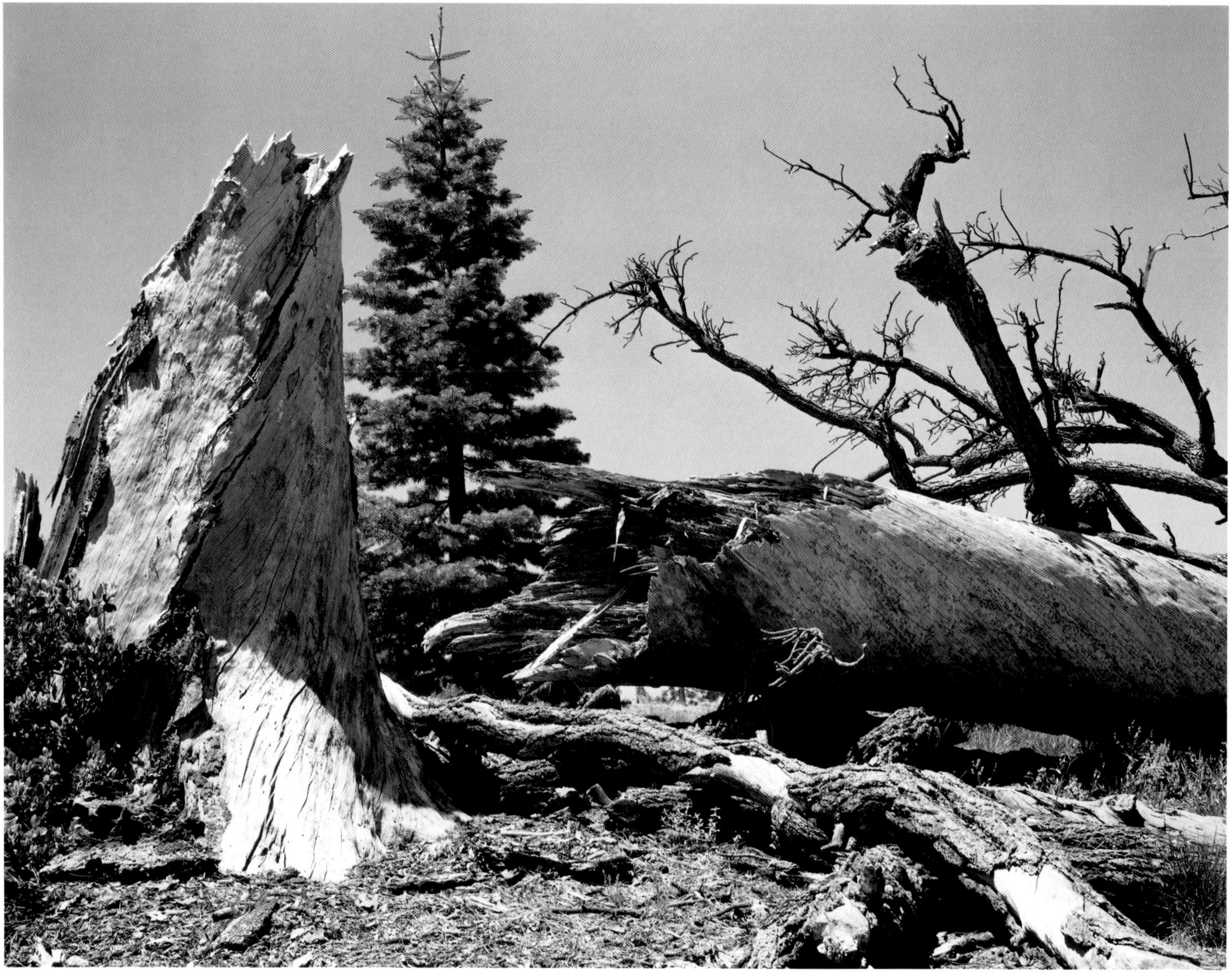

FALLEN TREE NEAR SENTINEL DOME, YOSEMITE NATIONAL PARK, CALIFORNIA, C. 1940

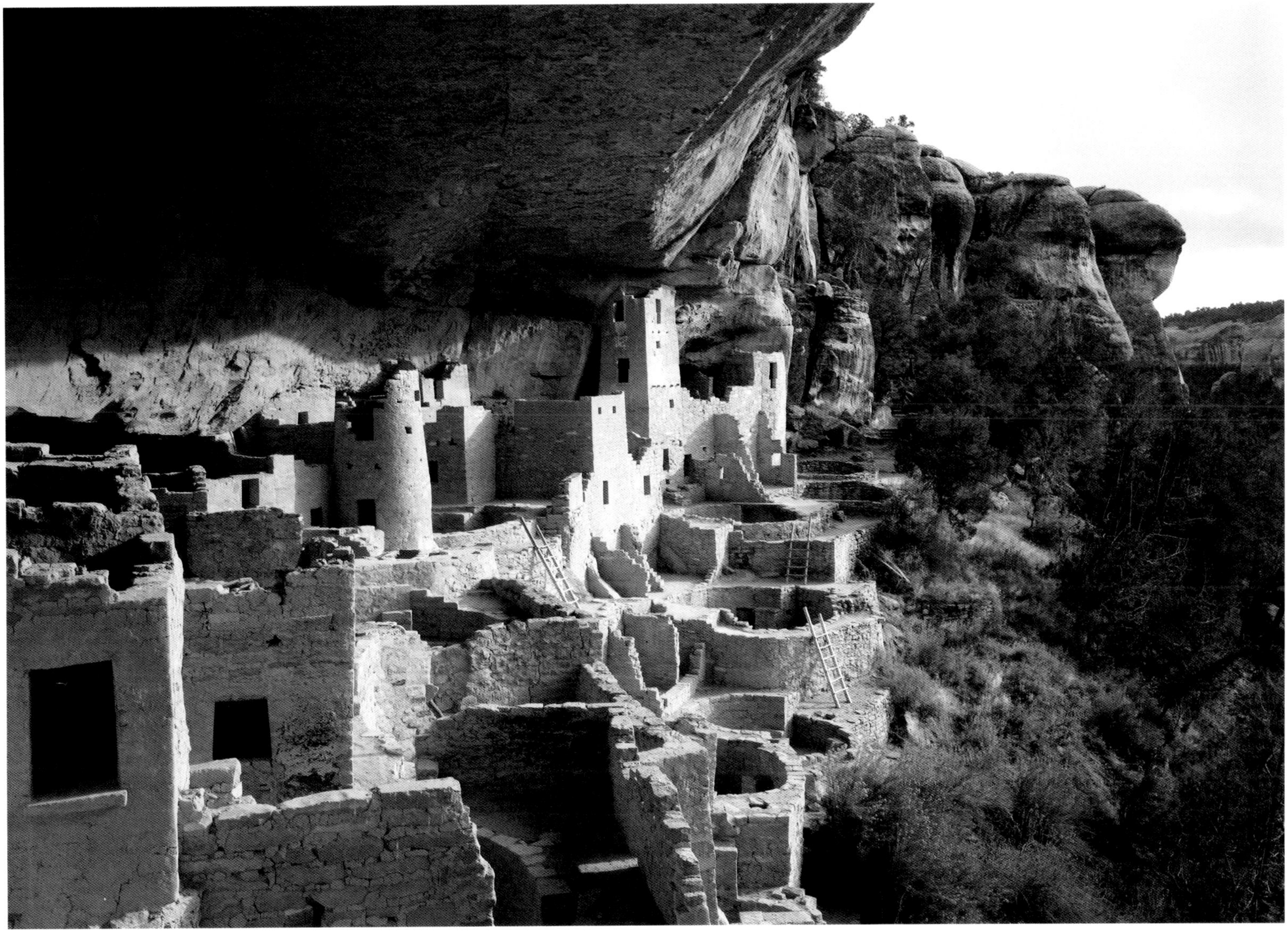

CLIFF PALACE RUIN, MESA VERDE NATIONAL PARK, COLORADO, 1942

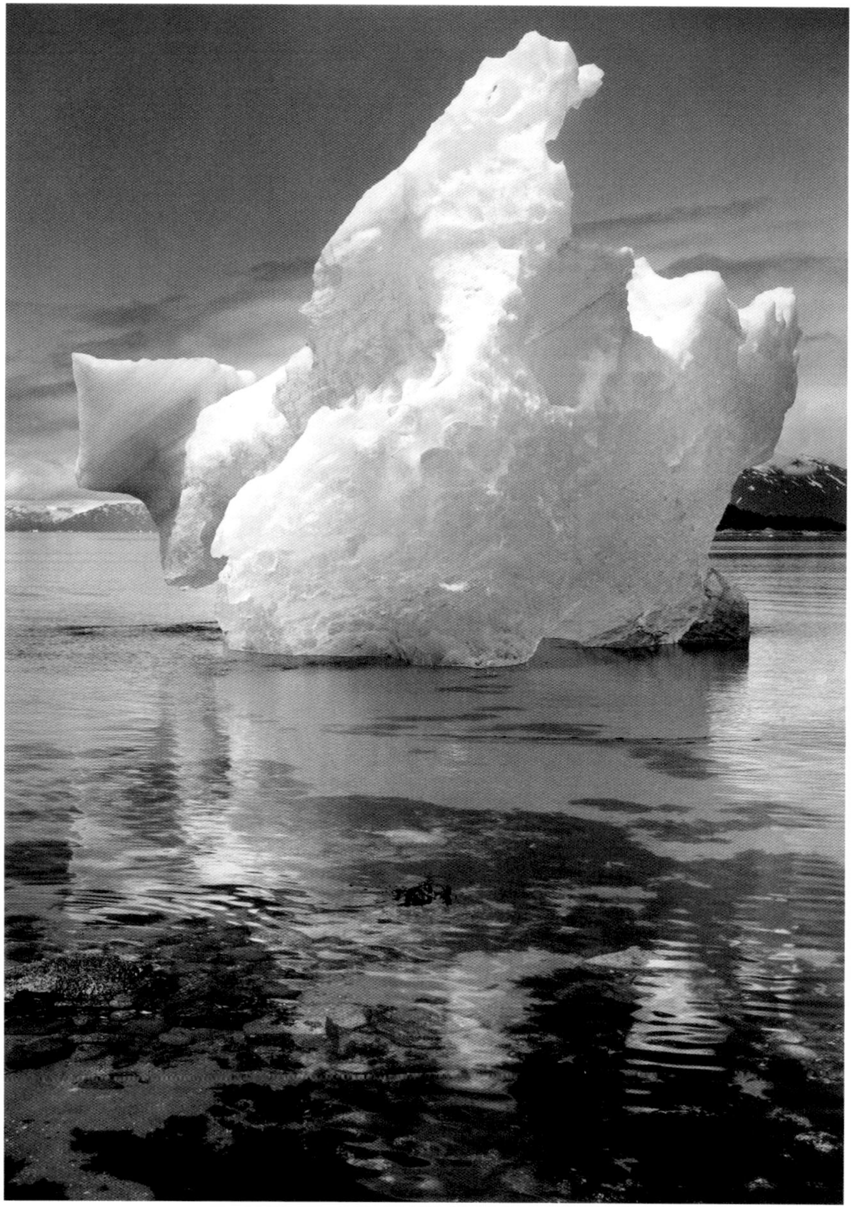

GROUNDED ICEBERG, GLACIER BAY NATIONAL PARK, ALASKA, 1948

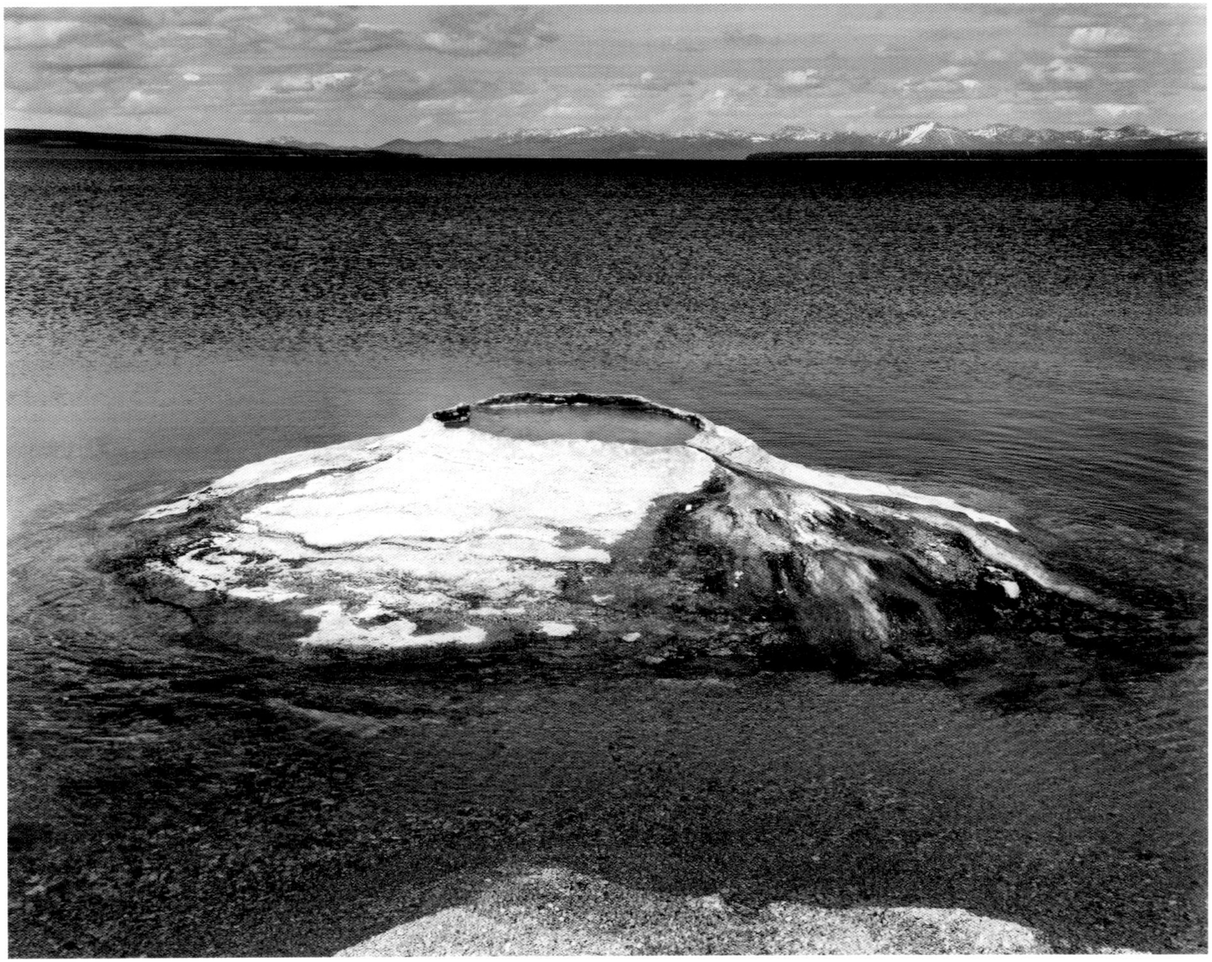

FISHING CONE, YELLOWSTONE NATIONAL PARK, WYOMING, 1942

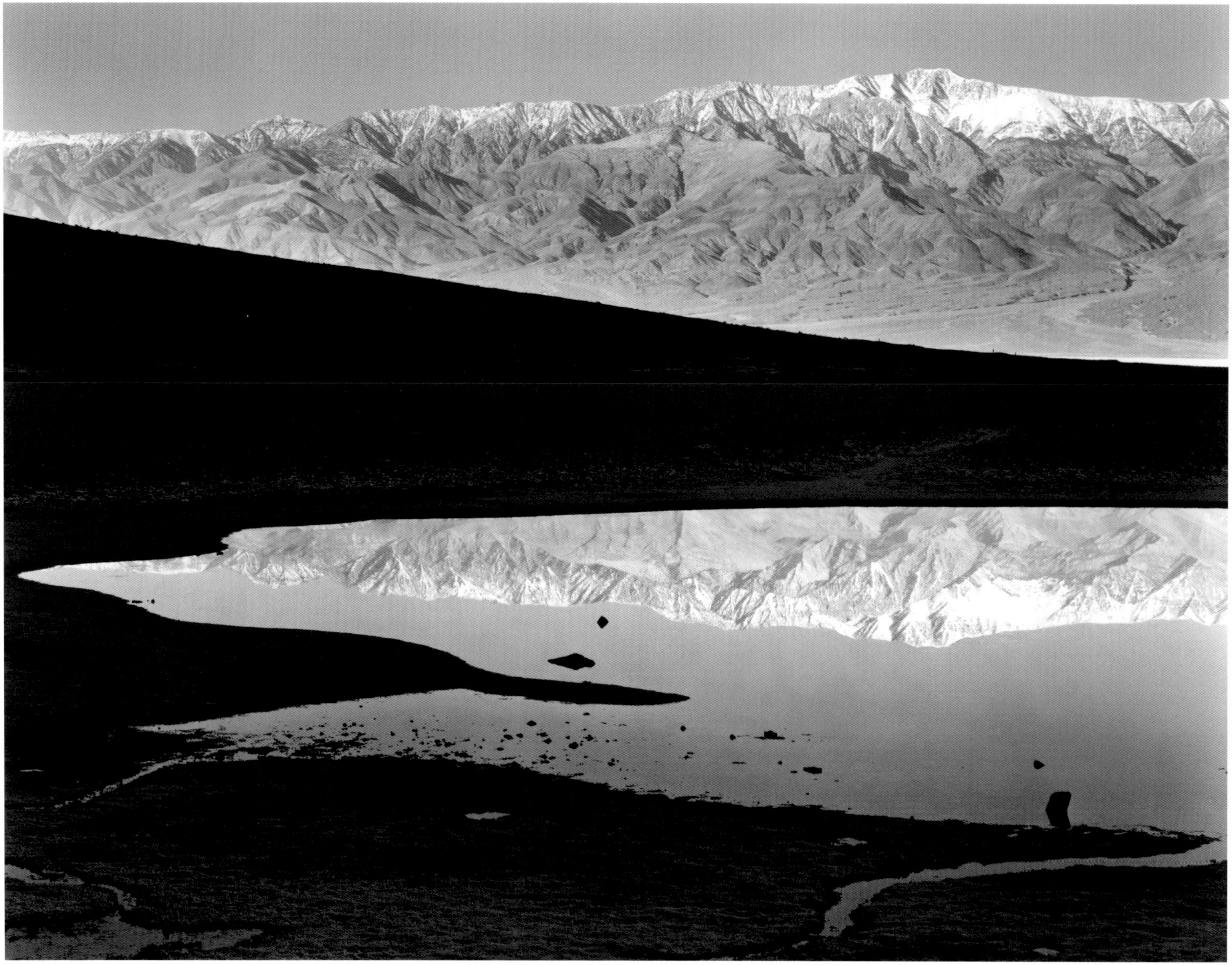

SUNRISE, BADWATER, DEATH VALLEY NATIONAL PARK, CALIFORNIA, 1948

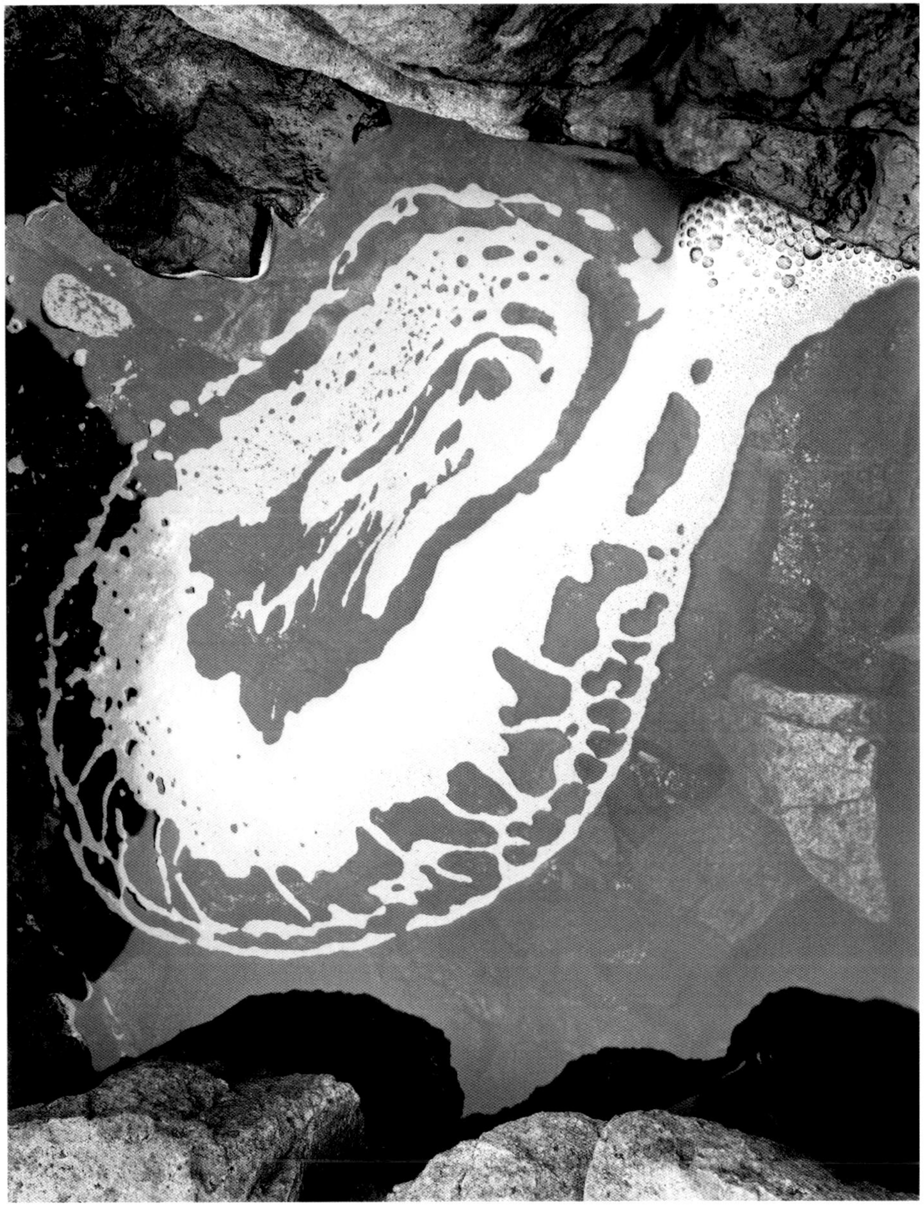

TIDE POOL, ACADIA NATIONAL PARK, MAINE, C. 1948

On the Sierra Club's annual High Trip in the summer of 1930, Ansel kept a small booklet titled "Record of Exposures, Sierra Club 1930," in which he recorded every negative he made on the trip. The entry for this image appears in his distinctive hand on the page for July 17. Made when Ansel was twenty-eight years old, this photograph exhibits characteristics of his mature work, with the isolation of a lone peak and the division of the composition into bands of light and dark.

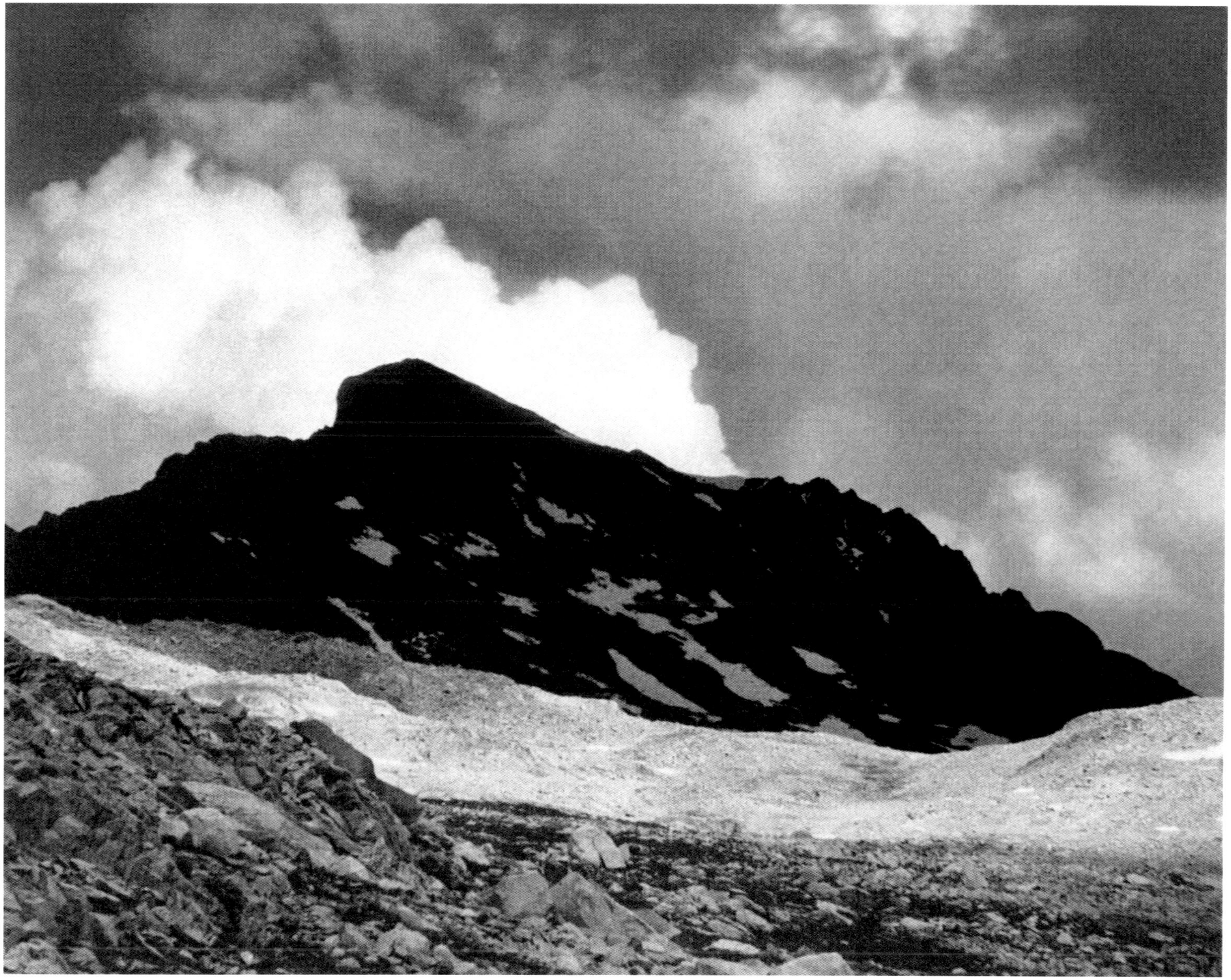

THE BLACK GIANT, MUIR PASS, KINGS CANYON NATIONAL PARK, CALIFORNIA, 1930

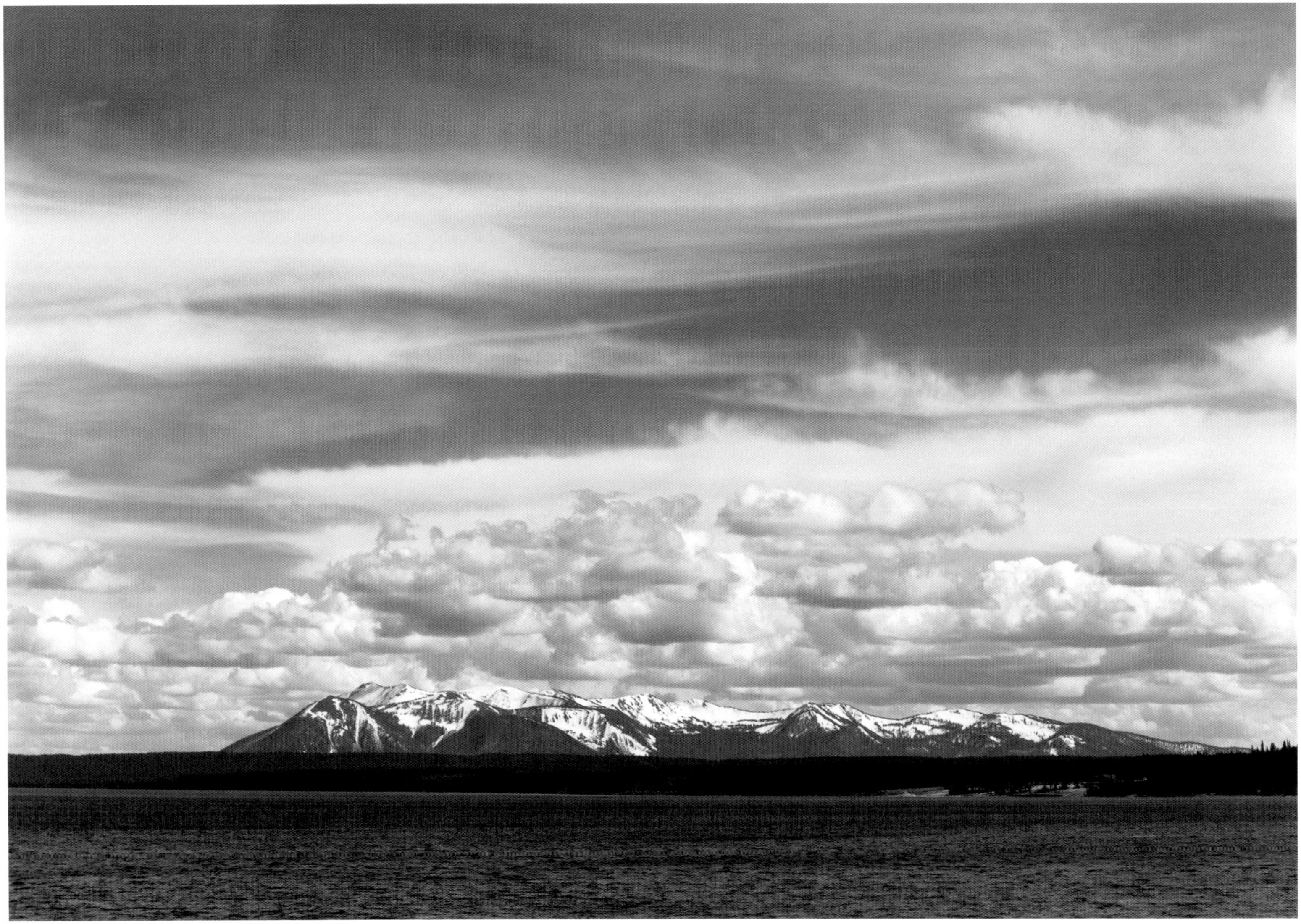

YELLOWSTONE LAKE, CLOUDS, YELLOWSTONE NATIONAL PARK, WYOMING, 1942

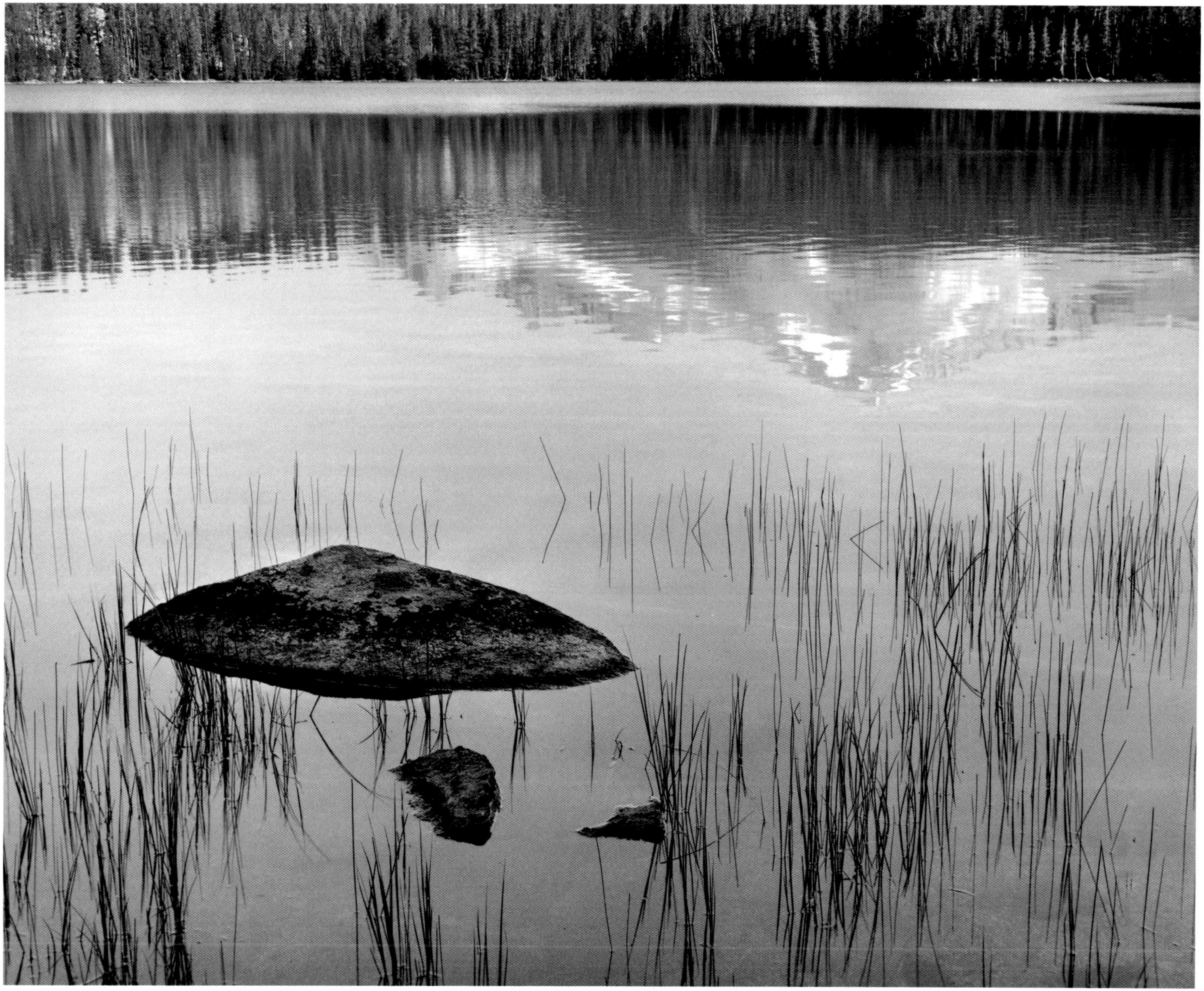

ROCK AND GRASS, MORAINE LAKE, SEQUOIA NATIONAL PARK, CALIFORNIA, 1936

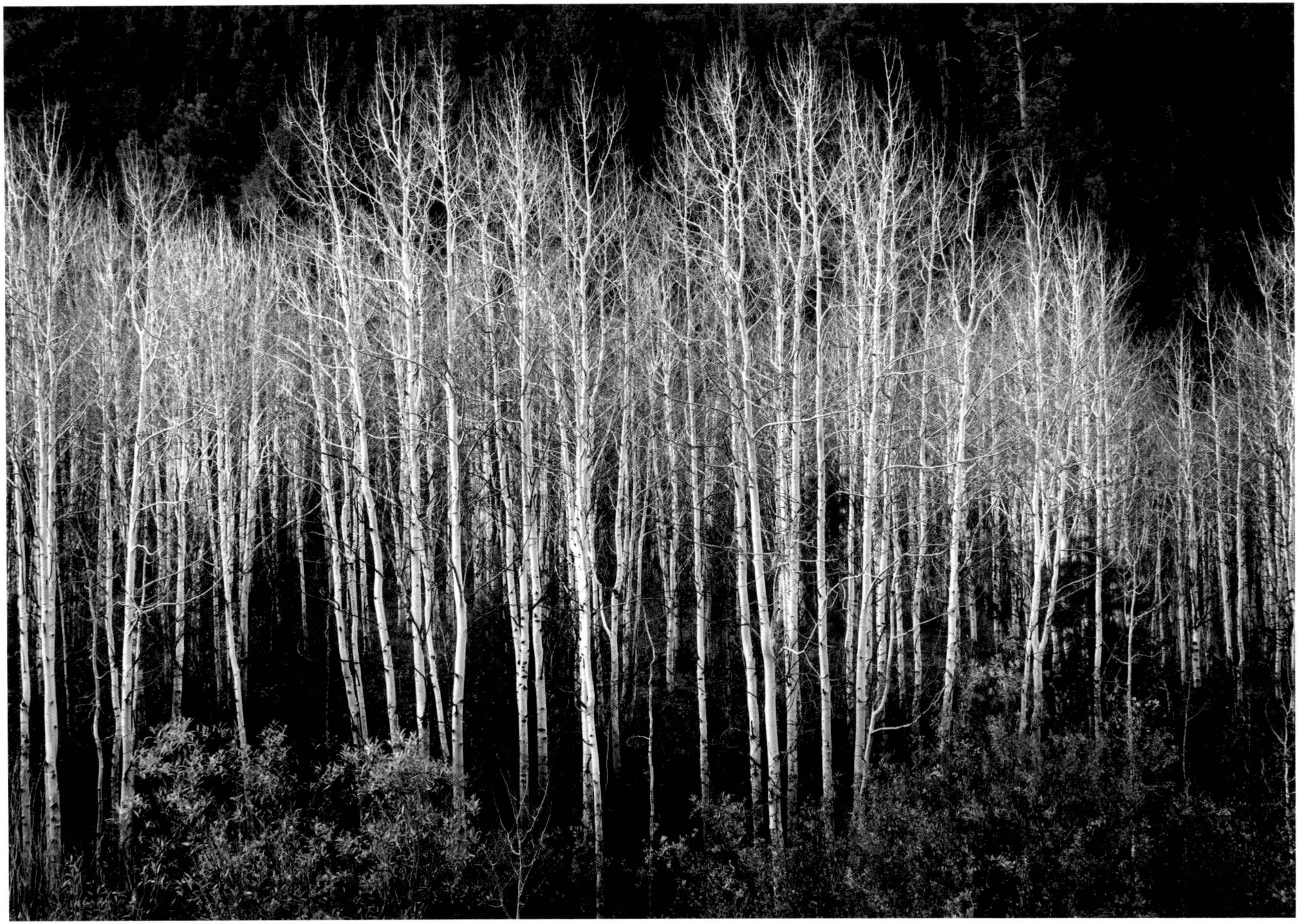

ASPENS, DAWN, AUTUMN, DOLORES RIVER CANYON, COLORADO, 1937

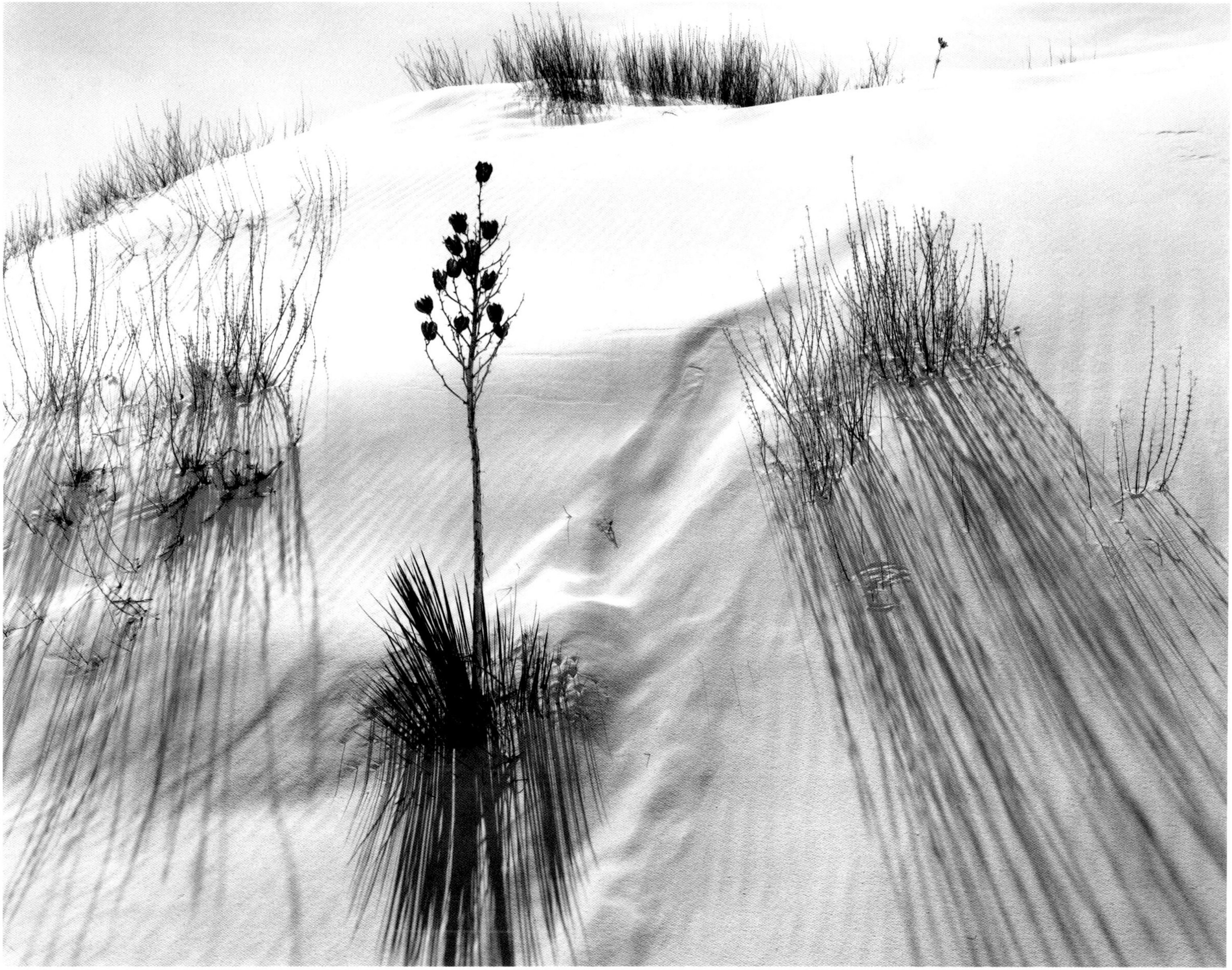

DUNE, WHITE SANDS NATIONAL MONUMENT, NEW MEXICO, 1948

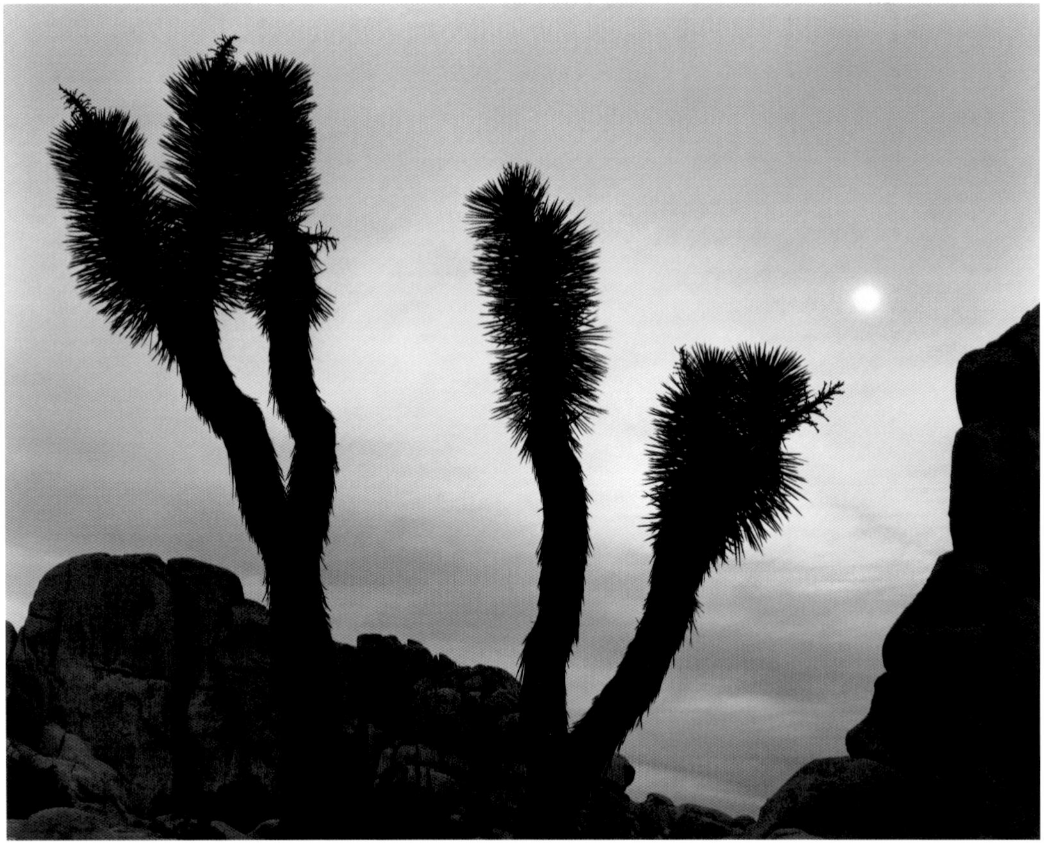

MOONRISE, JOSHUA TREE NATIONAL PARK, CALIFORNIA, 1948

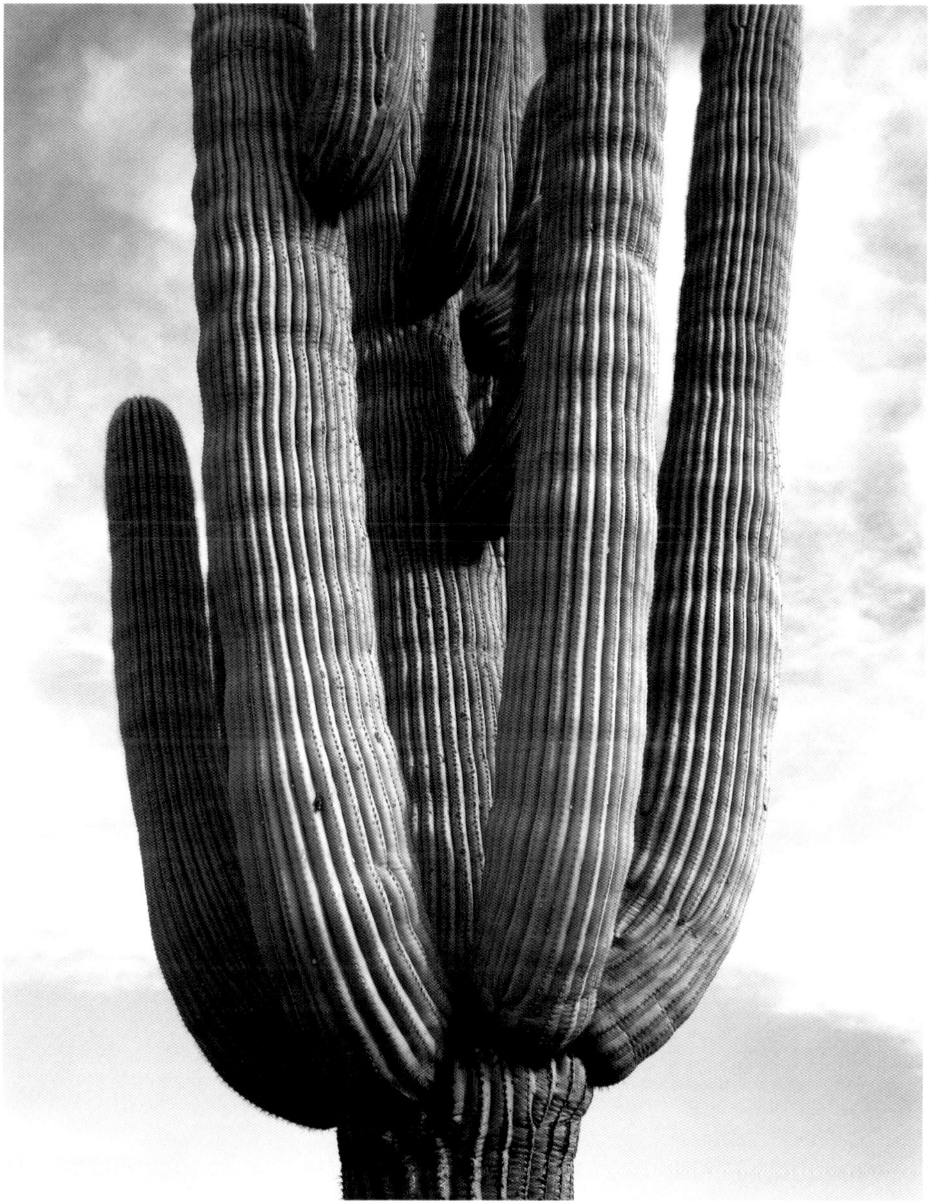

SAGUARO NATIONAL PARK, ARIZONA, 1942

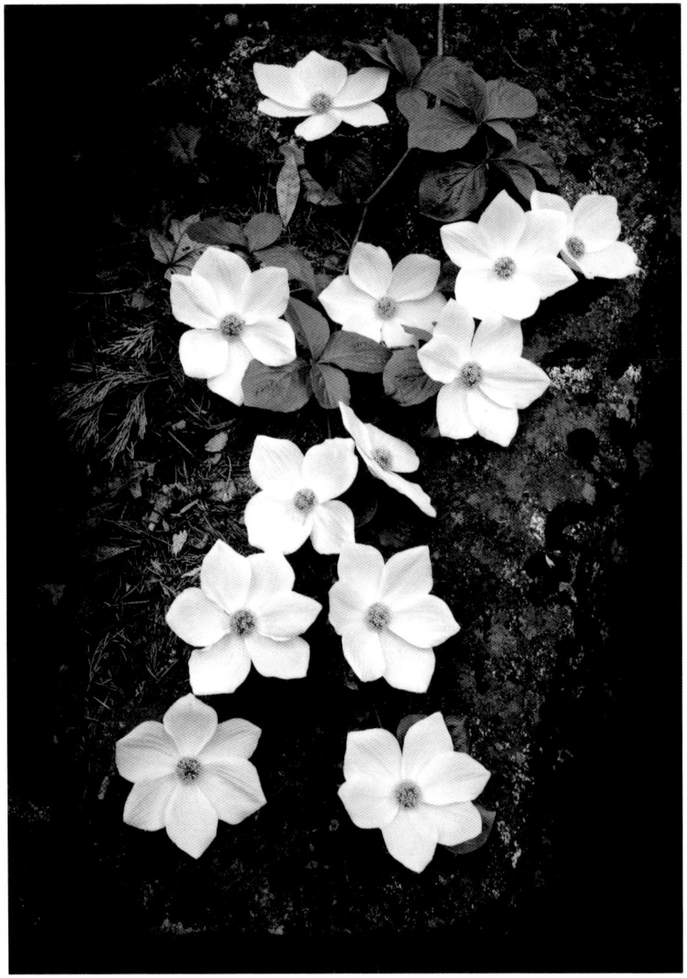

DOGWOOD, YOSEMITE NATIONAL PARK, CALIFORNIA, C. 1938

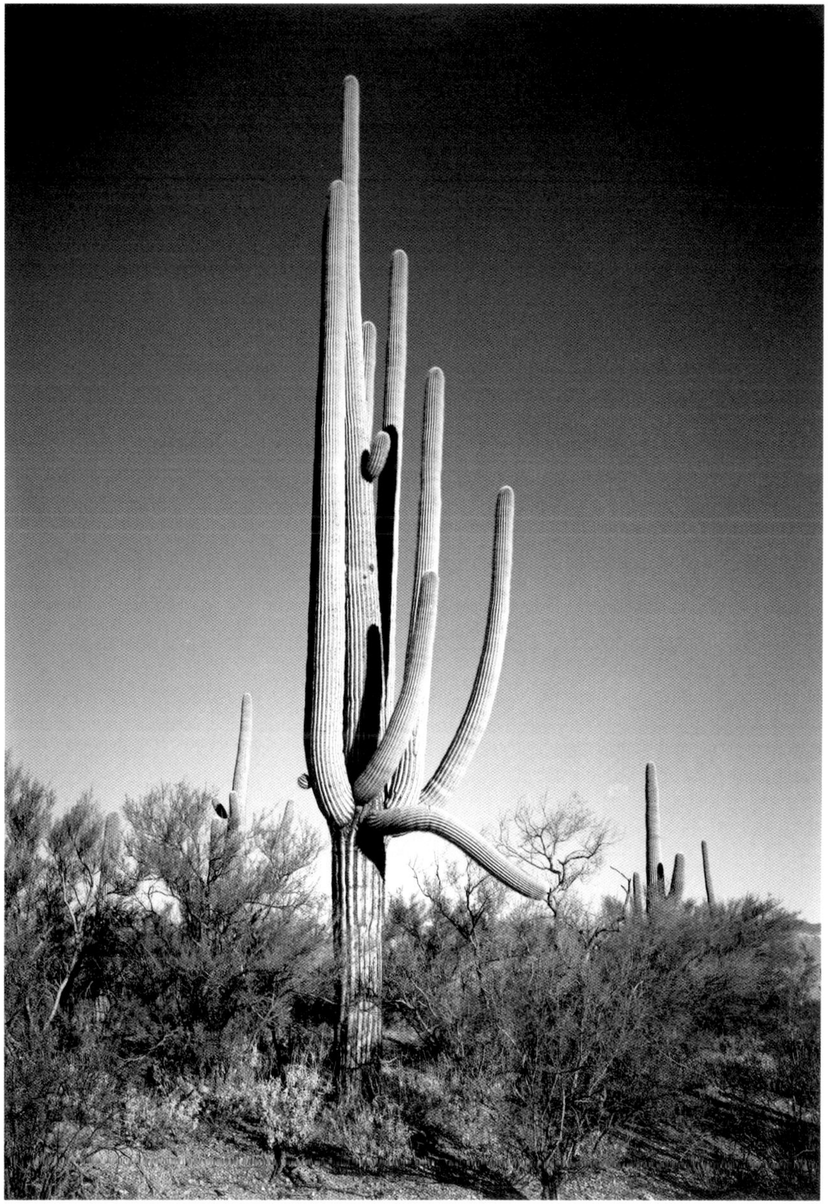

SAGUARO NATIONAL PARK, ARIZONA, 1942

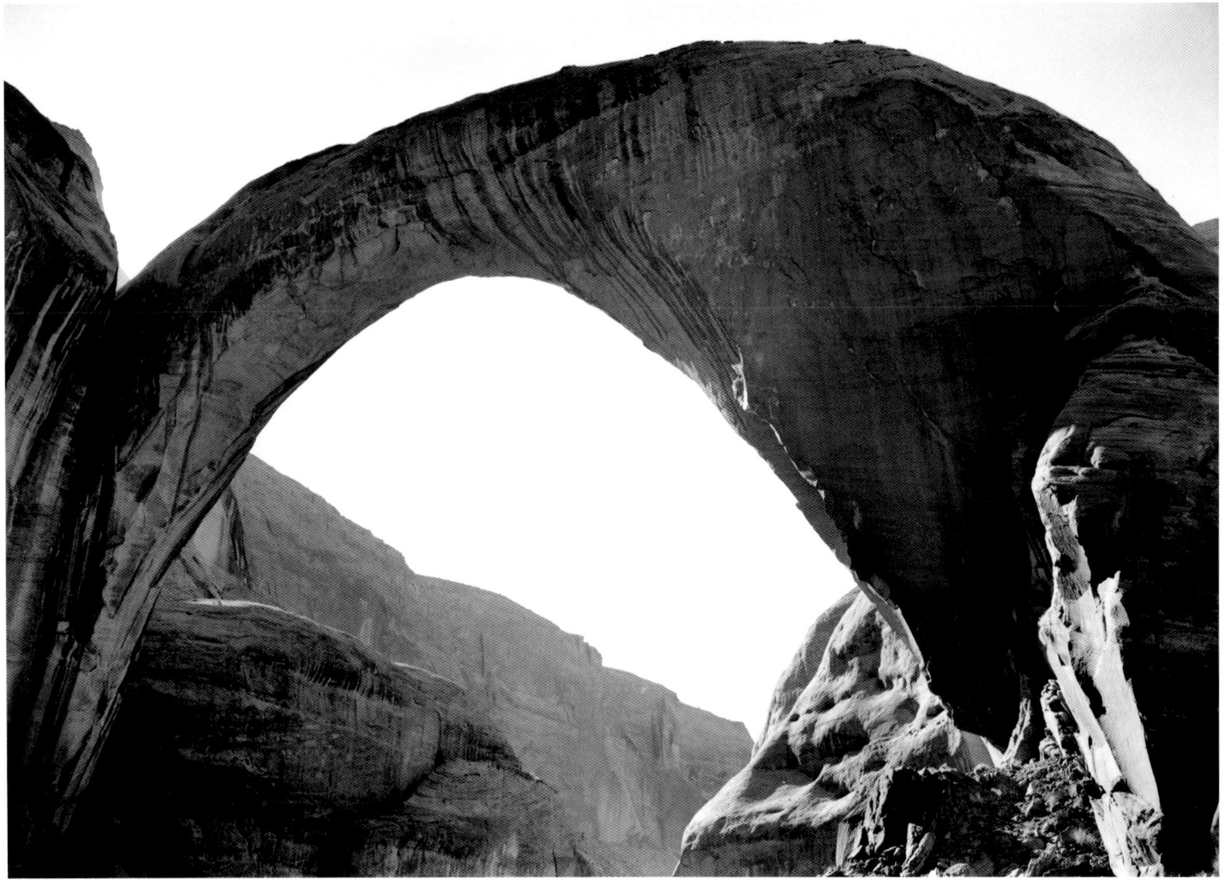

RAINBOW BRIDGE NATIONAL MONUMENT, UTAH, C. 1947

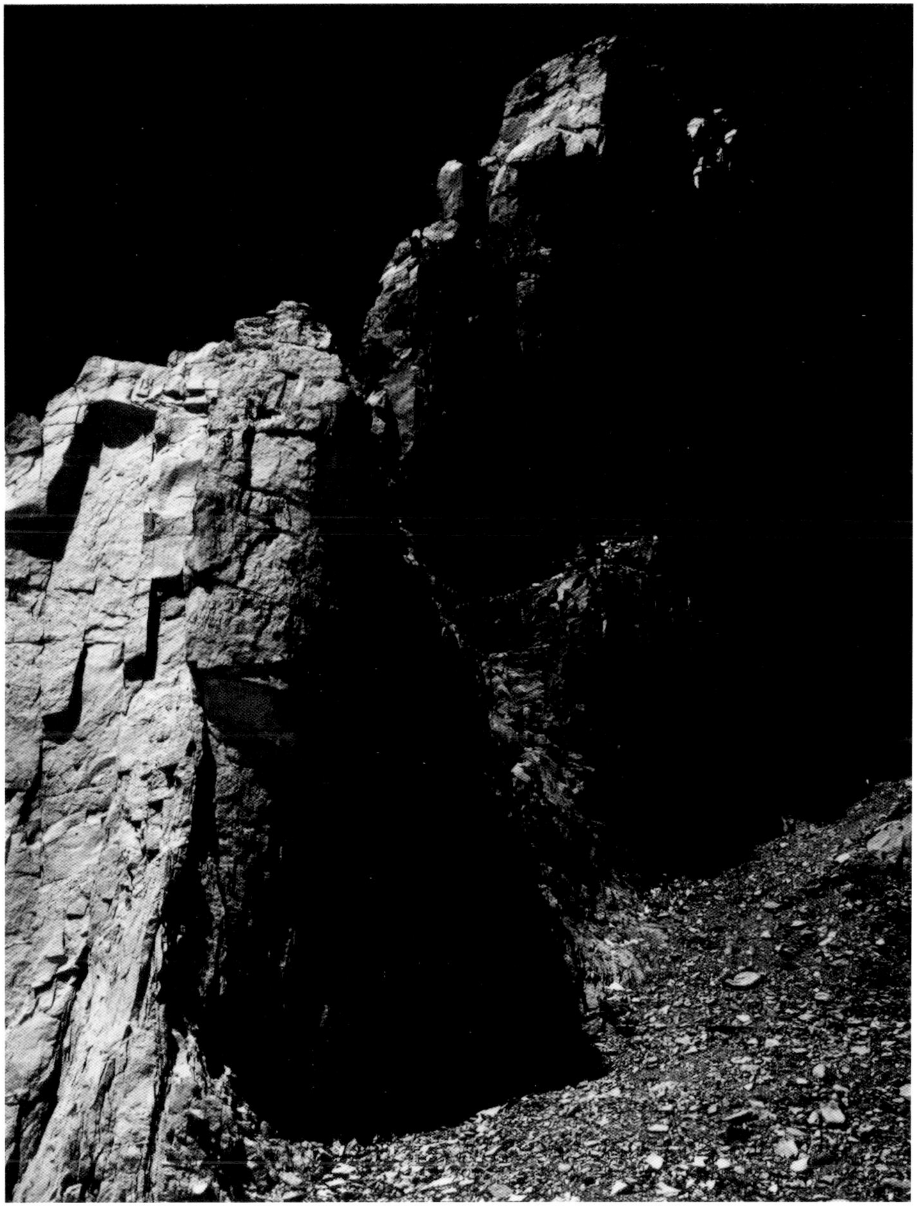

GRANITE RIDGE, MILESTONE MOUNTAIN, SEQUOIA NATIONAL PARK, CALIFORNIA, 1927

These images are known only through three unsigned proof prints in Ansel's archive at the Center for Creative Photography in Tucson, Arizona. There is no record of Ansel exhibiting or publishing any of the images. His only other known sequence includes five photographs of surf on the California coast (see *Ansel Adams: 400 Photographs*, pages 252–3).

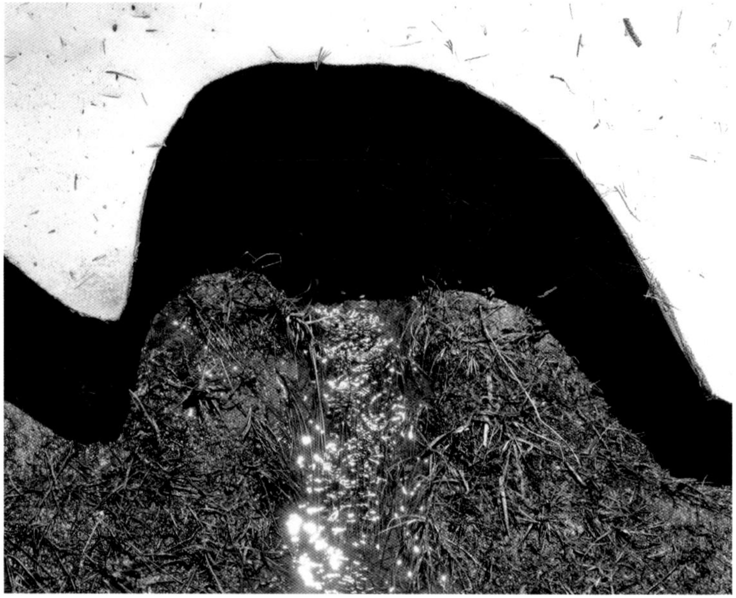

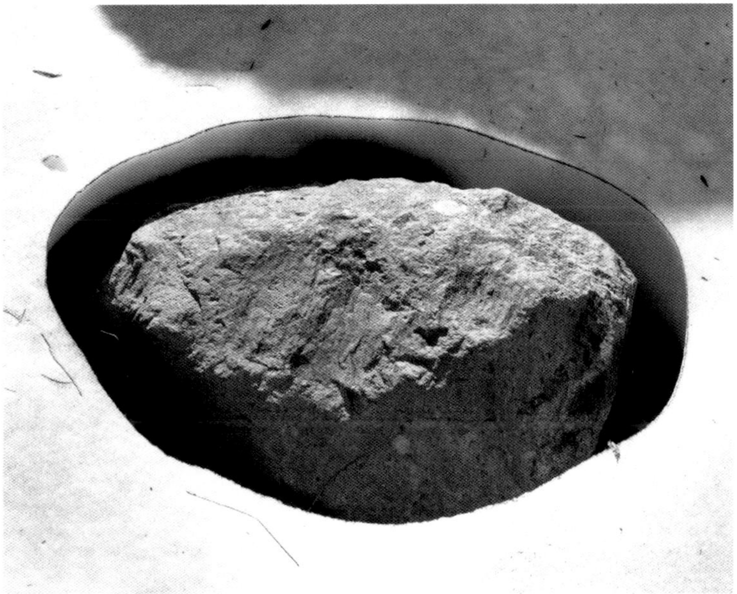

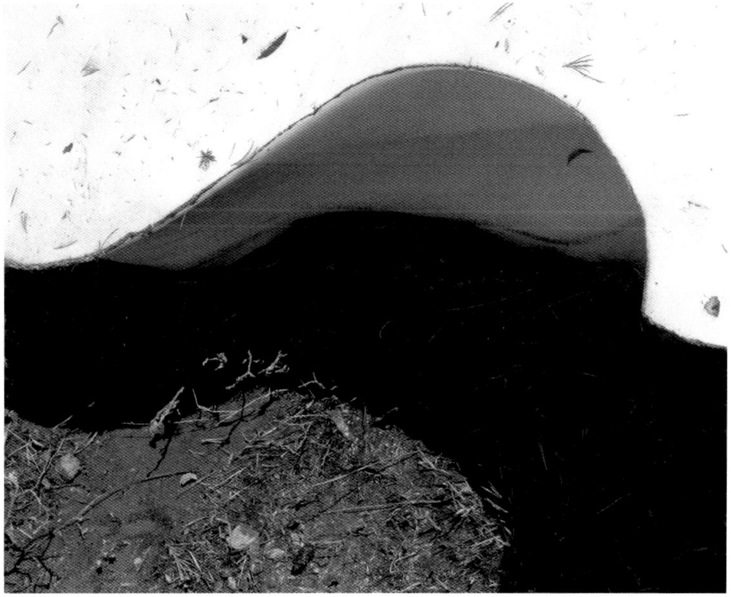

SNOW SEQUENCE, YOSEMITE NATIONAL PARK, CALIFORNIA, C. 1934

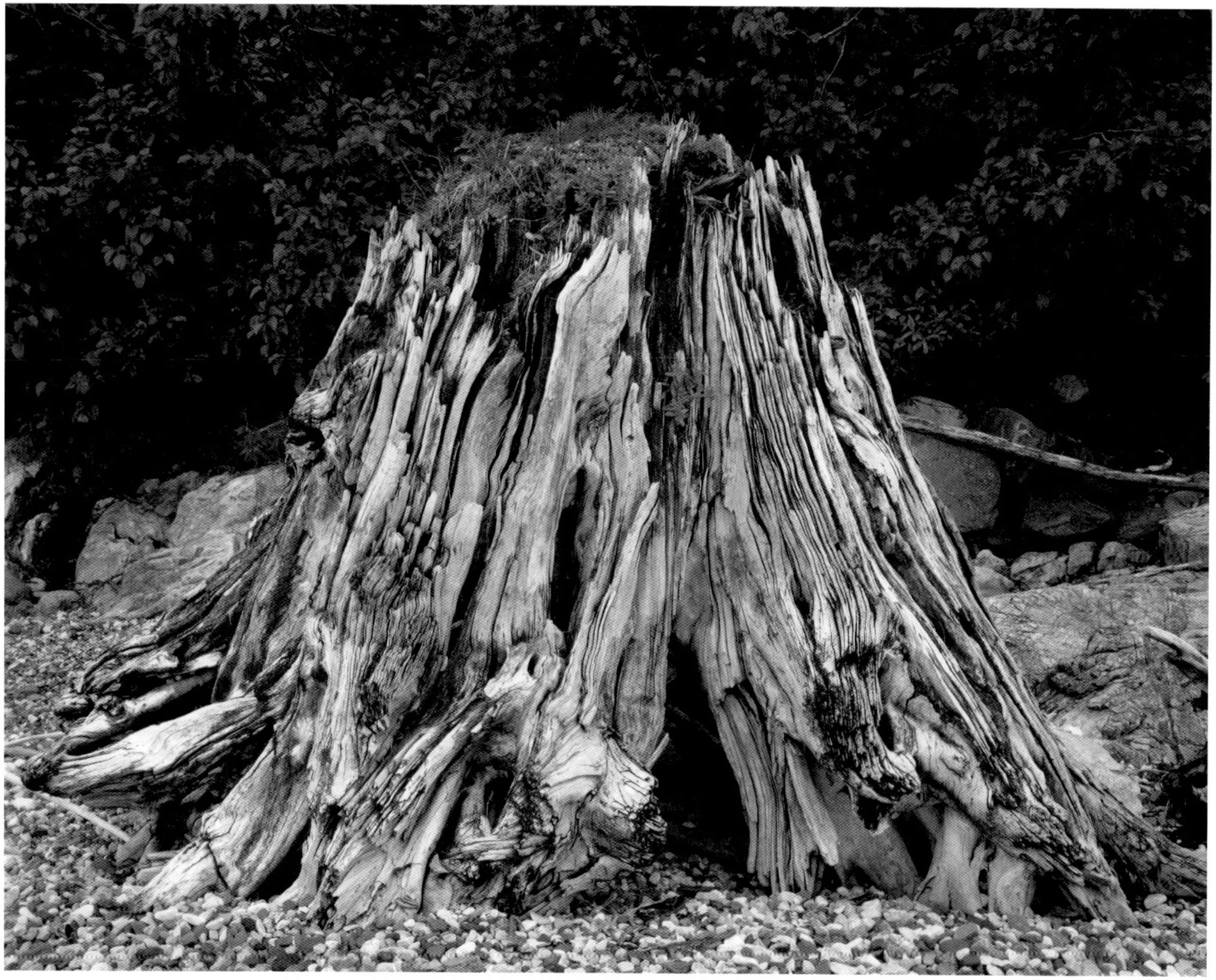

STUMP, INTERSTADIAL FOREST, GLACIER BAY NATIONAL PARK, ALASKA, C. 1948

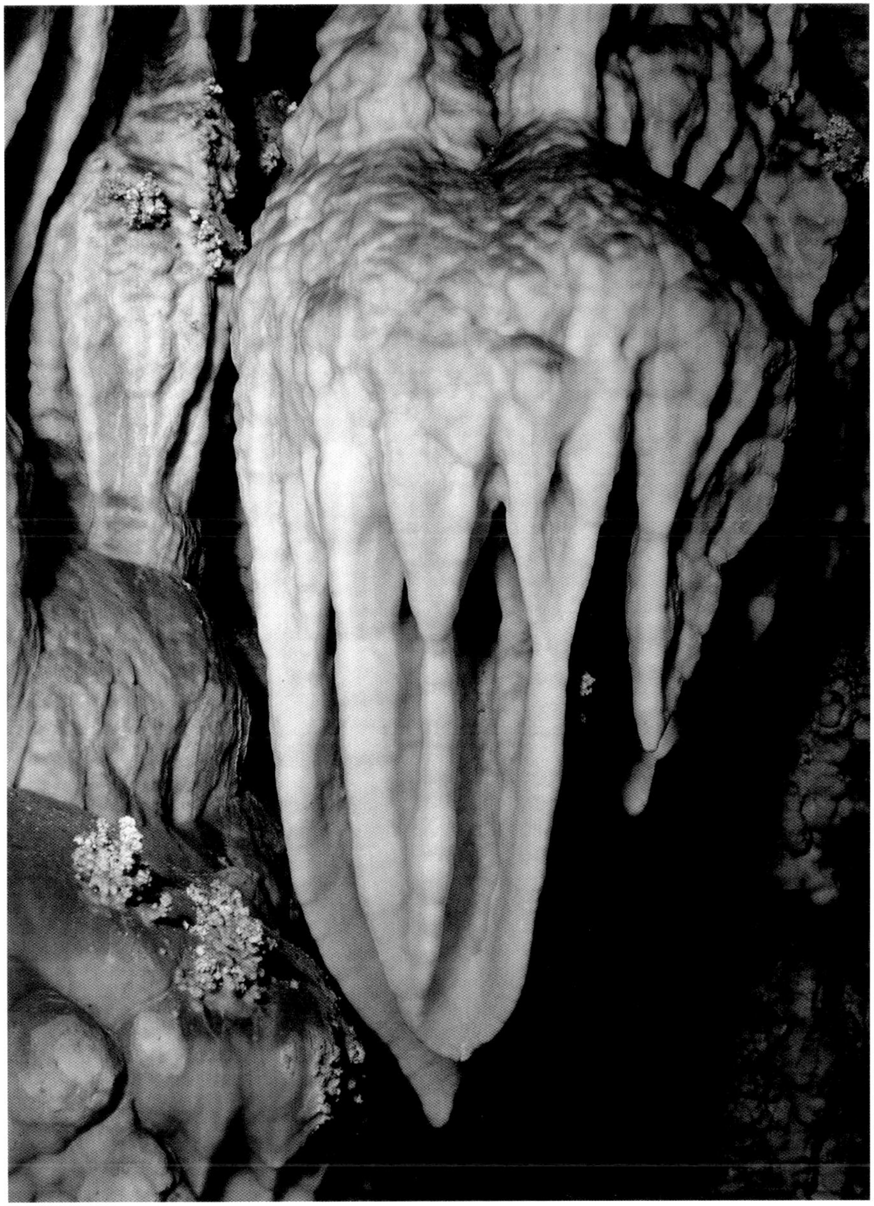

DETAIL, CARLSBAD CAVERNS NATIONAL PARK, NEW MEXICO, 1942

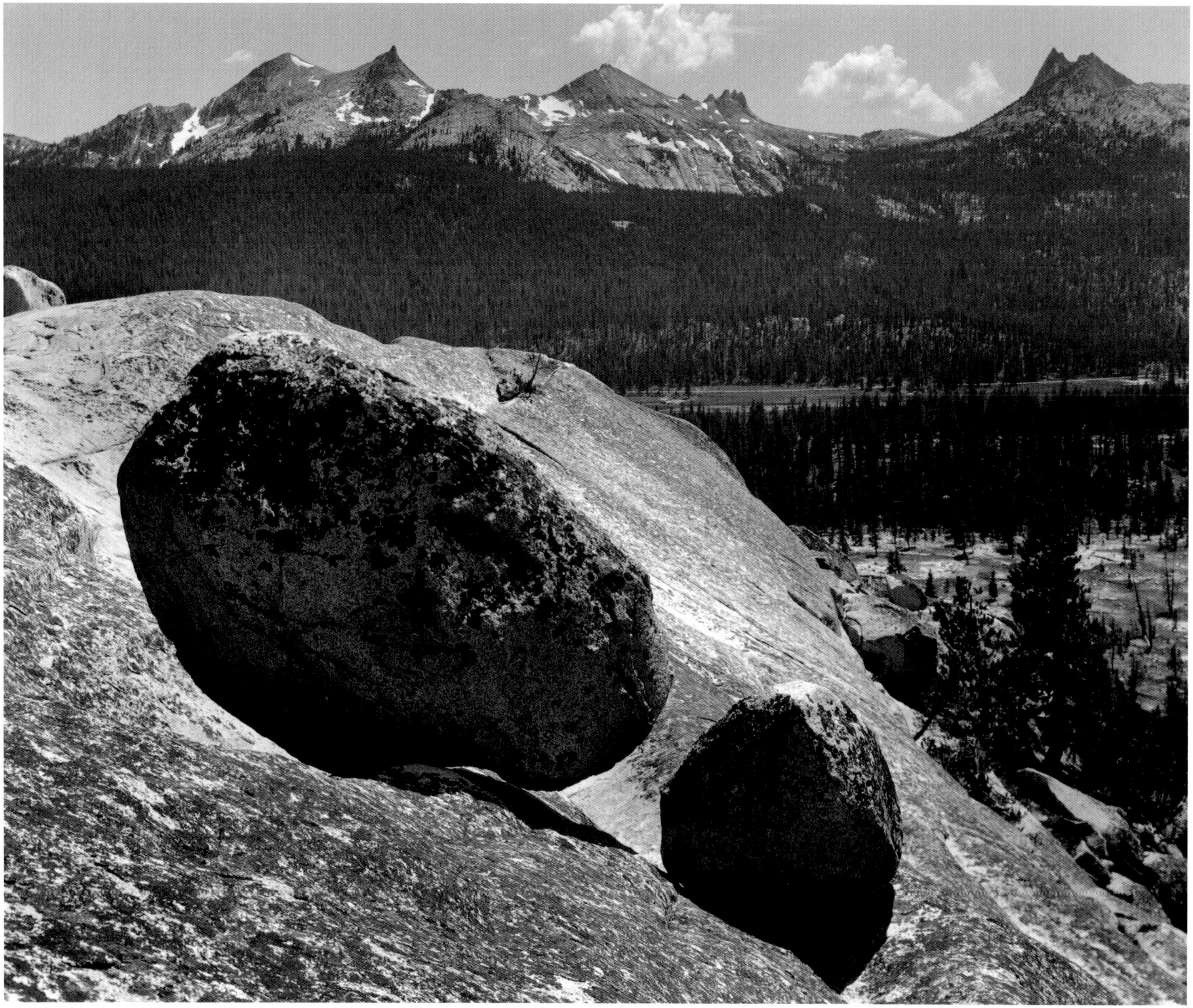

CATHEDRAL RANGE, ROCKS, SIERRA NEVADA, CALIFORNIA, C. 1945

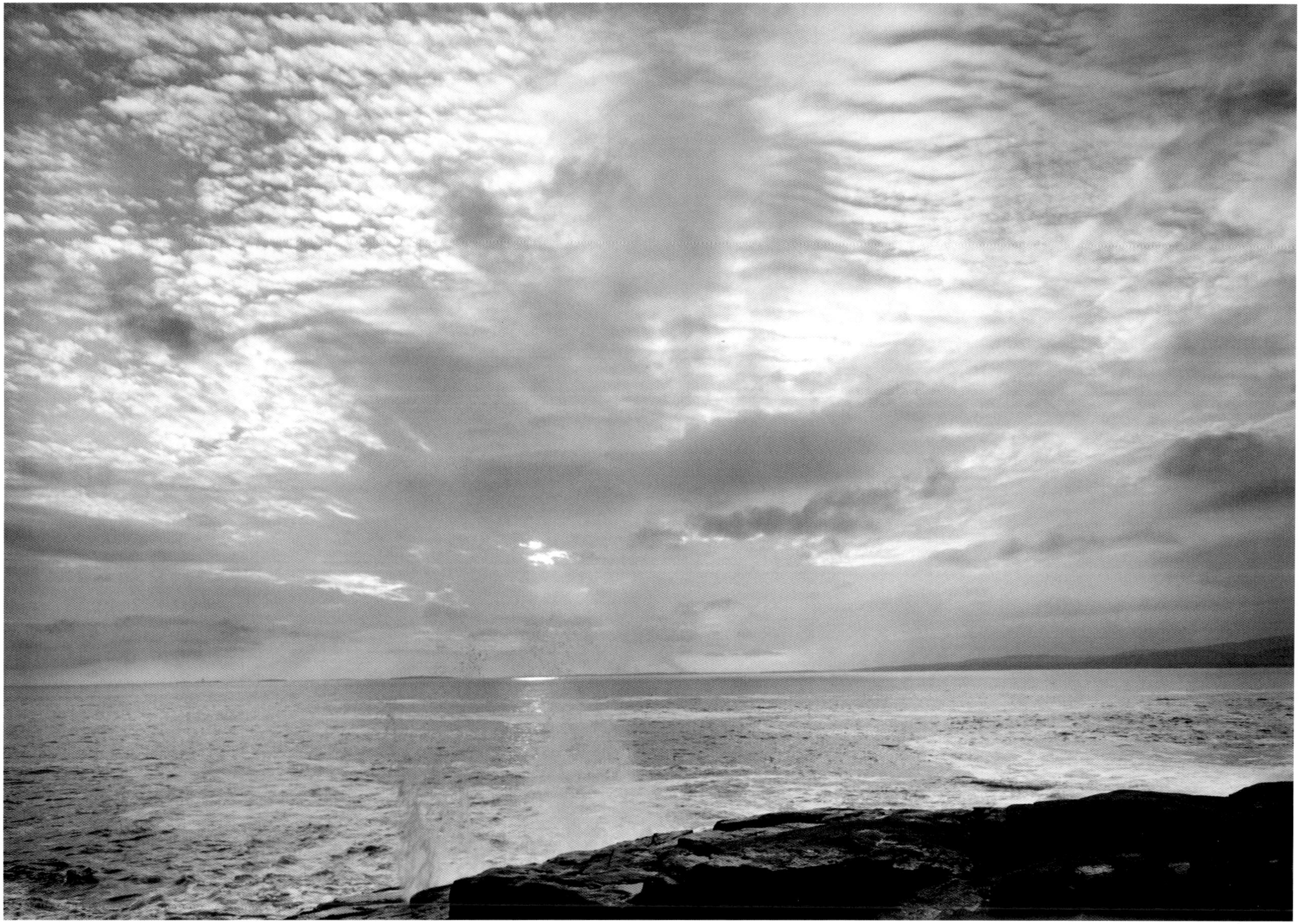

SCHOODIC POINT, SUNSET, ACADIA NATIONAL PARK, MAINE, 1948

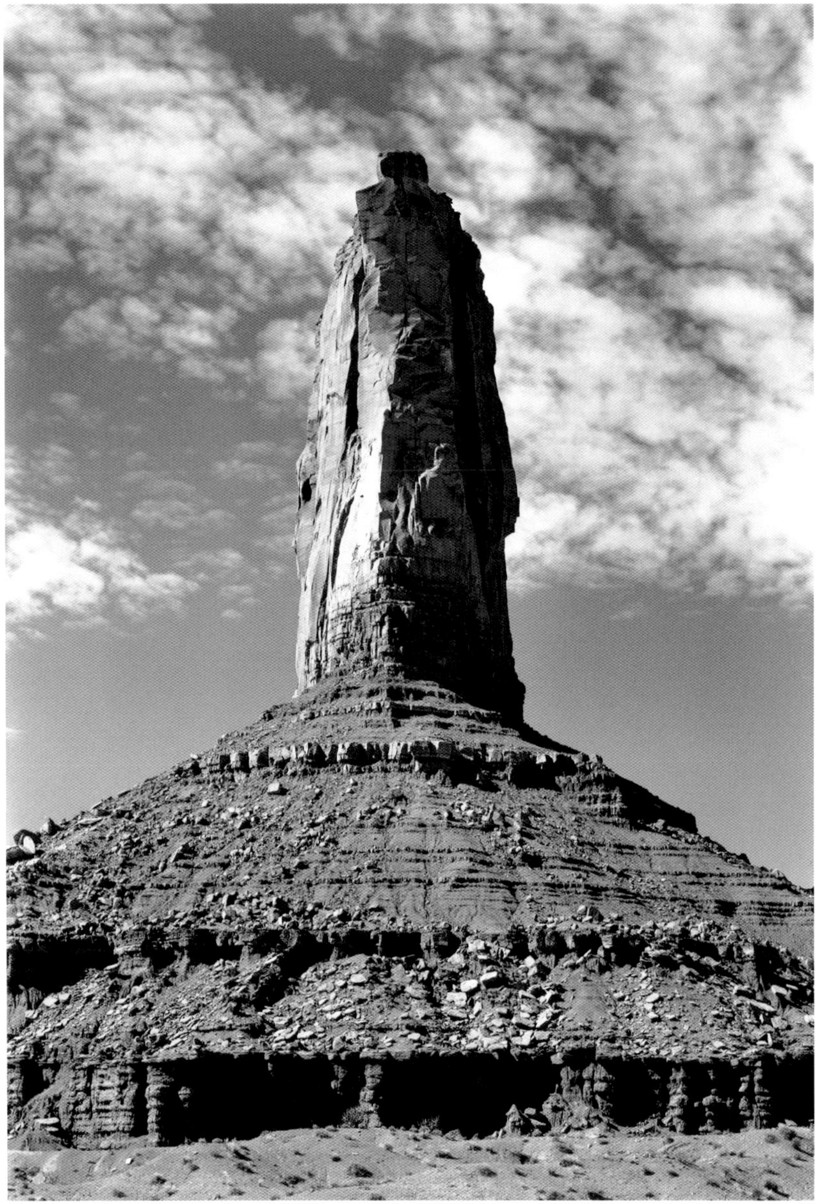

MONUMENT VALLEY NAVAJO TRIBAL PARK, ARIZONA, 1937

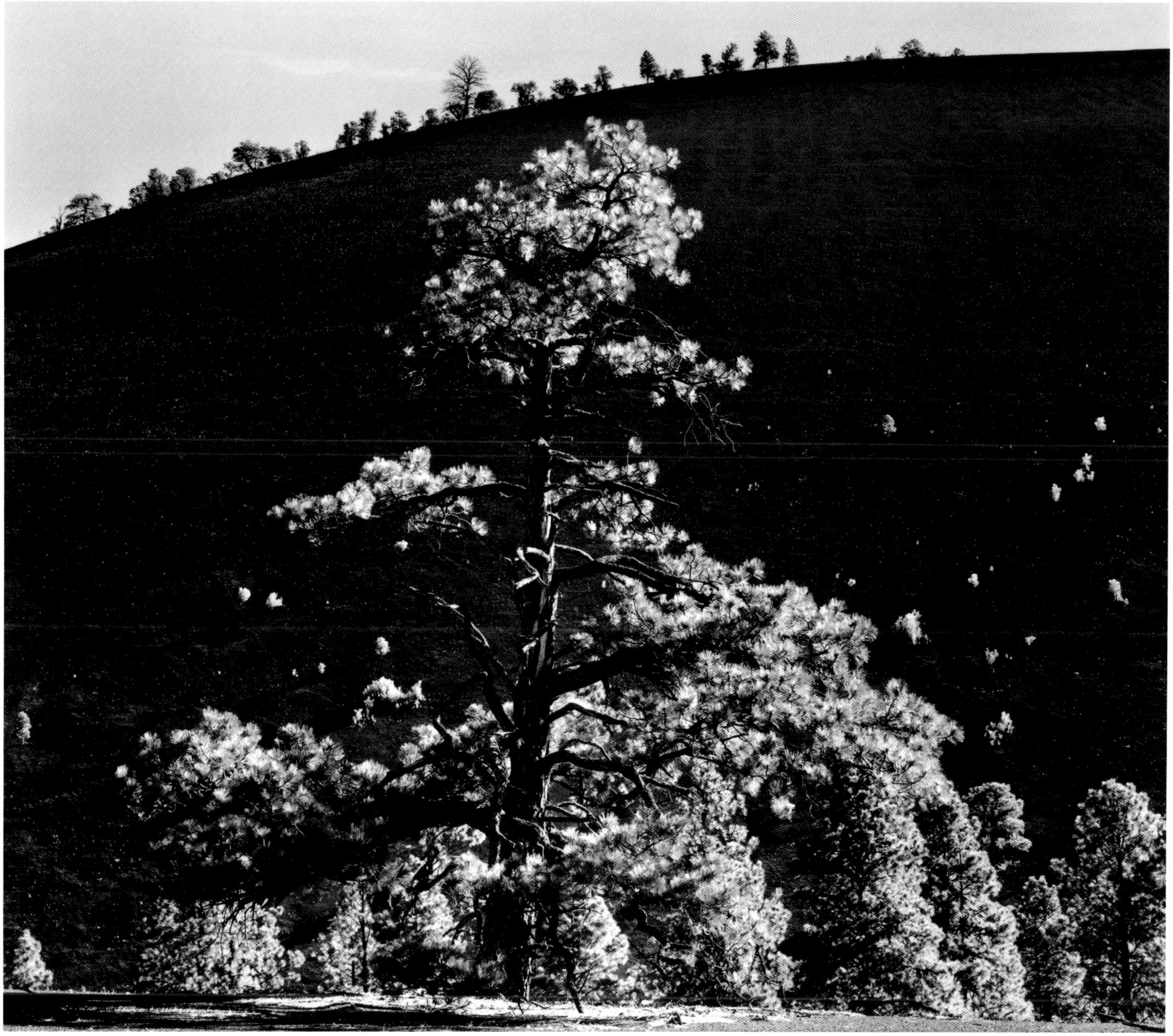

PUMICE SLOPE AND PINE TREES, SUNSET CRATER NATIONAL MONUMENT, ARIZONA, C. 1947

In the late 1970s, a gentleman wrote Ansel to place an order for a 16 x 20-inch print of this photograph. I replied to his request, he sent us his check, and I added the title to the list of images for Ansel to print. A few months later, after we had shipped the finished print, the buyer called to say that he was shocked that the photograph was not perfect. I inquired what was wrong, and he said that the image was not sharp, that some of the foliage on the trees was fuzzy, that he expected any photograph by Ansel Adams to be perfect, and that he wanted his money returned. I told him I would call him back and went to find Ansel, who laughed and explained that the photograph had been taken from a considerable distance, and that the wind had moved the foliage very slightly. I called the buyer to explain the circumstances and offered to return his money, but he decided to keep the photograph.

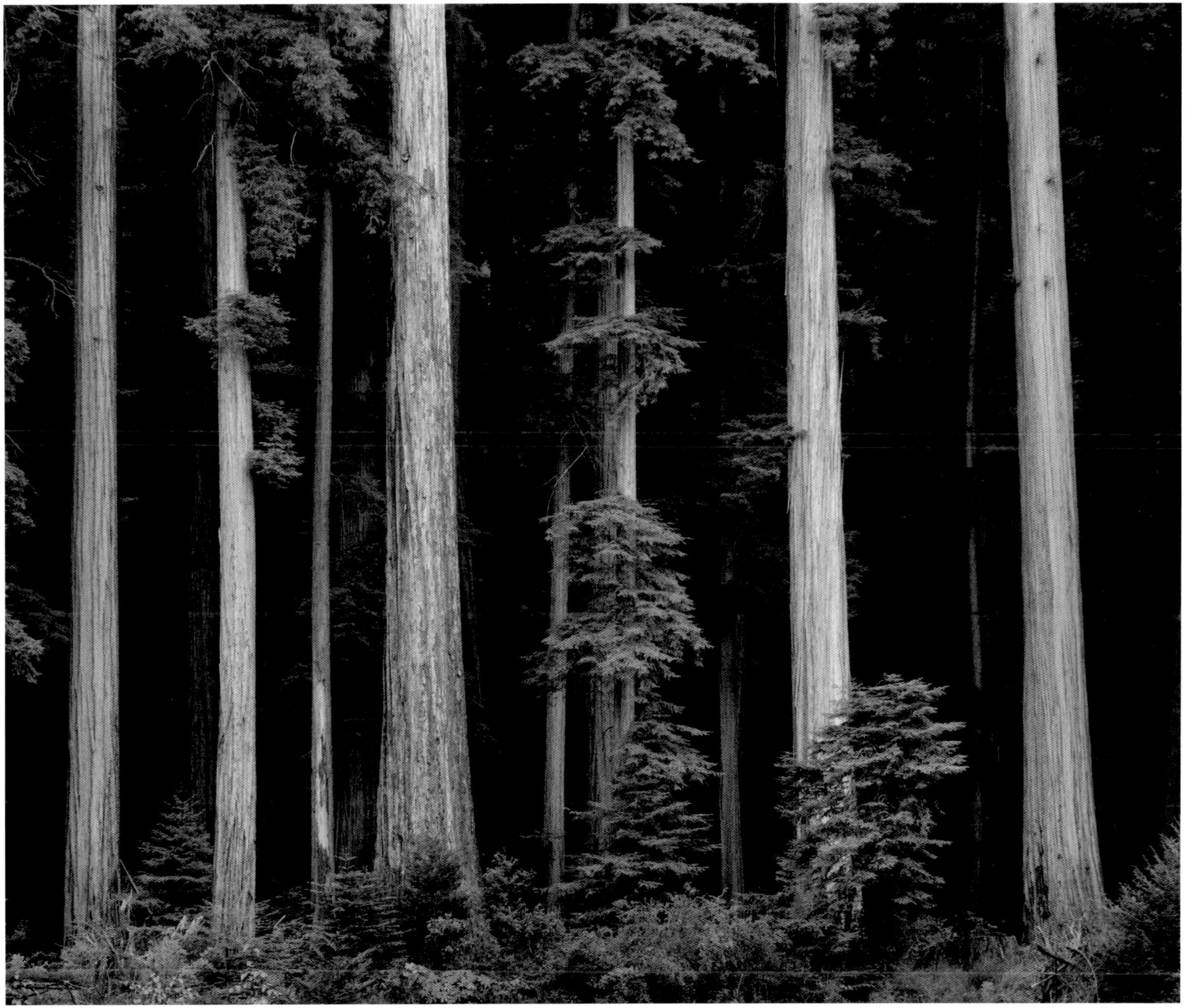

REDWOODS, BULL CREEK FLAT, SOUTH OF REDWOOD NATIONAL PARK, CALIFORNIA, 1960

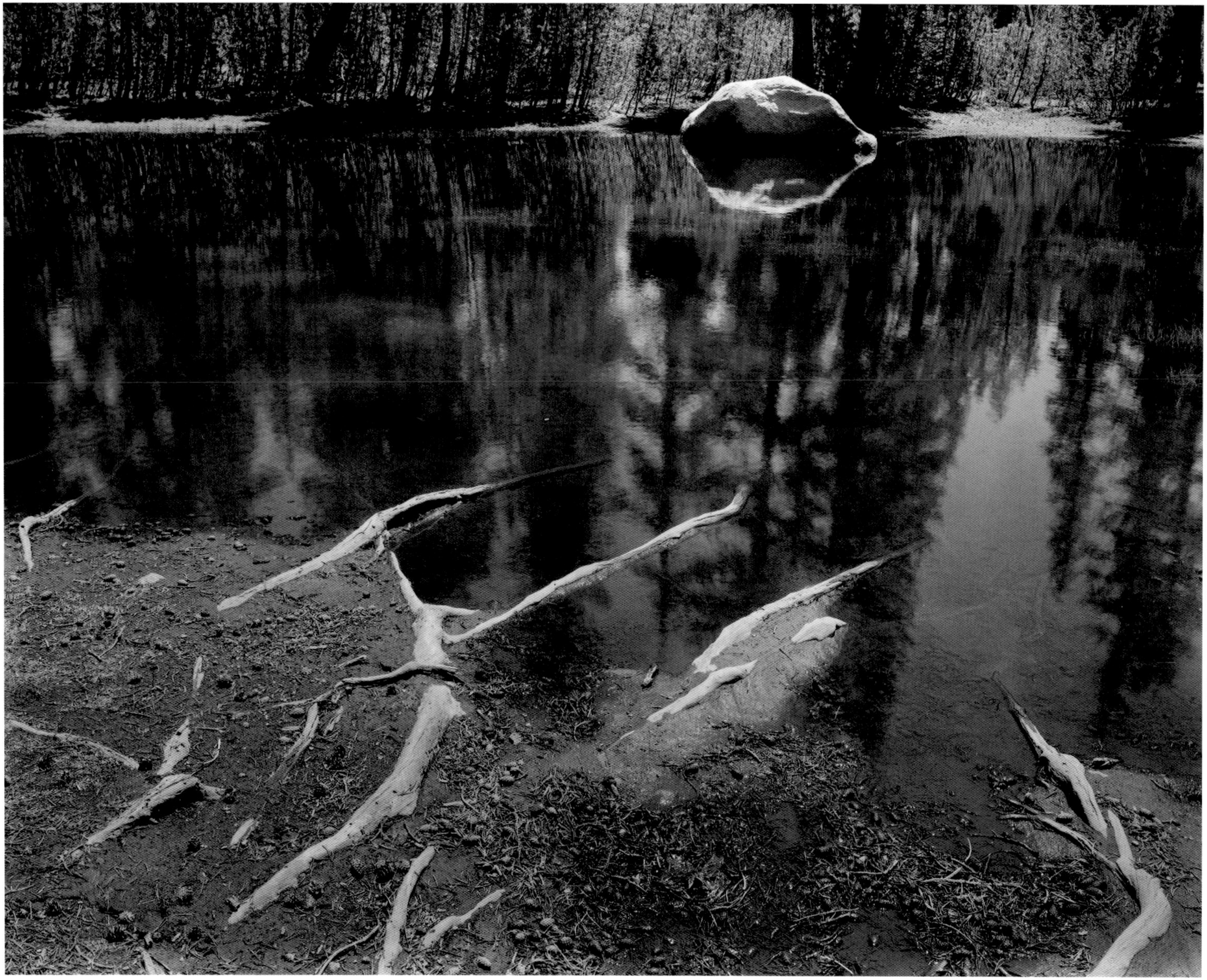

 ROOTS AND POOL NEAR TENAYA LAKE, YOSEMITE NATIONAL PARK, CALIFORNIA, 1955

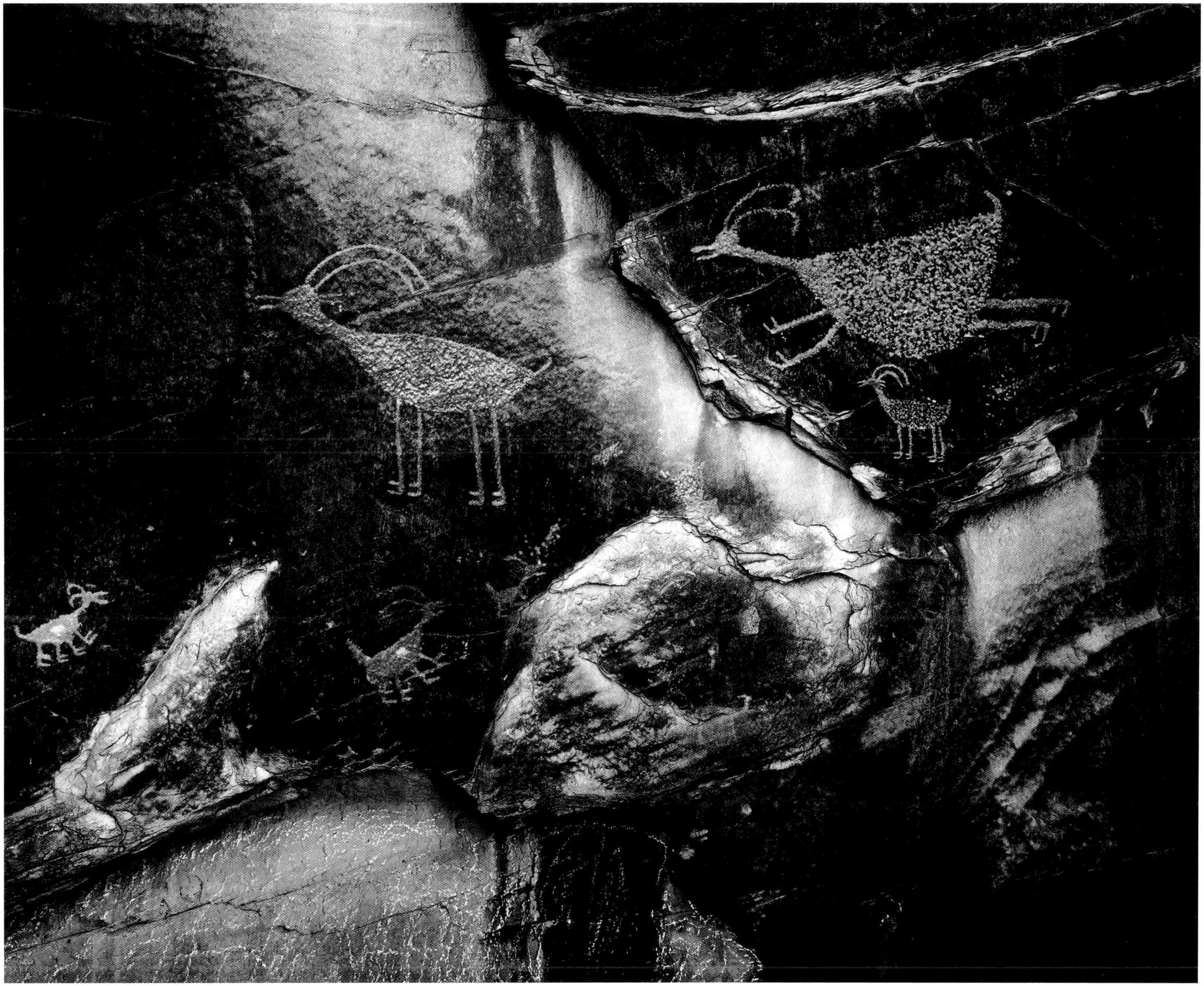

PETROGLYPHS, MONUMENT VALLEY NAVAJO TRIBAL PARK, UTAH, 1958

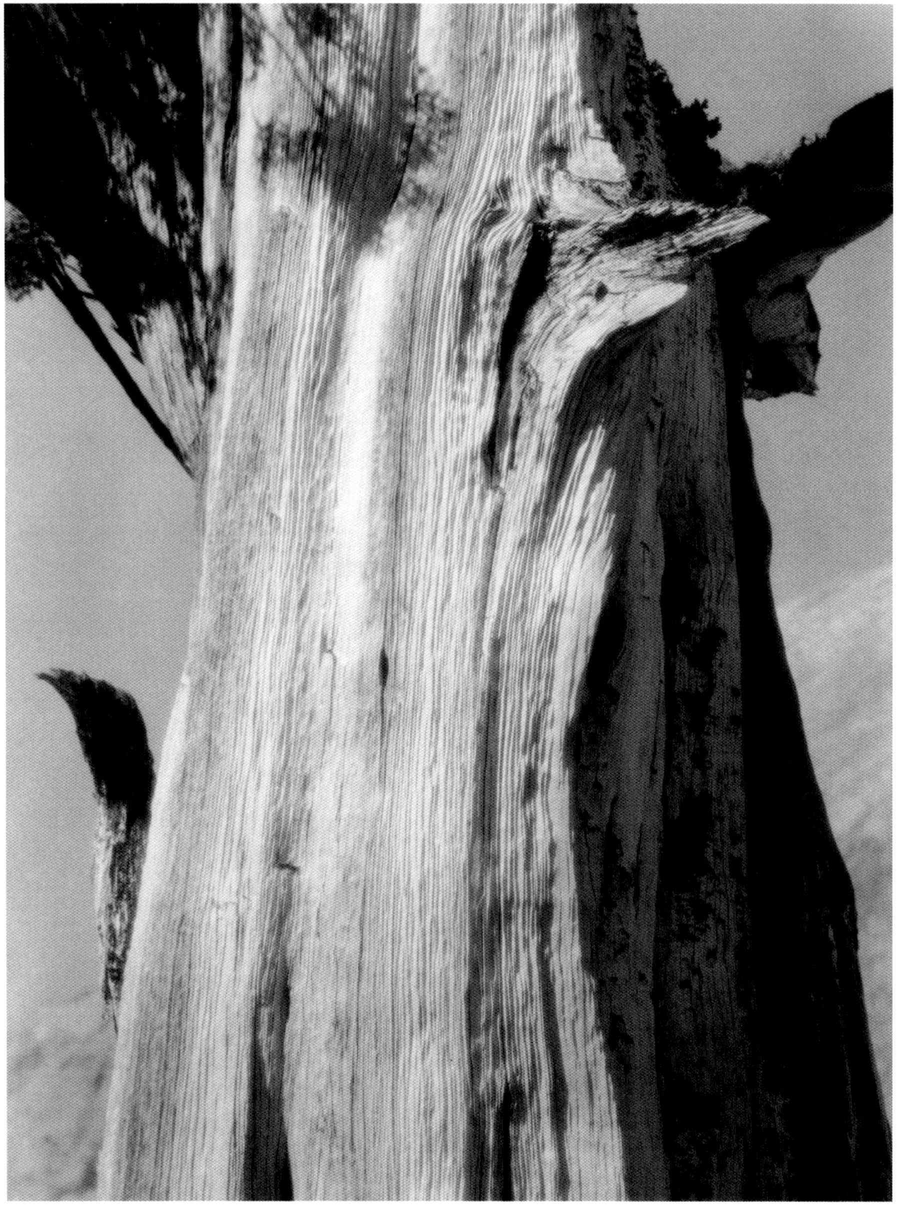

JUNIPER TREE, SEQUOIA NATIONAL PARK, CALIFORNIA, C. 1928

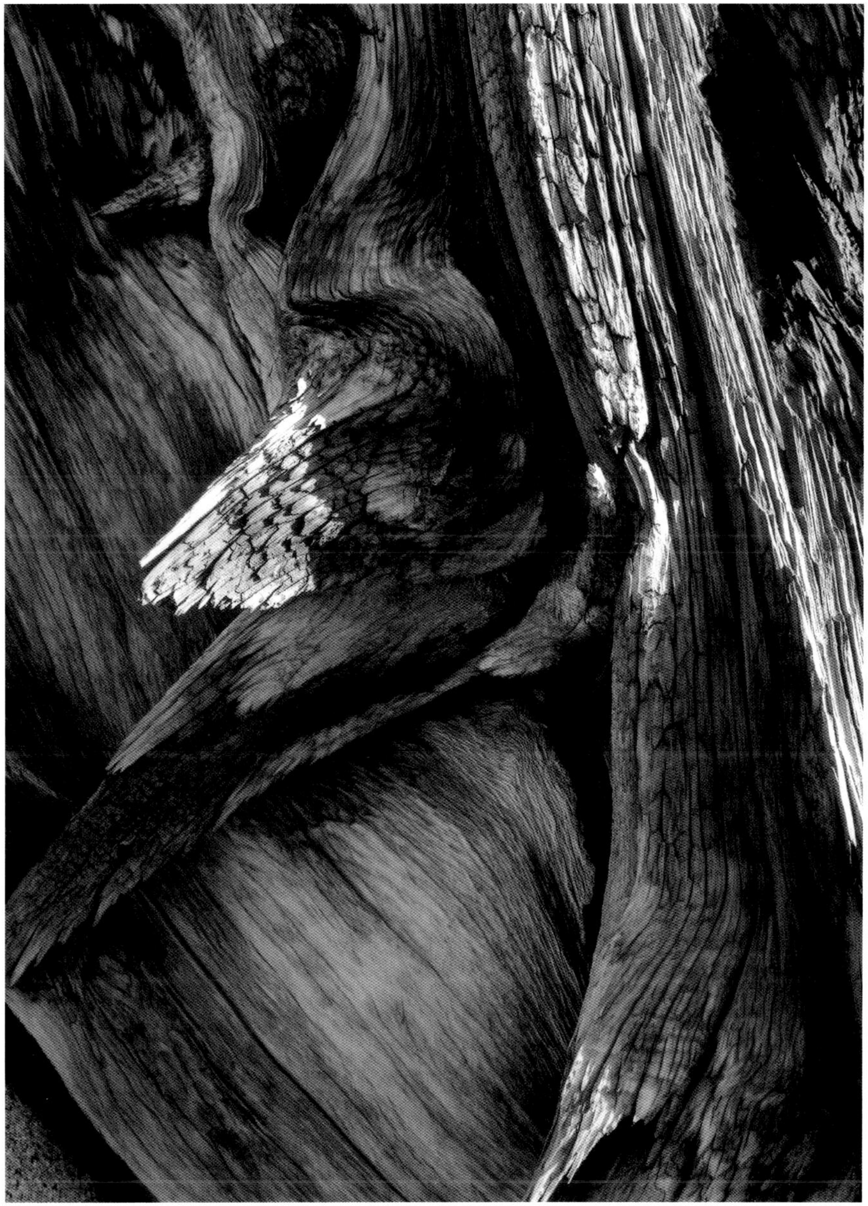

DETAIL, JUNIPER WOOD, SEQUOIA NATIONAL PARK, CALIFORNIA, C. 1927

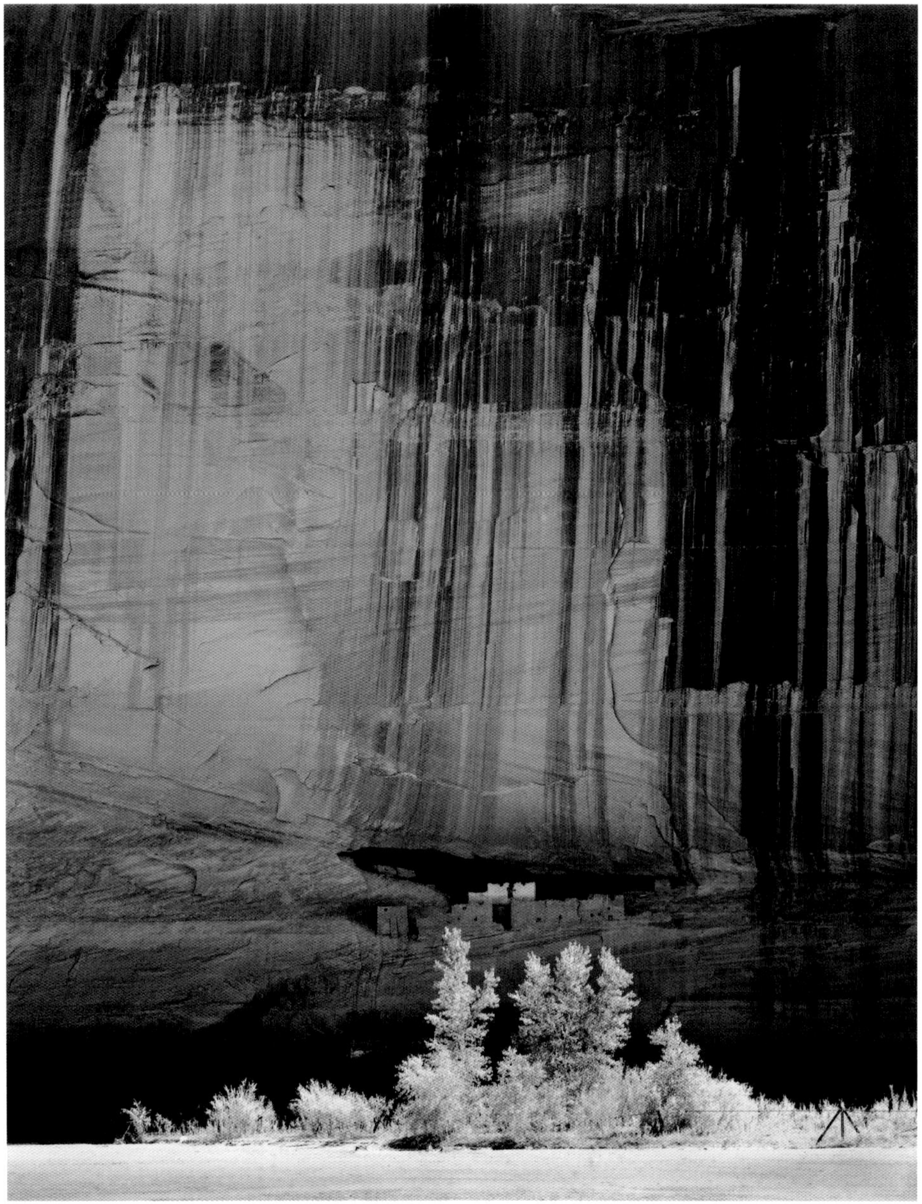

WHITE HOUSE RUIN, MORNING, CANYON DE CHELLY NATIONAL MONUMENT, ARIZONA, 1947

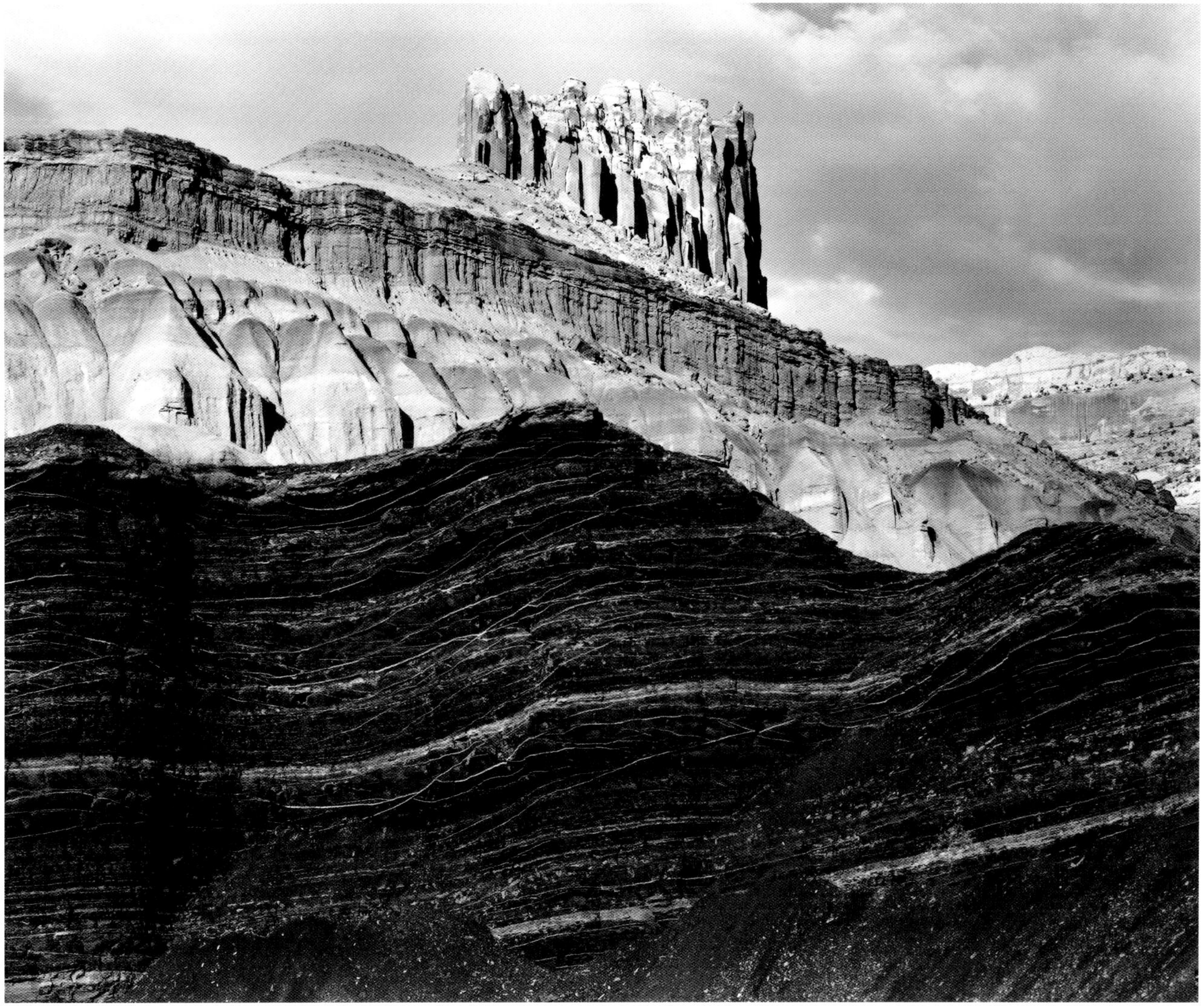

THE CASTLE, CAPITOL REEF NATIONAL PARK, UTAH, 1947

On a trip to the Southwest in 1937, Ansel wrote to Alfred Stieglitz:

> It is all very beautiful and magical here—a quality which cannot be described. You have to live it and breathe it, let the sun bake it into you. The skies and land are so enormous, and the detail so precise and exquisite that wherever you are you are isolated in a glowing world between the macro and the micro, where everything is sidewise under you and over you, and the clocks stopped long ago.

As early as 1928, on his second visit to the Southwest, Ansel considered spending several months a year in the area. "I have a strong feeling that this land is offering me a tremendous opportunity; no one has really photographed it," he wrote to a friend in 1928. Although those plans were unrealized, when he decided to leave San Francisco, the locations he considered were New Mexico and Carmel, California. Choosing the latter, in 1961 he built a house overlooking the Pacific, where he lived until his death in 1984.

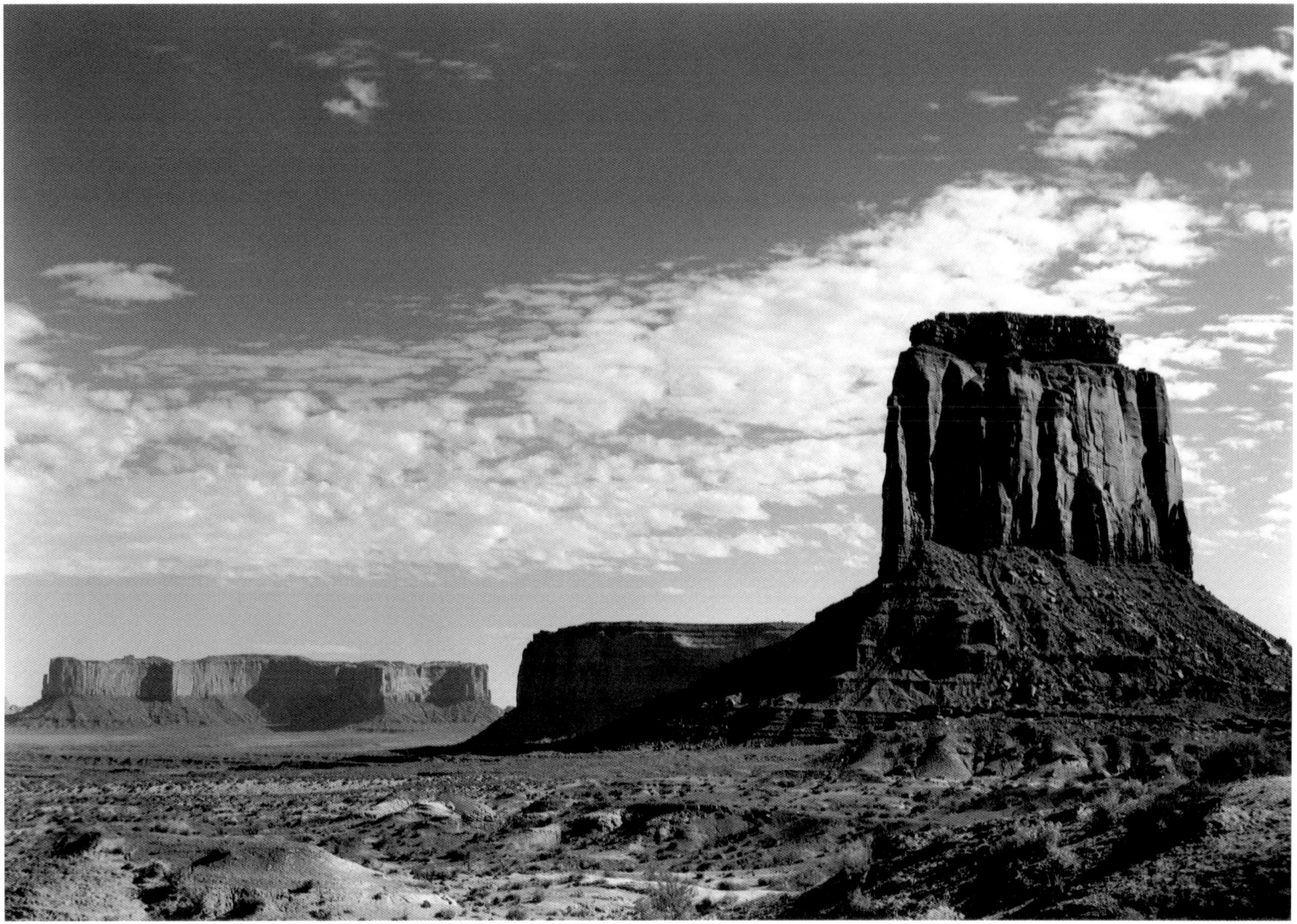

MESAS AND CLOUDS, MONUMENT VALLEY NAVAJO TRIBAL PARK, ARIZONA, 1947

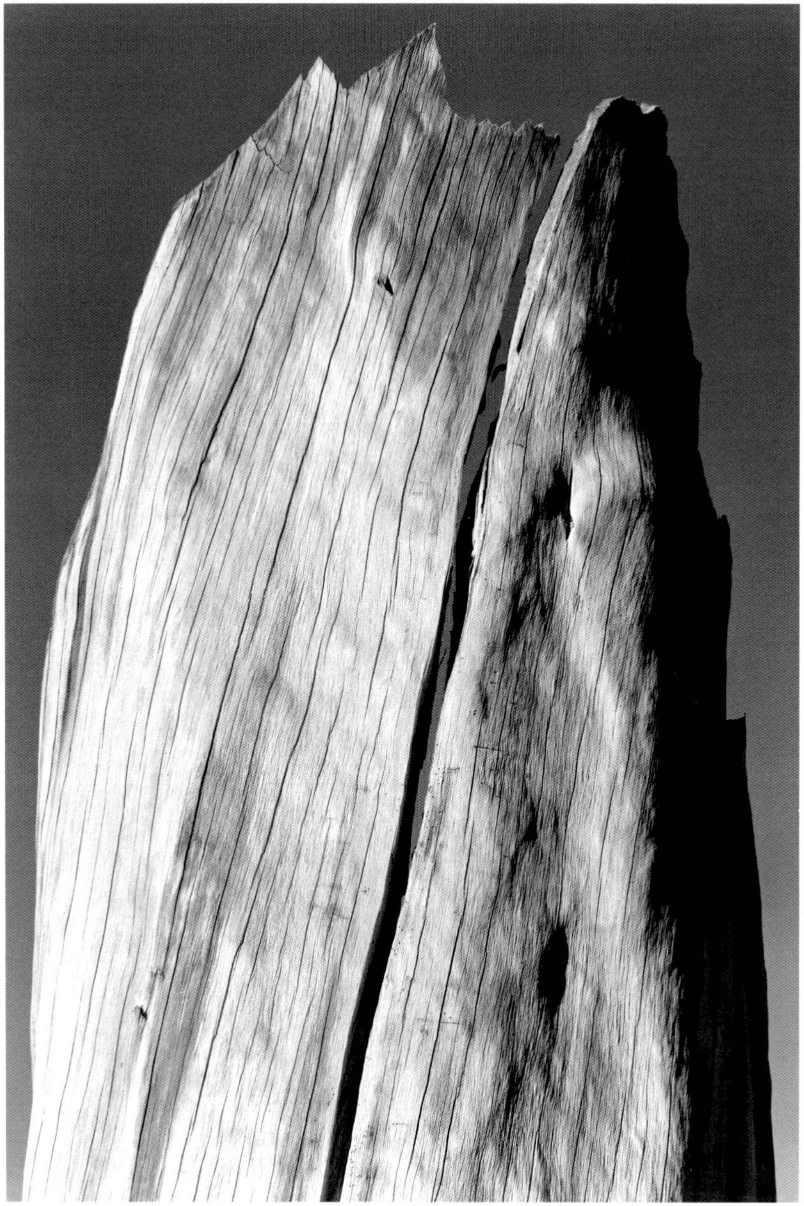

WHITE STUMP, SIERRA NEVADA, CALIFORNIA, 1936

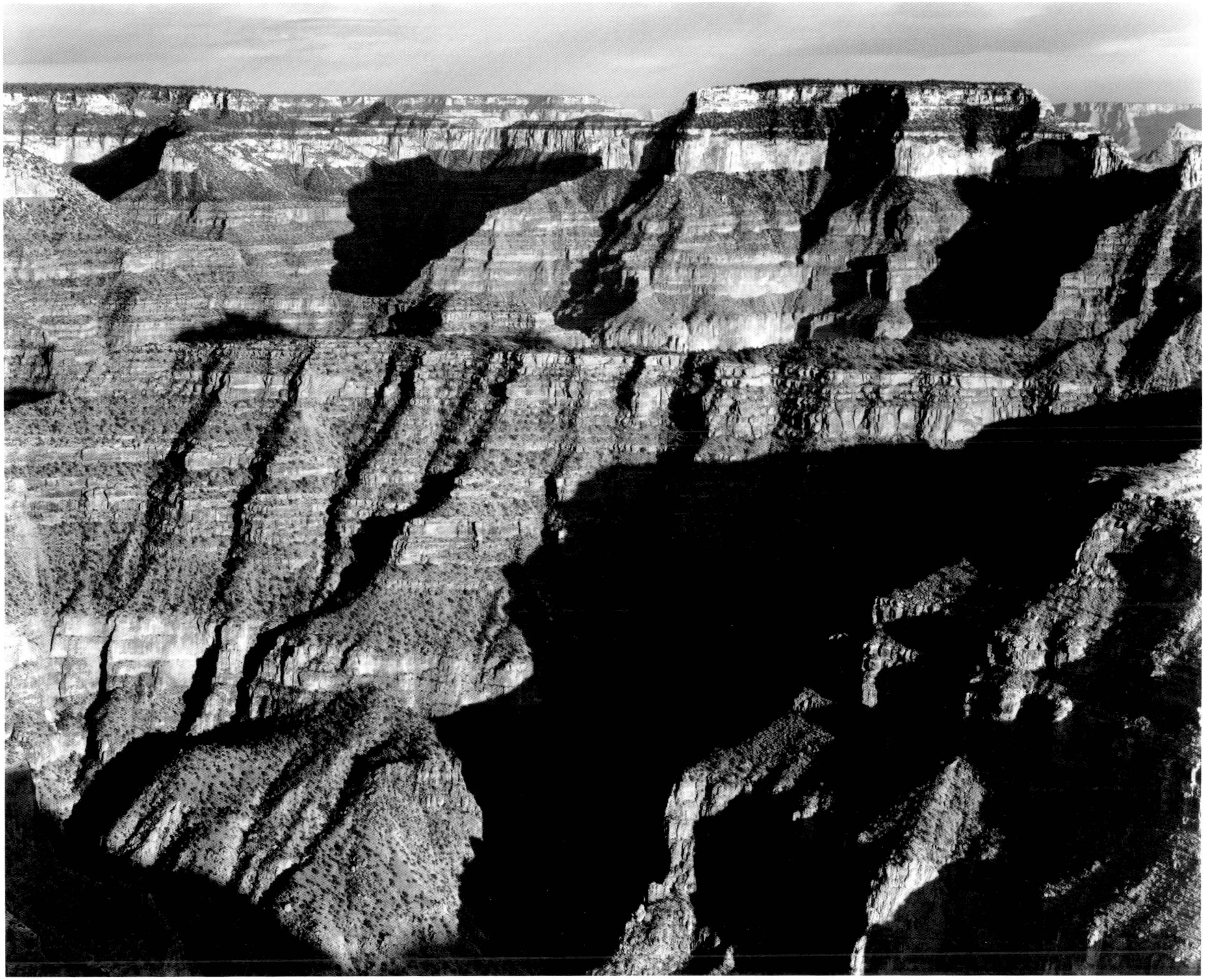

GRAND CANYON NATIONAL PARK, ARIZONA, 1942

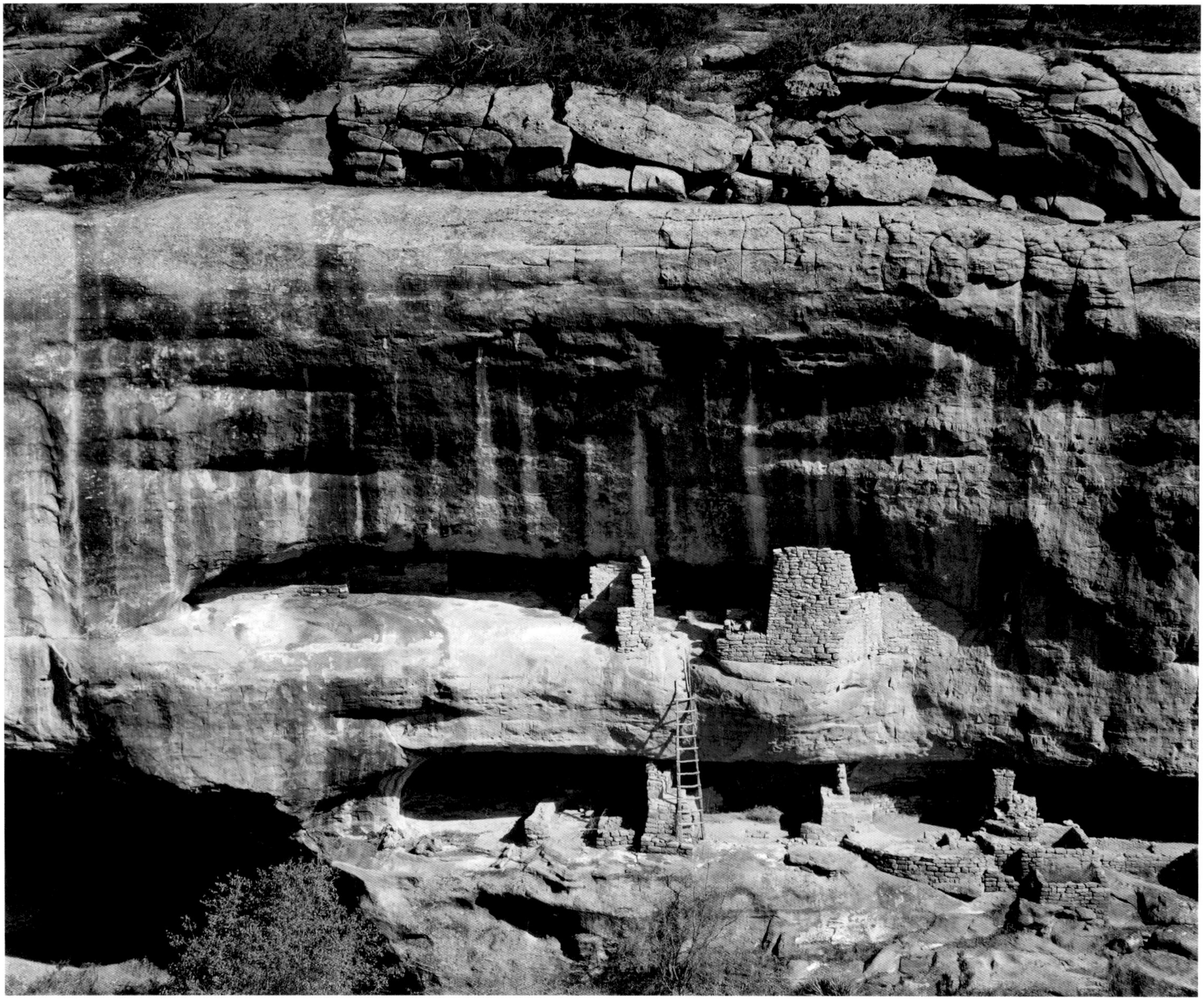

MESA VERDE NATIONAL PARK, COLORADO, 1942

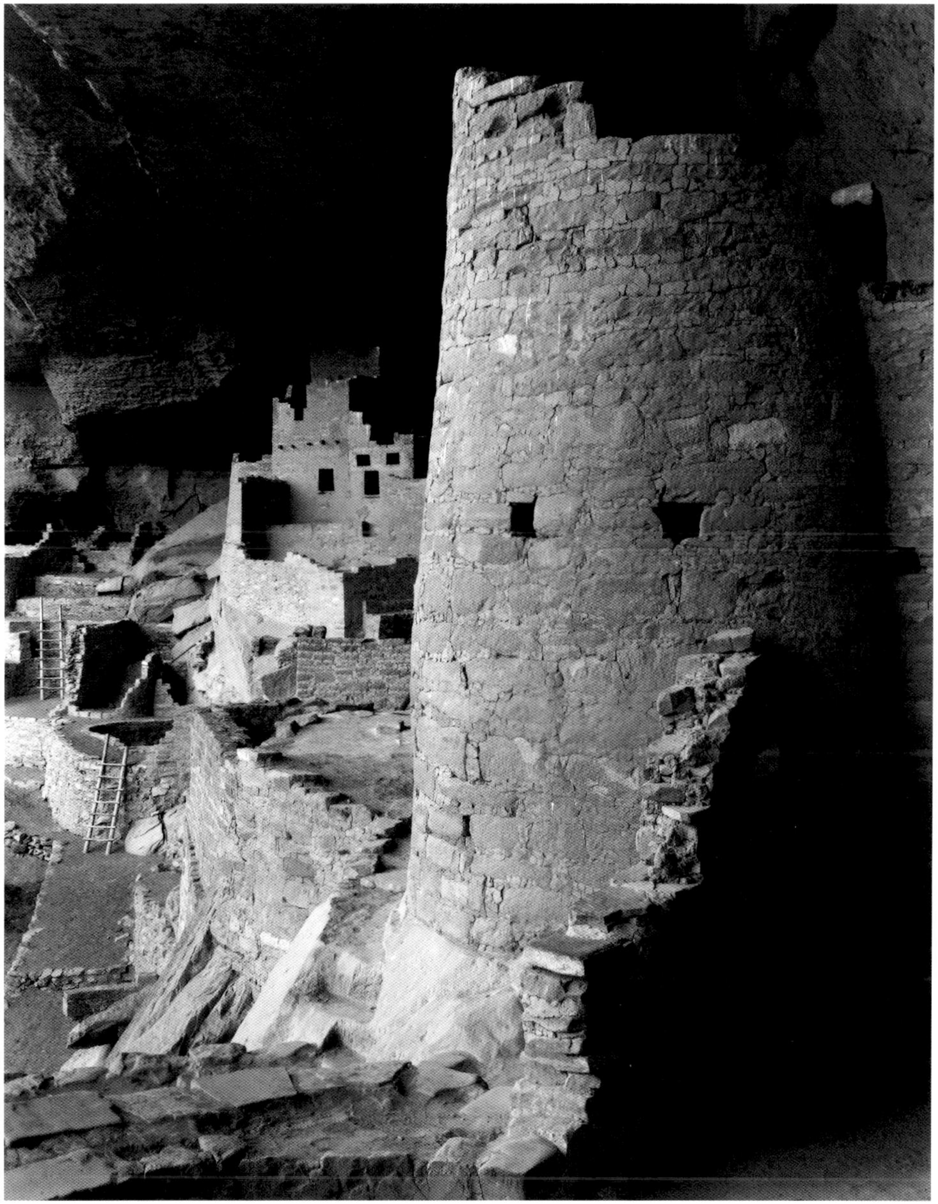

CLIFF PALACE DETAIL, MESA VERDE NATIONAL PARK, COLORADO, 1942

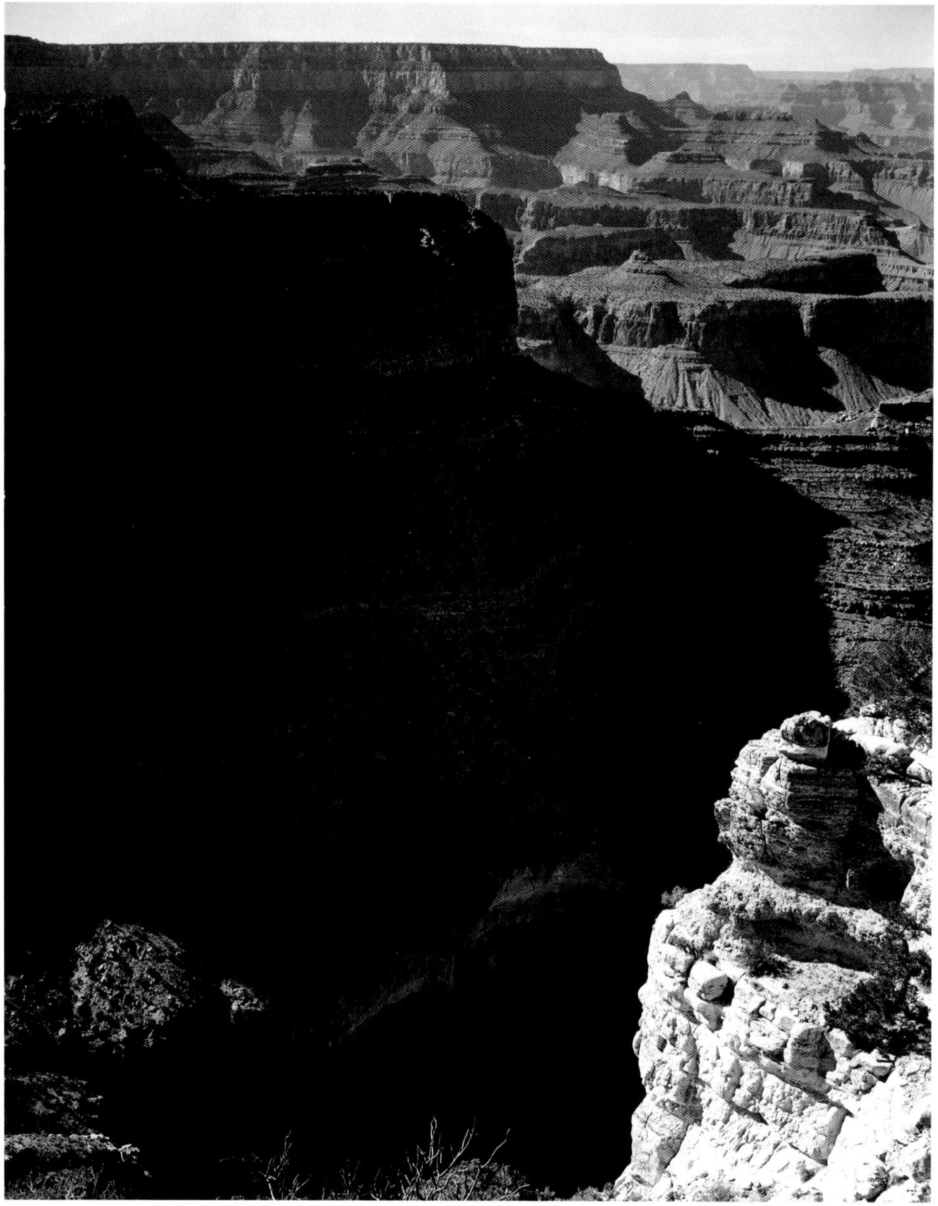

FROM POINT SUBLIME, GRAND CANYON NATIONAL PARK, ARIZONA, 1942

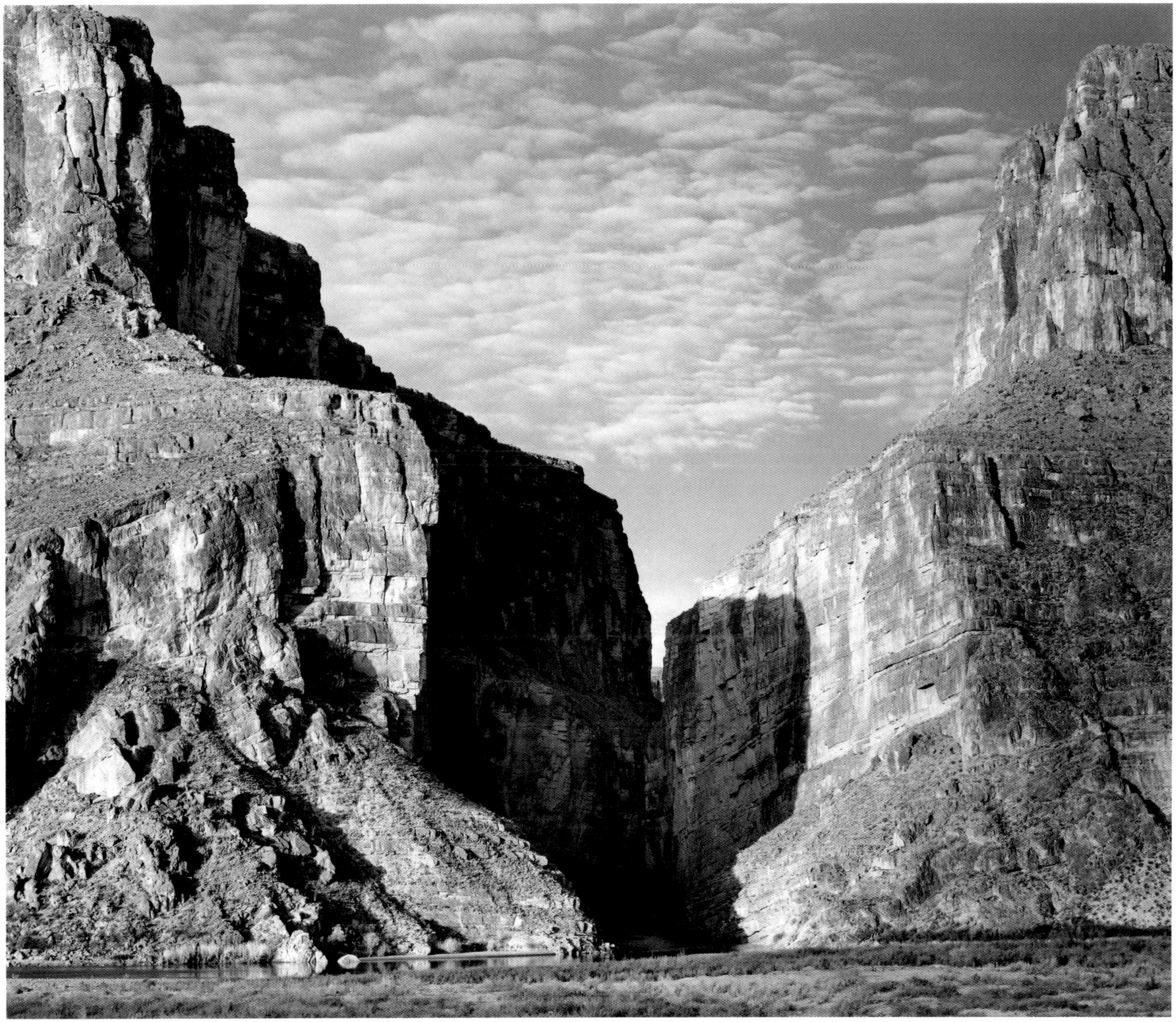

SANTA ELENA CANYON, BIG BEND NATIONAL PARK, TEXAS, 1947

In 1948, Ansel published *Yosemite and the Sierra Nevada,* a book that paired his photographs with the writings of John Muir. In the introduction, Ansel described his first visit to Yosemite Valley:

> Plans for a family visit to Yosemite in the spring of 1916 stirred a new and great expectancy. A month before the great event I was given [J. M.] Hutchings' *In the Heart of the Sierras,* and pored over it, building fantasies of Indians and bears, of huge waterfalls and precipices, of stagecoaches creaking on the edge of catastrophe, of remoteness and magic.... The days became prisons of impatience and restlessness. Finally, the train at Oakland! All day we rode, over the Coast Range, through Niles and Livermore, down across the heat-shimmering San Joaquin Valley, up through the even hotter foothills to the threshold of Yosemite.... And finally, in the bright morning, the grand, dusty, jolting ride in an open motor bus up the deepening, greening gorge to Yosemite.
>
> That first impression of the valley—white water, azaleas, cool fir caverns, tall pines and stolid oaks, cliffs rising to undreamed-of heights, the poignant sounds and smells of the Sierra...was a culmination of experience so intense as to be almost painful. From that day in 1916 my life has been colored and modulated by the great earth-gesture of the Sierra.

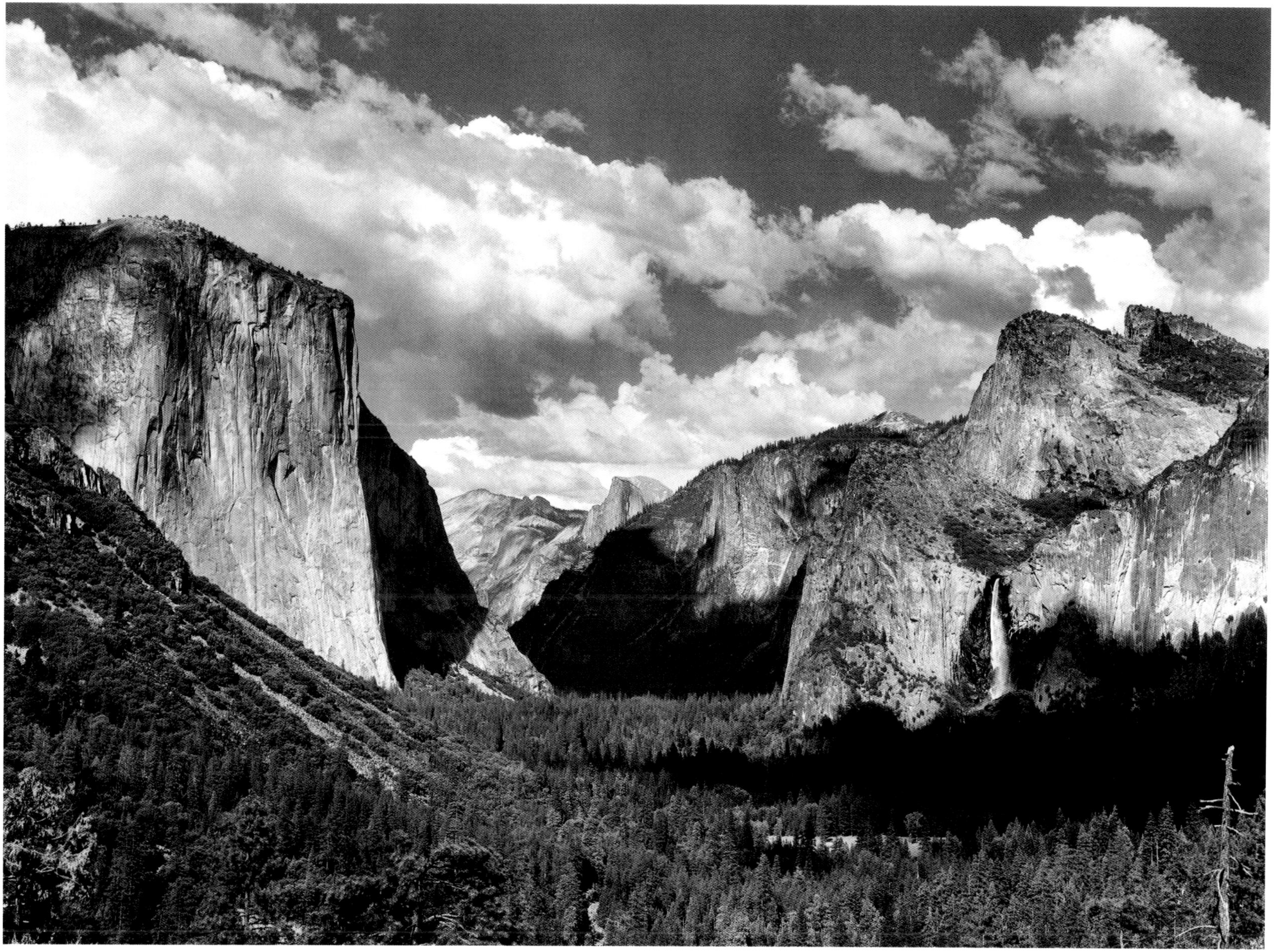

YOSEMITE VALLEY, SUMMER, YOSEMITE NATIONAL PARK, CALIFORNIA, C. 1935

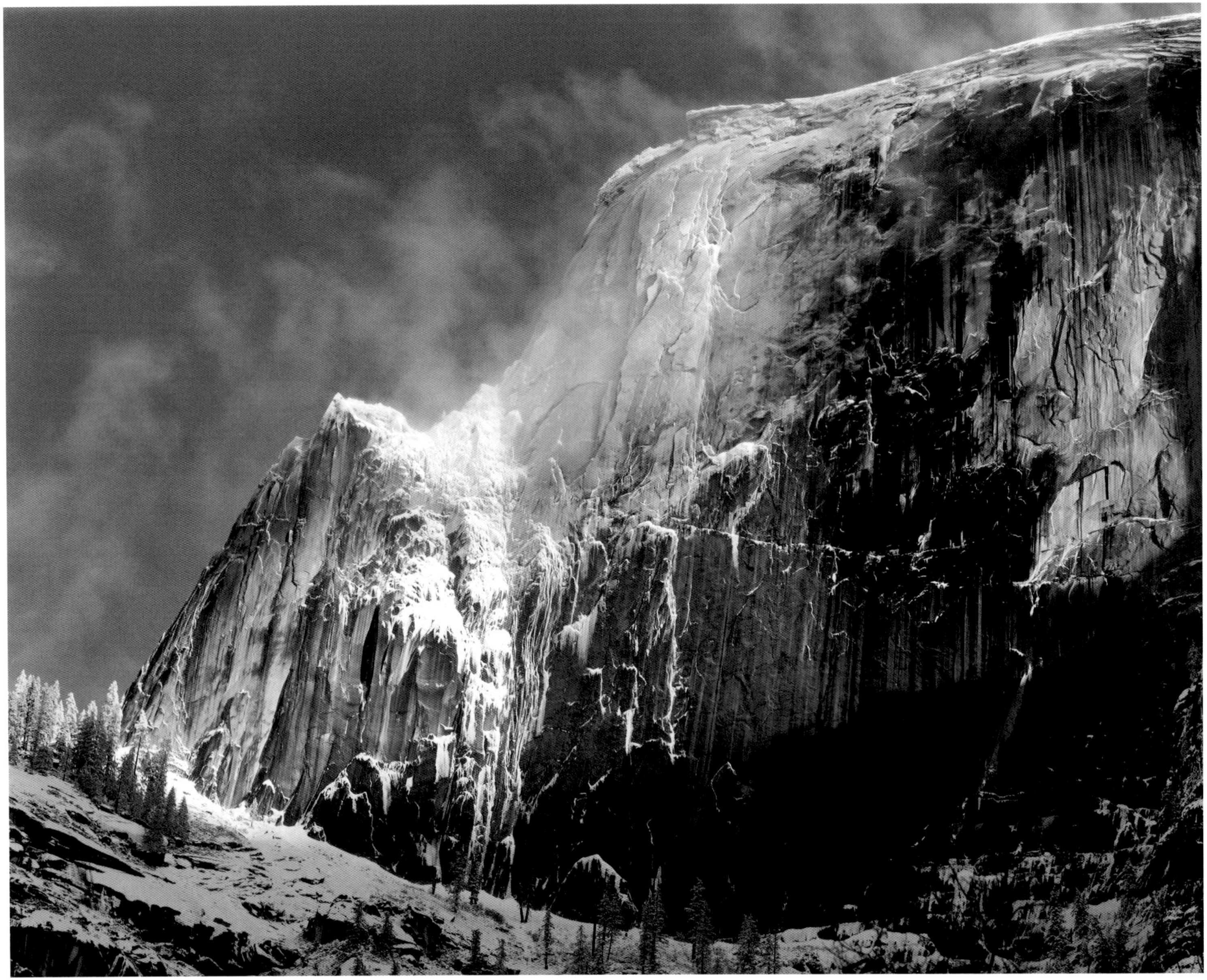

HALF DOME, BLOWING SNOW, YOSEMITE NATIONAL PARK, CALIFORNIA, C. 1955

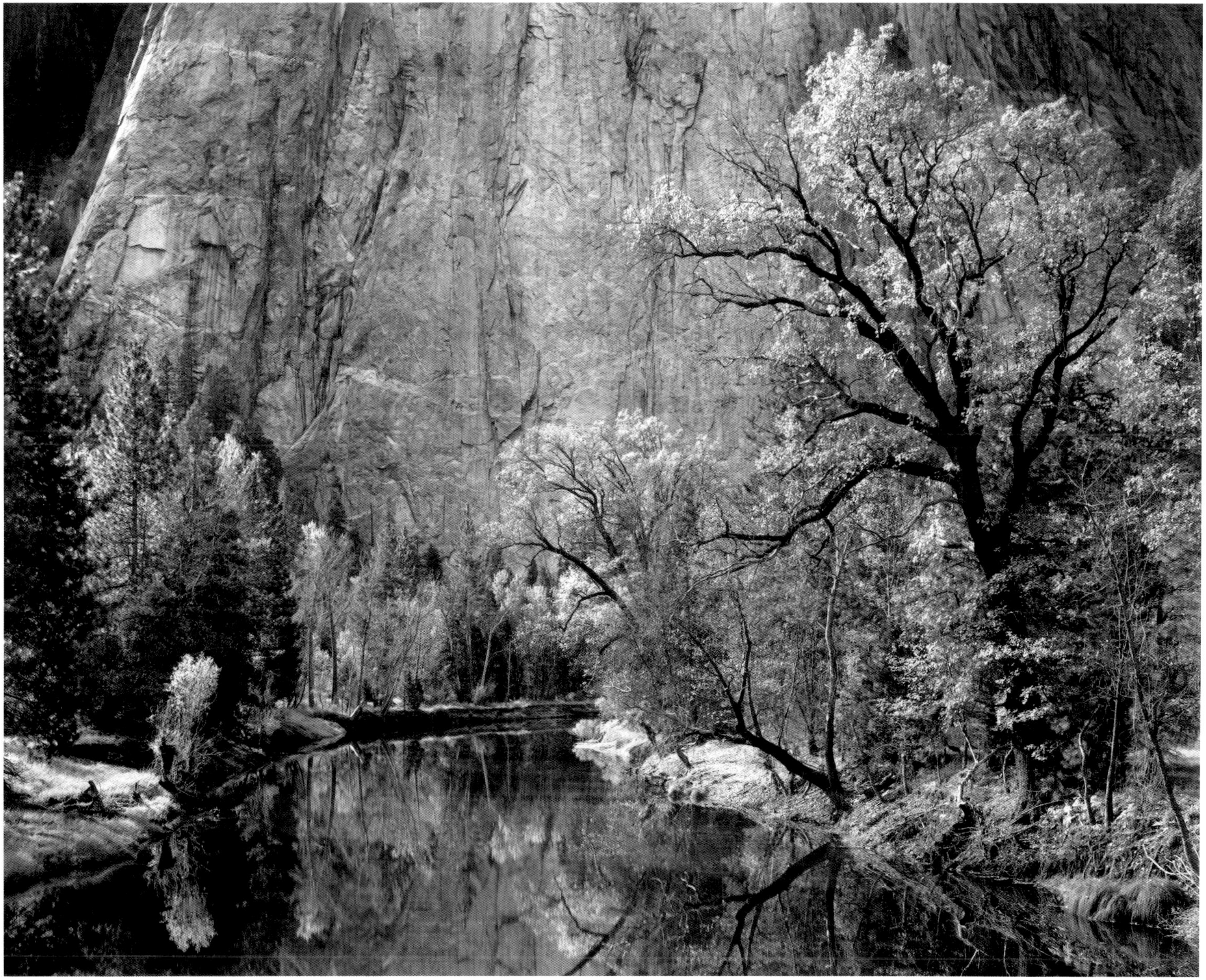

MERCED RIVER, CLIFFS OF CATHEDRAL ROCKS, AUTUMN, YOSEMITE NATIONAL PARK, CALIFORNIA, 1939

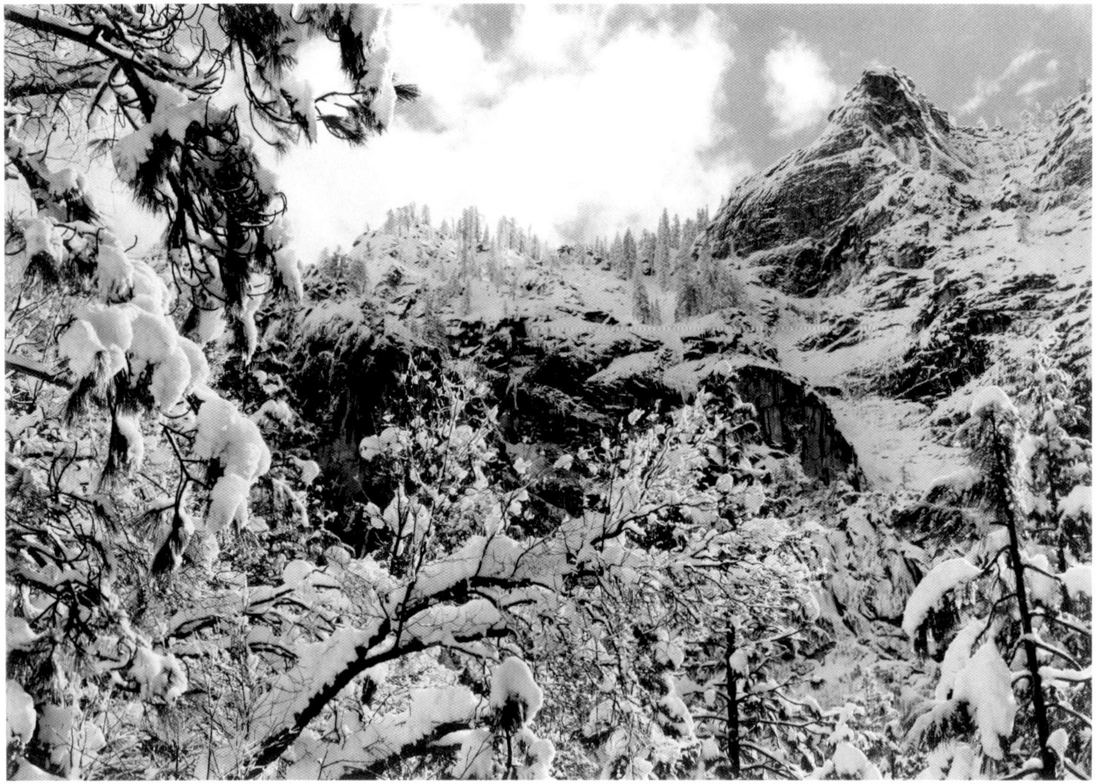

TREES AND CLIFFS IN SNOW, YOSEMITE NATIONAL PARK, CALIFORNIA, C. 1937

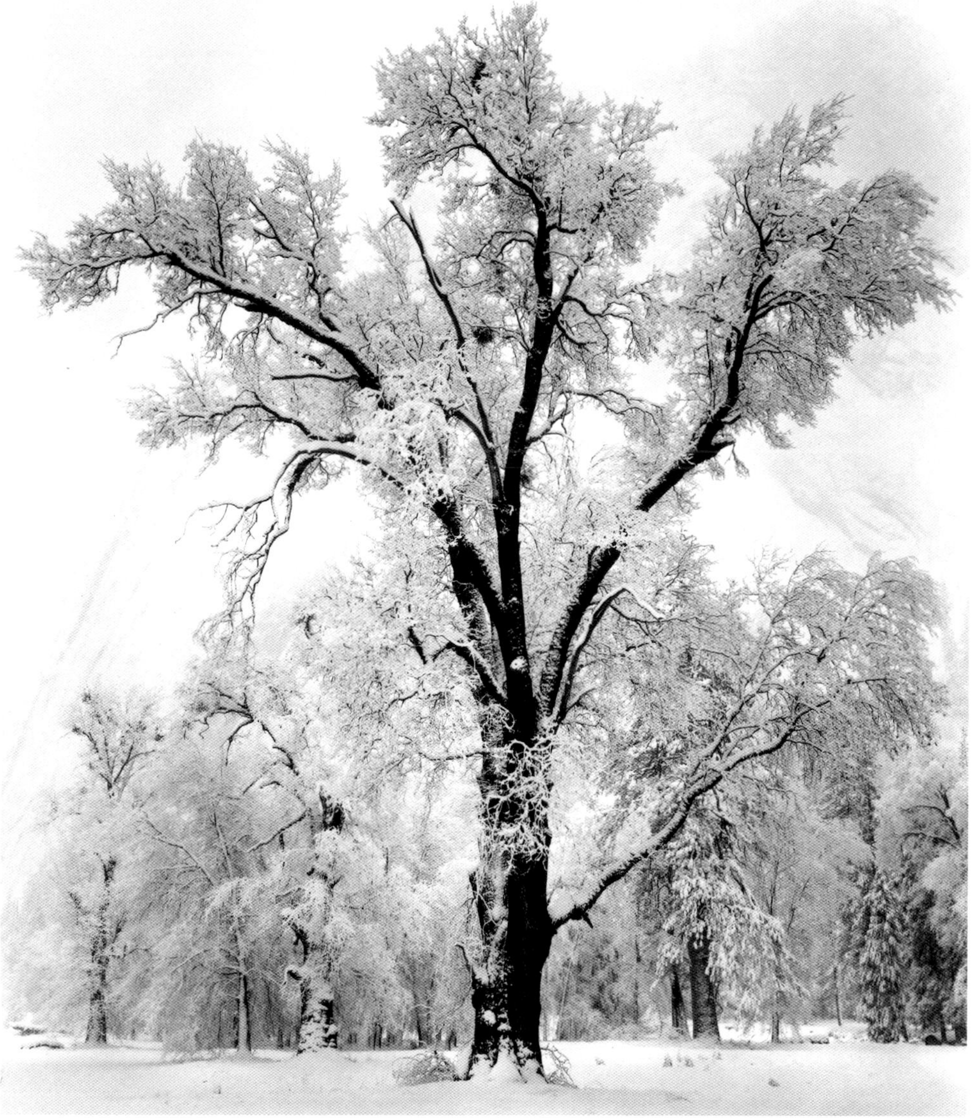

OAK TREE, SNOWSTORM, YOSEMITE NATIONAL PARK, CALIFORNIA, 1948

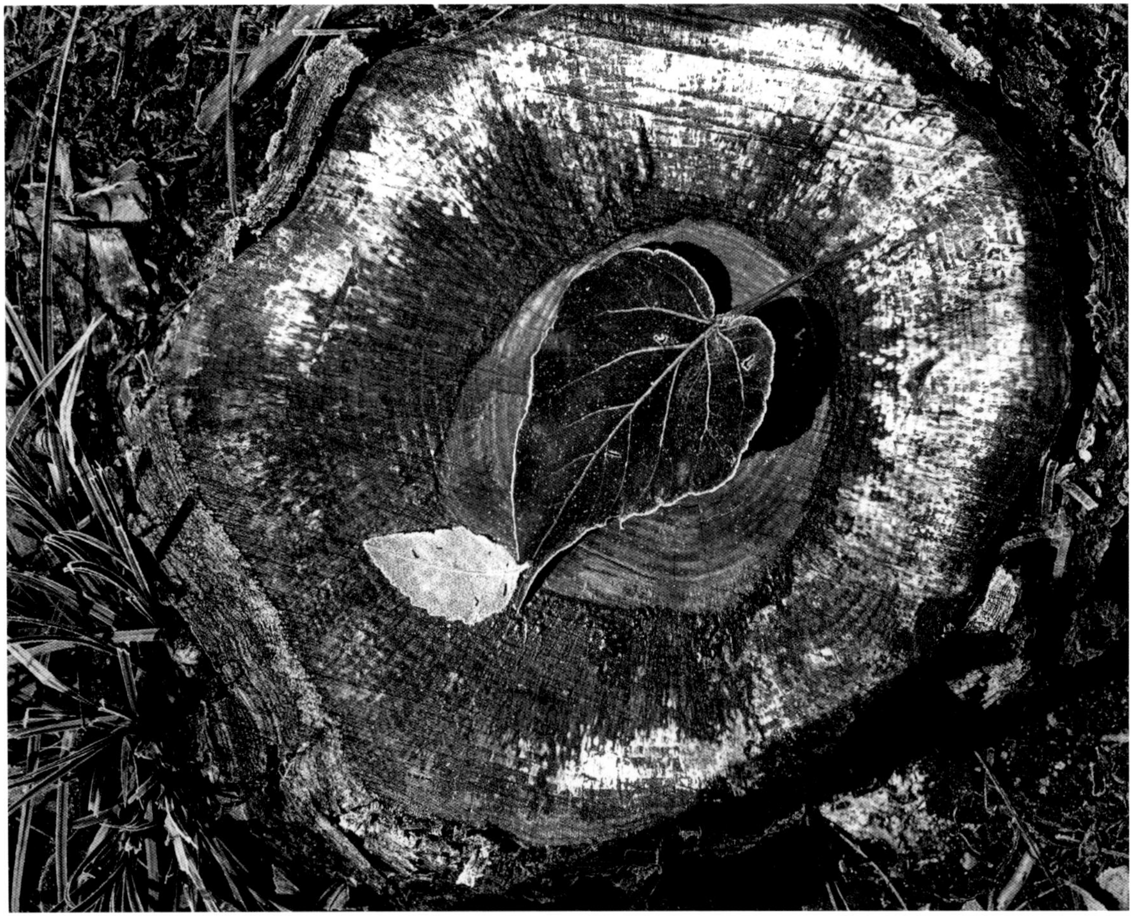

LEAVES, FROST, STUMP, OCTOBER MORNING, YOSEMITE NATIONAL PARK, CALIFORNIA, C. 1931

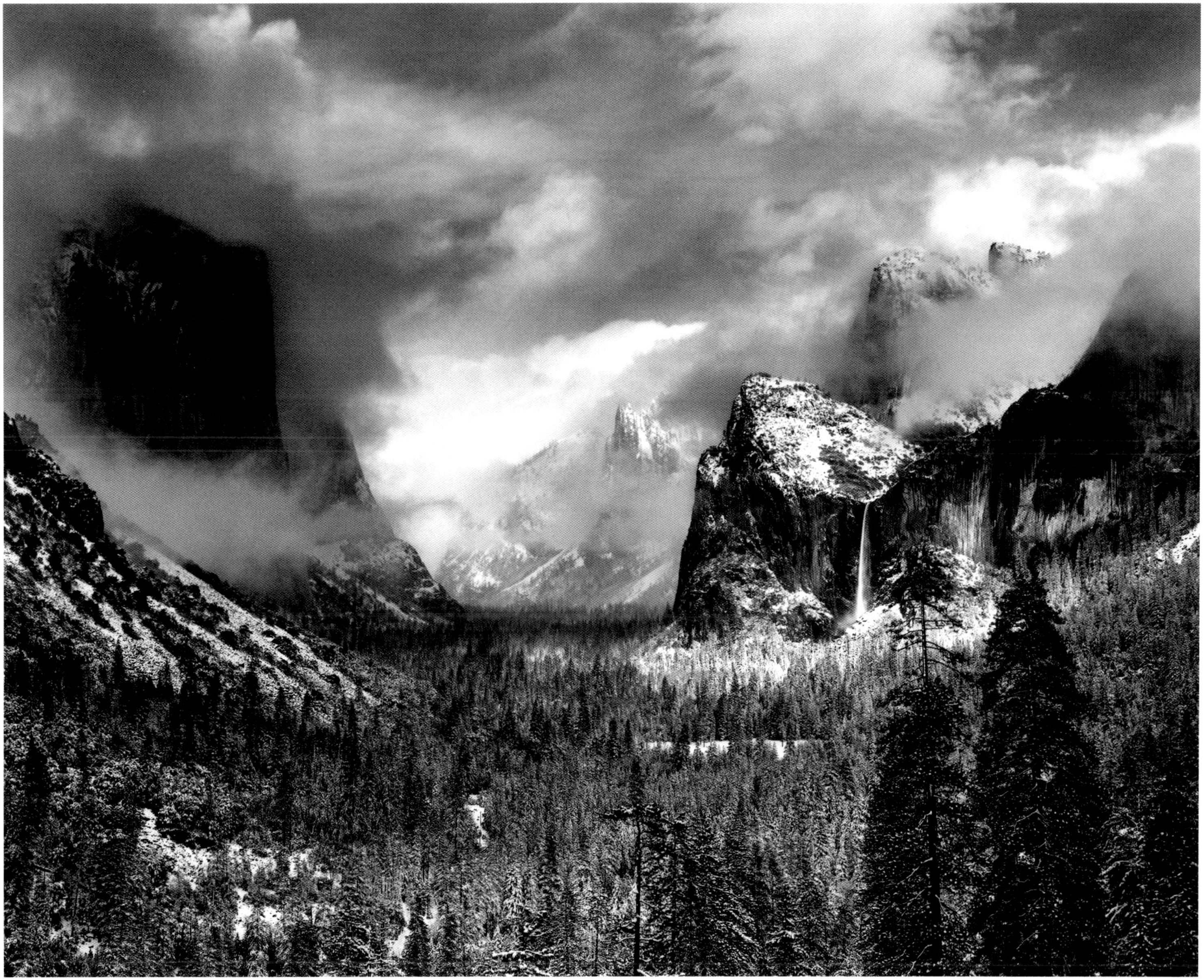

CLEARING WINTER STORM, YOSEMITE NATIONAL PARK, CALIFORNIA, C. 1937

"We are looking down through clear water to submerged rocks," Ansel said in an interview in 1978 describing this photograph. "This shows how pure that water was! It's very clear, and the sky was deep blue. If there had been clouds in the sky, you would have had a terrible time with the cloud reflections."

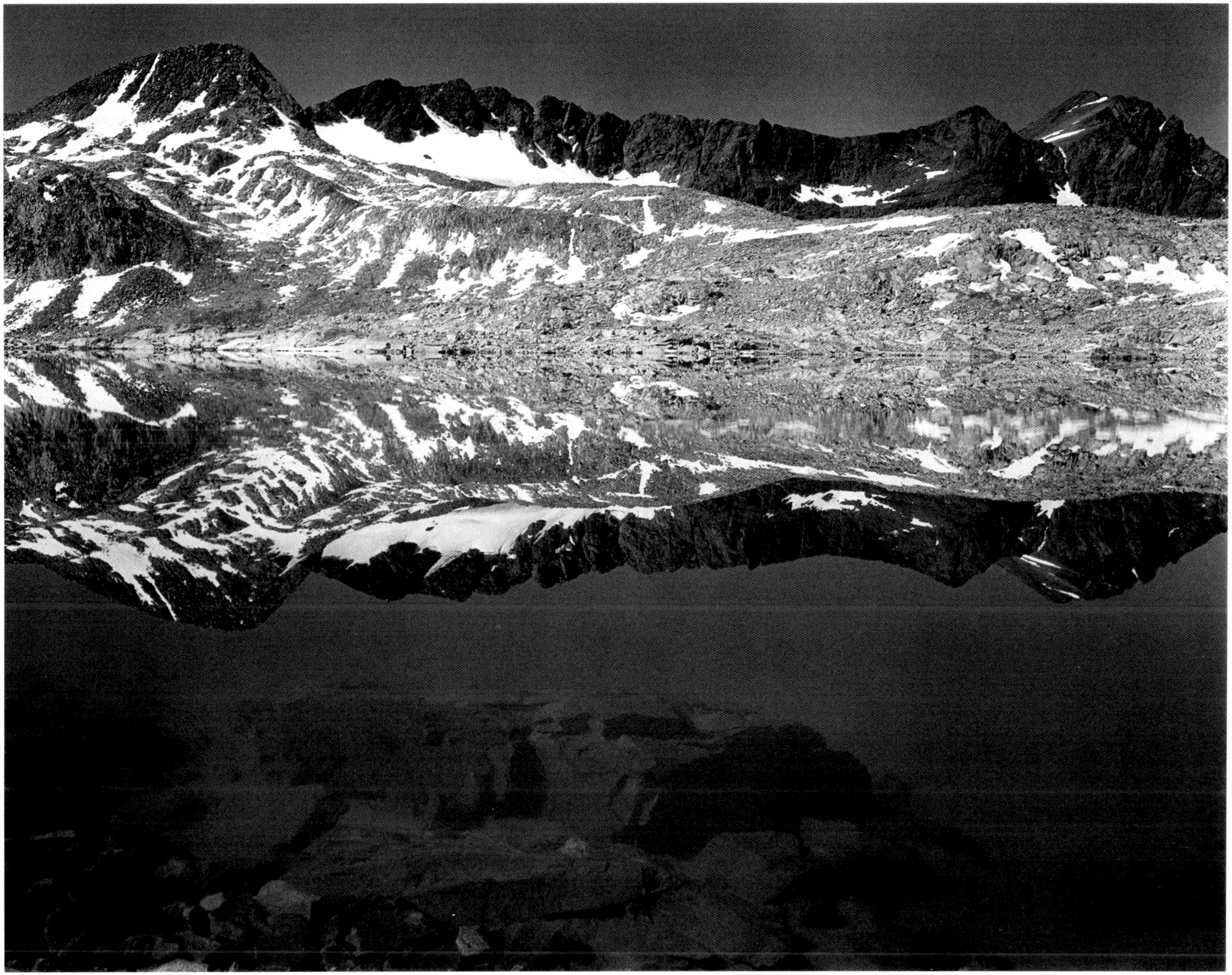

LAKE NEAR MUIR PASS, KINGS CANYON NATIONAL PARK, CALIFORNIA, 1934

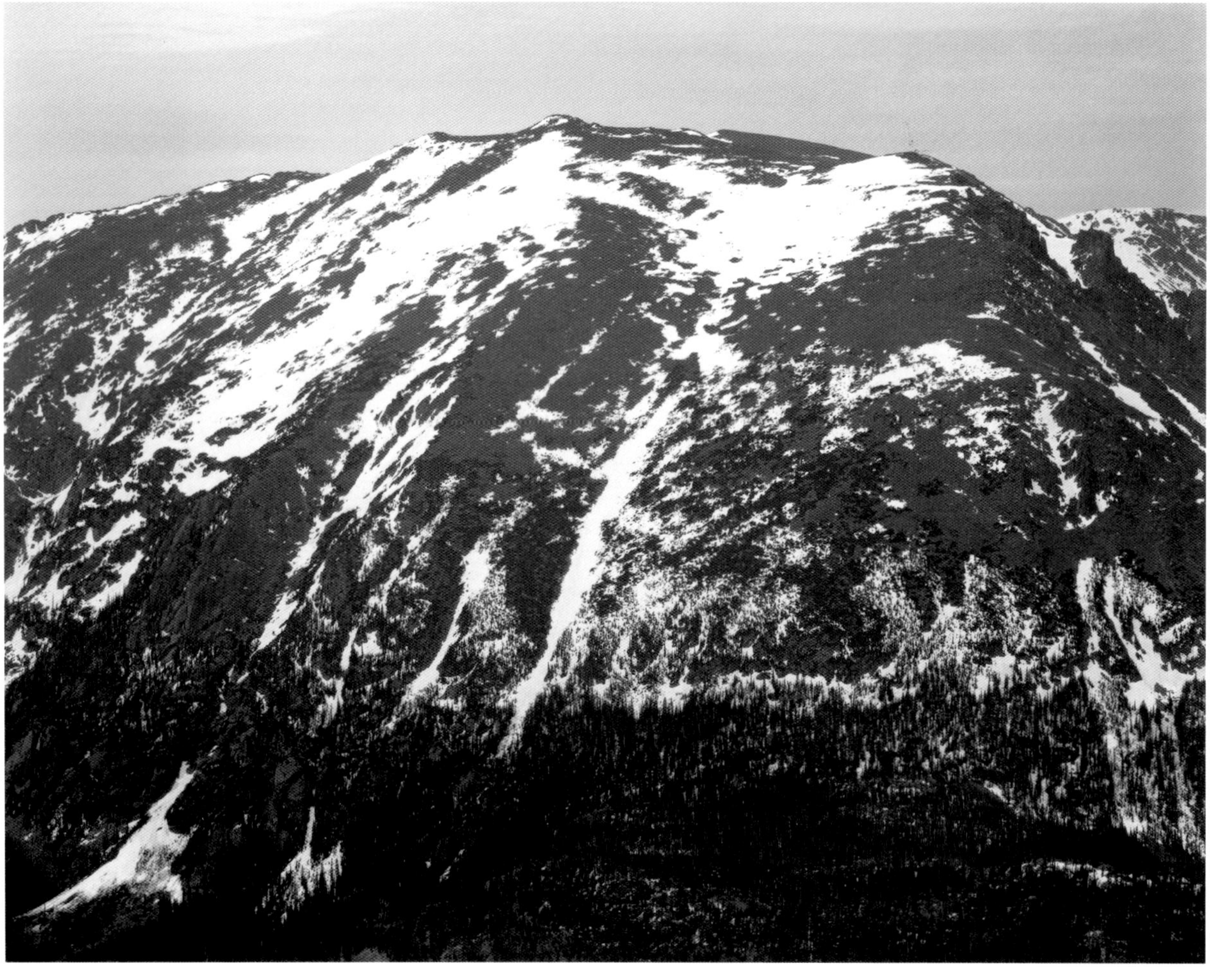

ROUNDED MOUNTAIN, DULL LIGHT, ROCKY MOUNTAIN NATIONAL PARK, COLORADO, 1942

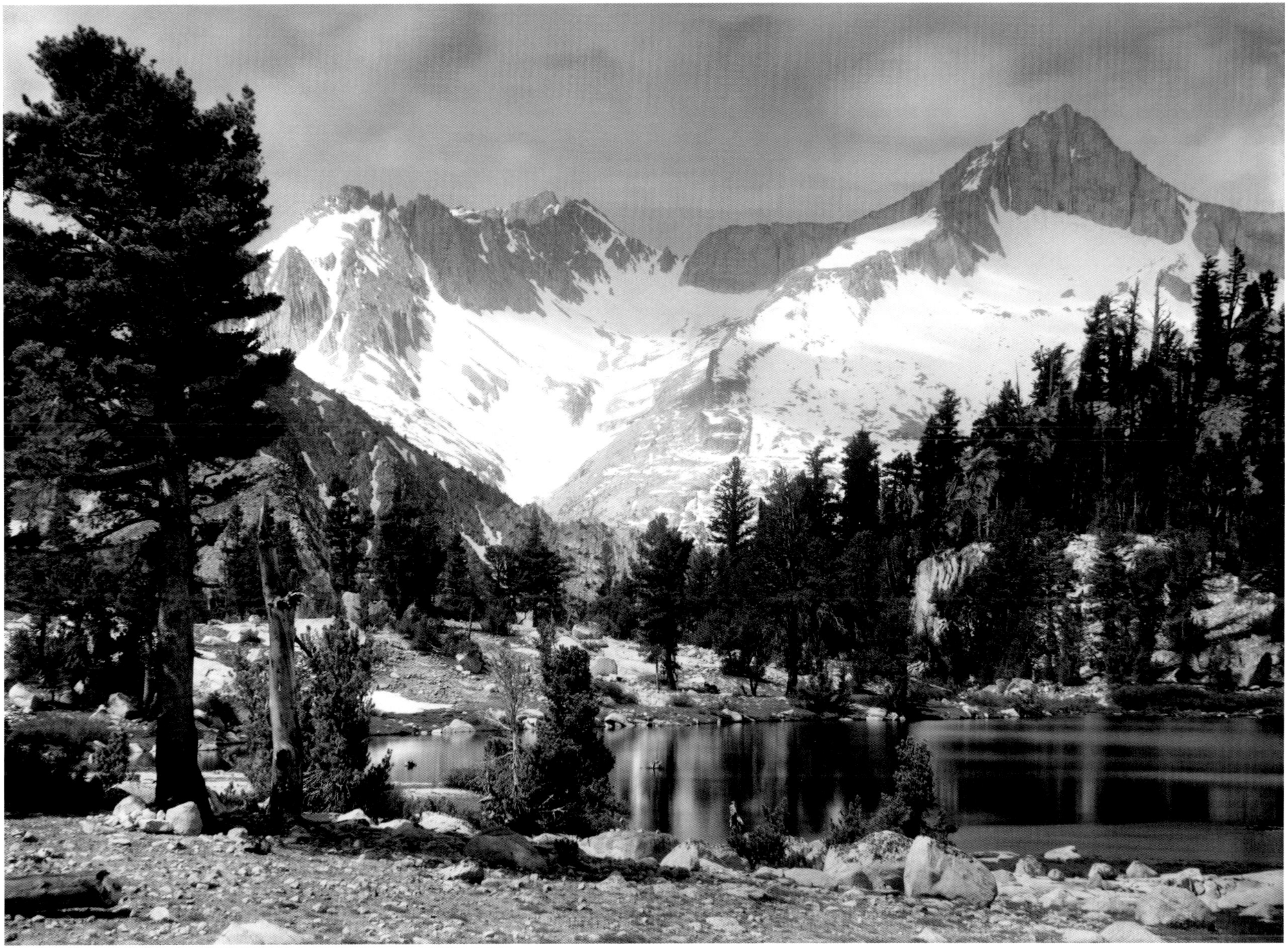

MOUNT BREWER AND BULLFROG LAKE, KINGS CANYON NATIONAL PARK, CALIFORNIA, C. 1925

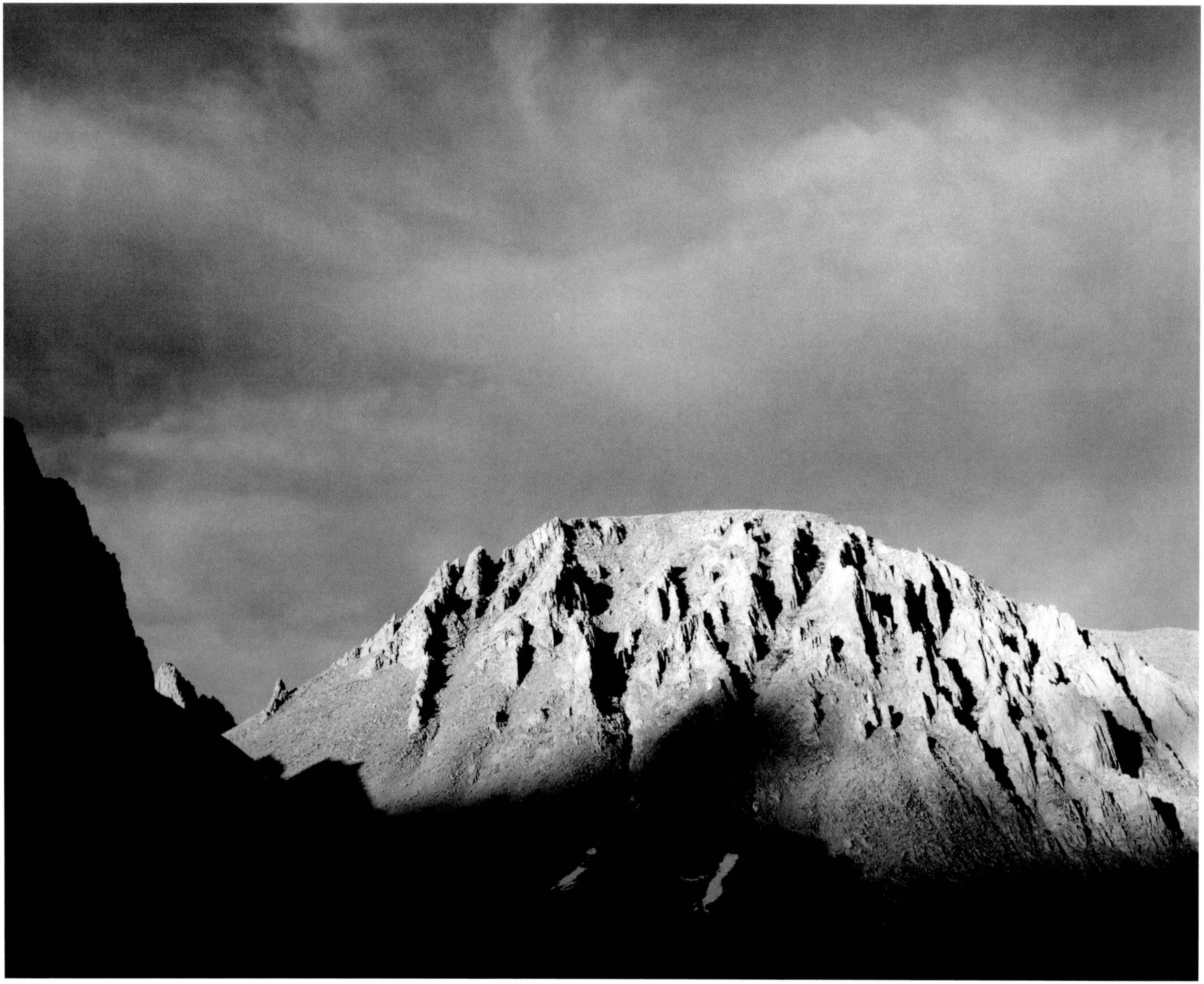

MOUNT WHITNEY FROM THE WEST, SIERRA NEVADA, CALIFORNIA, 1932

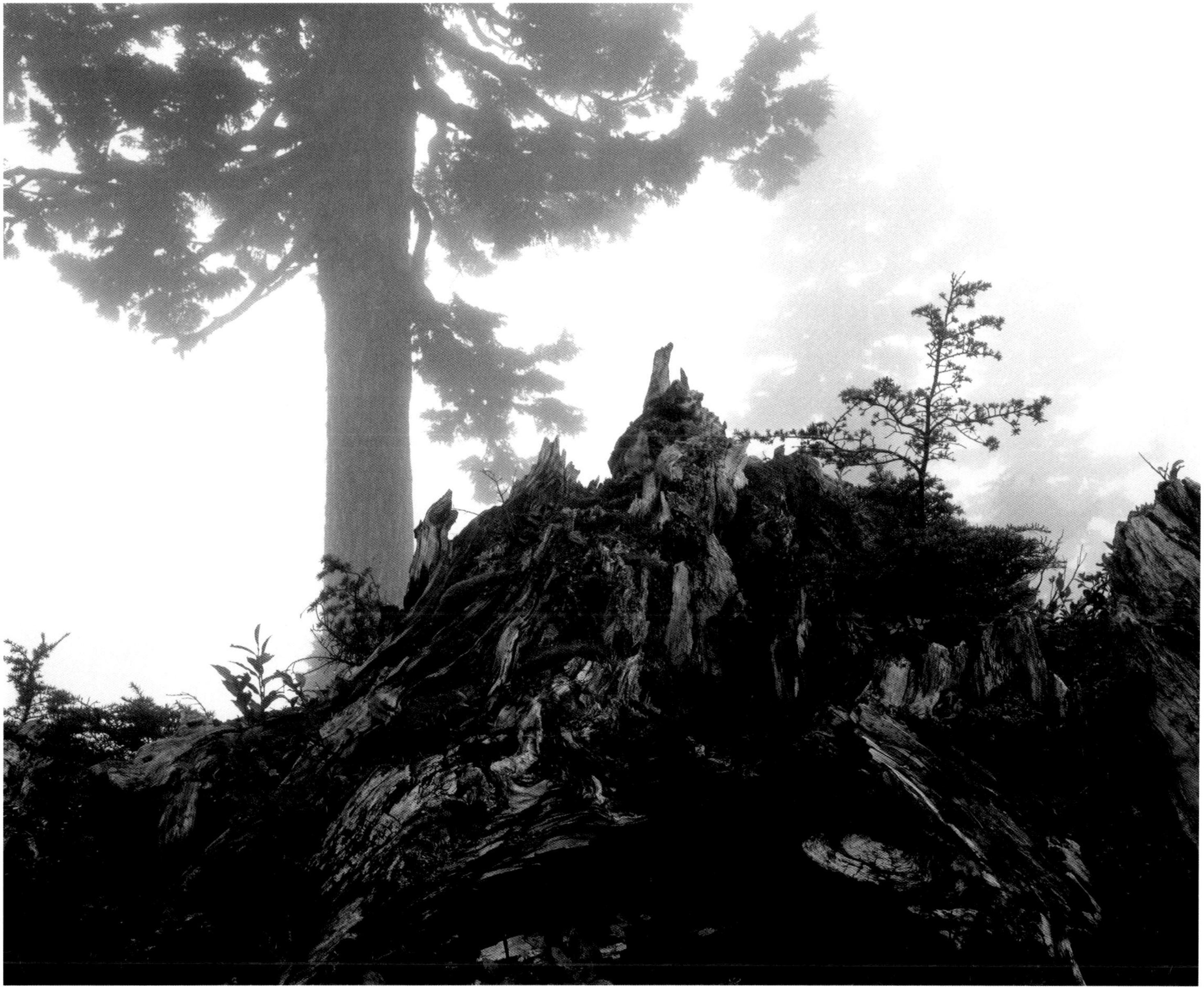

TREE, STUMP, AND MIST, NORTH CASCADES NATIONAL PARK, WASHINGTON, 1958

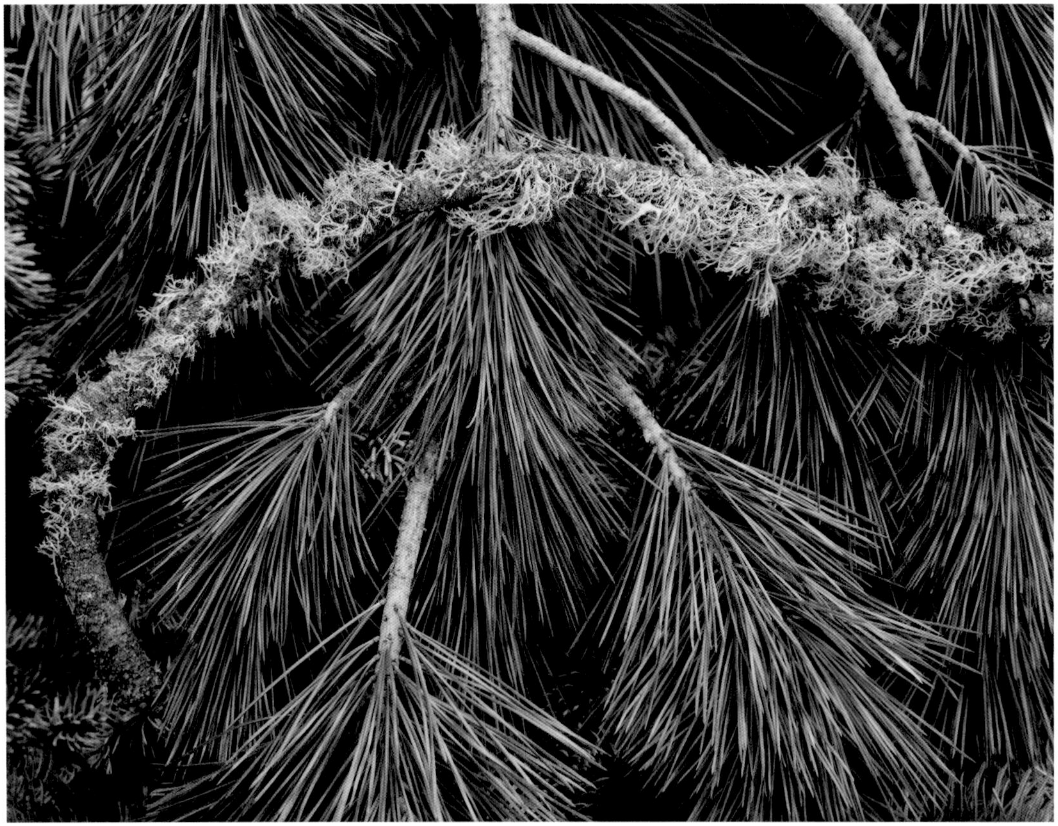

SUGAR PINE BOUGHS AND LICHEN, YOSEMITE NATIONAL PARK, CALIFORNIA, 1962

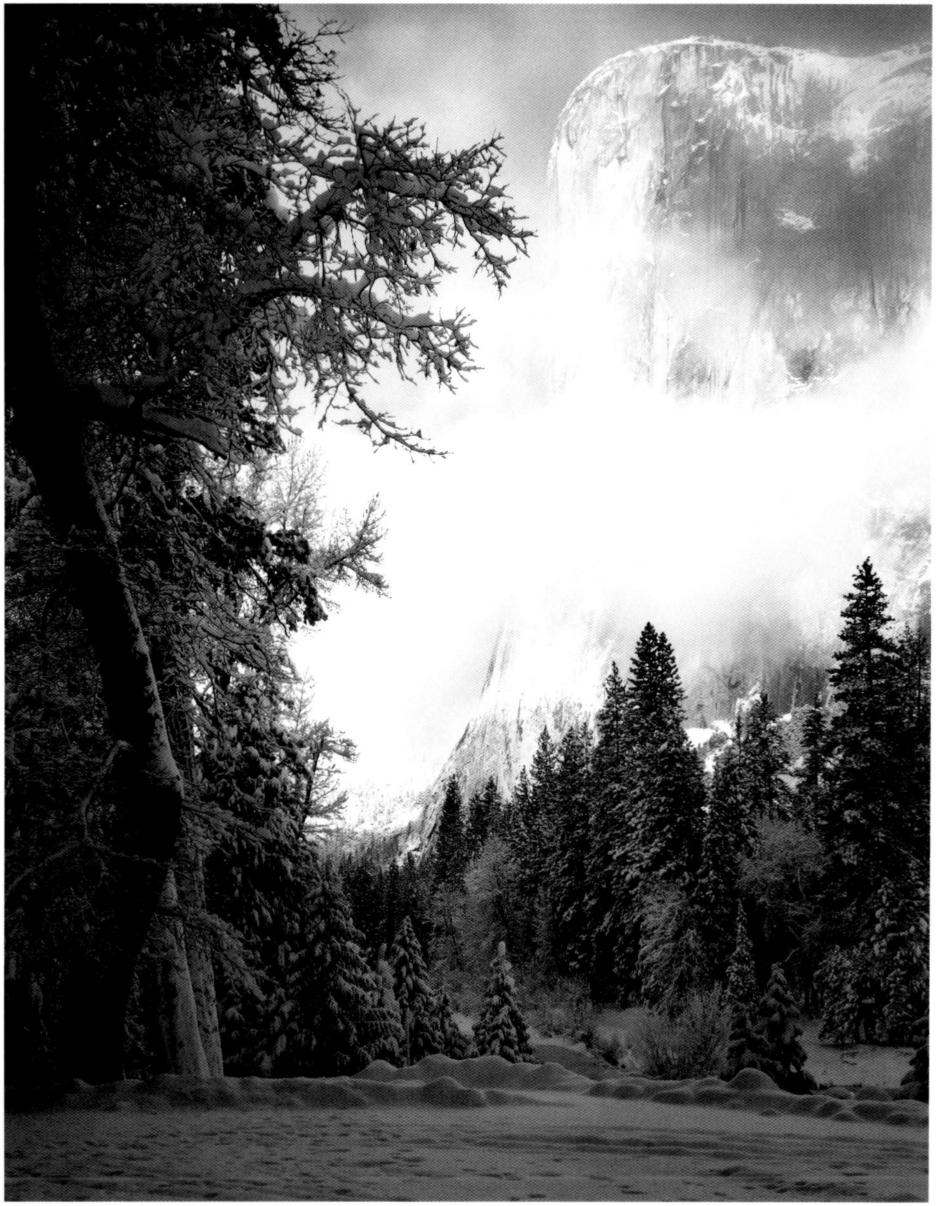

EL CAPITAN, WINTER, SUNRISE, YOSEMITE NATIONAL PARK, CALIFORNIA, 1968

El Capitan and Half Dome are two of the most imposing sights in Yosemite Valley. Ansel approached the huge granite monoliths with reverence and photographed them repeatedly over more than sixty years. He wrote: "The great rocks of Yosemite, expressing qualities of timeless, yet intimate grandeur, are the most compelling formations of their kind. We should not casually pass them by for they are the very heart of the earth speaking to us."

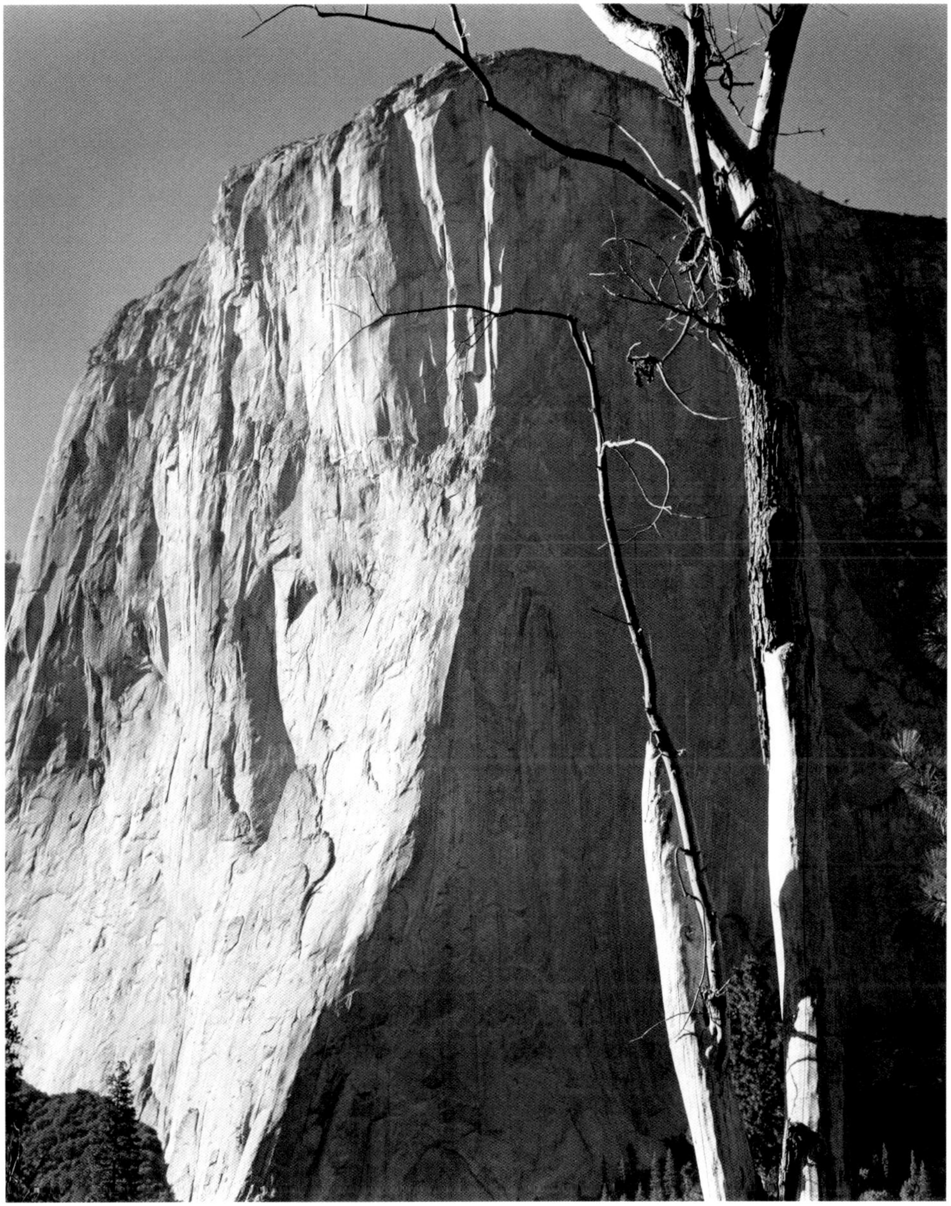

SUMMIT OF EL CAPITAN, DEAD TREE, YOSEMITE NATIONAL PARK, CALIFORNIA, C. 1950

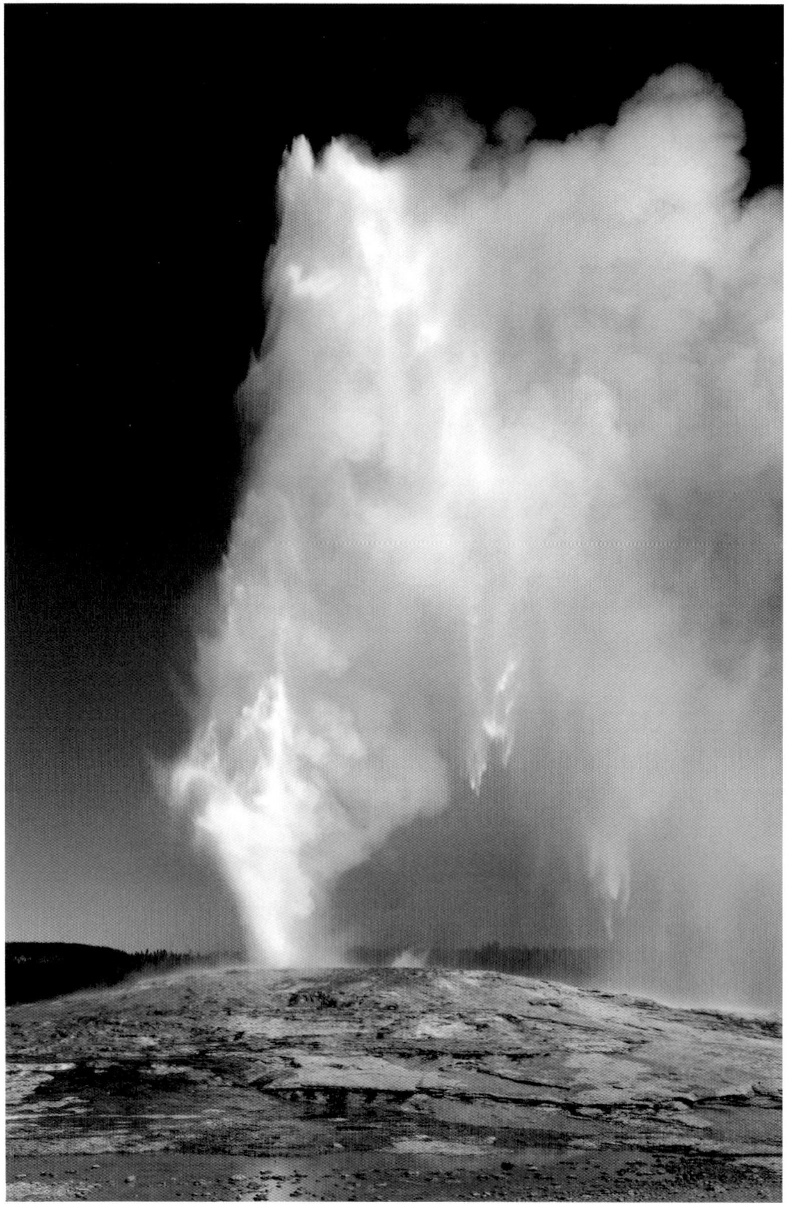

OLD FAITHFUL GEYSER, YELLOWSTONE NATIONAL PARK, WYOMING, 1942

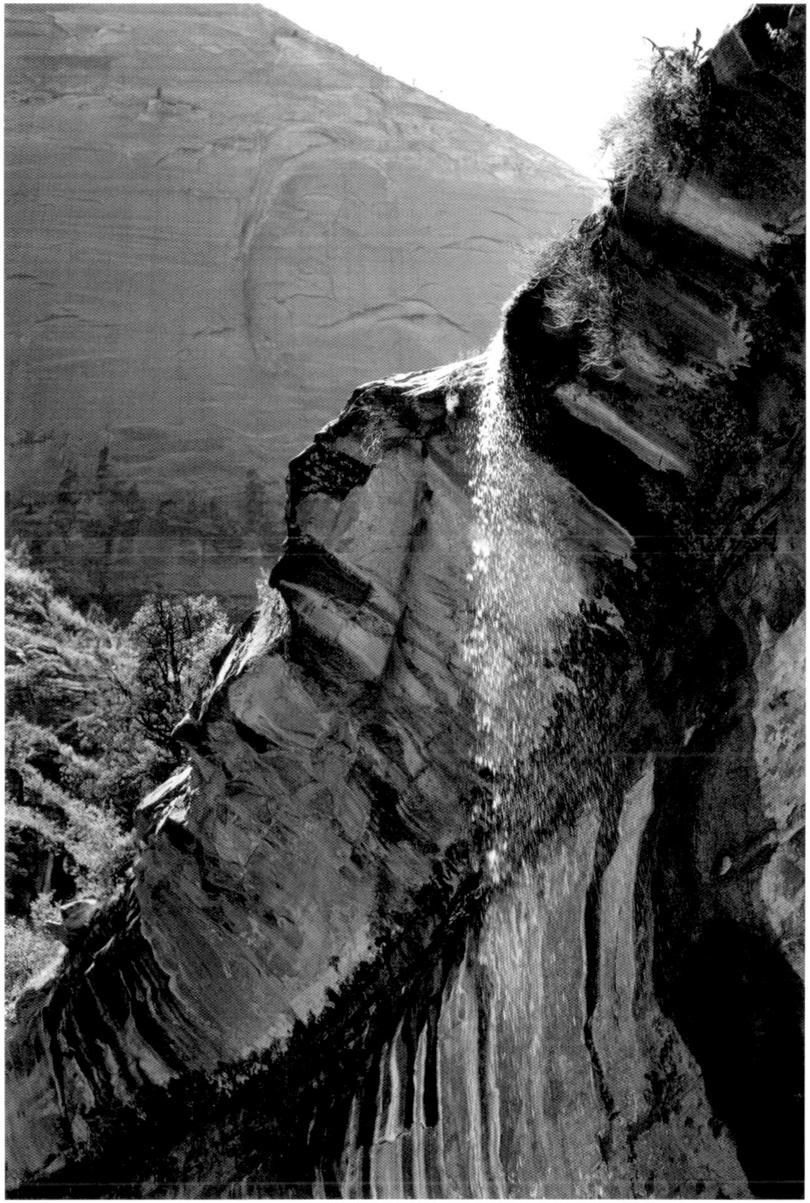

WATERFALL, ZION NATIONAL PARK, UTAH, 1947

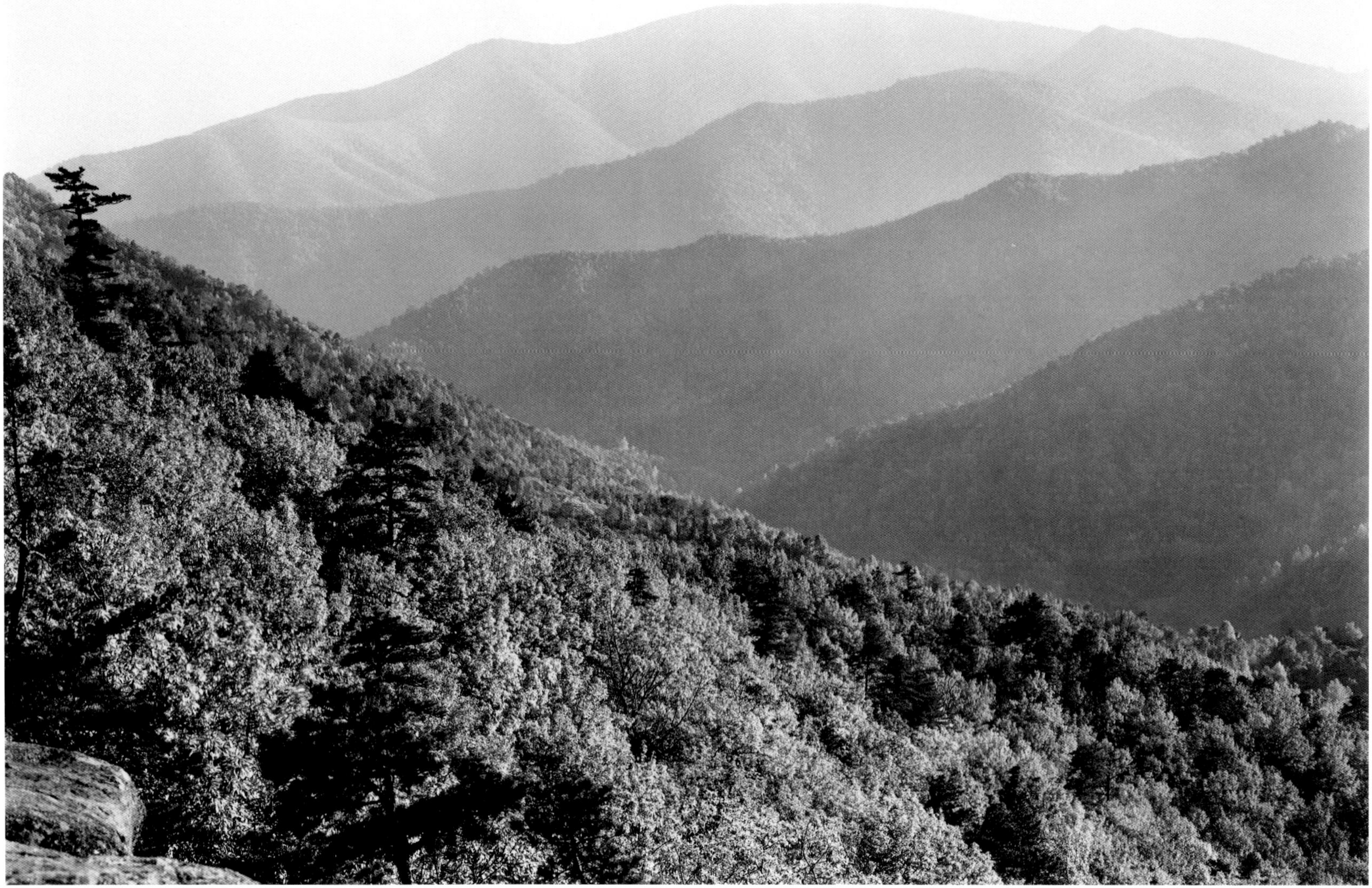

VIEW FROM THE ROAD, SHENANDOAH NATIONAL PARK, VIRGINIA, 1948

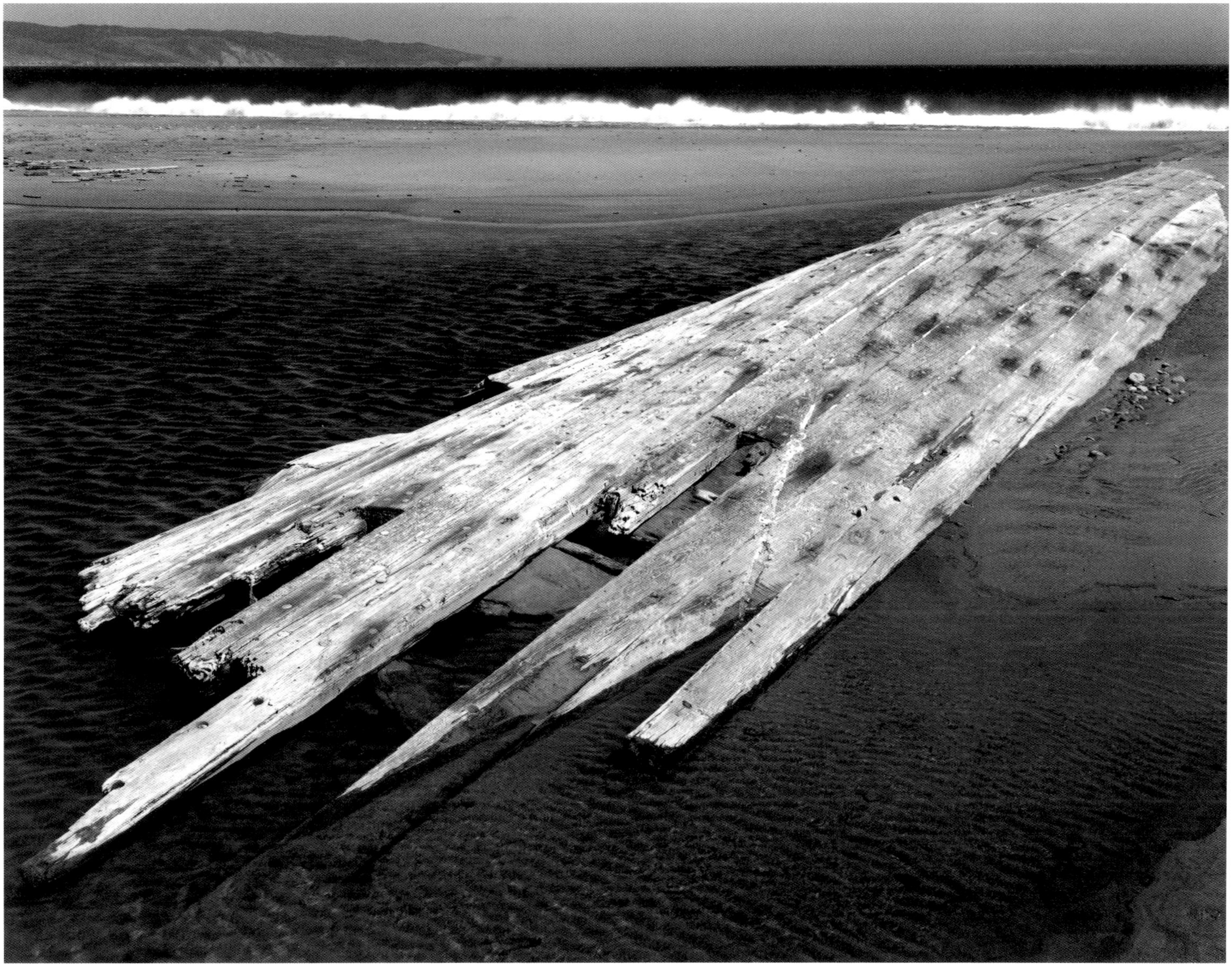

HULL OF WRECKED SHIP, DRAKE'S BAY, POINT REYES NATIONAL SEASHORE, CALIFORNIA, 1953

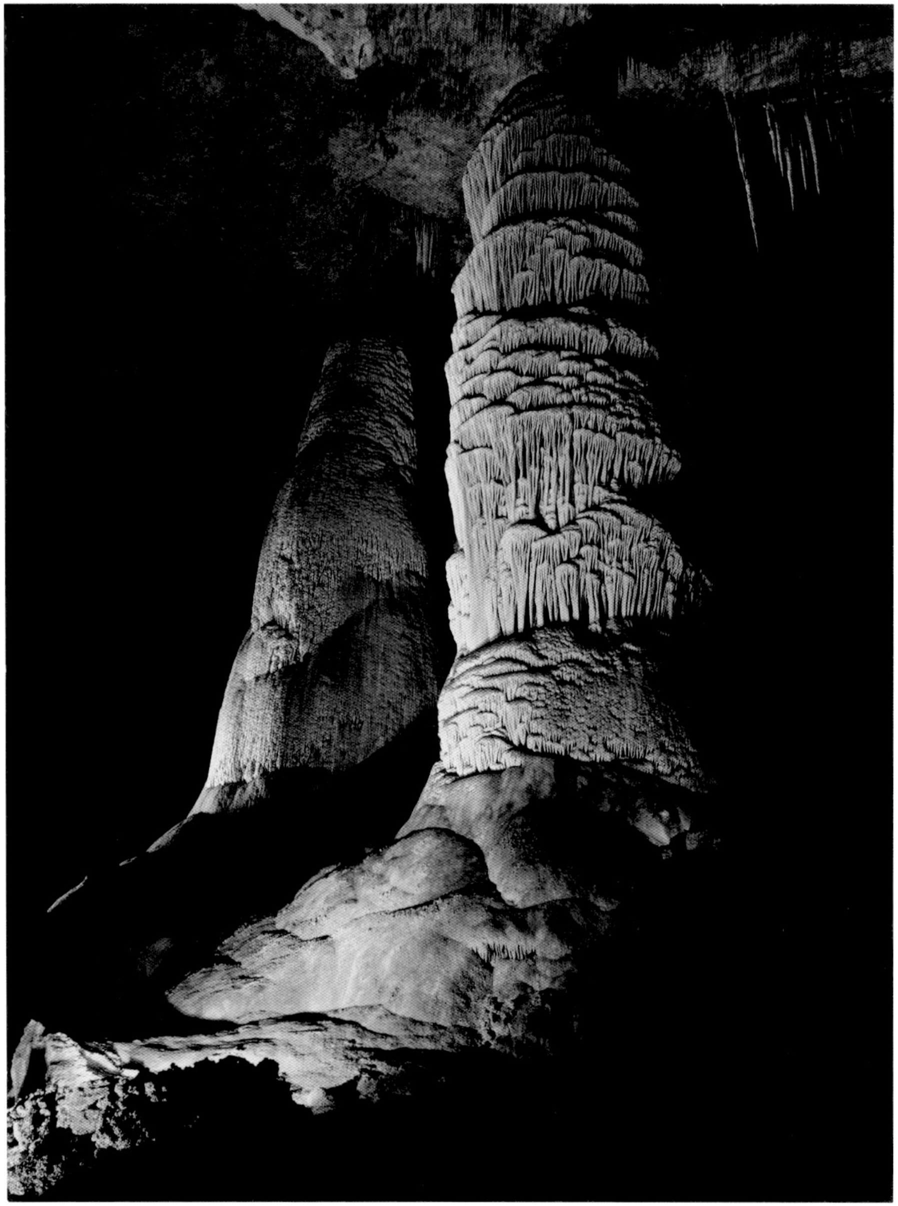

THE GIANT DOME, CARLSBAD CAVERNS NATIONAL PARK, NEW MEXICO, 1942

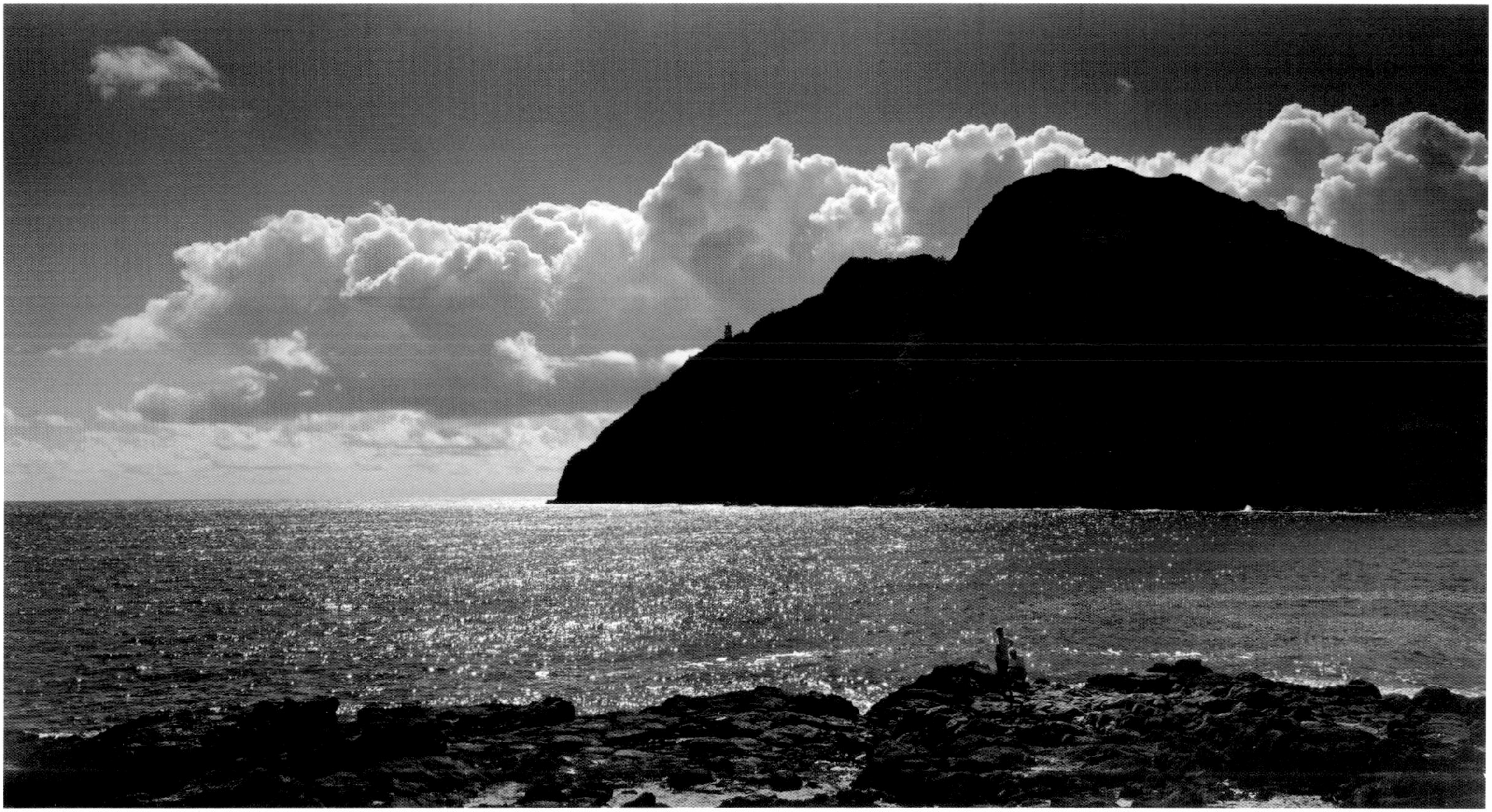

MAKAPU'U POINT, OAHU, HAWAII, 1957

"One spring morning in 1950," Ansel wrote, "Yosemite Fall was booming in flood, and I climbed to the base of the upper fall.... I was primarily interested in details of the falling water.... There was a constant change of fast-moving shapes in the water, and gusts of windy spray would frequently force me to keep the camera covered with my focusing cloth. When the spray disappeared, I would uncover the camera and await the precious moment."

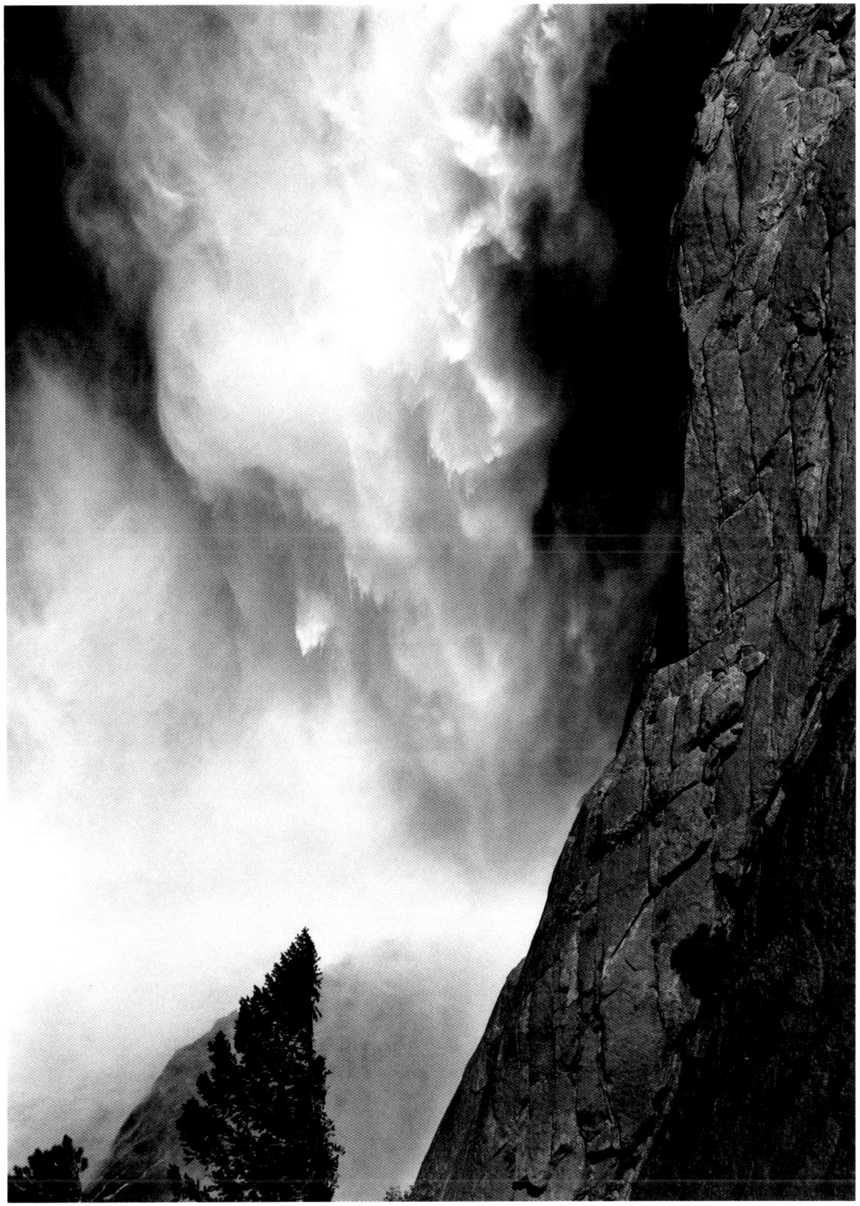

BASE OF UPPER YOSEMITE FALL, YOSEMITE NATIONAL PARK, CALIFORNIA, C. 1950

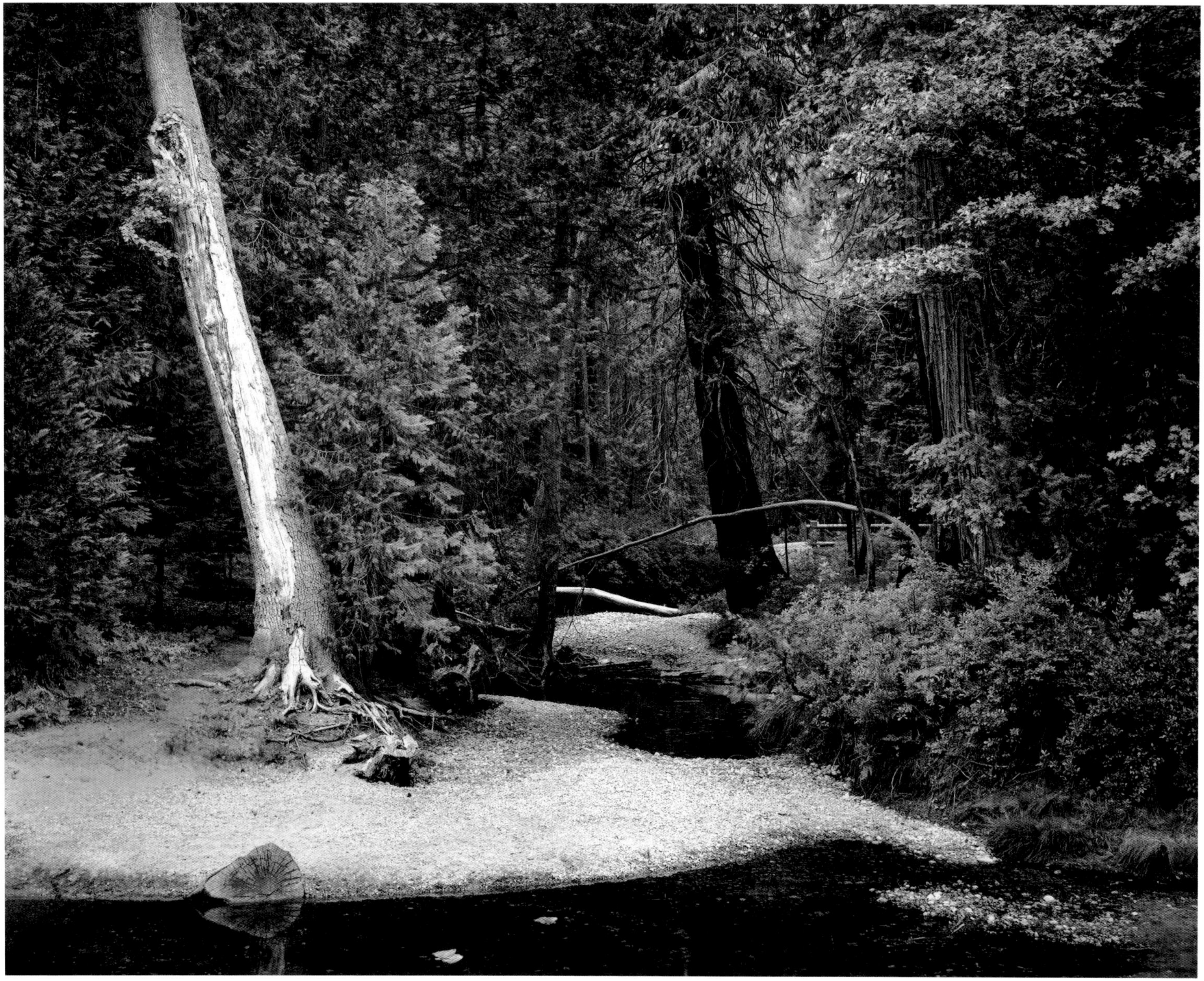

FOREST AND STREAM, LATE EVENING, YOSEMITE NATIONAL PARK, CALIFORNIA, C. 1936

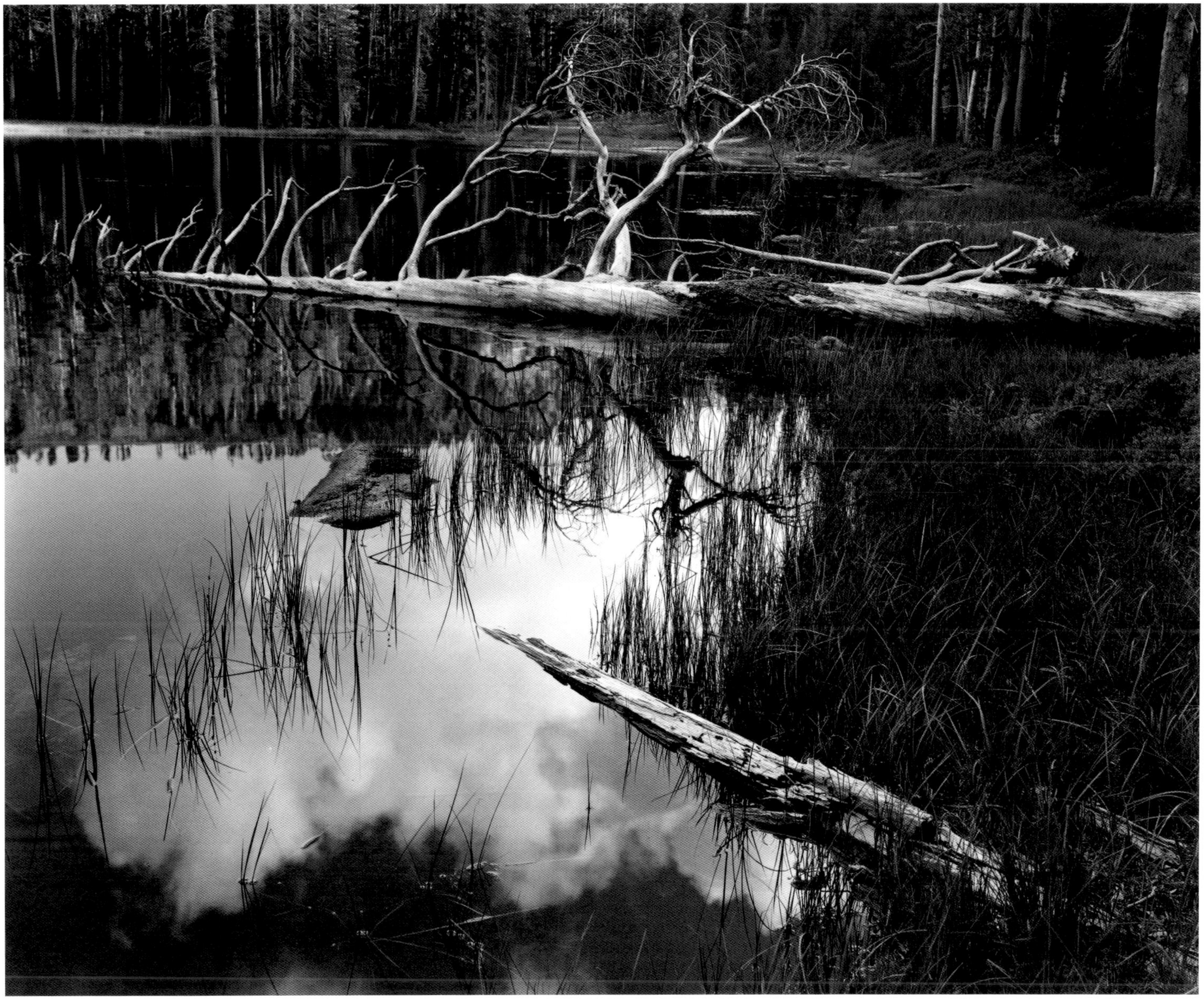

SIESTA LAKE, YOSEMITE NATIONAL PARK, CALIFORNIA, C. 1958

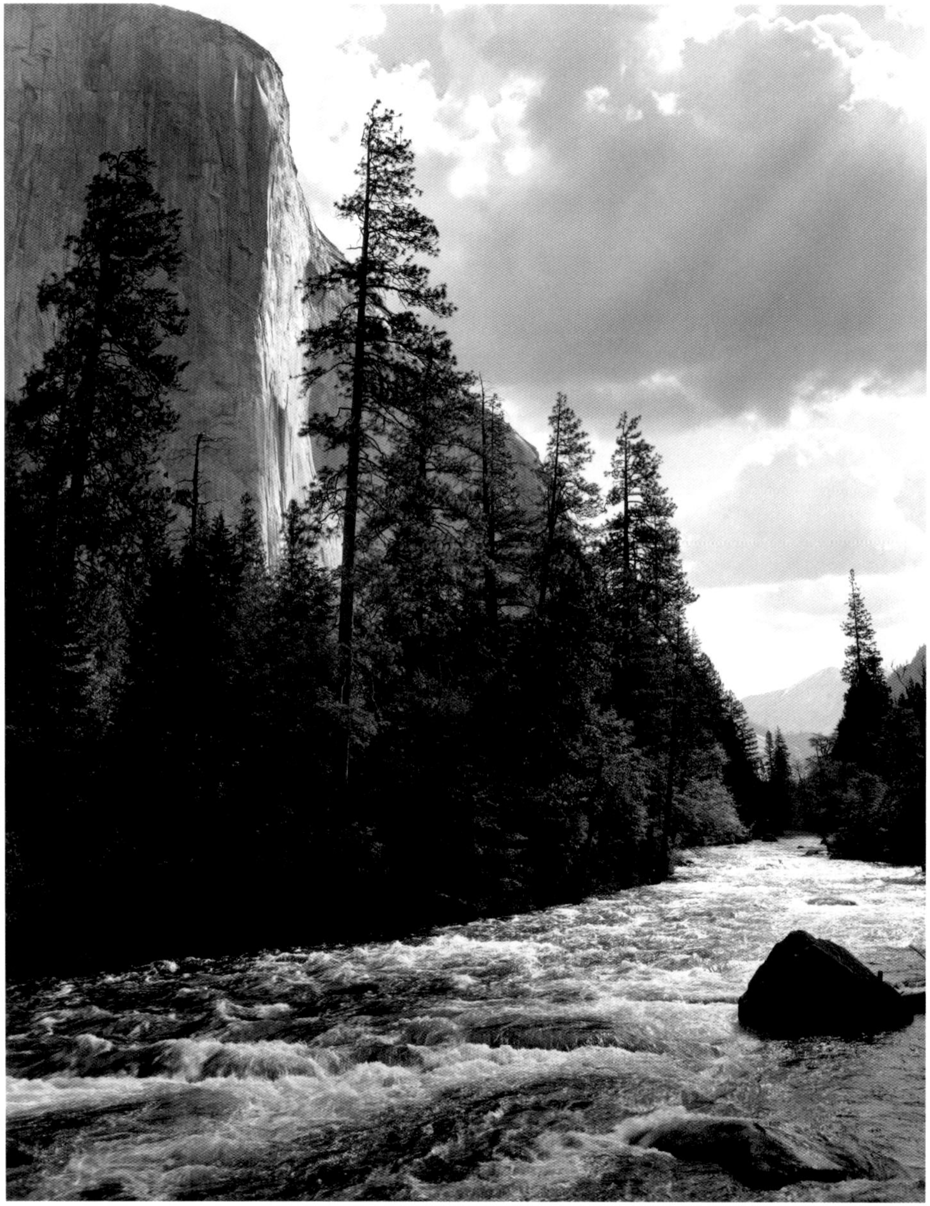

EL CAPITAN, MERCED RIVER, CLOUDS, YOSEMITE NATIONAL PARK, CALIFORNIA, 1948

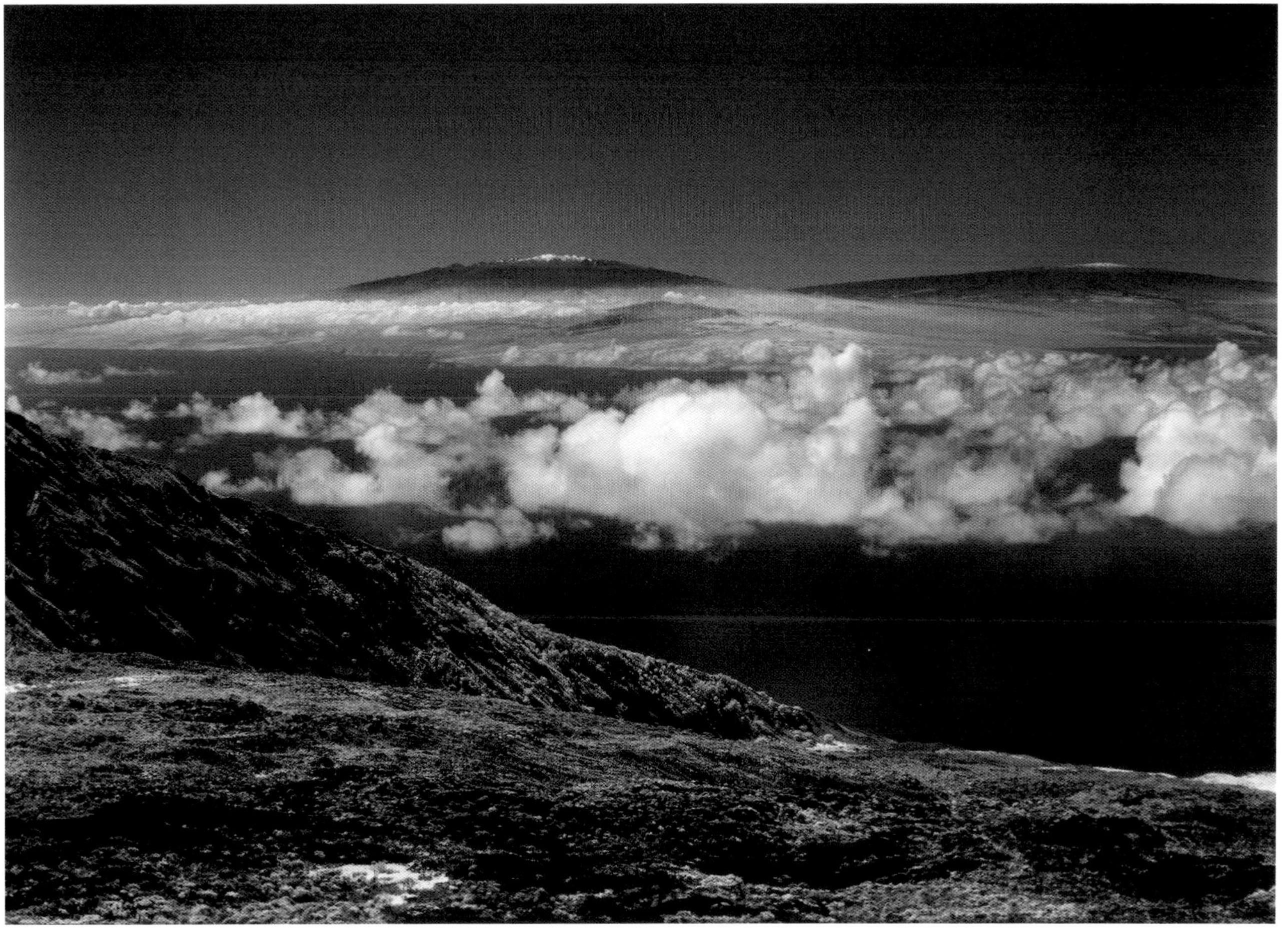

MAUNA KEA AND MAUNA LOA FROM HALEAKALA, HALEAKALA NATIONAL PARK, HAWAII, C. 1948

The spectacular beauty of the rugged and remote middle and south forks of the Kings River Sierra particularly appealed to Ansel, who photographed the area on repeated visits. He made this photograph (and the photographs on pages 111 and 144) on the annual High Sierra pack trip organized by the Sierra Club in 1934.

In 1936, the Sierra Club sent Ansel to Washington, DC, to lobby for the establishment of a Kings Canyon national park. "With total naivete," he wrote, "I ventured into the strange wilderness of our nation's capitol with a portfolio of photographs under my arm, visiting congressmen and senators in their lairs. I boldly proclaimed the glories of the High Sierra and showed my pictures with unabashed confidence that they would prove our contention." He left Washington without assurance that the campaign to protect Kings Canyon had succeeded.

Two years later, Ansel published a book of his photographs of the Sierra Nevada that included this image. He sent a copy of the book to the National Park Service, which forwarded it to Harold L. Ickes, the secretary of the interior. Ickes gave the book to President Franklin D. Roosevelt, who was greatly impressed and, in 1940, signed legislation creating Kings Canyon National Park. The director of the National Park Service, Arno Cammerer, wrote Ansel, "A silent but most effective voice in the campaign was your own book, *Sierra Nevada: The John Muir Trail.* So long as that book is in existence, it will go on justifying the Park." The five hundred books in the signed, limited edition published in 1938 are now rare collector's items; in 2006, Little, Brown and Company published a new deluxe edition, also limited to five hundred copies, as well as a smaller-format edition for wider distribution.

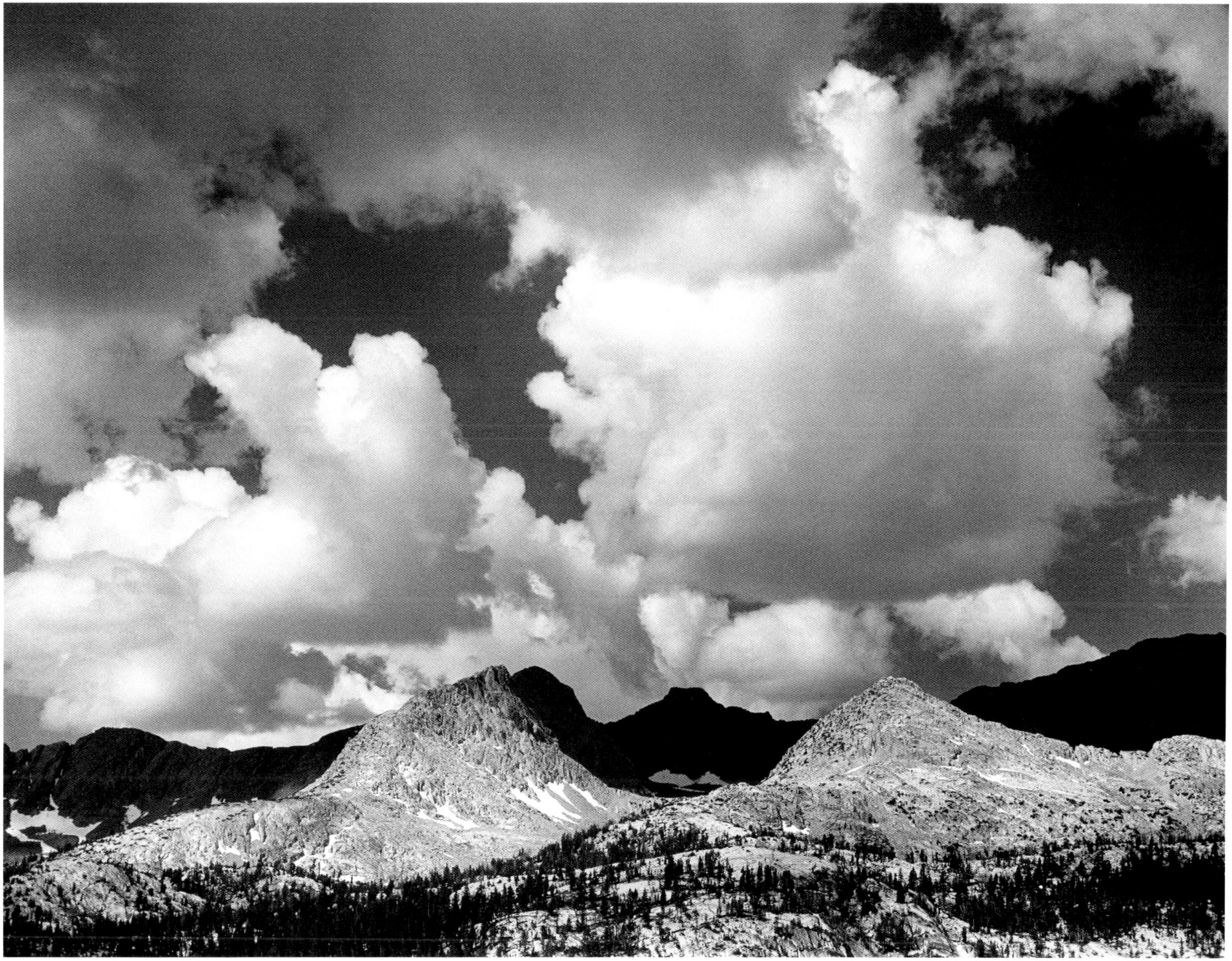

EMERALD PEAK, KINGS CANYON NATIONAL PARK, CALIFORNIA, 1934

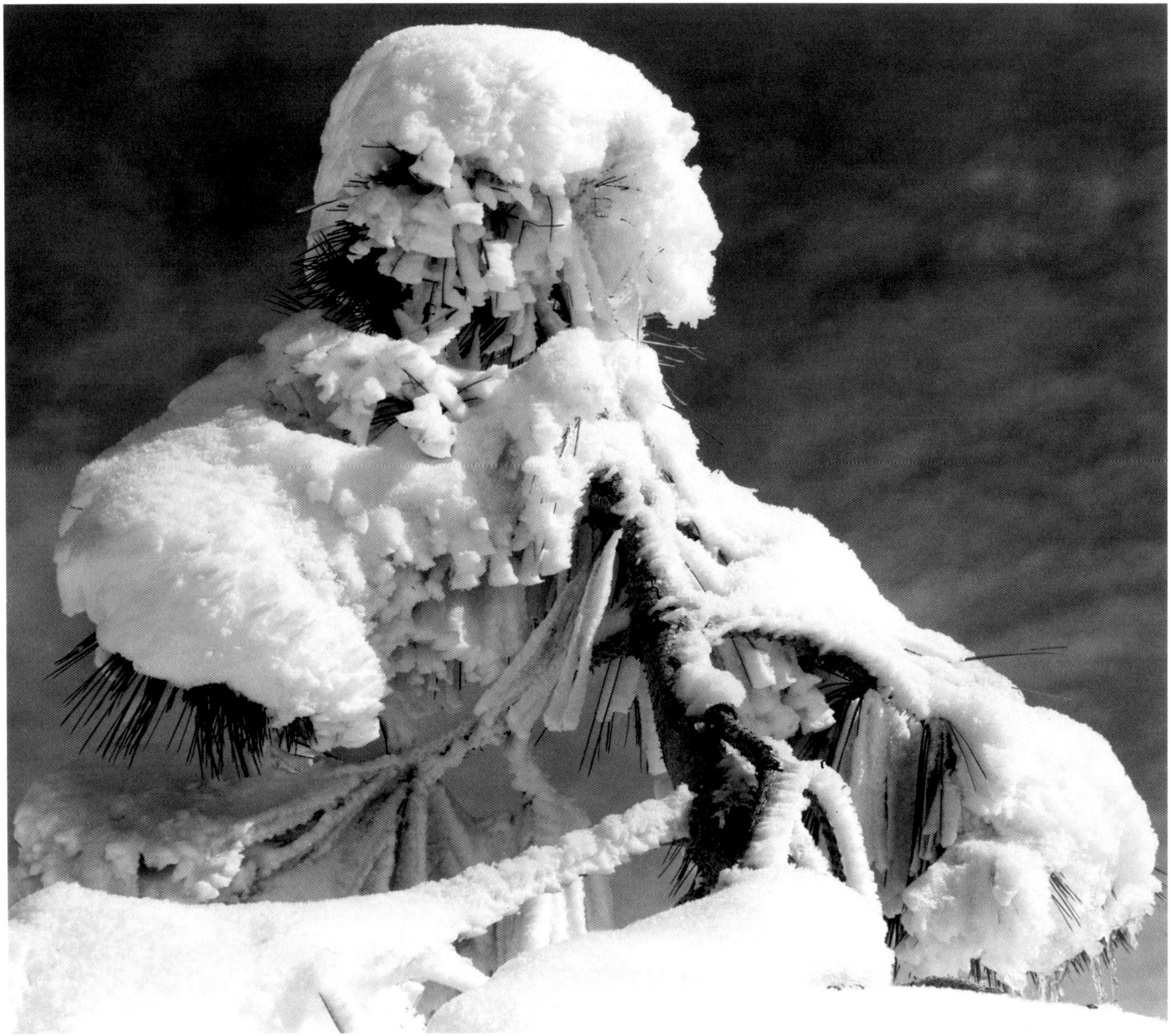

PINE TREE IN SNOW, YOSEMITE NATIONAL PARK, CALIFORNIA, C. 1937

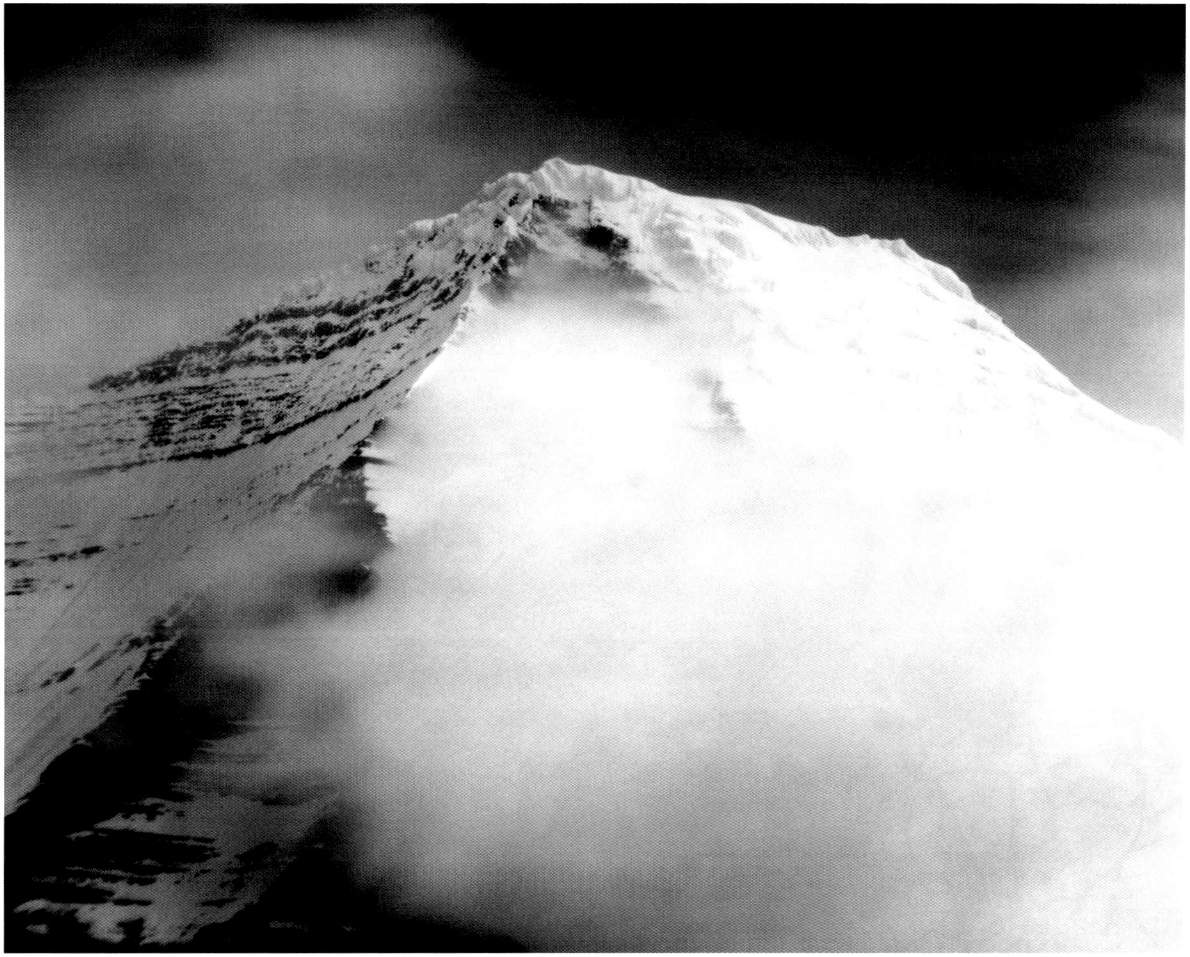

SUMMIT OF MOUNT ROBSON IN CLOUDS, JASPER NATIONAL PARK, CANADA, 1928

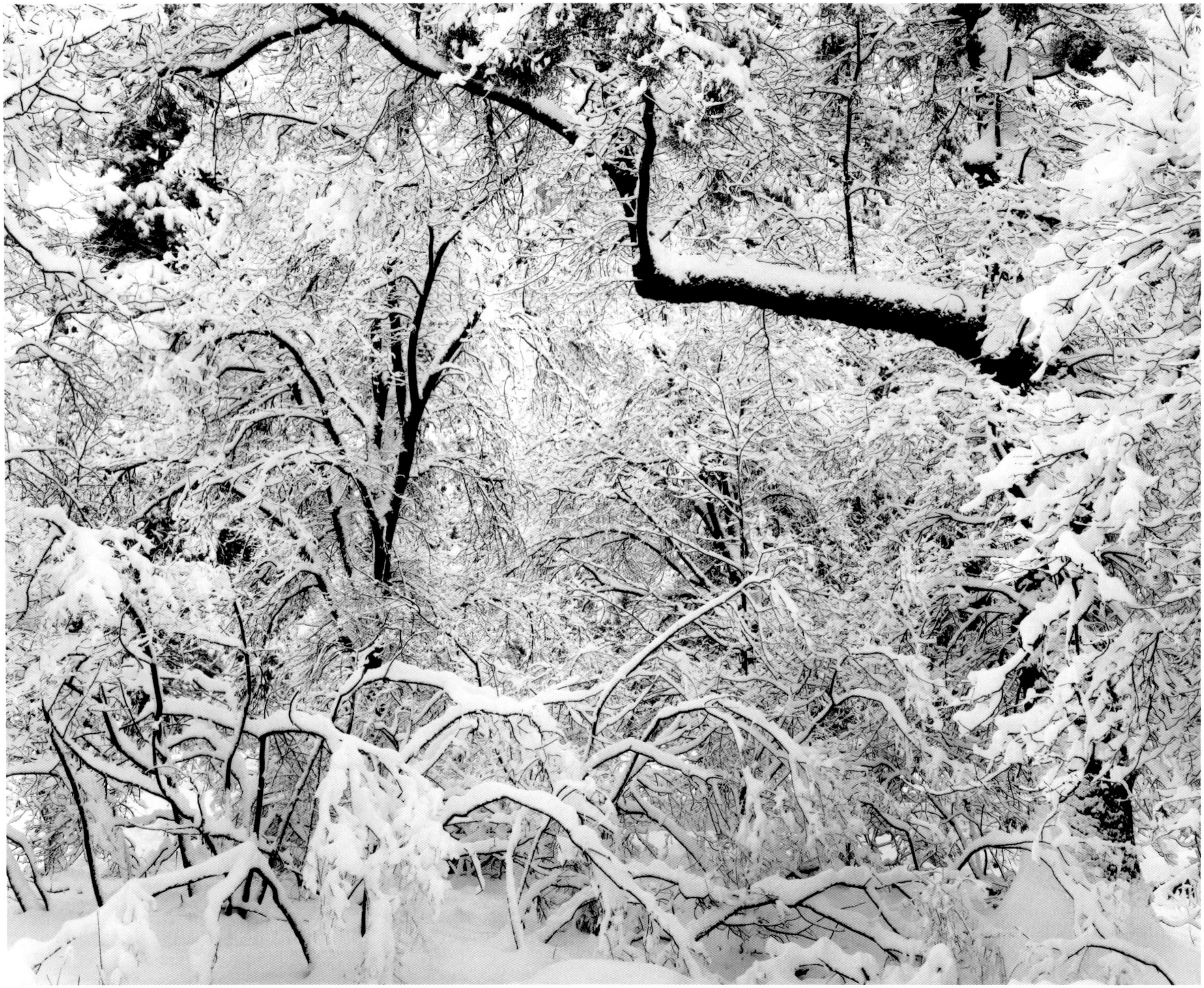

FRESH SNOW, YOSEMITE NATIONAL PARK, CALIFORNIA, C. 1947

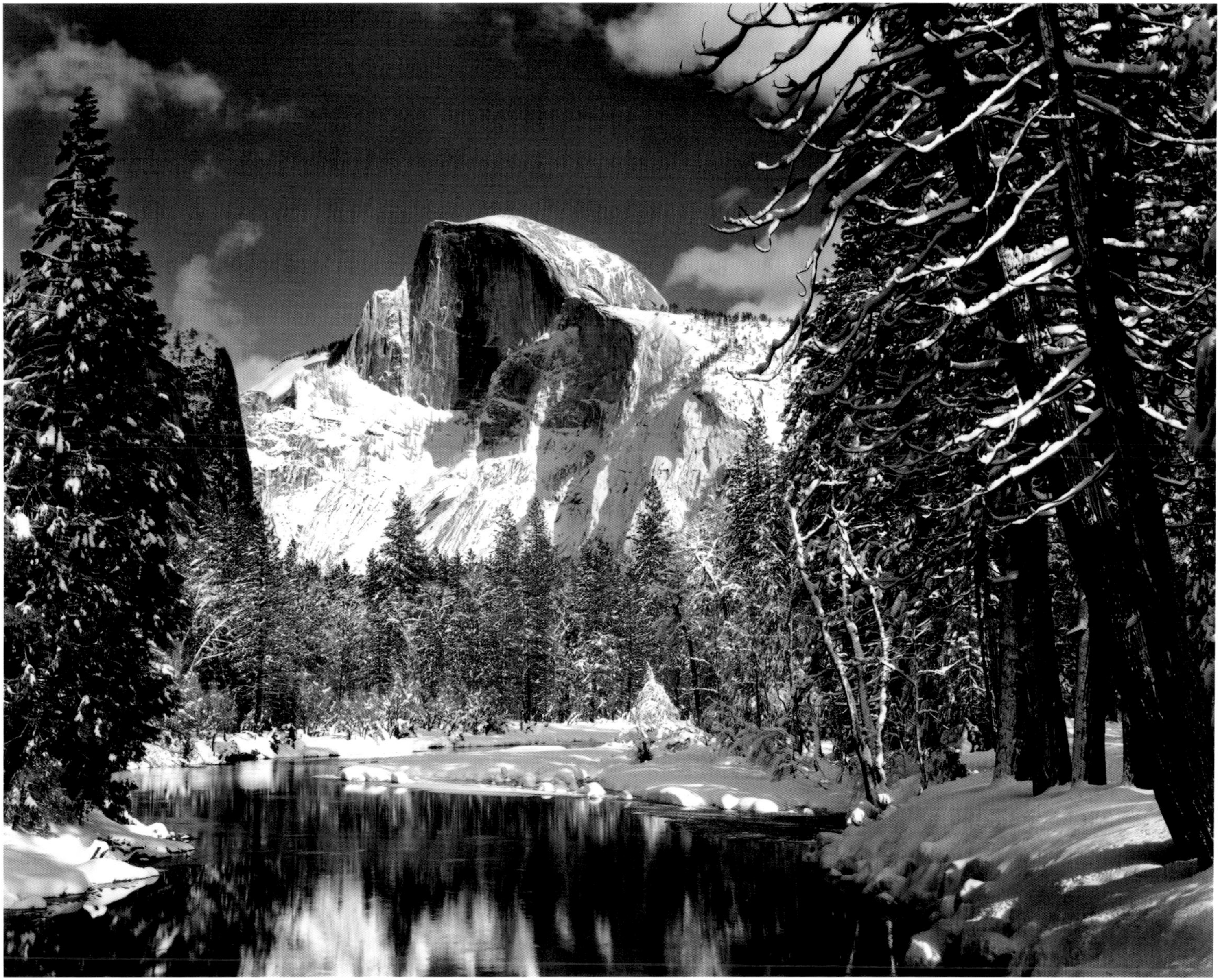

HALF DOME, MERCED RIVER, YOSEMITE NATIONAL PARK, CALIFORNIA, 1938

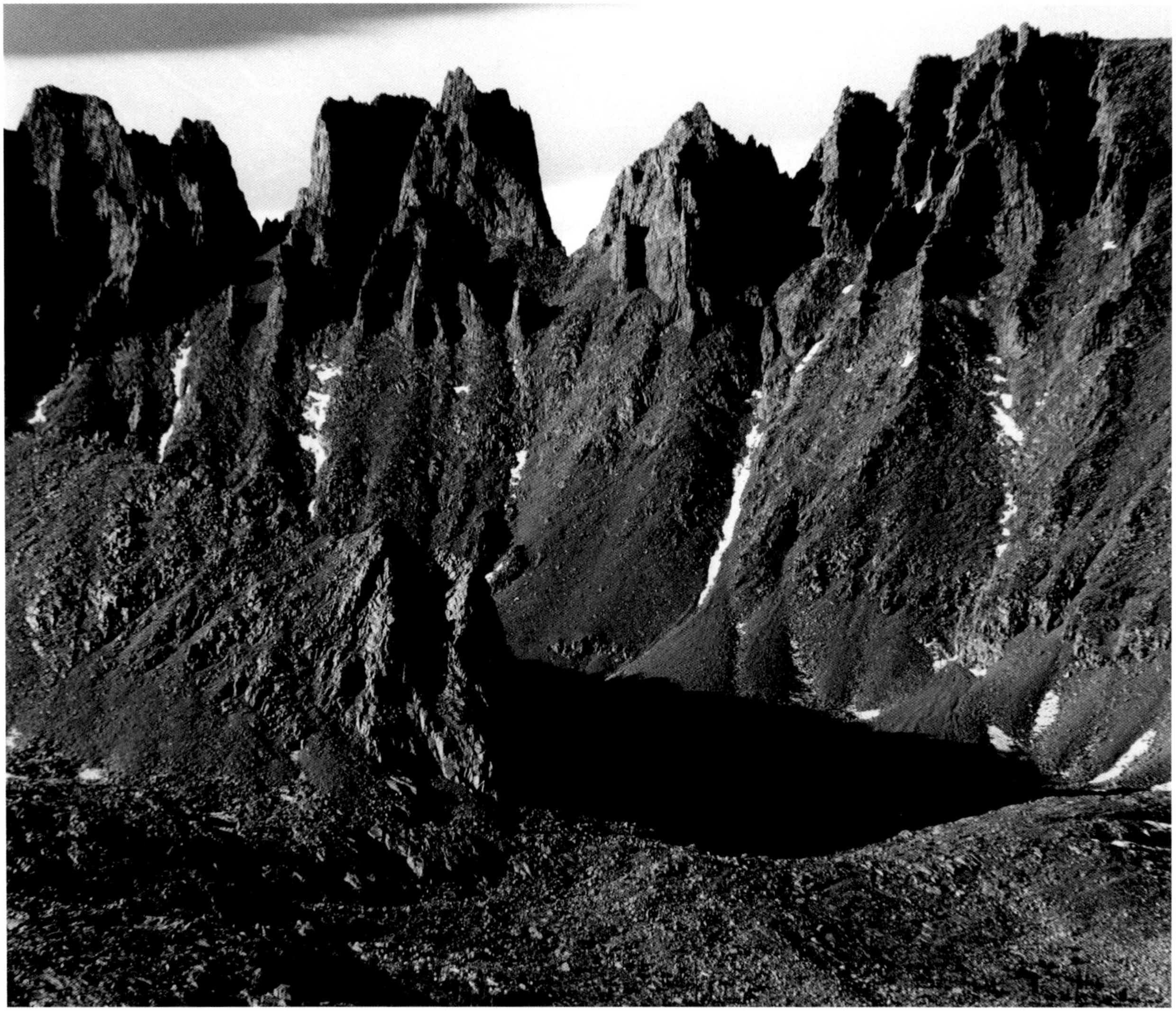

MIDDLE KAWEAH PEAKS, SEQUOIA NATIONAL PARK, CALIFORNIA, C. 1935

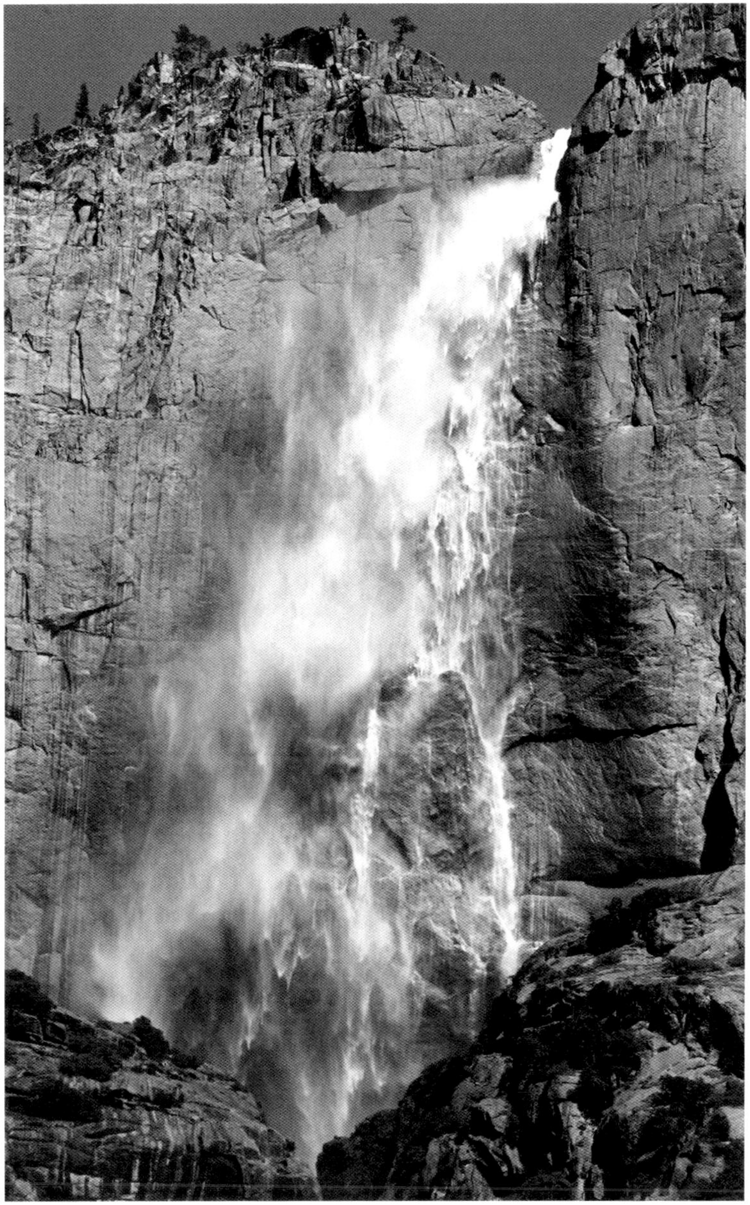

UPPER YOSEMITE FALL, YOSEMITE NATIONAL PARK, CALIFORNIA, C. 1938

One of the most popular ways to experience Glacier National Park is by driving the Going-to-the-Sun Road that runs through the center of the park. Many of the photographs Ansel made at Glacier were taken from this scenic road, including this view of Going-to-the-Sun Mountain. Ansel's photographs often appear to have been made in remote wilderness areas, but his vantage point was sometimes a much-visited spot. His iconic view of the Tetons (page 203) was made from a turnout on a main road traveled by many tourists. Likewise, many of his views of Yosemite Valley (see pages 103, 109, and 213) were made from the parking area on one of the principal routes into the park.

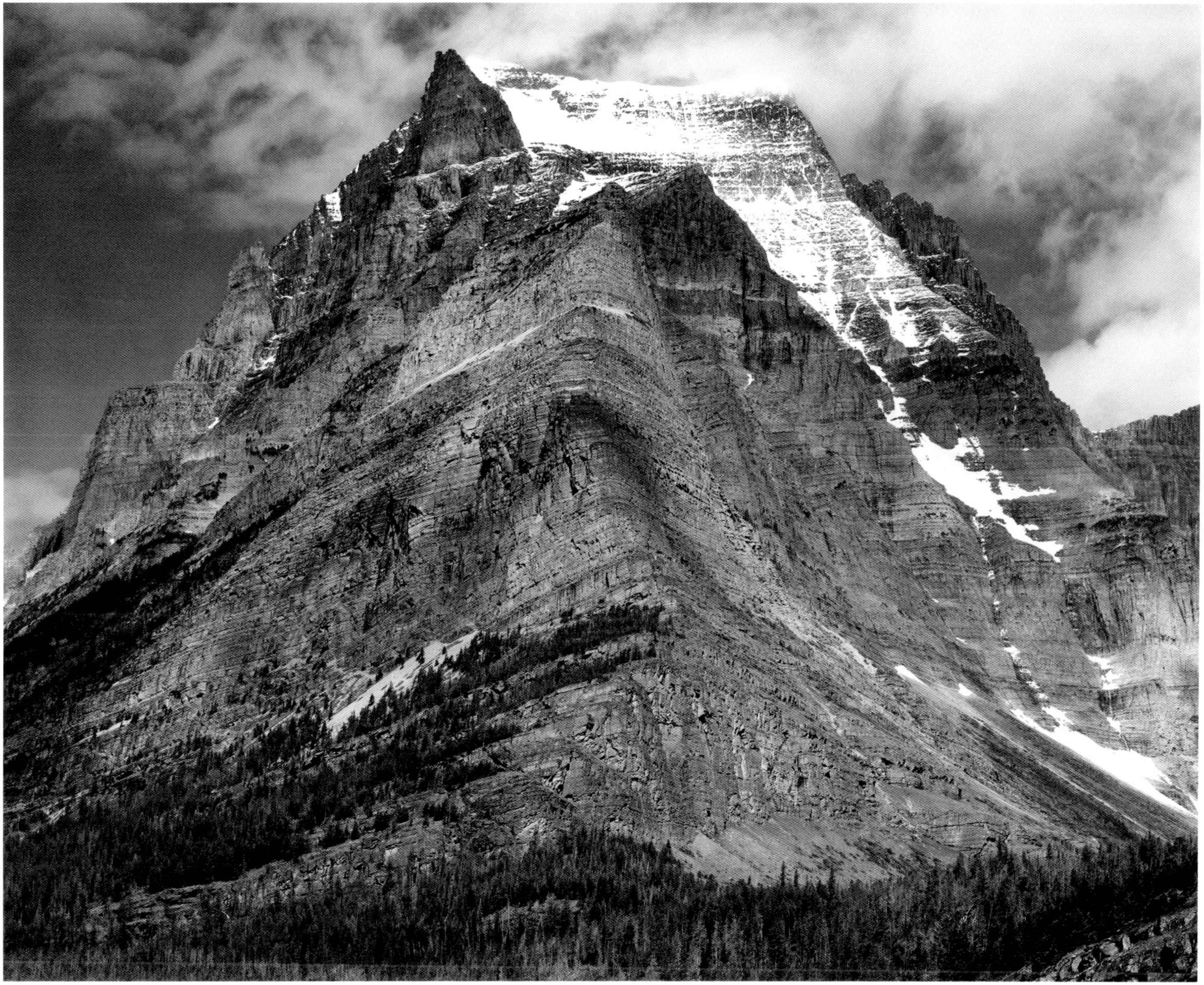

GOING-TO-THE-SUN MOUNTAIN, GLACIER NATIONAL PARK, MONTANA, 1942

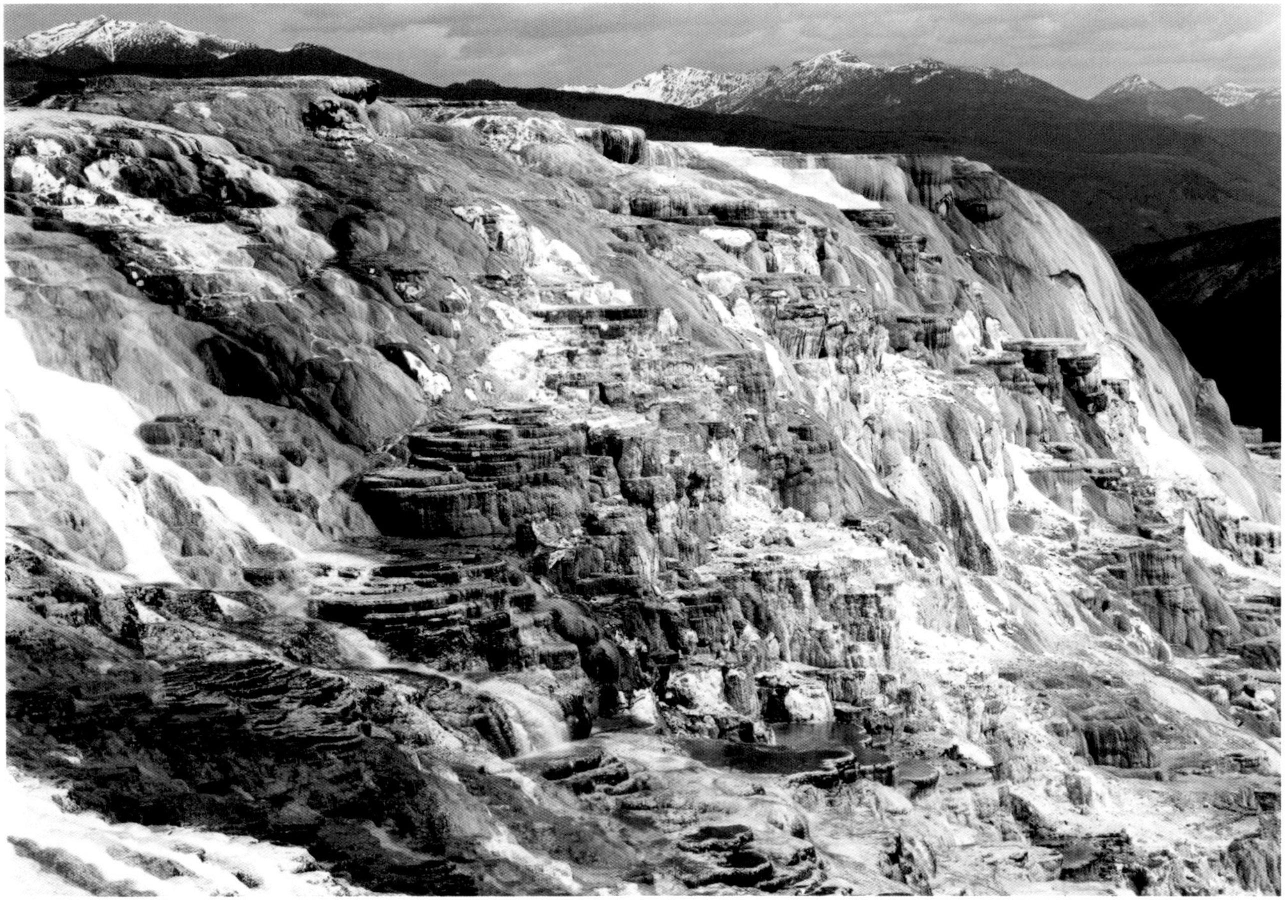

MAMMOTH HOT SPRINGS, YELLOWSTONE NATIONAL PARK, WYOMING, 1942

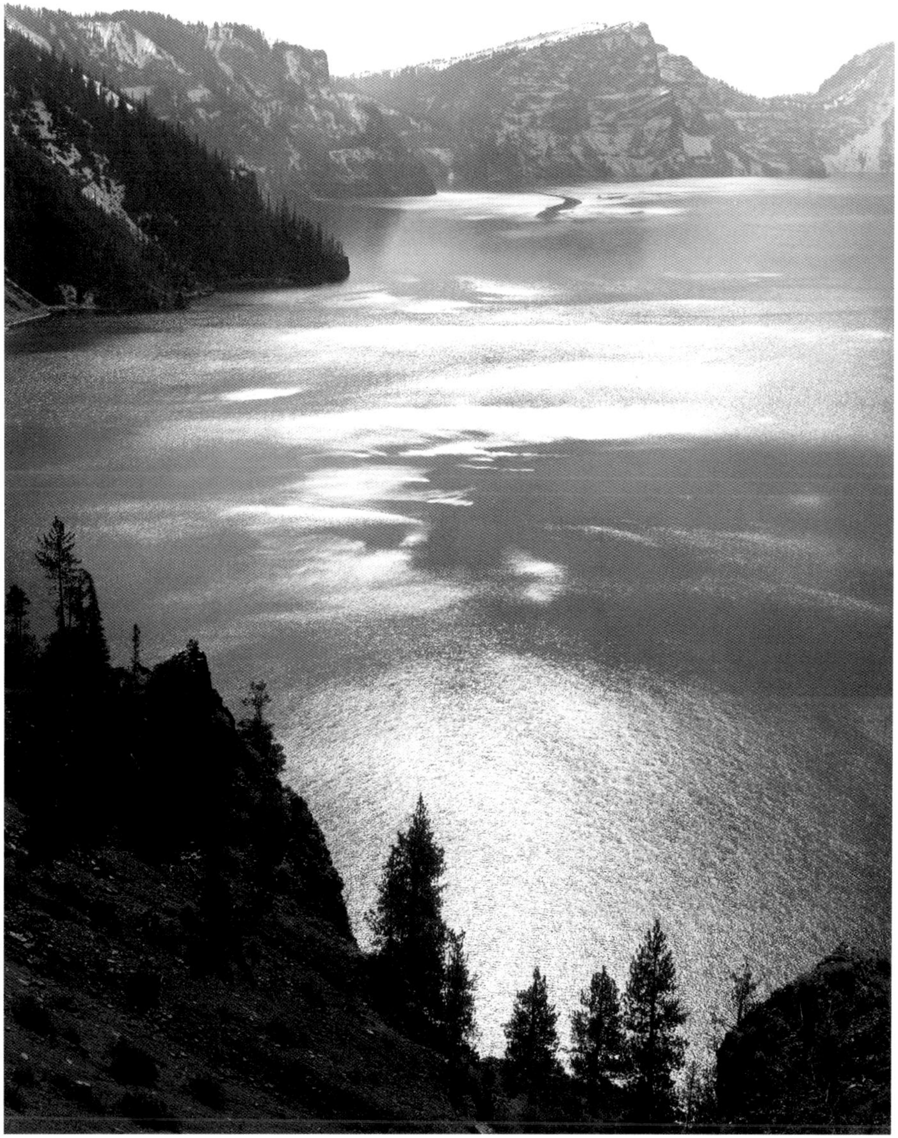

AFTERNOON SUN, CRATER LAKE NATIONAL PARK, OREGON, 1943

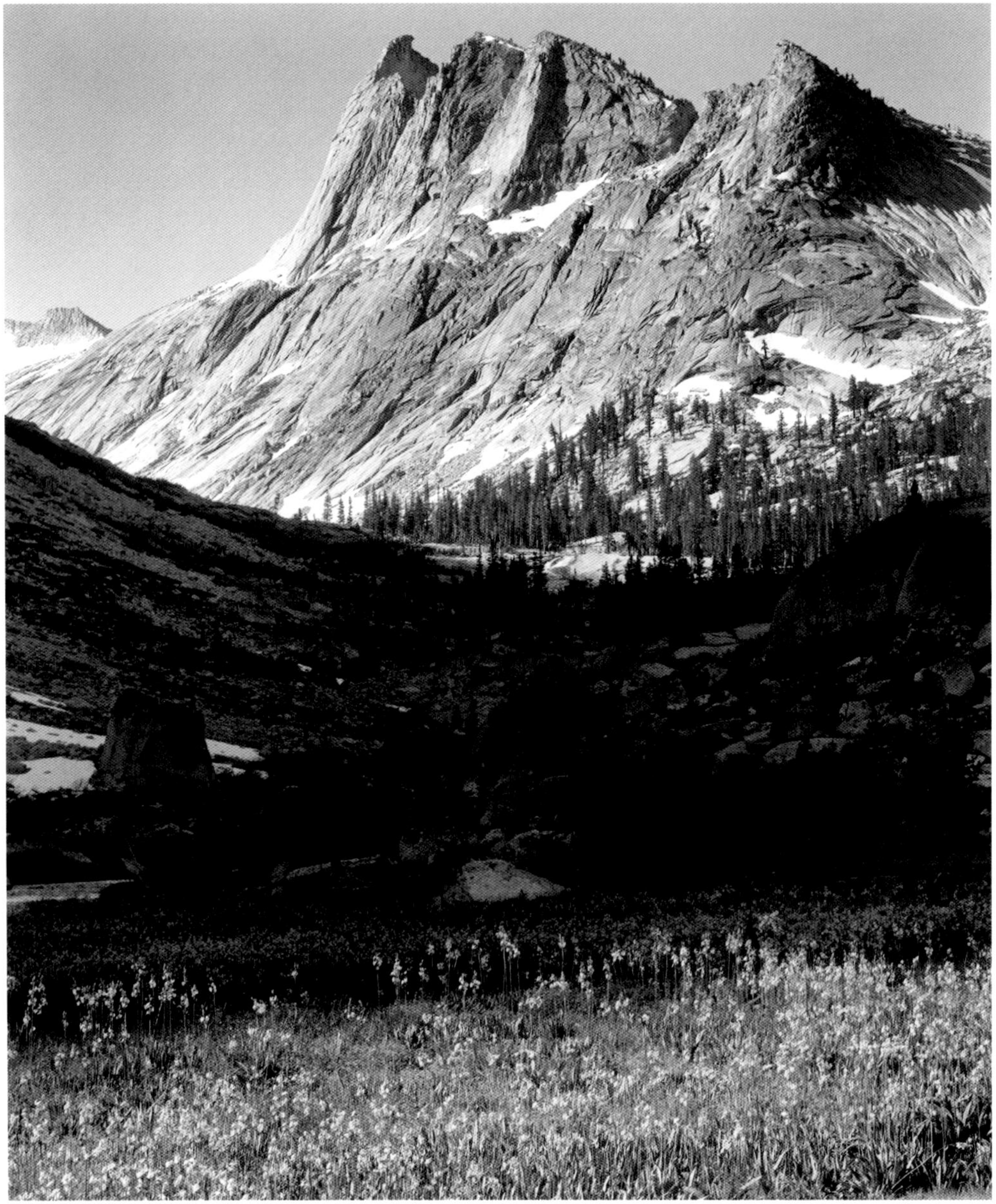

BIG BIRD PEAK, DEADMAN CANYON, KINGS CANYON NATIONAL PARK, CALIFORNIA, 1934

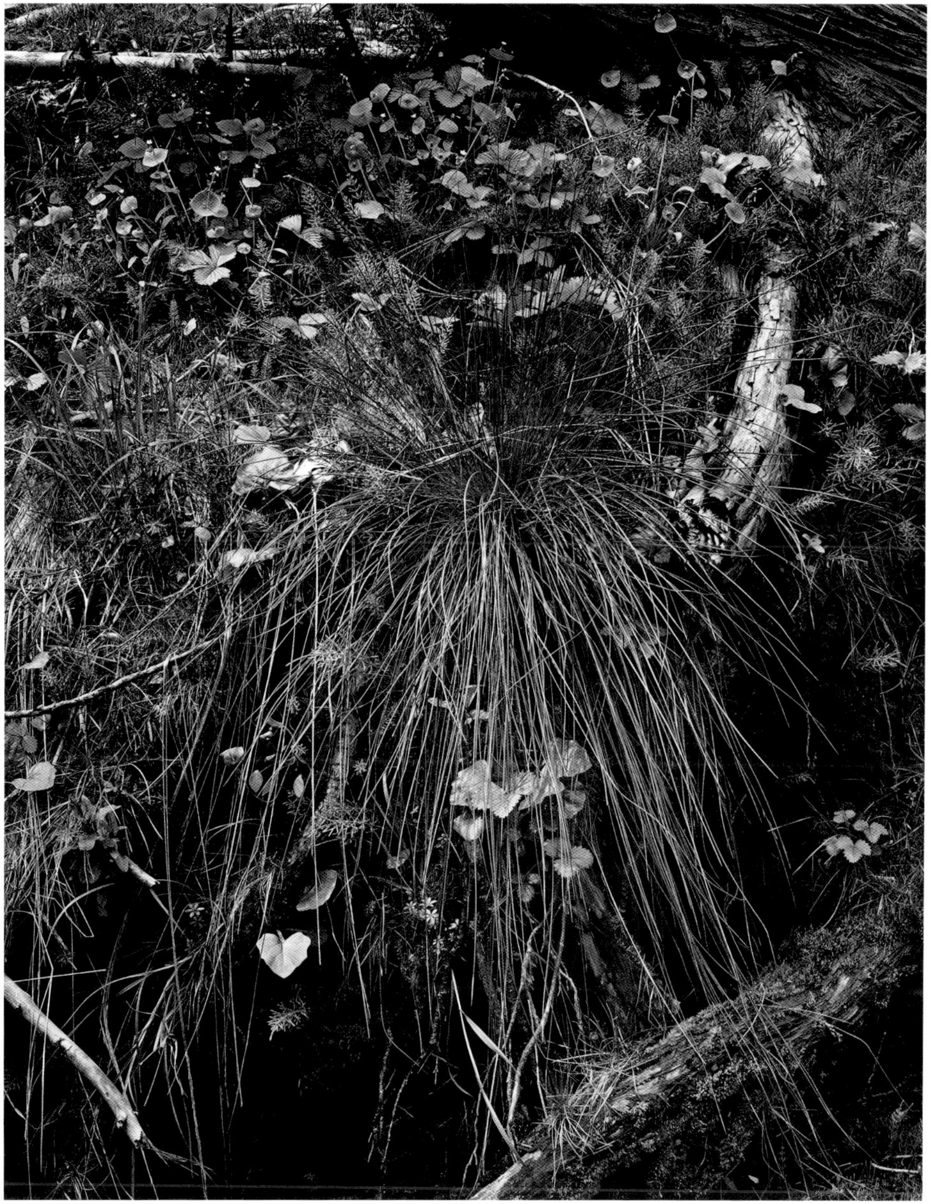

GRASS AND LEAVES, YOSEMITE NATIONAL PARK, CALIFORNIA, C. 1940

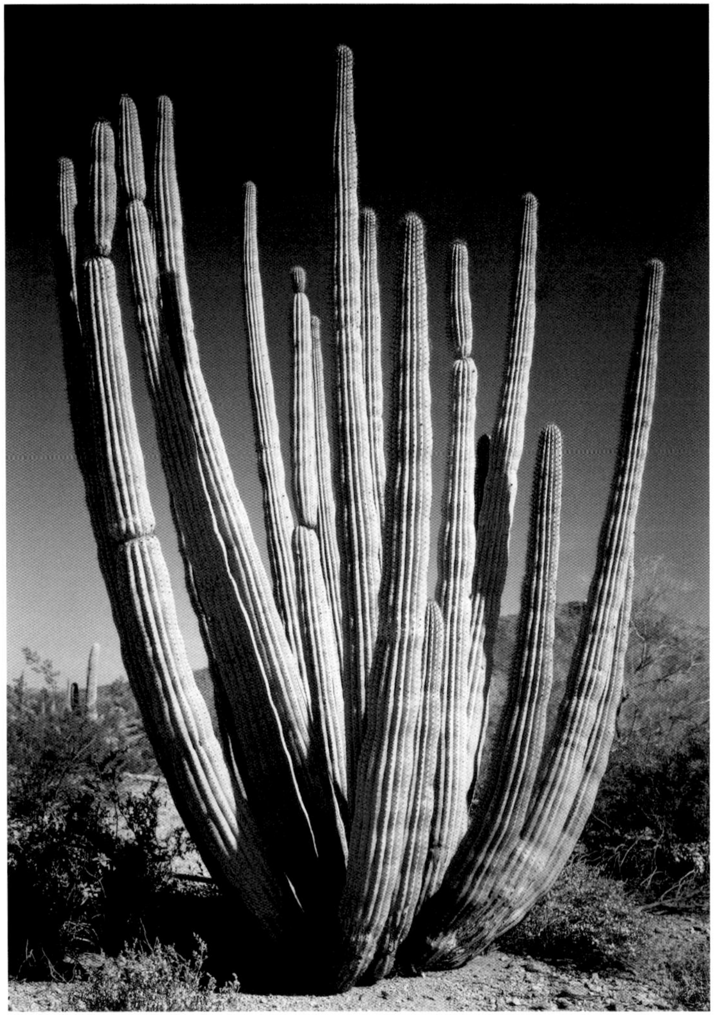

ORGAN PIPE CACTUS NATIONAL MONUMENT, ARIZONA, C. 1952

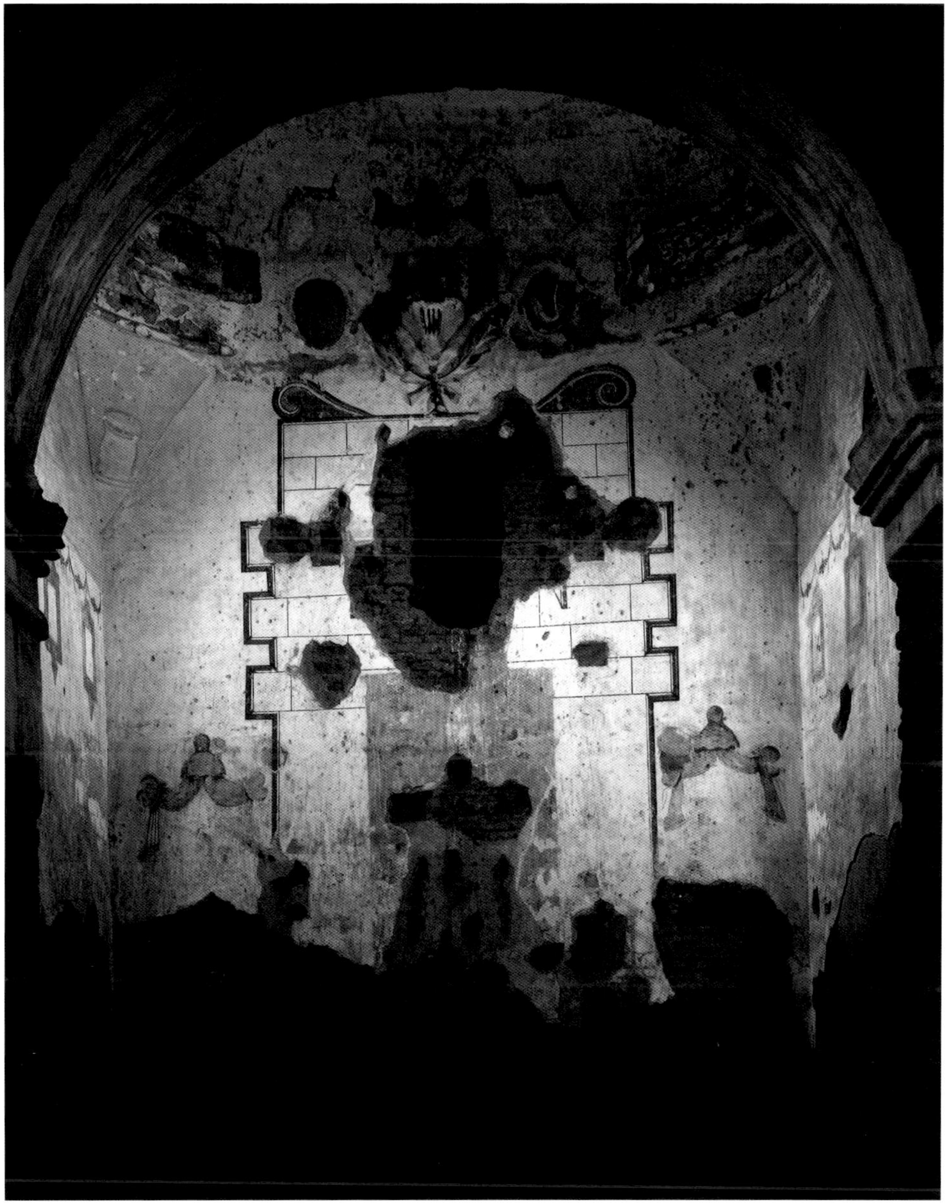

INTERIOR, TUMACACORI NATIONAL HISTORIC PARK, ARIZONA, 1952

Ansel photographed Carlsbad Caverns twice, in 1936 and 1942. It was a new experience to make photographs with artificial light deep underground. On the trip in 1936 he wrote his wife, Virginia: "The photography is interesting but difficult—the Caverns are larger and the problems rougher than I had supposed.... I am trying more for details than broad effects." He also wrote his photographic assistant, Patricia English:

> I am gradually becoming impressed with the Carlsbad Caverns; they are so strange and deep in the earth that I can never feel about them as I do with things in the sun—rocks, trees...surf and fog. The photographic problems are terrific; I start with a basic exposure of about ten minutes.... I then boost up the image and "drama" with photoflash. Some of the forms are beyond description for sheer beauty.... Twice a day I ride down in the elevator (just like an office building) for 750 feet, and then walk a mile through the caverns to the selected spot.... Today the elevators were not working in the morning and I carried the camera, tripod, reflector and lights all the way down the trail for the full 750 feet. My shoulders are a bit creaky tonight.

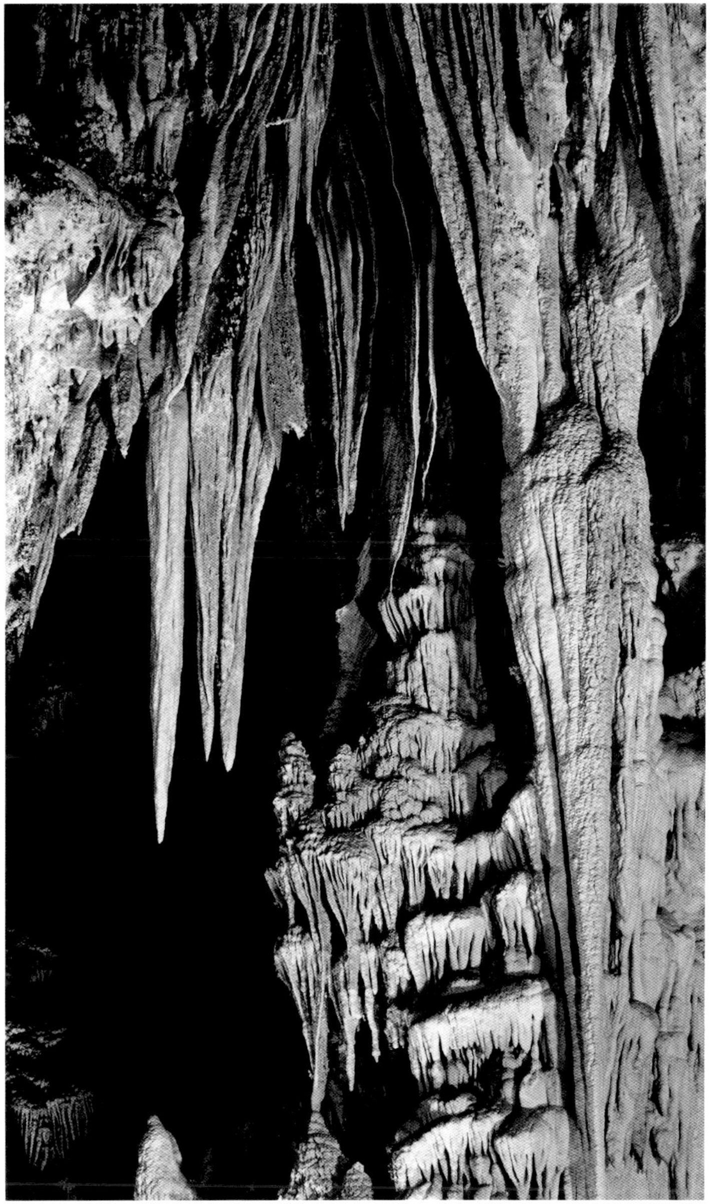

FORMATIONS, CARLSBAD CAVERNS NATIONAL PARK, NEW MEXICO, 1942

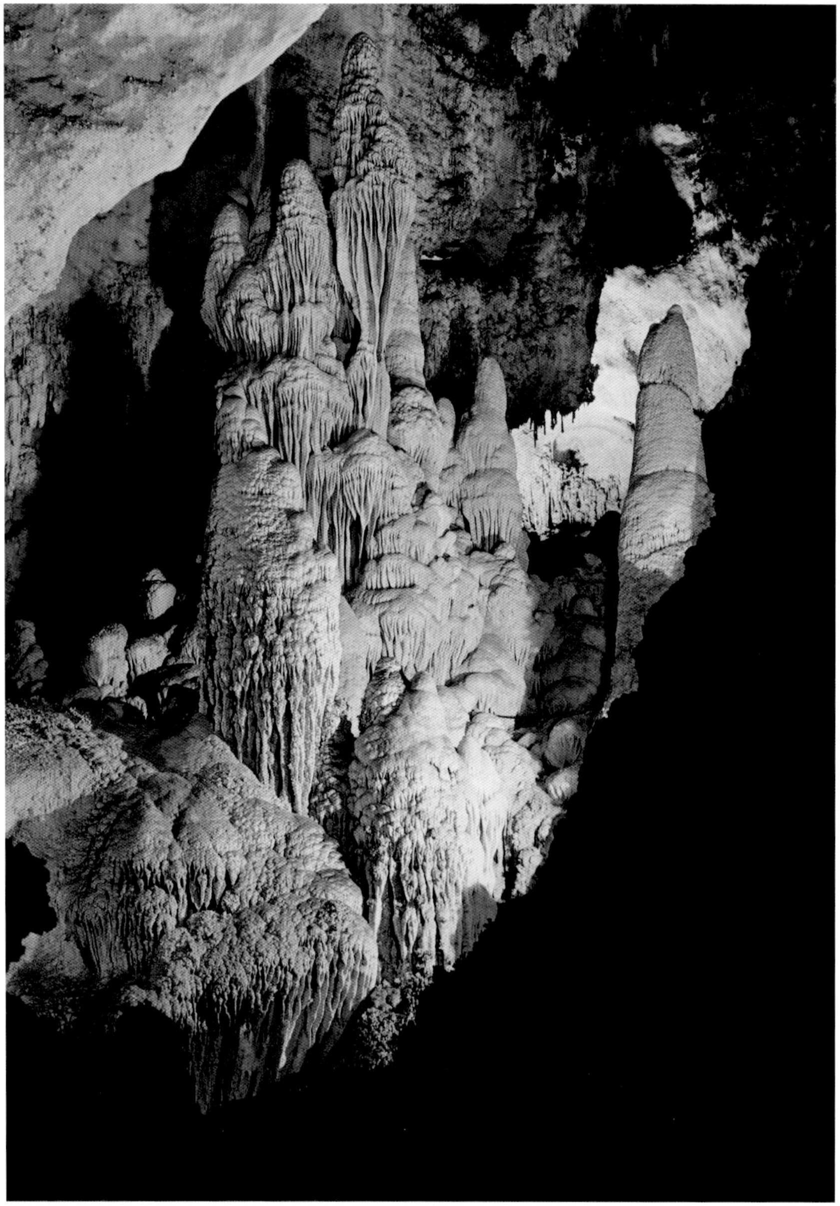

FORMATIONS, CARLSBAD CAVERNS NATIONAL PARK, NEW MEXICO, 1942

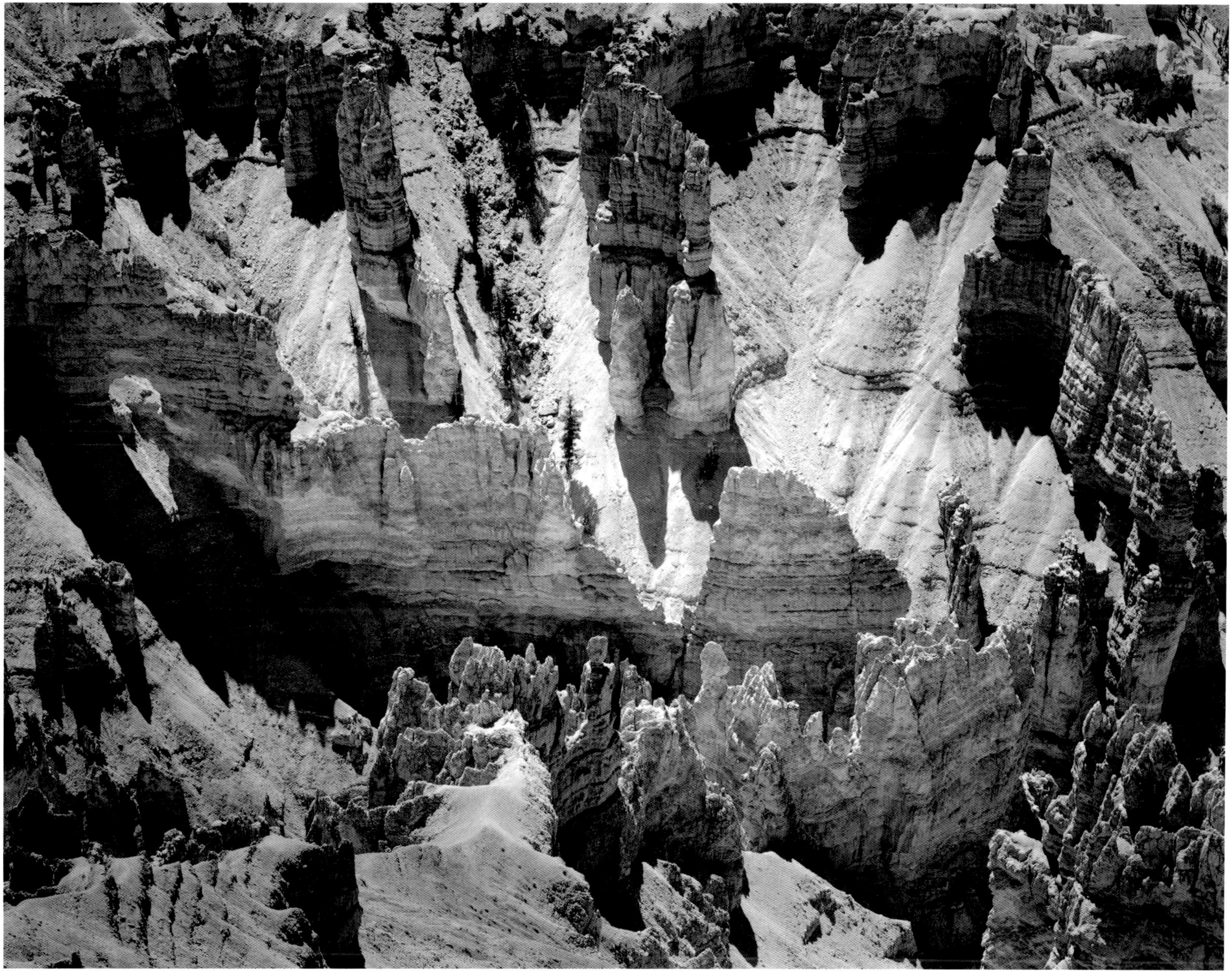

CEDAR BREAKS NATIONAL MONUMENT, UTAH, 1947

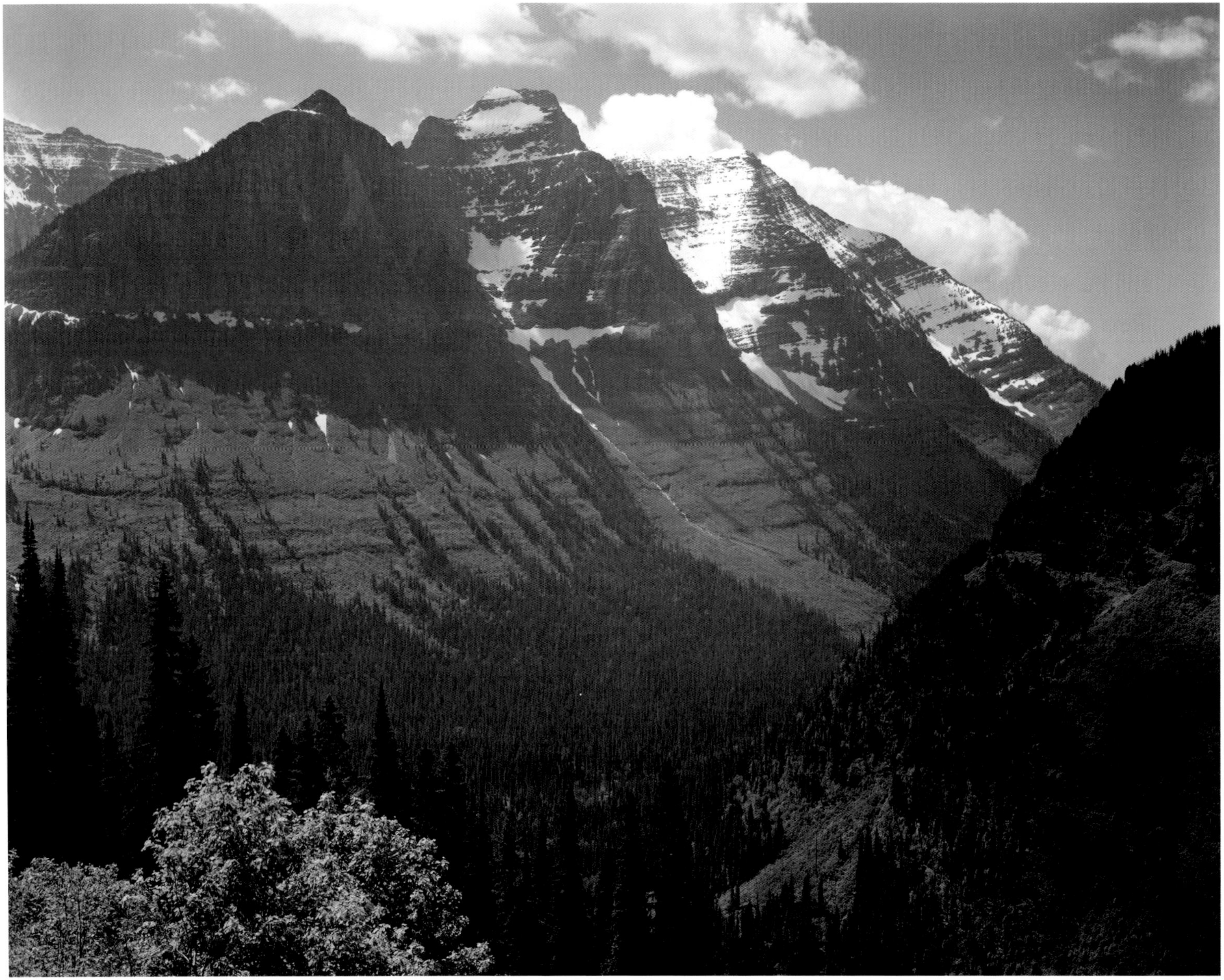

VIEW DOWN MCDONALD CREEK CANYON, GLACIER NATIONAL PARK, MONTANA, 1942

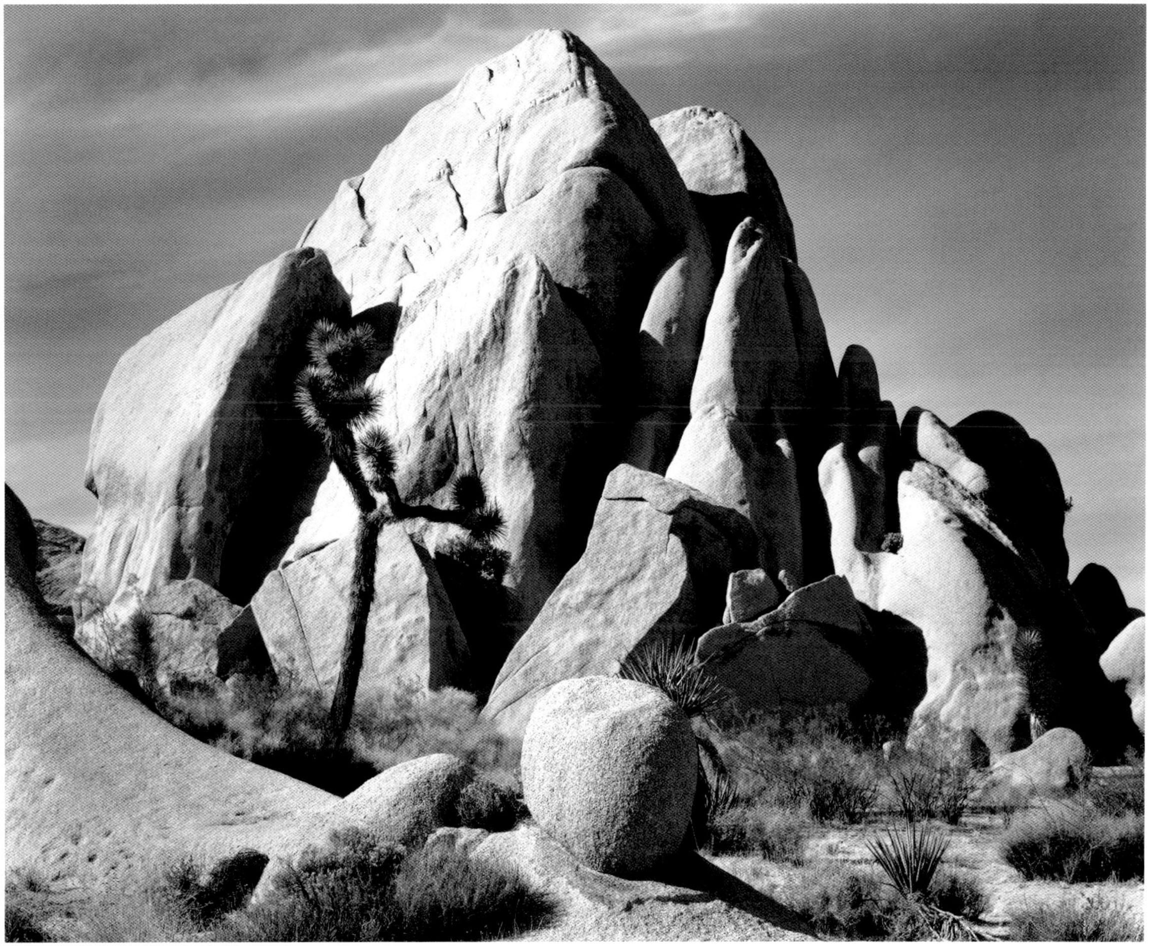

JOSHUA TREE NATIONAL PARK, CALIFORNIA, 1942

A devoted member of the Sierra Club since 1920, Ansel, with his future wife, Virginia Best, participated in the Sierra Club High Trip in the summer of 1927, at which time he made this image of a glacial cirque by moonlight. The photographs on pages 73, 91, and 235 were made on the same trip.

In the late 1920s, Ansel recorded his photographic prints in paperboard booklets. He listed eleven prints of this image, all made on the thick cream-colored paper custom made by William Dassonville that he then favored. When he printed this negative fifty years later, Dassonville paper was no longer available, and Ansel used contemporary glossy high-contrast photographic paper. The resulting prints were not as effective, lacking the mysterious smoky blacks and subtly raised texture of the 1920s paper.

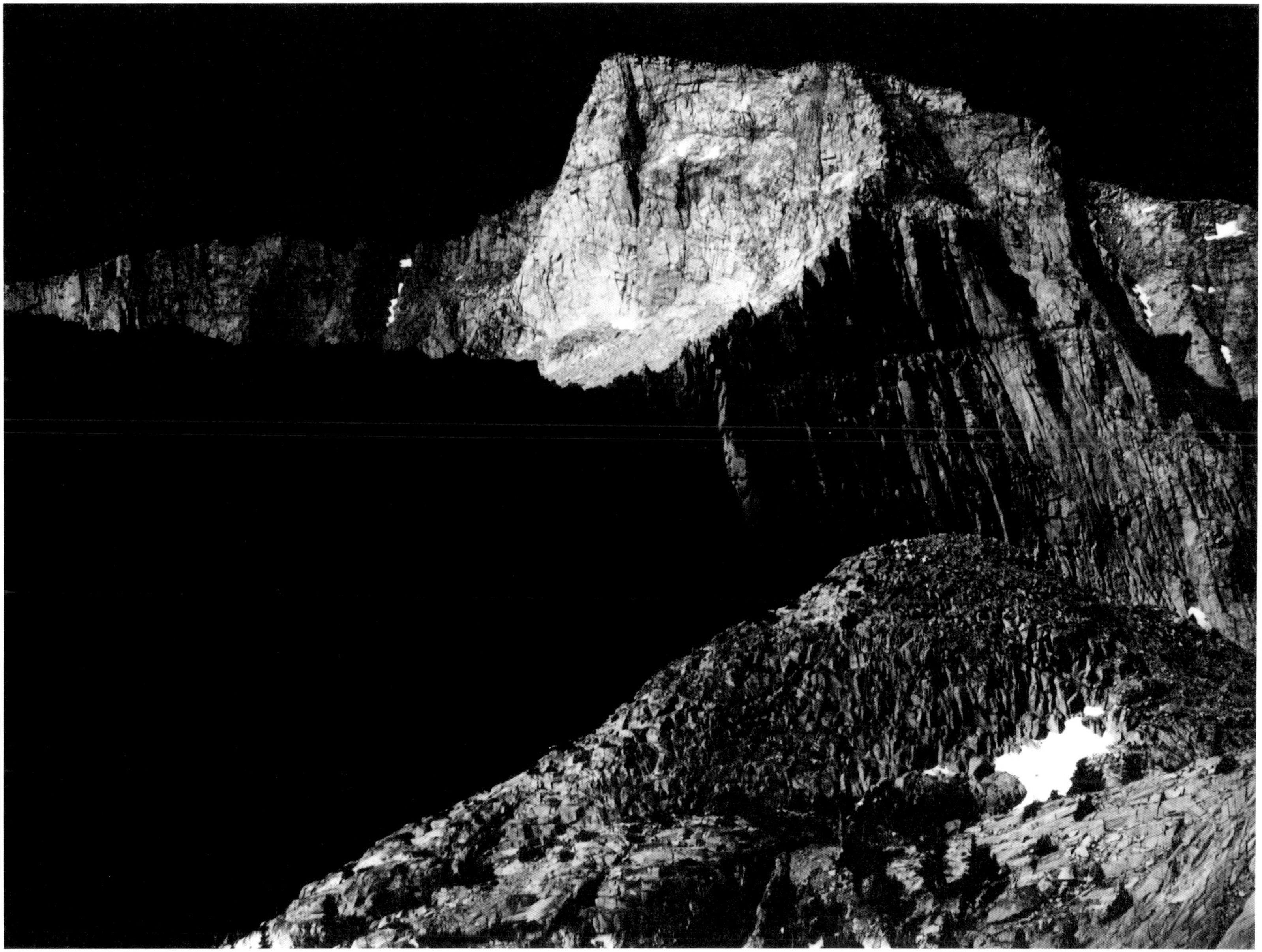

GLACIAL CIRQUE BY MOONLIGHT, MILESTONE RIDGE, SEQUOIA NATIONAL PARK, CALIFORNIA, 1927

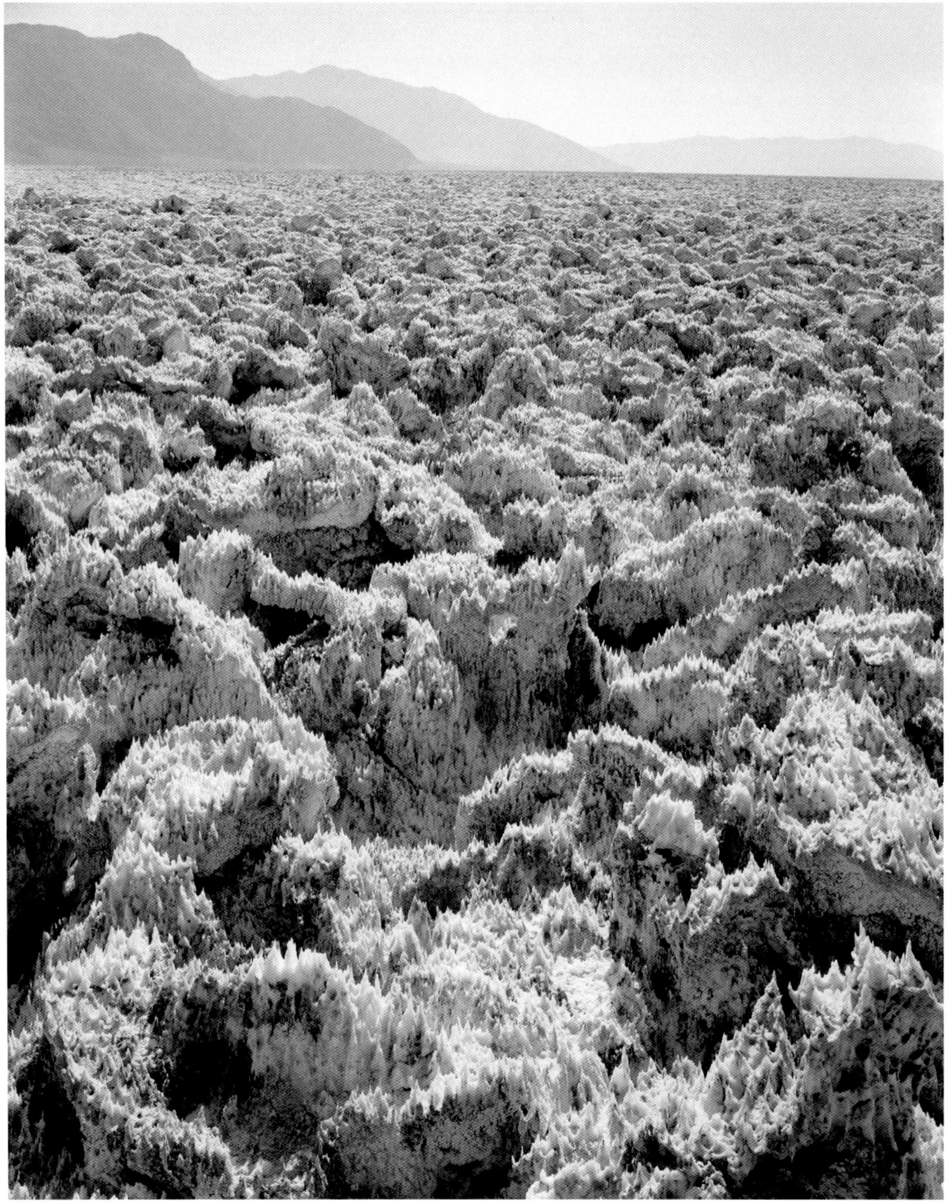

SALT FLATS, DEATH VALLEY NATIONAL PARK, CALIFORNIA, C. 1948

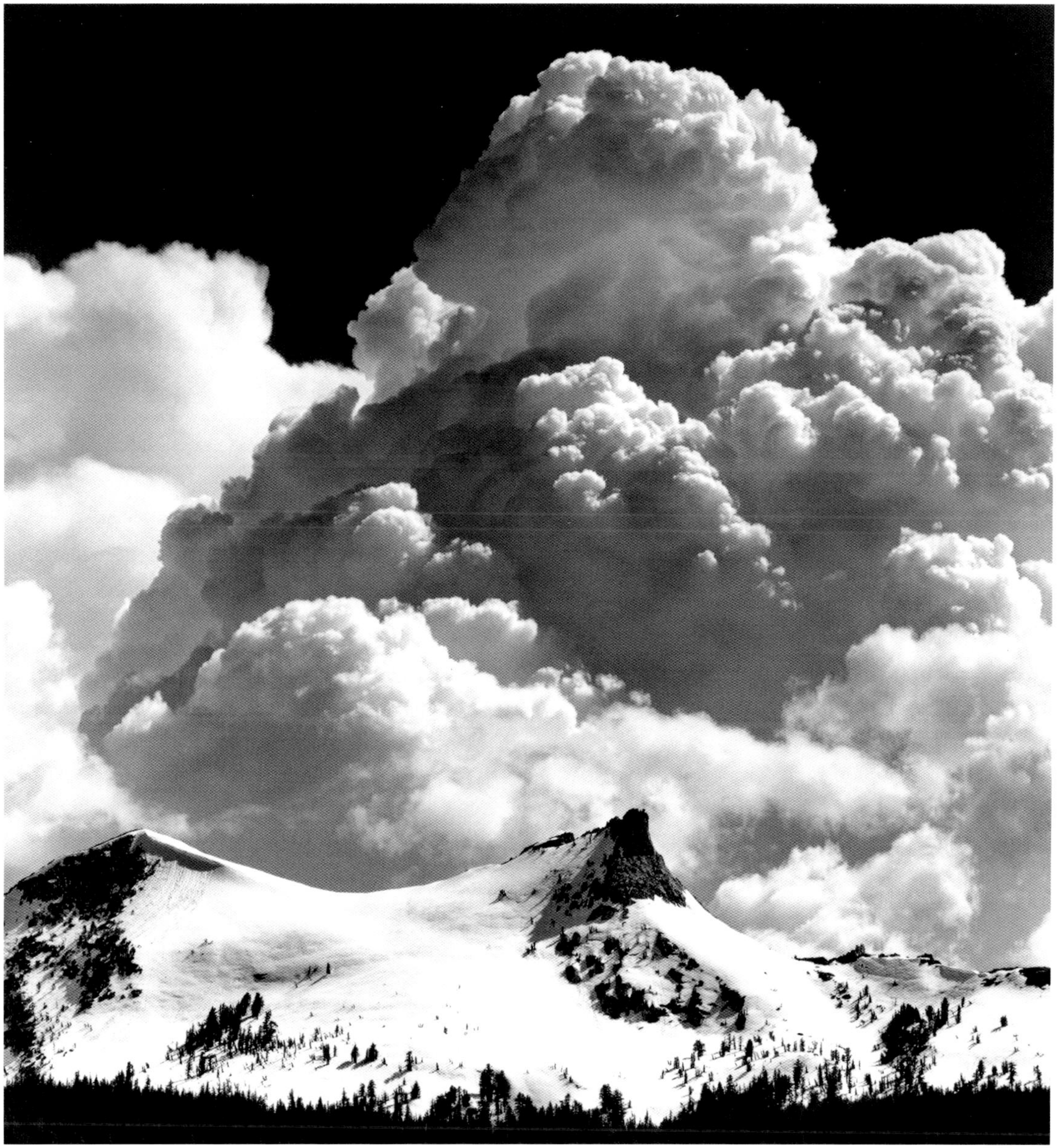

THUNDERCLOUD, UNICORN PEAK, YOSEMITE NATIONAL PARK, CALIFORNIA, C. 1967

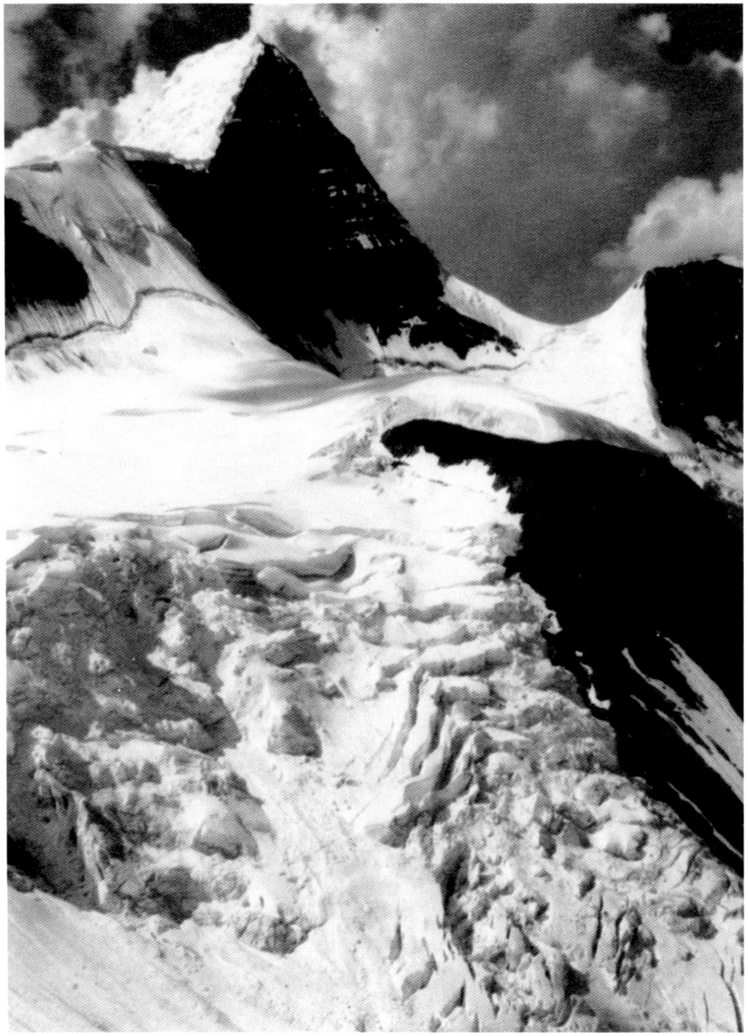

MOUNT ROBSON, JASPER NATIONAL PARK, CANADA, 1928

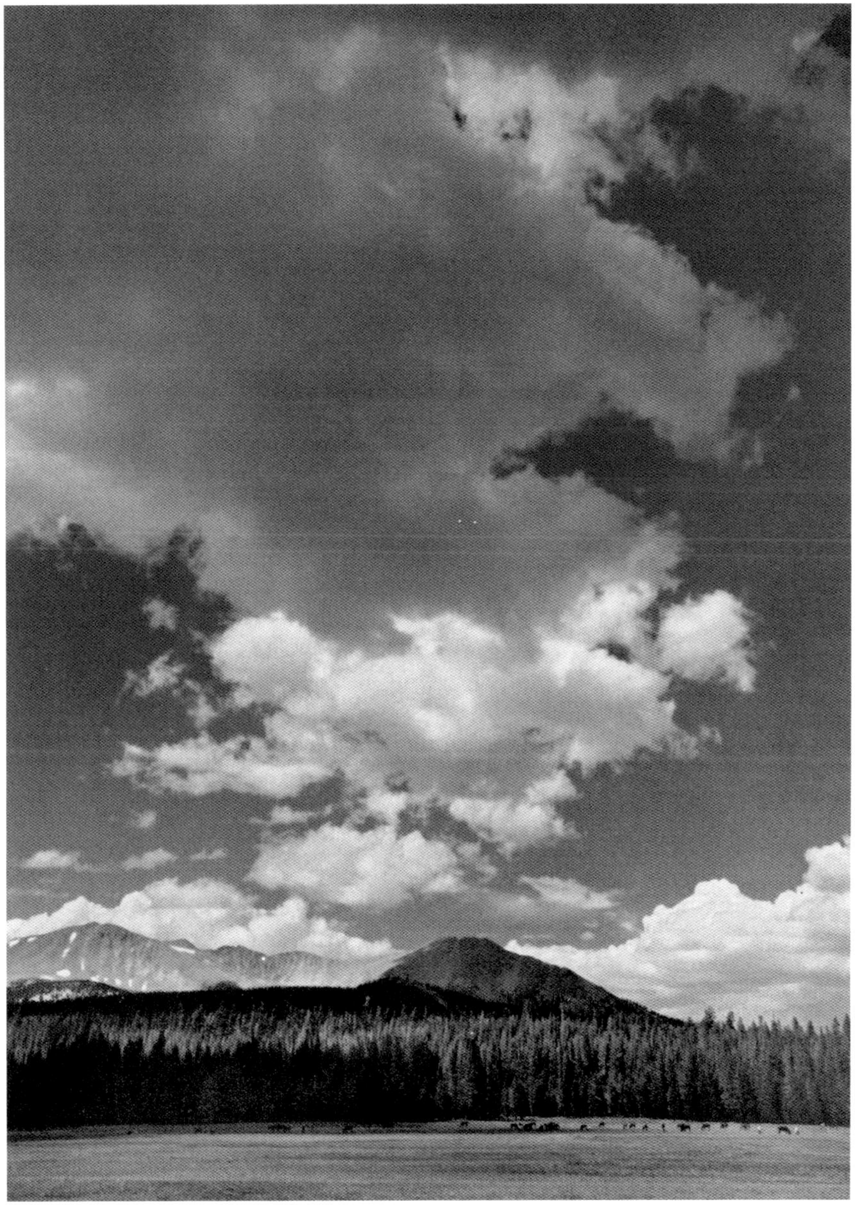

SKY PARLOR MEADOW, SEQUOIA NATIONAL PARK, CALIFORNIA, C. 1930

Beginning in 1901, the Sierra Club organized annual four-week pack trips into the High Sierra. Ansel participated in eleven of these trips and acted as the official photographer on many. Three of those "outings," as they were called, passed close to Mount Whitney. On the first, in 1927, Ansel wrote to Albert Bender, his friend and patron, "I wish you could see what I am seeing. It is the most wonderful country." Returning to the same area in 1932, Ansel rose before dawn and hiked in the dark to be ready to make this photograph of Mount Whitney at sunrise. The peak rises 14,505 feet above sea level and is the highest summit in the contiguous United States.

DAWN, MOUNT WHITNEY, SIERRA NEVADA, CALIFORNIA, 1932

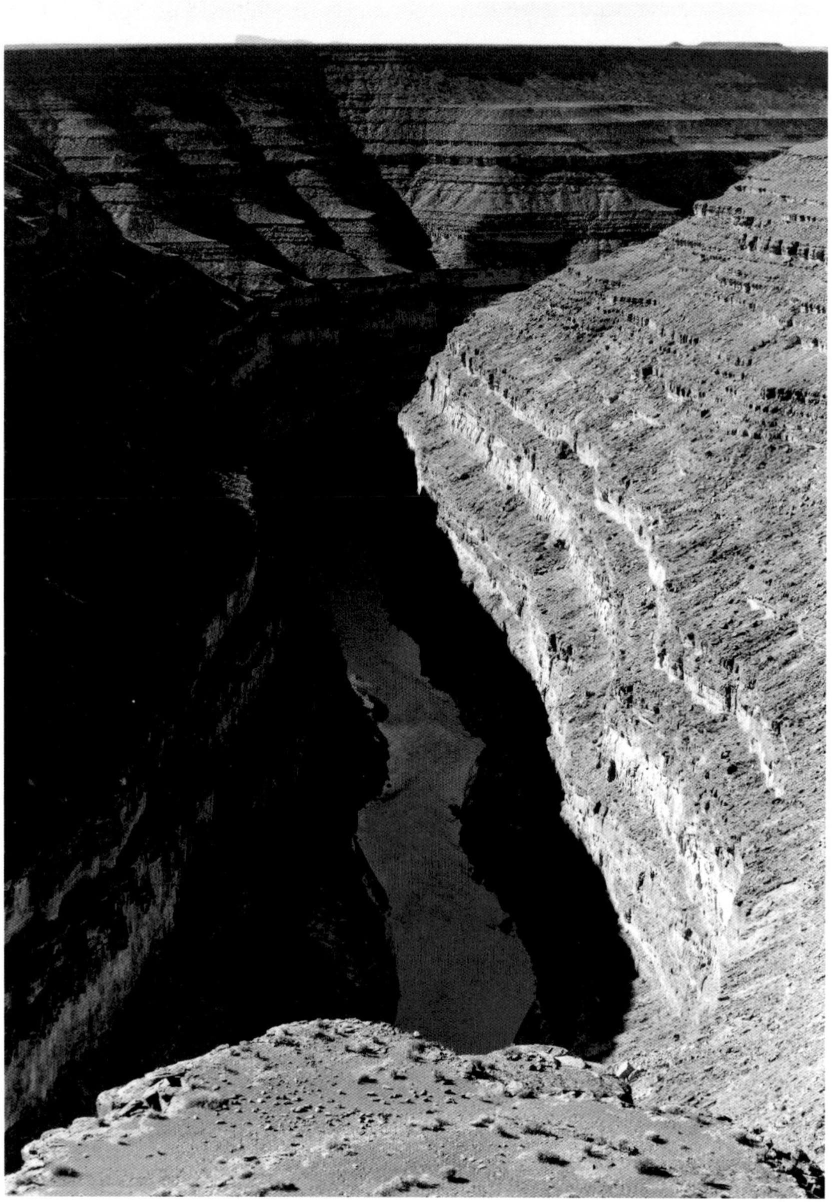

GOOSENECKS OF THE SAN JUAN RIVER, GOOSENECKS STATE PARK, UTAH, C. 1940

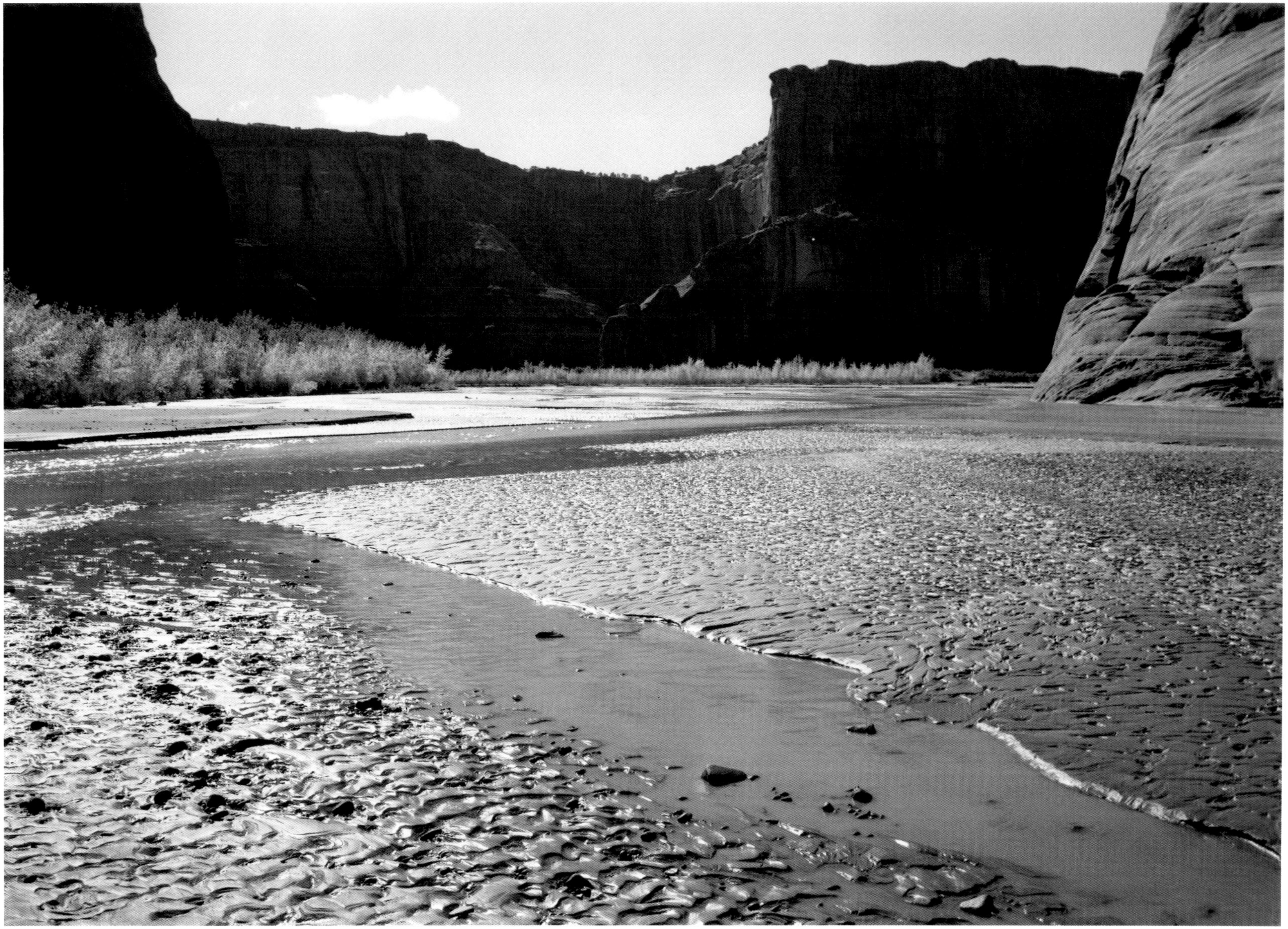

CANYON DE CHELLY NATIONAL MONUMENT, ARIZONA, C. 1949

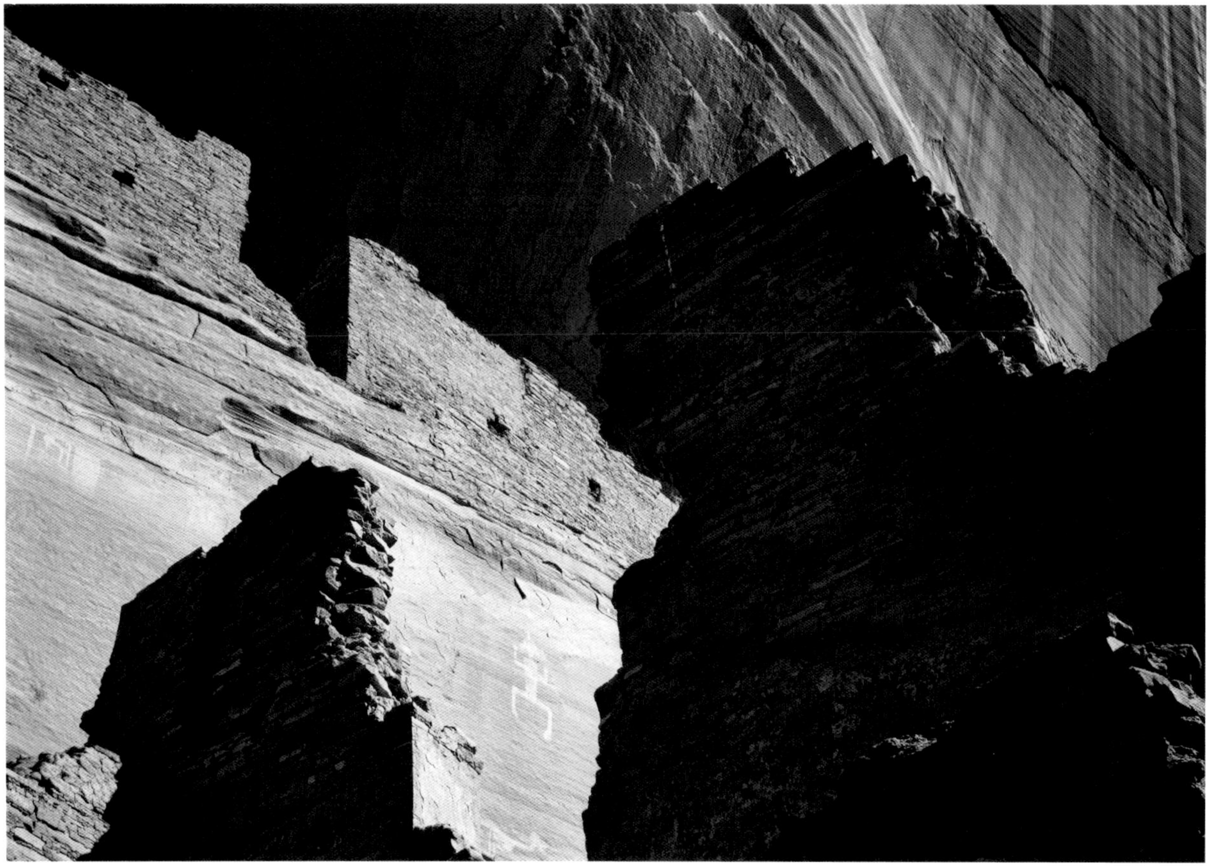

VIEW UP THROUGH LOWER RUINS, CANYON DE CHELLY NATIONAL MONUMENT, ARIZONA, C. 1947

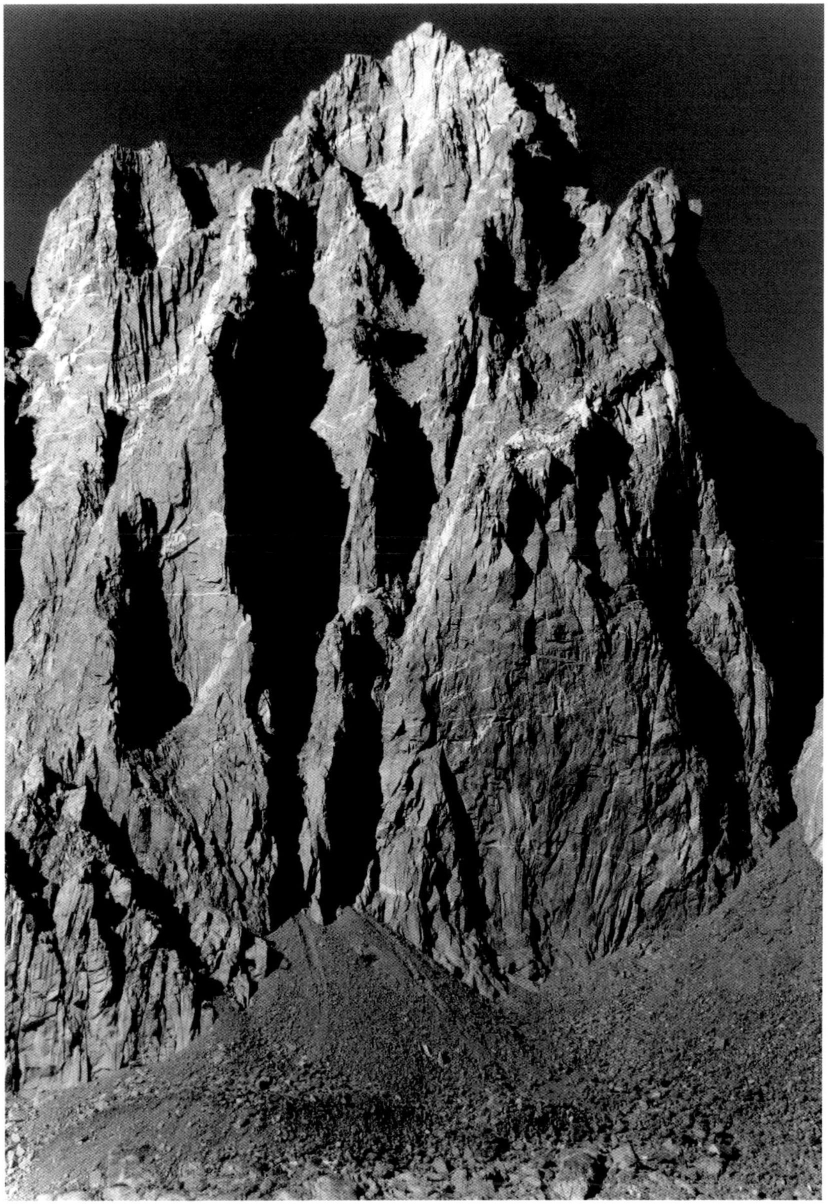

MOUNT WINCHELL, KINGS CANYON NATIONAL PARK, CALIFORNIA, C. 1932

ANSEL ADAMS IN THE NATIONAL PARKS

RICHARD B. WOODWARD

ANSEL ADAMS often drove alone on his Guggenheim-supported odyssey through the national parks in 1947 and 1948. When he did travel with others, his preferred companions (and, later, correspondents) were Beaumont and Nancy Newhall. All three were writers and photographers, and they rarely found themselves at a loss for the next topic of conversation. The Newhalls accompanied Adams on two trips during his Guggenheim Fellowships: to the Southwest (from Carmel, California, to Williams, Arizona, from May 25 to June 7, 1947); and to Maine and Massachusetts (from Acadia National Park to Boston, from November 19 to November 25, 1949). Beaumont's diaries of these journeys, especially the first, are the best records we have of the photographer at work in the field.[1]

"The Southwest Log" is clearly aimed at posterity. The seeds of several later books—Nancy's *The Eloquent Light,* the first volume of her unfinished biography of Ansel, as well as his own later *Examples: The Making of 40 Photographs*—can be found in the notes. Apart from the diary, which records events almost to the minute on certain days, an addendum of four pages lists all of the photographic equipment in Ansel's station wagon during the trip. But foremost, the log is a record of three people who appreciate one another immensely as they move through one of the most spectacular areas of the United States.

The trip began after the Newhalls had been alone with Edward Weston in his cabin for a week, a stay that included a day of photographing at Point Lobos nearby. Adams arrived on May 26 and whisked them away at three in the morning for the 225-mile drive to Yosemite. There, Virginia Adams greeted them and showed them her collection of historic materials on Yosemite, including stereographs and 18 x 24-inch prints by Muybridge.

"The thought has occurred to us that we might be able to do books on the West Coast," wrote Beaumont. "Perhaps a book on Yosemite itself, made up of old and new photographs. The history of the place does not seem to have been put down as dramatically as it might be."

After a dinner cooked by Harry, the Adamses' Japanese houseman, Ansel, dressed in his Chinese mandarin's robe, "composed music for an Emily Dickinson poem while we washed dishes, and then Ansel and Virginia went down to the big room and played piano and sang."

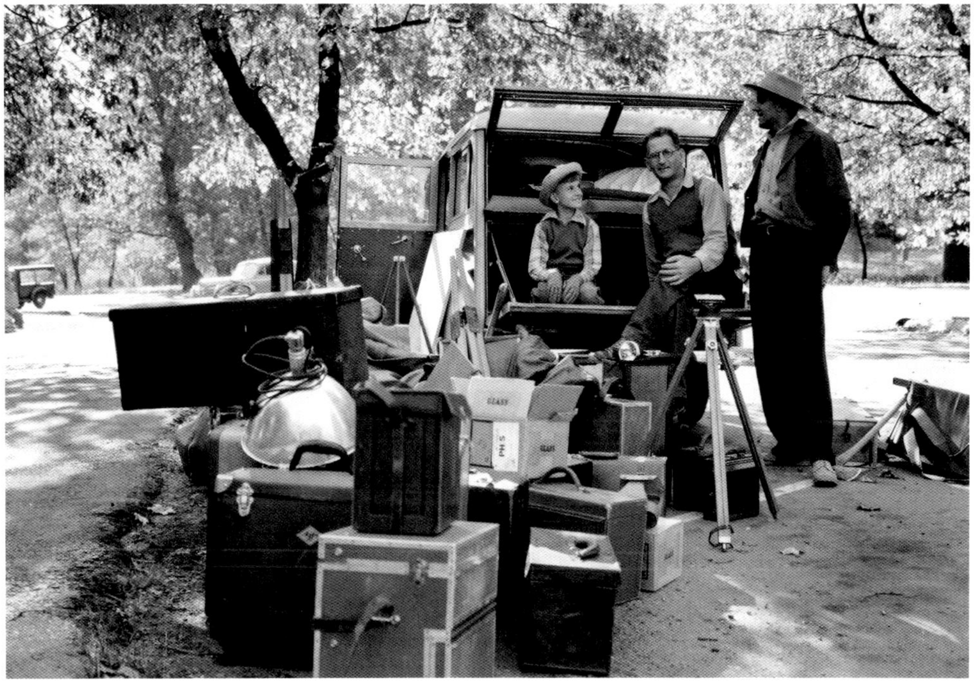

Ansel Adams packing the car before a Southwest trip with Cedric Wright and Michael Adams, 1941. By Virginia Adams

Two days later, Ansel and the Newhalls headed off to the Grand Canyon via Lake Tenaya in Yosemite, "where both Ansel and Nancy photographed the juniper tree which we call Edward Weston's because of his beautiful picture of it." Beaumont christened the car Helios, after the portable darkroom, "Helios, The Flying Studio," that Muybridge wheeled through Yosemite in 1867. Although both Nancy and Beaumont photographed—they sometimes rode on the aluminum platform installed on the roof—both were also watching Ansel.

He would have coffee for them when they woke up, his imitation of a braying jackass serving as their reveille at first light. "Both the 8 x 10 and 5 x 7 were already mounted on tripods." They were like a threesome in a movie about young lovers or criminals. "Ansel photographed sheer deep red pinnacles against blue sky and Nancy photographed Ansel and I photographed them both." During a rest stop in the desert Ansel would fire off a few rounds of his .22 rifle at tin cans.

On May 31, Beaumont showed the others what he had been writing, and "Ansel had the idea that it might be

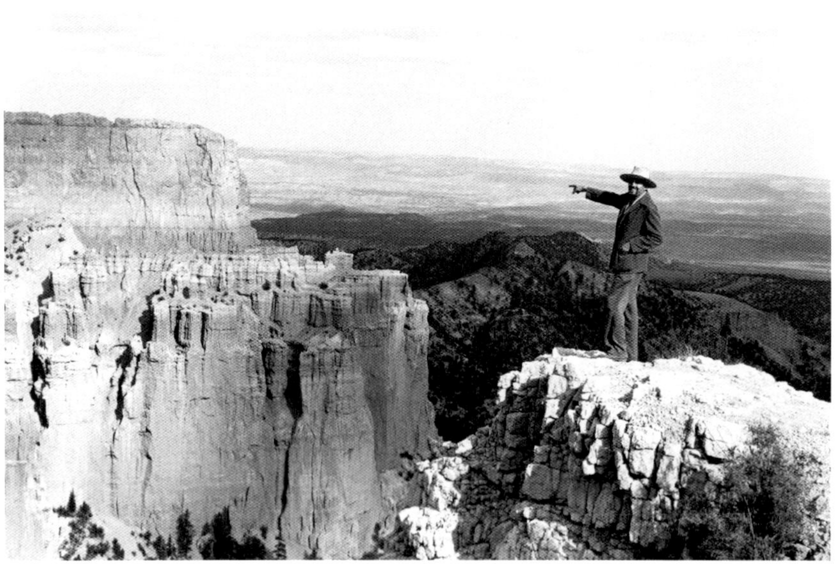

Ansel Adams at Bryce Canyon National Park, Utah, 1947. By Beaumont Newhall

interesting to slant the notes to the photographic problems and how they were overcome, with a view to possible publication. This is an interesting idea, and I shall see what can be done with it."

The log contains a detailed account of the customized interior of Ansel's four-wheeled studio:

> Across the station wagon, behind the front seat and level with its top, he has built a platform of plywood. Camera cases, tripods, and photographic equipment are stowed under the plywood from the back. Food is stowed under the plywood by the side door. Nancy's camera was under the platform on the left side. On top of the platform the sleeping bags and the mattresses were piled. Ansel has a couple of Coleman gasoline stoves—improved versions of the Primus—and a stock of canned foods and some cheese, a cooked ham, butter, eggs and other groceries. The dropped tailboard of Helios serves as kitchen table, stove and dining room. During the trip we have had excellent meals—steaks, chicken chasseur, ham with wine sauce, oysters in tomato sauce, good soups, tea, coffee and always a little something to drink.

By the time the threesome arrived at Bryce Canyon National Park on May 31, though, nerves had begun to fray. Ansel was discouraged the next day by the cloudy weather, and the normally unflappable Beaumont, after a week on the road, sleeping outdoors on the ground, could no longer exclaim over another stony landscape.

Even though he was standing at Bryce Point, one of the loveliest spots in the national parks, he "spontaneously burst forth, to the amazement and amusement of all, including myself: 'What, Nature again? I've never seen so much Nature: we sleep on it, we look at it in the morning and in the afternoon and by moonlight and by sunrise and sunset: I'm looked out!'" No more seems to have been said. After a nap in an actual bed in the cabin, and a quiet dinner together, Beaumont was revived and cheerful. The next day they drove off again.

Newhall's notes for June 4 and 5, as they hiked and photographed at the Grand Canyon, give a better sense than anything other than Ansel's own accounts of what he thought about as he went about his business. They are sufficiently technical that one suspects Ansel was consulted or looked them over before Beaumont typed them up.

After an afternoon in the forests of Point Sublime, where both Nancy and Ansel "went to work with great excitement," they retired to eat leftover stew and wait for sundown. Ansel was shooting both color and black-and-white and wanted to make a Kodachrome of the moonrise. Six years earlier, in Hernandez, New Mexico, he had photographed what is today the most familiar moonrise in American art. He had by now developed a method for solving this formidable technical problem.

> First, he photographed the landscape by the last feeble rays of light. Then he marked an X on the ground glass where the image of the moon was to be recorded when it rose. We feared that because of the overcast the sunset would be a disappointment, but at the last moment the under side of the clouds became vermillion and orange, spreading like fire. The red disk dropped; the peaks below our feet grew dim. We turned to the East: a glow on the horizon showed where the moon would rise, but not for half an hour did it finally appear sufficiently clear and brilliant for Ansel's purpose. In a state of great excitment [sic] he made the second exposure, using this time the 26 inch element of the Cooke convertible lens, in order to make the image of the moon relatively large.

Always concerned about violating his own principles of "straight photography," Ansel was especially concerned that his sleight-of-hand manipulation—a double exposure designed to exaggerate the size of the moon—might represent a moral and artistic transgression. Speaking for both, Beaumont wondered: "Where is the line between double exposure (as made by Stieglitz in his night views of skyscrapers) and combination prints (as made by [Henry Peach] Robinson)?"

The June 5 entry, even more lush with terminology that Ansel was imparting in his how-to books on photography, shows Beaumont acknowledging his friend's mastery.

> At five o'clock I tried to light the stoves to make coffee, but they wouldn't seem to work, so I brought them down to Ansel on the ledge a hundred yards or so beyond the road where Helios was parked. He had already made three exposures; of course the stoves were all right. I had not positioned the needle valve correctly, and soon we had coffee. Until seven Ansel

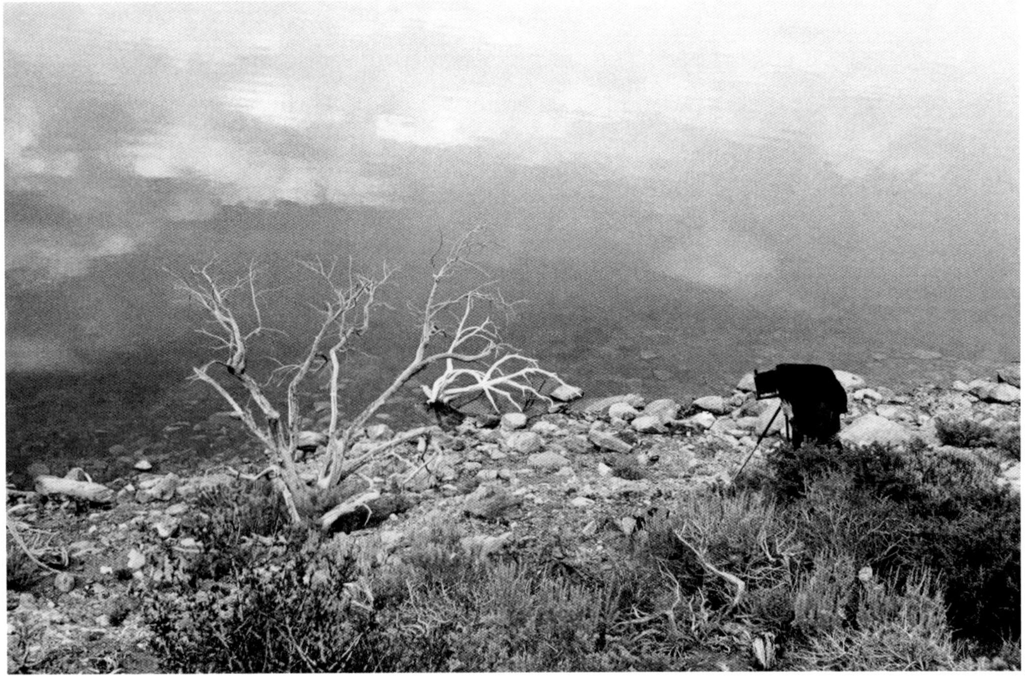

Ansel Adams photographing white branches at Mono Lake, 1947. By Nancy Newhall

photographed the crags with great speed and intensity, taking advantage of every change of light. Then we packed and made the journey to the South Rim.

Our progress through the wondrous forest was slow. We stopped for pictures of the silver trunks of the aspens and the dark emerald of the pines and the fire. I have seen many photographers at work, but none have worked more deftly and with more assurance than Ansel. He discovers a subject, stops the wagon, jumps out and studies the picture possibilities, looking thought [sic] the rough frame of his hands. If the subject can be "rectangled," as Ansel once said, then he breaks out one of the three cameras—8 x 10, 5 x 7, 3¼ x 4¼. He studies the ground glass image in a state of great excitement—because he knows before he sets up that a picture is possible. Almost invariably he wants to share this revelation of the image with us. While we put our heads under the focusing cloth he calculates the exposure.

Emotional impact now gives place to cold scientific reasoning. Ansel has a rationale. Until this trip I had felt that his system was complicated, with exaggerated emphasis on sensitometric theory. But I soon saw that it was, in the fullest sense of the word, brilliant technique.

Experience has taught him to judge many values without measurement; a favorite game was to challenge Ansel to give the Weston [meter] reading of a tree trunk, a patch of ground, the sky: always his estimate matched exactly the meter reading.

Rigid control of processing is part of this rationale, for the "placement" on Zones is determined by development. Flat subjects in which the amounts of light are closely spaced, may be recorded brilliantly by long development: excessively contrasty subjects, in which the range of tones exceeds the limit of the film, may be compressed by short development or "water bath"—soaking the film alternately in water and developer.

Therefore Ansel records the light conditions for each exposure in a notebook and indicated the developing technique to be used to bring out the previsioned image.

Not only does this system assure successful exposures: it enables Ansel to make deviations for expressive purposes. In the moon picture he was able to calculate each of the separate exposures so that the two would produce a cumulative effect.

As the Guggenheim stipend would not come close to paying all the bills for himself, his family, and a transcontinental three-year project, Ansel had lined up commercial assignments from magazines (*Fortune* and *Life* were clients) and companies (Eastman Kodak). As he traveled through the national parks, he would often make photographs in color and black-and-white of the same prospect, the color pictures to satisfy his clients.

On the last day of the trip, June 7, needing to take pictures for Kodak of models enjoying America's scenery and having no one else on hand except his companions, he asked the Newhalls to pose. With Beaumont in gabardine pants and yellow sport shirt and Nancy wearing a skirt and red sweater, Ansel photographed them with his 5 x 7 at Sunset Crater National Monument in Arizona. Beaumont found the black dunes ("negative Westons") and volcanic mountain "the most spectacular sight of all we have seen." The Newhalls then boarded a train in the dark and waved good-bye while Ansel and Helios continued on their way.

NOTE

1. Both of these documents can be found in the Ansel Adams archive at the Center for Creative Photography in Tucson, Arizona.

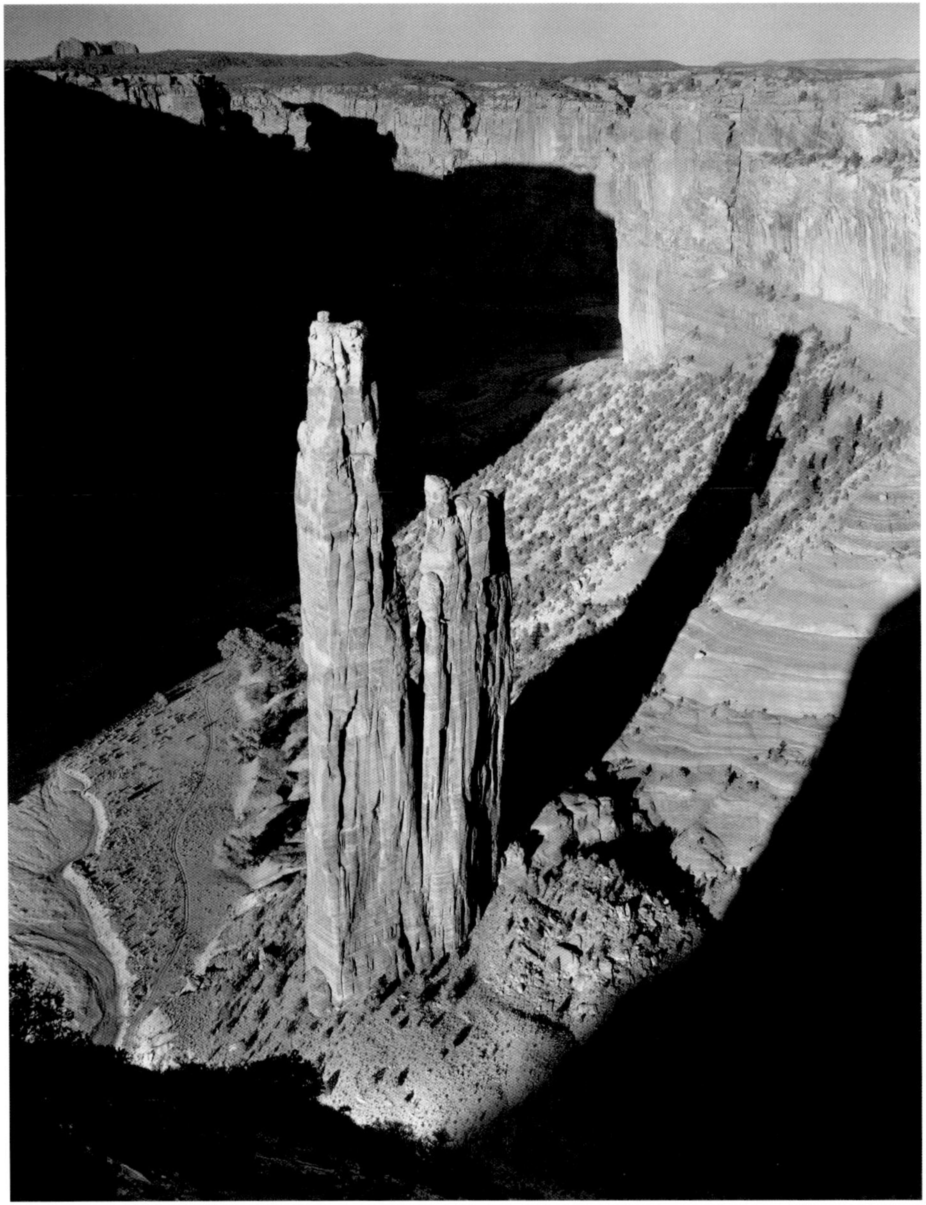

SPIDER ROCK FROM RIM, CANYON DE CHELLY NATIONAL MONUMENT, ARIZONA, 1949

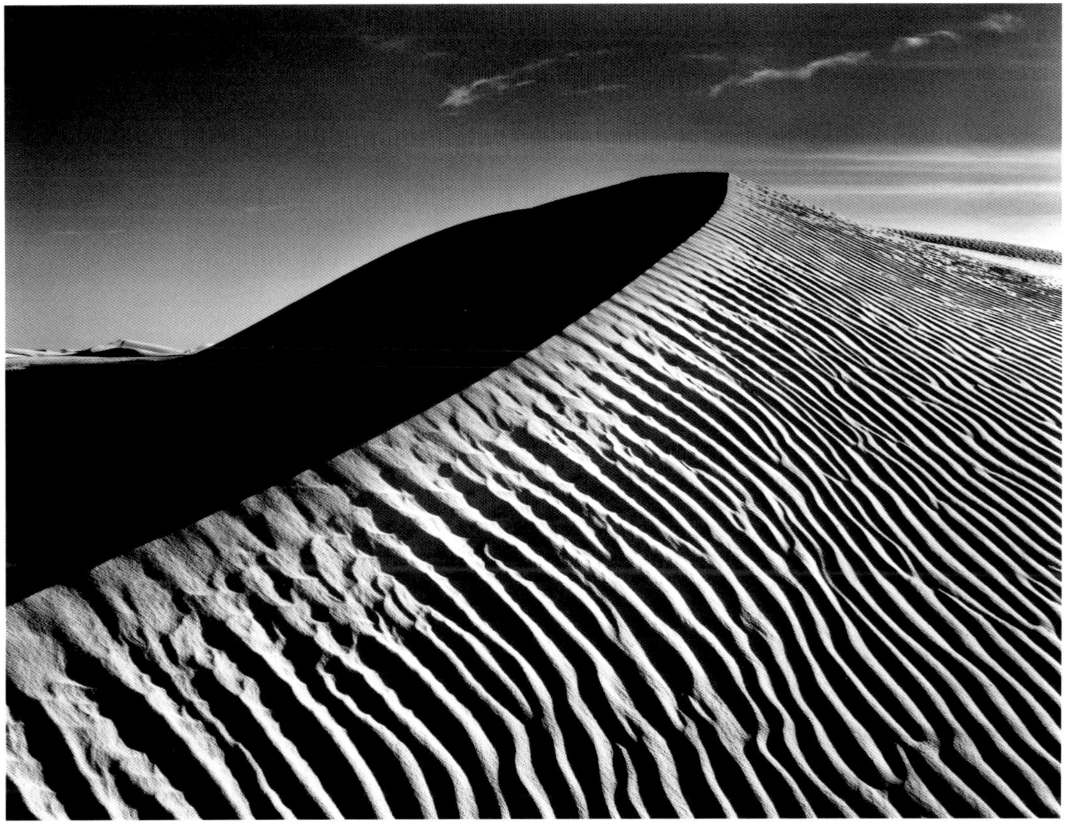

SAND DUNES, WHITE SANDS NATIONAL MONUMENT, NEW MEXICO, C. 1942

Each time Ansel clicked the shutter he "visualized" the final photographic print and calculated the exposure necessary to produce the best possible negative. But in spite of this visualization and his impressive technical abilities, his negatives were often challenging to print. This negative was by far the most difficult, and Ansel used to groan when he saw the title on the weekly list of images to print.

Each print required more than seven minutes of continuous moves: ten seconds for the basic exposure, followed by more than seven minutes of burning and dodging, a dance-like sequence using various implements to admit or withhold light to targeted areas of the print. This process darkened and lightened specific areas of the image.

To watch Ansel in the darkroom was to watch a carefully choreographed ballet. John Sexton, a fine photographer and Ansel's photographic assistant in the 1970s, said: "The level of concentration necessary to execute all the motions is intense. You have to blend the moves properly, and if even one goes wrong, you have to start over. Most of Ansel's iconic images required greater printing skills than most photographers possess. For Ansel, the creative process began at the camera but did not end until he felt a sense of satisfaction in the darkroom. His photographic prints are a personal intensification of what was in front of the camera. They reveal not only the photographic process, but also the photographer."

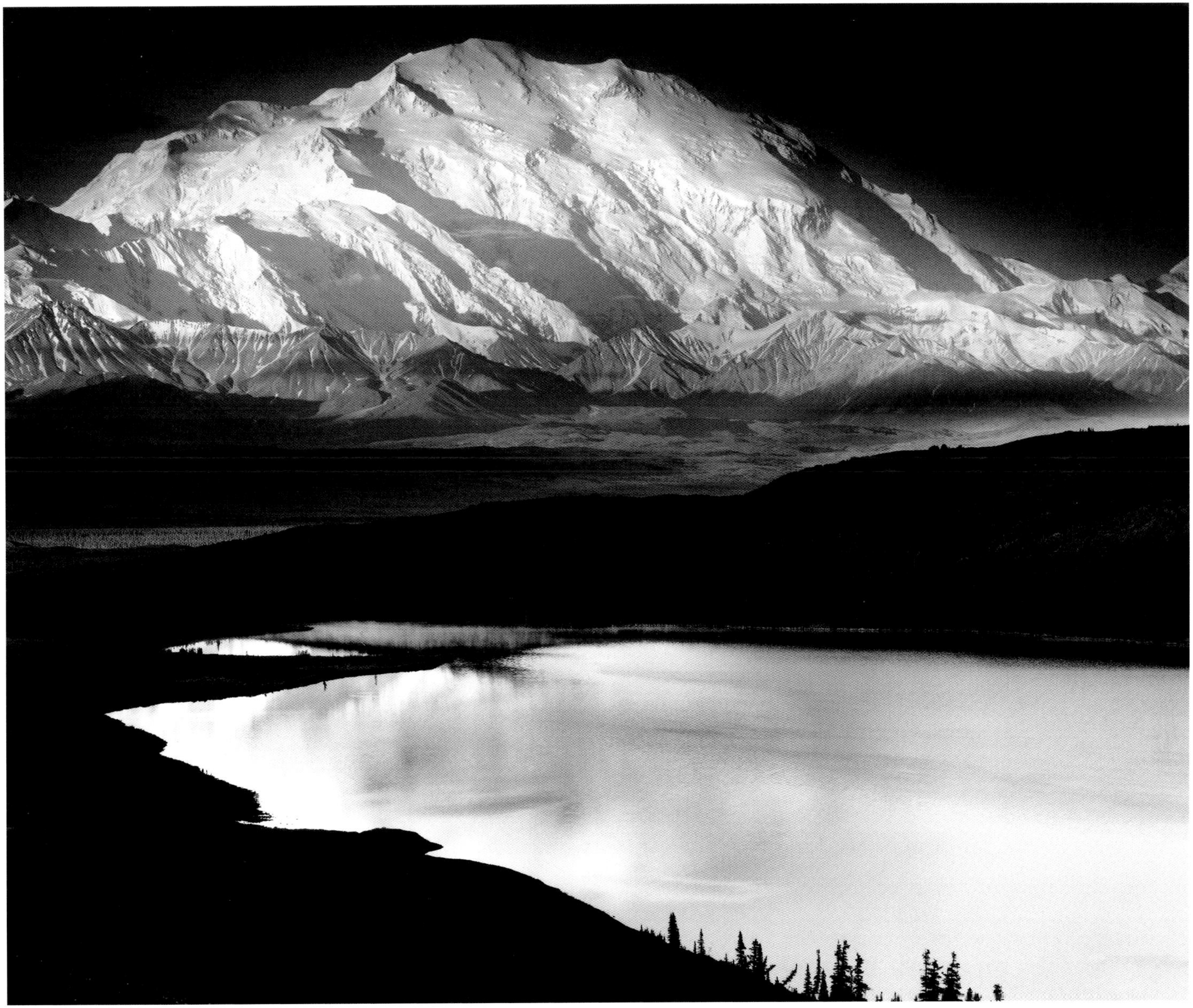

MOUNT MCKINLEY AND WONDER LAKE, DENALI NATIONAL PARK AND PRESERVE, ALASKA, 1947

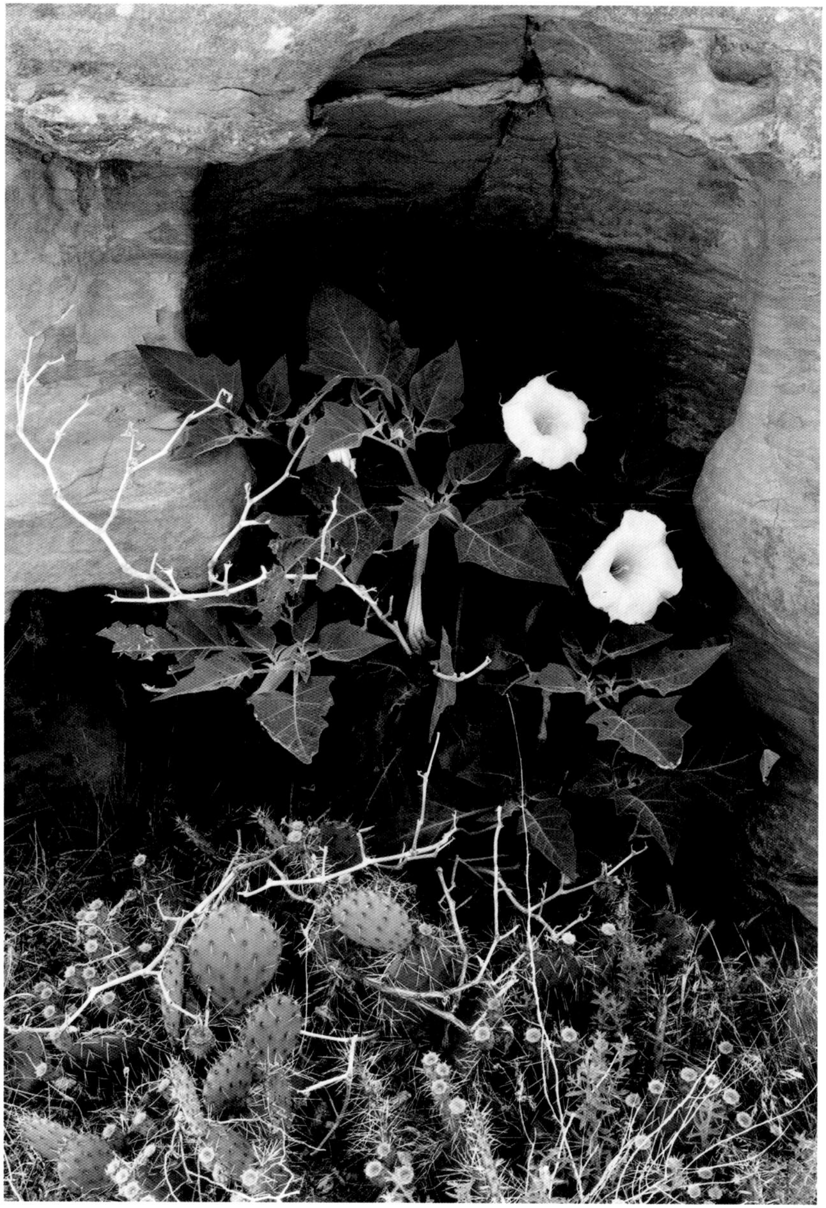

DATURA FLOWER, CANYON DE CHELLY NATIONAL MONUMENT, ARIZONA, 1947

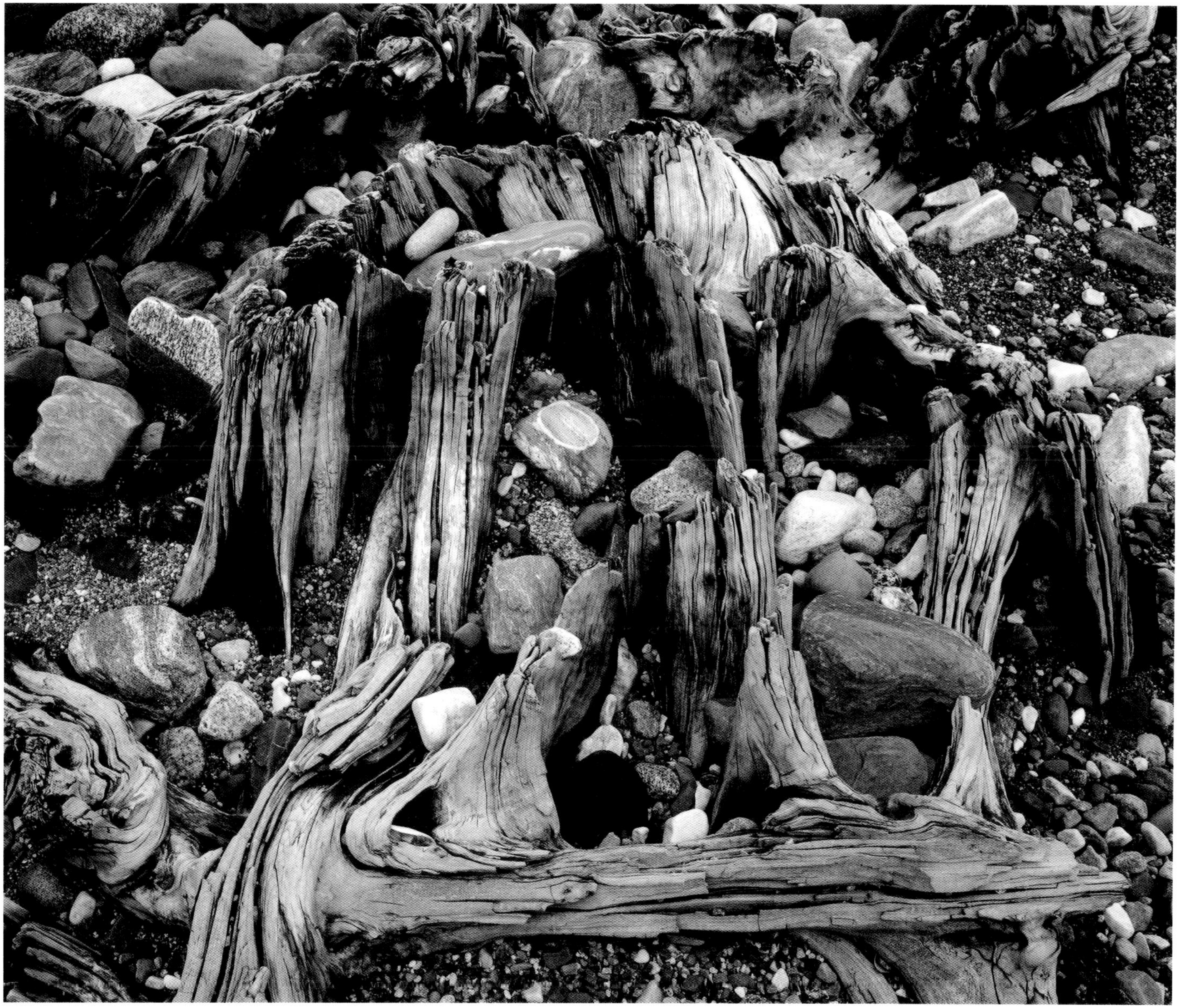

INTERSTADIAL FOREST DETAIL, GLACIER BAY NATIONAL PARK, ALASKA, 1947

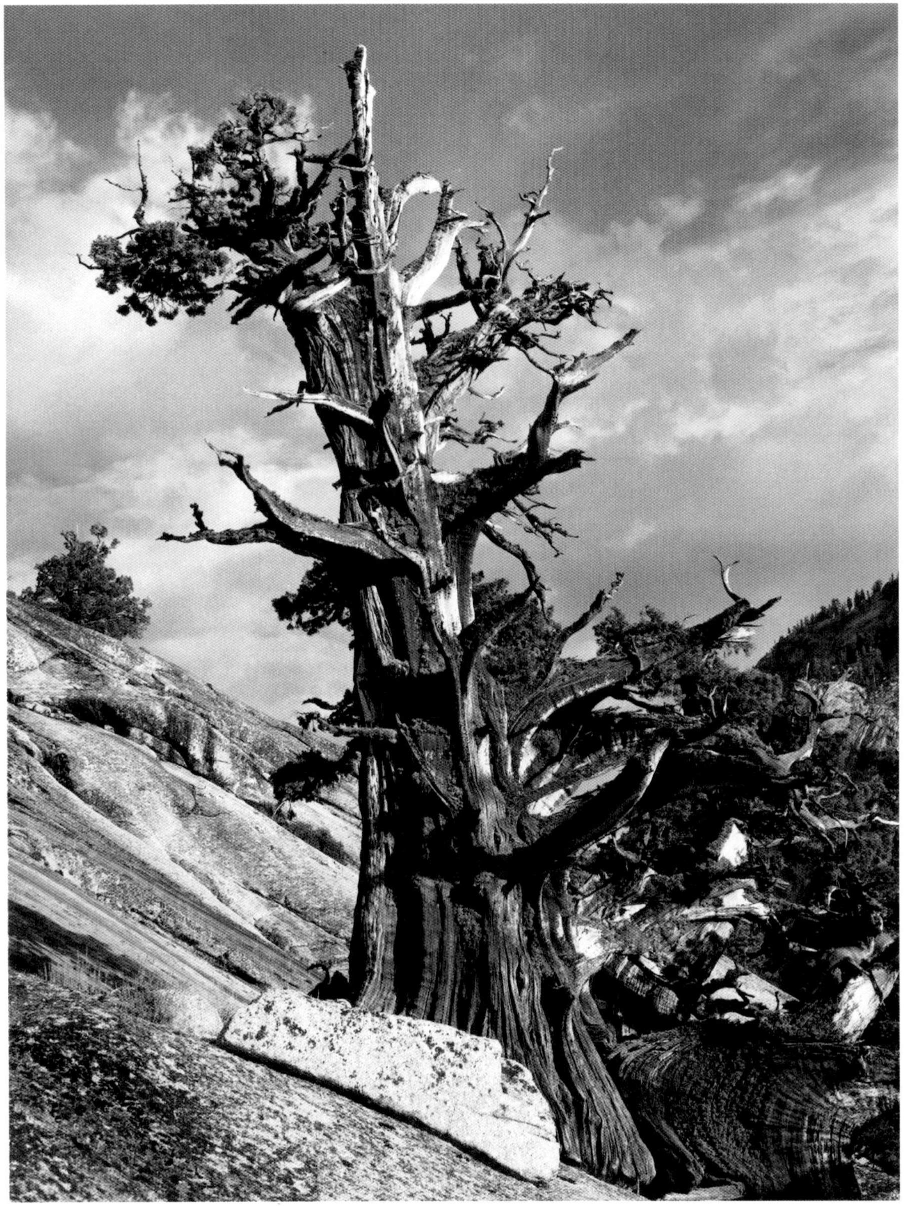

JUNIPER TREE, TRIPLE PEAK FORK, UPPER MERCED RIVER CANYON, YOSEMITE NATIONAL PARK, CALIFORNIA, C. 1940

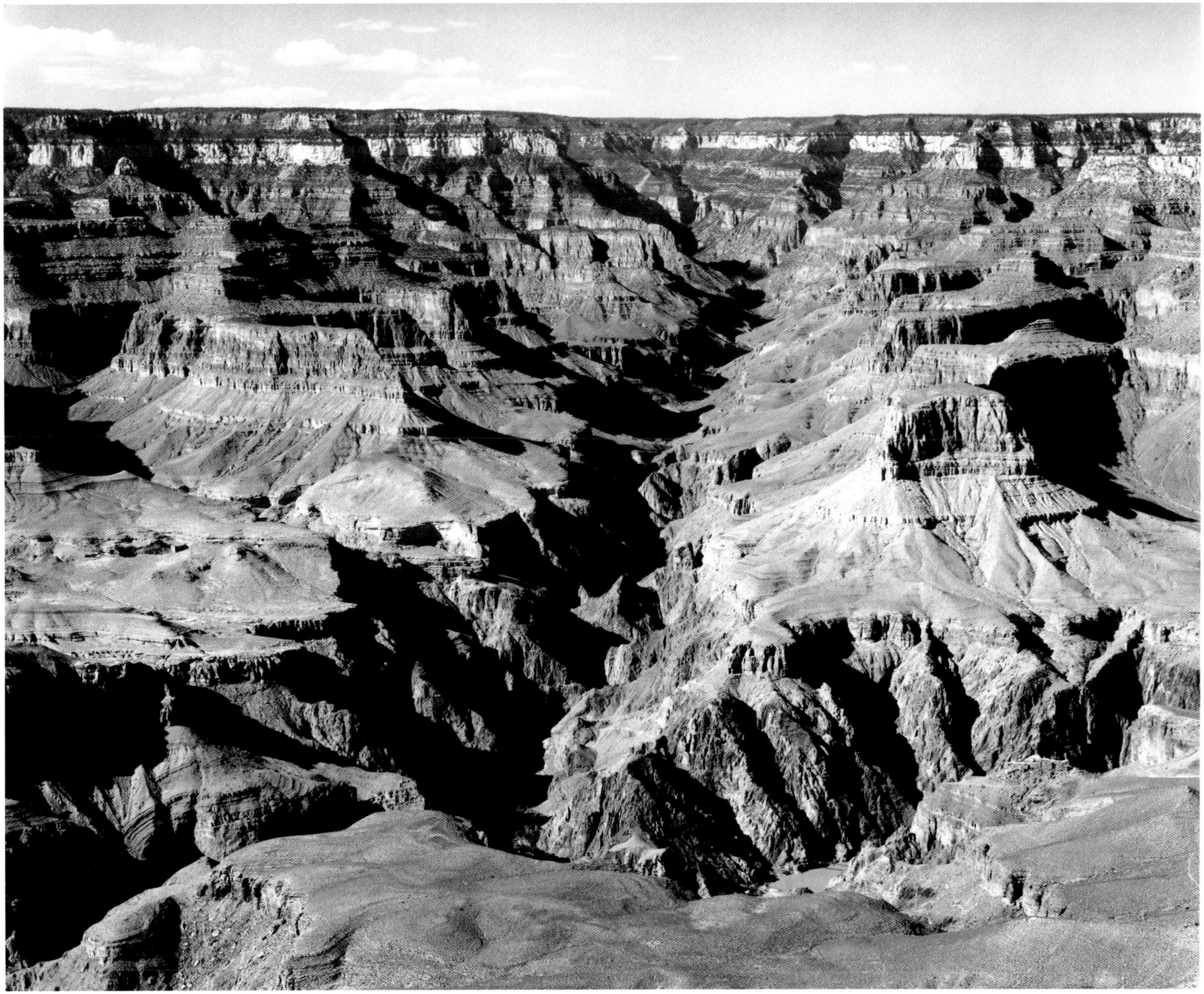

BRIGHT ANGEL CANYON, FROM YAVAPAI POINT, GRAND CANYON NATIONAL PARK, ARIZONA, 1942

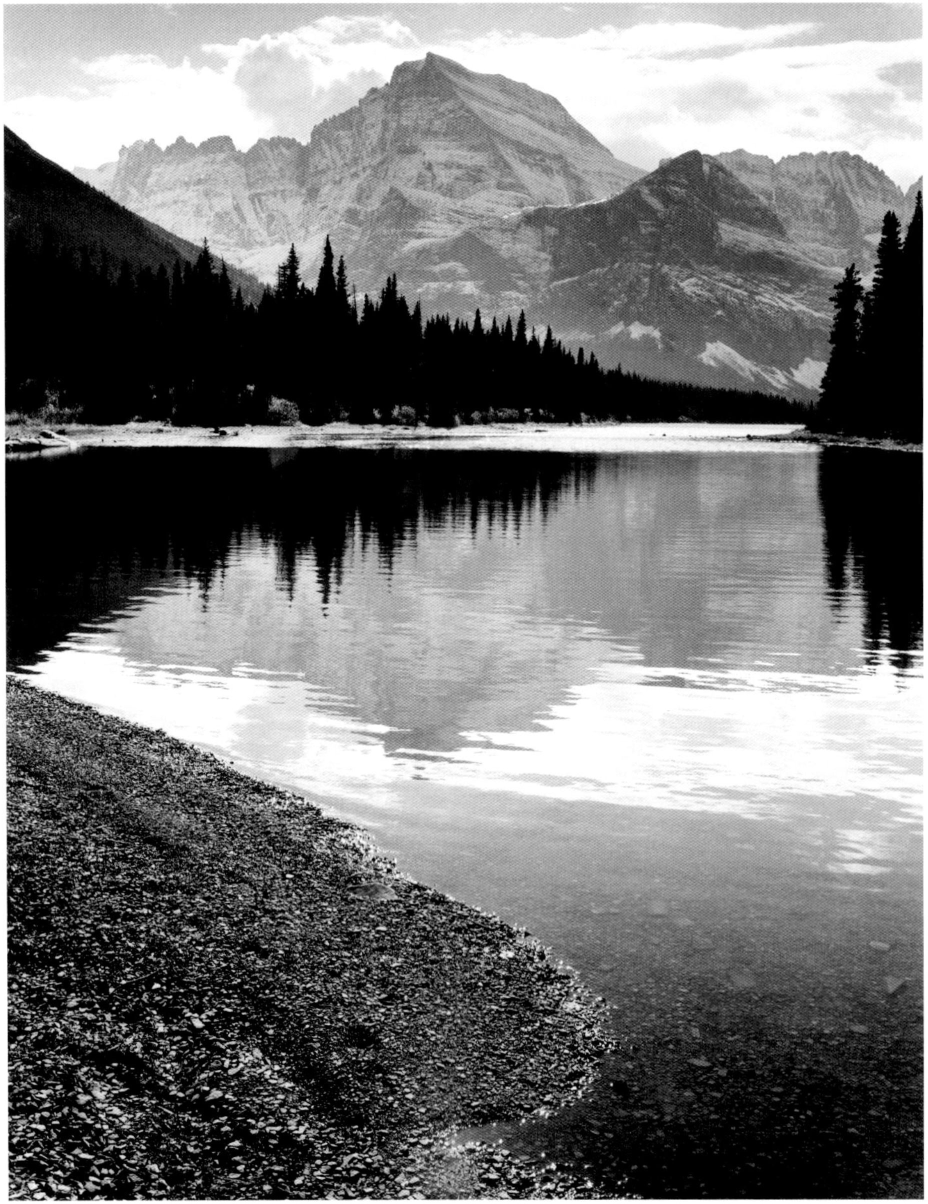

JOSEPHINE LAKE, GLACIER NATIONAL PARK, MONTANA, C. 1948

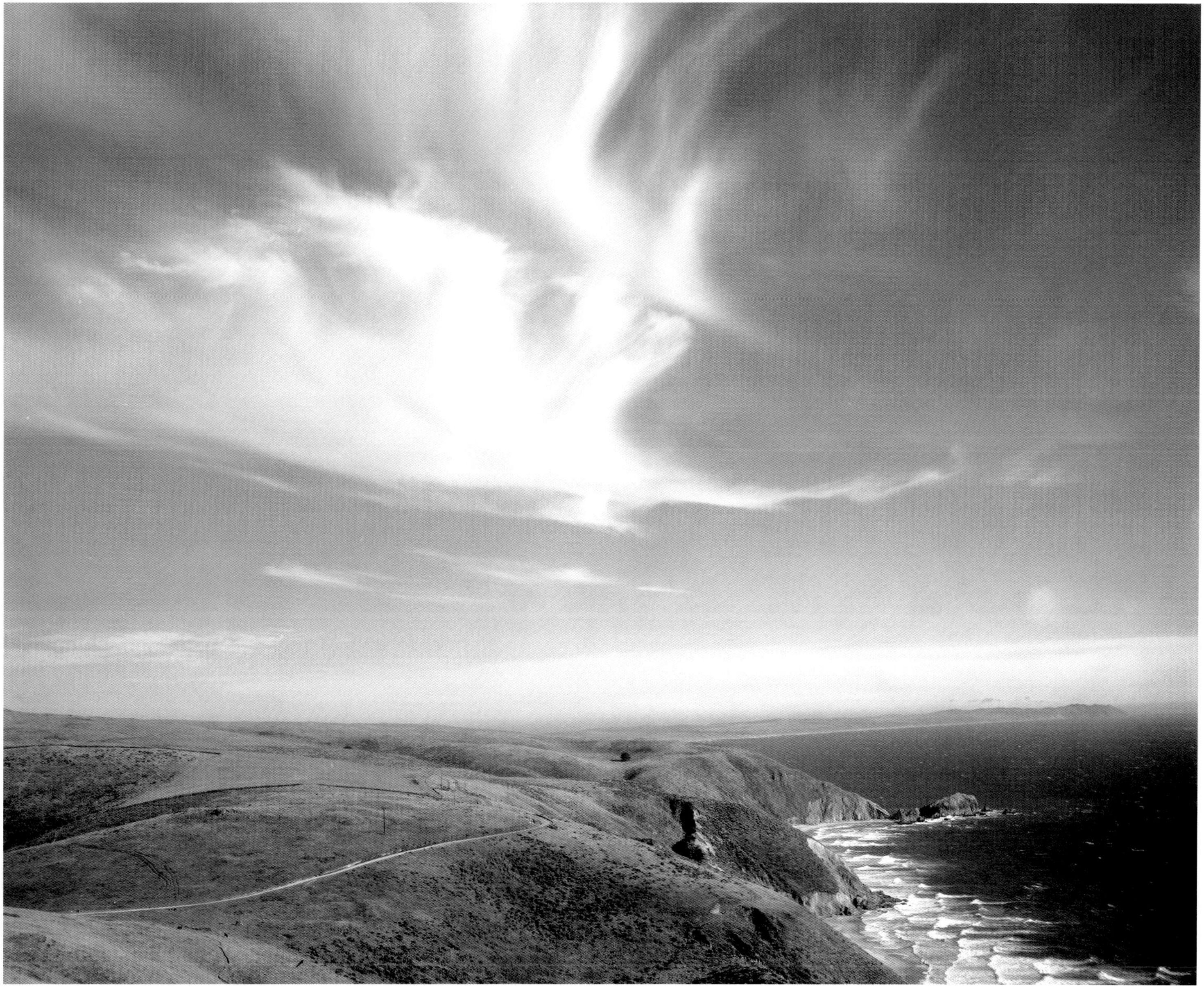

COAST LOOKING SOUTH TOWARD POINT REYES, POINT REYES NATIONAL SEASHORE, CALIFORNIA, 1958

In 1949, Ansel visited Maine "to photograph storms and great waves along the Atlantic shore." Nancy and Beaumont Newhall accompanied him, and on November 21, Beaumont recorded: "By 7:45 AM we were on the road from Bar Harbor to Schoodic Point. It was overcast when we arrived, but the surf was pounding fiercely on the rocks and we all photographed.... Ansel worked like mad—I think he said he made 36 exposures during the morning."

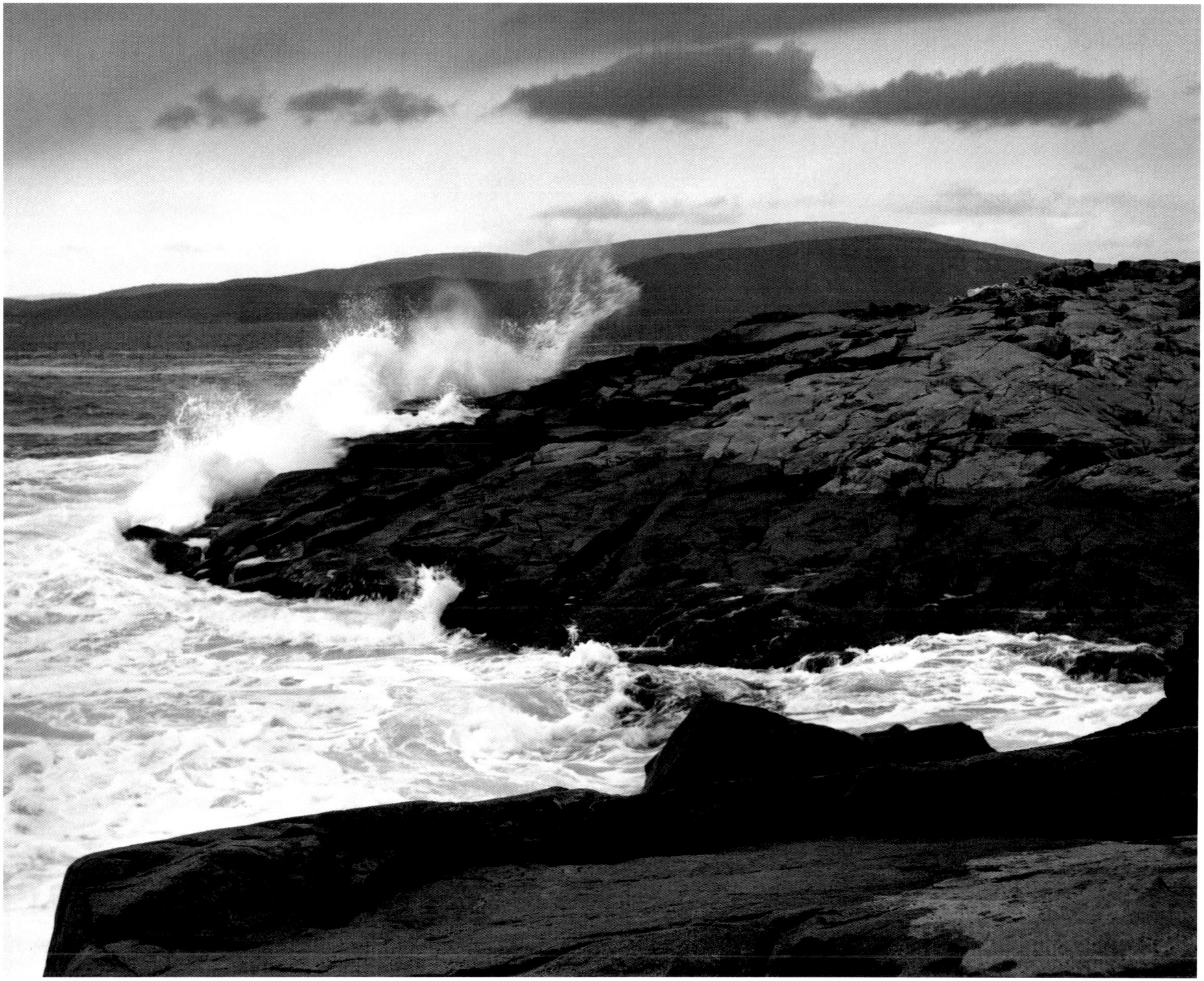

SEA AND ROCKS, STORM, SCHOODIC POINT, ACADIA NATIONAL PARK, MAINE, 1949

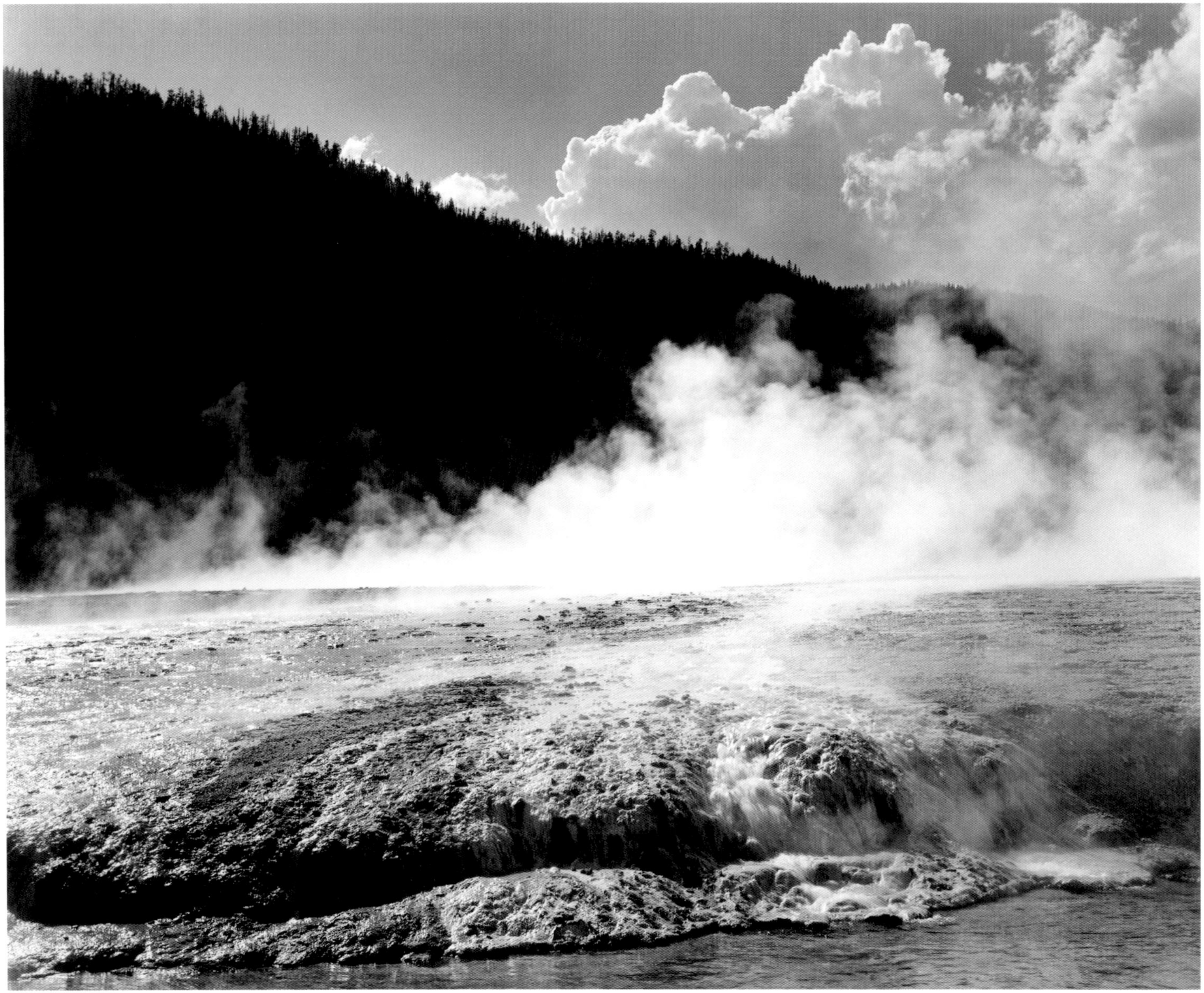

VIEW ON NORTHEAST ROAD, YELLOWSTONE NATIONAL PARK, WYOMING, 1942

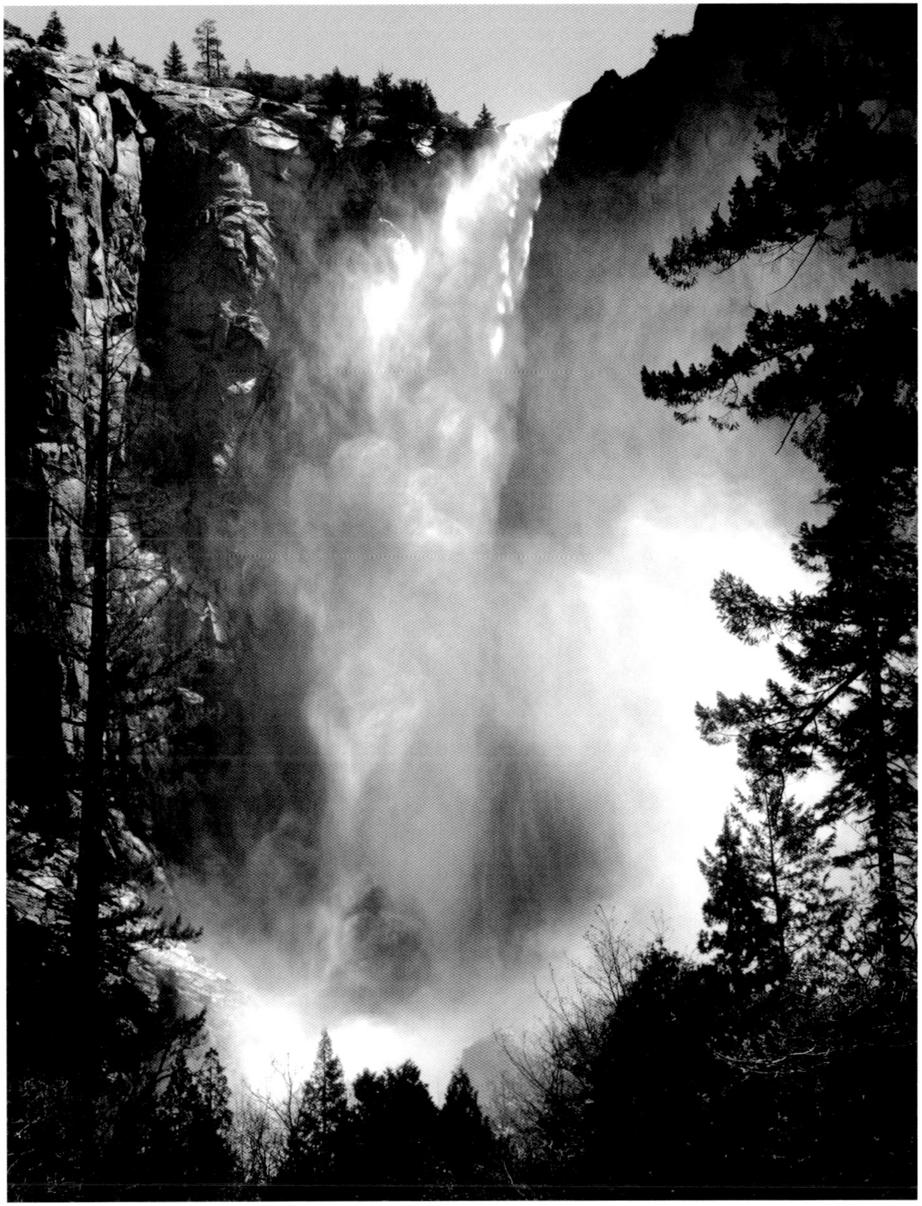

BRIDALVEIL FALL, YOSEMITE NATIONAL PARK, CALIFORNIA, 1927

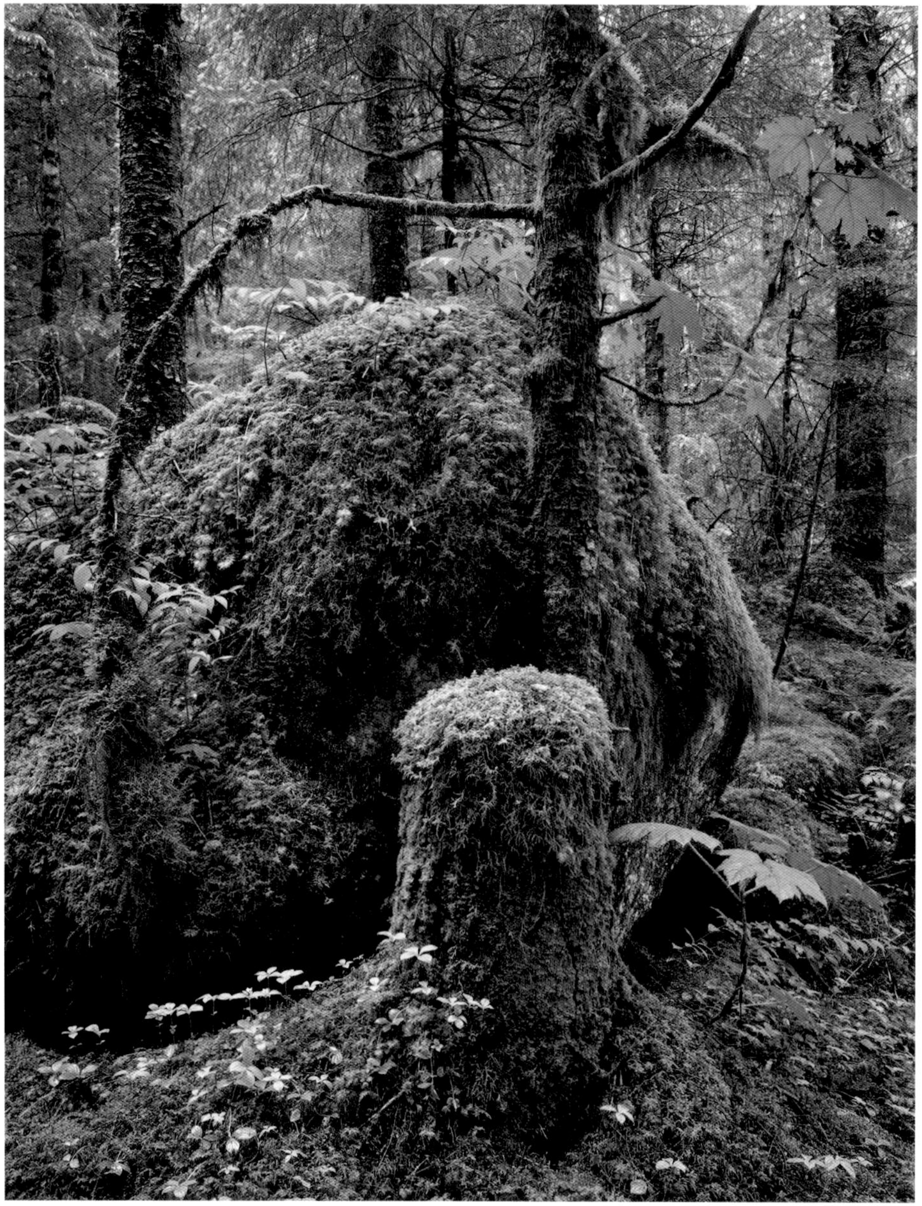

FOREST, BEARTRACK COVE, GLACIER BAY NATIONAL PARK, ALASKA, 1948

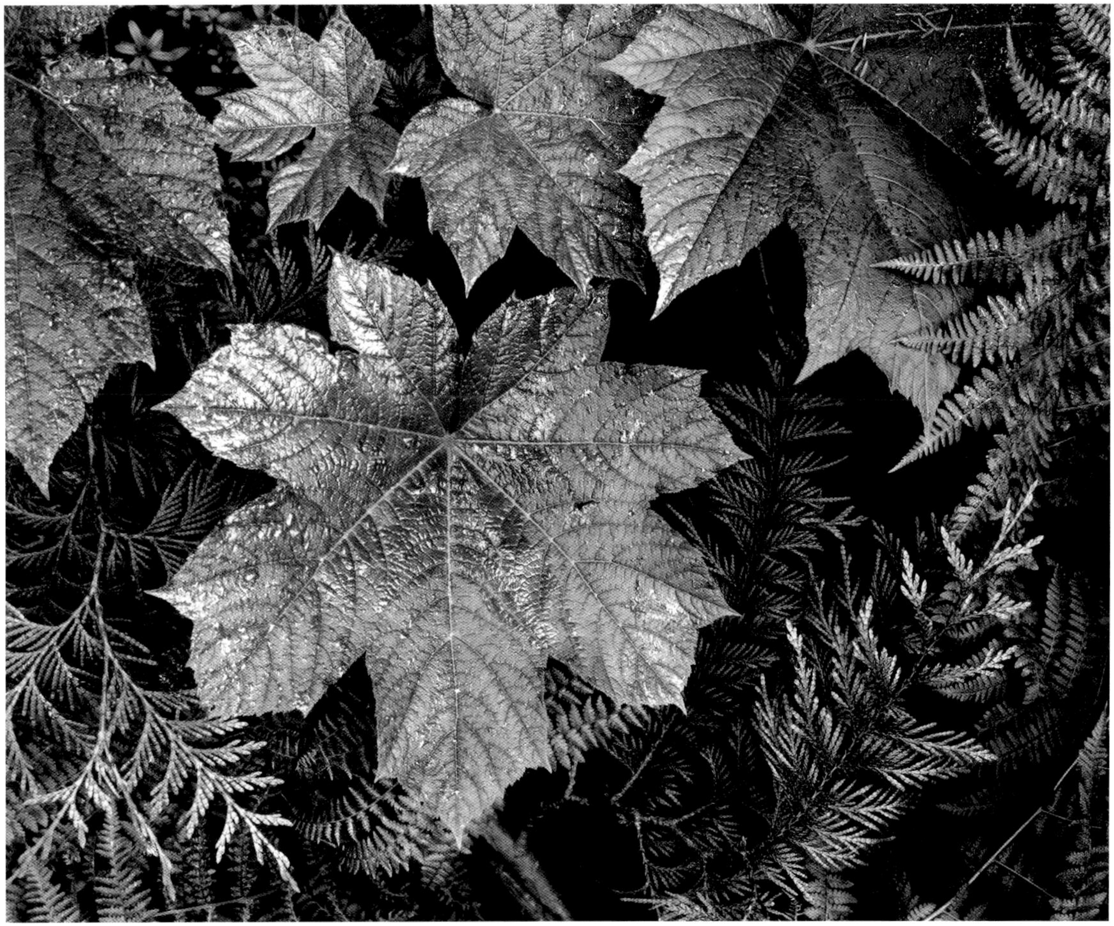

LEAVES, GLACIER NATIONAL PARK, MONTANA, 1942

Ansel visited Yellowstone National Park several times and made many photographs there, particularly a series of dazzling portraits of Old Faithful Geyser (see pages 81 and 120). But the park failed to capture his imagination in the same way his beloved Sierra Nevada or the nearby Tetons did. He described Yellowstone as a collection of curios: geysers, bubbling mud pools, oozing terraces, herds of captive buffalo. He disliked the tourist mentality of the visitors in long caravans of cars with windows rolled down to see the sights. His best photographs in the park were made in the summer of 1942. Perhaps the park was emptier then, just after the beginning of World War II; when he visited again in 1948, he had a different experience. In a letter to Nancy Newhall of August 1948, he complained, "Yellowstone is simply horrible. Millions of people, cars, bears, garbage. Ah Wilderness!"

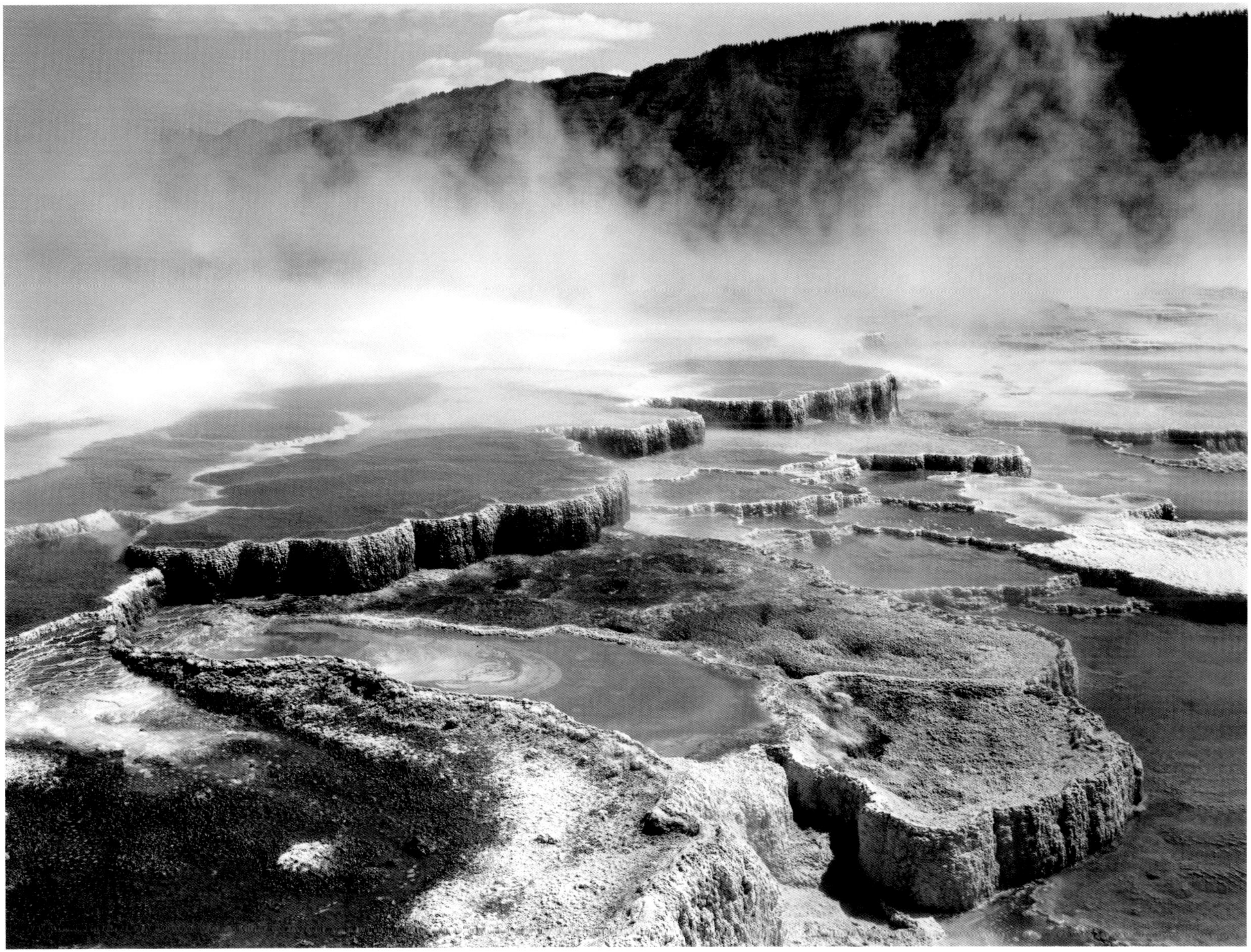

JUPITER TERRACE, MAMMOTH HOT SPRINGS, YELLOWSTONE NATIONAL PARK, WYOMING, 1942

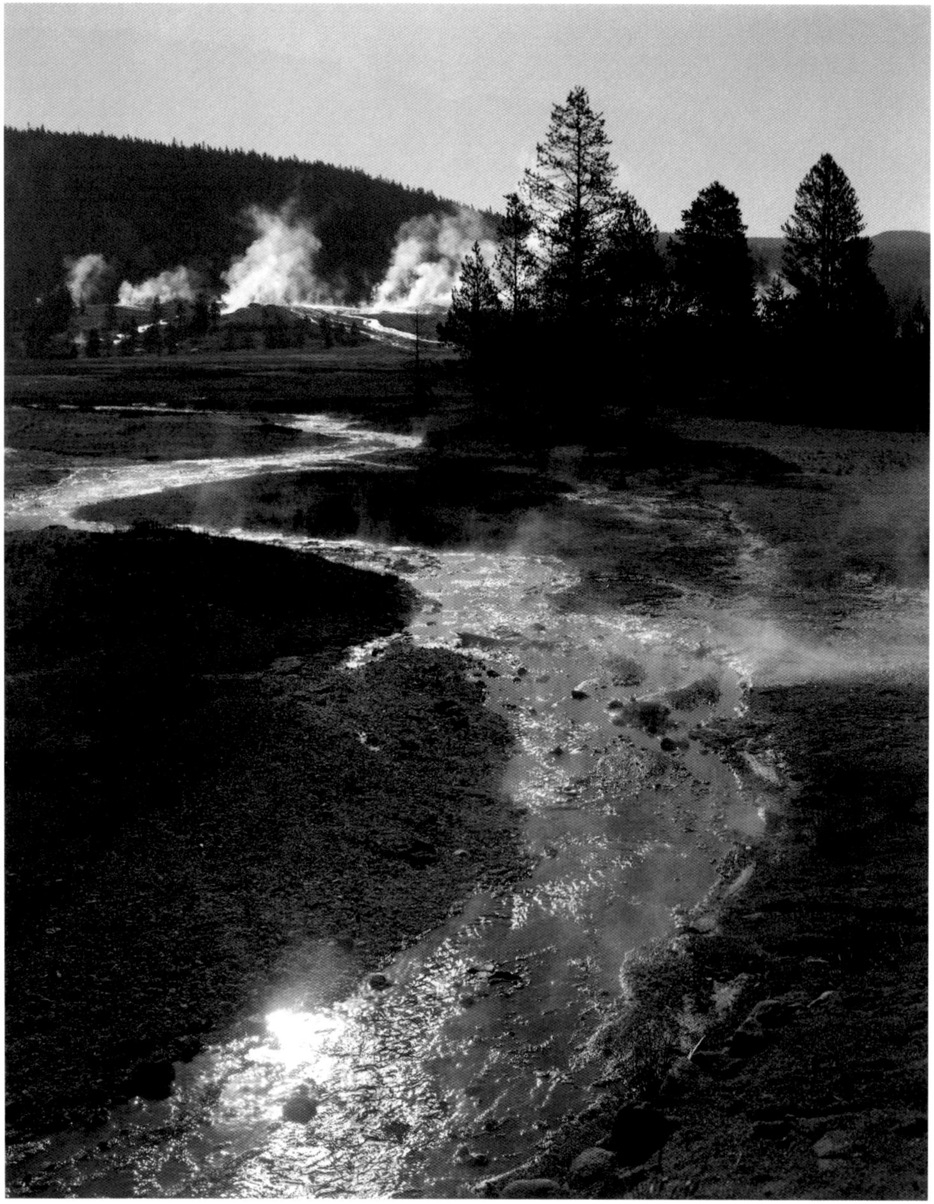

FIREHOLE RIVER TRIBUTARY, YELLOWSTONE NATIONAL PARK, WYOMING, 1942

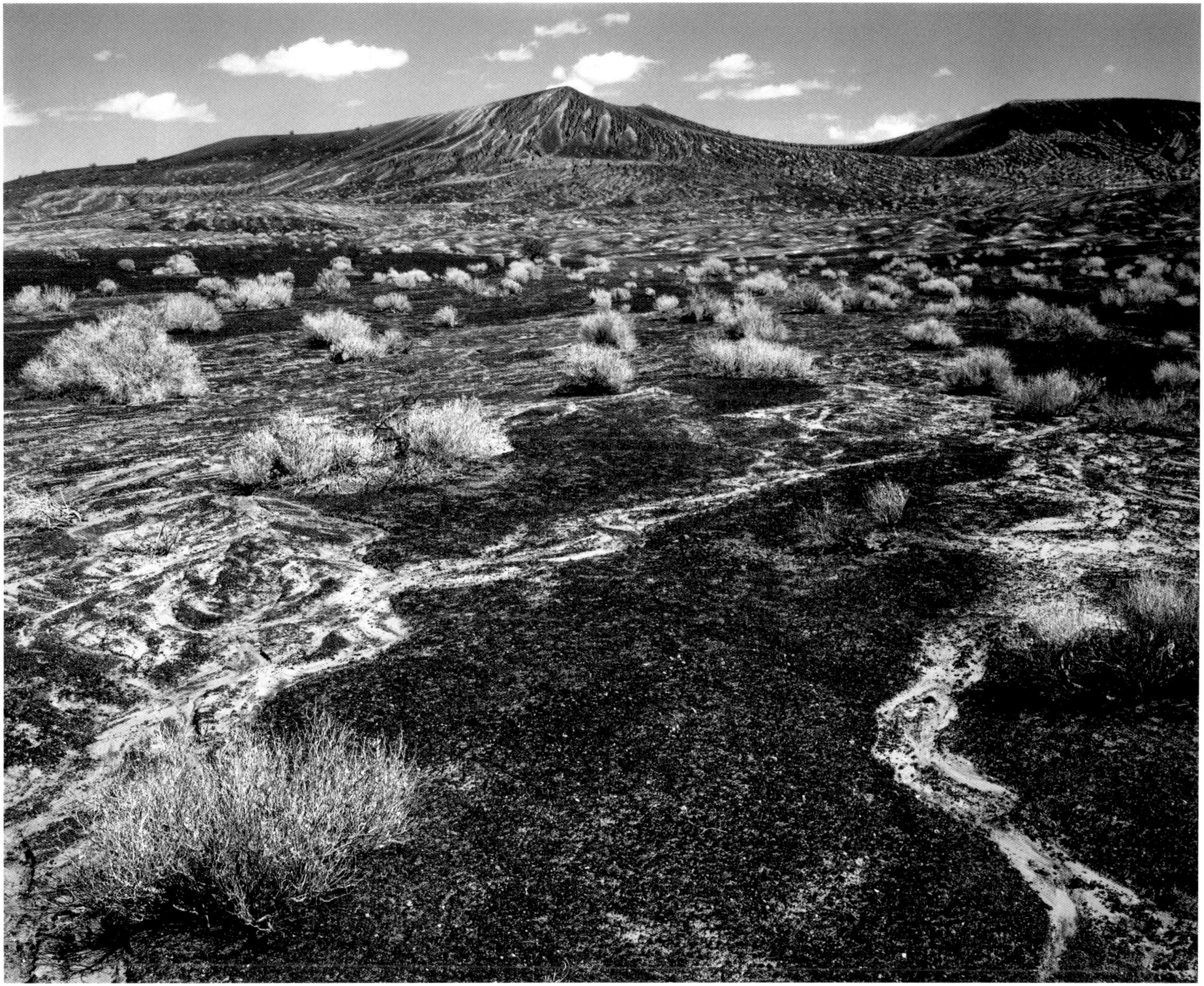

UBEHEBE CRATER, DEATH VALLEY NATIONAL PARK, CALIFORNIA, 1952

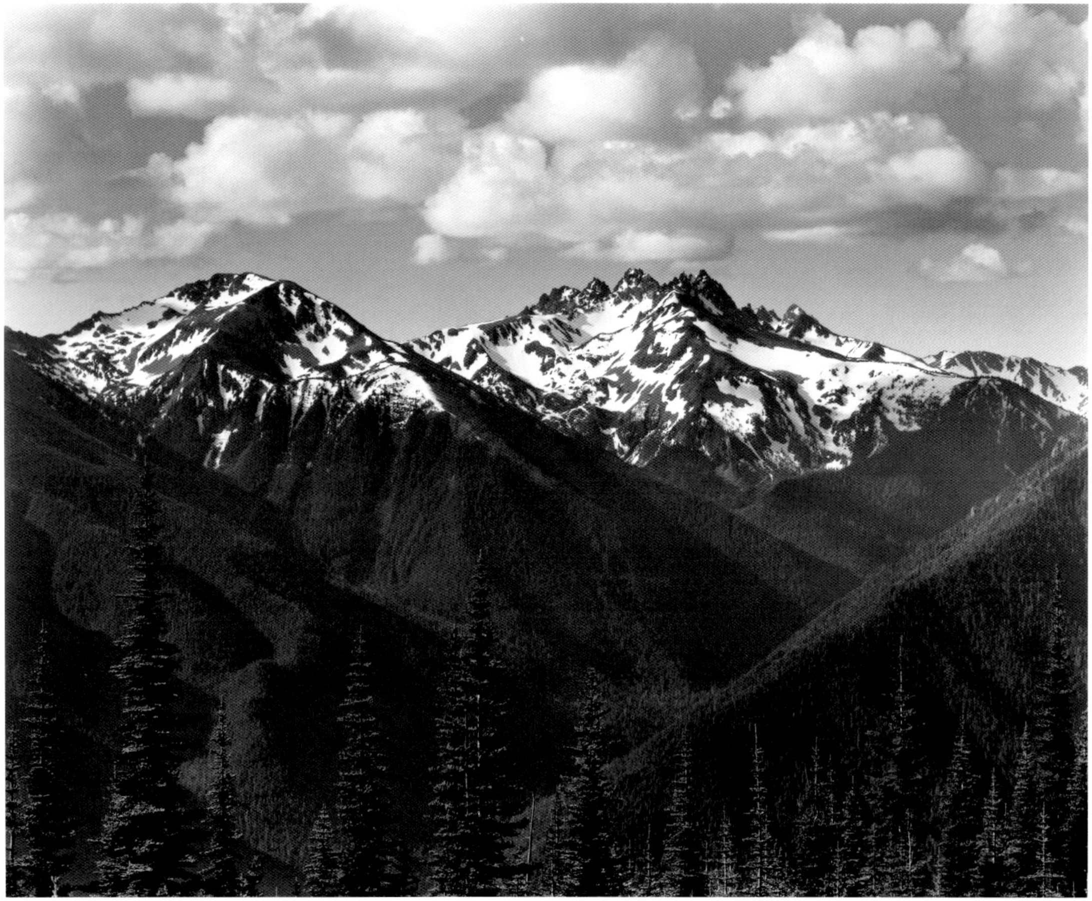

FROM HURRICANE HILL, OLYMPIC NATIONAL PARK, WASHINGTON, C. 1950

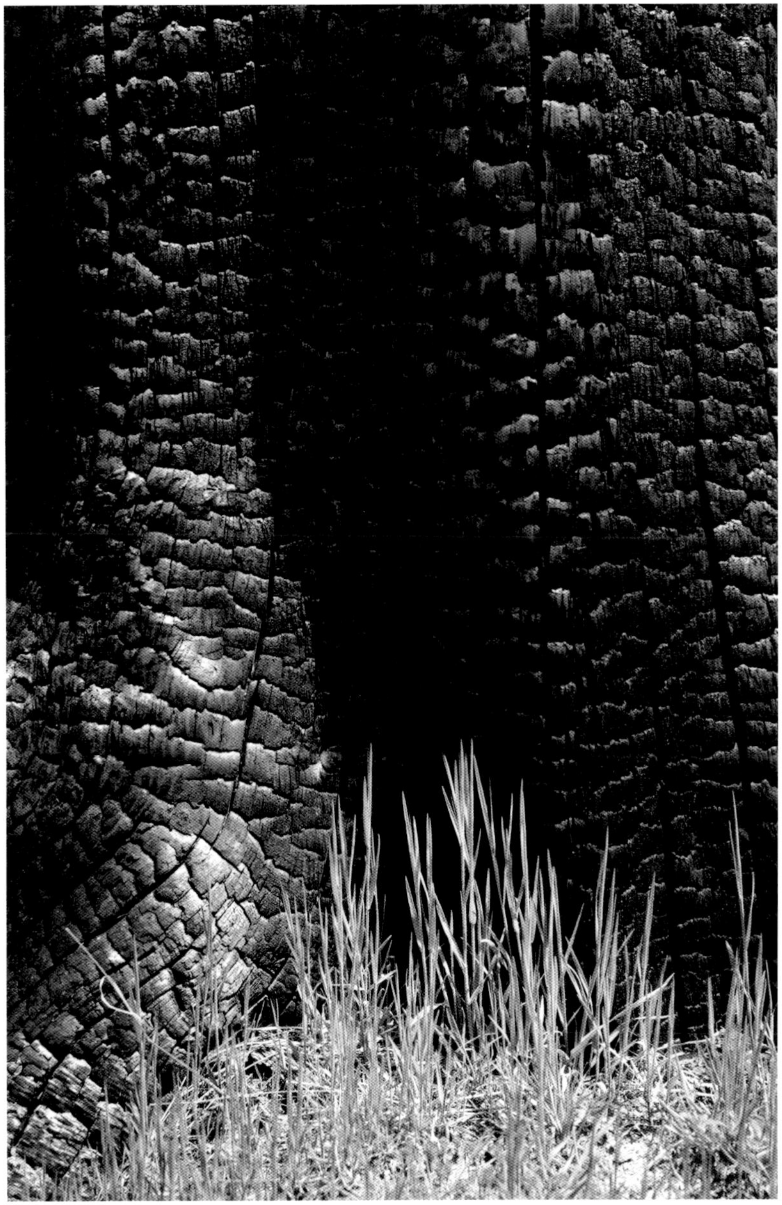

BURNT STUMP AND NEW GRASS, SIERRA NEVADA, CALIFORNIA, 1935

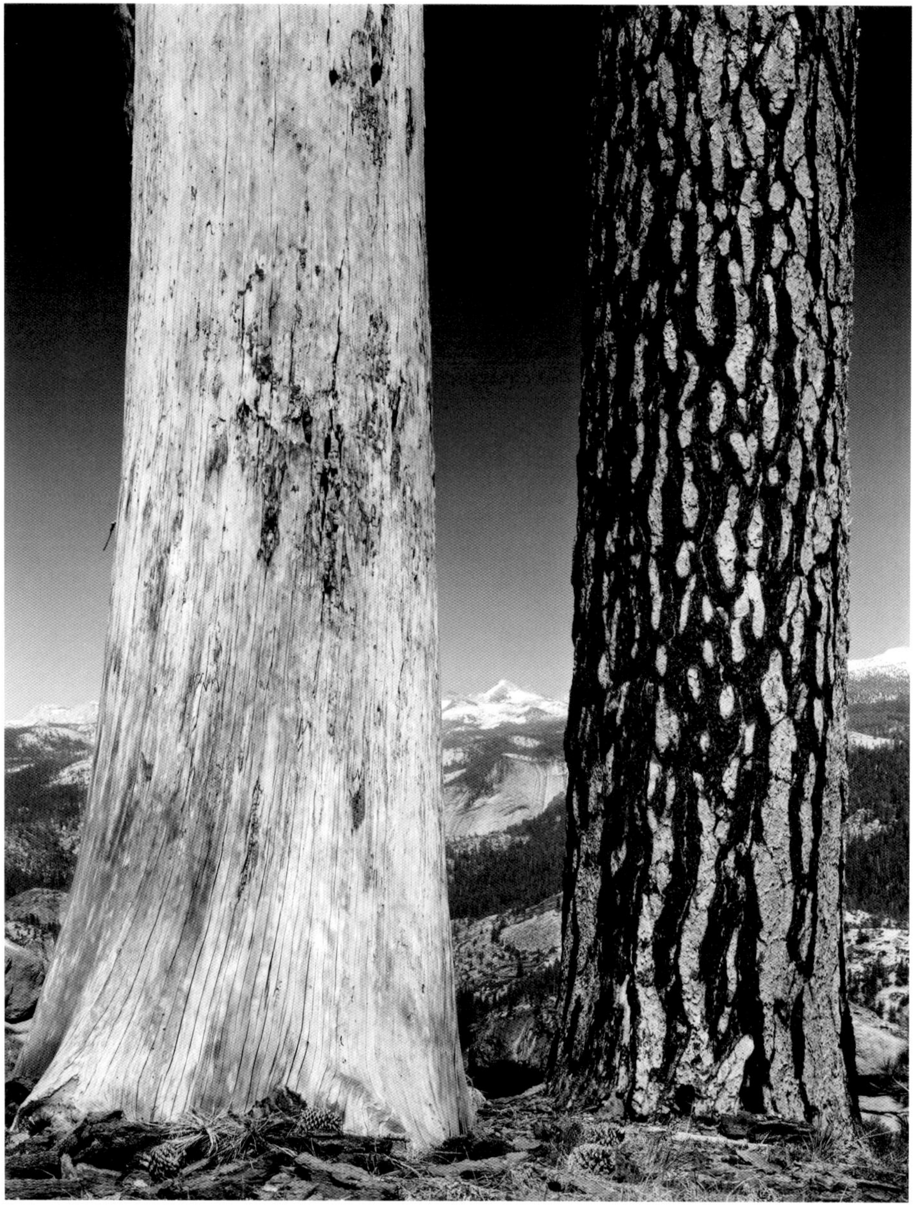

TREES, ILLILOUETTE RIDGE, YOSEMITE NATIONAL PARK, CALIFORNIA, 1945

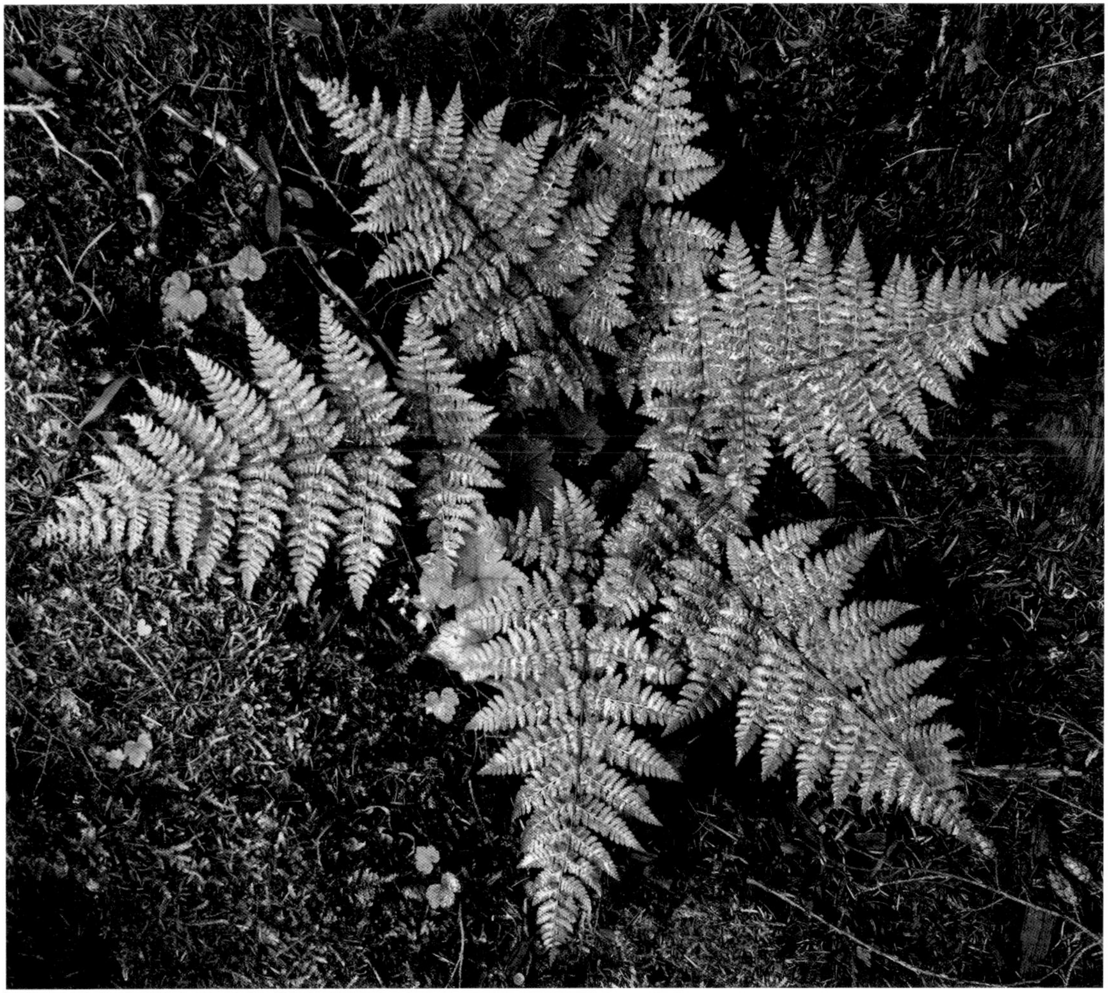

FERNS, GLACIER NATIONAL PARK, MONTANA, 1942

In *The Camera,* volume one of his renowned technical series, Ansel wrote about this image: "The camera configuration causes exaggeration of the foreground stream, but with interesting compositional effect. Note that the horizon appears slightly curved; this is due to a slight curvature in the film, exaggerated by the short focal length of the lens."

This image was made using one of Ansel's favorite Polaroid products, Polaroid Type 55 Land film, introduced in 1961, which simultaneously produced both an instant print and a negative. He served as a consultant for the Polaroid Corporation for more than thirty years and relished reporting on their film and cameras. For the last twenty years of his life, as the creative urge lessened, he spent more and more time working on tests of Polaroid materials, which he discussed in several thousand memoranda to the company.

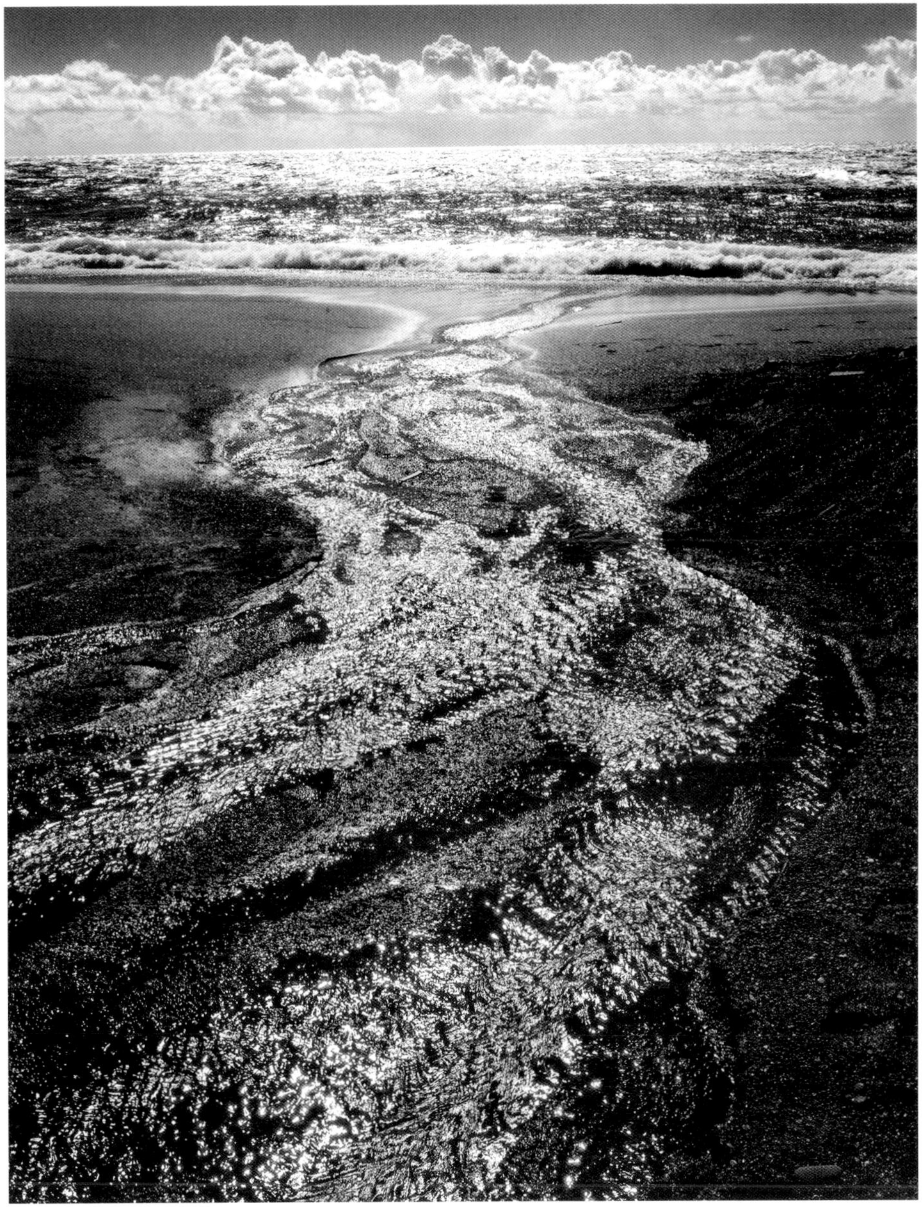

STREAM, SEA, CLOUDS, RODEO LAGOON, GOLDEN GATE NATIONAL RECREATION AREA, CALIFORNIA, 1962

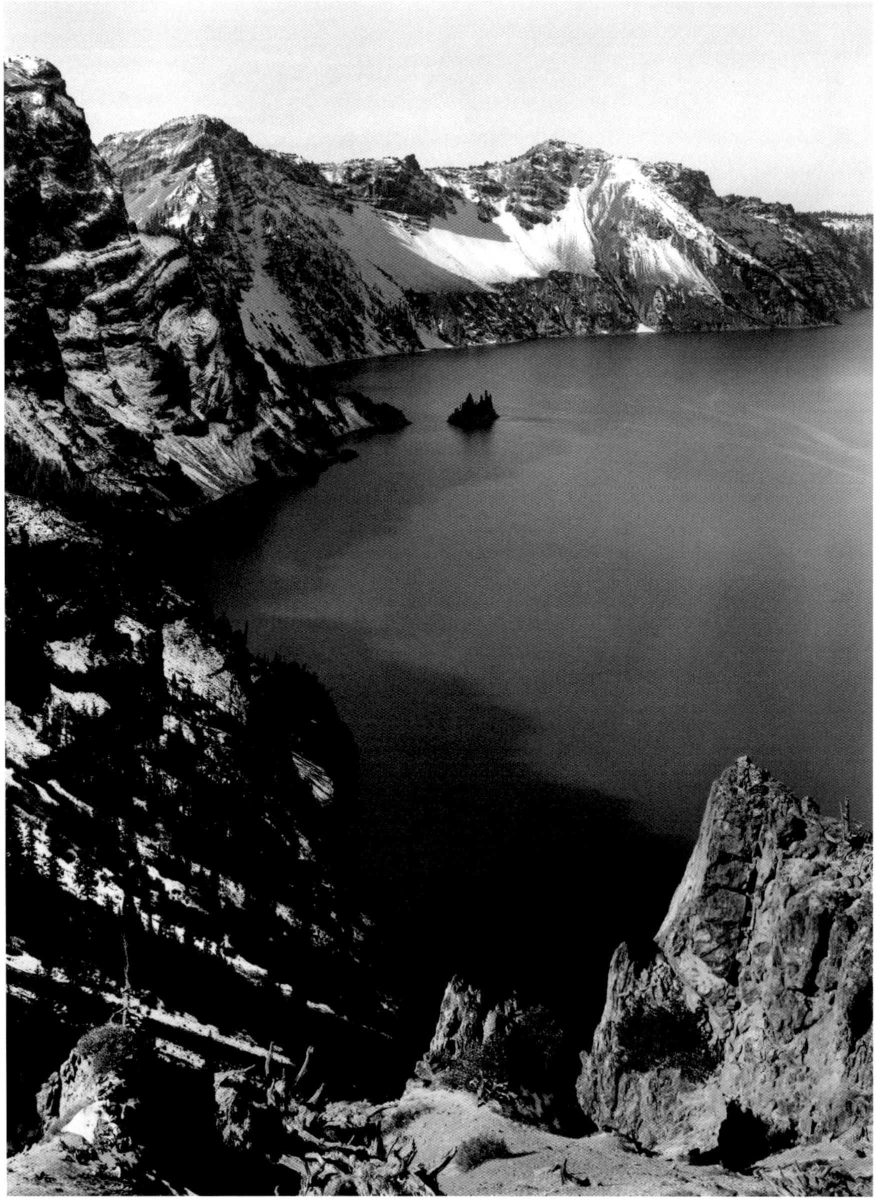

CRATER LAKE AND SNOW, CRATER LAKE NATIONAL PARK, OREGON, 1943

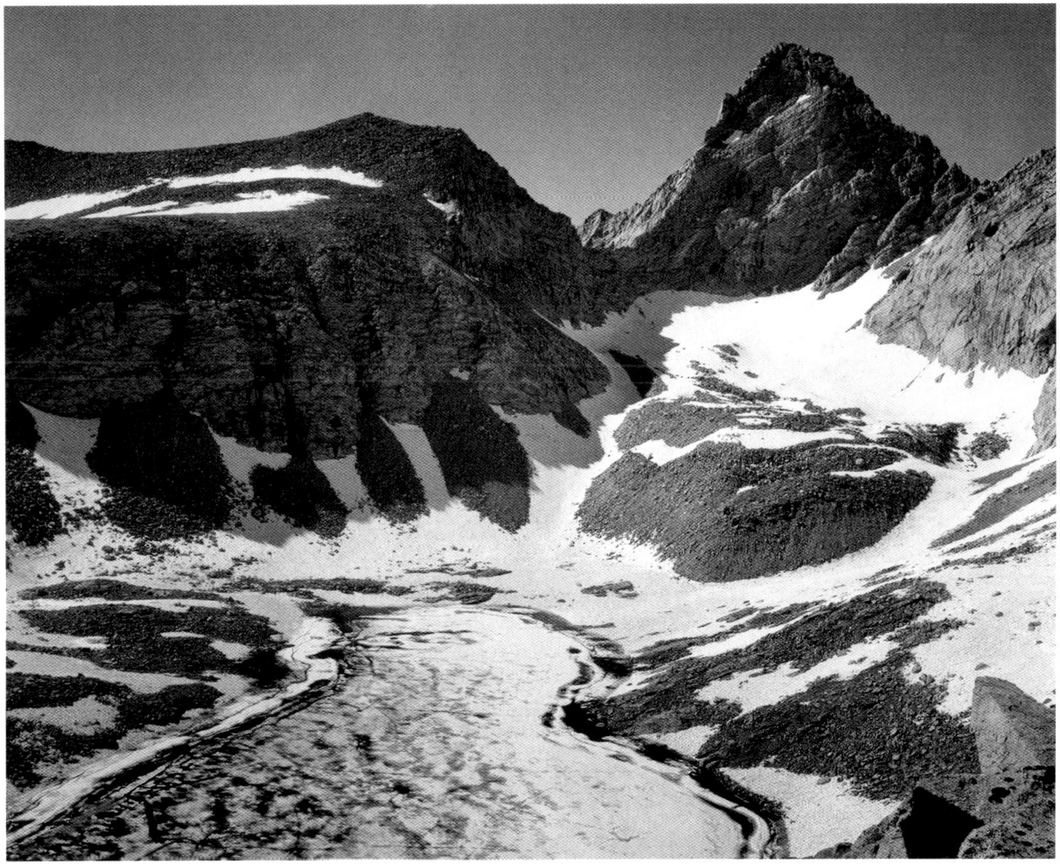

JUNCTION PEAK, KINGS CANYON NATIONAL PARK, CALIFORNIA, C. 1932

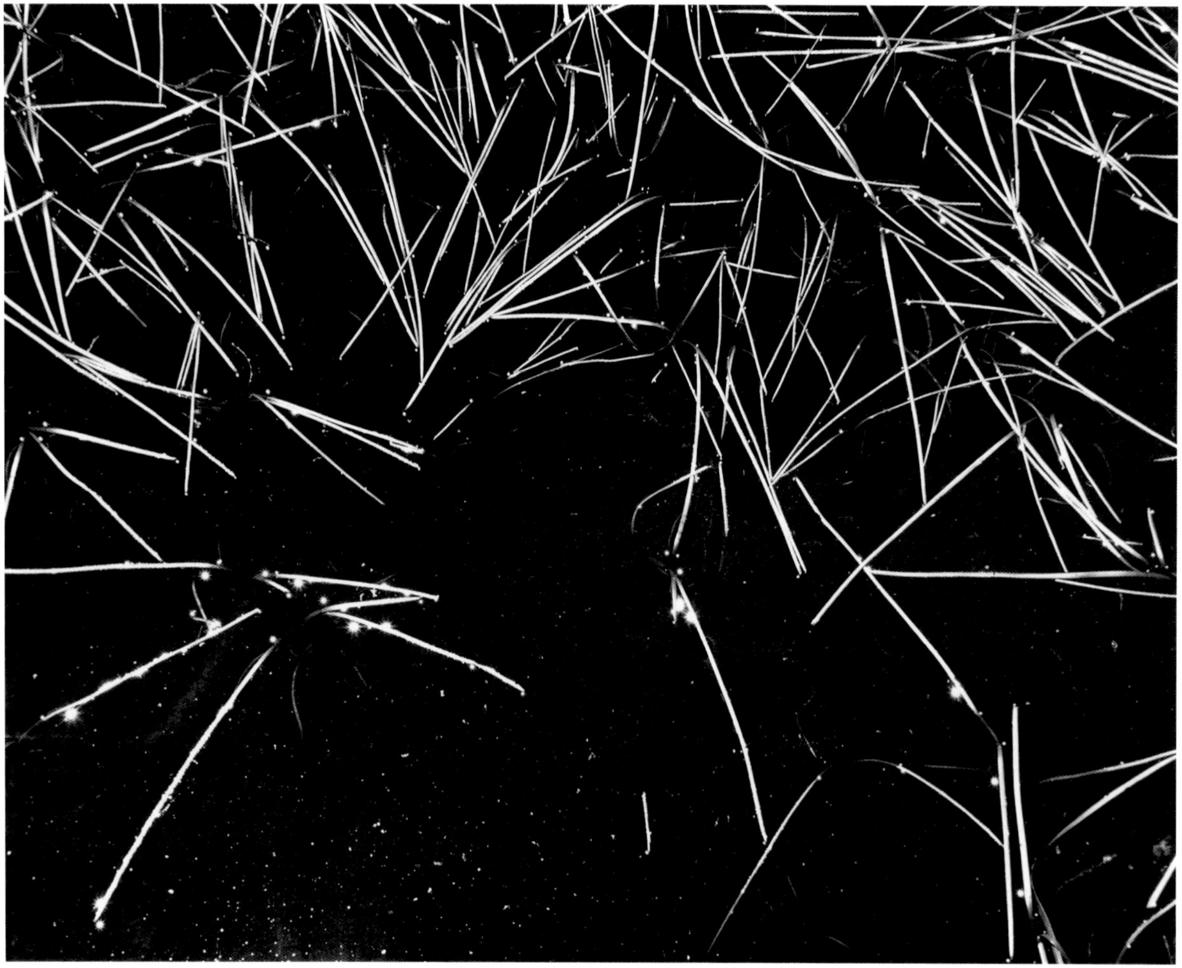

GRASS AND POOL, TUOLUMNE MEADOWS, YOSEMITE NATIONAL PARK, CALIFORNIA, C. 1935

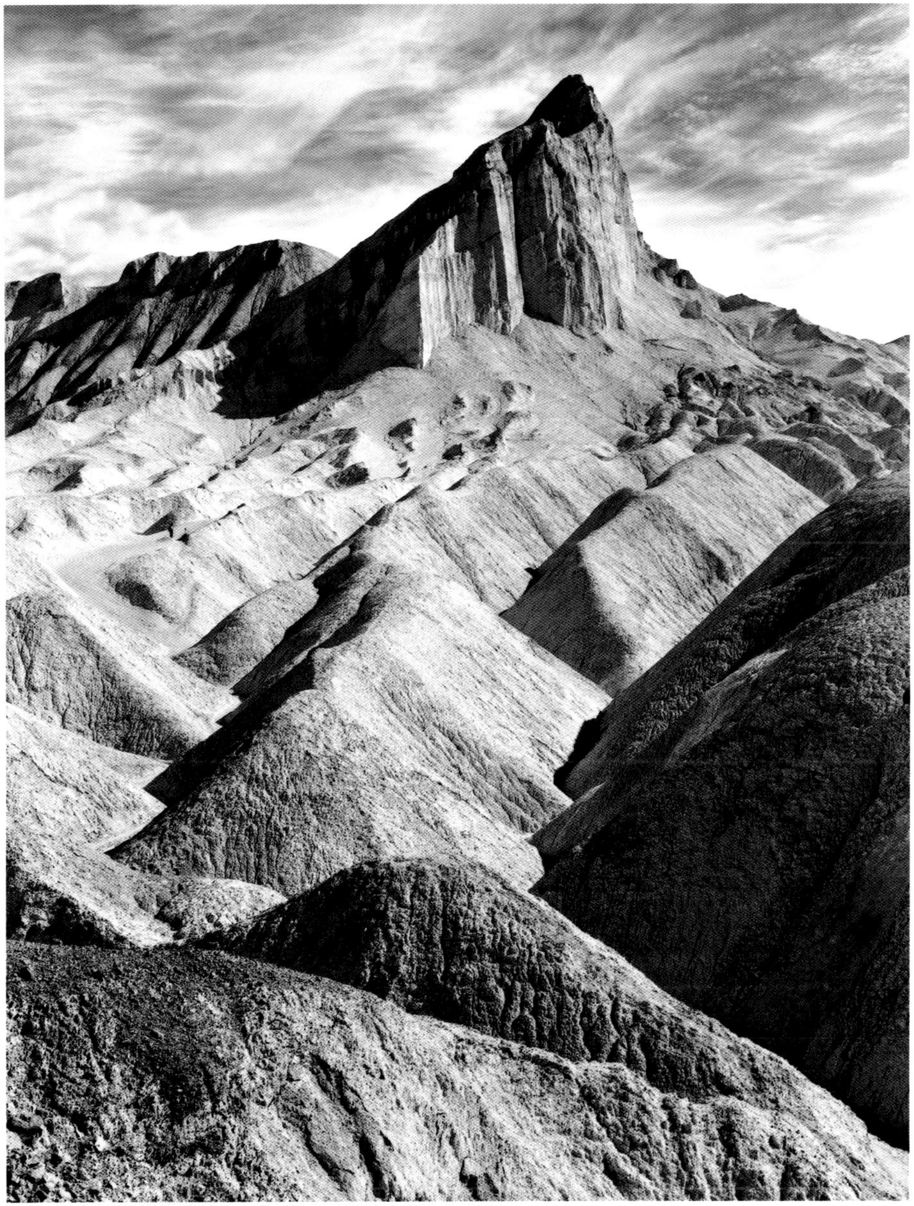

MANLY BEACON, DEATH VALLEY NATIONAL PARK, CALIFORNIA, C. 1948

In 1941, Ansel was appointed by Secretary of the Interior Harold Ickes as a photographic muralist to record the national parks and monuments. The resulting photographs were to be enlarged into murals to decorate the Department of the Interior's new headquarters in Washington, DC. Ansel was paid $22.22 a day plus five dollars for room and board and four cents a mile. This stipend allowed him to explore areas of the country that he had never visited before, such as the Rockies and the Pacific Northwest. With America's entry into World War II, the project was necessarily discontinued. Ansel was thus able to make only one trip in the fall of 1941 and a second trip in the summer of 1942—when this photograph was made.

"This is one of a sequence of five photographs of the Tetons in a thunder storm," wrote Ansel. "All were made with rather ample exposure and development in order to assure rich values in the clouds and shadowed areas. As no blue sky shows, the effect of the K2 yellow filter was only to clarify the distance, as there was a slight haze over all."

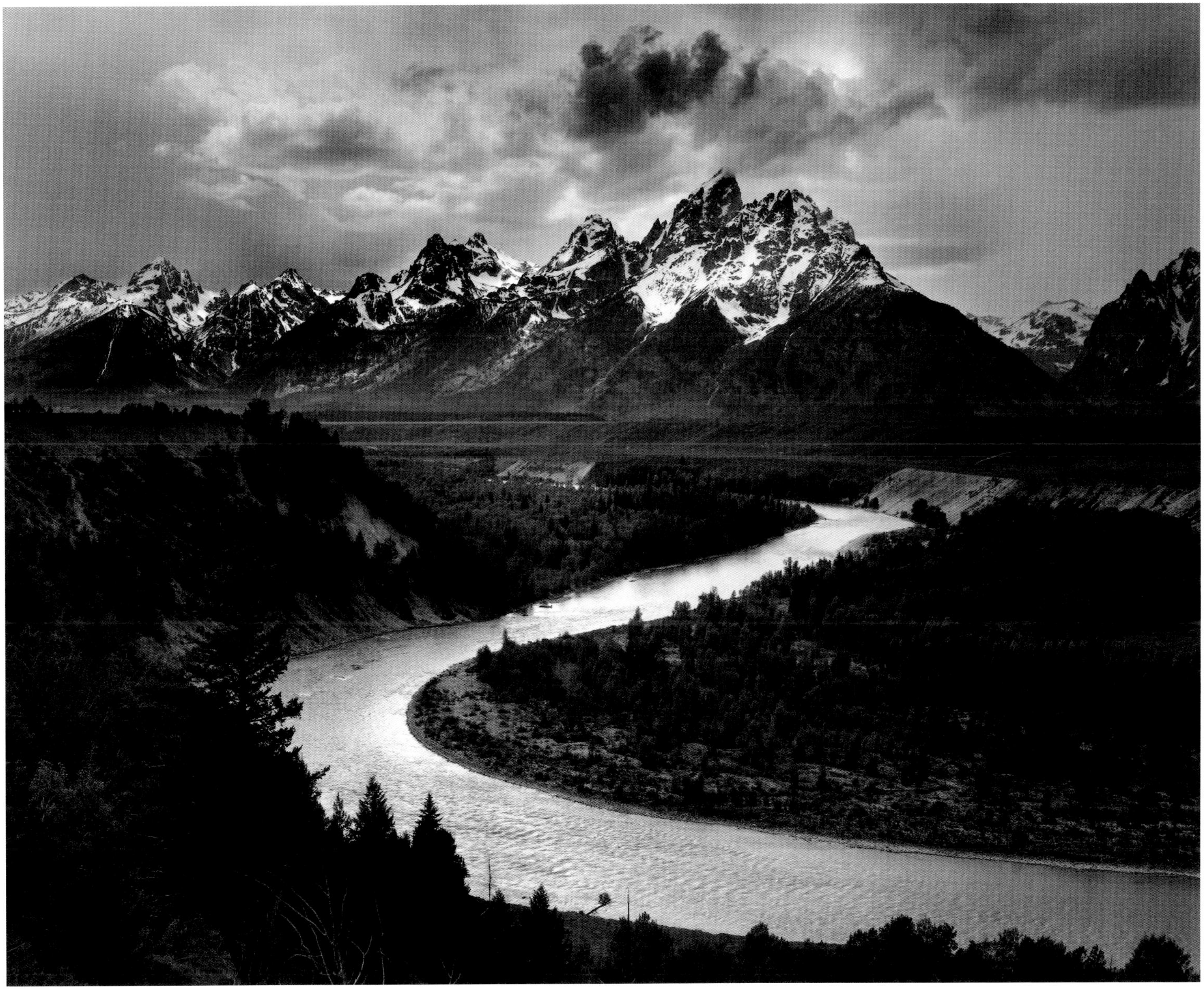

THE TETONS AND THE SNAKE RIVER, GRAND TETON NATIONAL PARK, WYOMING, 1942

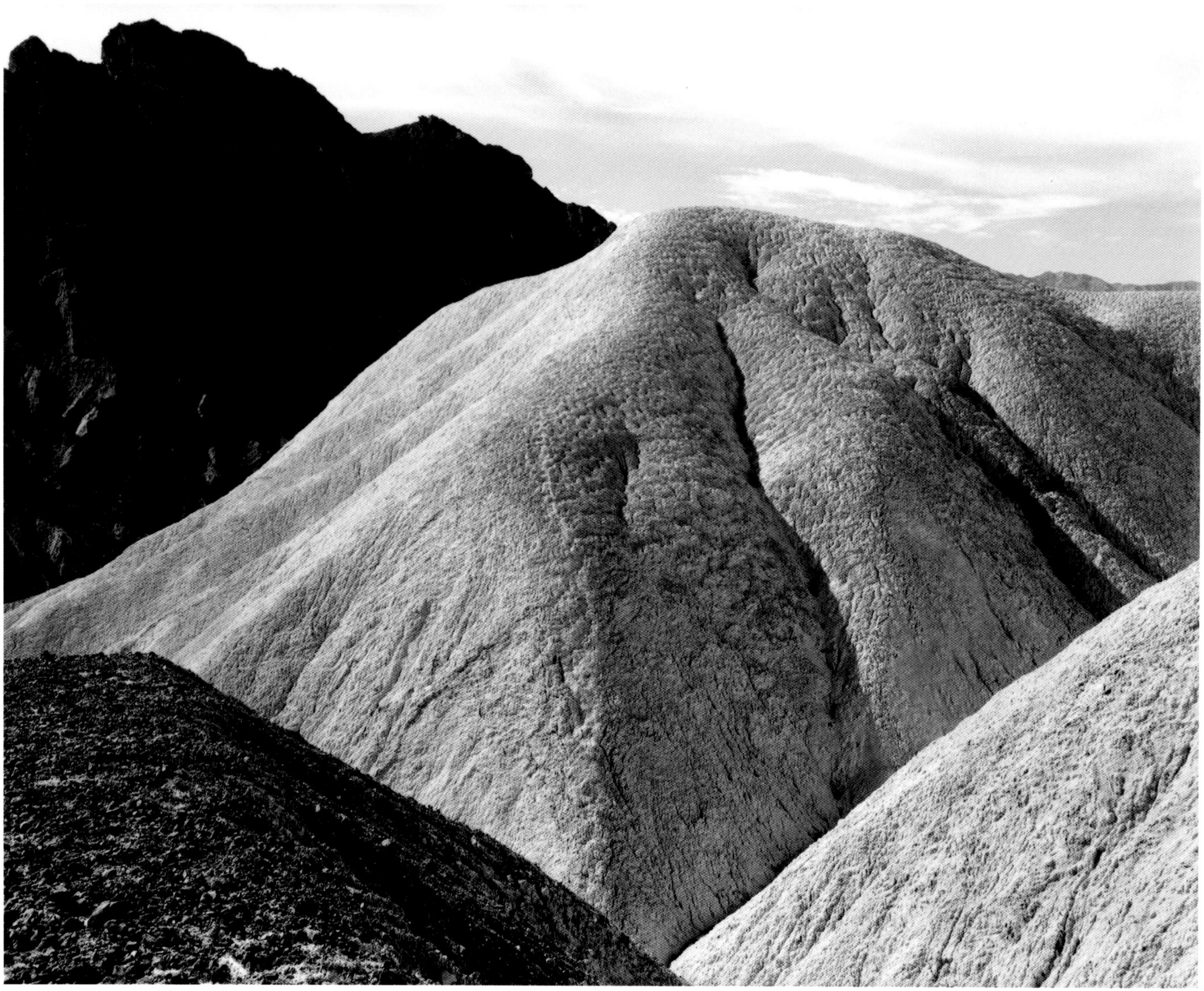

IN GOLDEN CANYON, DEATH VALLEY NATIONAL PARK, CALIFORNIA, C. 1946

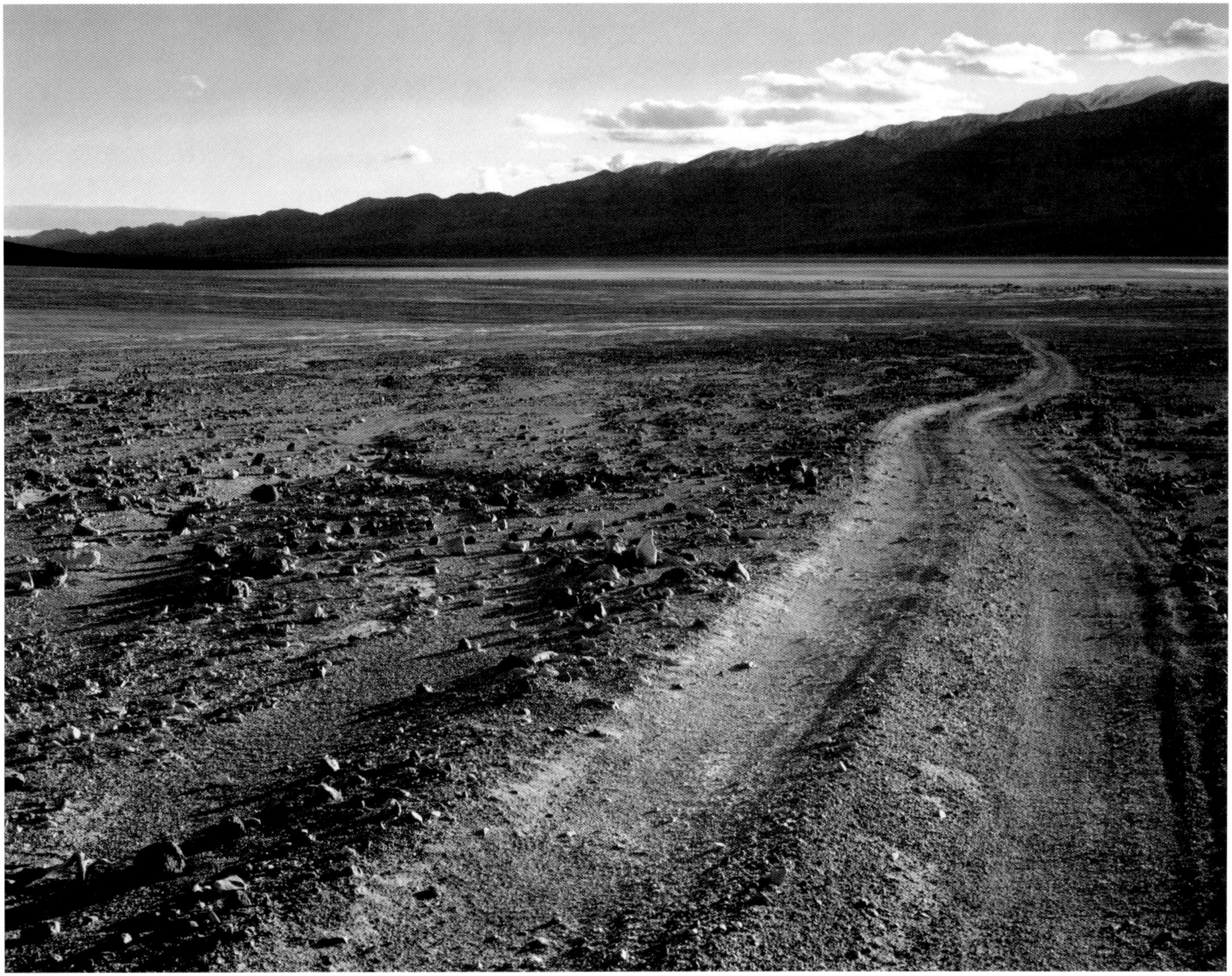

ROAD TO SALT FLATS, EVENING, DEATH VALLEY NATIONAL PARK, CALIFORNIA, C. 1947

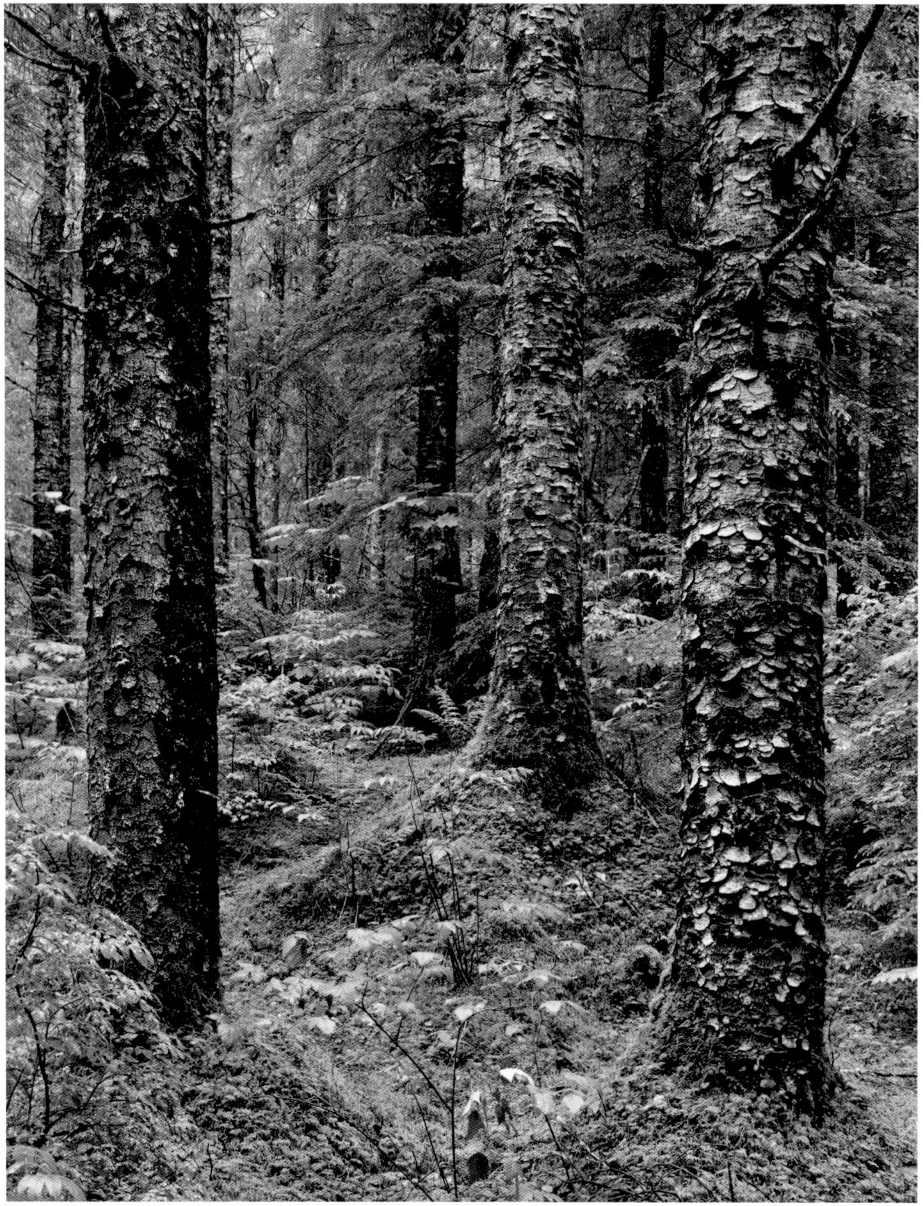

FOREST, BEARTRACK COVE, GLACIER BAY NATIONAL PARK, ALASKA, 1948

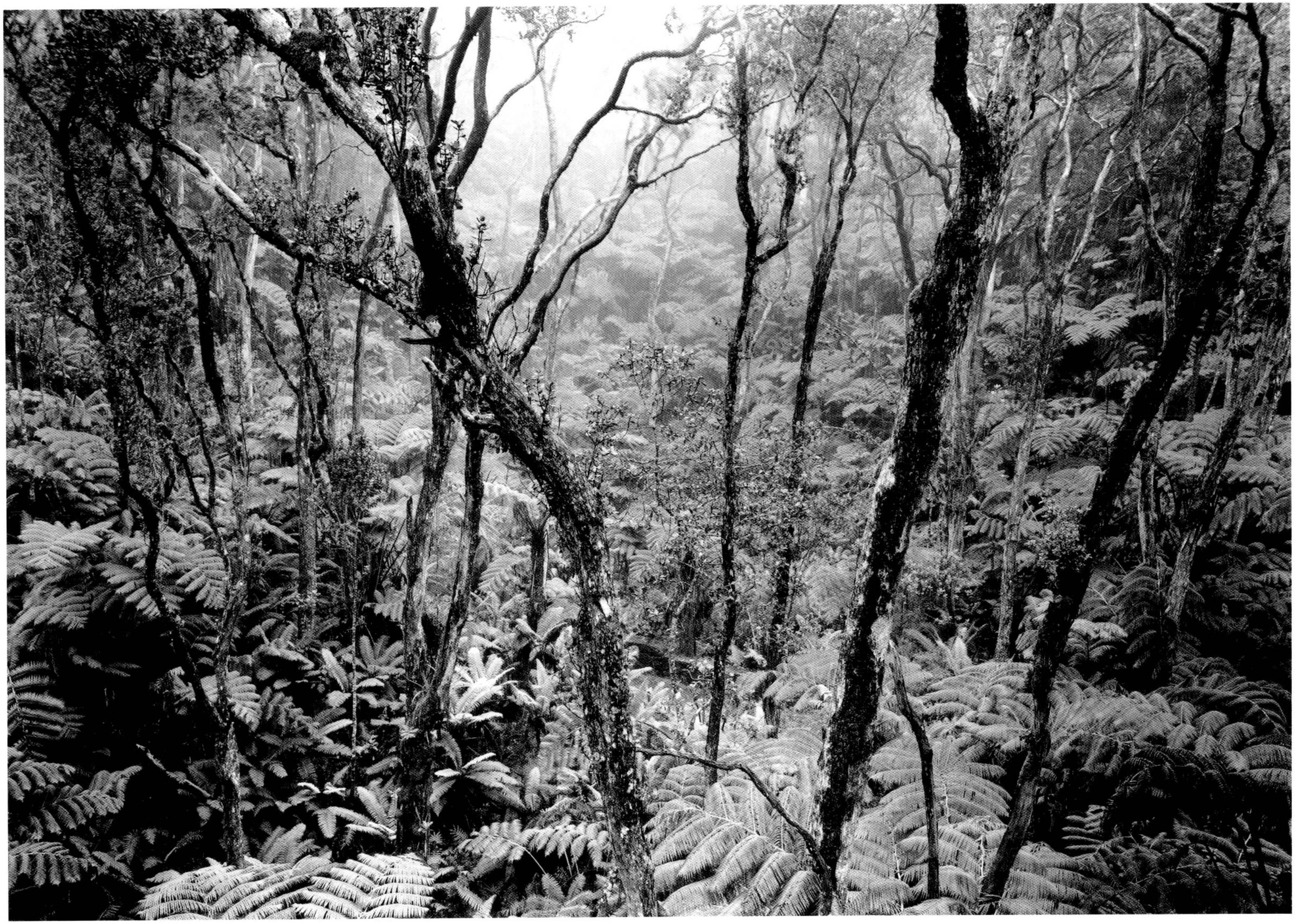

FERN FOREST, KILAUEA CRATER, HAWAII VOLCANOES NATIONAL PARK, HAWAII, 1948

Ansel found photographing in Hawaii difficult. There were two principal reasons. First, the extraordinary brightness, even harshness, of the sunlight made photographing in black and white extremely challenging. Things tended to look washed out. Second, Hawaii, with its intense rainbow hues, is a place that was "made" to be photographed in color. Ansel produced spectacular color transparencies there for commercial use. But after six weeks in Hawaii in 1948 (when he made this photograph), he was happy to return to the dramatic granite peaks and towering thunderheads of the Sierra Nevada.

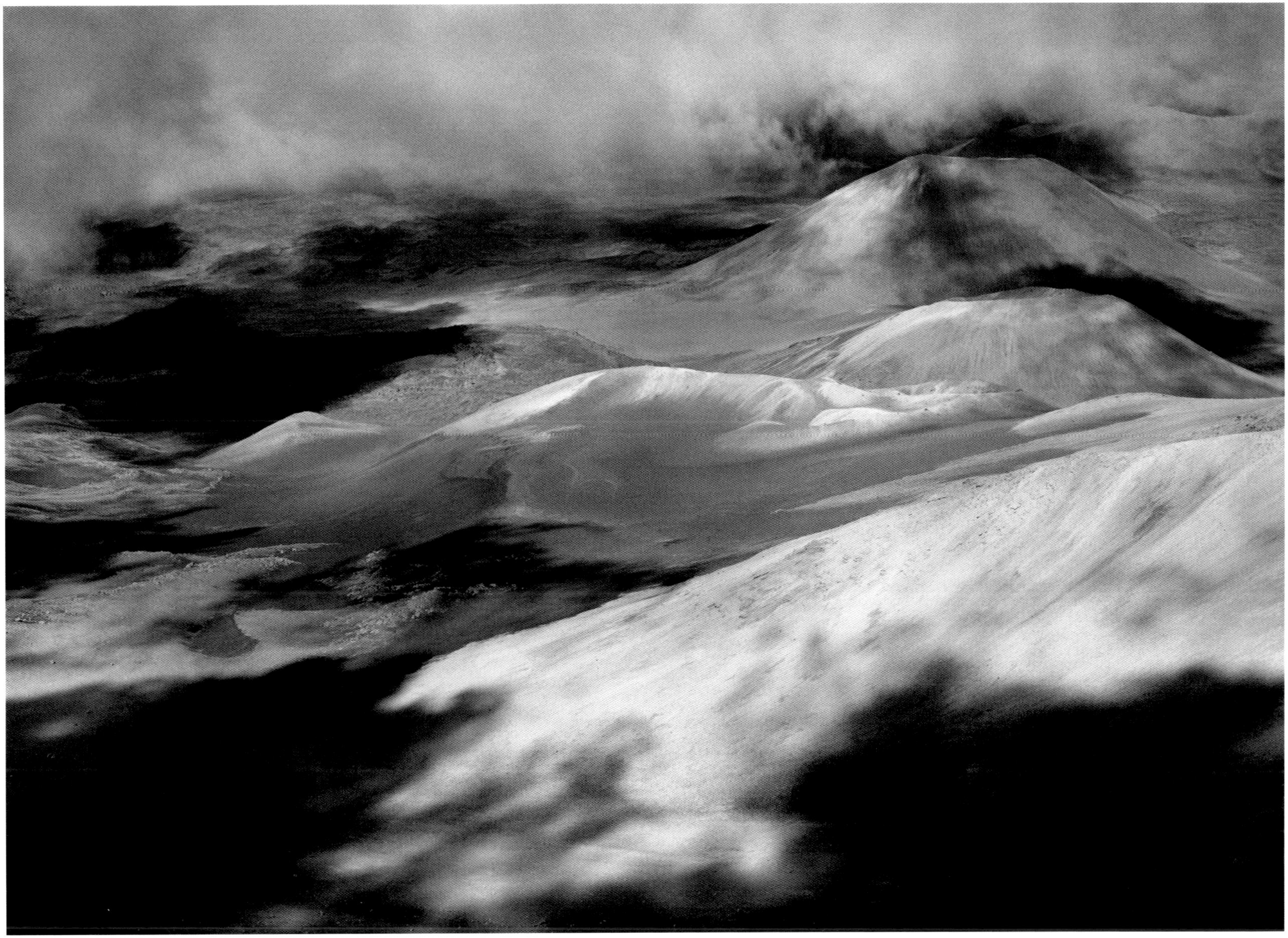

IN THE CRATER OF HALEAKALA, CLOUDS, HALEAKALA NATIONAL PARK, HAWAII, 1948

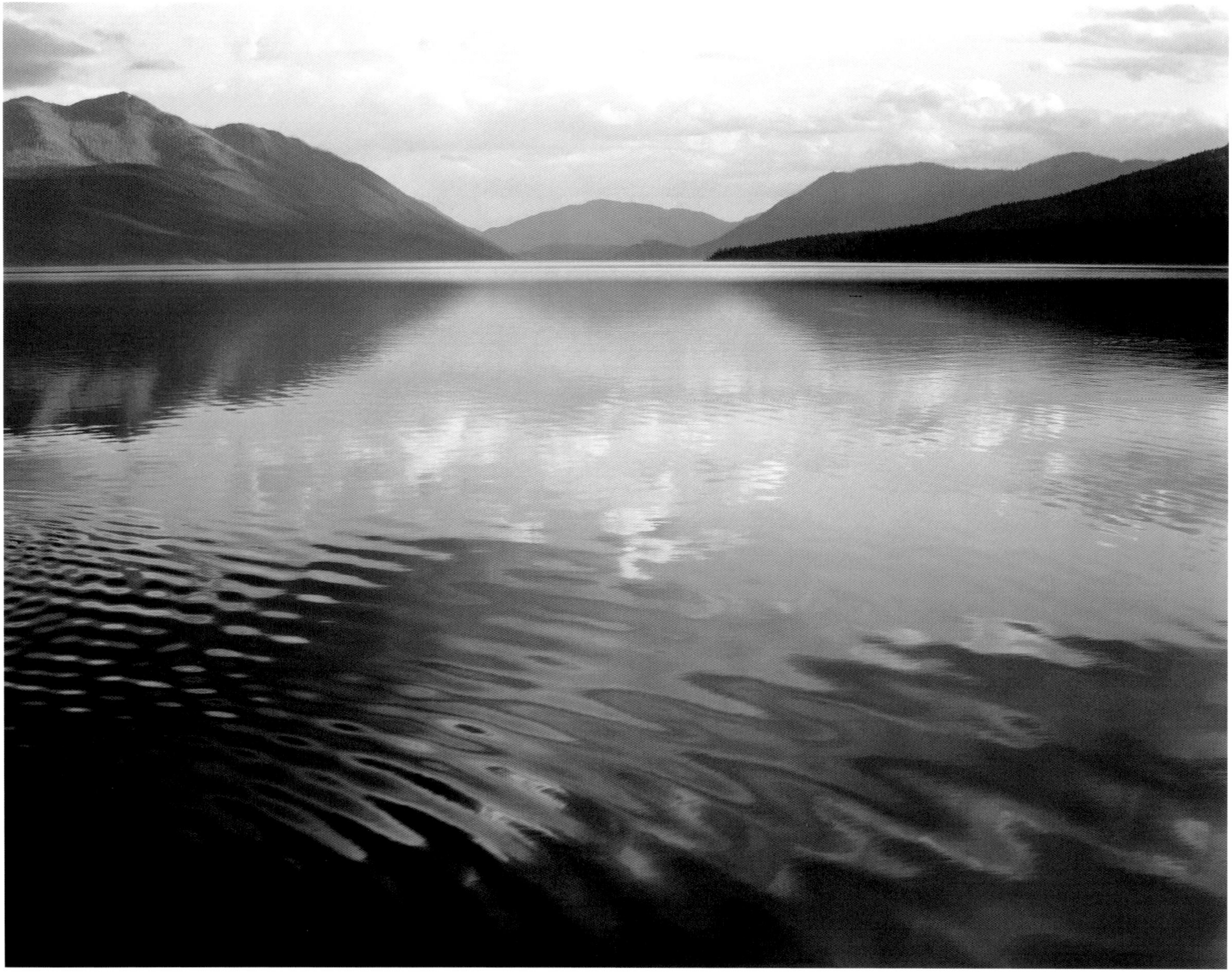

LAKE MCDONALD, EVENING, GLACIER NATIONAL PARK, MONTANA, 1942

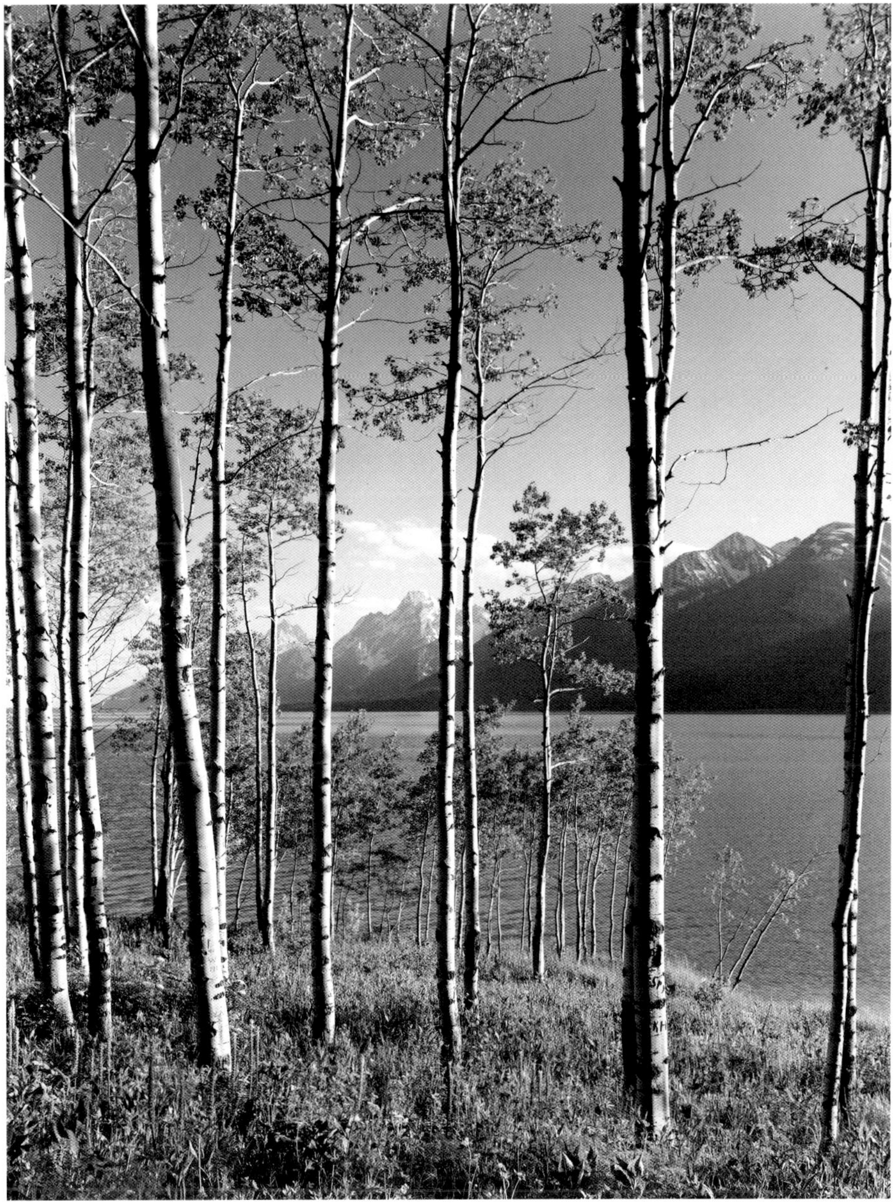

ASPEN GROVE, JACKSON LAKE, GRAND TETON NATIONAL PARK, WYOMING, C. 1948

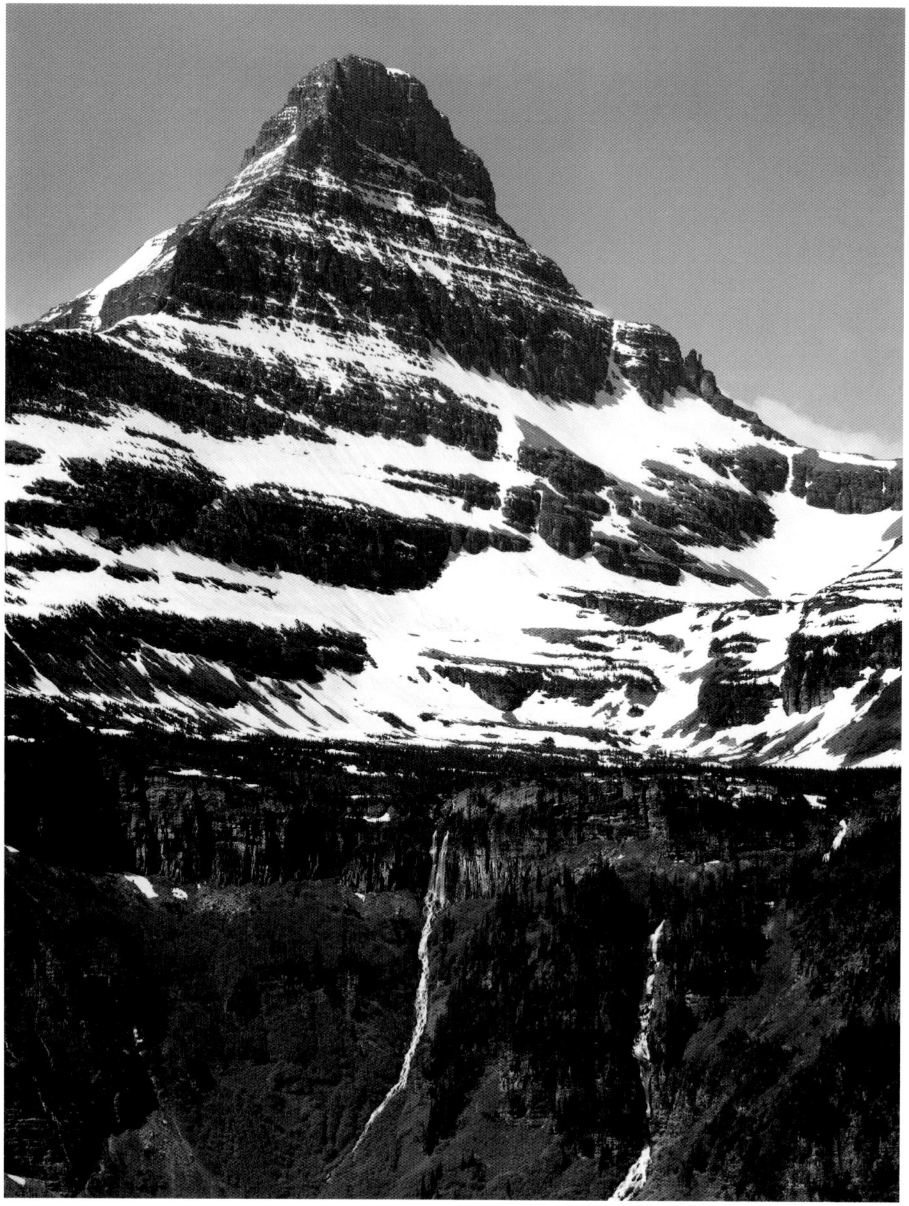

PEAK FROM LOGAN PASS, GLACIER NATIONAL PARK, MONTANA, 1942

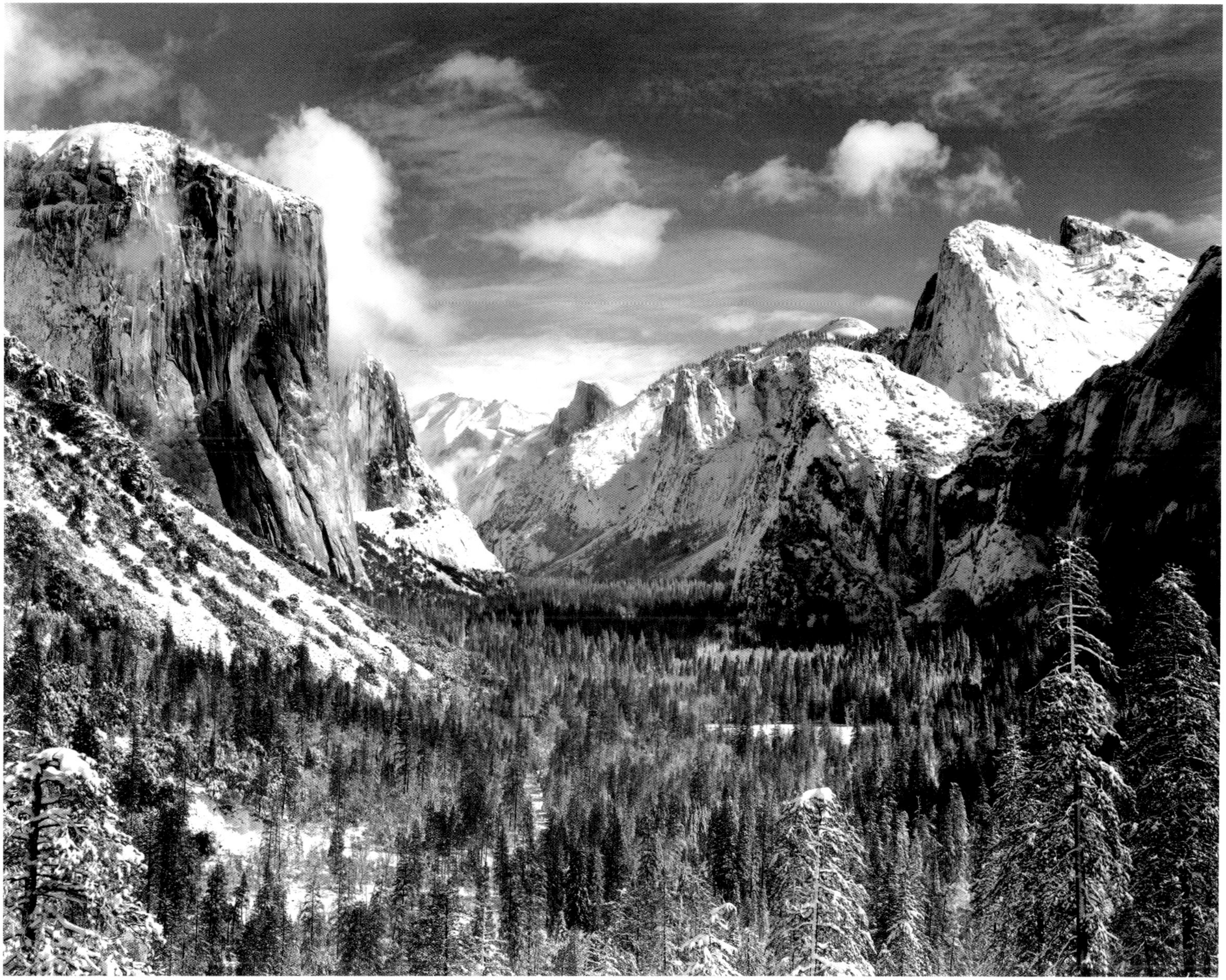

YOSEMITE VALLEY, WINTER, YOSEMITE NATIONAL PARK, CALIFORNIA, C. 1940

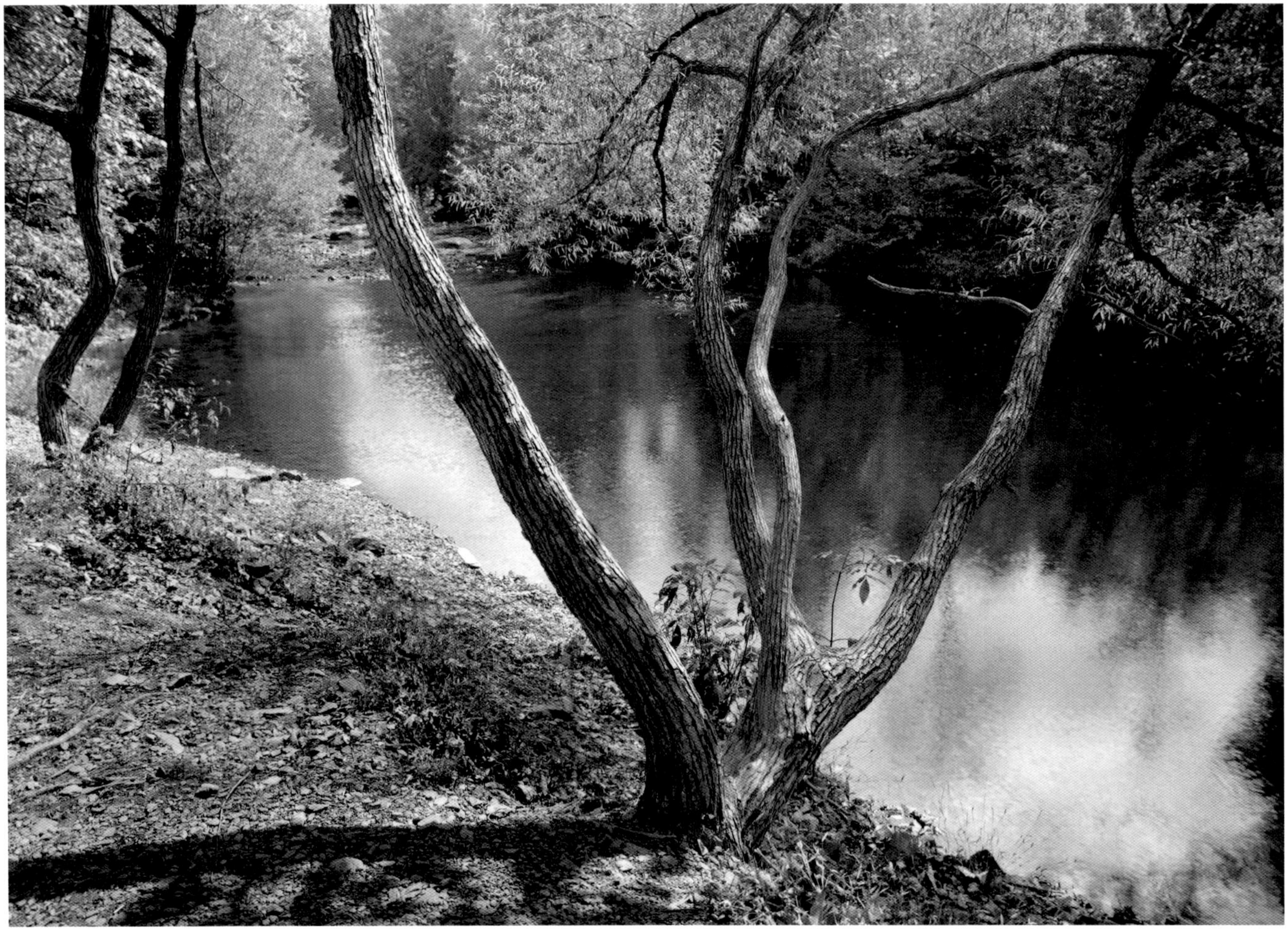

STREAM AND TREE TRUNK, GREAT SMOKY MOUNTAINS NATIONAL PARK, TENNESSEE, 1948

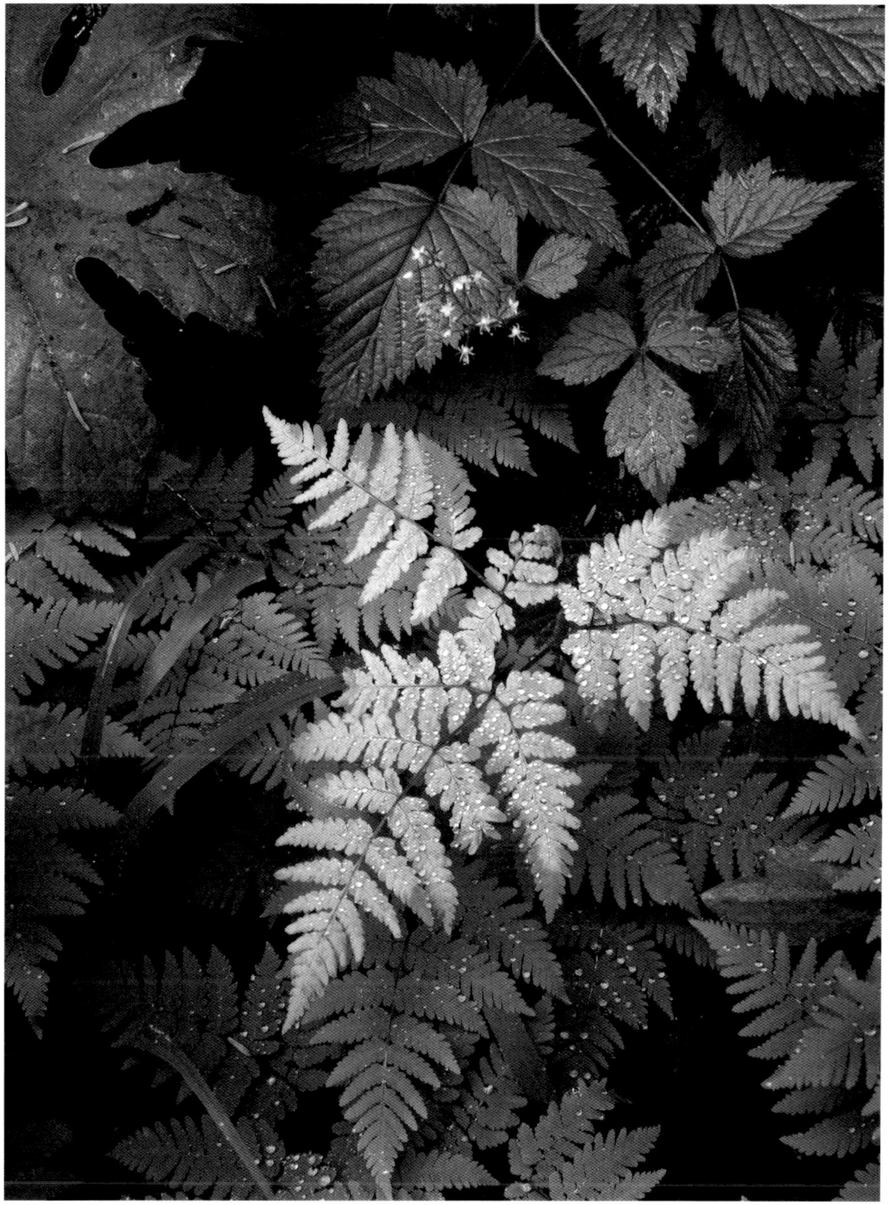

LEAVES, MOUNT RAINIER NATIONAL PARK, WASHINGTON, C. 1942

In June 1942, Ansel made a marathon trip to the Southwest and Pacific Northwest. During a brief stop in Estes Park, Colorado, he wrote a rambling letter to his friend Cedric Wright:

> Wait until you see. I have 26 8 x 10s!!!!!! Tomorrow I go to Yellowstone: takes two days!! Will do Guysars, Teatons, Fallz. Then to Glacier Park. Then to Rainier. Then to Kratur Lake. Then to S.F. Jezuz, Jezuz Krispe ulmity. Wot a trip.... I confess I have had two drinks, but I don't feel them. I got up at five, drove 20 miles, made six 8 x 10s, developed those and twelve from the Grand Canyon, completed the notes, took a one hour rest, and started off again for the Falls River Road stuff—40 miles! I got back here at 8:30—twelve 8 x 10s, 3 5 x 7 Kodachromes. Took a bath, waiting for the phone, have to load filums. Up at five in the morning again to get another angle of the Park. Then at 3:30 off to Denver and Yellowstone....
>
> Yours in the spirit of Hypo,* Ansel

*Hypo is a thiosulfate solution applied in the final development of a negative to remove undeveloped silver salts and "fix" the image.

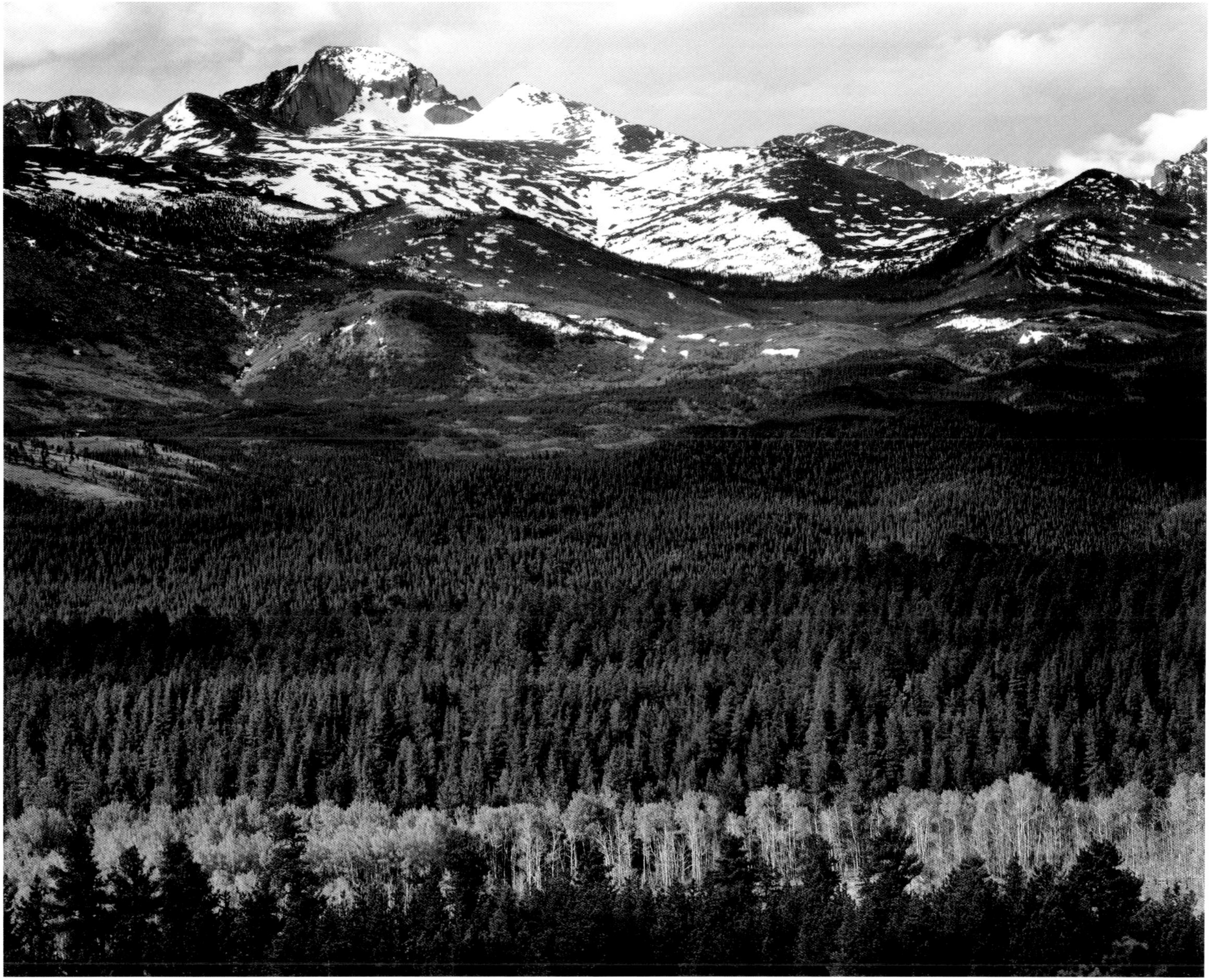

LONG'S PEAK FROM ROAD, ROCKY MOUNTAIN NATIONAL PARK, COLORADO, 1942

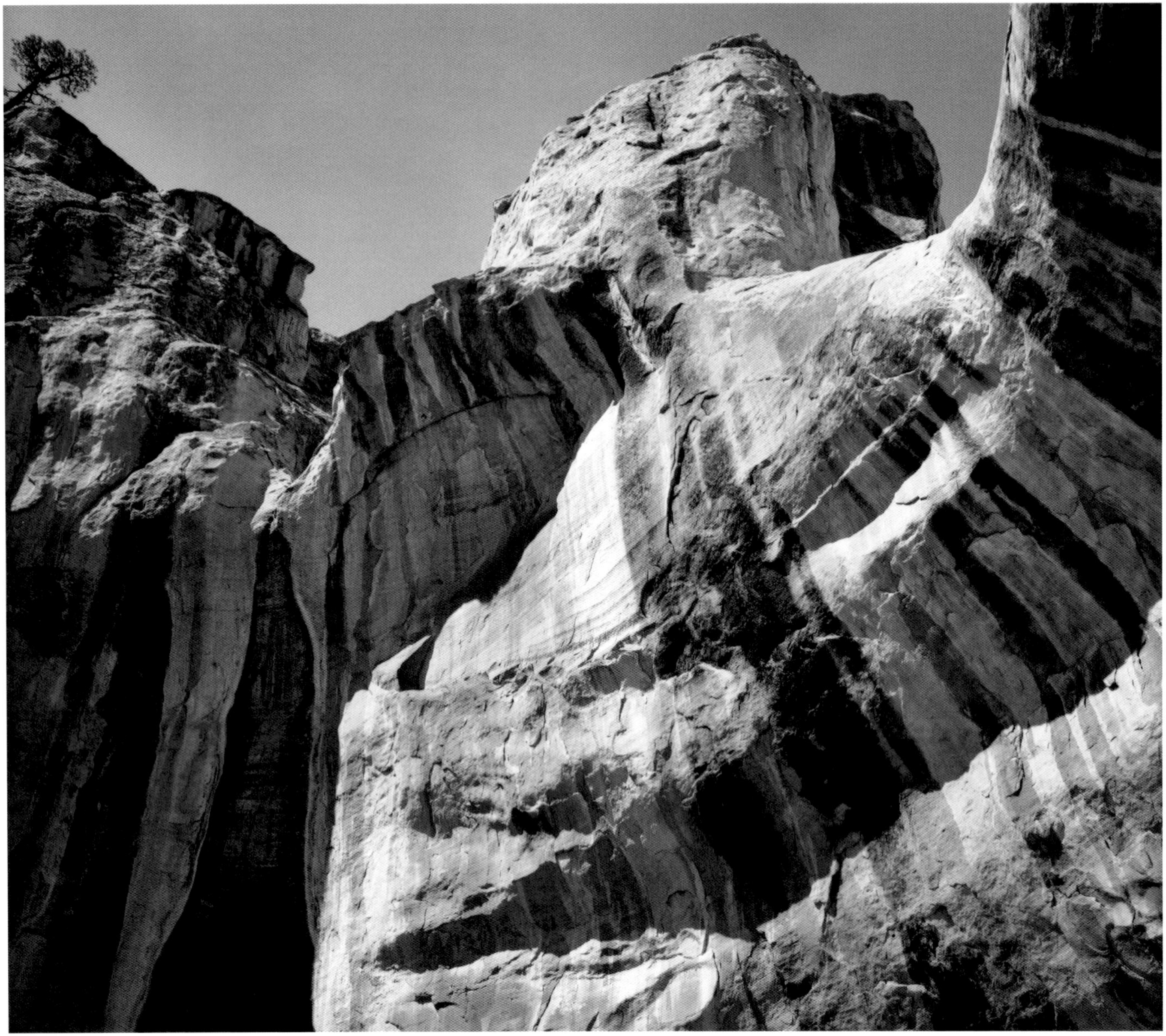

CLIFFS, EL MORRO NATIONAL MONUMENT, NEW MEXICO, C. 1950

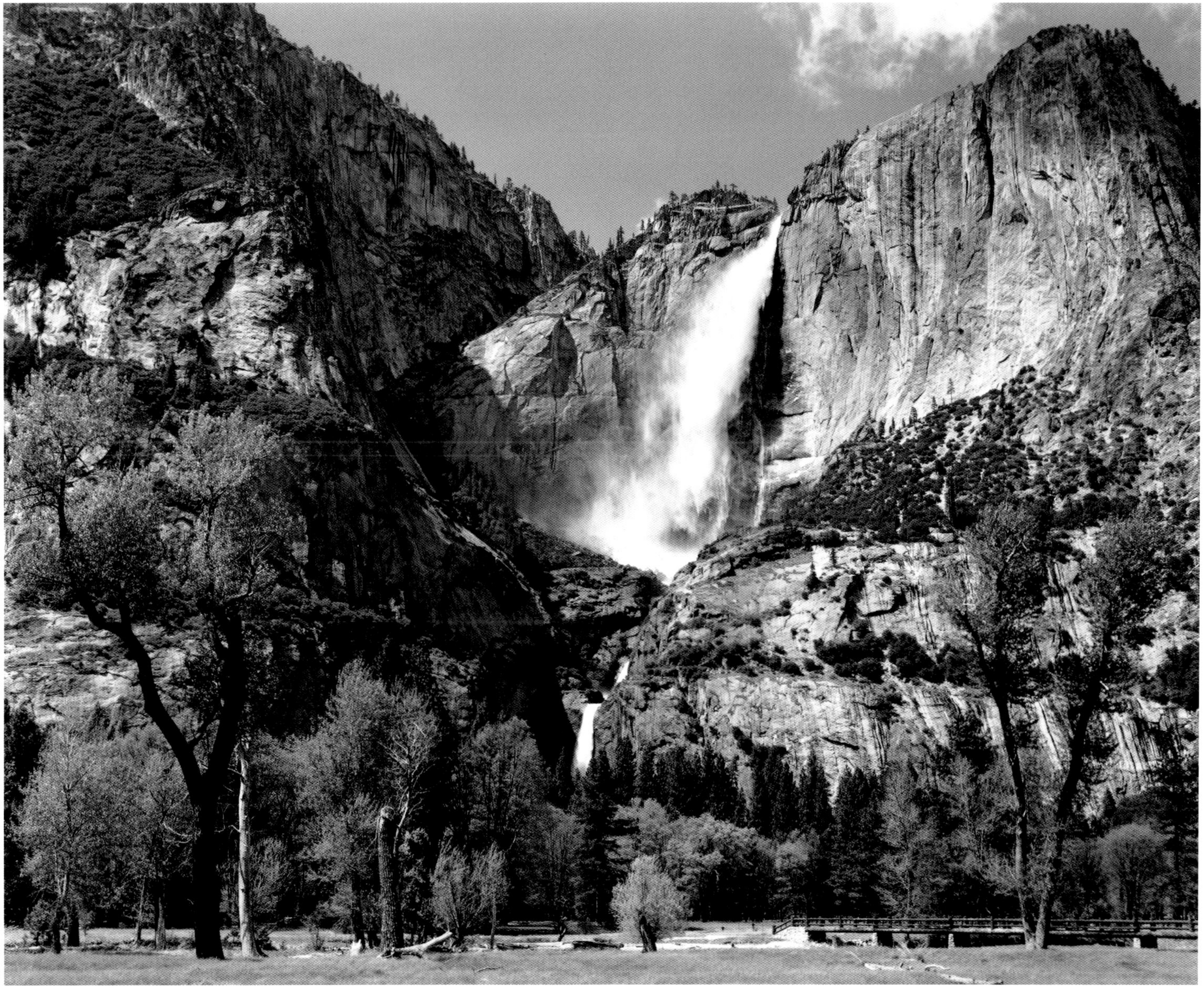

YOSEMITE FALLS AND MEADOW, YOSEMITE NATIONAL PARK, CALIFORNIA, 1953

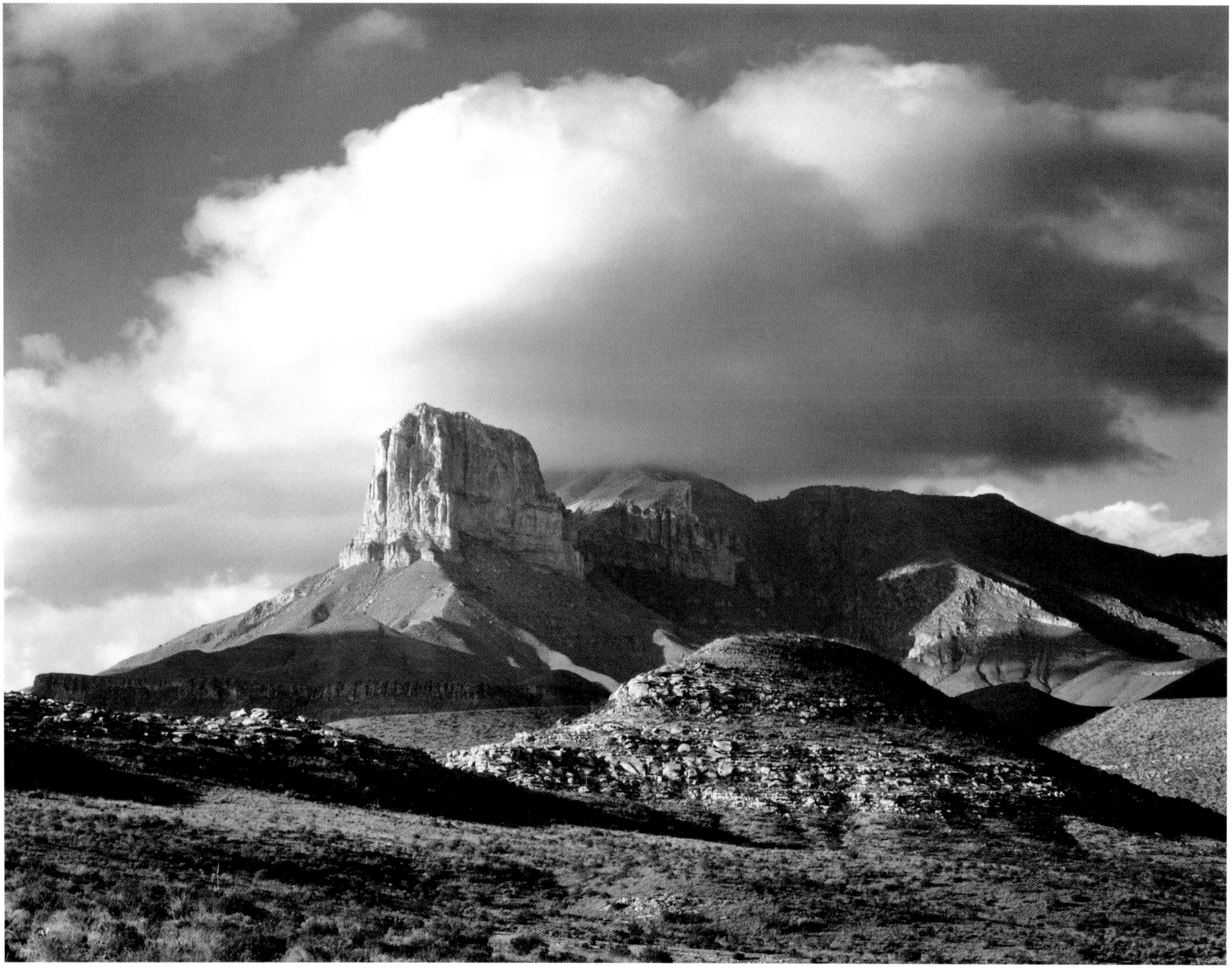

EL CAPITAN PEAK, GUADALUPE MOUNTAINS NATIONAL PARK, TEXAS, 1947

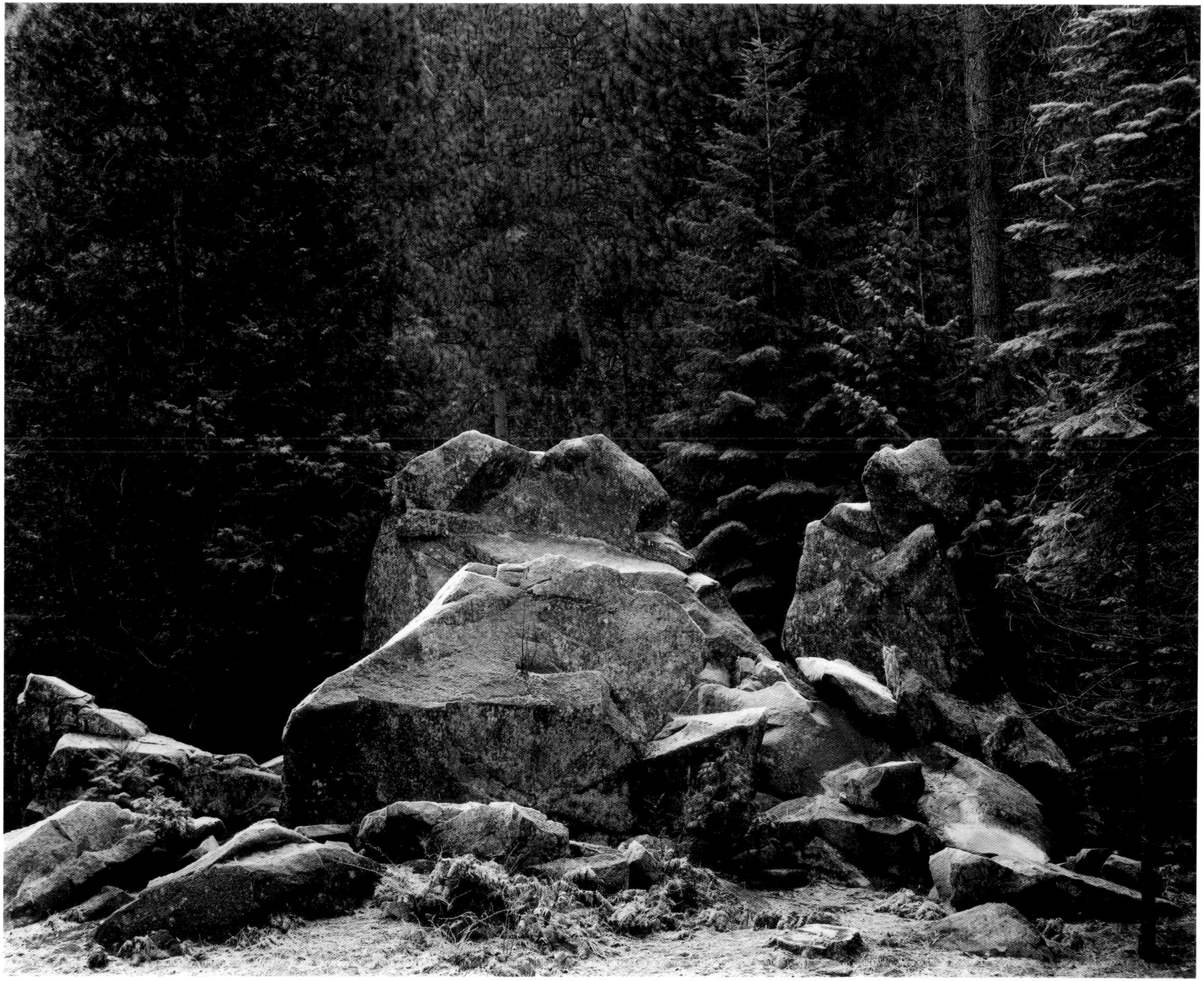

ROCKS, YOSEMITE VALLEY, YOSEMITE NATIONAL PARK, CALIFORNIA, C. 1940

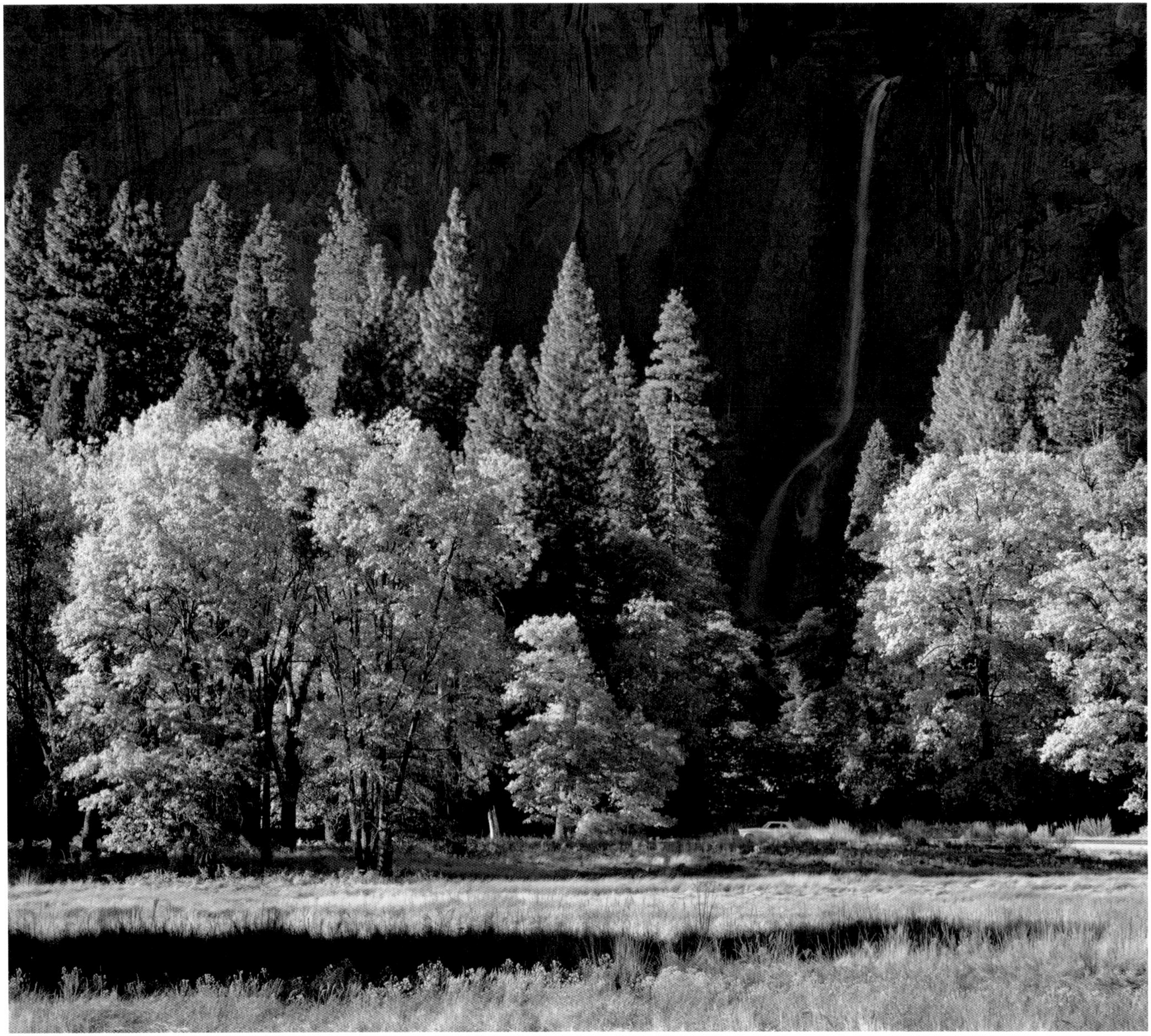

LOWER YOSEMITE FALLS, AUTUMN, YOSEMITE NATIONAL PARK, CALIFORNIA, C. 1945

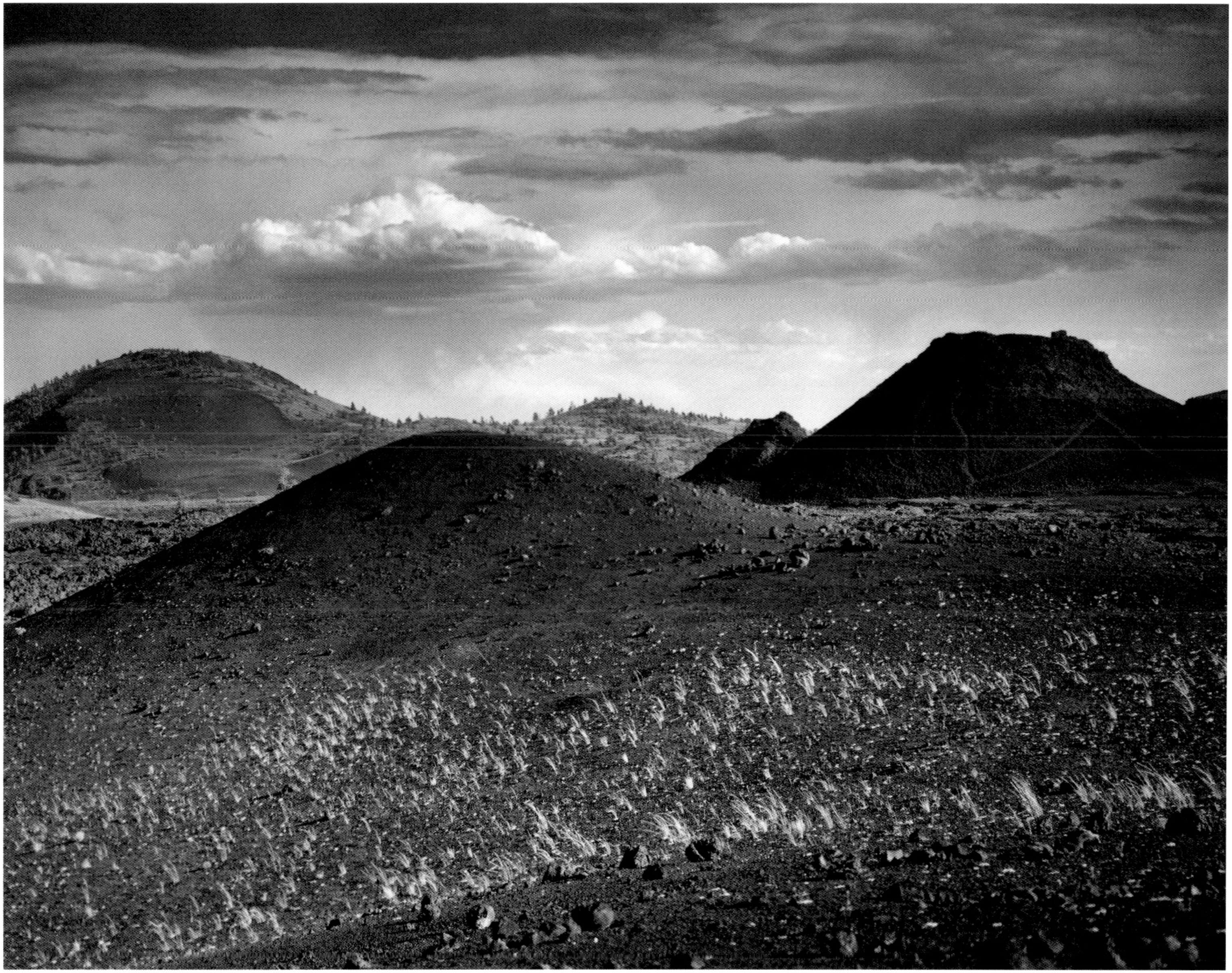

CRATERS OF THE MOON NATIONAL MONUMENT AND PRESERVE, IDAHO, C. 1950

The Guggenheim Foundation made two yearlong grants to Ansel to complete his project on the national parks and monuments. "Upon receiving the [first] Guggenheim," he wrote, "I decided to travel to Glacier Bay and Mount McKinley [now called Denali] National Parks in Alaska. Since a trip to the state of Washington in 1942, I had sensed that this northwest country was only the threshold of a certain mystery.... I felt Alaska might be close to the wilderness perfection I continuously sought."

Reflecting further, Ansel wrote that his visits to Alaska in 1947, 1948, and 1949 "clarified my own concepts of re-creation versus recreation. I saw more clearly the value of true wilderness and the danger of diluting its finest areas," and he "resolved to dedicate as much of my time and energy to it as I could." In the ensuing years, Ansel felt that a day had been wasted if he did not write or telephone at least one influential individual about the need to protect America's wilderness.

A crowning achievement for Ansel was the passage of the Alaska National Interest Lands Conservation Act, the most substantial wildlands protective legislation ever to be enacted by Congress. It was signed into law by President Jimmy Carter in 1980. Ansel had spent a few days in Washington the year before to make the president's official portrait. Ansel's photographs and his frequent and personal letters and persuasive arguments reinforced President Carter's commitment to the protection of America's wildlands.

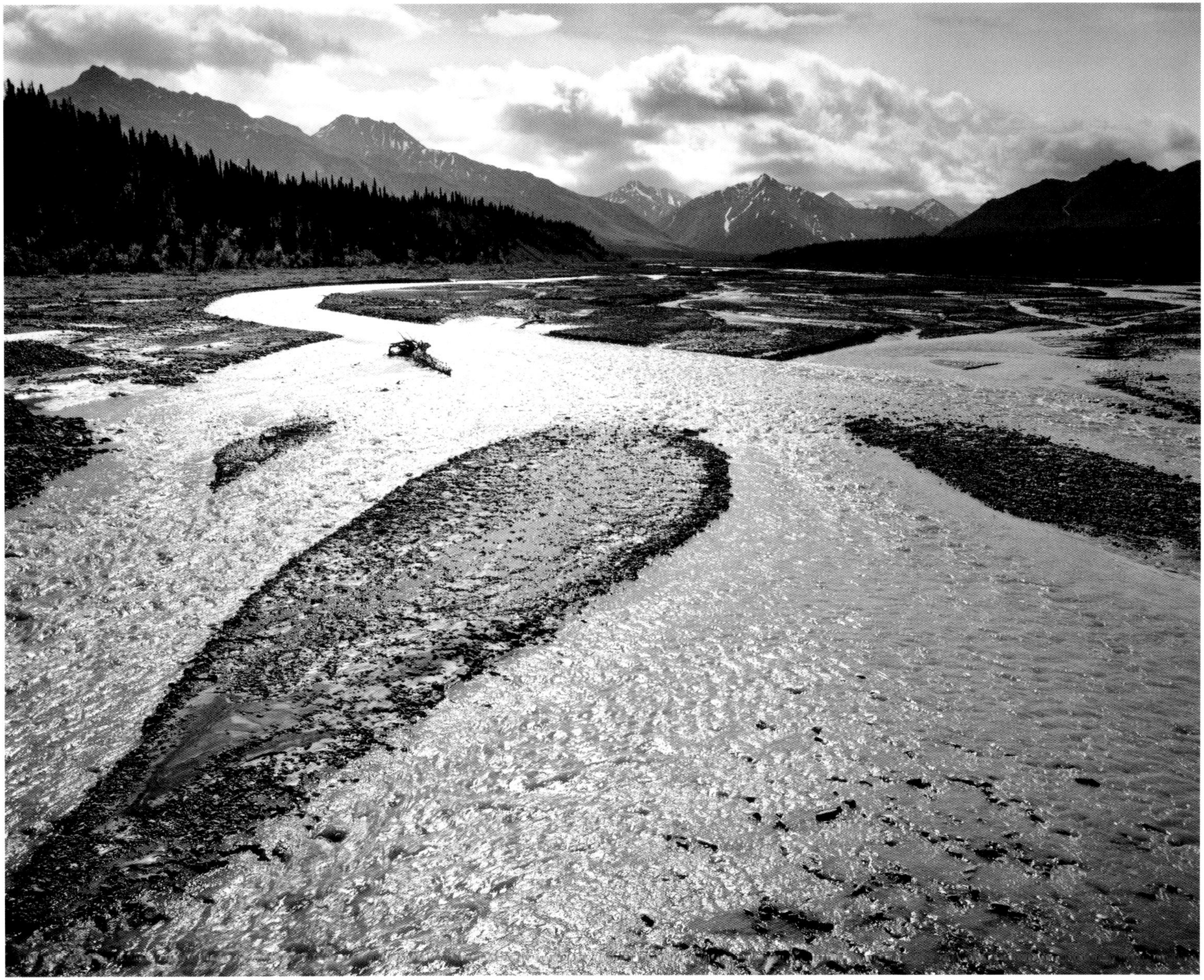

TEKLANIKA RIVER, DENALI NATIONAL PARK AND PRESERVE, ALASKA, 1947

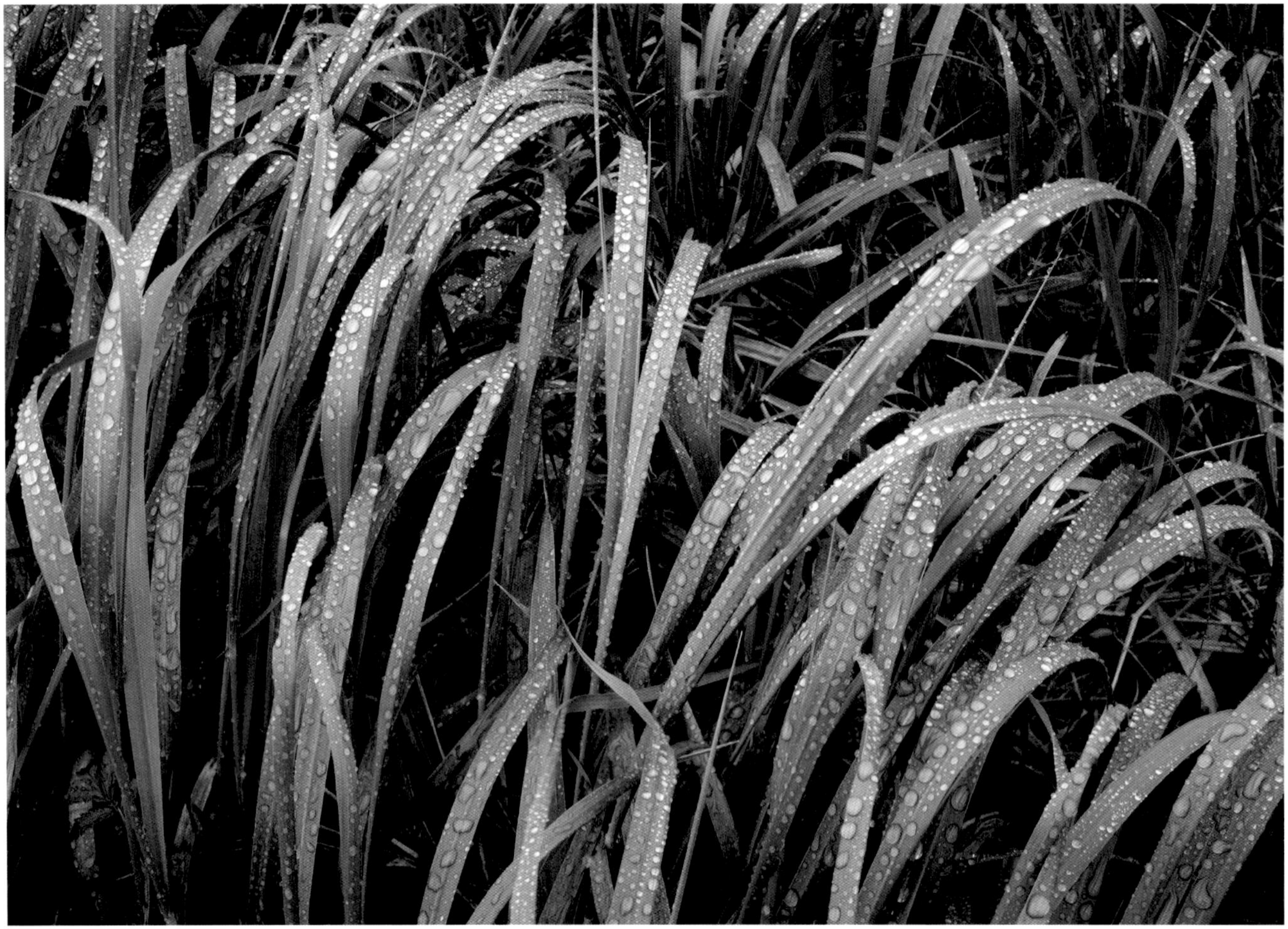

GRASS IN RAIN, GLACIER BAY NATIONAL PARK, ALASKA, 1948

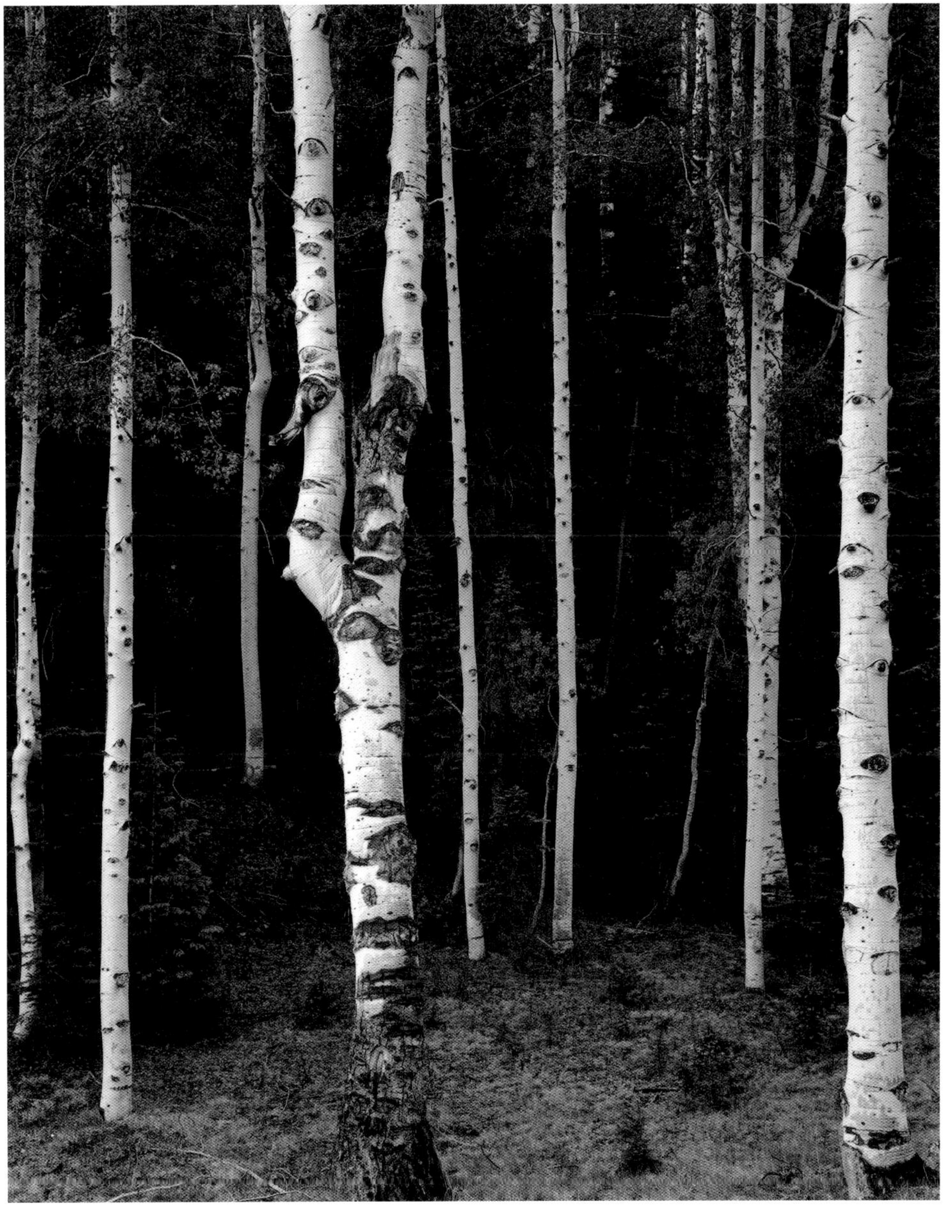

ASPEN GROVE, NORTH RIM, GRAND CANYON NATIONAL PARK, ARIZONA, C. 1947

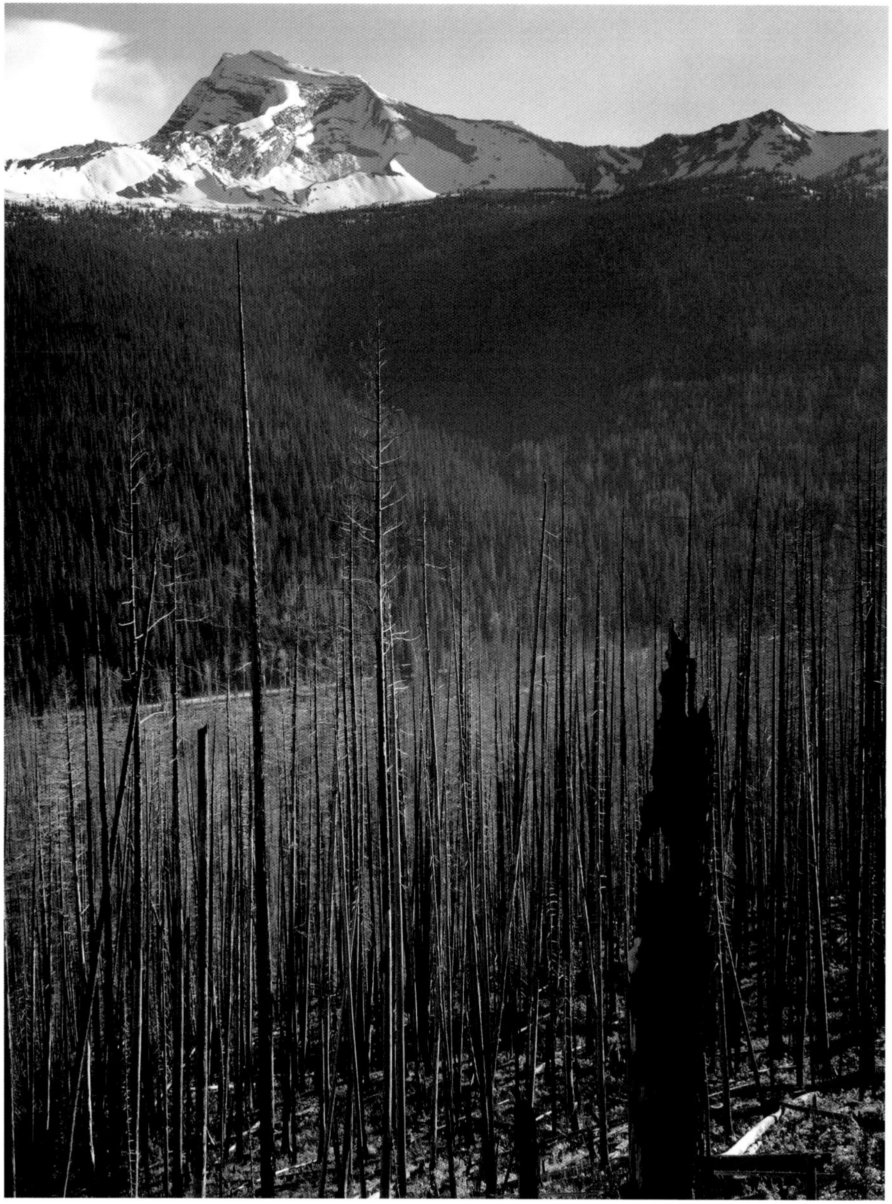

HEAVEN'S PEAK, BURNED AREA, GLACIER NATIONAL PARK, MONTANA, 1942

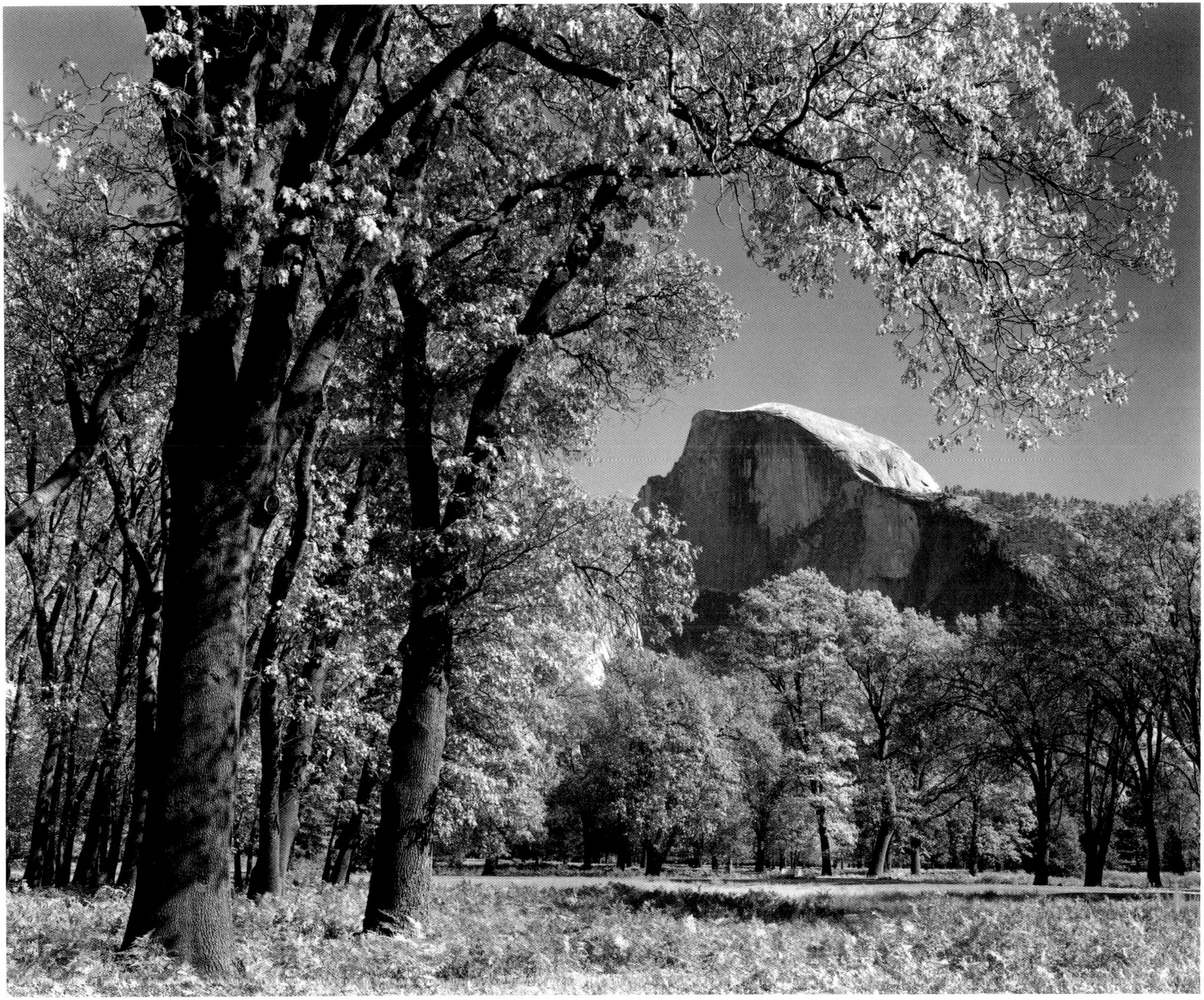

HALF DOME, OAK TREES, AUTUMN, YOSEMITE NATIONAL PARK, CALIFORNIA, 1938

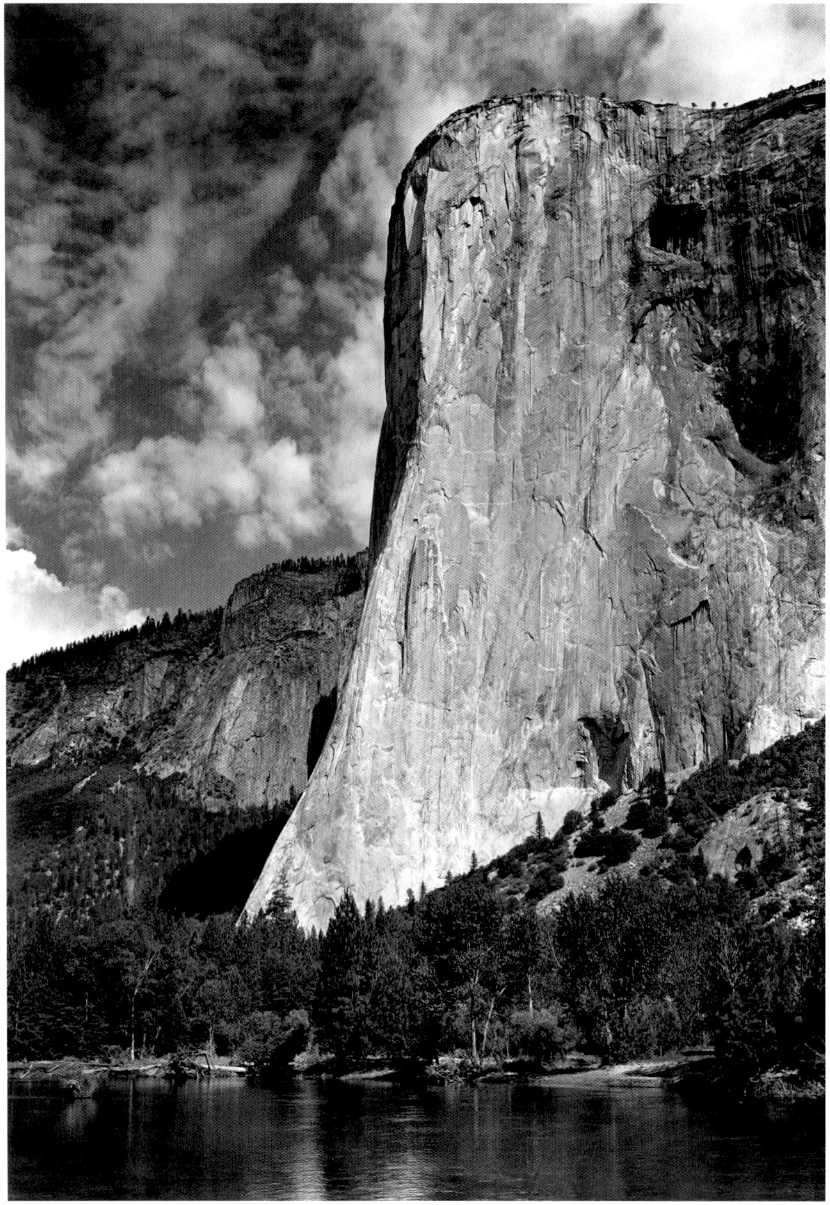

EL CAPITAN, MERCED RIVER, CLOUDS, YOSEMITE NATIONAL PARK, CALIFORNIA, 1948

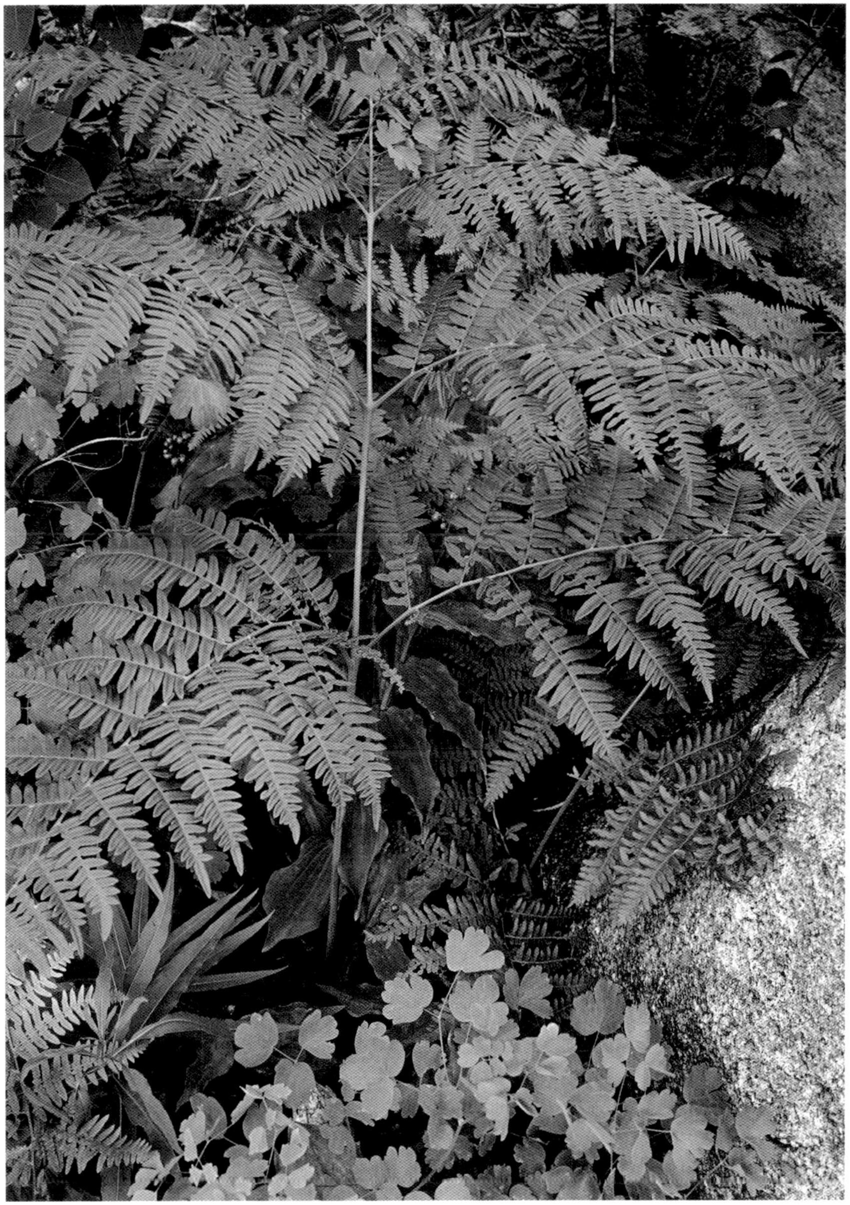

LEAVES AND FERNS, SIERRA NEVADA, CALIFORNIA, C. 1930

In 1934, the art gallery at Mills College in Oakland, California, planned an exhibition entitled "Leading American Photographers." Ansel helped to refine the list of photographers (which included prominent artists of the day such as Charles Sheeler and Edward Weston) who would be asked to submit ten photographs each. This image of an oak tree in snow was among Ansel's submissions. Glenn Wessels reviewed the show in the February 16, 1934, issue of *The Argonaut* and singled out Ansel for special praise: "Of the artists in this group I think Ansel Adams shows the greatest mastery of the medium. His accuracy in detail and texture is marvelous to see; the snow glistens on every twig of his trees with beautiful luminosity, and his work seems entirely free of any camera trickery or dark-room manipulation."

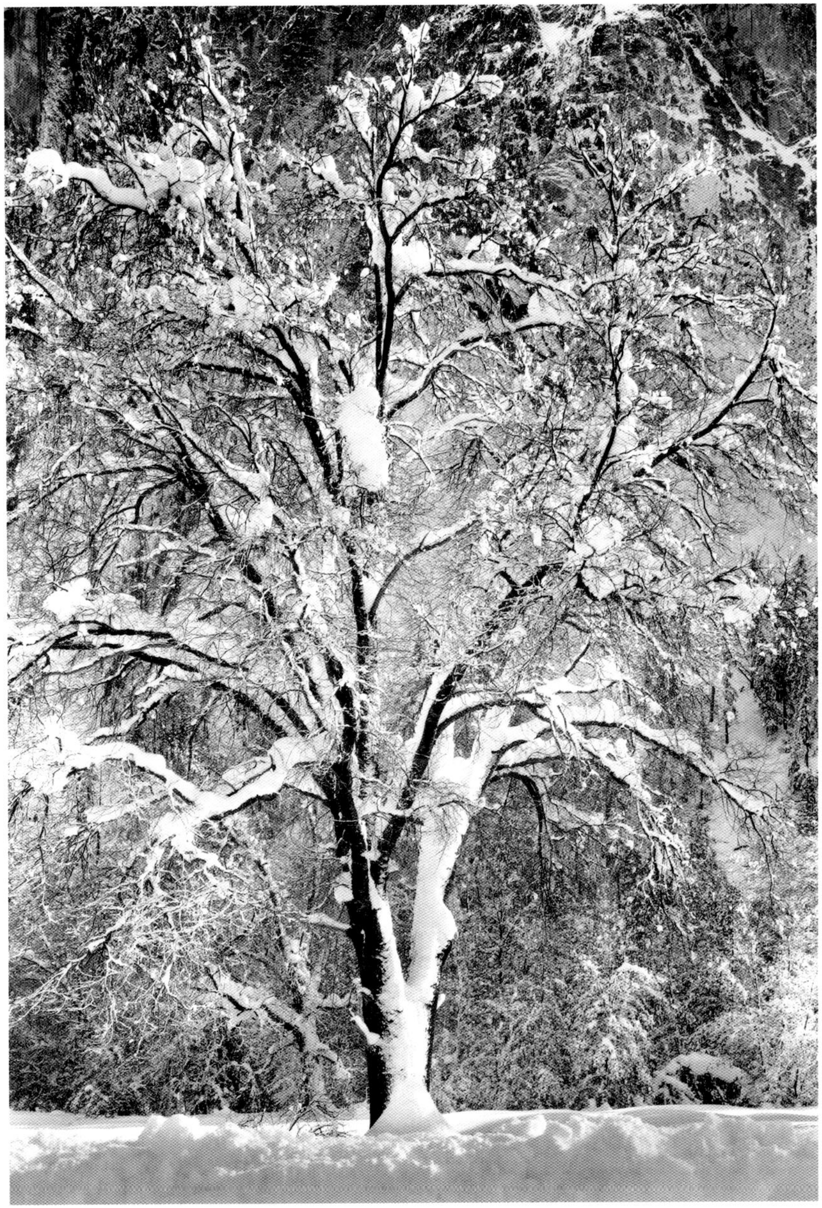

OAK TREE IN SNOW, YOSEMITE NATIONAL PARK, CALIFORNIA, C. 1933

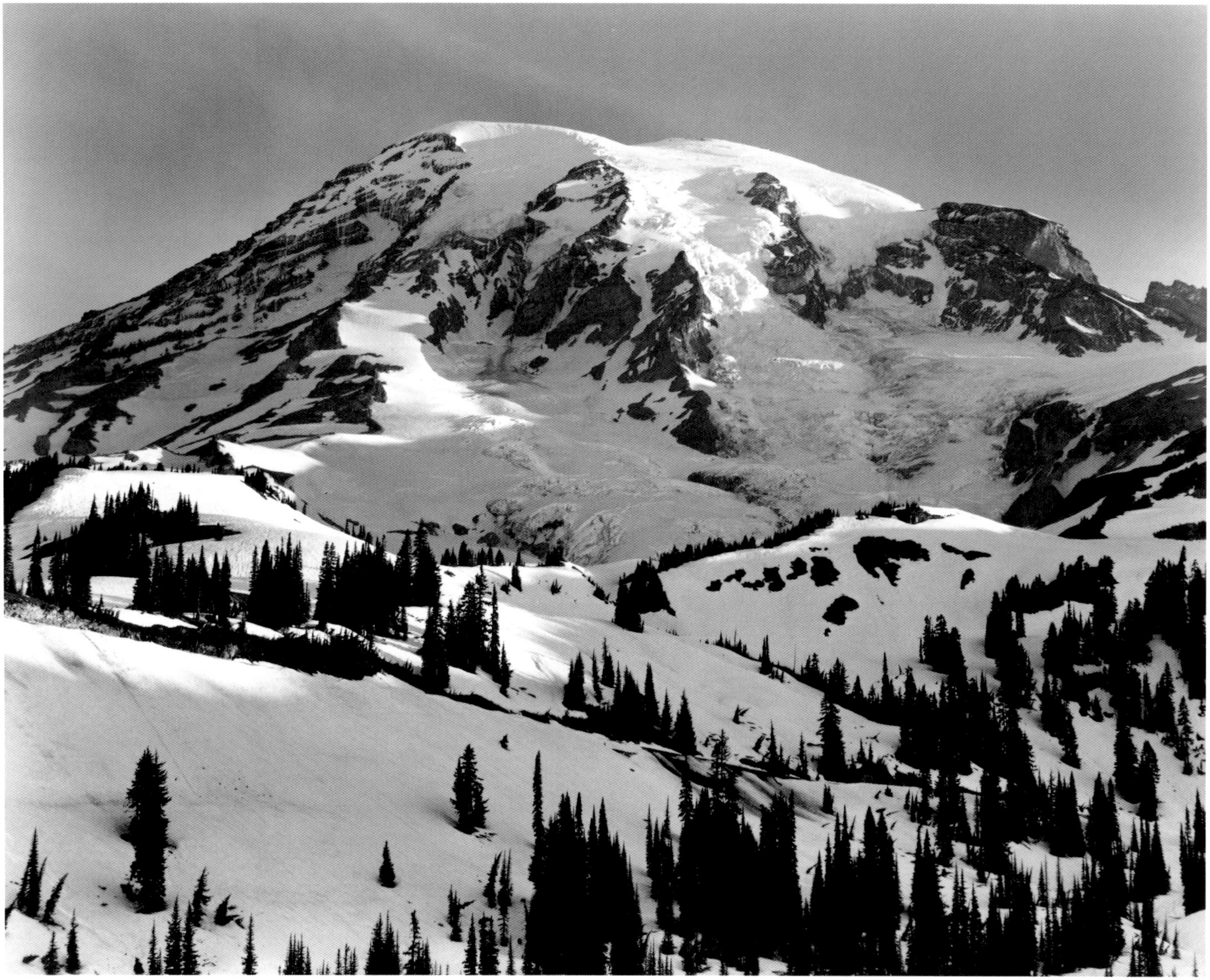

MOUNT RAINIER, SUNRISE, MOUNT RAINIER NATIONAL PARK, WASHINGTON, C. 1950

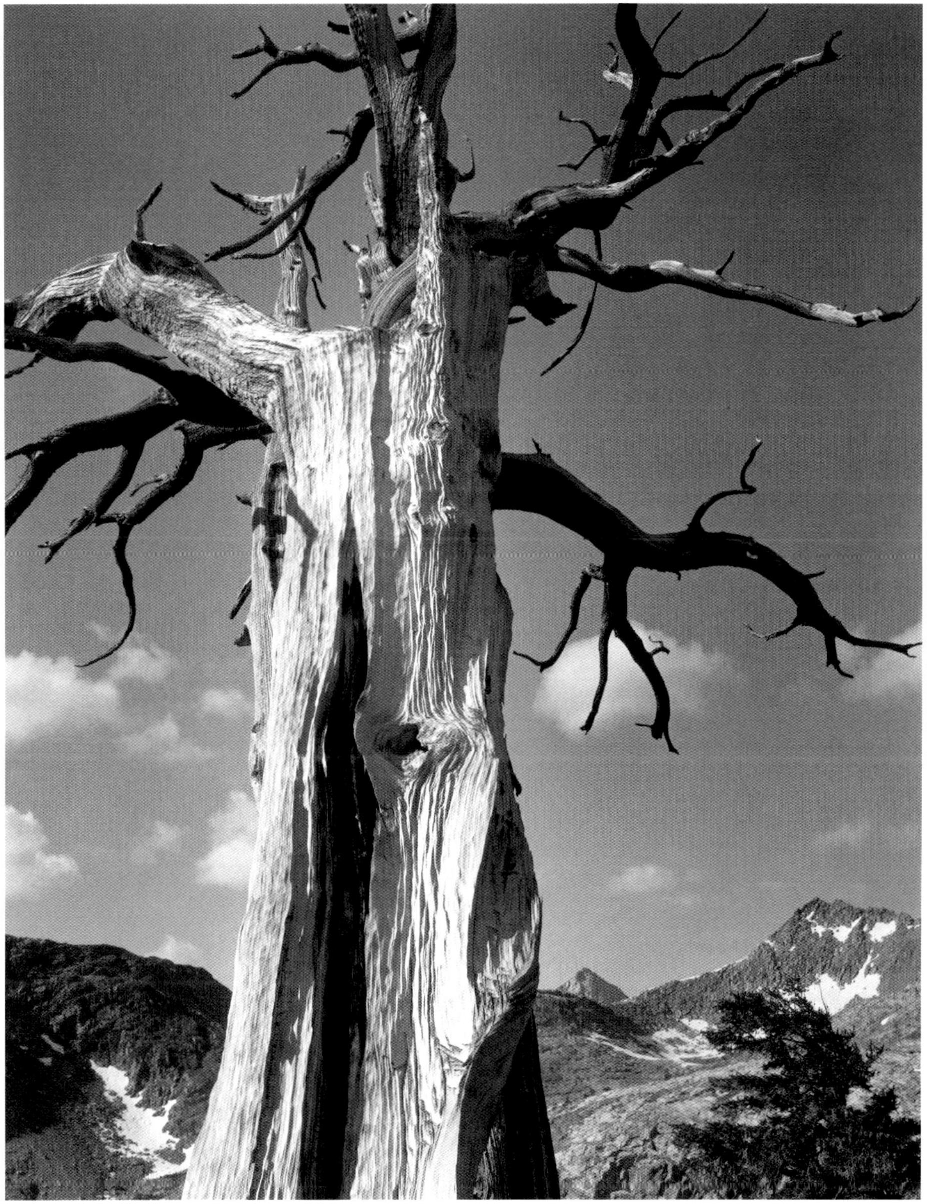

DEAD TREE, NEAR LITTLE FIVE LAKES, SEQUOIA NATIONAL PARK, CALIFORNIA, 1927

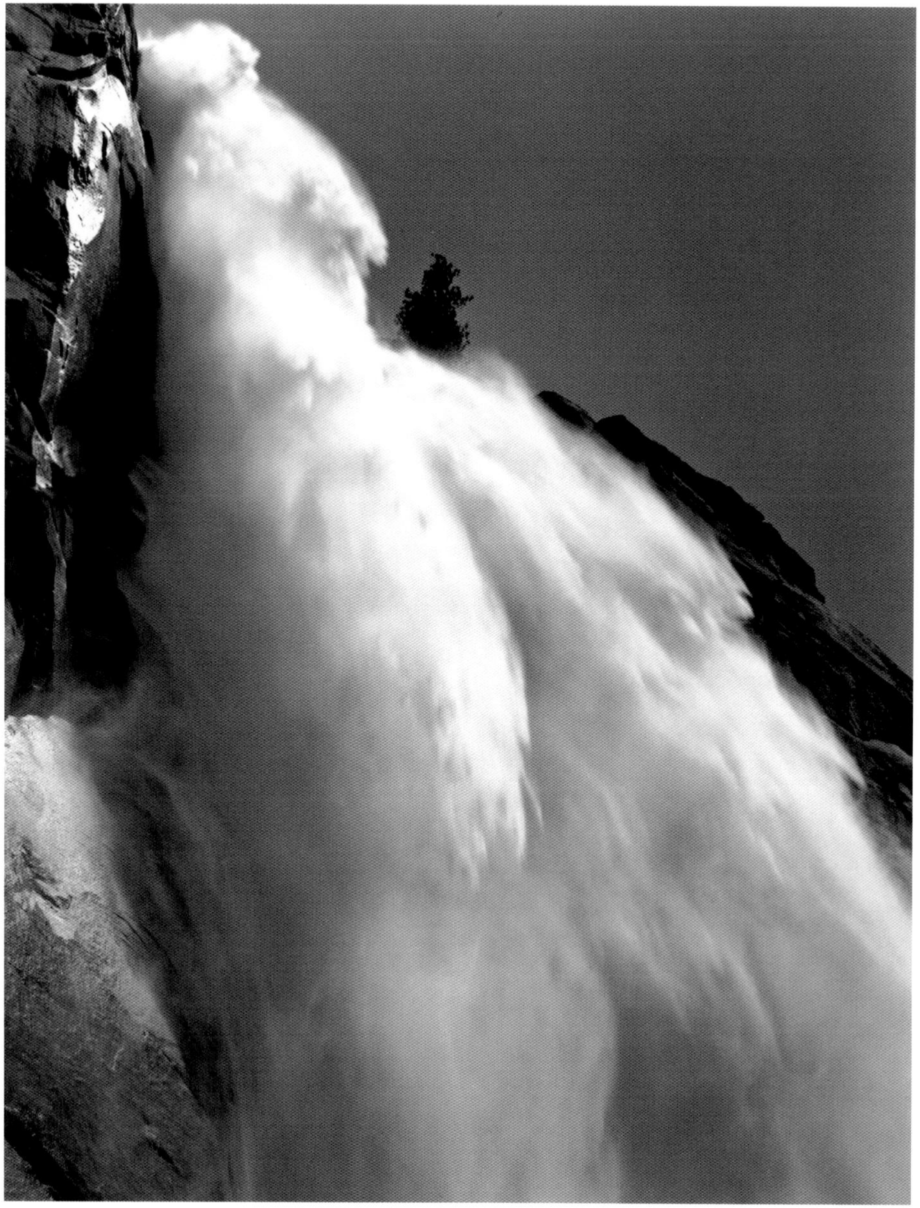

NEVADA FALL, UPPER SECTION, YOSEMITE NATIONAL PARK, CALIFORNIA, C. 1957

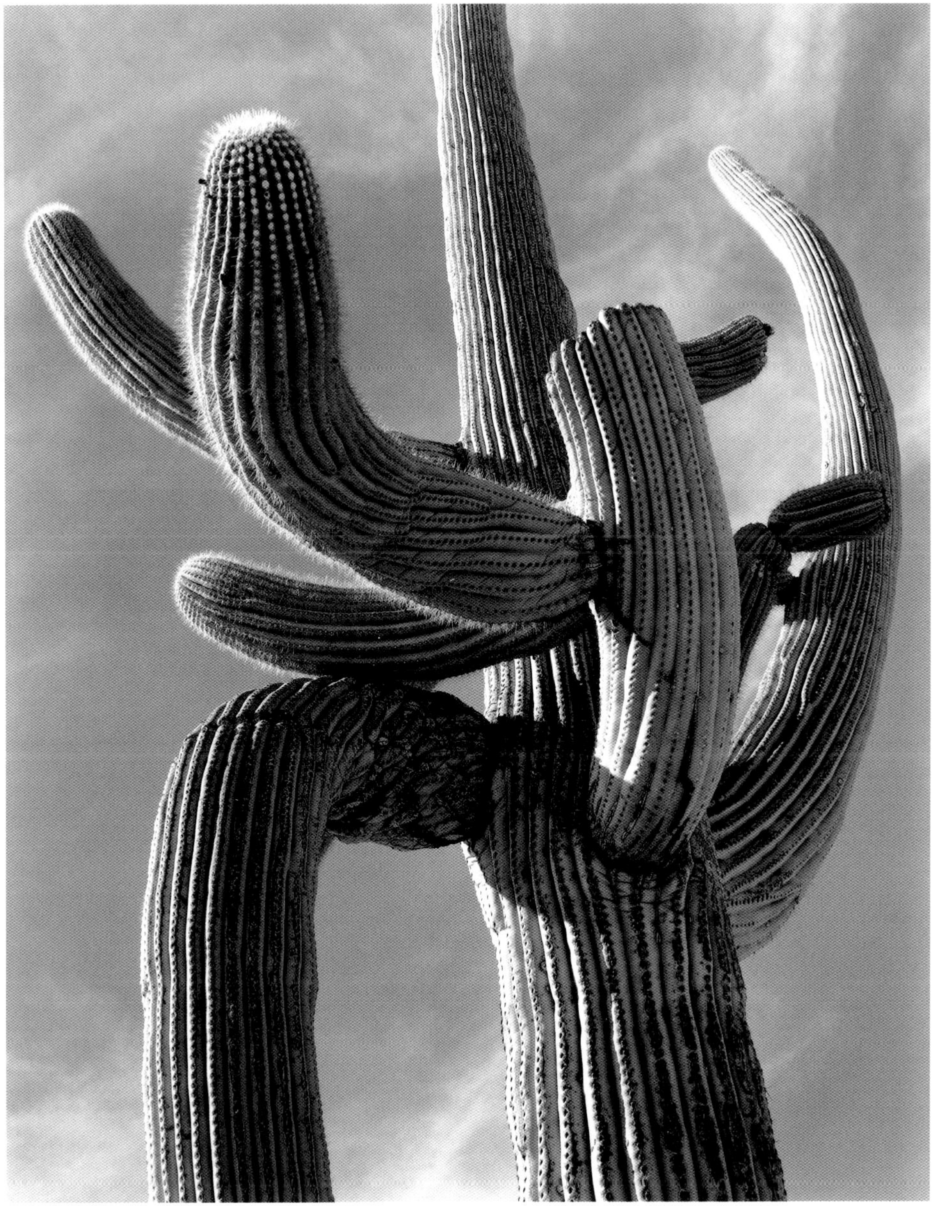

INVOLUTE CACTUS, ORGAN PIPE CACTUS NATIONAL MONUMENT, ARIZONA, C. 1948

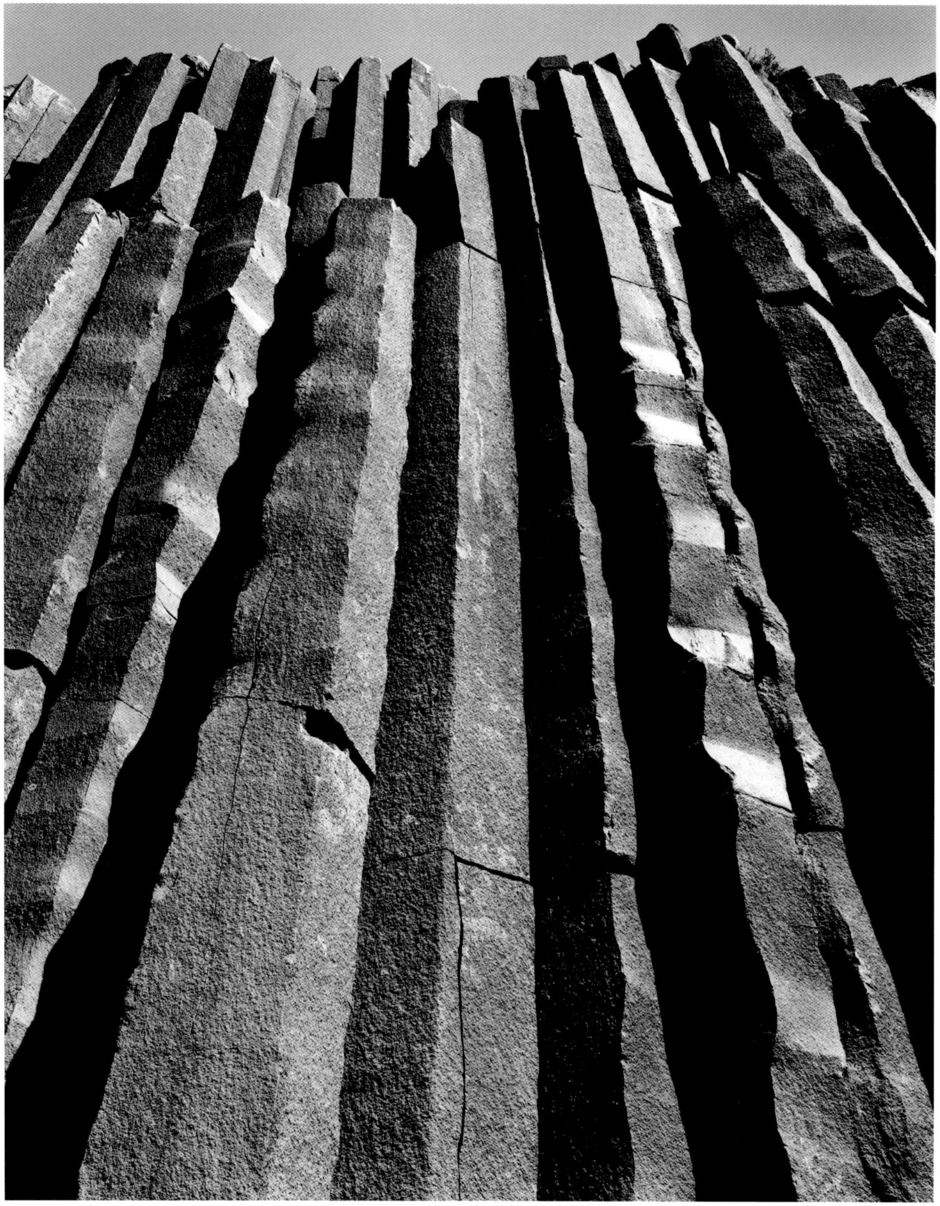

DETAIL, DEVILS POSTPILE NATIONAL MONUMENT, CALIFORNIA, 1946

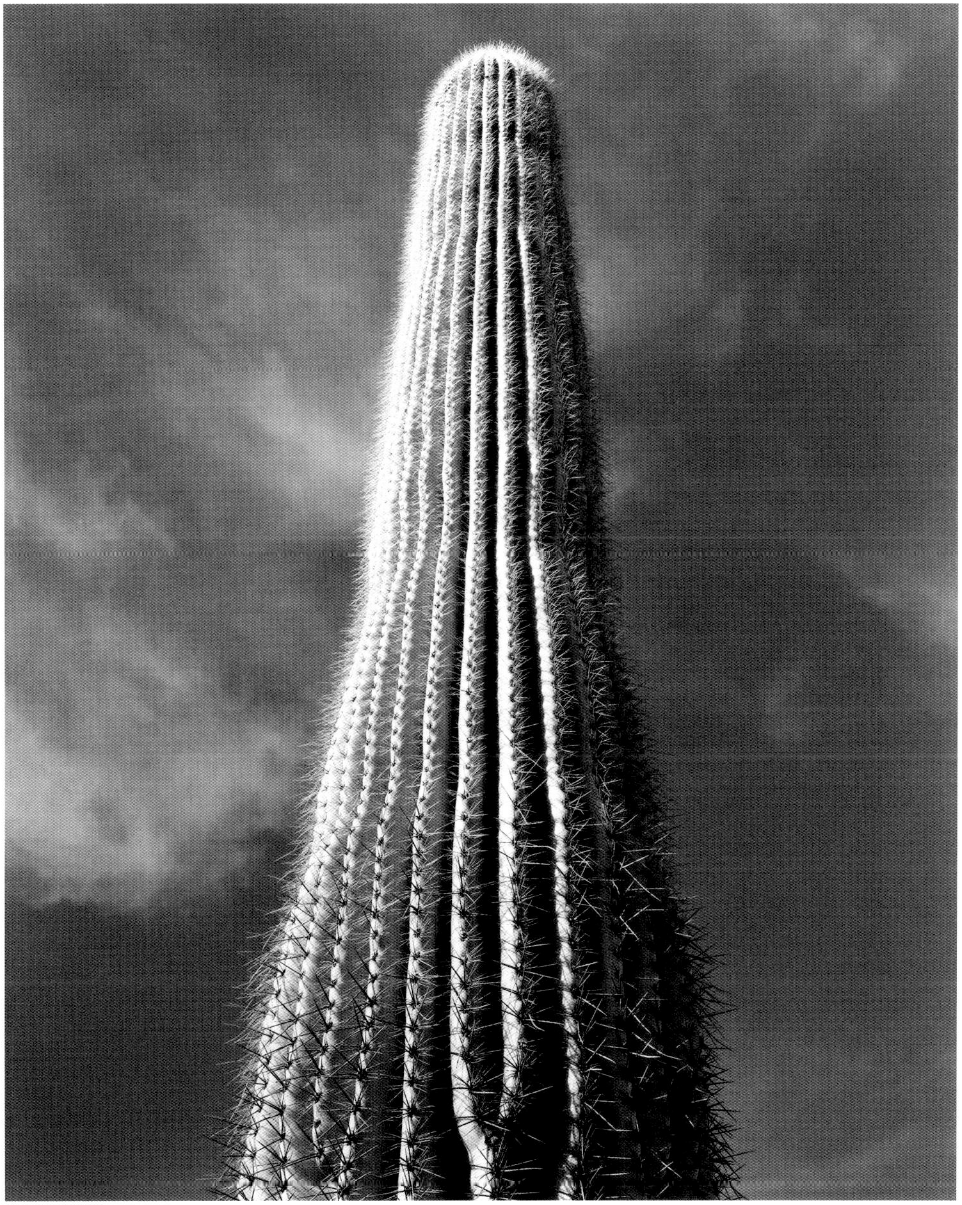

SAGUARO CACTUS, SAGUARO NATIONAL PARK, ARIZONA, 1942

On a trip with Ansel to the Southwest in 1947, Beaumont Newhall recorded in his log for June 1:

> We arrived at Bryce at the end of the day. There was nothing particularly spectacular about the approach, but when we got out of the car and went over to the rim of the canyon and looked down, we saw a most amazing spectacle. The limestone had eroded in such a way that thousands of tall spindles had been left standing "like men," as the Indians said.

On the same photographic trip, Ansel recorded similar erosion in nearby Cedar Breaks National Monument (see page 151), the result of millions of years of erosion by wind and water.

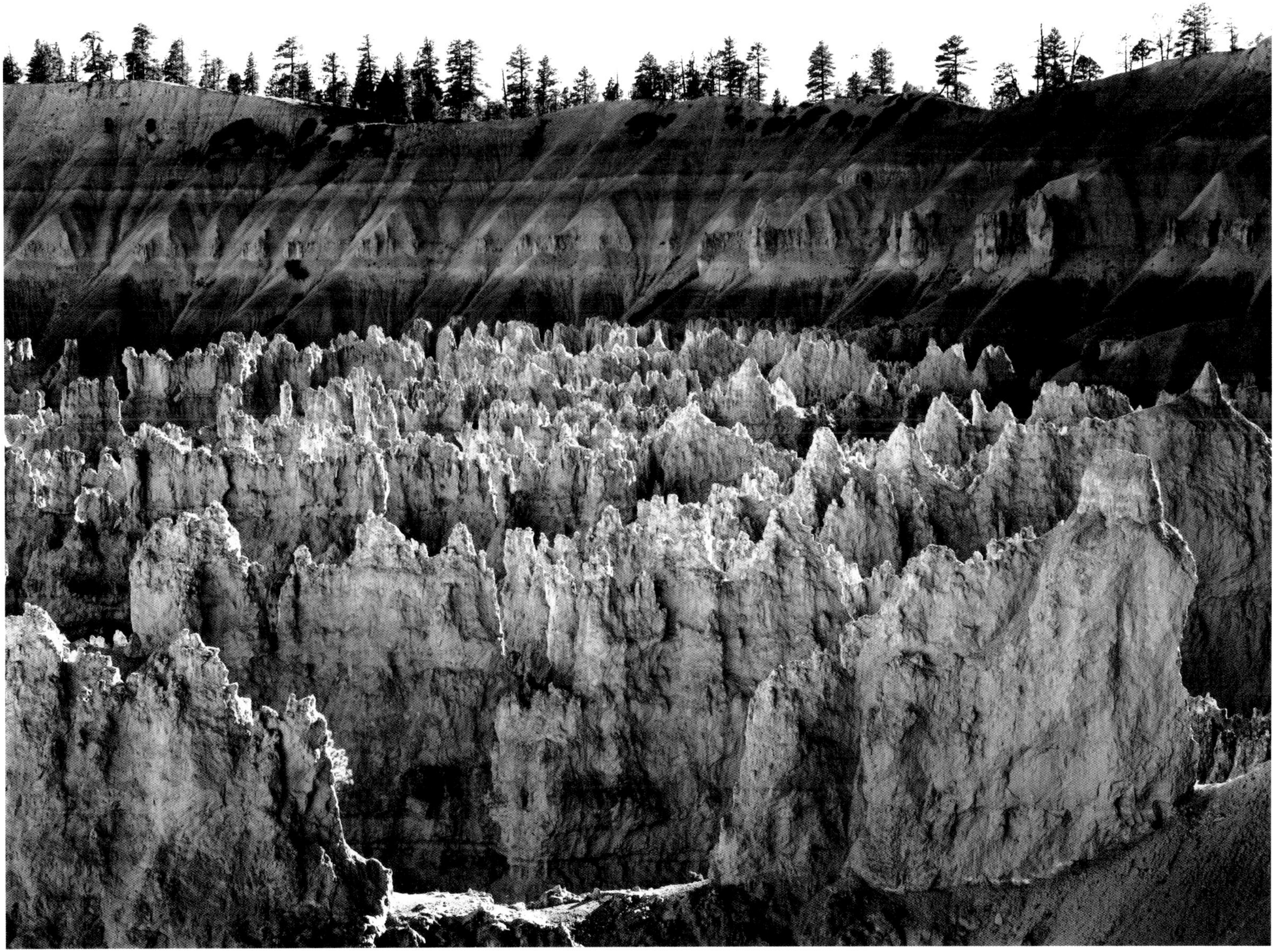

FORMATIONS, BRYCE CANYON NATIONAL PARK, UTAH, 1947

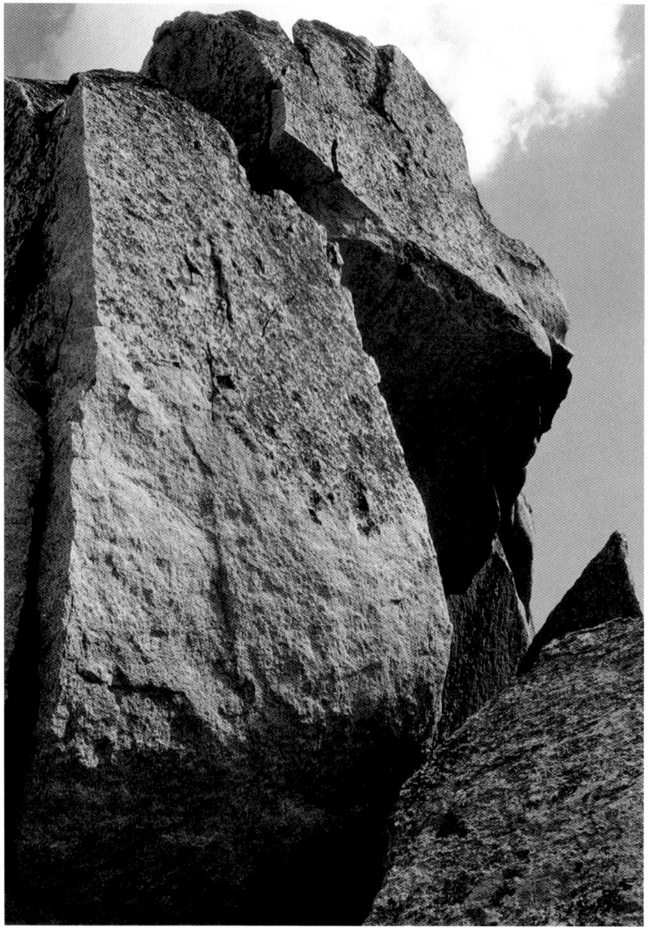

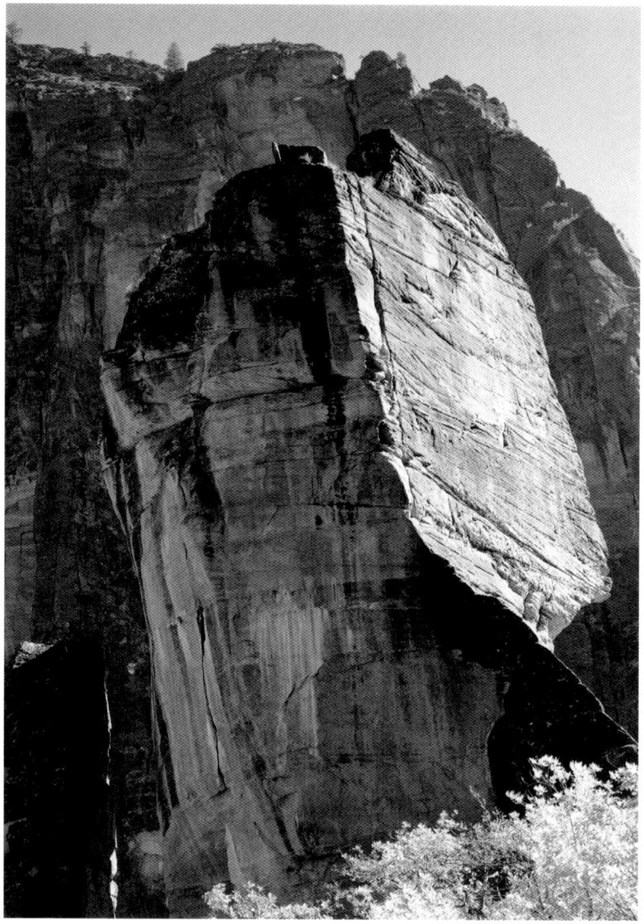

ROCKS, SIERRA NEVADA, CALIFORNIA, C. 1927

DETAIL, THE GREAT WHITE THRONE, ZION NATIONAL PARK, UTAH, 1942

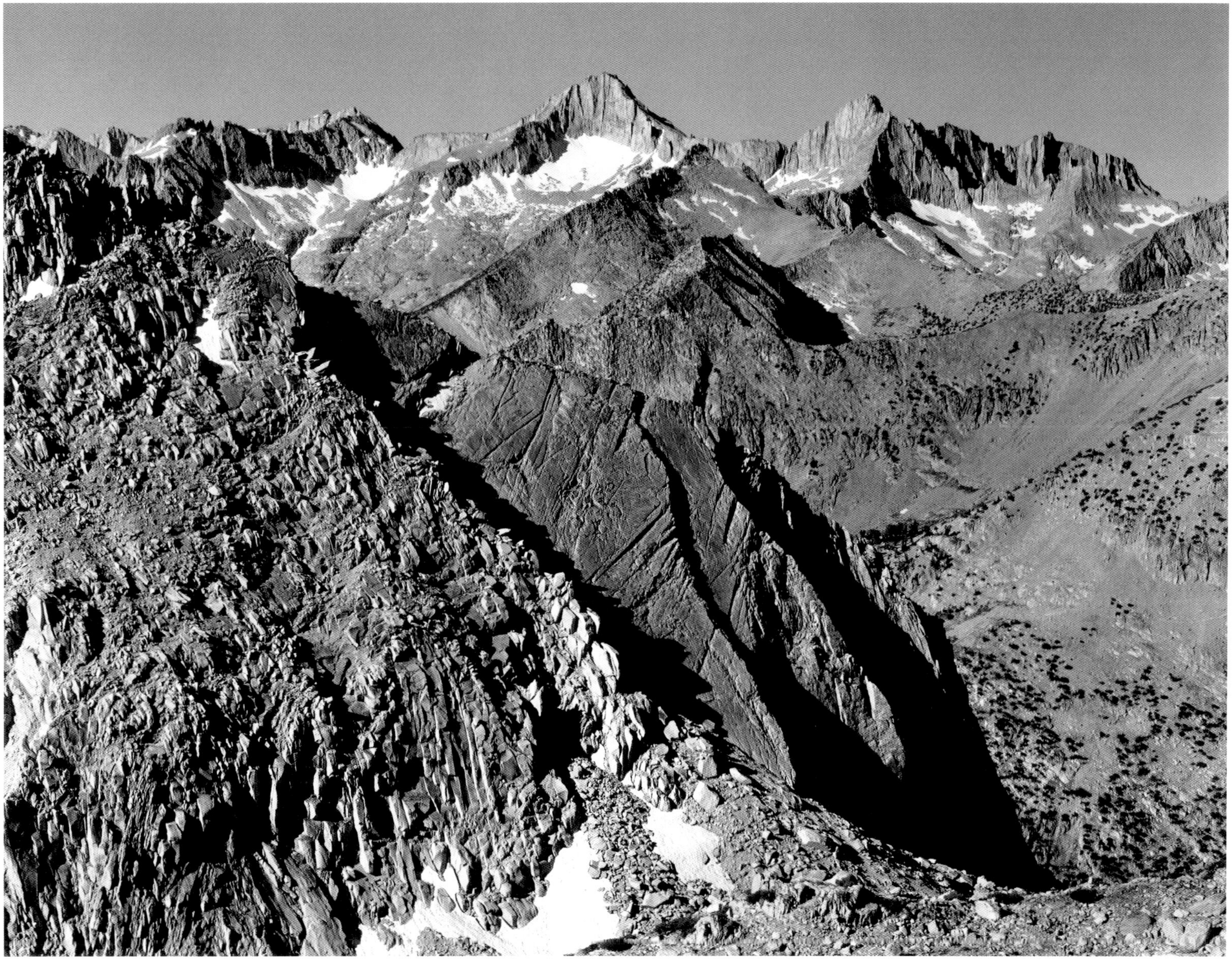

MOUNT BREWER GROUP FROM GLEN PASS, SIERRA NEVADA, CALIFORNIA, 1935

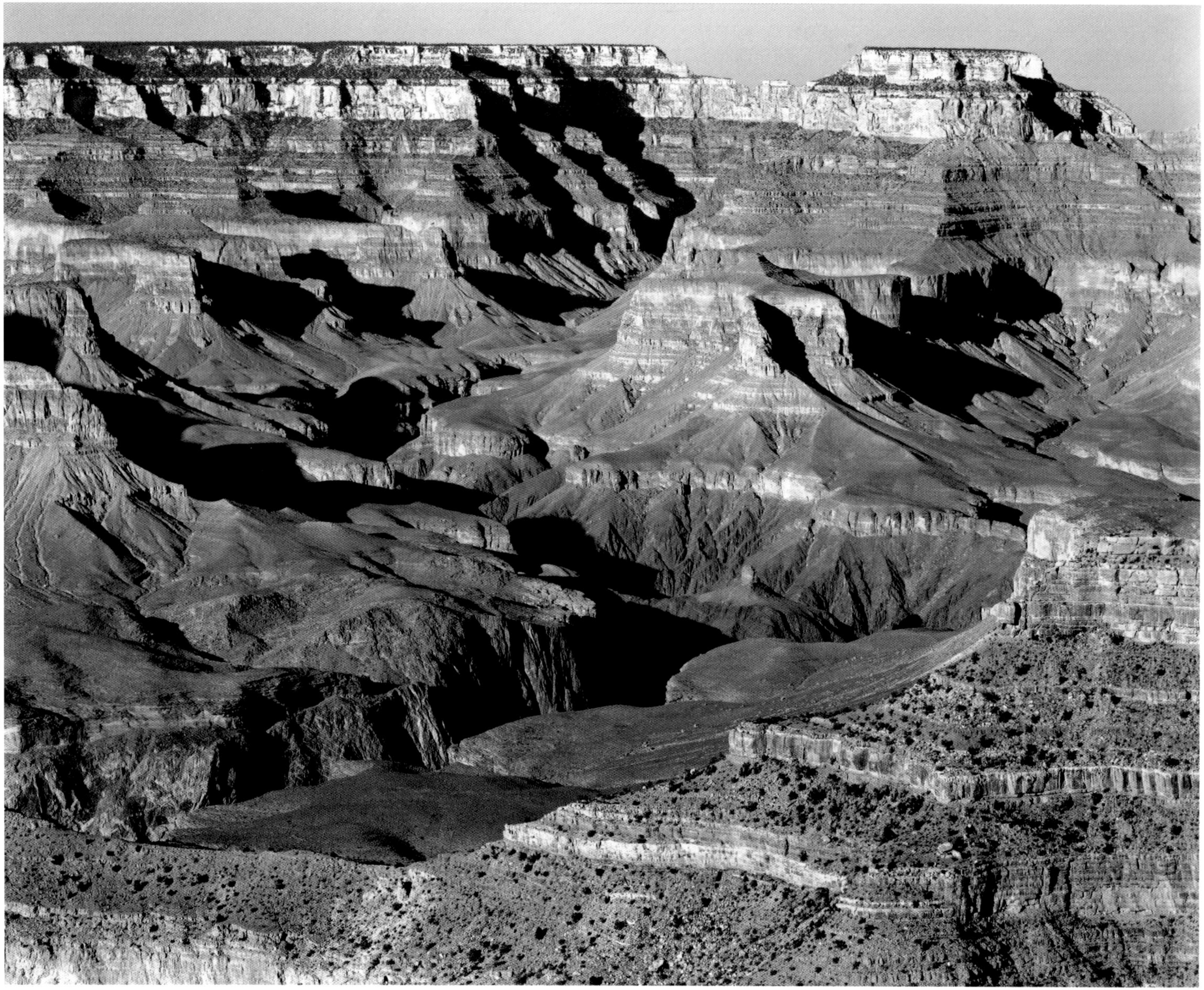

GRAND CANYON FROM YAVAPAI POINT, GRAND CANYON NATIONAL PARK, ARIZONA, 1942

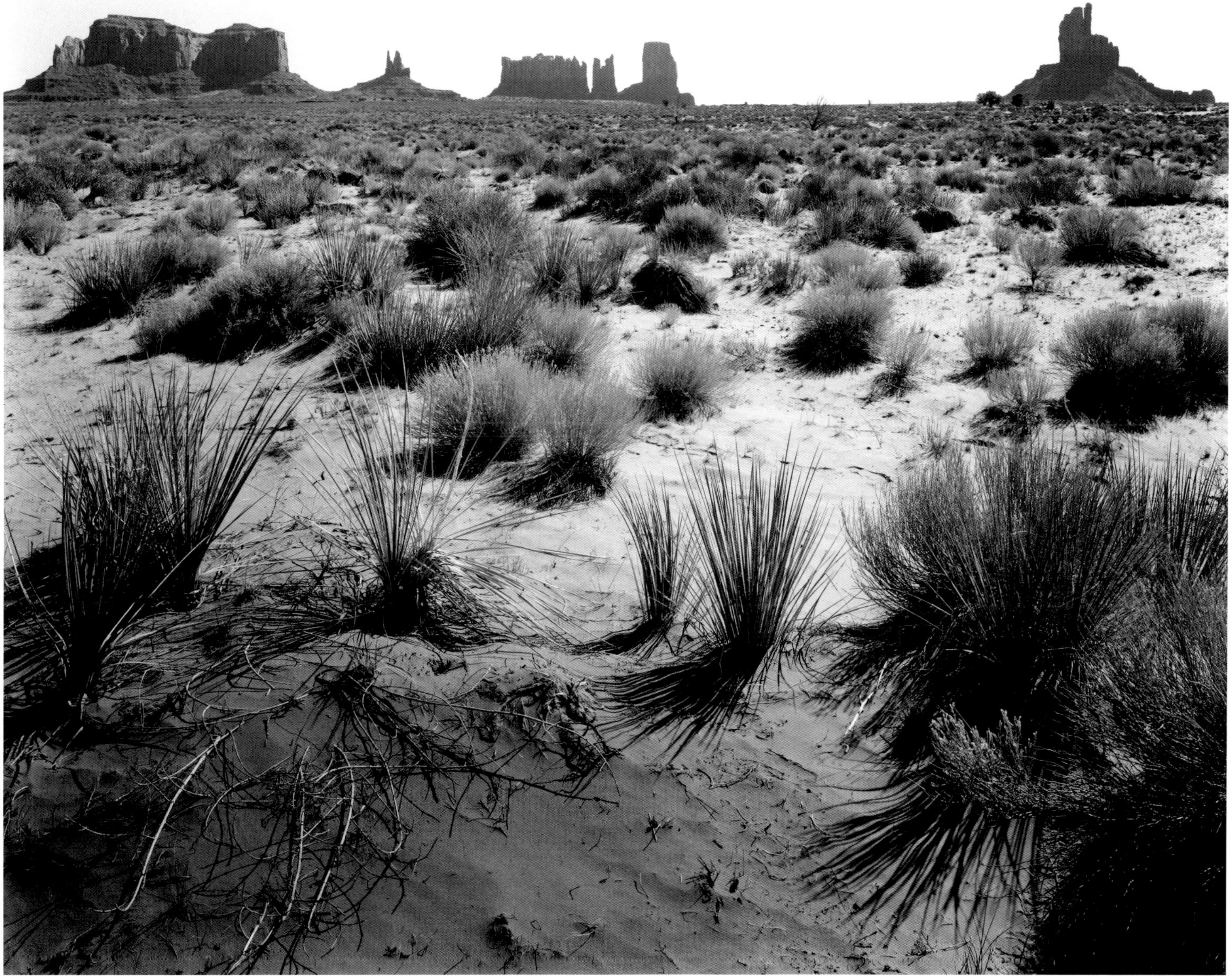

MONUMENT VALLEY NAVAJO TRIBAL PARK, ARIZONA, C. 1947

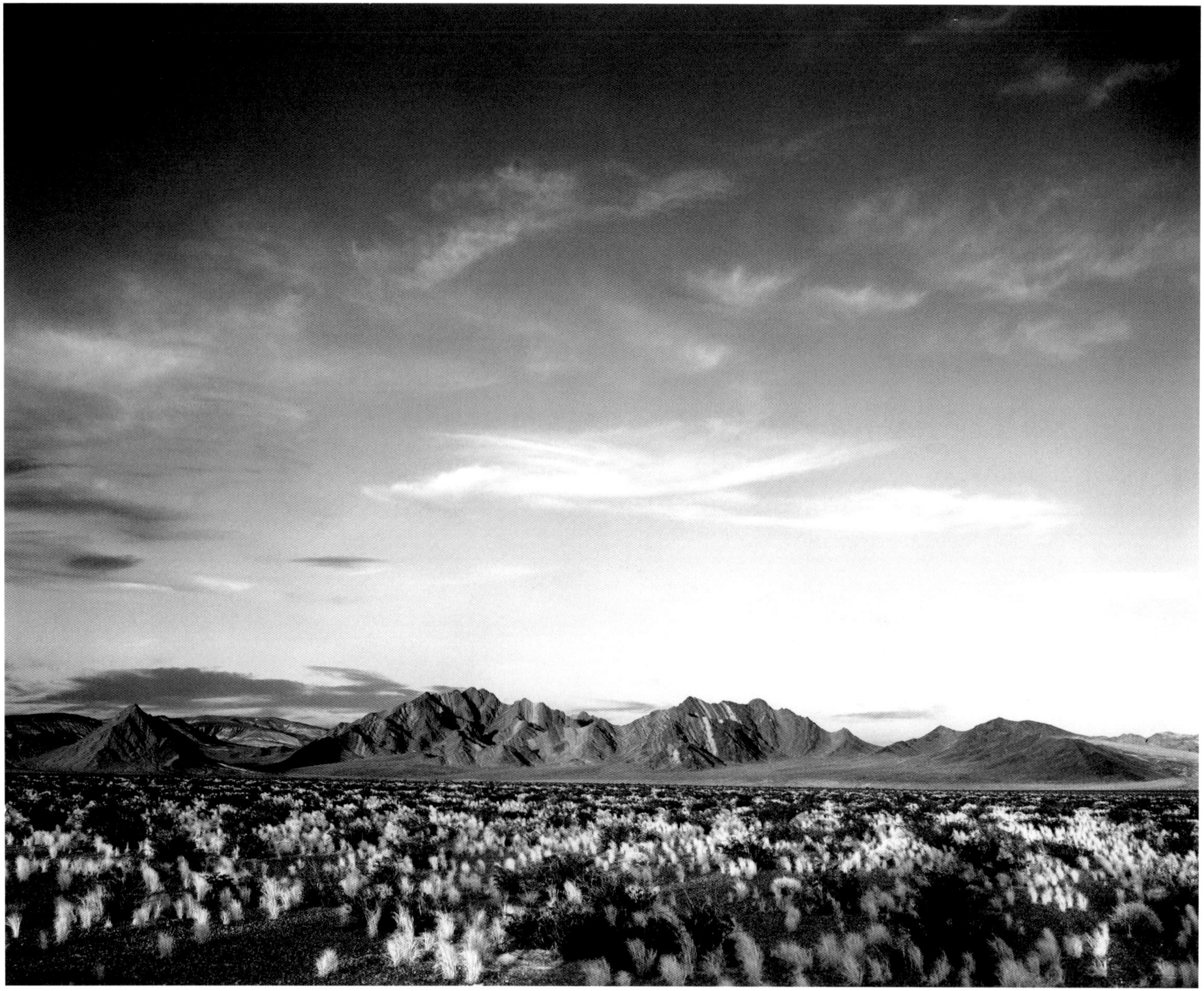

DESERT EAST OF DEATH VALLEY, DEATH VALLEY NATIONAL PARK, CALIFORNIA, C. 1942

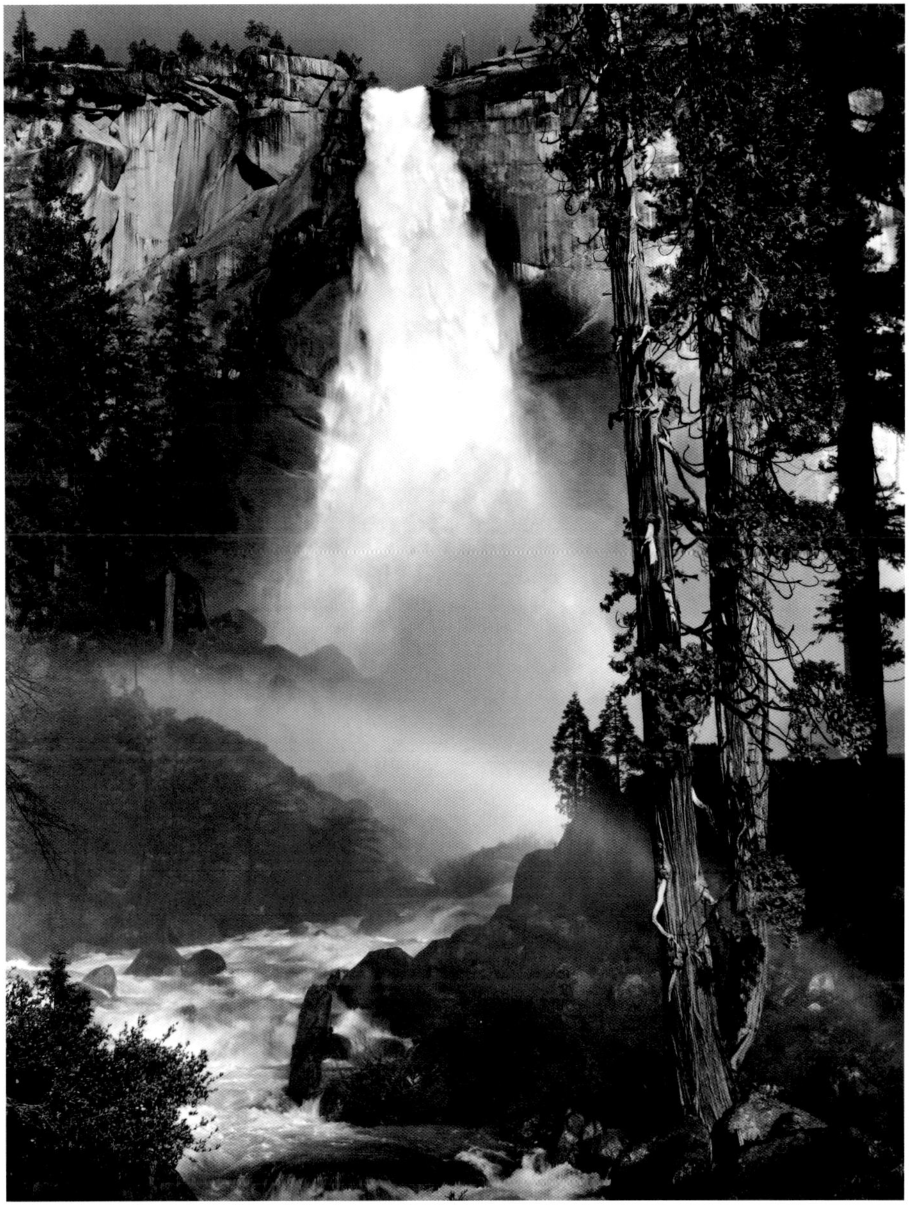

NEVADA FALL, RAINBOW, YOSEMITE NATIONAL PARK, CALIFORNIA, C. 1947

No matter how remote his travels, Ansel kept up a lively correspondence using his portable typewriter. On the first of two Guggenheim Fellowships, he spent a few days in Big Bend National Park, and on his forty-fifth birthday, he wrote his friends Beaumont and Nancy Newhall:

> Big Bend National Park, Texas
> February 20th, 1947
> My Birthday, by Gawd!
>
> Dear Nancy and Beaumont,
> Three letters from youse guys arrived today! This is a hell of a remote place, and the mail comes about as infrequently as the rain. But it's really wonderful—one of the great Parks! The roads are terrible—I ruined two tires yesterday—completely blasted.… Am getting some swell stuff.

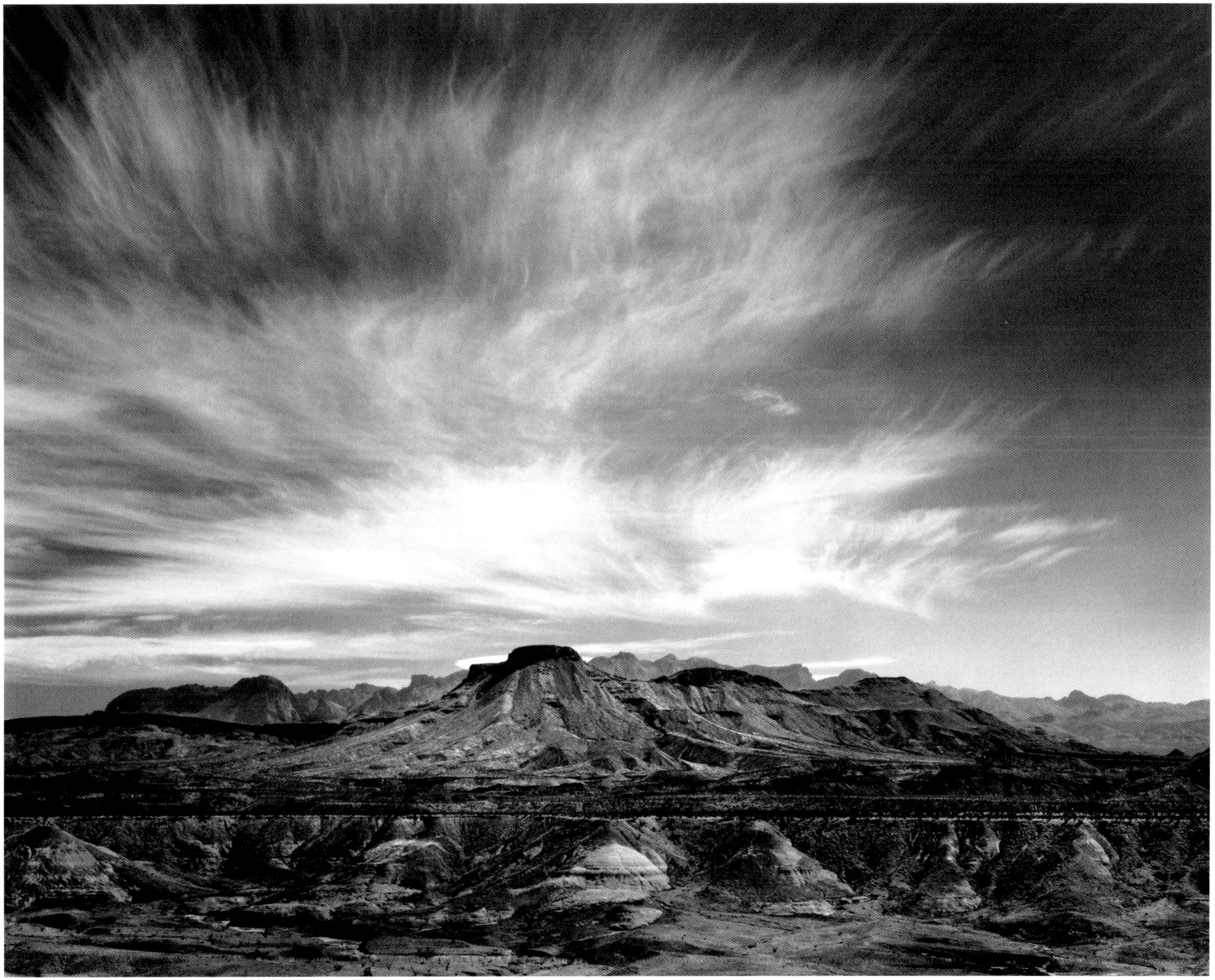

BURRO MESA AND THE CHISOS MOUNTAINS, BIG BEND NATIONAL PARK, TEXAS, 1947

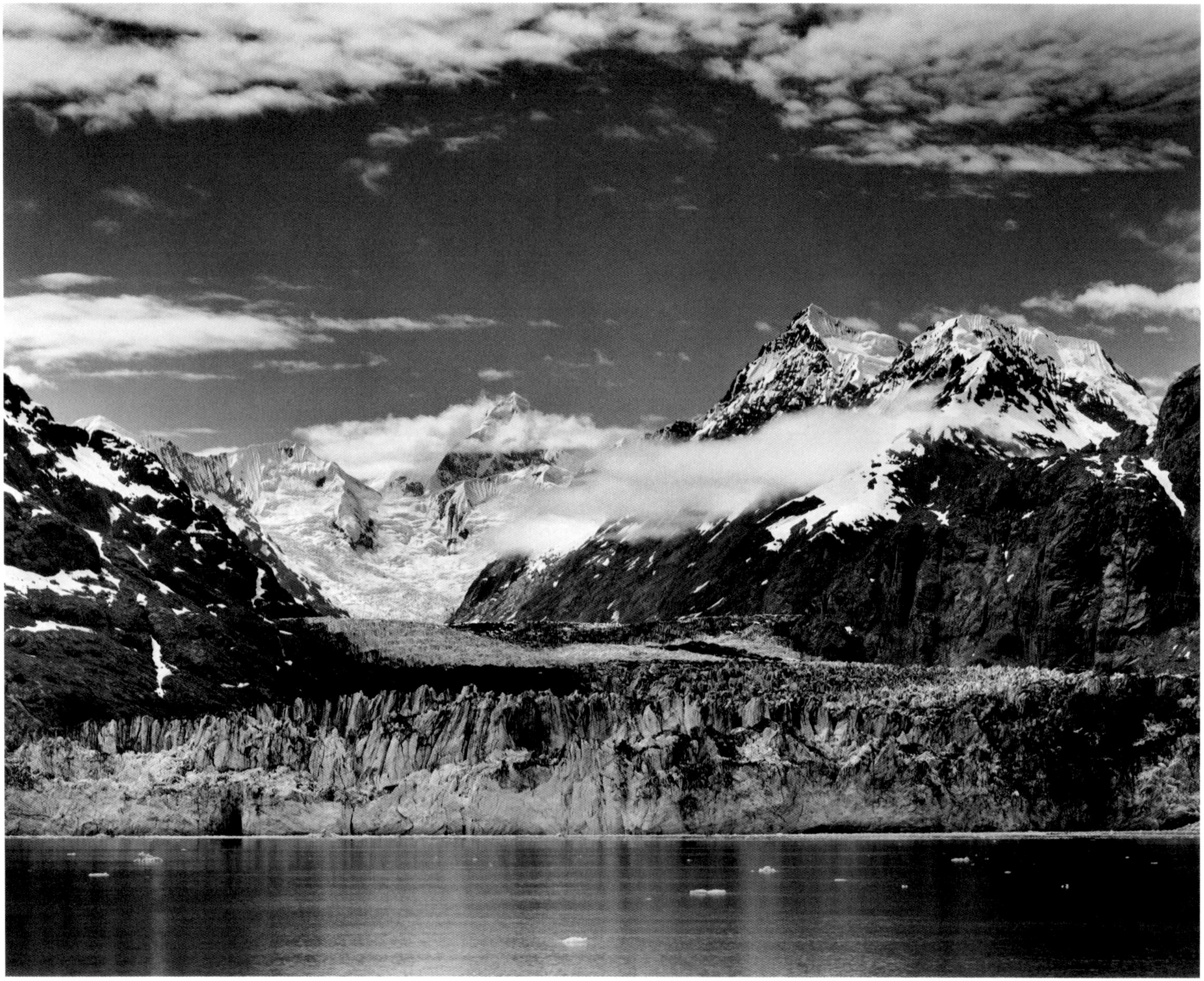

MARJORIE GLACIER, PEAKS AND CLOUDS, GLACIER BAY NATIONAL PARK, ALASKA, 1942

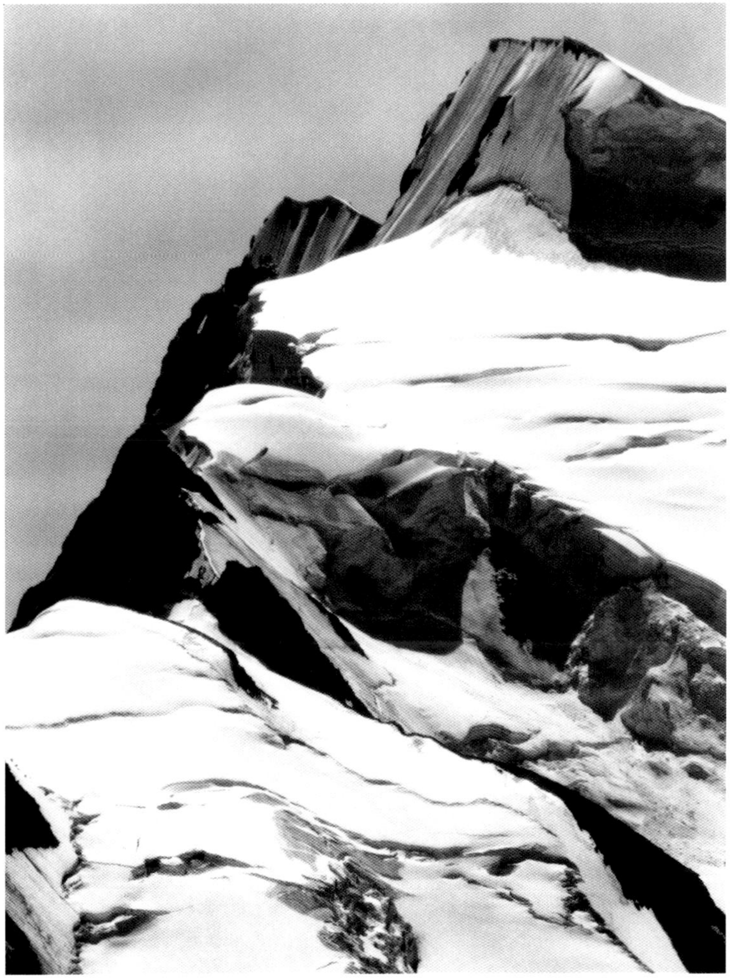

MOUNT RESPLENDENT, MOUNT ROBSON PROVINCIAL PARK, CANADA, 1928

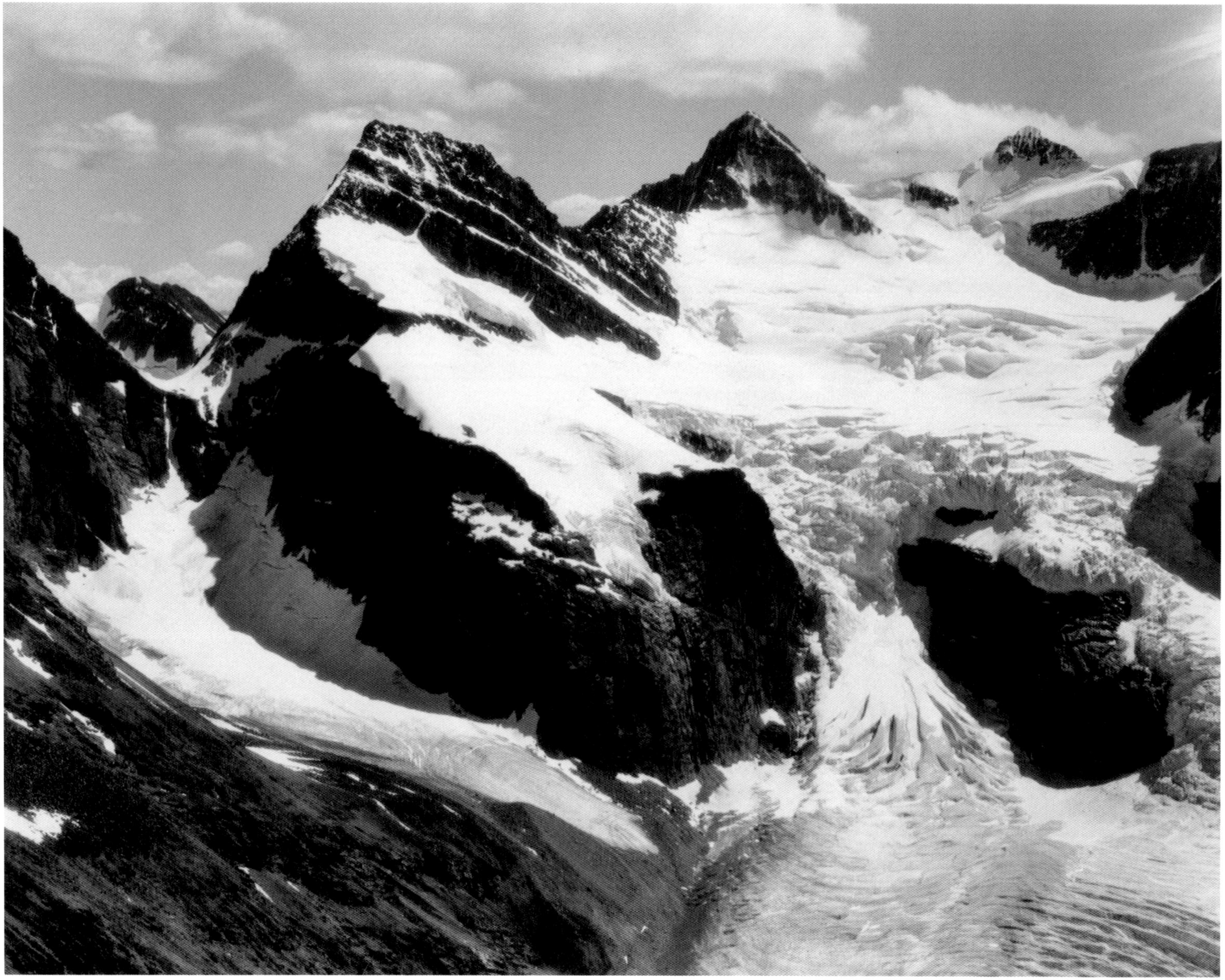

PEAKS, MOUNT ROBSON PROVINCIAL PARK, CANADA, 1928

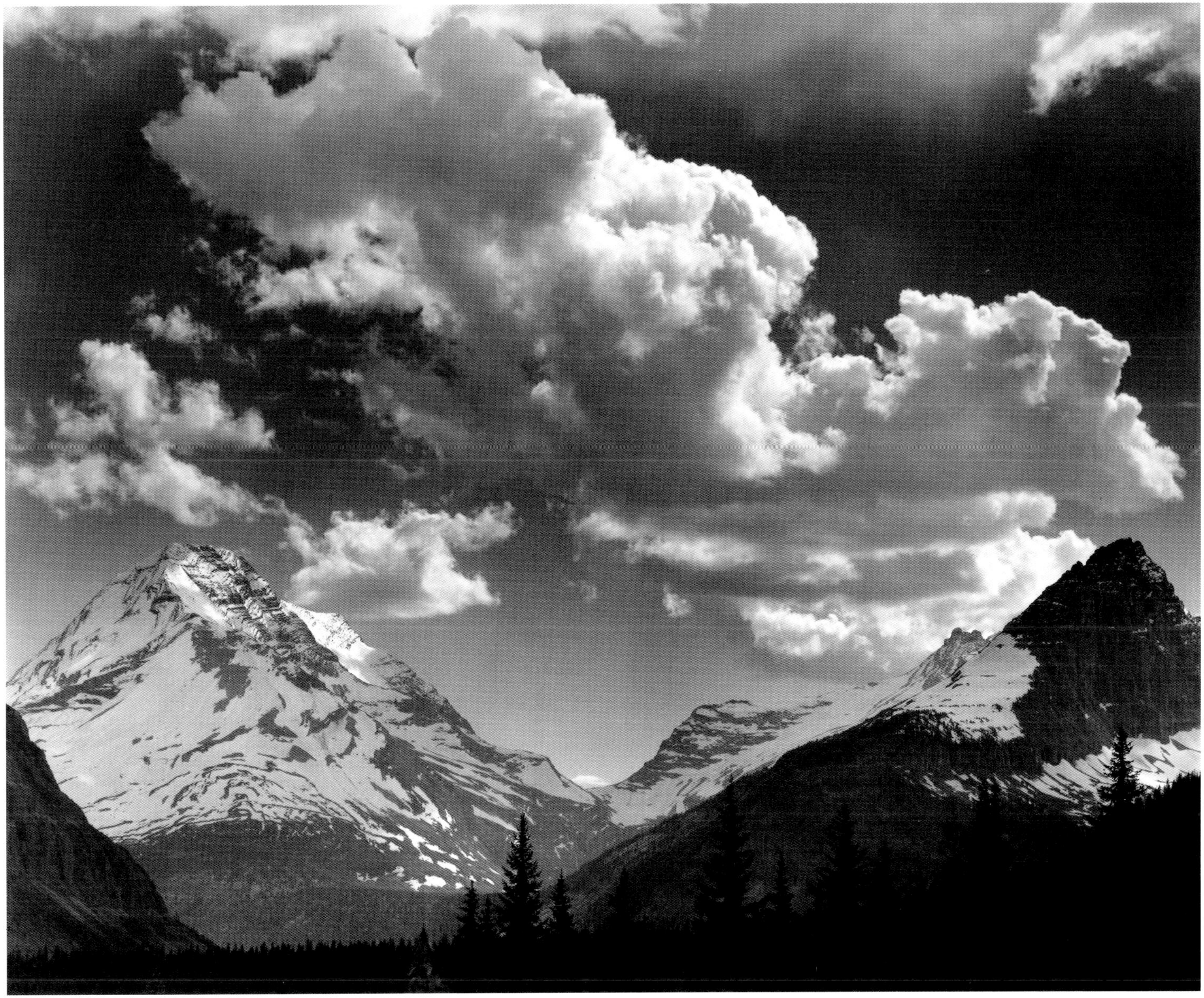

NOON CLOUDS, MOUNT JACKSON AND FUSILLADE MOUNTAIN, GLACIER NATIONAL PARK, MONTANA, 1942

At the age of seventy-seven, Ansel wrote, "Since June 1916 the Sierra has dominated my mind, art and spirit." Although he photographed the great ranges of North America, including the Rockies, the Tetons, and the Cascades, as well as, briefly, the Swiss and French Alps, he preferred the Sierra Nevada. He never tired of photographing the Sierra's granite peaks, which he saw as "sculptures in stone." The Sierra photographs in this book are but a minute selection from the thousands of images he made there between 1916 and 1980.

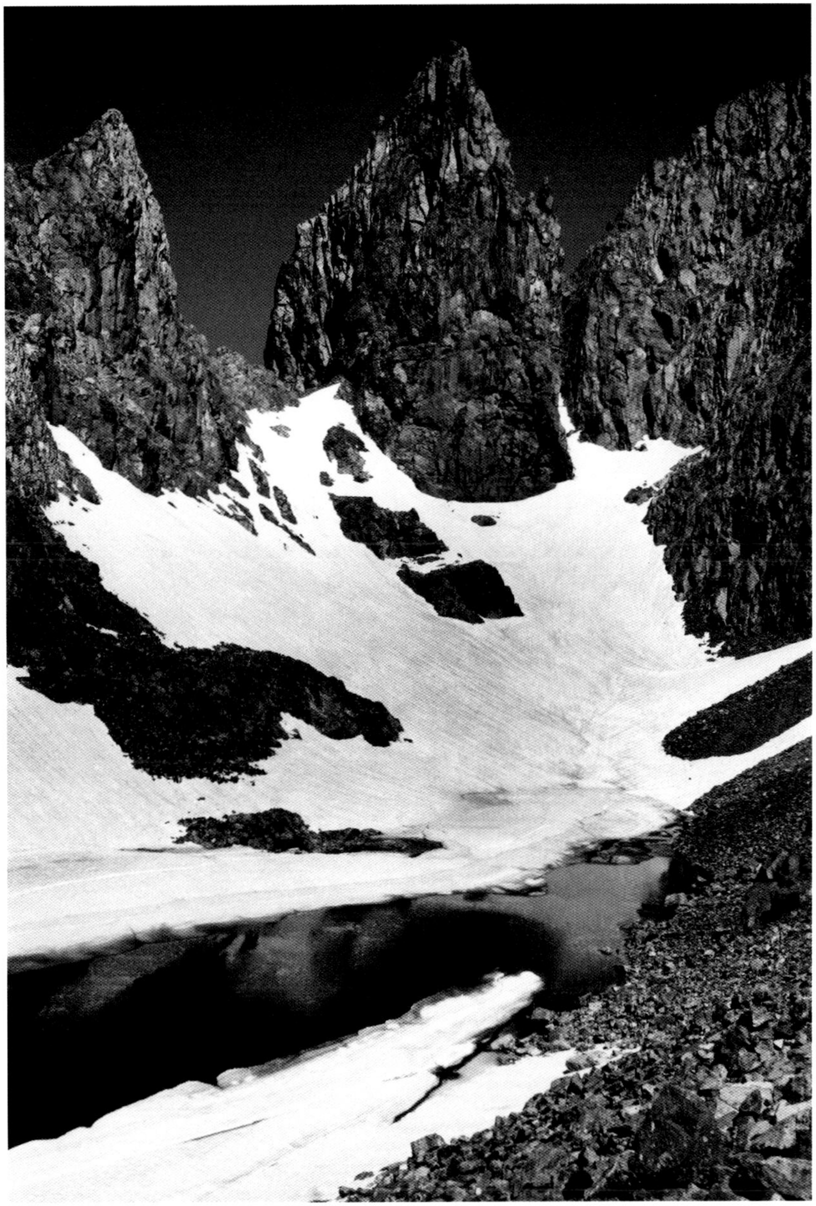

MICHAEL'S MINARET, SIERRA NEVADA, CALIFORNIA, C. 1930

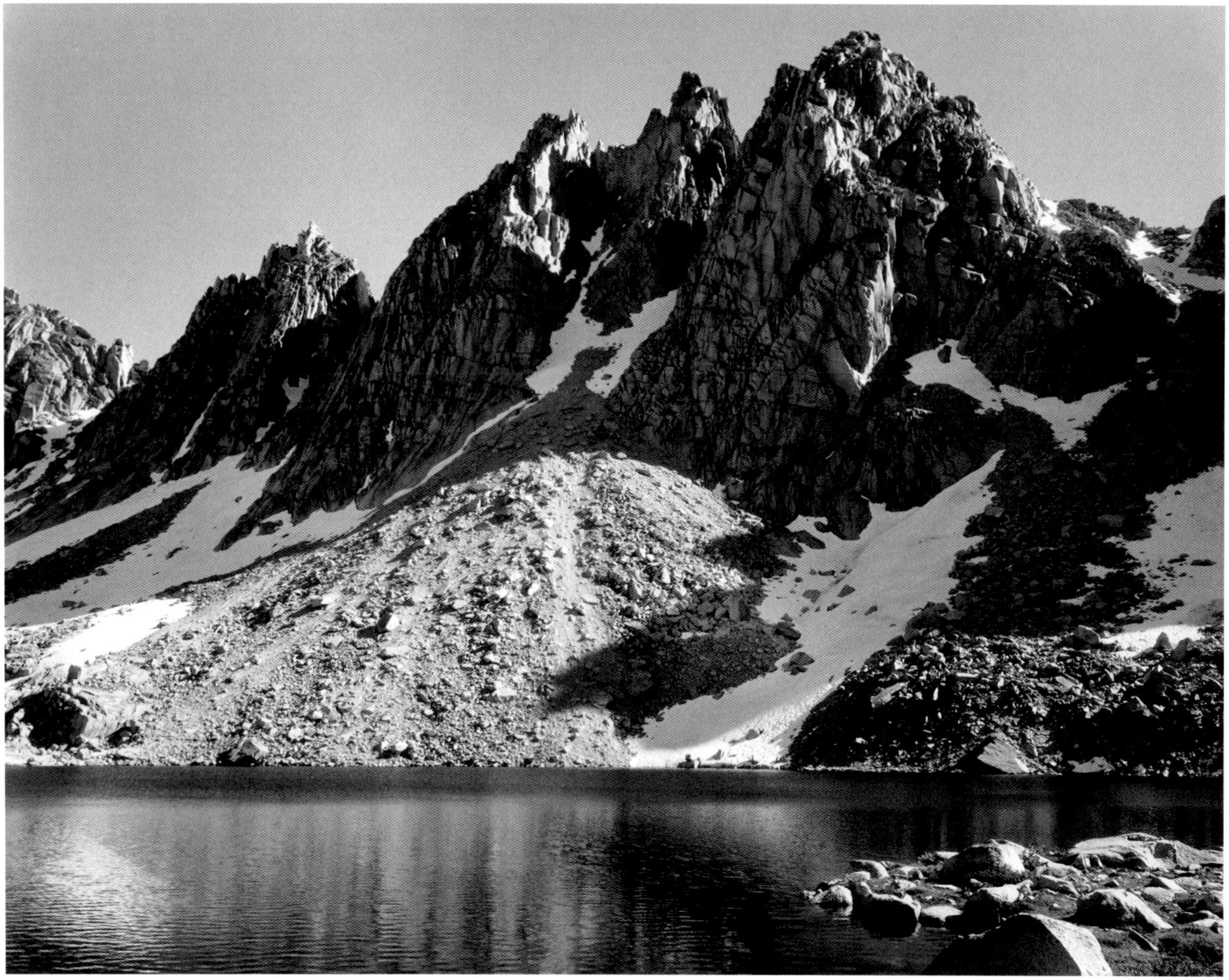

KEARSARGE PINNACLES, KINGS CANYON NATIONAL PARK, CALIFORNIA, C. 1932

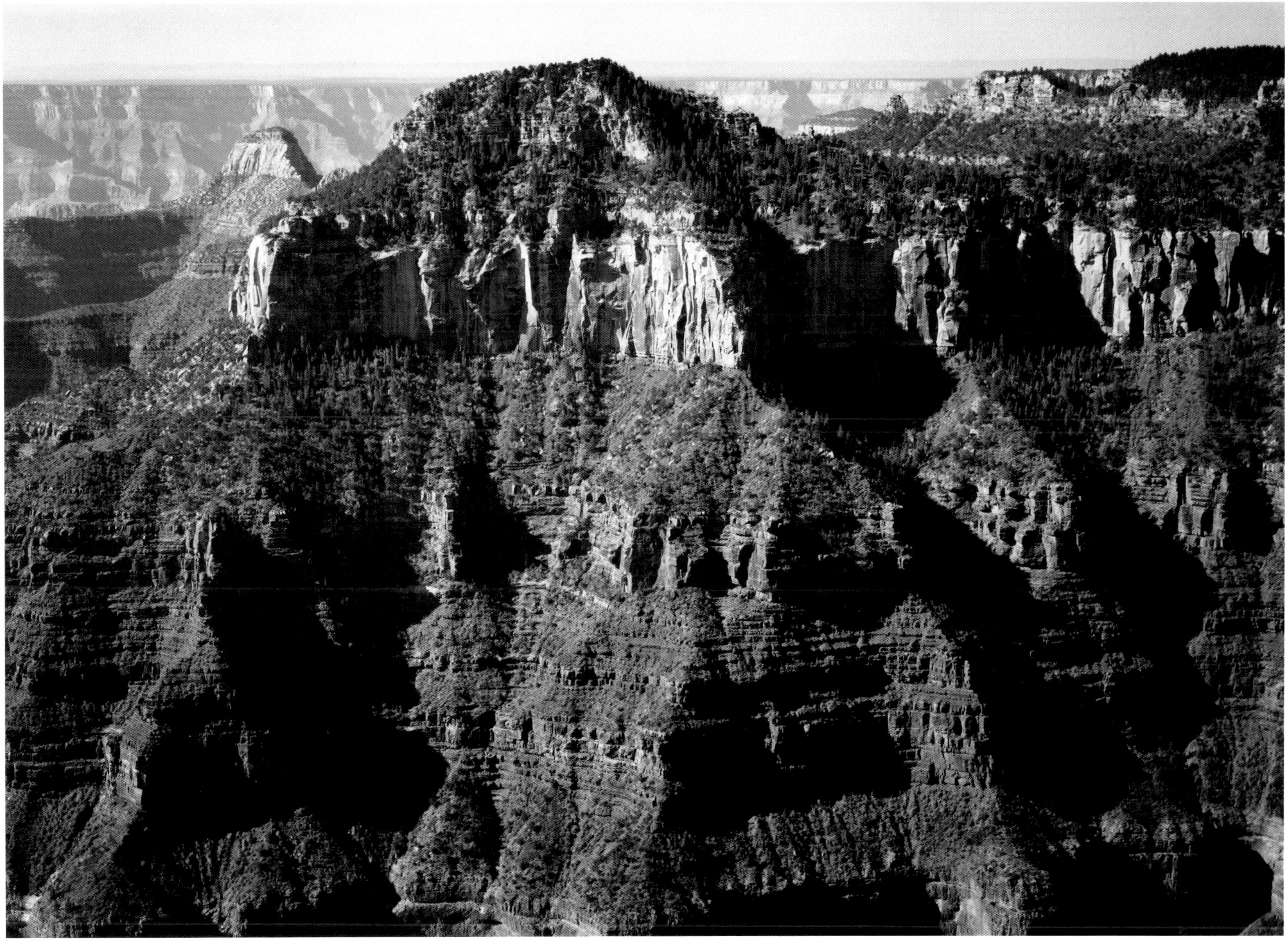

POINT SUBLIME, GRAND CANYON NATIONAL PARK, ARIZONA, 1942

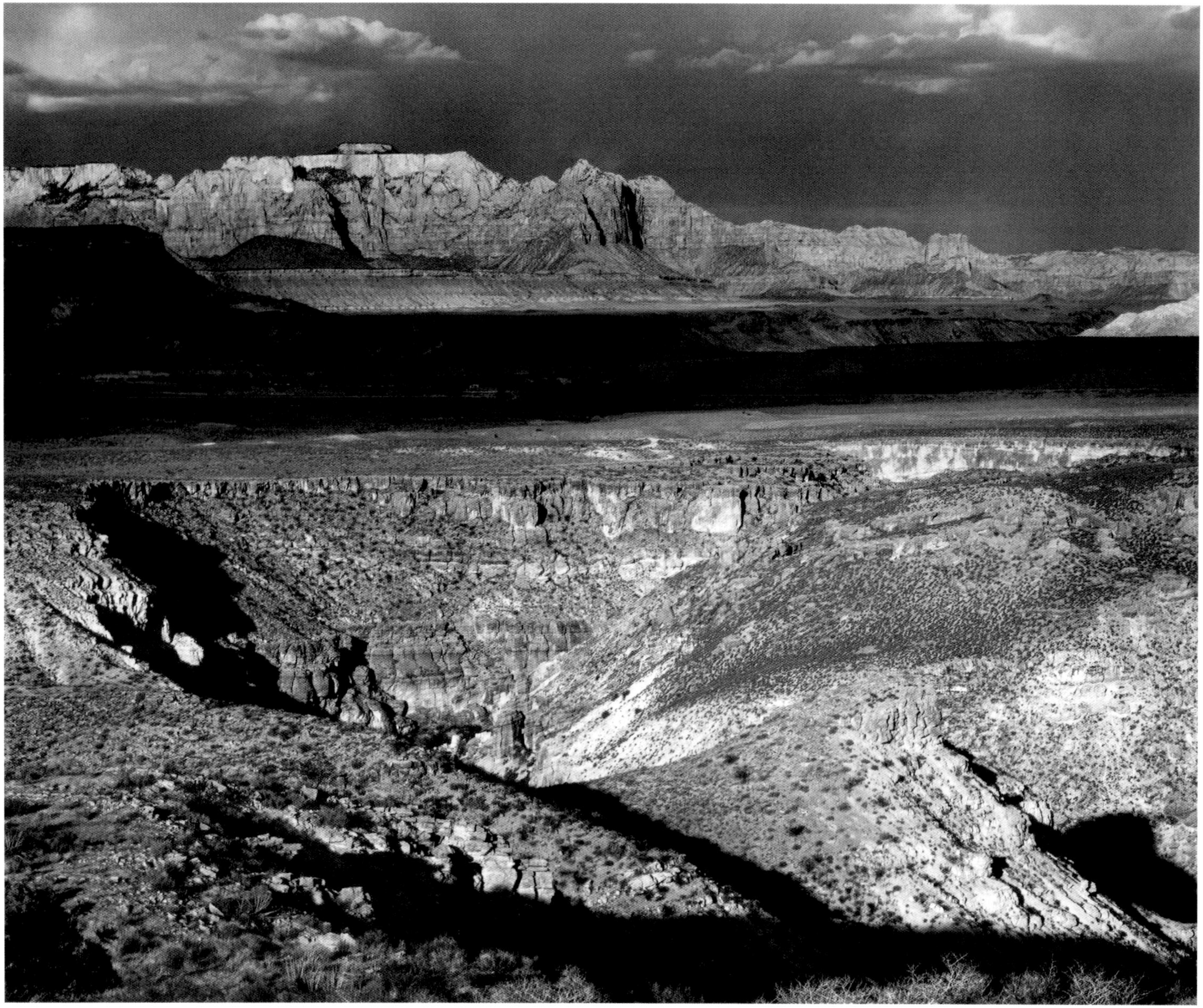

WEST TEMPLE, ZION NATIONAL PARK, UTAH, 1961

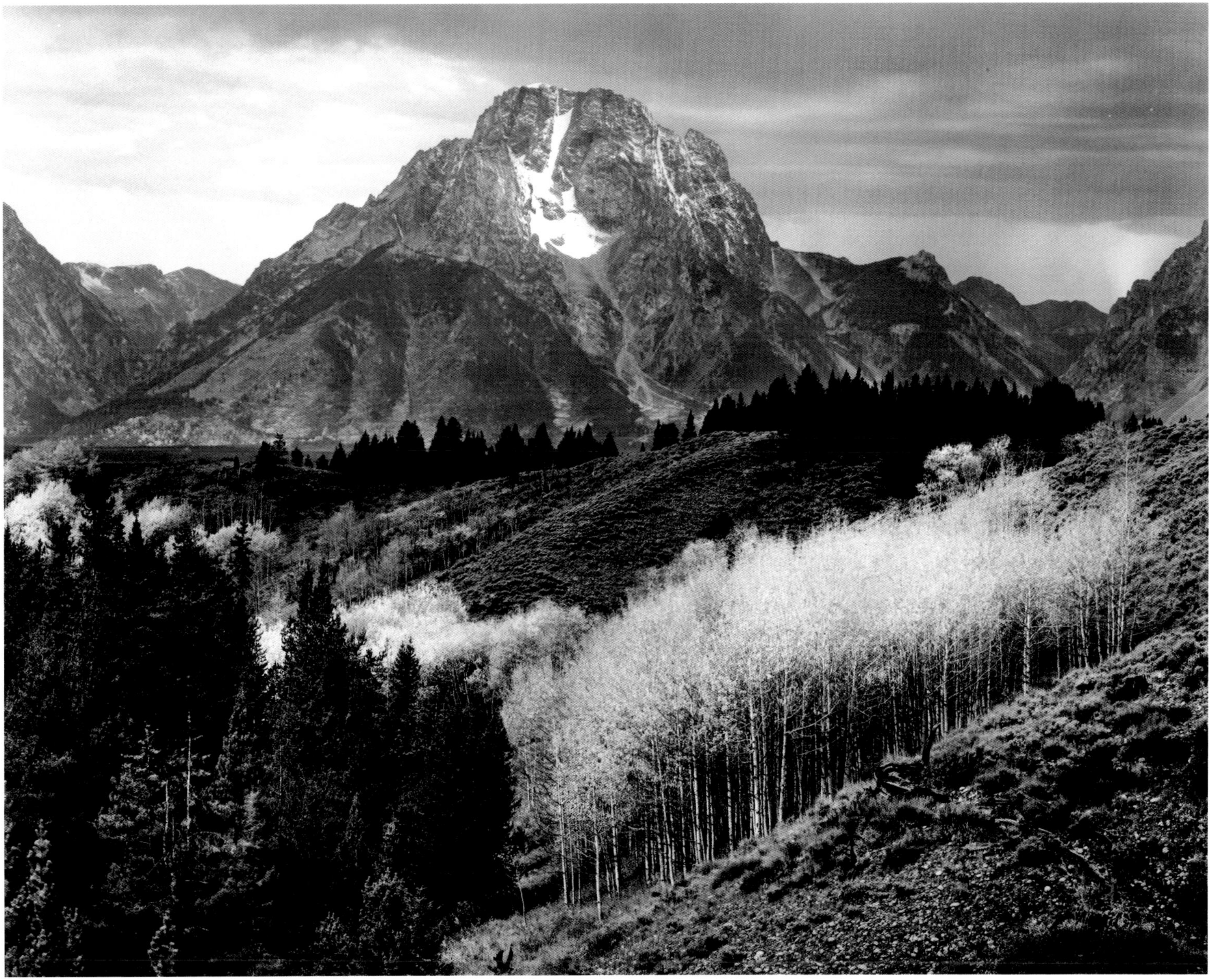

MOUNT MORAN, AUTUMN, GRAND TETON NATIONAL PARK, WYOMING, 1948

Ansel wrote to Virginia Best, his future wife, on October 20, 1924: "I have been very busy since you left, but I found several hours of spare time in which I made a Bromoil. It is a scene near Muir Woods—one that I took when we made the trip in the car. It is my masterpiece to date. I am anxious that you see it. I would like to show it to you at Christmas time.... With the deepest love Ansel." Two months later, Ansel gave a bromoil print of Muir Woods to Virginia inscribed, "With love to Virginia from Ansel."

To make a bromoil, the photographer bleaches and tans a black-and-white photograph, soaks it in water, and then applies lithographic ink, often with a brush. Ansel waxed enthusiastic about the process in 1923: "Bromoil is the most magnificent photographic process I have ever seen.... It *is* mussy—but more than worth-while." Bromoils were popular in the early twentieth century, but for Ansel they were a passing fancy, and he made only a few. They were usually printed on heavily textured cream-colored paper, quite different from the sharp, glossy black-and-white photographs we associate with his name.

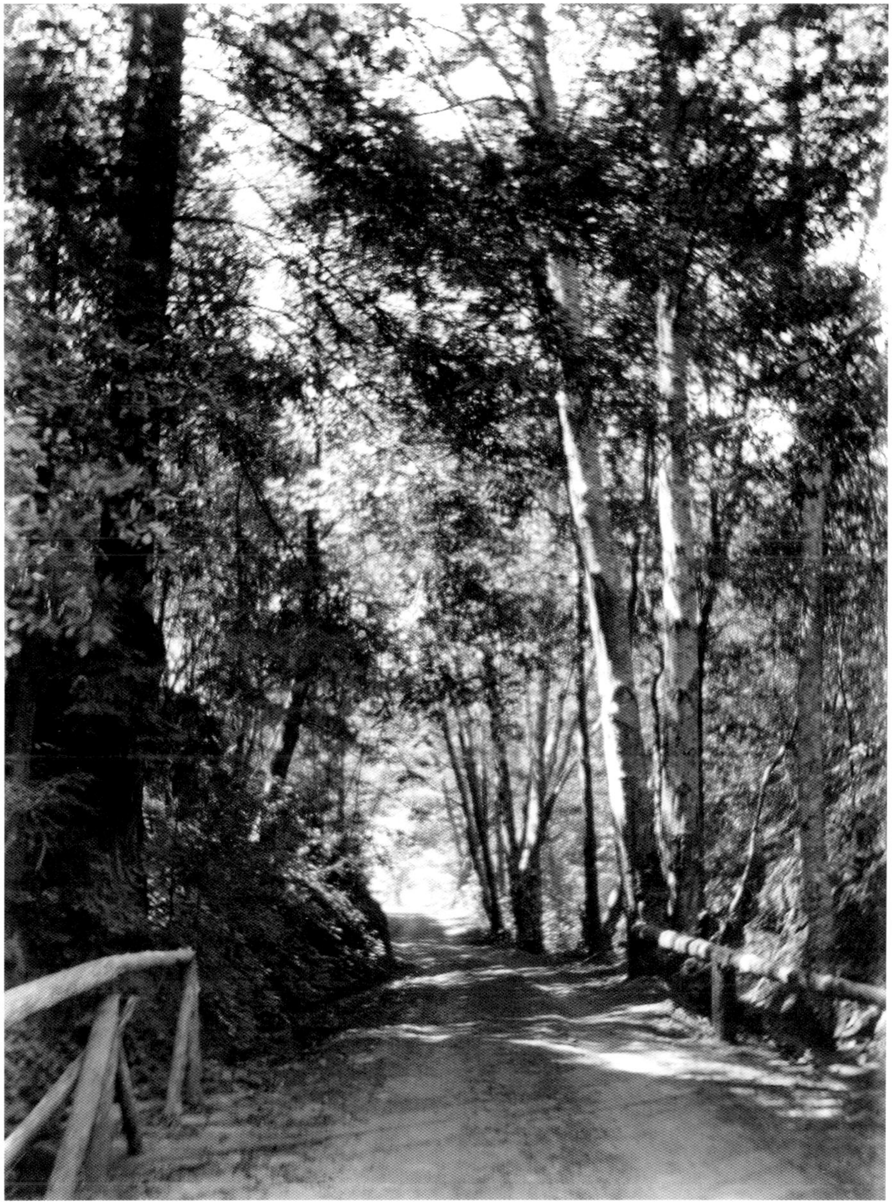

IN MUIR WOODS NATIONAL MONUMENT, CALIFORNIA, 1924

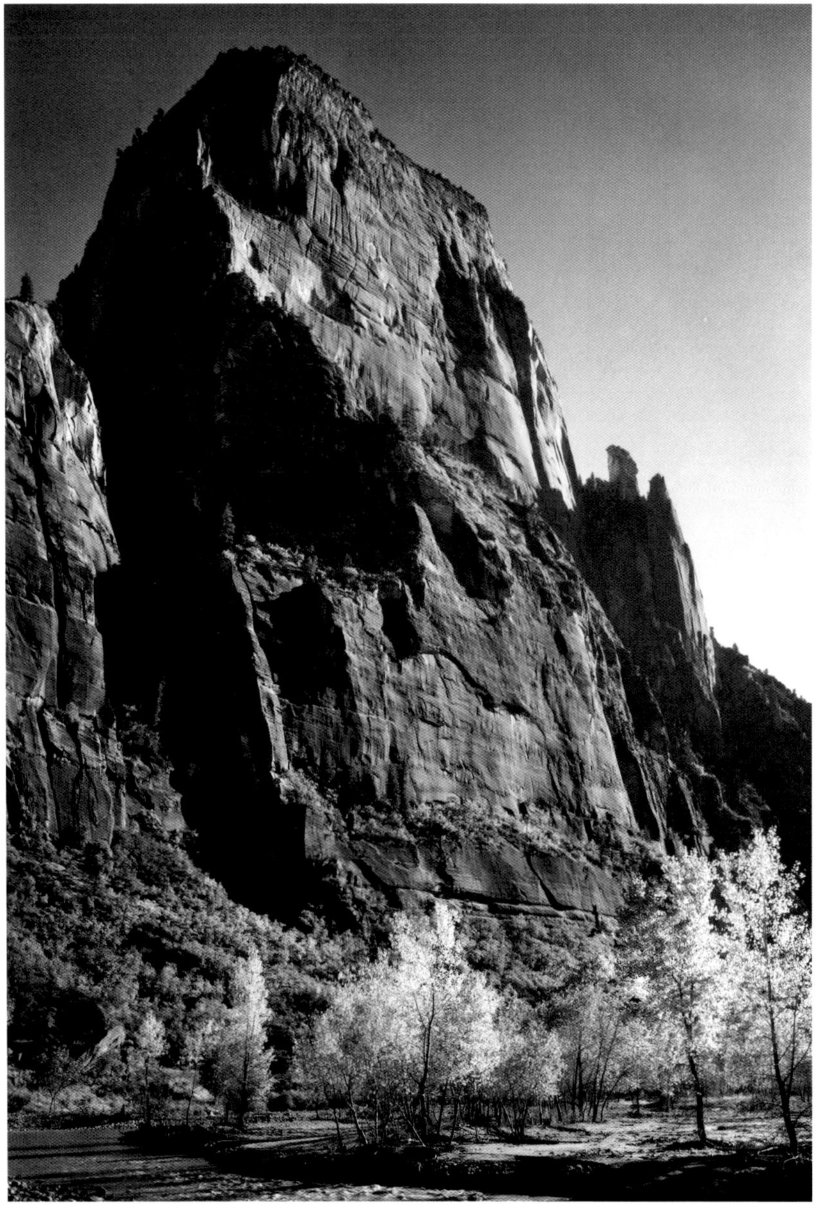

THE GREAT WHITE THRONE, ZION NATIONAL PARK, UTAH, 1942

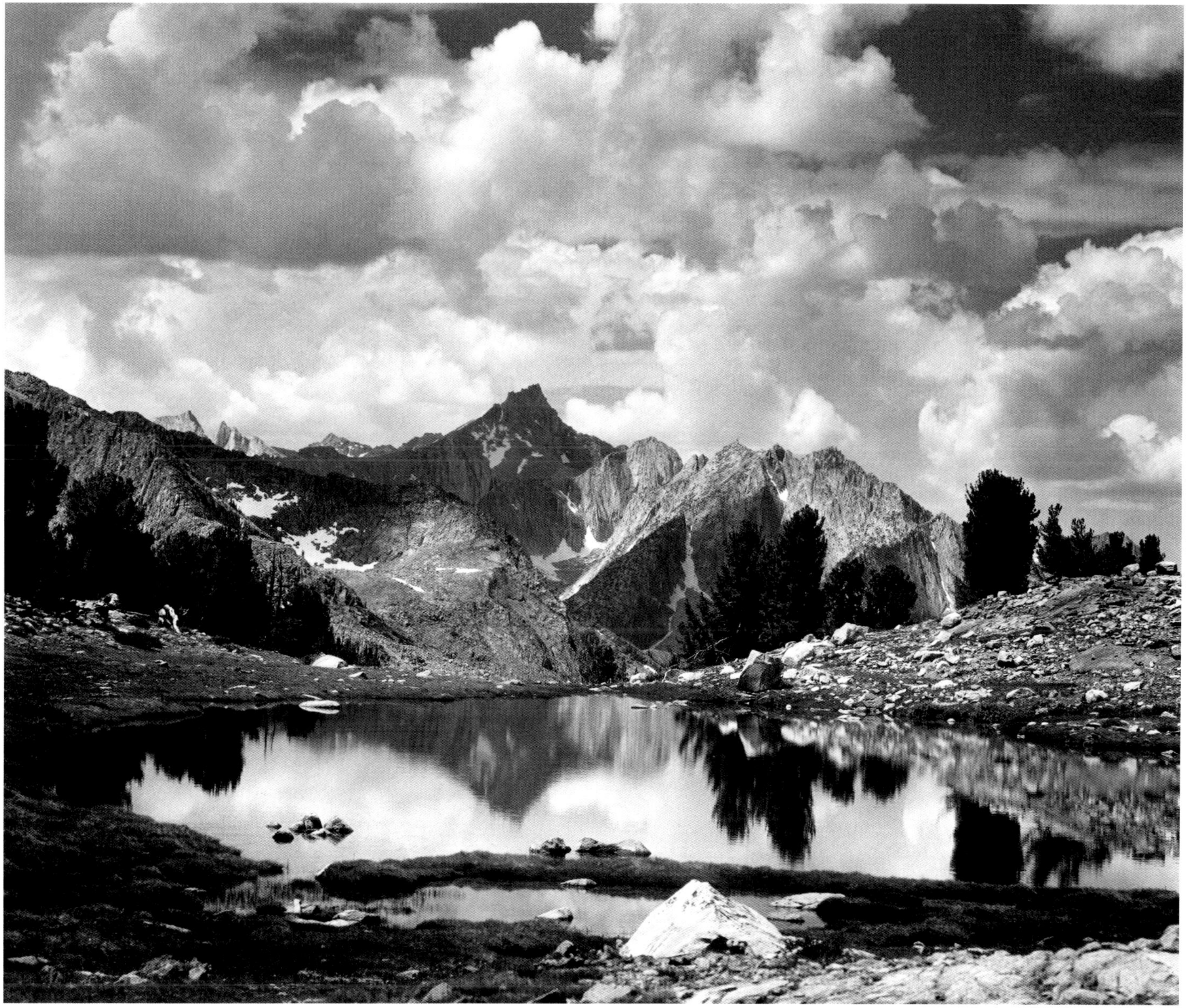

MOUNT CLARENCE KING, POOL, KINGS CANYON NATIONAL PARK, CALIFORNIA, C. 1925

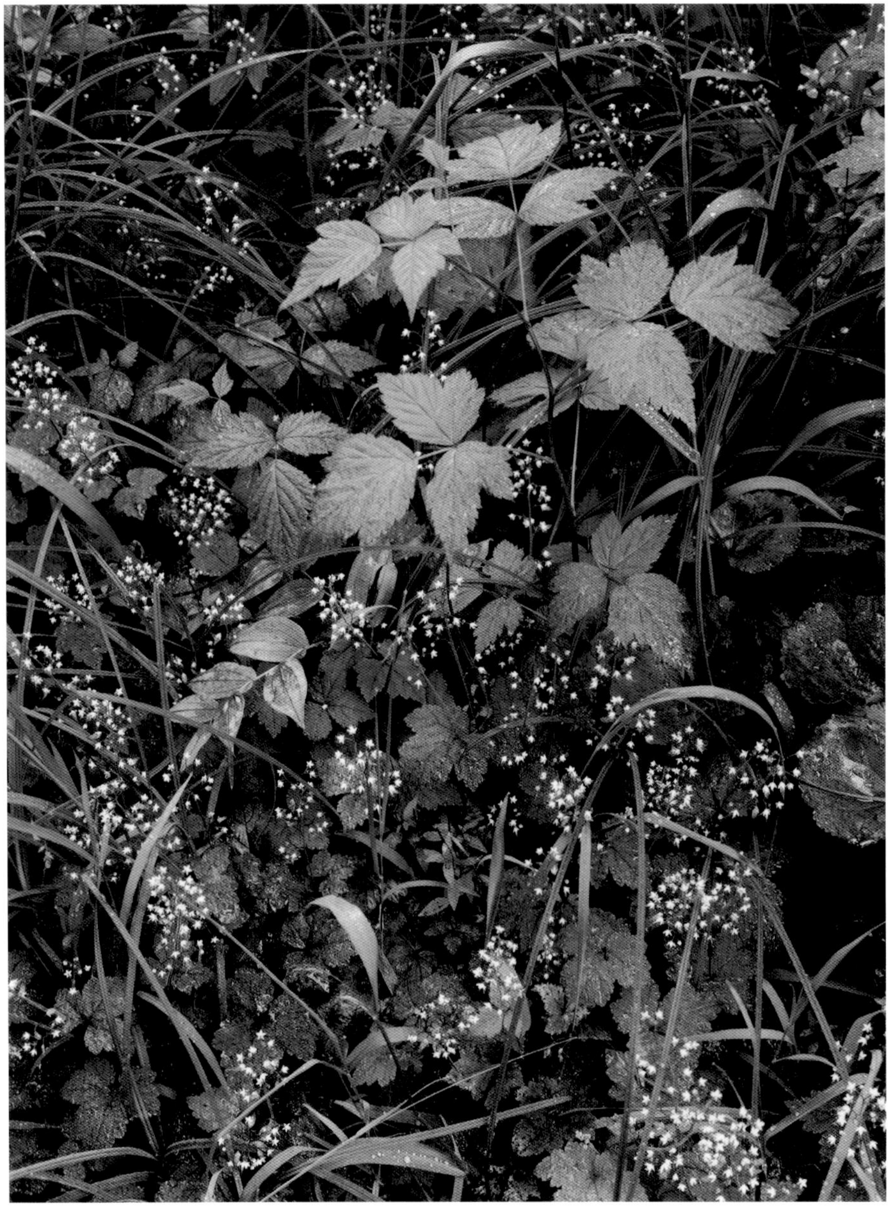

TRAILSIDE, NEAR JUNEAU, ALASKA, 1947

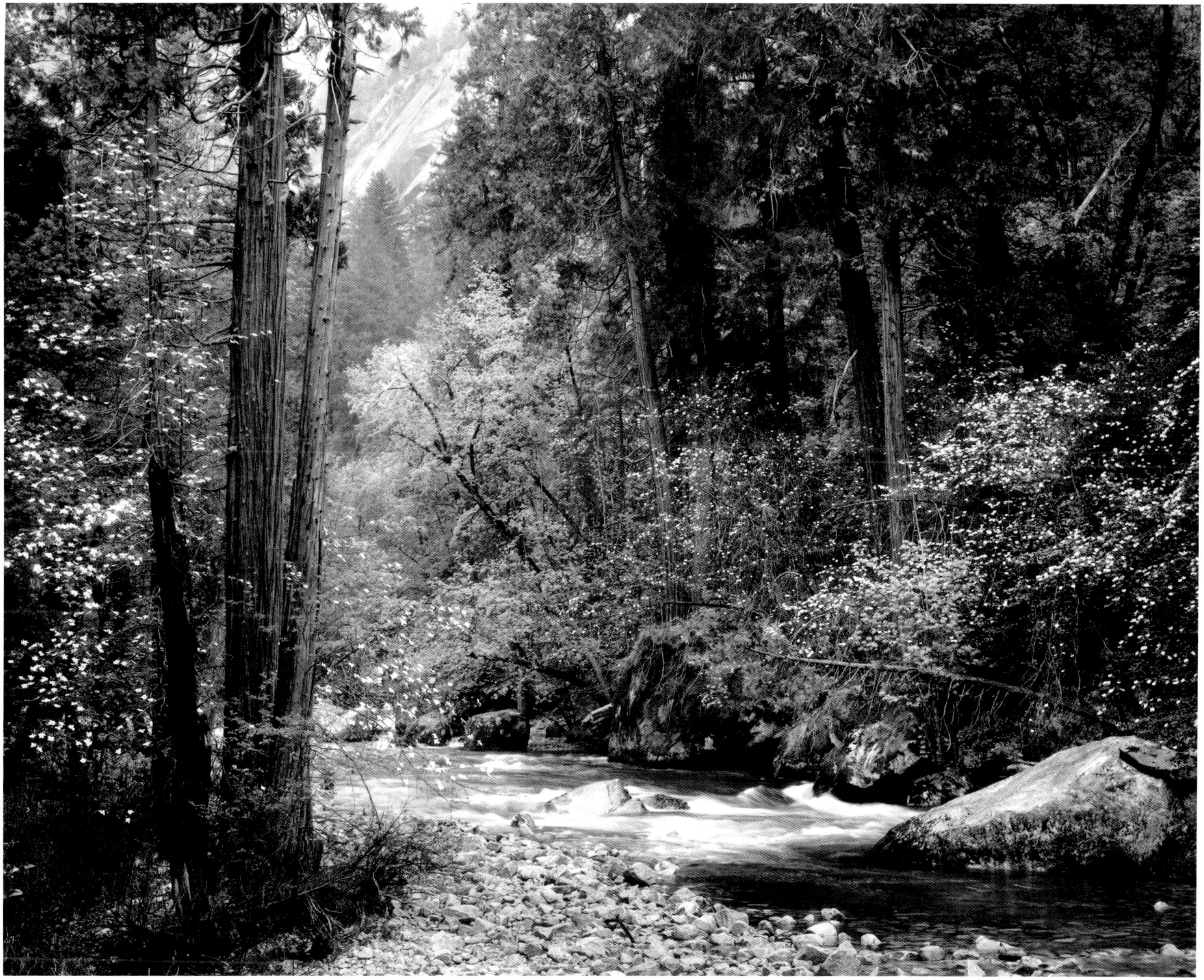

TENAYA CREEK, DOGWOOD, RAIN, YOSEMITE NATIONAL PARK, CALIFORNIA, C. 1948

Few people realize that for most of his life, Ansel relied on commercial work to "keep the wolf from the door" (one of his favorite expressions). Kodak was among his biggest clients, and he produced hundreds of color transparencies that were reproduced in their advertisements in *Life, Time,* and *Fortune*. They were also blown up to gigantic scale—18 x 60 feet—and displayed as backlit transparencies called "Coloramas" in the vaulted halls of New York's Grand Central Station.

In August of 1958, Ansel traveled to the Cascades on assignment for Kodak, but the weather did not cooperate. He bemoaned his lack of success in a letter of September 1 to Nancy Newhall:

> I had a Hell of a trip—the worst drought in the history of the Northwest! Dust (we say the horse trails are covered with SHUST!), forest-fire smoke, heat and no snow—just nice glaciers melting furiously. I (and others) were prepared with tents, warm longies, heavy shirts, etc.—there was not one cool shirt in the bunch. NO pictures worth their hypo! Never did I carry so many pounds of cameras for such a slight result! Ah Wilderness. Better luck next time! No Colorama, of course!

In spite of the adverse weather, Ansel made two photographs that he exhibited and published, the forest detail opposite and the image on page 115.

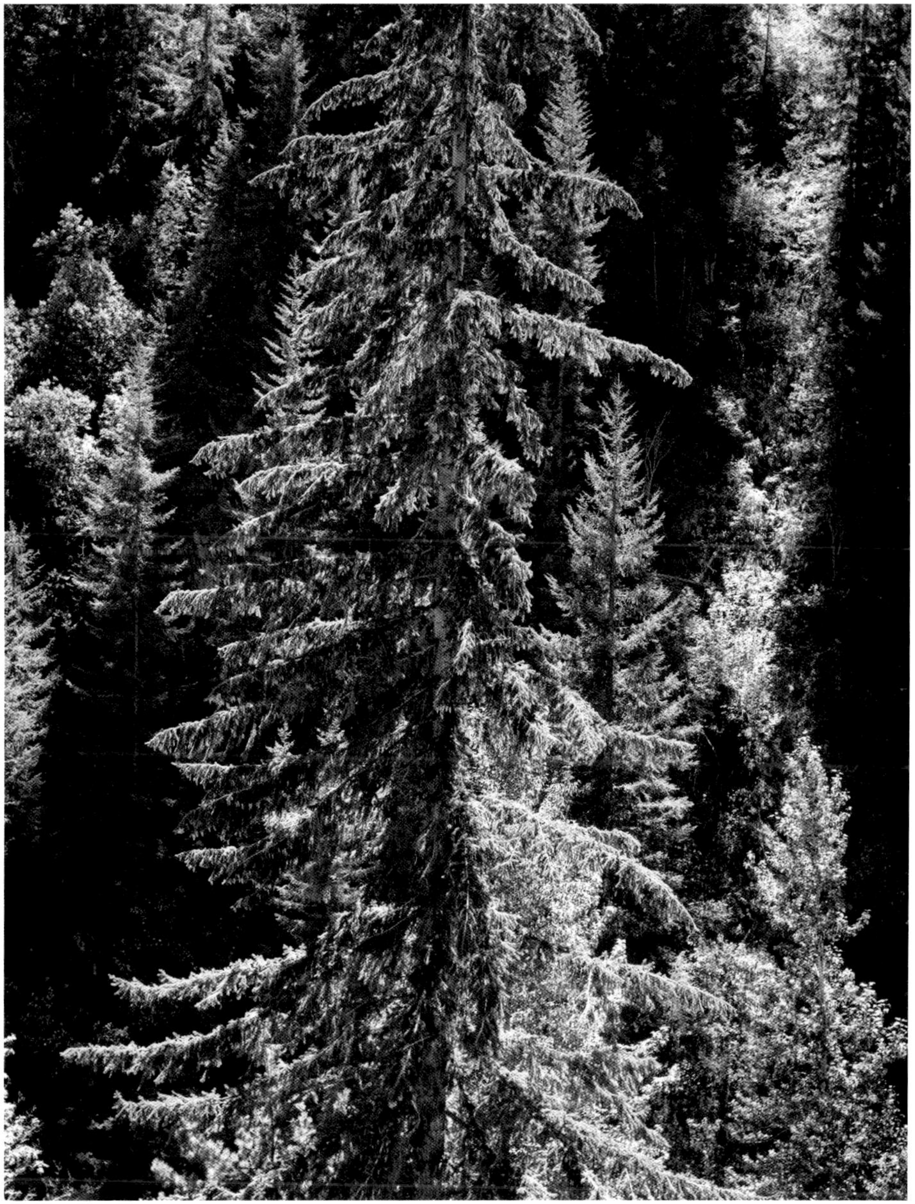

STEHEKIN RIVER FOREST, NORTH CASCADES NATIONAL PARK, WASHINGTON, 1958

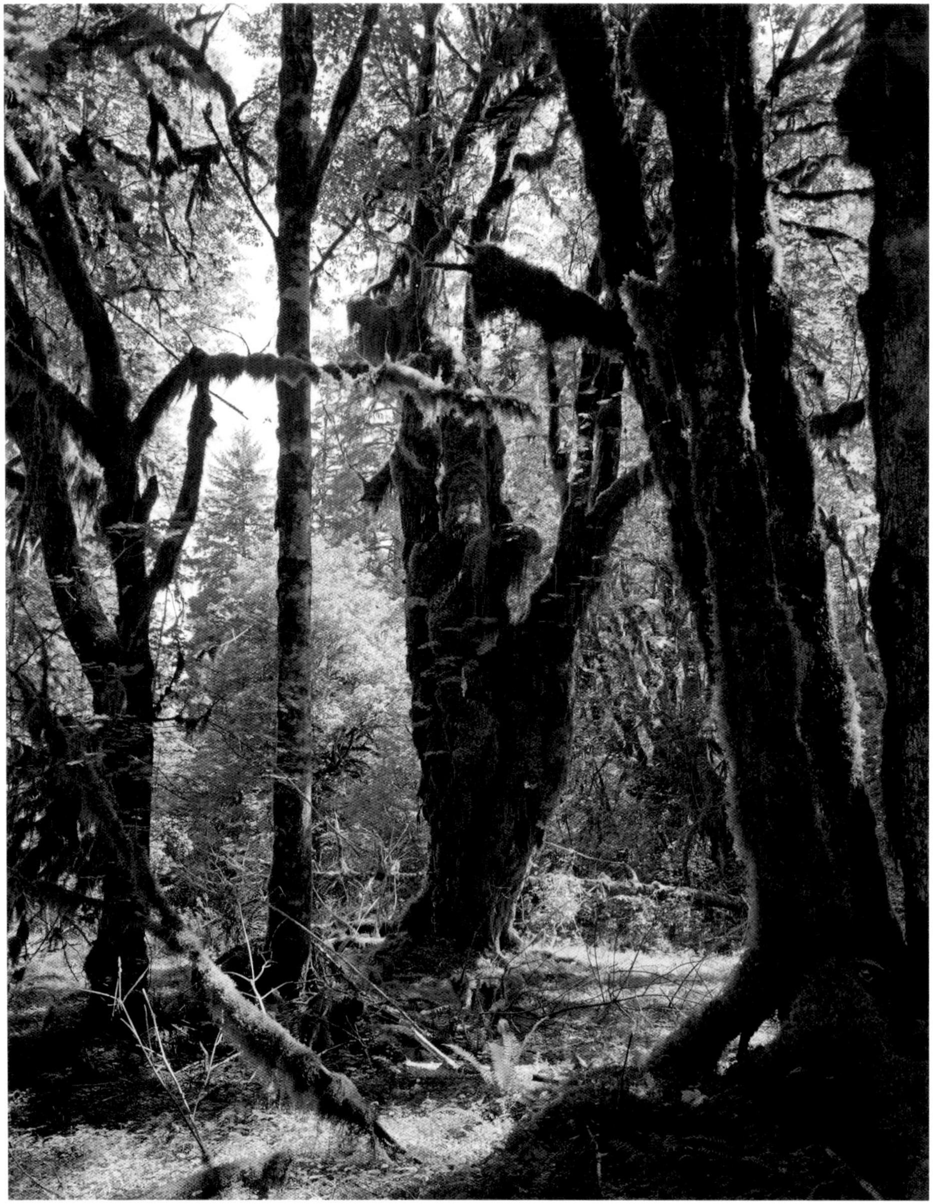

RAIN FOREST, OLYMPIC NATIONAL PARK, WASHINGTON, C. 1948

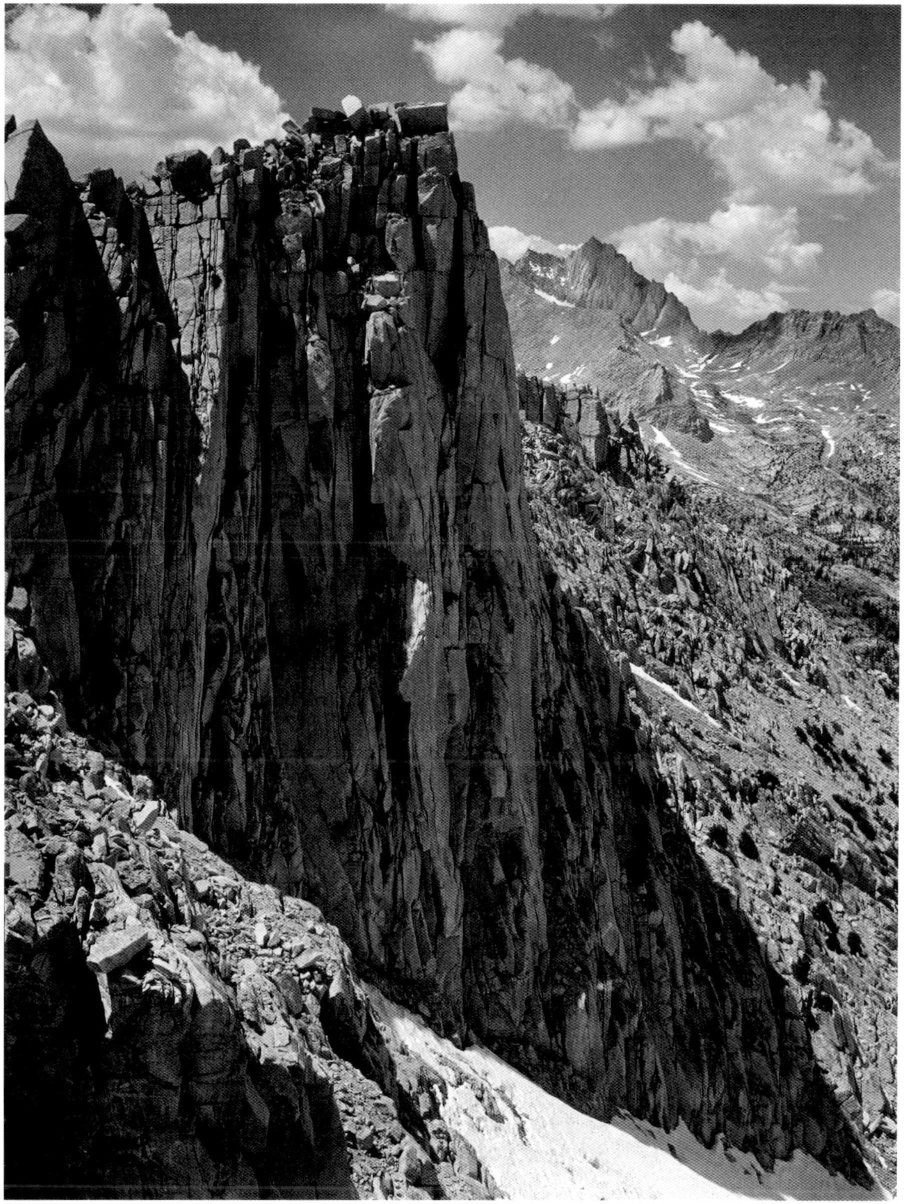

PEAKS, SIERRA NEVADA, CALIFORNIA, C. 1932

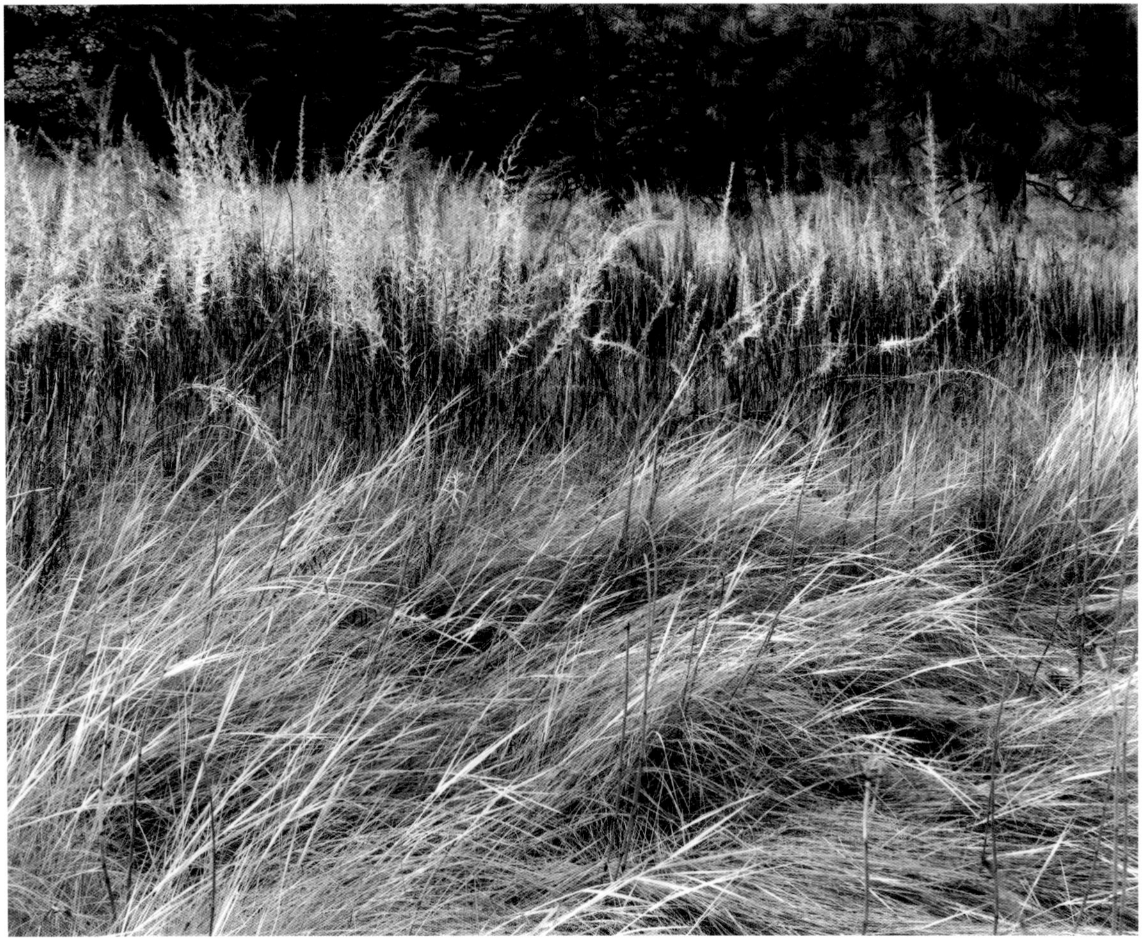

GRASS, YOSEMITE NATIONAL PARK, CALIFORNIA, 1944

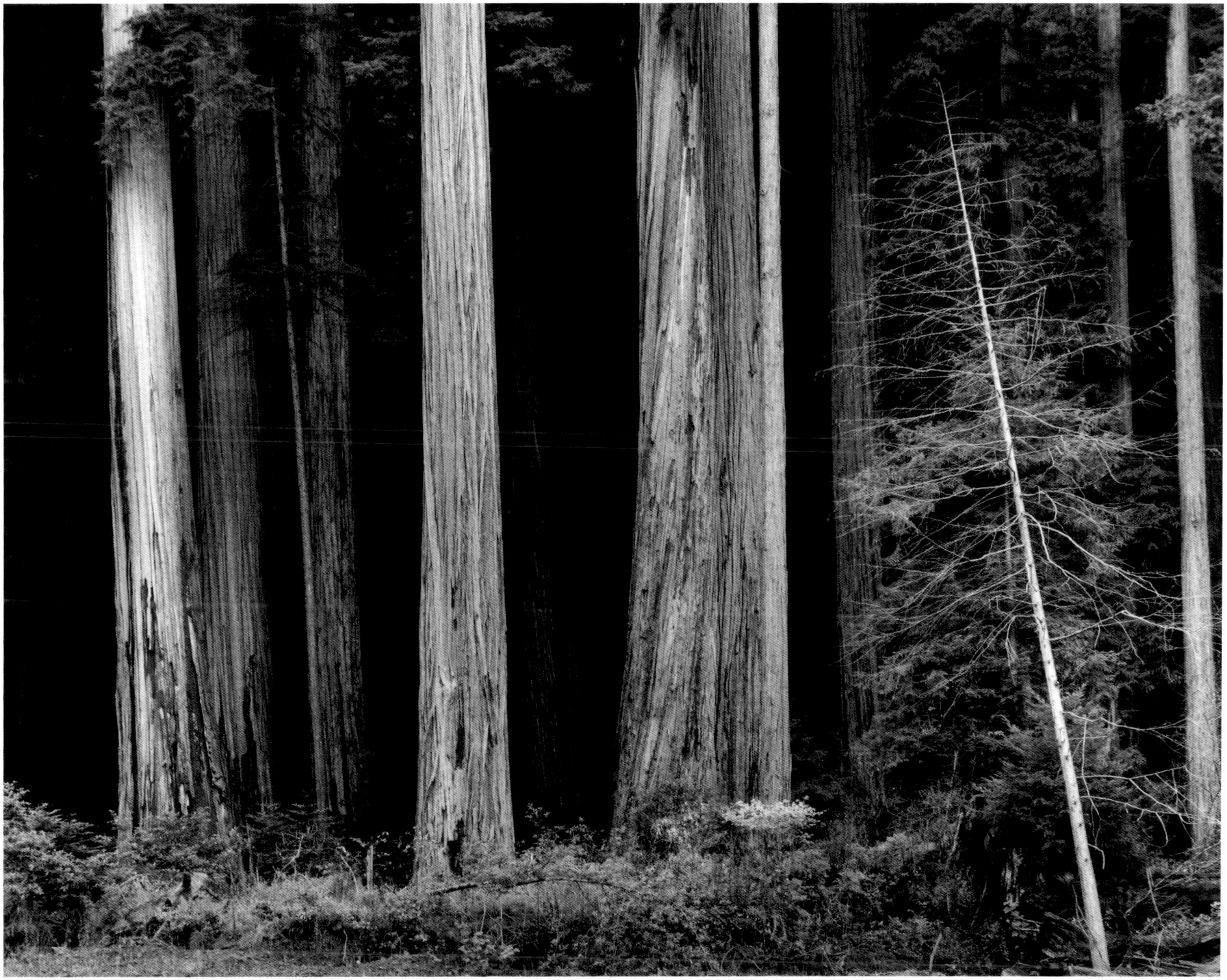

REDWOODS, BULL CREEK FLAT, SOUTH OF REDWOOD NATIONAL PARK, CALIFORNIA, C. 1960

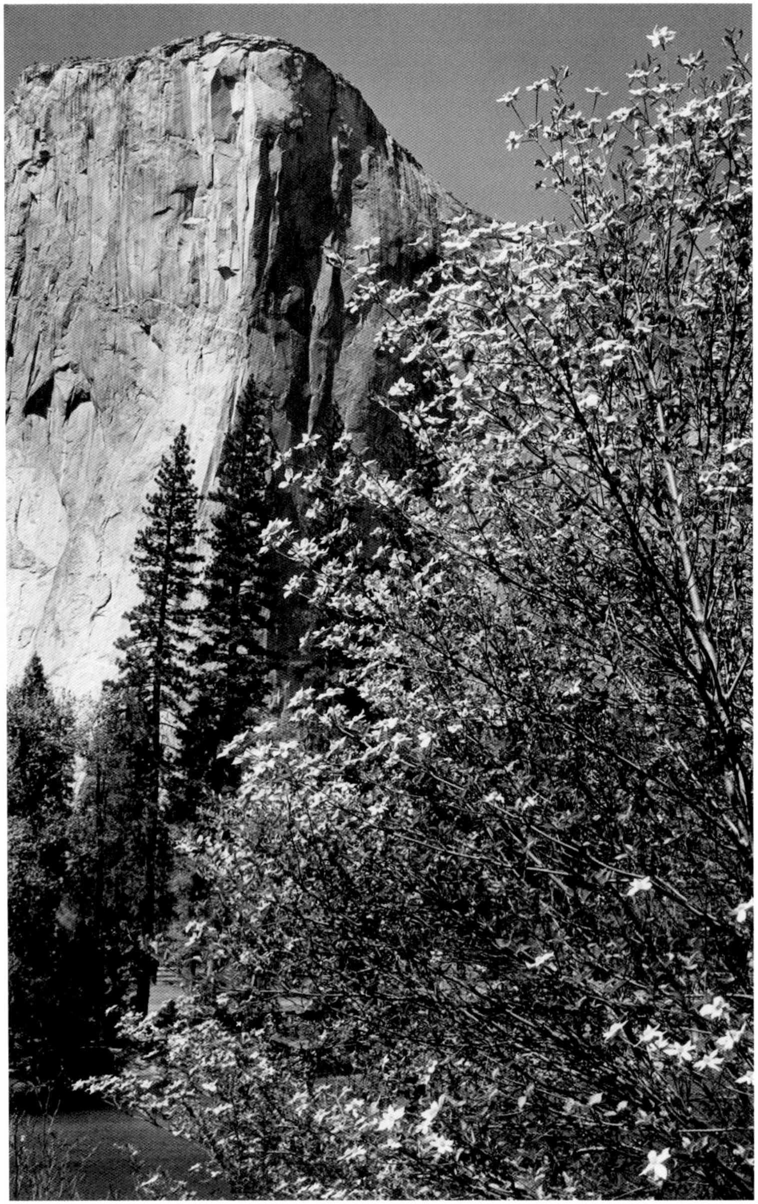

EL CAPITAN, DOGWOOD, YOSEMITE NATIONAL PARK, CALIFORNIA, C. 1940

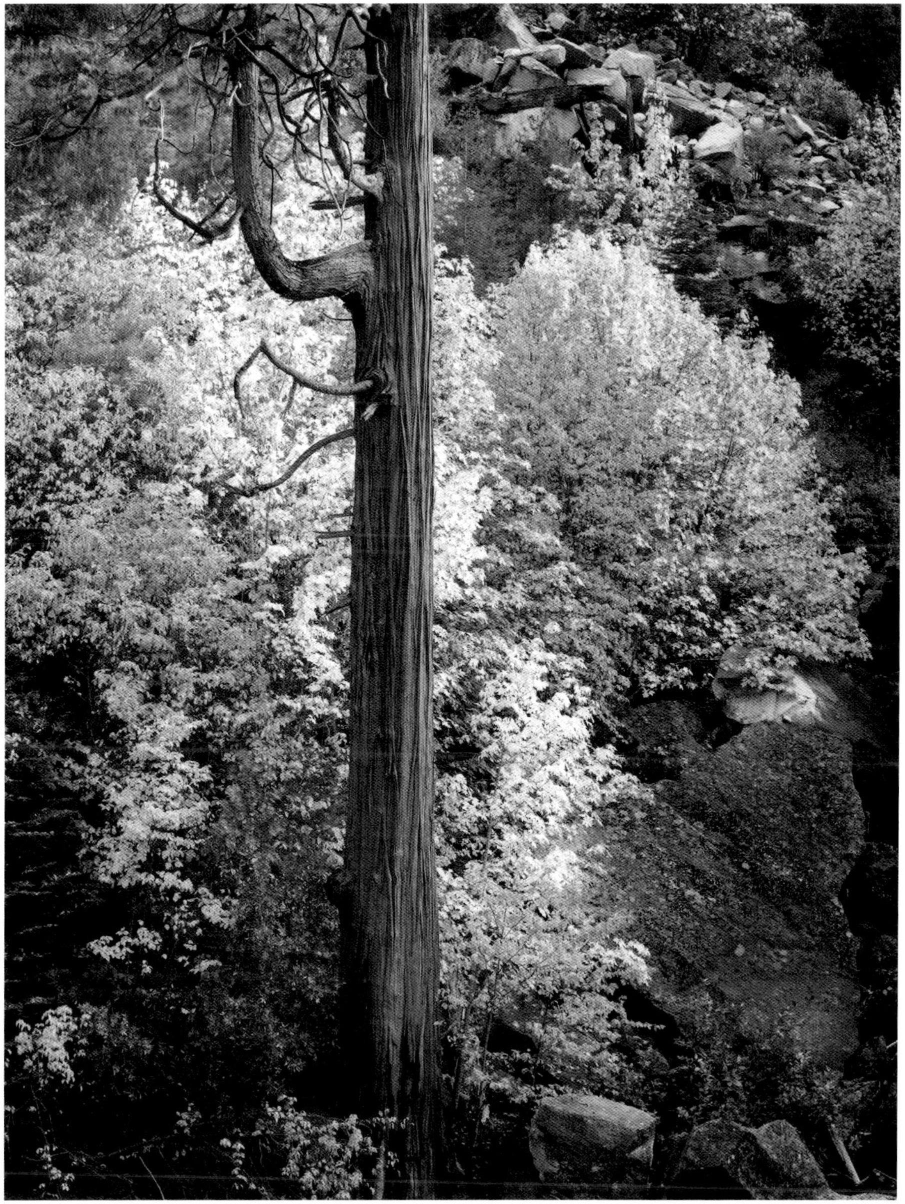

FOREST, AUTUMN, YOSEMITE NATIONAL PARK, CALIFORNIA, 1965

In the search for photographs that merited inclusion in this book, it was a joy to discover a vintage print of this hitherto unknown image. Ansel originally gave the print to his wife, Virginia; it is now in The David Arrington Collection. The photograph on page 56 reproduces another unusual image by Ansel, of a fallen tree near Sentinel Dome, known only through a proof print at the Center for Creative Photography in Tucson, Arizona.

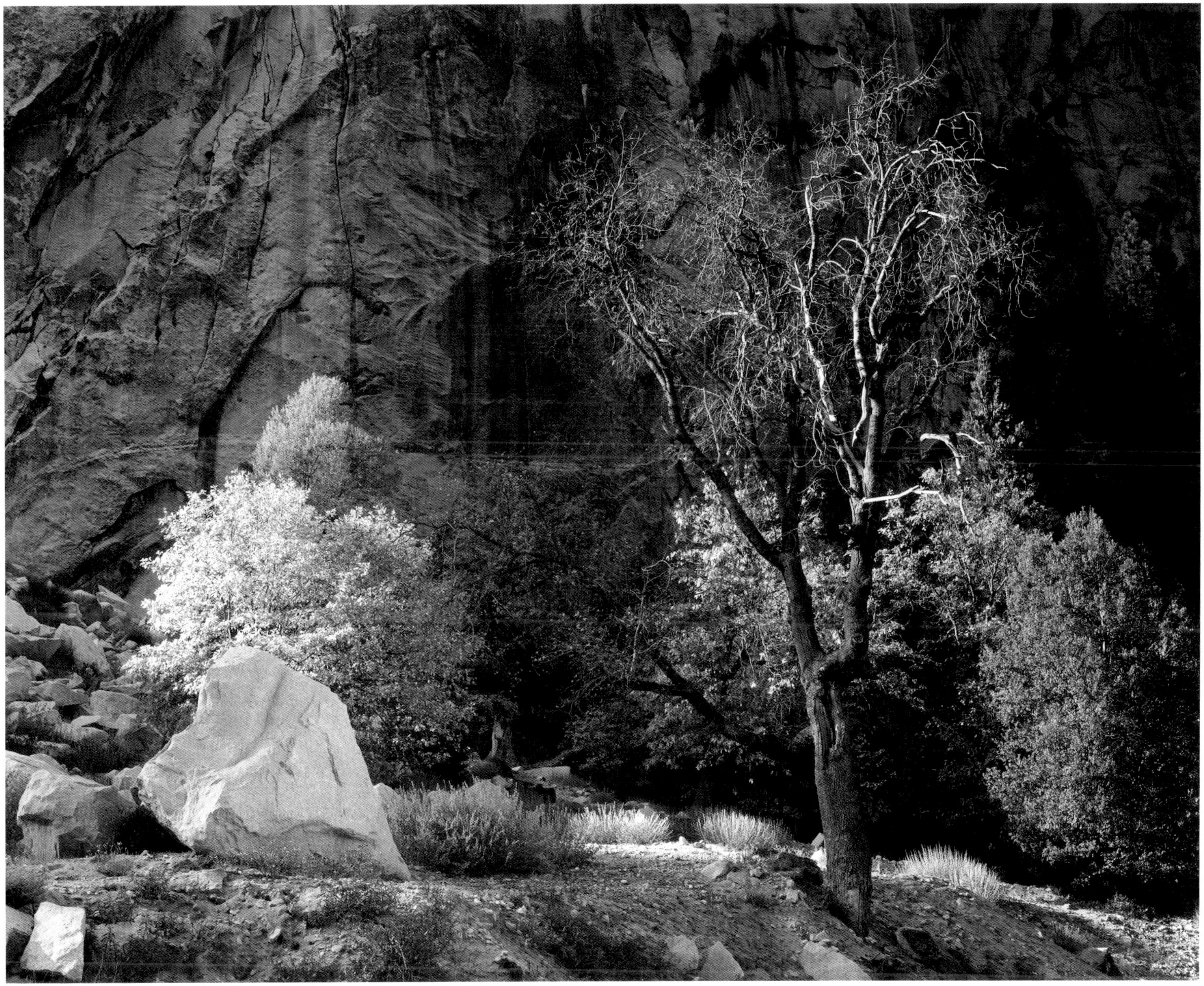

BOULDER AND TREES, AUTUMN, YOSEMITE NATIONAL PARK, CALIFORNIA, C. 1950

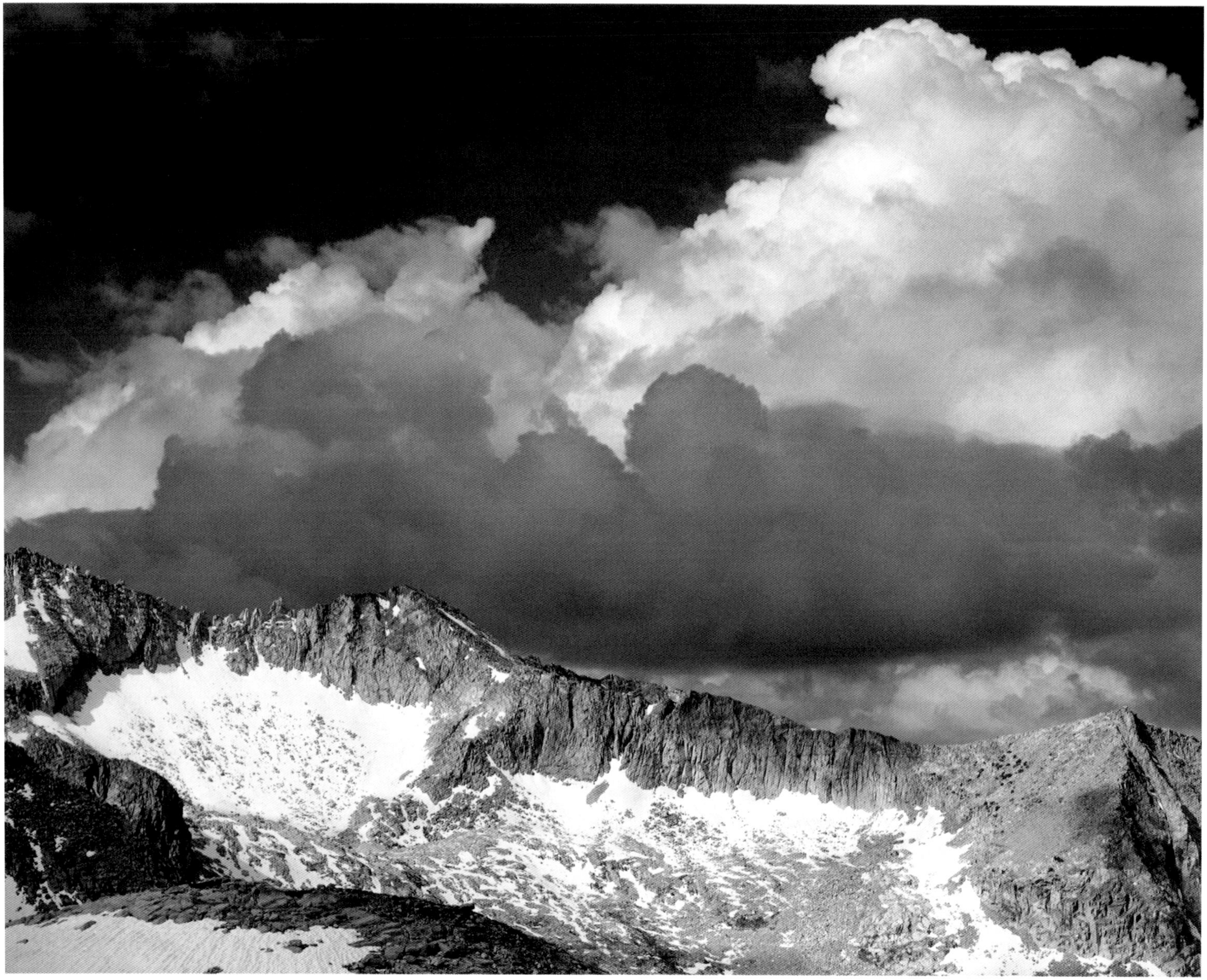

CLOUDS, KINGS RIVER DIVIDE, SIERRA NEVADA, CALIFORNIA, C. 1932

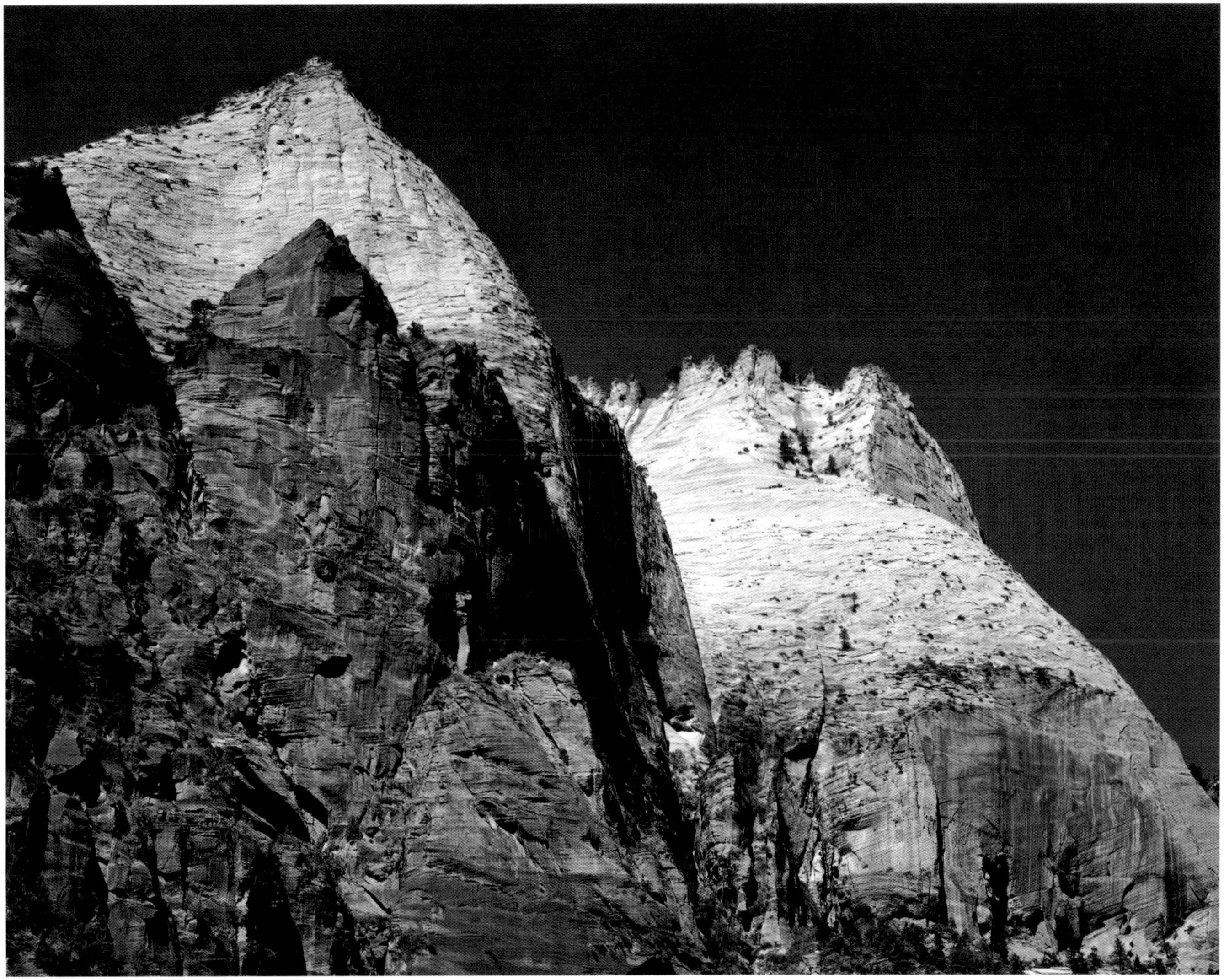

ZION NATIONAL PARK, UTAH, C. 1942

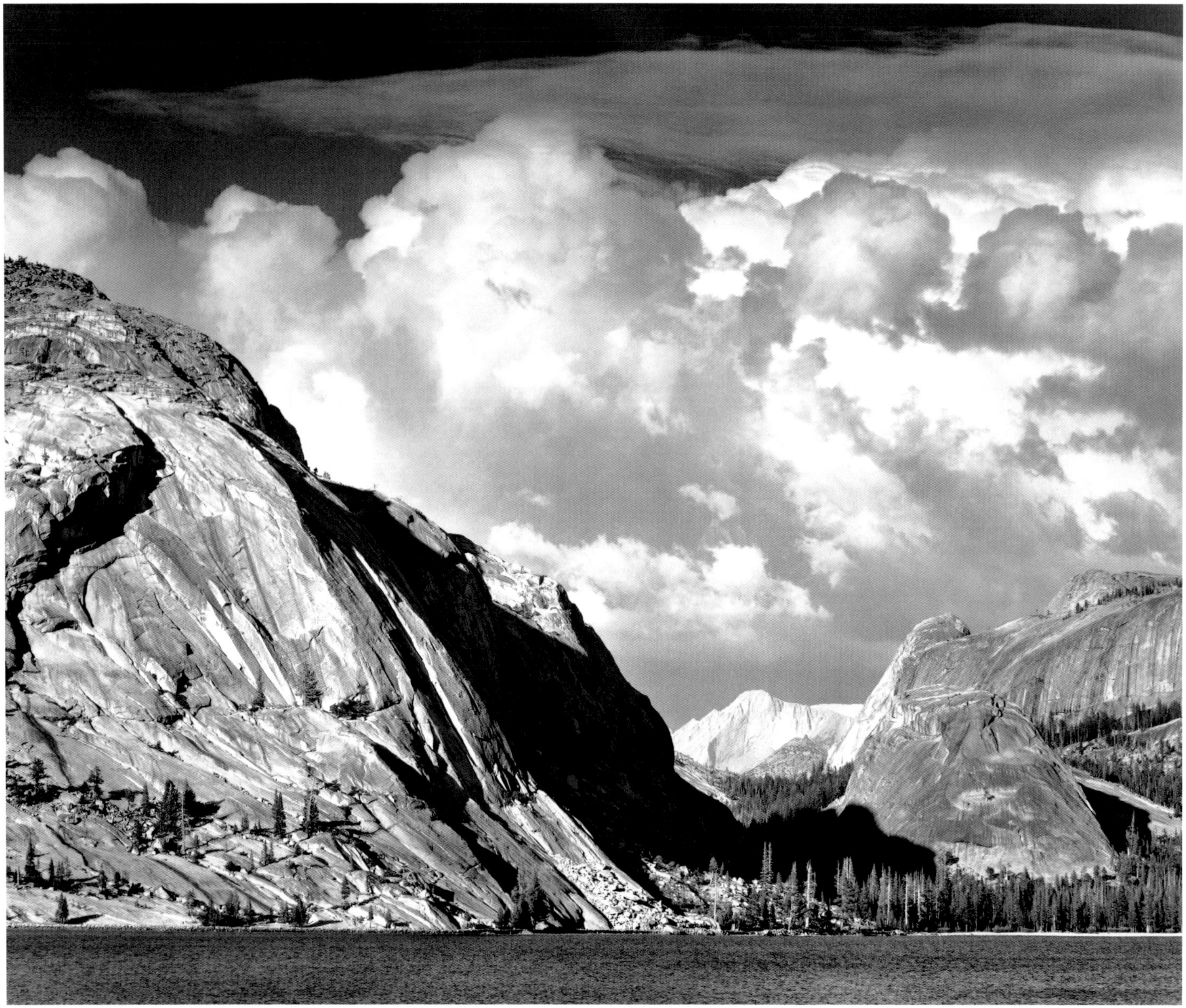

TENAYA LAKE, MOUNT CONNESS, YOSEMITE NATIONAL PARK, CALIFORNIA, C. 1946

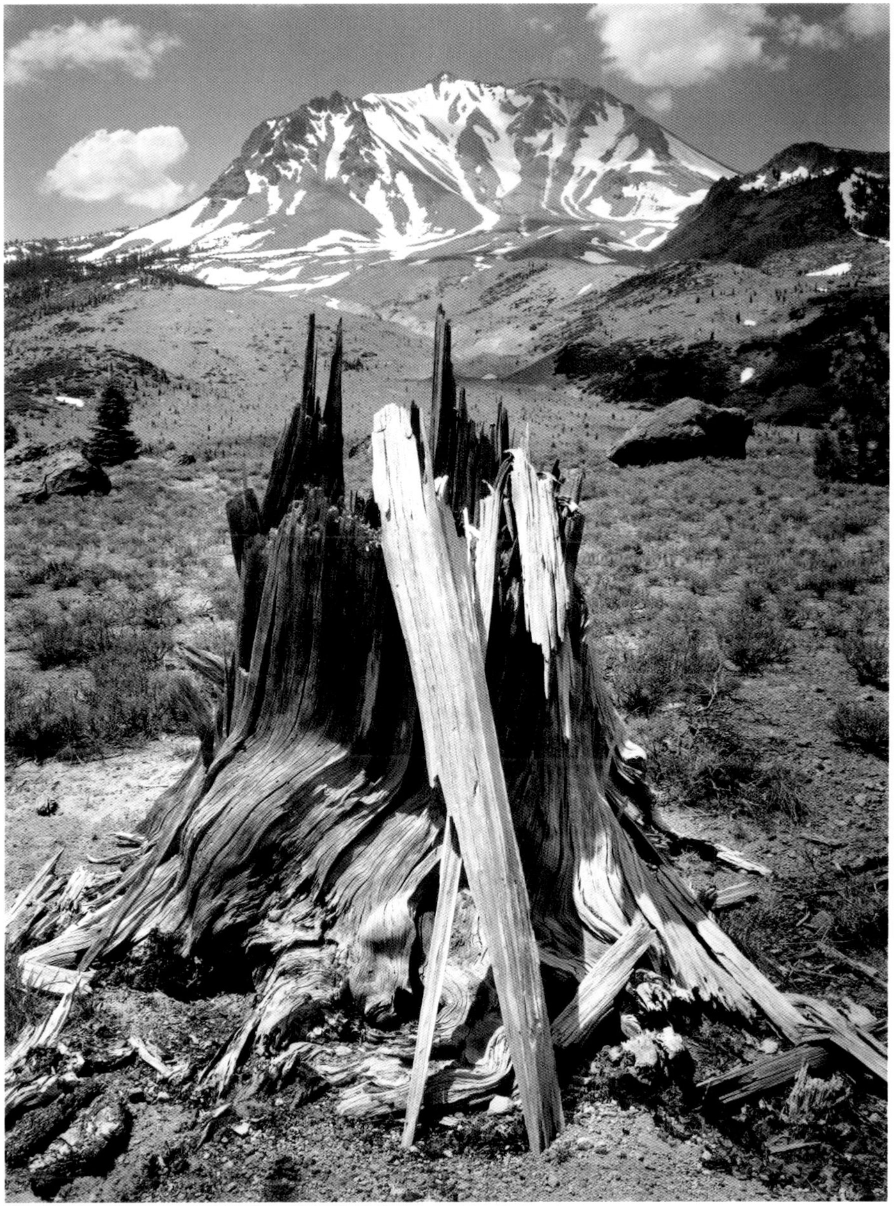

MOUNT LASSEN FROM DEVASTATED AREA, LASSEN VOLCANIC NATIONAL PARK, CALIFORNIA, 1949

On his arrival in October 1948 in Gatlinburg, Tennessee, at the western entrance to the Great Smoky Mountains, Ansel wrote his friend Beaumont Newhall, "The Smokys [sic] are OK in their way, but they are going to be devilish hard to photograph." After five days photographing in the area, Ansel wrote Newhall's wife, Nancy, "I think I have some good things of the Smokies." Of the photographs made in the Smokies, he was enthusiastic about two, this image and a view of Mount LeConte (see page 82).

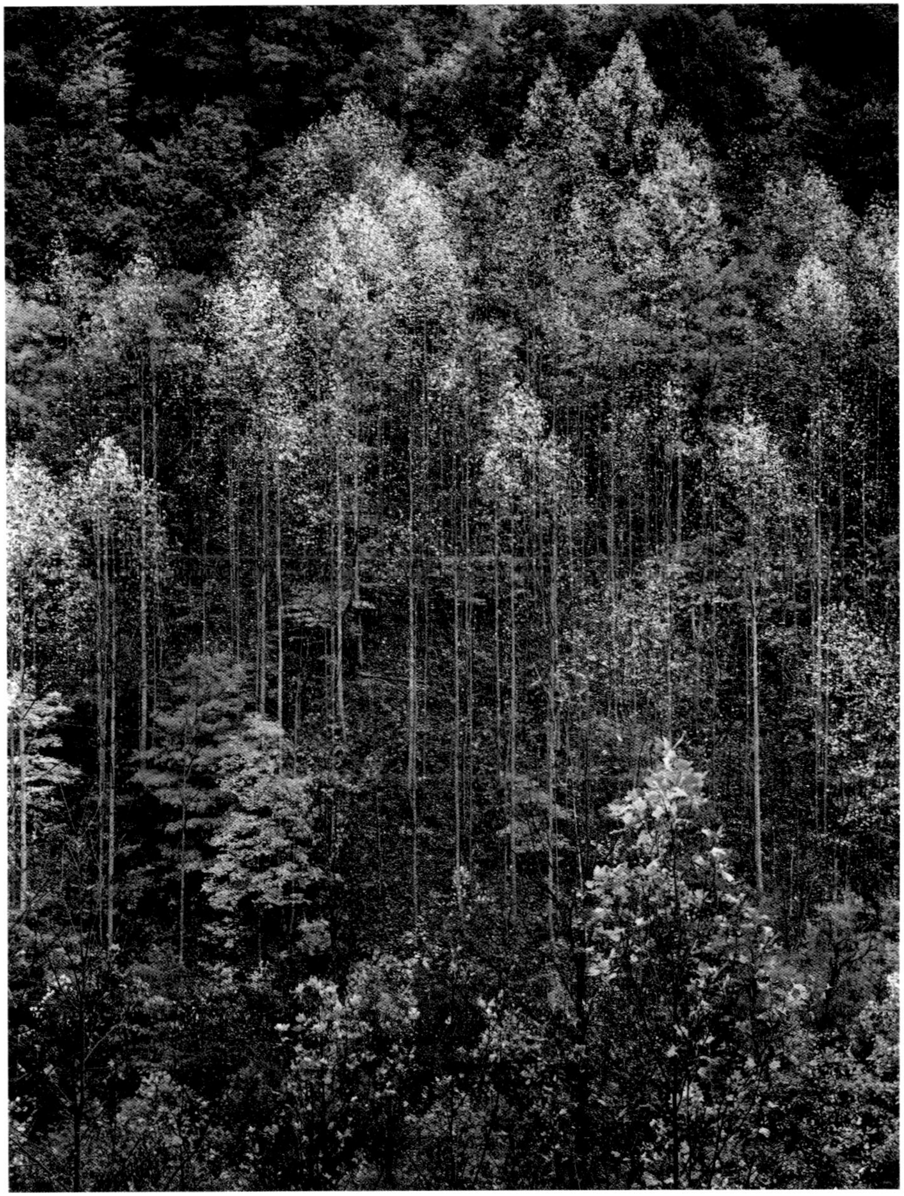

DAWN, AUTUMN, GREAT SMOKY MOUNTAINS NATIONAL PARK, TENNESSEE, 1948

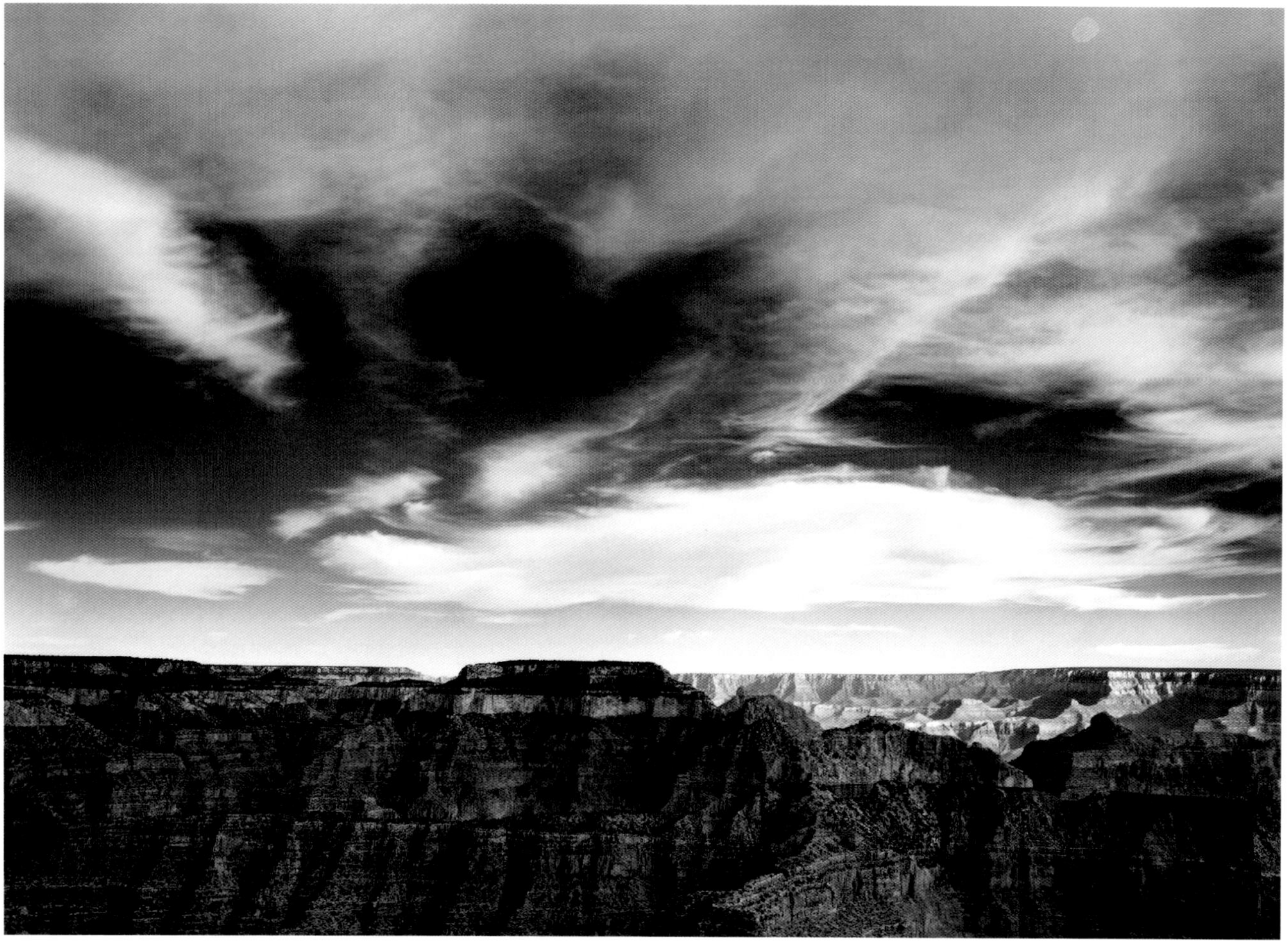

CLIFFS AND CLOUDS, GRAND CANYON NATIONAL PARK, ARIZONA, 1942

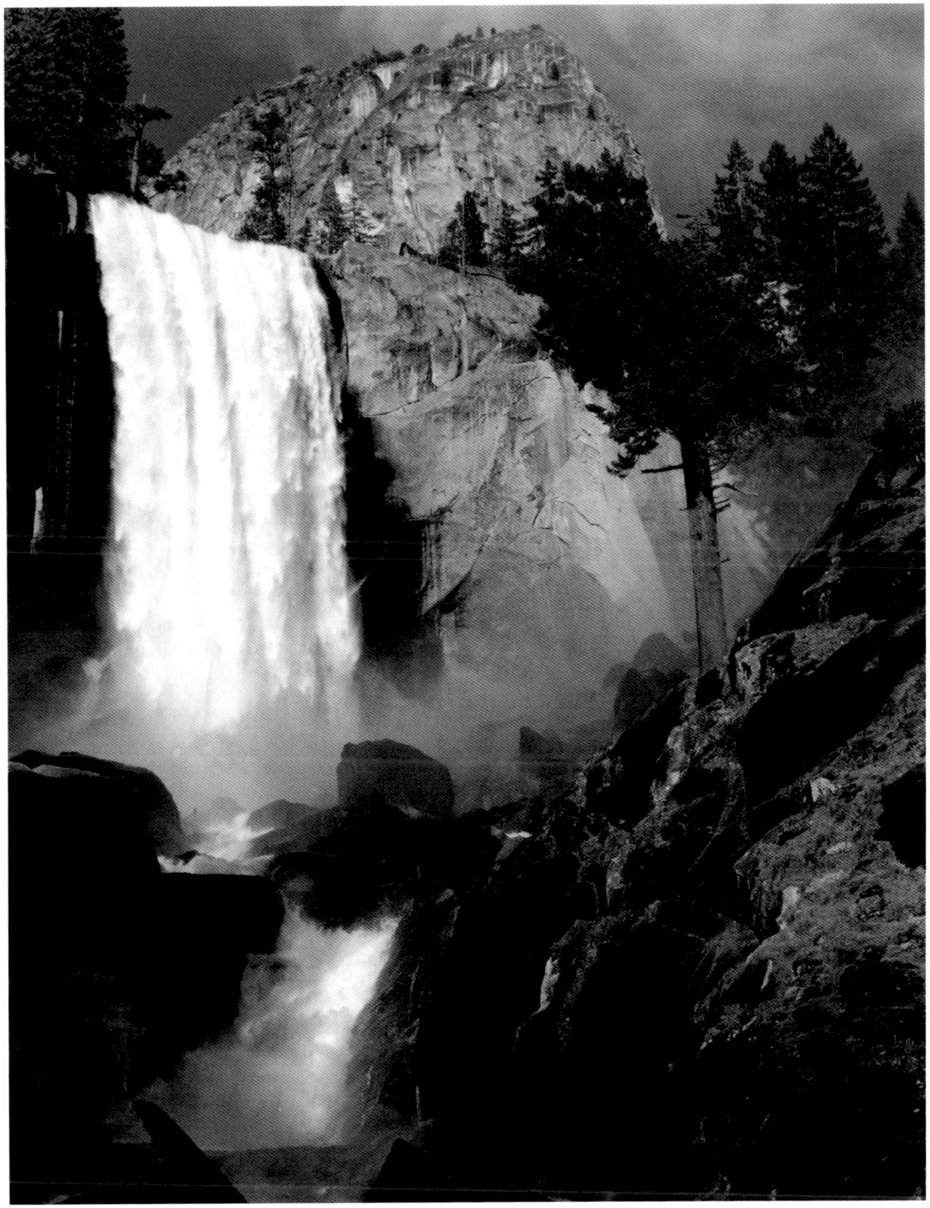

VERNAL FALL, YOSEMITE VALLEY, YOSEMITE NATIONAL PARK, CALIFORNIA, C. 1948

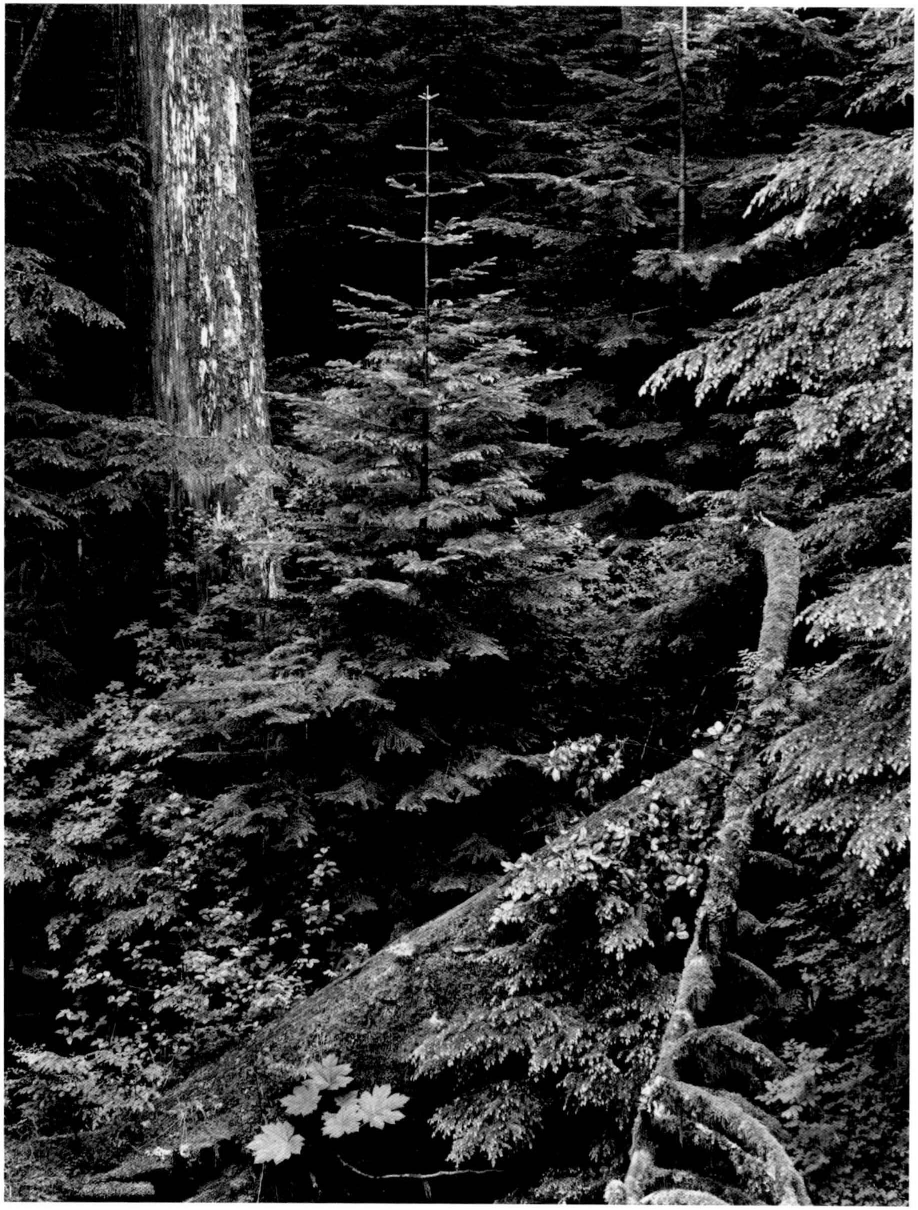

FOREST, EARLY MORNING, MOUNT RAINIER NATIONAL PARK, WASHINGTON, 1949

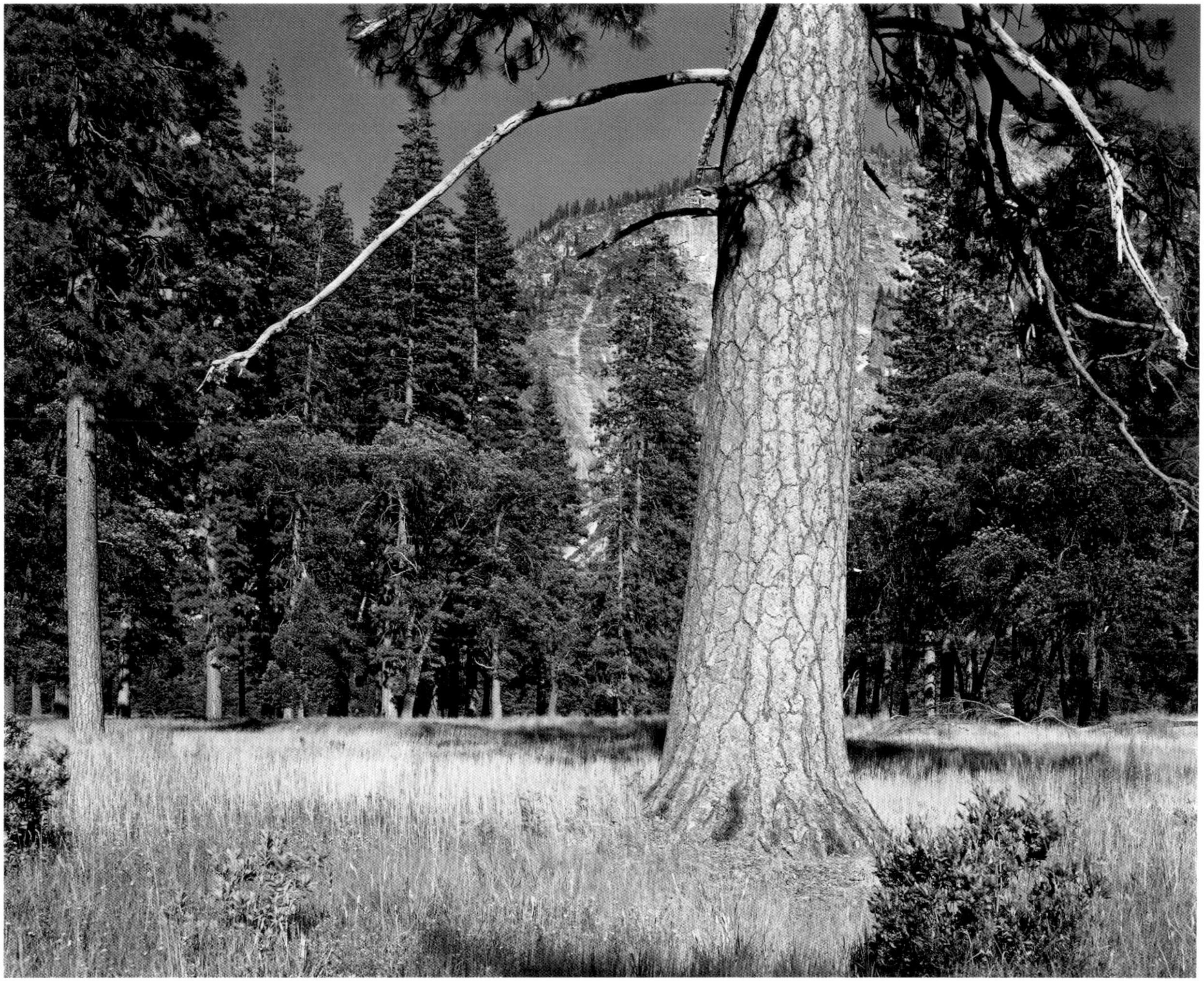

YELLOW PINE TREE, EL CAPITAN MEADOW, YOSEMITE NATIONAL PARK, CALIFORNIA, 1940

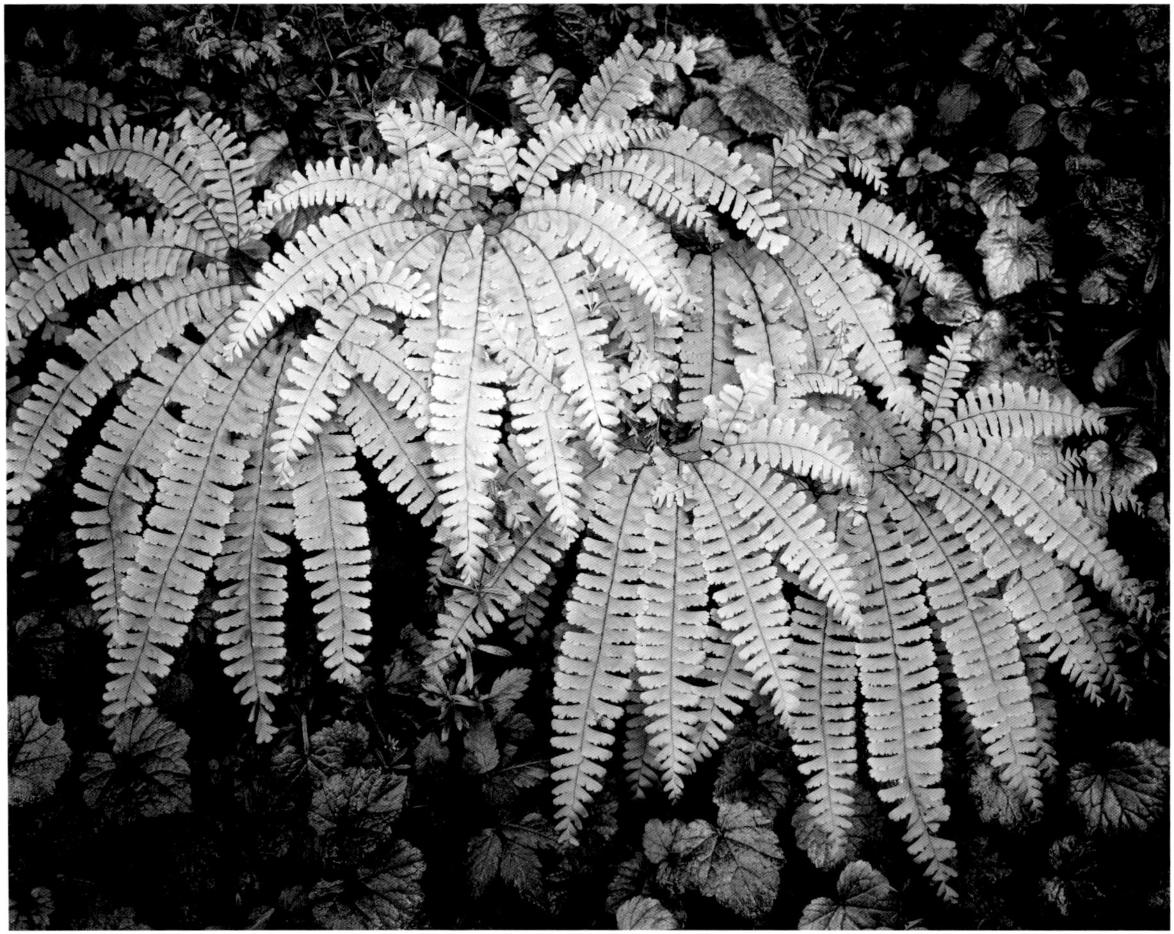

FERN DETAIL, MOUNT RAINIER NATIONAL PARK, WASHINGTON, 1942

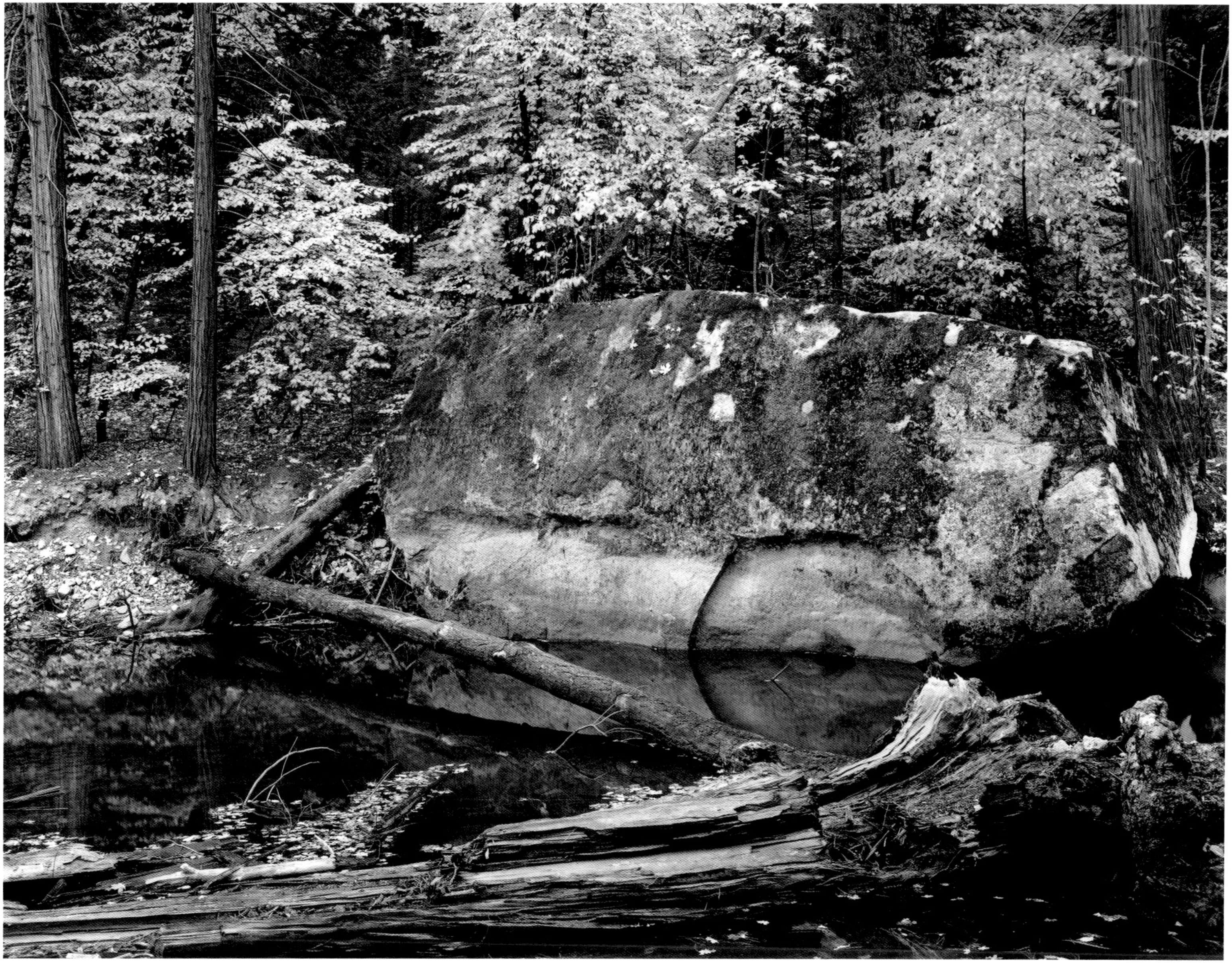

TENAYA CREEK, AUTUMN FOREST, YOSEMITE NATIONAL PARK, CALIFORNIA, C. 1952

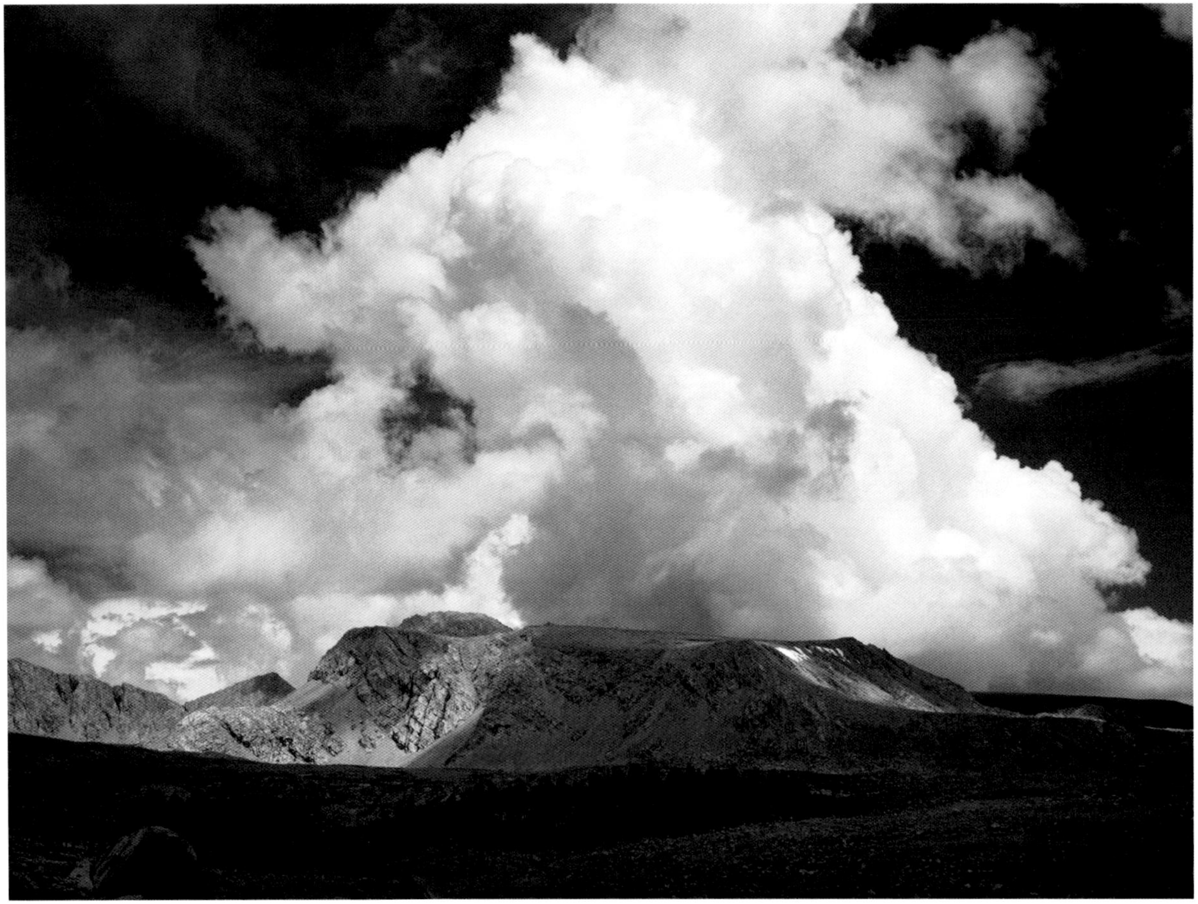

AFTERNOON CLOUDS, NEAR THE KINGS-KERN DIVIDE, SEQUOIA NATIONAL PARK, CALIFORNIA, C. 1936

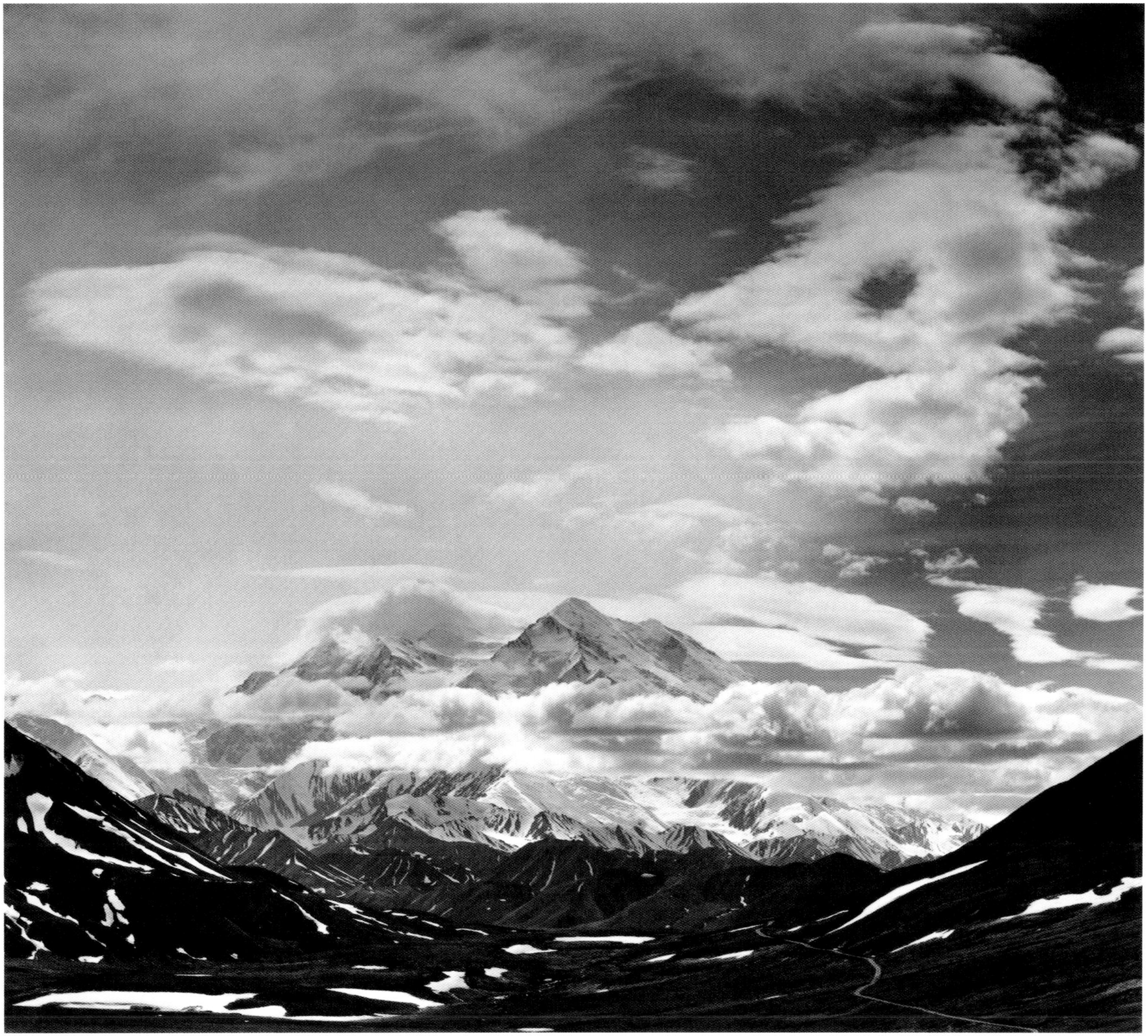

MOUNT MCKINLEY FROM STONEY PASS, DENALI NATIONAL PARK AND PRESERVE, ALASKA, 1948

Alfred Stieglitz, photographer and legendary proponent of modern art, was an inspiration for Ansel. Stieglitz made a number of small jewel-like photographs called "equivalents," of which many were cloud studies. In a letter to Beaumont Newhall in 1949, Ansel described this image of clouds over Golden Canyon as "a sort of Apotheosis of Stieglitz; an equivalent of an equivalent." Ansel often said, "I go out into the world, I make a photograph, and I give it to you as the equivalent of what I saw and felt." He included the image in Portfolio I, produced in 1949, and dedicated the portfolio to Stieglitz, who had died in 1946.

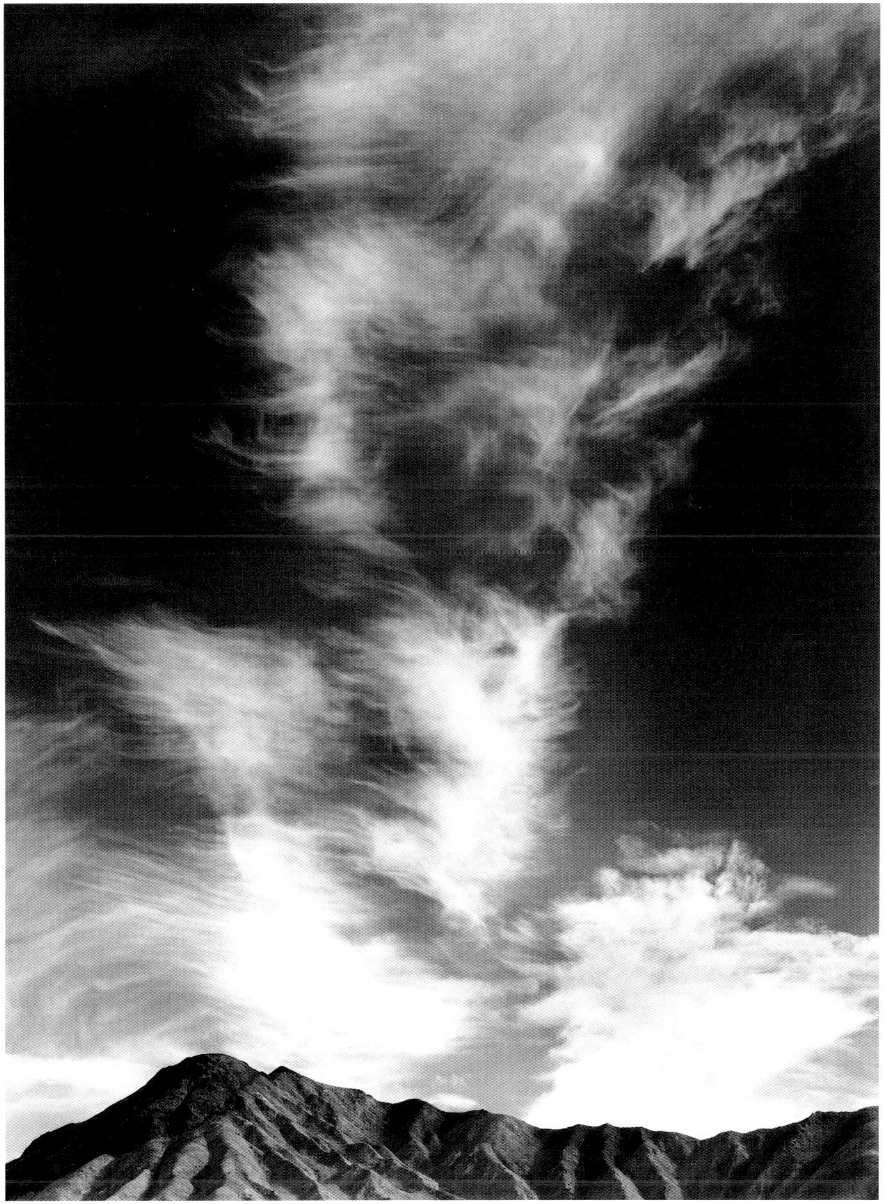

CLOUDS ABOVE GOLDEN CANYON, DEATH VALLEY NATIONAL PARK, CALIFORNIA, 1946

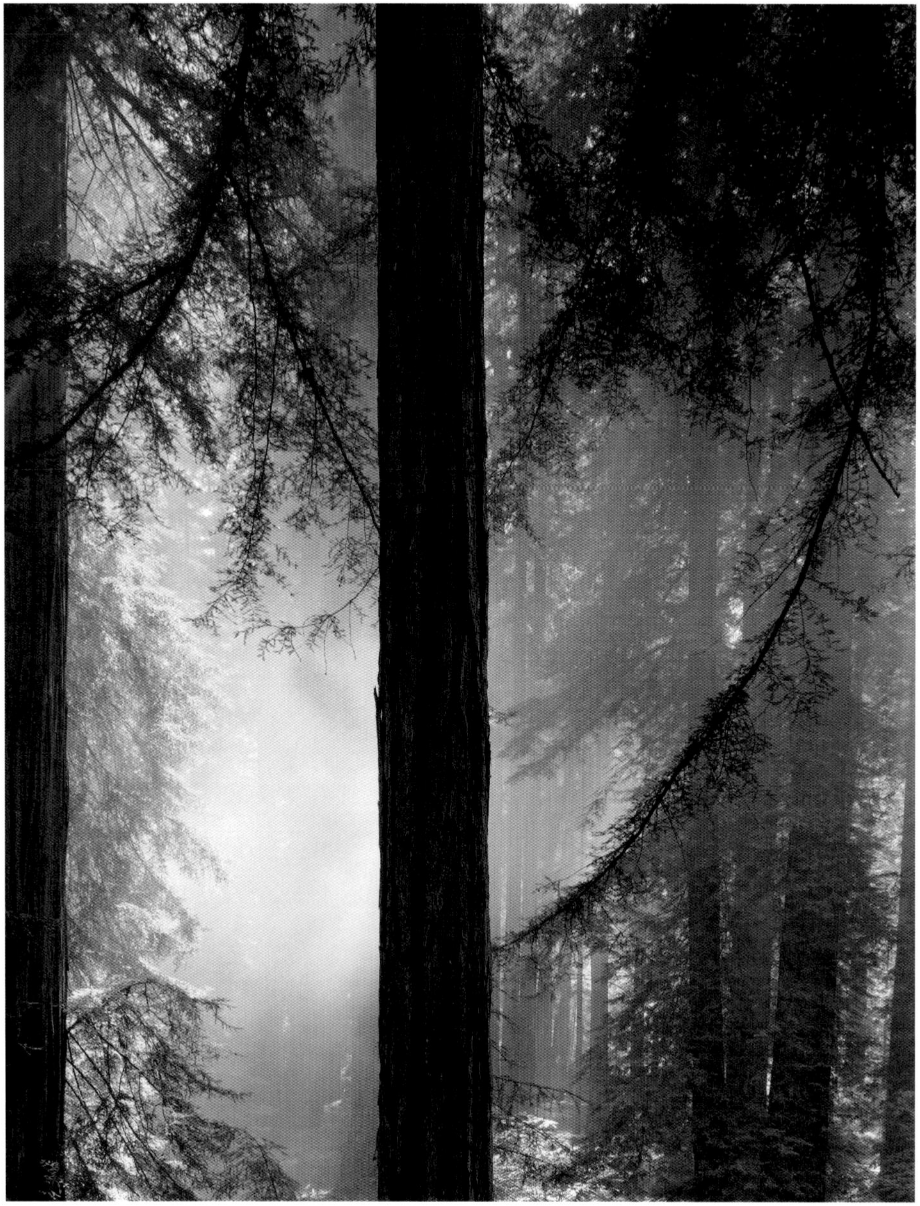

REDWOODS IN FOG, BOHEMIAN GROVE, CALIFORNIA, 1963

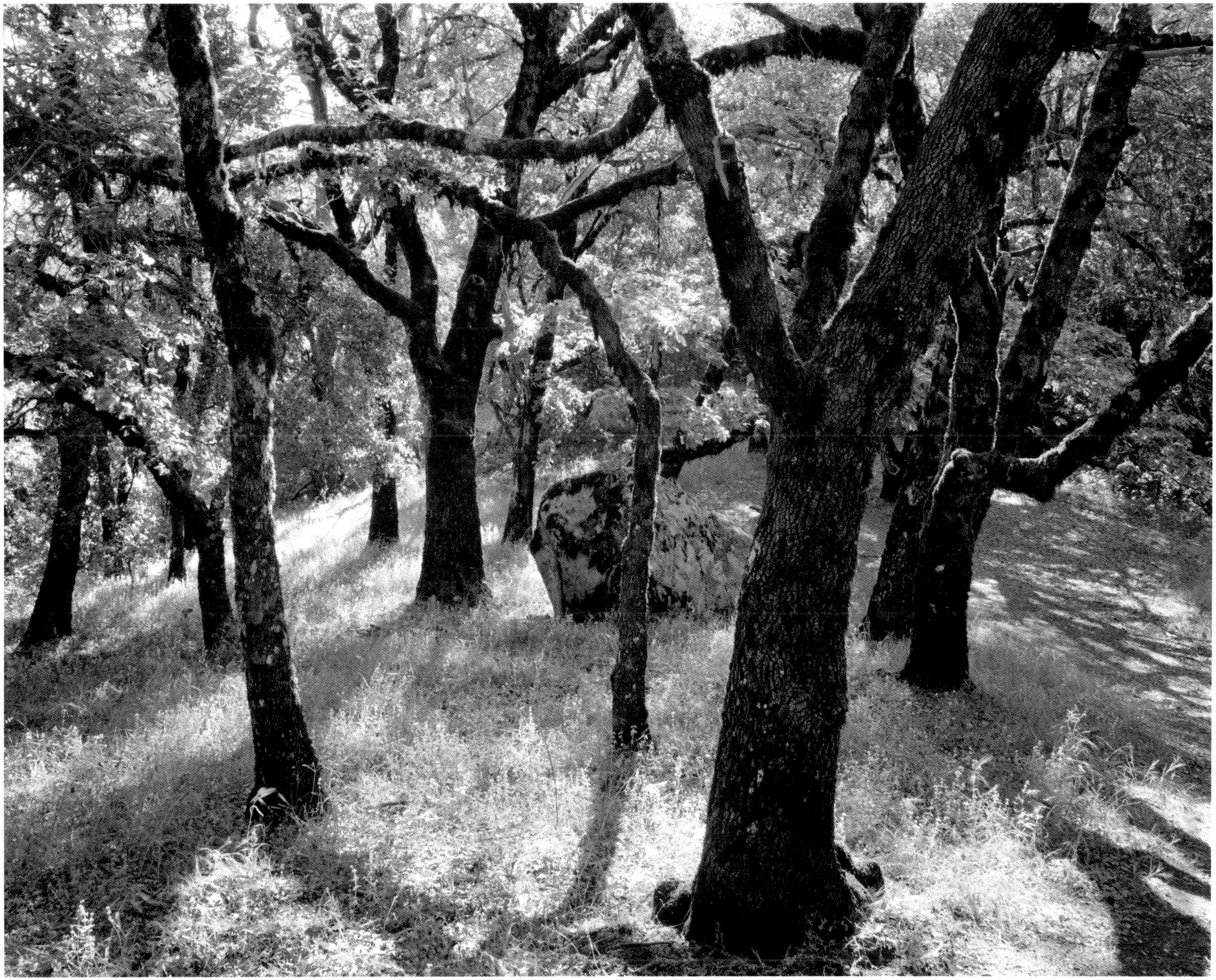

FOREST, CASTLE ROCK STATE PARK, CALIFORNIA, 1962

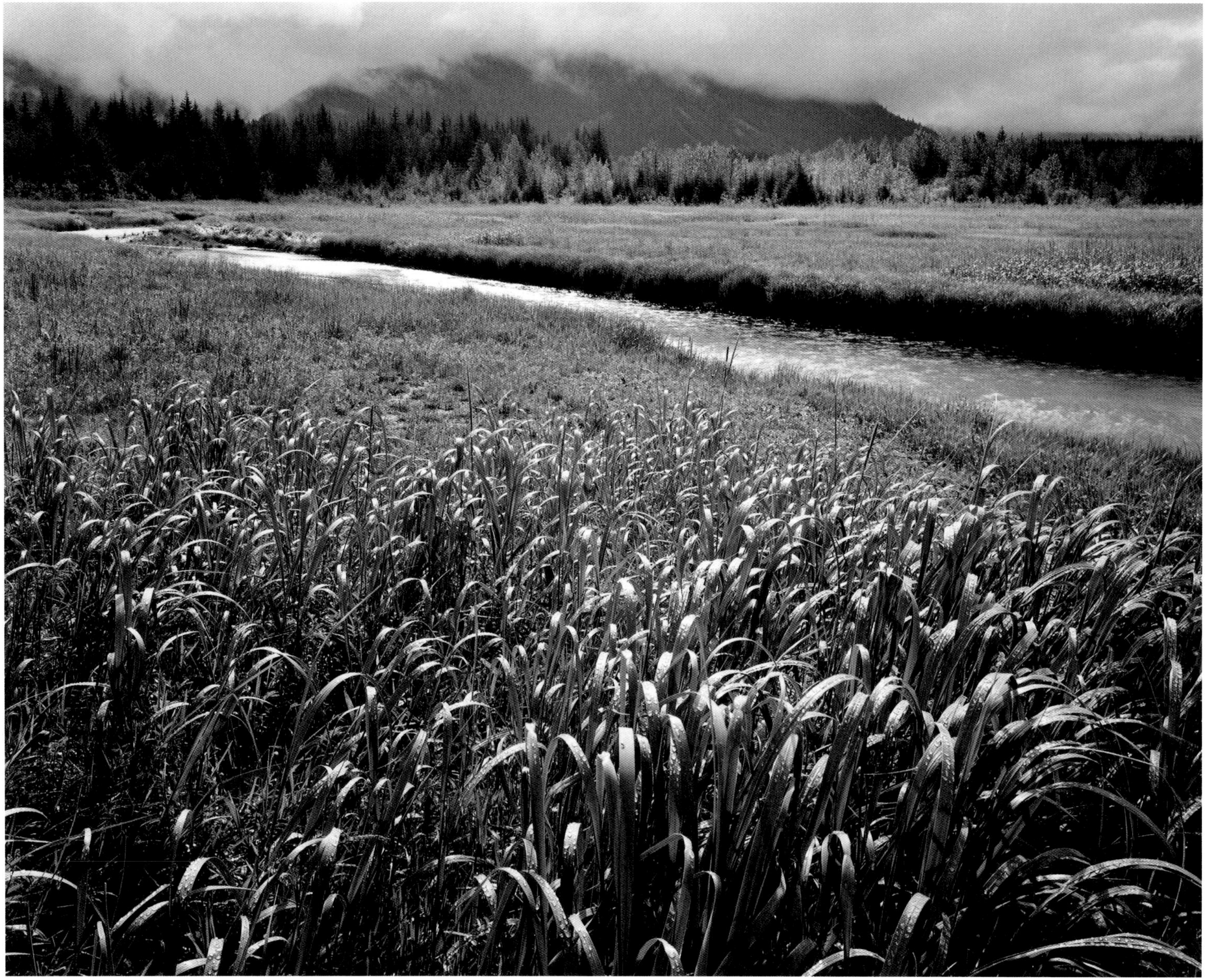

RAIN, BEARTRACK COVE, GLACIER BAY NATIONAL PARK, ALASKA, 1949

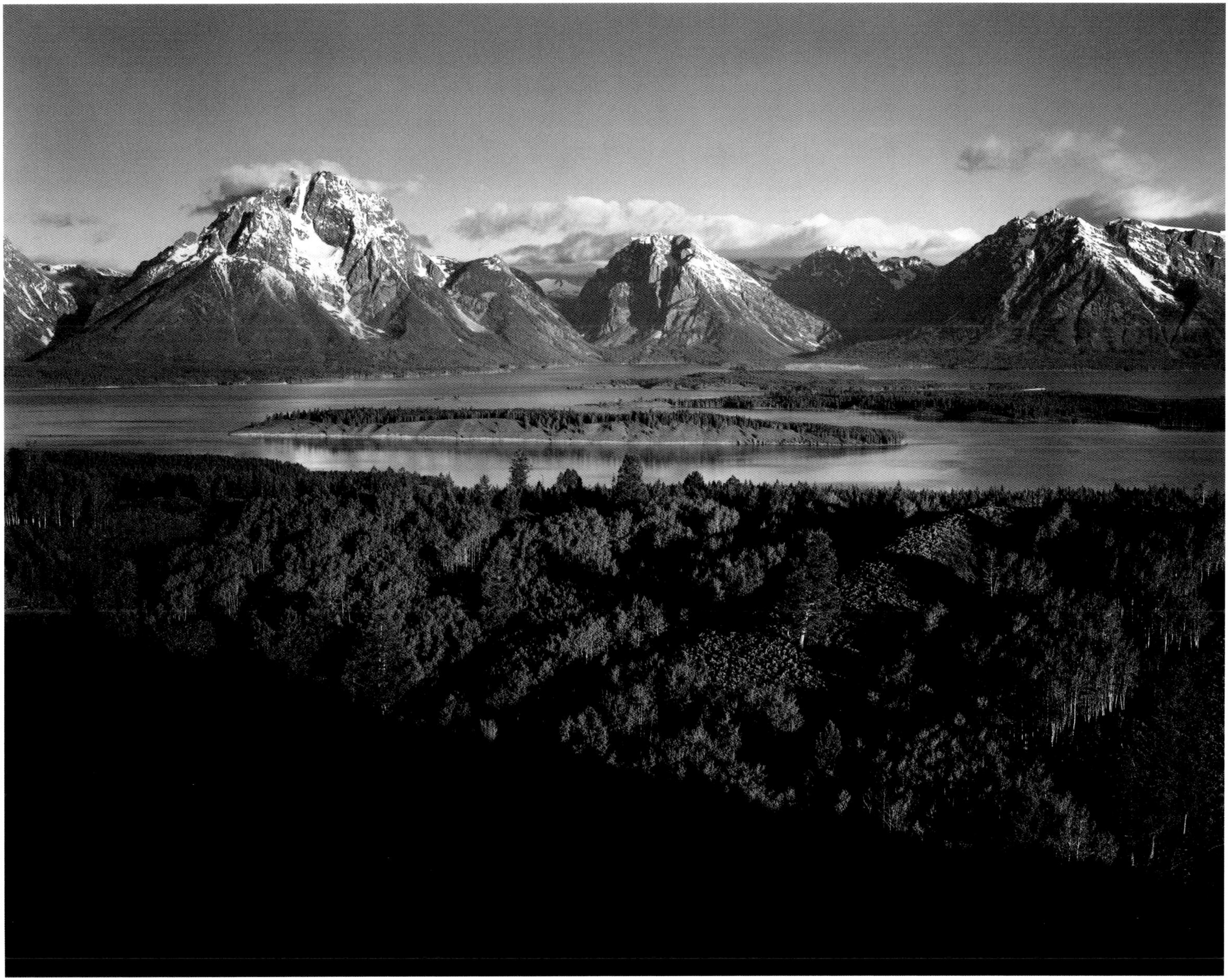

MOUNT MORAN FROM SIGNAL HILL, GRAND TETON NATIONAL PARK, WYOMING, 1942

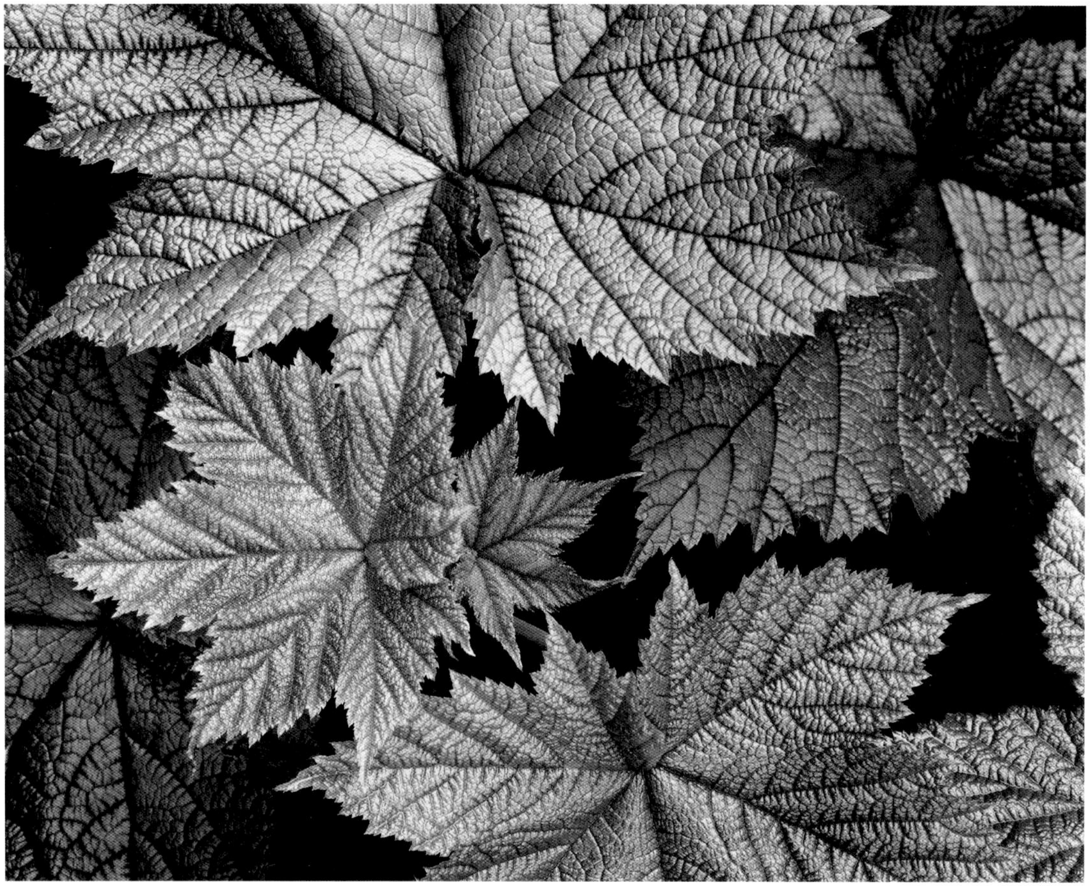

LEAVES, GLACIER NATIONAL PARK, MONTANA, 1942

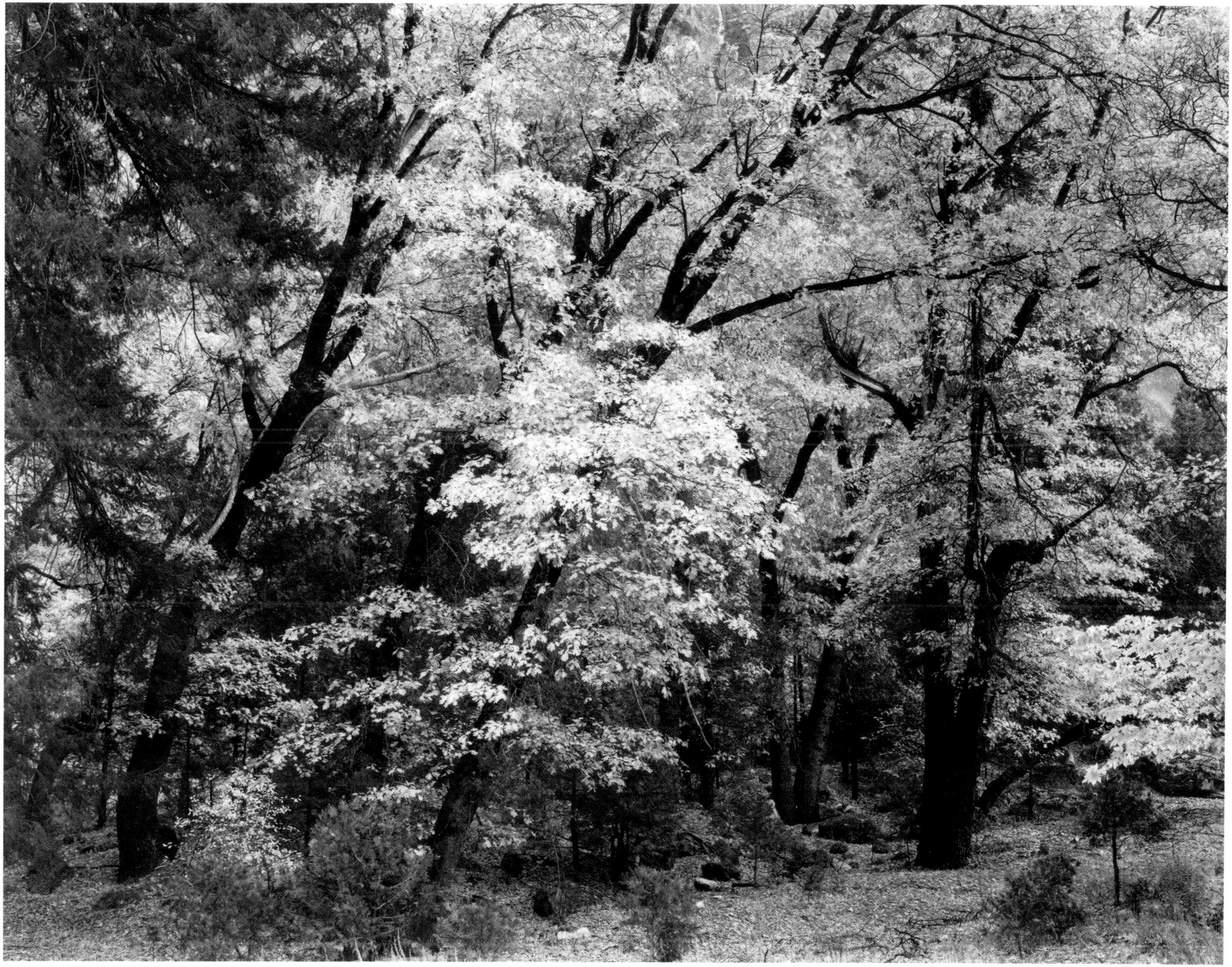

AUTUMN, YOSEMITE VALLEY, YOSEMITE NATIONAL PARK, CALIFORNIA, C. 1933

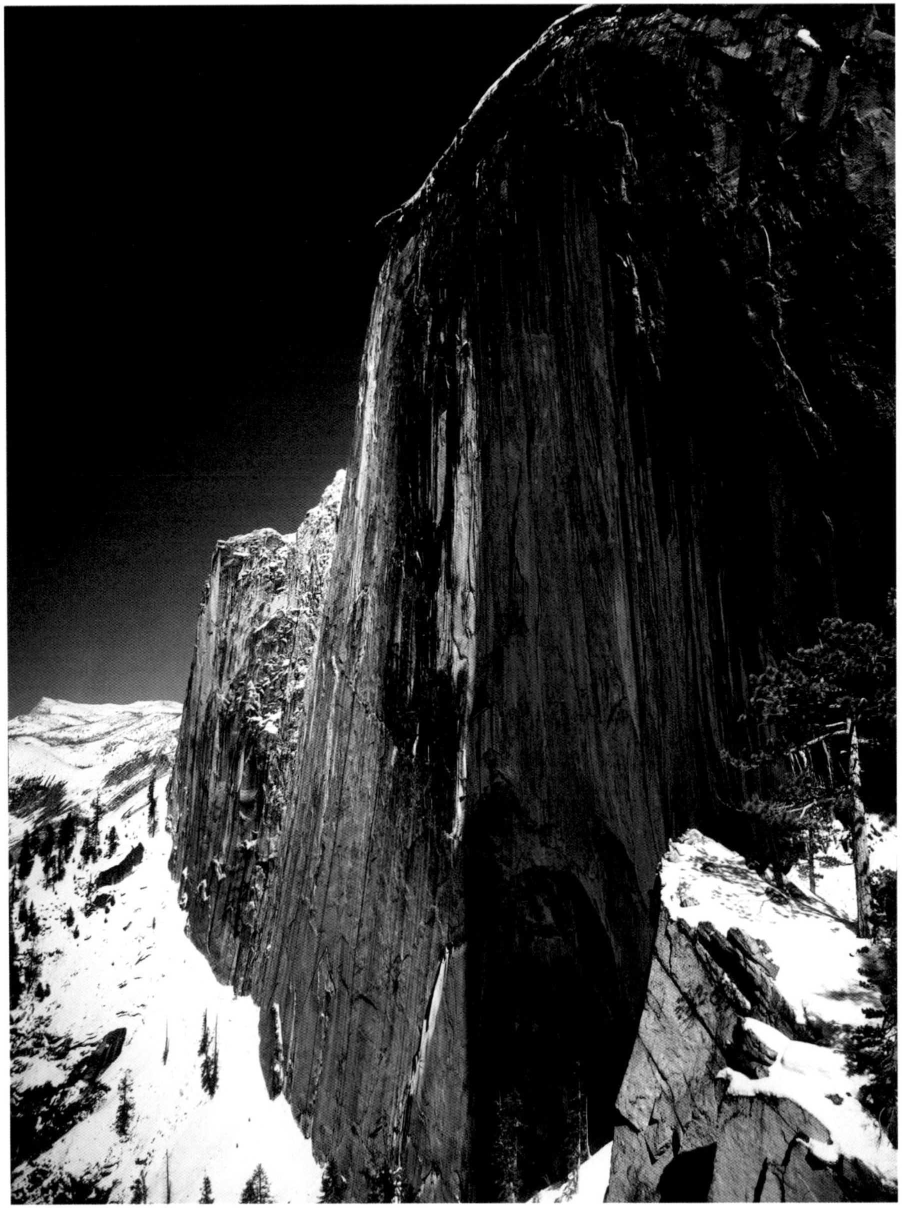

MONOLITH, THE FACE OF HALF DOME, YOSEMITE NATIONAL PARK, CALIFORNIA, 1927

NOTES ON SELECTED PHOTOGRAPHS

ANDREA G. STILLMAN

Frozen Lake and Cliffs, Kaweah Gap, Sierra Nevada, California, 1932

Surrounded by more than a hundred intrepid hikers, Virginia Adams and a few hardy souls swam in the glacier melt of this lake in the Kaweah Gap and sunned on rocks while Ansel set up his tripod and 4 x 5-inch Korona view camera. He made six exposures, some more similar than others. He singled out the first image reproduced here as the best, and it was this photograph that he included in many of his books and exhibitions.

John Szarkowski, the late director of the department of photography at New York's Museum of Modern Art, wrote:

> I will assume that we agree that Adams made the right choice; Kaweah Gap [or Frozen Lake and Cliffs] seems to me not only the best of these six pictures but one of the most memorable of his career. Nevertheless, the other five negatives are not negligible, and might be brought back as trophies by most excellent photographers.

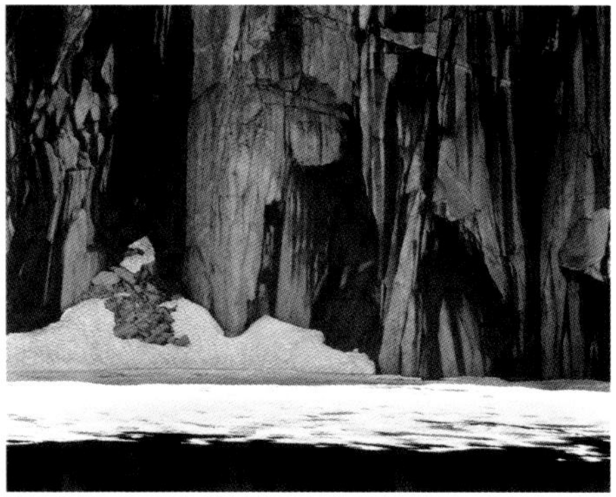

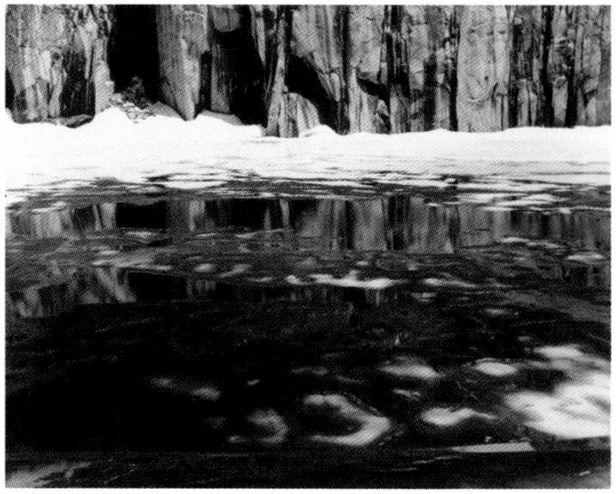

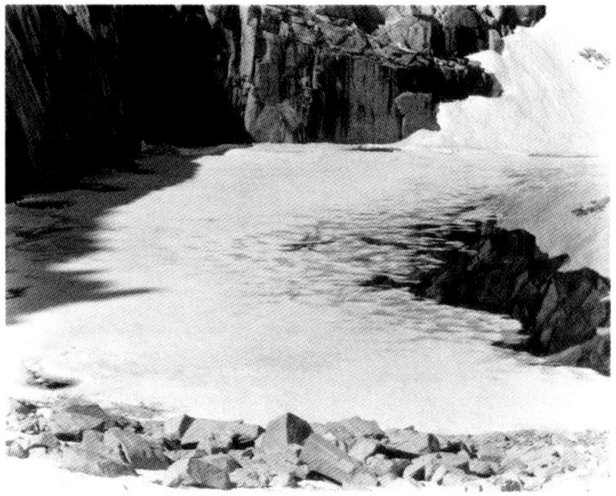

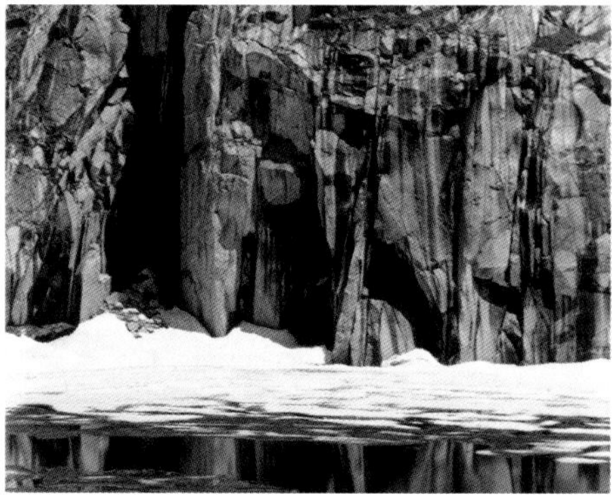

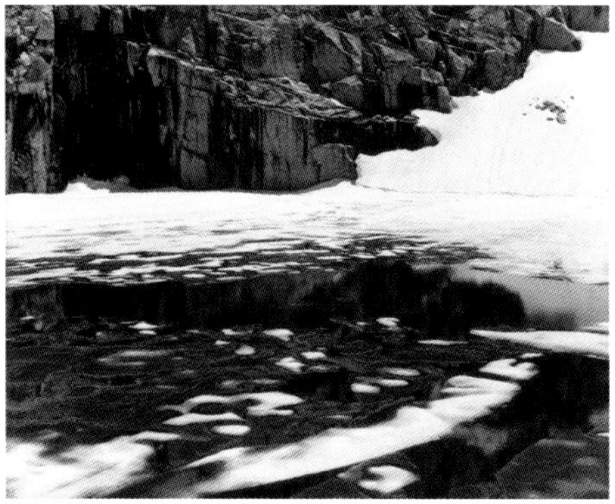

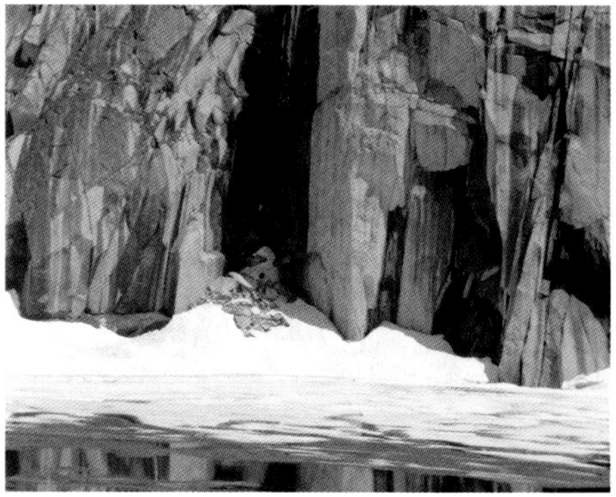

Sand Dunes, Sunrise, Death Valley National Park, California, c. 1948

On a visit to Death Valley in 1948, Ansel made the photograph on the right and the variants shown below. Later he wrote:

> I was camped in my car near Stovepipe Wells, usually sleeping on top of my car on the camera platform, which measured about 5 x 9 feet. Arising long before dawn, I made some coffee and reheated some beans, then gathered my equipment and started on the rather arduous walk through the dunes to capture the legendary dune sunrise....
>
> A searing sun rose over the Funeral Range, and I knew it was to be a hot day. Fortunately I had just arrived at a location where an exciting composition was unfolding. The red-golden light struck the dunes, and their crests became slightly diffuse with sand gently blowing in the early wind. To take advantage of the sunrise colors on the dunes I worked first with 4 x 5 Kodachrome.... Then, without moving the camera, I made several exposures with black-and-white film.

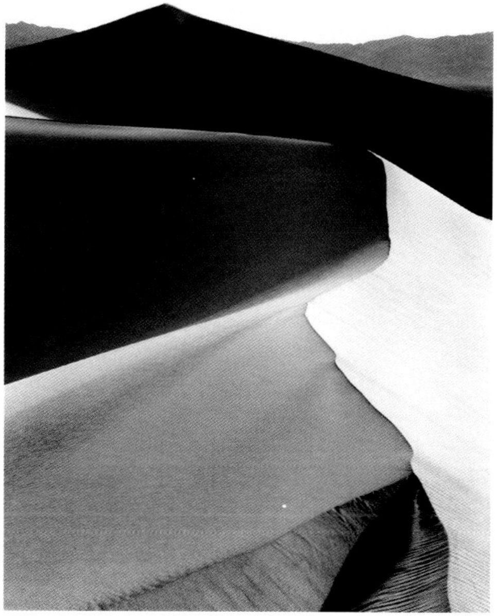

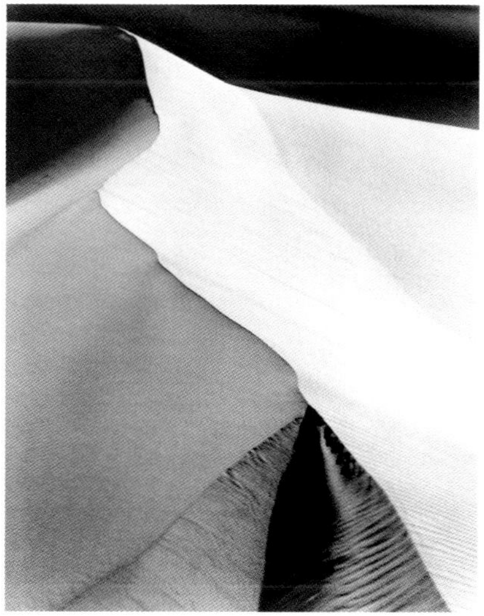

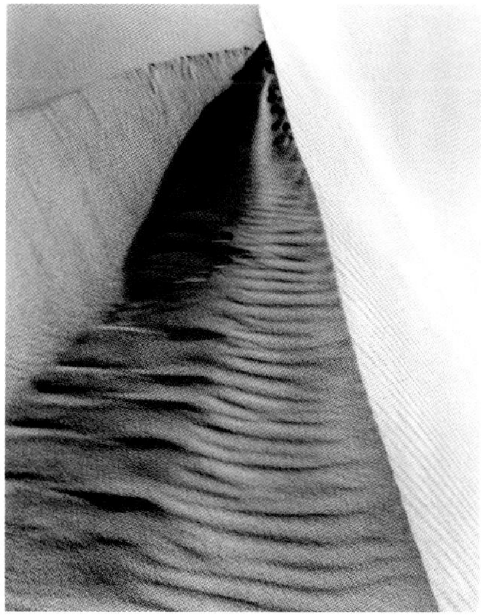

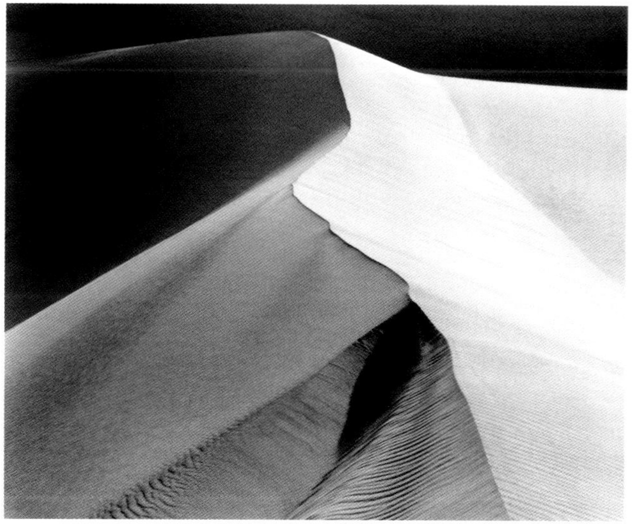

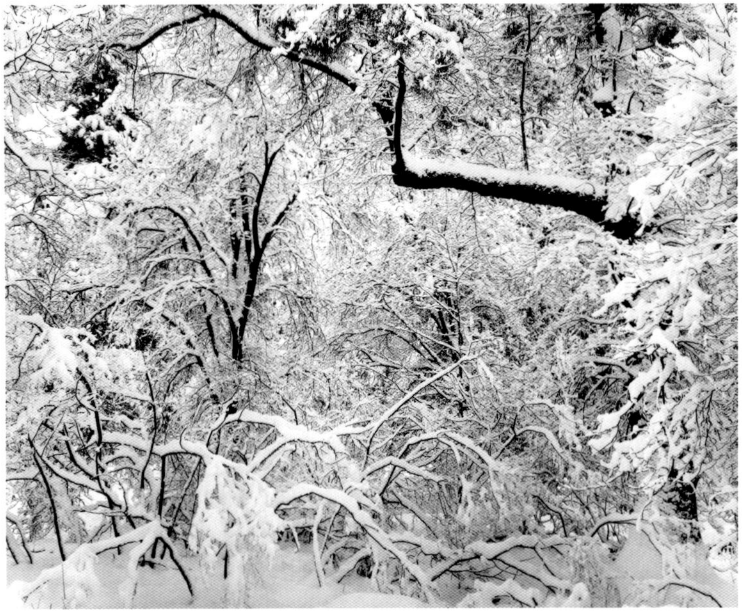

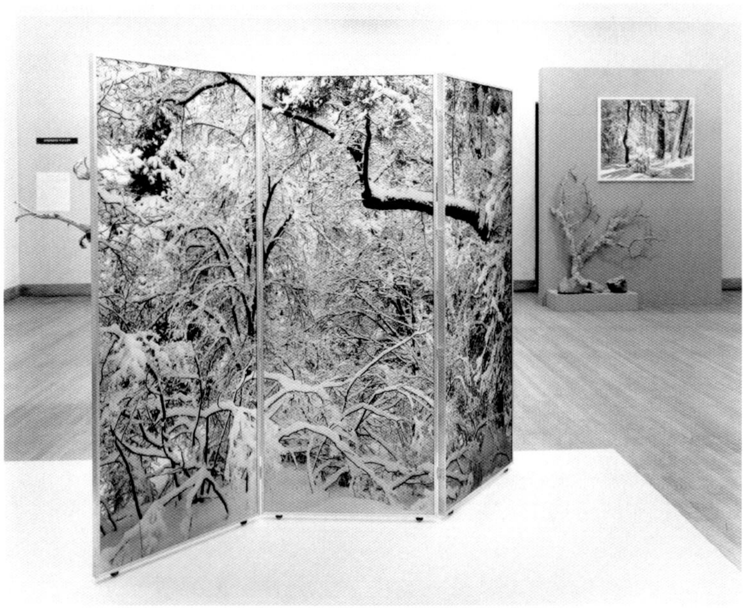

Fresh Snow, Yosemite National Park, California, c. 1947

Ansel loved the challenge of printing oversized photographs. "In 1935 Yosemite Park and Curry Company commissioned me to make large murals (prints up to forty-by-sixty inches) for display at the upcoming San Diego Fair. I was fascinated with the challenge of making a photographic print in grand scale." In 1948, after he made what he described as "A GORJEZUZ NEW 8 x 10 segment of snowy forest," he made two screens of the new image. "Three separate large prints were made of slightly overlapping segments of the single 8 x 10 negative, carefully balancing and matching the tonal values.... These prints were mounted on sealed plywood and framed with aluminum molding to which piano hinges were attached." At the same time that Ansel photographed the scene in black-and-white, he also made a 5 x 7-inch Ektachrome photograph that is reproduced on page 99 in the revised edition of *Ansel Adams in Color.*

In 1949, one of the screens was exhibited at the San Francisco Museum of Art, and the reviewer from the *San Francisco Chronicle* wrote: "This is a most handsome and sumptuous affair and suggests new uses for photography." When the same screen was included in an exhibition in 1979, a New York art critic described the show as "not without a certain touch of vulgarity—oh, that terrible Japanese-type screen made up of panels of pictures."

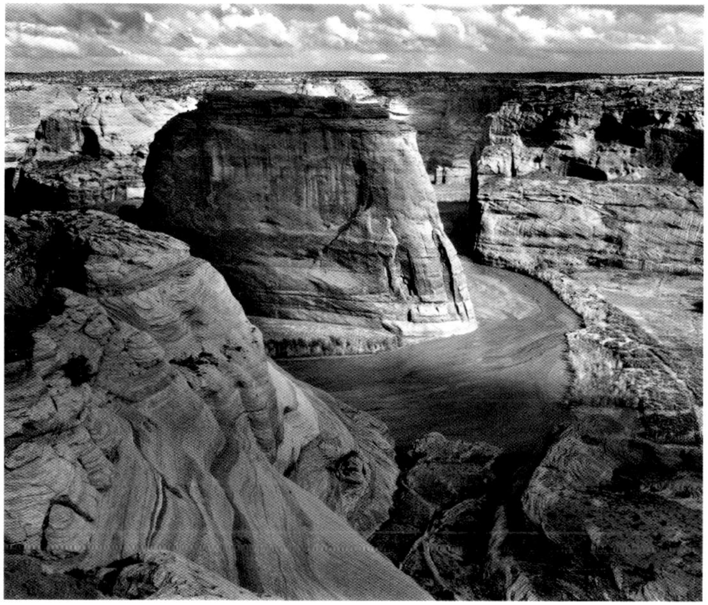

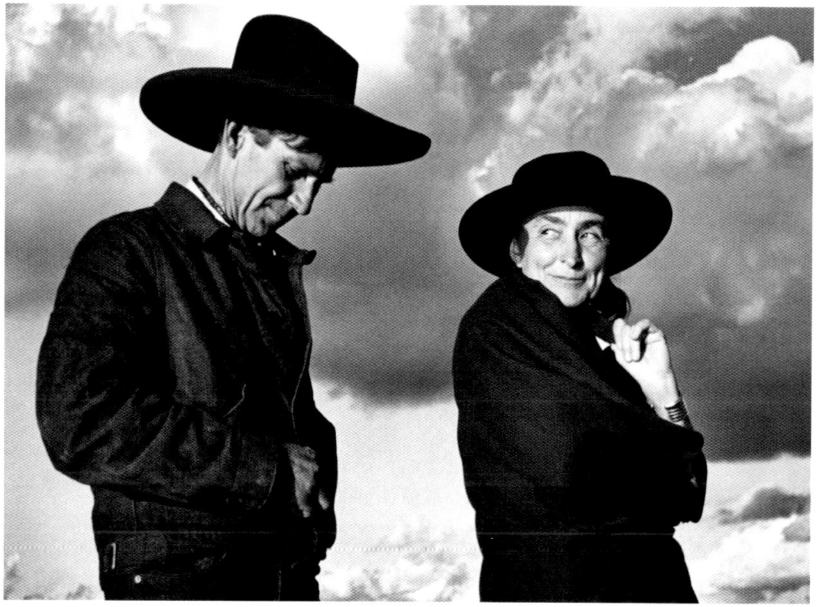

Canyon de Chelly from White House Overlook, Canyon de Chelly National Monument, Arizona, 1942; Georgia O'Keeffe and Orville Cox, Canyon de Chelly National Monument, Arizona, 1937

On his first trip to Canyon de Chelly in September 1937, Ansel was drawn to the "beautiful, flowing patterns" of the solidified sand dunes clearly visible in the lower left corner of this photograph. He wrote to his wife, Virginia, "The Canyon de Chelly exceeds anything I have imagined at any time!" On another occasion he enthused, "Some of my best photographs have been made in and on the rim of the canyon," perhaps referring to the well-known portrait he made of Georgia O'Keeffe and their guide on an earlier trip.

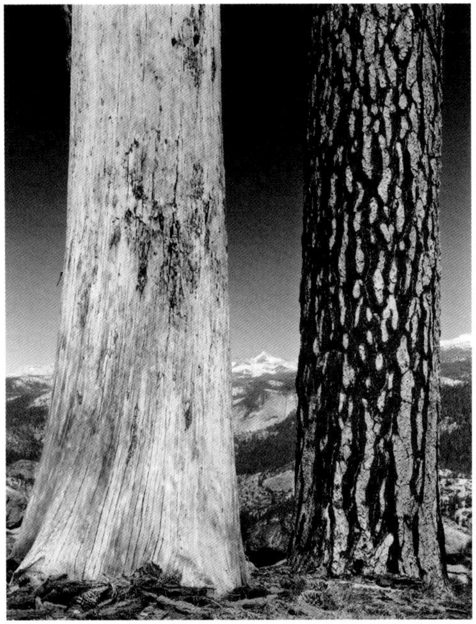

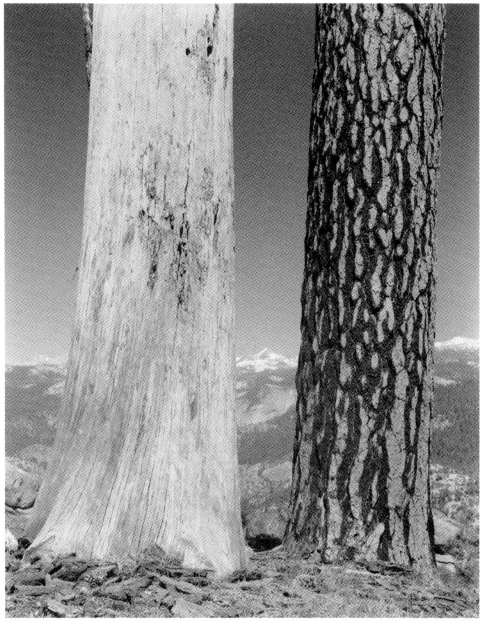

Trees, Illilouette Ridge, Yosemite National Park, 1945

Precise cropping was a hallmark of Ansel's photographs. Consider the photograph of two trees on Illilouette Ridge as Ansel composed it on the ground glass of his 8 x 10-inch camera (above right). Now compare that original composition with the final cropped version (above left). Ansel removed the white rock at the base of the tree on the left, and he removed part of the top of the image to show less of the small branch that protrudes from the same tree. His goal was to remove distractions so that the viewer could focus on the main subject, in this case the tree trunks and their beautiful textured wood and bark.

In Ansel's workroom there was a large paper cutter that he used for cropping. I remember the first time I saw him take a gorgeous 16 x 20-inch photograph and start whacking away at it as he turned it round and round, gradually taking a little off each side. I was stunned!

When students came to visit him with their portfolios, Ansel often suggested ways to improve a composition through cropping. He was remarkably consistent in the way he cropped his photographs, and he considered his decisions inviolate. If a publisher imposed its own cropping on one of his photographs for a magazine or book, he would protest vigorously.

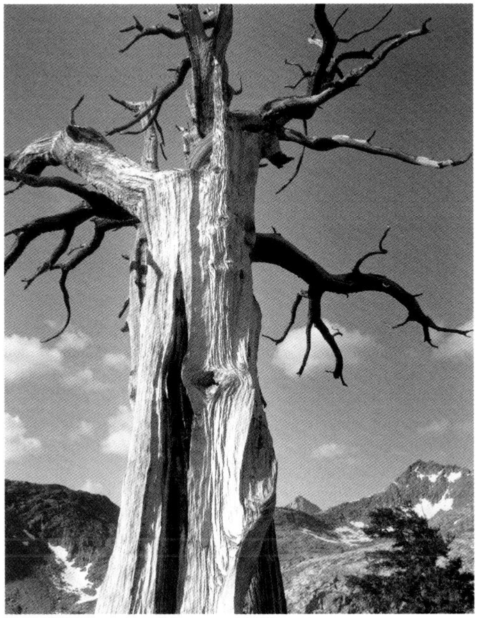

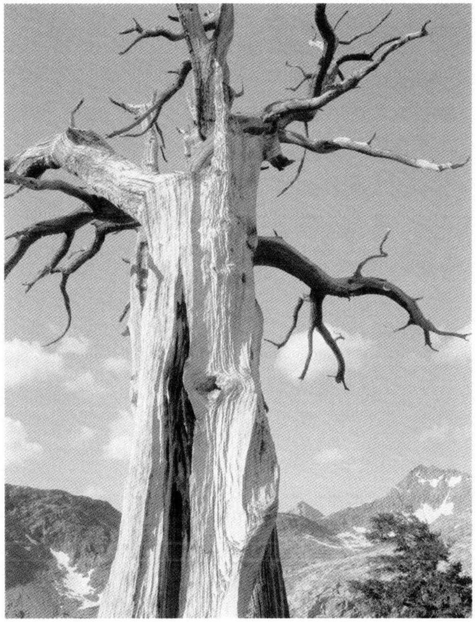

Dead Tree near Little Five Lakes, Sequoia National Park, California, 1927

"This is an example of nearly perfect exposure," wrote Ansel, describing the negative for this image in his technical book *The Negative*. Nevertheless, when printing the negative, Ansel felt the need to darken the edges through extra exposure (called "burning"). Compare the straight print without burning (above right) with the final print (above left). "Judicious edge-burning," wrote Adams, "equalized the values. The left and right sides were burned down to balance the flare [on the left from the sun]. The top left corner received some burning, and the bottom corner areas were lowered in value by the edge burning. A short burning along the bottom edge gave some solidity to the image." Adams was recognized as one of the great photographic printers of the twentieth century, and he looked forward to working in the darkroom, a crucial part of his creative process. He felt no regret at leaving the breathtaking view of the Pacific Ocean from his living room windows to spend several hours in the dark.

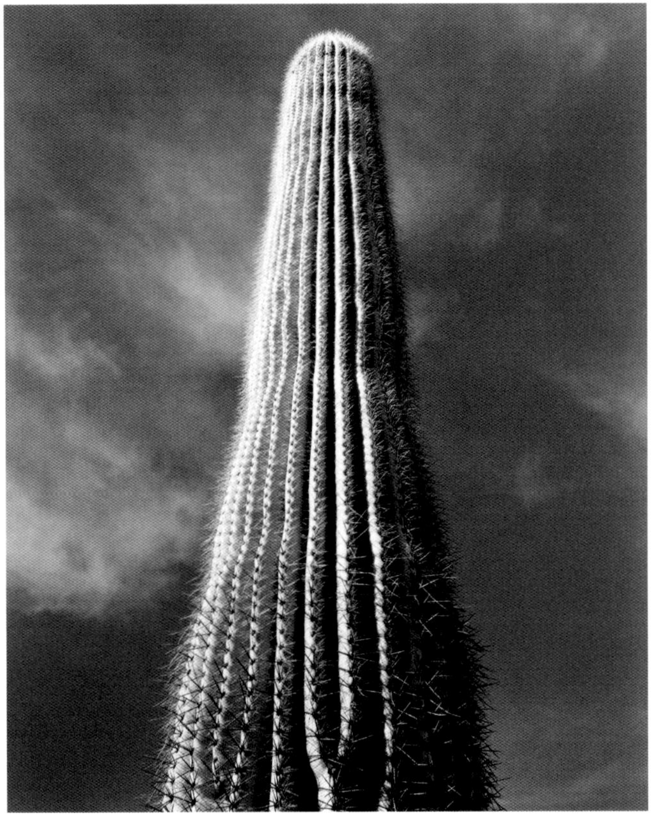

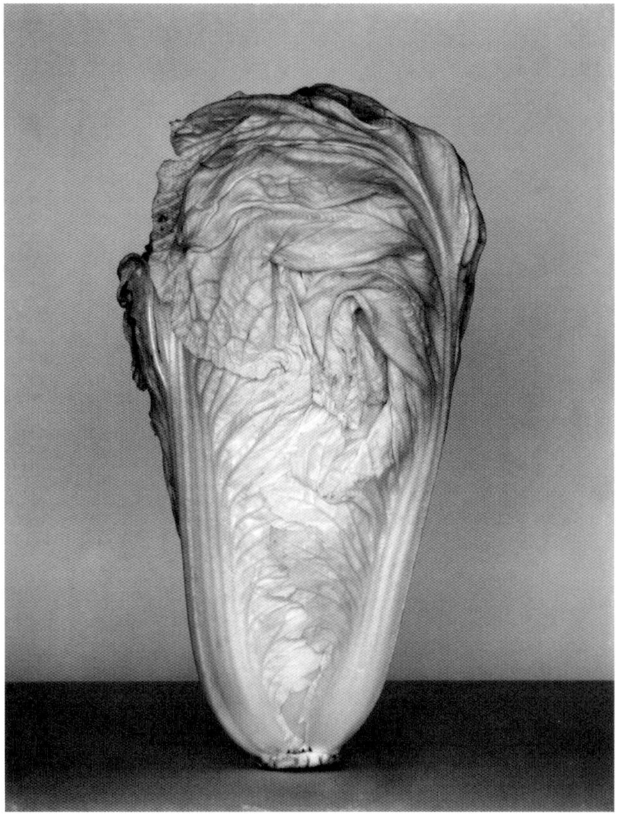

Saguaro Cactus, Saguaro National Park, Arizona, 1942; Chard, 1927, by Edward Weston

Ansel commiserated with friend and fellow photographer Edward Weston about the erotic connotations attributed by critics to their work. In the December 18, 1931, issue of *The Fortnightly,* a popular West Coast art publication, Ansel reviewed an exhibition of Weston's photographs: "He is often accused of direct symbolism—pathologic, phallic, and erotic.... In discussion with Weston on this very point I became convinced that there is no conscious attempt to imply symbolism of any sort in his work. In deference to him as an artist I must accept his word that he is not conscious of any effort in this direction." Weston wrote to Ansel in response on January 28, 1932: "The discussion of phallic symbolism should at least clear me of intention, though the disciples of Freud will not be convinced."

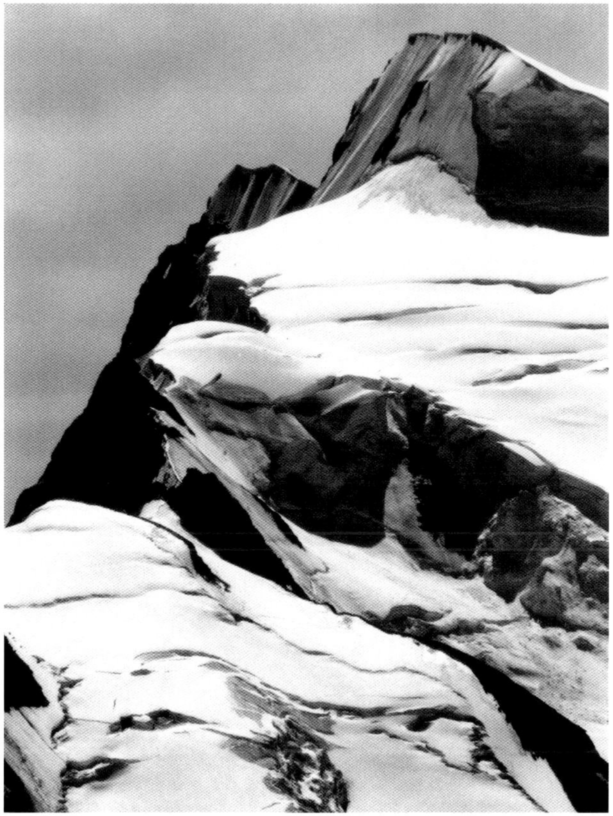

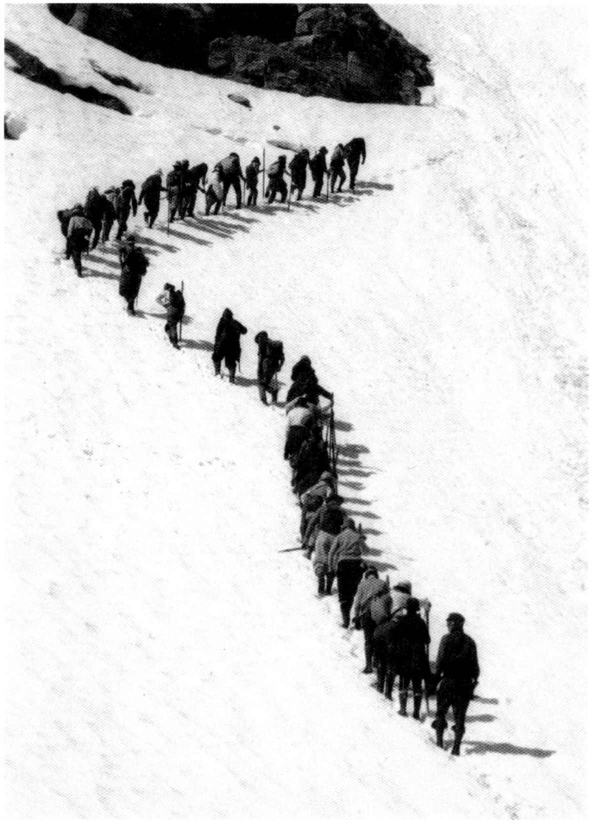

Mount Resplendent, Mount Robson Provincial Park, Canada, 1928

"The Canadian Rockies are another world: spectacular and difficult," recalled Ansel. "Daylight lingered long and dawn came in the small hours. On a climbing day our Swiss guides would call us at two-thirty A.M., breakfast at three, and we were on the trail shortly thereafter" (see photograph above right). At the end of a daylong ascent of Mount Resplendent, he wrote, "The guides took several large parties to its summit. The glacier we traversed was shattered with crevices, and the guides were in a frenzy to keep us in safe areas. The main groups were tied together with ropes, but I was on the loose with my camera." Shortly before Ansel took this photograph, he paused to clean his lens and noticed several pinholes in the lens board. He immediately applied opaque black tape, but the negatives he had made on the trip up until that moment were ruined by light leaks.

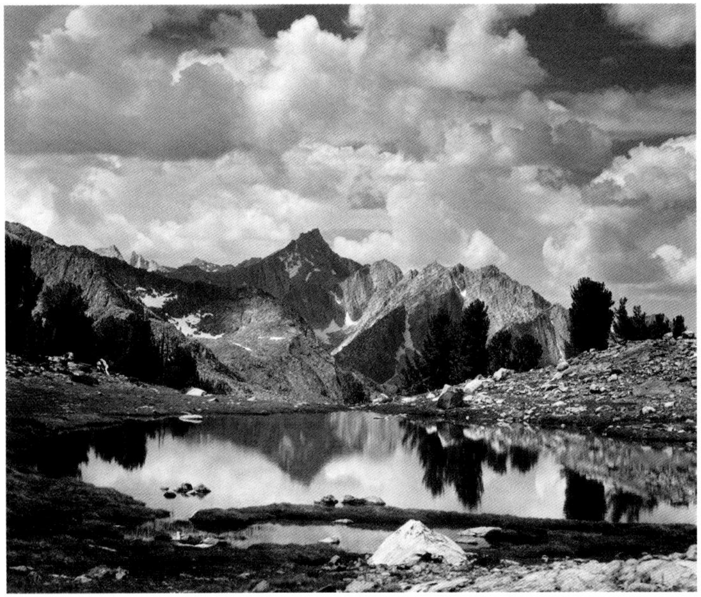

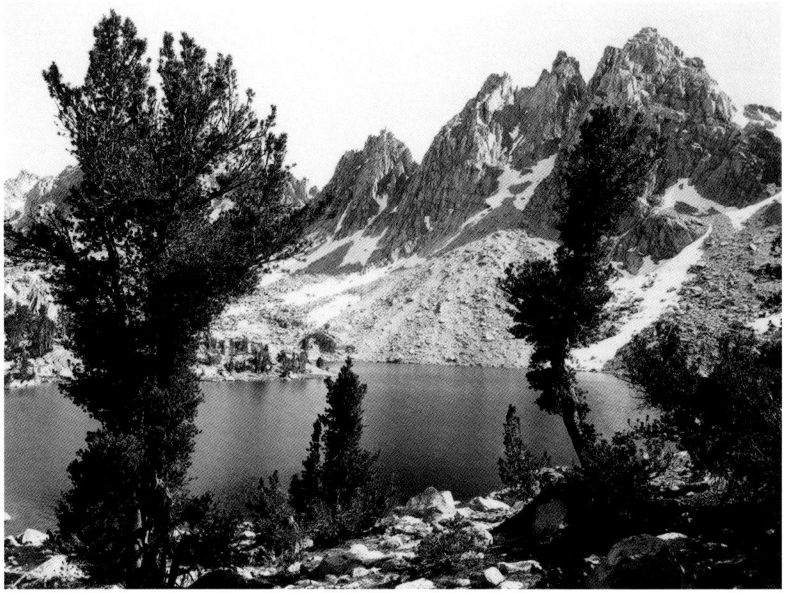

Mount Clarence King, Pool, Kings Canyon National Park, California, c. 1925; Kearsarge Pinnacles, Kings Canyon National Park, California, c. 1925

"The clouds are the cool voices of the sky and winds," Ansel wrote in a poem around 1925. Dramatic clouds are a hallmark of many of Ansel's photographs. This is one of the first photographs he made with a panchromatic glass plate. The emulsion on a panchromatic plate is sensitive to all colors and can therefore reproduce clouds. Compare the glorious clouds in the Mount Clarence King image (above left) with the empty sky in a photograph of the Kearsarge Pinnacles made on an orthochromatic plate around the same time (above right). The emulsion on an orthochromatic plate is not sensitive to red light, only to blue and green, and therefore cannot reproduce clouds. Panchromatic plates were more expensive, and it was a few years before Ansel could justify the extra expenditure.

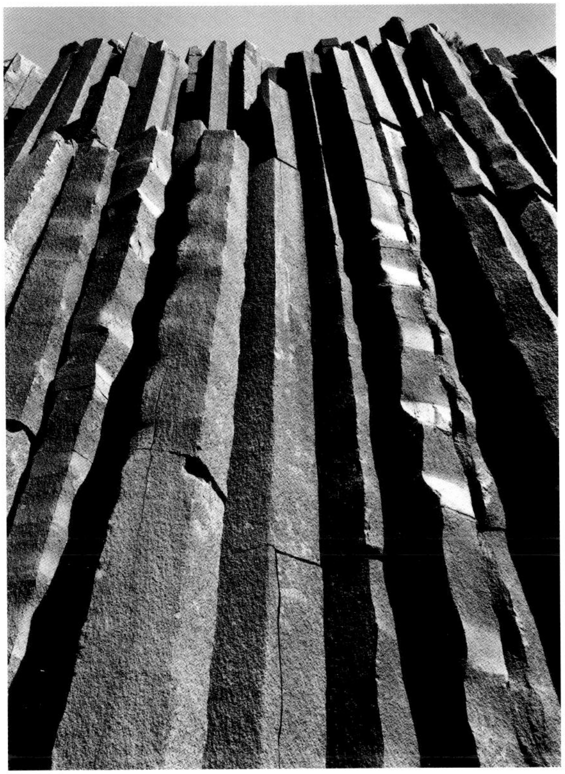

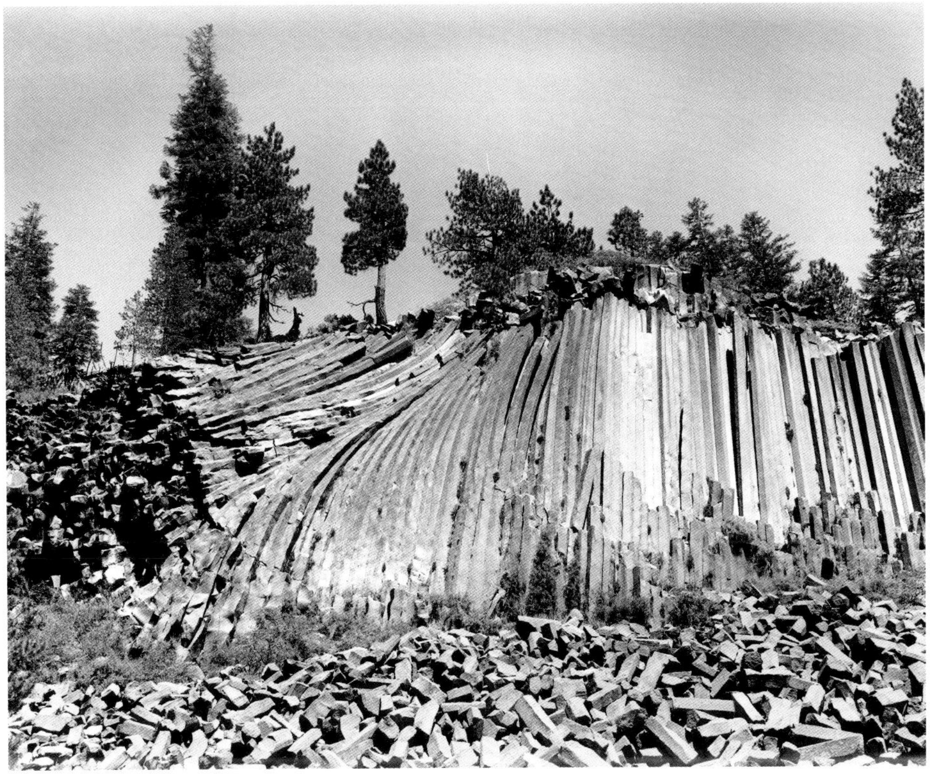

Detail, Devils Postpile National Monument, California, 1946

To make this photograph (above left), Ansel pointed his camera up at a wall of exfoliating basalt columns formed thousands of years ago. By choosing not to correct the "convergence" of the columns (the optical illusion that makes the columns appear to converge at the top), he created a dramatic image altogether different from a more traditional view (above right) made at the same time.

Adams was—by strength of will, if not by nature—an optimist. As an optimist he saw the forces of environmental responsibility as ascendant, and the minds and hearts of the people moving steadily toward the understanding that something similar to reverence for our planet was the essential precondition to ethical life on it. He could point to many victories in support of this optimistic view: new parks, new laws, burgeoning memberships for environmental organizations, etc., and these victories were undeniably real. . . .

As Adams' audience we are grateful to him for enlarging our emotional knowledge of the natural world, the knowledge of its constant mutability—that it is (one might say) alive. If we avert our eyes for a moment, we will return them to a different world, a constant source of wonder and deep surprise, which we love not only as an aesthetic delight but as a deep moral cryptogram to which we have no key.

John Szarkowski, from Ansel Adams at 100

ANSEL ADAMS AND THE PRESERVATION OF WILDERNESS

RICHARD B. WOODWARD

"In the United States there is more space where nobody is than where anybody is. This is what makes America what it is."

Gertrude Stein, The Geographic History of America

THROUGHOUT his long career, Ansel Adams was dedicated to and embodied the Sierra Club's present-day motto: "Explore, enjoy, and protect the planet." His decision to communicate that principle in photographs, and to do his utmost to ensure they were printed expertly and published widely, grew out of his sense of professionalism and public duty as well as a firm set of artistic convictions. The profound impact of his work and life on the environmental movement of his day derived from the contagious enthusiasm for his self-directed mission. No one has done a more persuasive job of making comprehensible to more people through the lens of a camera the majesty of wilderness and what is at stake in its loss.

It is often said that Adams in his photographs portrays the timelessness of the American West: the silence of towering mountains, the weight of massy granite, the forest primeval, and the light eternal. But it is just as true that his pictures, whether on the wall of a museum or in the pages of a book, do what the finest photographs have always done: they convey the fragility of time, of moments or eras that are going or already gone, and in so doing start the viewer wondering if a piece of the world should be, and even might be, saved.

Photography was from its beginnings innately allied with maternal forces of preservation. Cameras are in the sealed chambers of their hearts instruments for conserving the past. Each moment caught in one of these light traps is unique. Whatever the camera is aimed at, from a landscape out a car window to a rare specimen of life, may be saved and recalled for study later. As our sense of what happened yesterday or decades ago is often as muddled and contentious as our plans for the future, a mechanical process that provides more or less realistic evidence of the world as it once was can be of immense practical and political value.

If the runaway locomotive of progress could not be halted by photography—the medium was, after all, inseparable from the scientific-industrial matrix that gave it birth—the lineaments of change could at least be framed and appreciated. By appearing to "stop time," the picture machine even fostered the illusion that time might be reversed.

Architecture historians in several European countries understood this vital function of photography soon after Daguerre took credit for inventing it in 1839. In France, the government had already founded the Commission des monuments historiques in 1837 and assigned it to compile a list of decaying medieval and Renaissance structures—cathedrals, parks, chateaus, villages—imperiled by neglect. The organization's first director, the novelist and man of letters Prosper Mérimée, rejected a suggestion that the daguerreotype could aid the group in its task. As a process that yielded only a single, unreproducible image on a small metal plate, it would have been ineffective in awakening the public to what he and his confrères regarded as a cultural emergency.

Only when shown a group of prints on paper, products of the rival calotype process developed by the English inventor William Henry Fox Talbot, did Mérimée reverse himself. That photography could more easily and faithfully perform the job previously done with drawings by hand was intriguing. What's more, Talbot's calotypes could also generate multiple prints from the same negative, thus allowing the government to increase the volume on the message it hoped to convey.

In 1851, the Commission selected five photographers—Édouard-Denis Baldus, Hippolyte Bayard, Gustave Le Gray, Henri Le Secq, and O. Mestral—for an elite unit that operated under the name La mission héliographique. It was perhaps the first time, though by no means the last, that photographers were hired in a noble-minded effort to preserve valuable parts of the world, in this case a centuries-old heritage that France was in danger of forfeiting unless quick action was taken to save these crumbling and irreplaceable sites.

Many of the three hundred or so paper negatives and the higher number of prints generated by La mission héliographique are now regarded as supreme works of photographic art. In the rare cases when a superb example comes up for auction, they are priced at hundreds of thousands of dollars. It should not be forgotten, though, that the mission was organized to aggrandize as well as to document, and that the five men, now viewed as artists, took their stirring pictures of Norman castle ruins and Gothic sculpture in support of a propaganda campaign dreamed up by historians and bankrolled by the French government.

Throughout the nineteenth century, photographs by individuals and institutions in Great Britain, Germany, Italy,[1] and elsewhere were enlisted to identify traditions threatened by the relentless pace of modern life and, by extension, to urge a more vigilant custodianship over the past. The British widened the scope of this memorializing application by establishing the National Photographic Record Association in 1897. The stated objectives of the project, which lasted until 1910, were "to leave to posterity a permanent pictorial record of contemporary life, to portray for the benefit of future generations the manners and customs, the festivals and pageants, the historic buildings and places of our time."[2]

The United States during the nineteenth century did not present the same set of concerns for preservationists that sent European photographers into cities, towns, and fields. The North American continent was still in many respects the New World. Its historic monuments were younger and fewer than most of those in France, at least in the eyes of white settlers, and the customs of its population were not as uniform or as eroded by the upheavals of the industrial revolution as was the case in the British Isles.

The historic way of life most under siege in the United States was that of the American Indian, and the national heirlooms thought to be worthiest of protection—before, during, and after the bloody interruption of the Civil War—were not Massachusetts wooden churches or Virginia plantations, but the country's spectacular natural resources, notably the forests, mountains, and valleys in the western third of the country that were already by the 1850s being denuded of trees and dotted with miners' camps.

Photographers played a decisive role in the Yosemite Grant of 1864, the first time any government had conserved a vast swath of land in the public interest. Shortly after gold prospectors entered the valley in the 1850s, artists had begun to make extraordinary pictures of this extraordinary place. The draftsmen Thomas Ayres and Adolph Schwartz were the pioneers, their sketches and lithographs from 1855 to 1856 of Yosemite Falls and other landmarks alerting their colleagues to its rich potential as a popular subject.[3]

They were followed by Clarence Leander Weed in 1859. The first photographer in Yosemite Valley, he exhibited prints of Bridalveil Fall and other sites from his trip before crowds in San Francisco that same year. Tourists on horseback were already being guided along former Indian trails, drawn by tales of the area's glories recounted by the English author and publisher J. M. Hutchings in his pamphlets and books.

The prospect of beholding the highest waterfall on the continent and other scenic attractions promoted by

Hutchings brought the German American painter Albert Bierstadt from New York City to Yosemite in 1863. He saw the valley floor as the perfect stage on which to celebrate the American wilderness that, by implication, needed people to look at and be astonished by it. In a series of panoramic canvases, some measuring fifteen feet across, the light of providence appears to shine on the country's natural beauty.

But the most persuasive celebrant of Yosemite as a national sublime to rival Niagara Falls may have been the photographer Carleton Watkins. Another refugee from New York state who came to California during the gold rush, he had taken his boxes of glass plates and array of cameras to Yosemite in 1861. His stereo views of its vertiginous heights and titanic rock formations quickly gained favor with armchair travelers, and a set of his mammoth plate prints were attached with a private petition sent to US Senator John Conness of California, who ultimately introduced the 1864 bill. Signed by President Lincoln, who never saw the region his pen was protecting, it granted 39,000 acres of Yosemite Valley and the Mariposa Grove of Big Trees to the stewardship of California, for "public use, resort, and recreation… inalienable for future generations."

Other photographers contributed to the emerging idea that America's natural resources were exceptional and should be preserved in a thoughtful fashion for later generations. The English photographer Eadweard Muybridge, eyeing the accomplishment of Watkins, went to Yosemite in 1867 and made pictures from many of the same places as his predecessor. William Henry Jackson, a Civil War veteran from Keeseville, New York, had accompanied Ferdinand V. Hayden's geologic expedition to the Yellowstone region in 1871. Jackson's large-scale photographs of Yellowstone Lake, Riverside Geyser, and Mammoth Hot Springs were widely admired by the public and, together with Thomas Moran's operatic paintings of the area and Hayden's report,

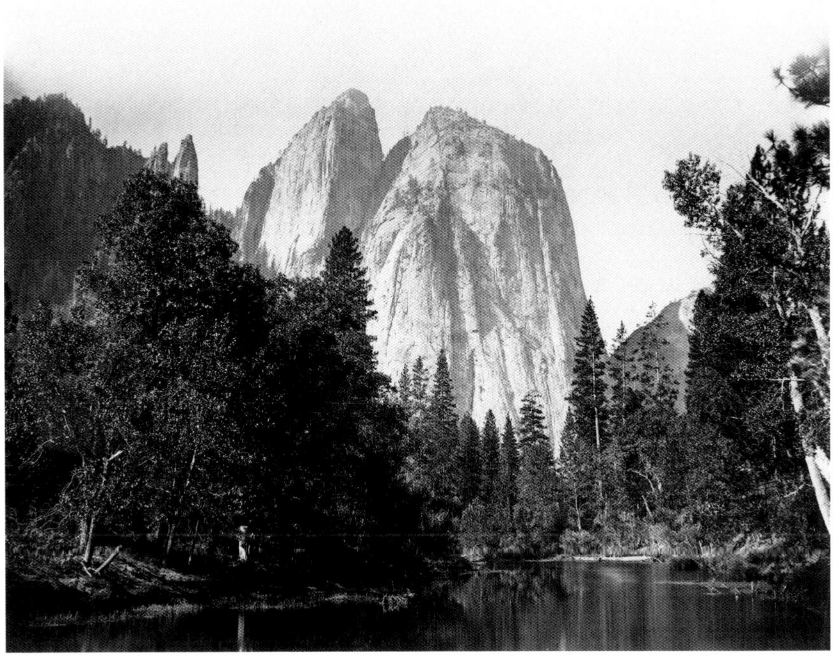

Merced River and Cathedral Rocks, Yosemite National Park, c. 1860s. By Carleton Emmons Watkins

influenced the US Congress to create Yellowstone National Park in 1872, the first in the country's history and another milestone in the conservation movement.

During these same years, Timothy O'Sullivan ventured with his view camera and glass-plate negatives into the American deserts of the Southwest. An Irish immigrant who worked at Mathew Brady's studio in New York City and was later hired as one of his cameramen to patrol the battlefields of the Civil War, he signed on from 1871 to 1874 with Lieutenant George M. Wheeler's survey west of the one hundredth meridian. The photographs he brought back from these trips revealed to the public a number of unfamiliar places, including Canyon de Chelly and the edges of Grand Canyon, many of which were eventually designated as national parks and monuments. O'Sullivan's photographic documents were among the first[4] to suggest that these remote, little-known landscapes might be as historic and precious as the country's tall fir trees, geysers, and cloud-capped mountain peaks.

Ansel Adams is the most recognized descendant of this American landscape tradition in photography, and the most accomplished. The feats of virtuosity and reverence for nature evident in the prints of Weed, Watkins, Muybridge, Jackson, O'Sullivan, and their contemporaries were matched and in many cases exceeded by Adams, whose energies as an artist and a conservationist outdid all of his predecessors combined in keeping alive the Edenic ideal of America.

At the same time, by being born when he was, history granted Adams opportunities inconceivable in the calotype and glass-plate era. Not only did he take advantage of technological improvements, a number of which he instigated, to enhance the fidelity of reproductions on the printed page, he also positioned his images for maximum impact in the public arena. His pictures may show a continuity with nineteenth-century photographers, but as a public figure he represents a new species of American artist.

Born in San Francisco, he was, first of all, of the American West. During his early childhood, examples of unspoiled nature were never far from hand. The house his father built in 1902 on dunes overlooking San Francisco Bay had windows opening toward the fabled Golden Gate, a breathtaking stretch of water and land not arched over by the Golden Gate Bridge until the 1930s. For a native son, an only child who remembered spending much of his time either practicing the piano (he was a prodigy) or walking on the beach, preserving the western landscape and way of life was personal.

A series of episodes from Adams' life, especially during boyhood, bound him to Yosemite and the High Sierra, giving him a profound stake in seeing that his "spiritual home," and the inspiration for so many of his photographs, would be preserved. The expedition photographers, men from New York who traveled across America to fulfill terms of a contract, arguably had less of an emotional investment in the lands they photographed.

> I am sending you two pictures of Yosemite Valley that I have taken. Films are expensive to develop and I expect to be broke if I keep up the rate I am taking pictures. I have taken 30 already.
> —Letter from Ansel Adams to his aunt Mary, June 23, 1916[5]

Landscape photographers have a deserved reputation as a footloose, itinerant bunch. After a few years, if not a few days or hours, most will have exhausted the picture opportunities of the most resplendent place. Aiming their cameras at a distant prospect that catches their eye and grabbing a shot or two that keeps them happy, most are then ready to be on their way to a promising view around the bend. Economic incentives may also carry them onward: impatient editors or art dealers expect new material from new locations.

Watkins had returned several times to Yosemite Valley in the 1860s and 1870s after his mammoth plate photographs had helped to persuade the US Congress to save it from private exploitation, and Jackson, after watching demand for his 1871 pictures of Yellowstone boost his income, undertook a number of even more profitable trips around the West, where by one estimate he made approximately eighty

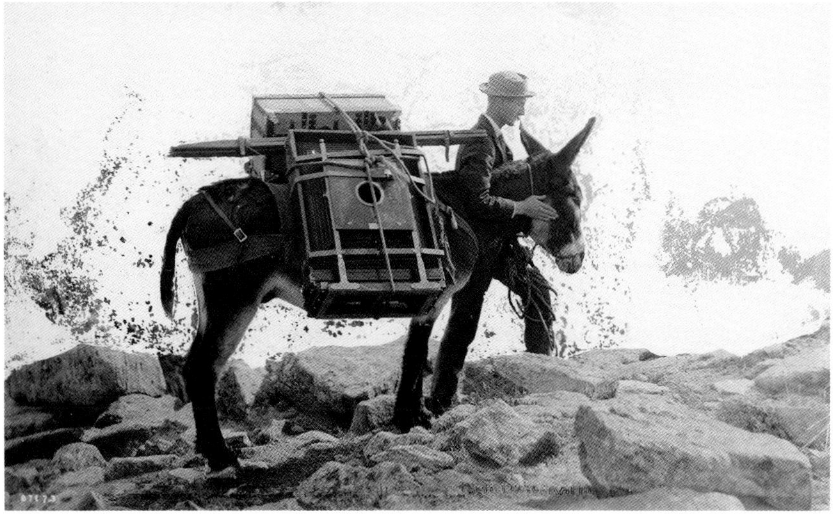

The Photographer's Assistants, c. 1873. By William Henry Jackson

thousand negatives. But many of their contemporaries, including O'Sullivan, seldom went back to the amazing places where they had taken pictures.[6]

Adams was an exception. He first saw Yosemite as a thirteen-year-old, and the enchantment of the visit never really left him. According to his posthumously published autobiography—a sometimes photoshopped version of his personal history that John Szarkowski once called "the life Ansel wishes he had lived"[7]—the first photograph he made of anything was of Half Dome, taken in 1916 from the valley floor with a Kodak #1 Box Brownie given to him by his parents. It would be almost fifteen years before the aspiring classical pianist from San Francisco abandoned his

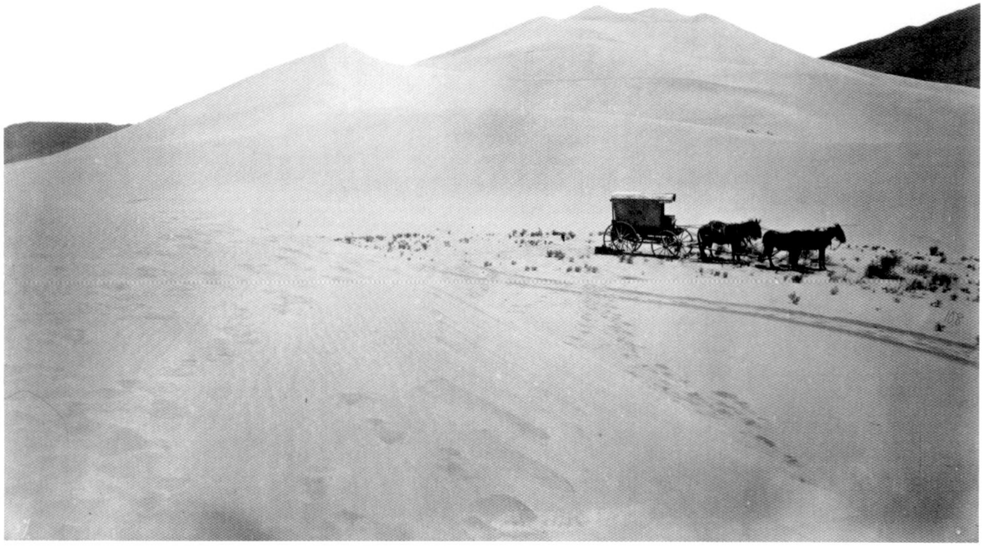

Ambulance Wagon in the Desert, King Geological Survey, Carson Desert, Nevada, 1867. By Timothy H. O'Sullivan

youthful dreams of a concert career to devote himself full-time to photography. But during that interim, regular trips to Yosemite never ceased.

The vital importance of the park and the surrounding High Sierra for both the person and the photographer is hard to exaggerate. What Cézanne found during his stays in the mountains and forests of his native Provence, and the aging Monet in his constructed garden at Giverny, Adams gained from being in and around Yosemite: daily contact with the moods of nature and light, and a set of complex formal and technical problems to solve—enough to complete his soul and occupy his mind for a lifetime.

Of the more than two thousand photographs Adams published in his lifetime (not counting the many that did not meet his standards), thirty-one were of Half Dome, fifteen of El Capitan, and thirteen of Yosemite Valley. A large number (but not all) are from the same vantage point. He photographed from Inspiration Point during his first trip in 1916 and dozens of times thereafter over the next half century. Perhaps one-tenth of the estimated forty thousand negatives in his archive were taken in Yosemite. In the book you are holding, 45 of the 236 photographs, dating between 1920 and 1968, are views of the national park that was dearer to him than any of the others. And Yosemite was where he met his wife, Virginia Best.

Adams' activism started early on, and in an outstanding instance, he helped persuade Congress and the president to create the Kings Canyon National Park in California, the second of the so-called wilderness parks in the country. The legislation that set its boundaries into law in 1940 was the result of intense lobbying by the Sierra Club. The publication of Adams' classic book of photographs *Sierra Nevada: The John Muir Trail* in 1938 was simultaneously "one of the true landmarks in the history of photomechanical reproduction,"[8] according to Szarkowski, and "a silent but most effective voice"[9] in the political rumble over Kings Canyon, according to Arno B. Cammerer, associate director of the National Park Service.

What five Frenchmen in the 1850s were assigned to do for their country with La mission héliographique—sound the alarm about a heritage at risk of being squandered—Adams single-handedly tried to accomplish with his life's work as a photographer and conservationist. An artist who seldom took a picture except to please himself, he nonetheless had a flair for publicity and an acute political conscience that led him to engage repeatedly in group actions. Like many prominent twentieth-century activists, he leveraged his own fame to promote social change. His photographs are now widely known in no small part because he allowed them to be used in advancing causes he believed in, mainly but not limited to conservation. If one artist can be said to have raised public awareness over the fragility of the earth during the 1960s and 1970s, it was Ansel Adams.

His writings on nature profess many of the same tenets uttered by Emerson, Thoreau, Muir, and their disciples Whitman and Edward Carpenter, specifically a faith in the healing power of wilderness. His photographs, too, display a kinship with the painters of the Hudson River School and American Luminism. The visual rhetoric of Bierstadt and Moran, which seeks to reduce the viewer to a sense of awe, left an impression on Adams, notwithstanding his expressed disdain for their grandiloquence.

But though some of his most beloved landscapes, such as "Clearing Winter Storm," seem to refer back fondly to a pictorial tradition formulated prior to his birth, to a more bucolic and untamed America before the machine had entered the garden, Adams was also a self-conscious modernist who by 1930 had aligned himself with the teachings of Alfred Stieglitz. Disparaging the soft, moody, blurred outlines that had dominated art photography at the turn of the century, Stieglitz in his manifestos and photographs favored a clear, direct, sharp-focused approach to subjects. As long as a picture was presented without fussy obfuscation, it could be of anything.

His repertoire of views is more varied than Bierstadt's or Moran's. The close-ups of stones, tree stumps, ocean waves, blades of grass, thin stands of trees, mountaintops on a cloudy day, are the result of patient observation rather than theatrical urges. As Szarkowski has written, "He was certainly among those who sketched the outlines of a new sense of the meaning of the natural landscape, an understanding based on the earth's intimate detail, its unnoted cases, its ephemeral gestures." By organizing the exhibition Group f.64 in 1932—with Edward Weston, Imogen Cunningham, and others—Adams became an eloquent spokesman for "straight photography" in San Francisco and far beyond.

His preferred equipment until the late 1950s—the large-format camera on a tripod—may appear to be an homage to an earlier time. The choice was certainly out of step with modernist-minded Europeans in the 1930s and '40s. Their Leicas and Contaxes exploited the handheld camera's facility at capturing rapid action and fleeting expressions. But as the view camera gave Adams what he wanted—a larger negative that optimized chances for sharper detail and tonal range in photographing a landscape—he could ignore the trend. He was intrigued by smaller cameras and sometimes used them on assignments. They just didn't often suit his needs as an artist.

Finally, no photographer except Stieglitz did more to win acceptance for photography as a fine art. In 1940, when the Museum of Modern Art in New York created a separate department of photography, the first in the world, Adams became one of its founding fathers. Without training as a scholar or curator, he was nonetheless instrumental in the rediscovery of Watkins, Jackson, and O'Sullivan. By extolling their achievements to Beaumont Newhall and others in the museum community, he helped to construct a nascent art historical continuum for landscape photography.

His own international prominence as an artist toward the end of his life altered the material conditions for those choosing to take the medium in that direction. In the 1970s, prints by Adams became one of the pillars of an emerging market for photographs as an art collectible, for sale in galleries and auction houses. The select but not inconsiderable number of photographers lucky enough to earn a living today from sales of their prints have Adams to thank for proving this could be done. Despite an altered context and a newfound respect for photographers within the realm of contemporary art, his pictures remain basic to the photography market and show no sign of diminishing in prevalence twenty-five years after his death.

The majority of Adams' iconic images date from his many years in Yosemite, from numerous trips to the Southwest, and from his more far-flung excursions in the national parks during the 1940s, projects first undertaken on commission for the US Department of the Interior and then with funding from a pair of Guggenheim Fellowships. It is from these two bodies of work, one rooted in his California backyard, the other from more peripatetic adventures, that the overwhelming number of pictures in this book were drawn. These were the years he prepared his books *My Camera in Yosemite Valley* and *My Camera in the National Parks,* published in 1949 and 1950 respectively.

Adams is by now such a national treasure himself, it's easy to forget that his photographs were not always everywhere and that he worked methodically to achieve his sizeable portion of renown. His independence from money worries in his final decade, along with his standing as a genial and passionate spokesman for wilderness, were hard earned and not attained without sacrifice. He was a more driven, pragmatic, and complicated man than might be imagined from viewing the serene grandeur of "Winter Sunrise, the Sierra Nevada, from Lone Pine" or "The Tetons and the Snake River" in a history of photography.

The closer you look at Ansel Adams, and the farther away in the historical mirror he gets, the more he appears to be inimitable, the sort of photographer and public figure that could have appeared at no other time and nowhere else but during the twentieth century on the West Coast of the United States.

NOTES

1. Beginning in 1858, when he became the official photographer of the city of Paris, Charles Marville recorded its rapidly changing architecture, especially those areas being razed under the Baron Haussmann's radical plans. In Great Britain, the photographers A. and J. Bool performed a similar function. In 1867 The Society for Photographing the Relics of Old London asked them to survey neighborhoods in London threatened with demolition. The results were published in a series of volumes published by Henry Dixon, the first appearing in 1867. See *Architecture Transformed: A History of the Photography of Buildings from 1839 to the Present* by Cervin Robinson and Joel Herschman (Cambridge, MA, and London: MIT Press, 1987). Efforts in Germany and Italy were less systematic. But even when undertaken by individuals who sold their pictures of ruins as tourist curios, the photographs carried the sense of preserving a valuable past. See *Voir l'Italie et mourir: Photographie et peinture dans l'Italie du XIXe siècle; sur une idée d'Ulrich Pohlmann et de Guy Cogeval* (Paris: Musée d'Orsay, 2009).

2. *The Oxford Companion to the Photograph,* edited by Robin Lenman (Oxford and New York: Oxford University Press, 2005), page 434.

3. *Yosemite: Art of an American Icon,* by Amy Scott (Berkeley: University of California Press, 2006), the catalog for a 2006 exhibition at the Museum of the American West in Los Angeles, traces the long and varied history of Yosemite's depiction by illustrators, painters, and photographers.

4. E. O. Beaman and John K. Hillers were two other photographers in the Southwest during the 1870s. Both of them worked for John Wesley Powell on his 1871–72 survey, and Hillers continued to explore the area with his camera for the next twenty years.

5. *Ansel Adams: Letters and Images 1916–1984*, edited by Mary Street Alinder and Andrea Gray Stillman (Boston: Little, Brown, 1988), page 1.

6. One exception in the case of O'Sullivan was Shoshone Falls in Idaho, which he visited in 1868 with the King survey and then again in 1874 as one of his final trips on the Wheeler survey. See *Framing the West: The Survey Photographs of Timothy H. O'Sullivan,* by Toby Jurovics, Carol M. Johnson, Glenn Willumson, and William F. Staff (New Haven: Yale University Press, 2010).

7. Conversation with the author in the 1990s.

8. From the introduction by William Turnage to the reissue of *Sierra Nevada: The John Muir Trail* by Ansel Adams, originally published in 1938 (New York: Little, Brown, 2006), unpaginated.

9. Ibid.

ANSEL ADAMS, ENVIRONMENTALIST

WILLIAM A. TURNAGE

INTRODUCTION TO *THE AMERICAN WILDERNESS* • 1990

"As each returning day brought with it no tangible evidence of the arrival of the Yo Semites, it was resolved that they should be sought after in their boasted stronghold; and, notwithstanding the discouraging pictures so graphically painted, in both language and gesture, by Ten-ie-ya [their aged chief], of the difficulties and dangers to be encountered on the way, coupled with assurances of the early arrival of his people, AN EXPEDITION TO THE MYSTIC VALLEY WAS RESOLVED UPON."

J. M. Hutchings, In the Heart of the Sierras *(1886)*

YOSEMITE, the Sierra Nevada, the rolling sand dunes of the San Francisco coast, the myth and mood of these wild places became the wellspring of Ansel Adams' consciousness. His childhood was devoted to daily, solitary exploration of the dunes and beaches of the Golden Gate. His youth was shaped and dominated by the great walls and falling waters of the incomparable Yosemite Valley. Young manhood saw him walking, climbing, photographing the High Sierra, from Tuolumne to Kings Canyon, from Thousand Island Lake to the Minaret Summits in what is today the magnificent Ansel Adams Wilderness. It would be difficult indeed to exaggerate the impact of nature and natural beauty on Adams' life, work, beliefs, and accomplishments. The mountains and the wilderness were so very much a part of him and his life that, as some individuals come to look like their mates, and others like their pets, Adams came, in later life, to look like his beloved mountains, like society's spiritual artifact in nature. His great white beard was of Muir, his stout physique of the giant sequoia, his joyous exuberance of Yosemite Falls, his intensity and integrity of El Capitan itself.

Adams grew up in the newly built family home on the dunes beyond the Golden Gate, above Baker Beach, a mile west of the urban limits of San Francisco. In his early childhood, the house stood alone and Adams' "backyard" ran unfettered to the ocean and the bay, the view across a bridgeless Golden Gate to the rugged bluffs of the Marin Headlands. At the age of four, he was thrown to the ground by a severe aftershock of the first great San Francisco earthquake, badly breaking his nose. Rushing him to the doctor, his mother was told that the nose should not be surgically straightened until the youngster matured. As the nose retained a rather dramatic bend to the left throughout his long life, Adams delighted in explaining that it was due to the fact that he had never matured!

Born into a wealthy, upperclass Bay Area family, Adams saw the financial panic of 1907, shipwrecks, and fin-de-siècle corporate raiders cause the loss of the family mills and ships. Thereafter, the Adamses lived with what might be termed "genteel frugality." Despite the economic setbacks, the heritage of patrician, nineteenth-century values and manners had a lasting impact. His personality and life were marked by an unfailing and rather elaborate courtesy, as well as genuine concern for others. Ansel Adams was a gentleman—and a remarkably gentle man. As part of this "noblesse oblige" came a deep sense of larger societal obligations and responsibilities. He could never learn or discover or own something without wanting to share it for the greater good.

In the spring of 1916, when he was fourteen and bedridden by influenza, Adams was given a copy of J. M. Hutchings' romantic paean, *In the Heart of the Sierras*. He "became hopelessly enthralled with the descriptions and illustrations of Yosemite and the romance and adventure of the cowboys and Indians . . . [and] devoured every word and pored over the pages many times."[1] Bowing to insistent pleading, his parents agreed to a family vacation in Yosemite. The effect of that summer holiday was overwhelming, complete, life-altering: "I *knew* my destiny when I first experienced Yosemite."[2] The vacation occurred just two years after the death of John Muir and the same year the National Park Service was established. Adams would spend time in Yosemite for sixty-seven consecutive years. He hiked, climbed, explored, worked, taught, wrote, and most important, photographed. His creative work was inspired by the peaks and streams and valleys of the California Sierra, the fabled "range of light." His vocation was photography; his absolute passion, natural beauty. While he was to become a legend and leader of modern environmentalism, he was always an artist first and an activist second. But the source, the inspiration, the motivation was one and the same: nature and its infinite, ever-changing, indefinable beauty. For passion and purpose, vocation and avocation to have such harmony was

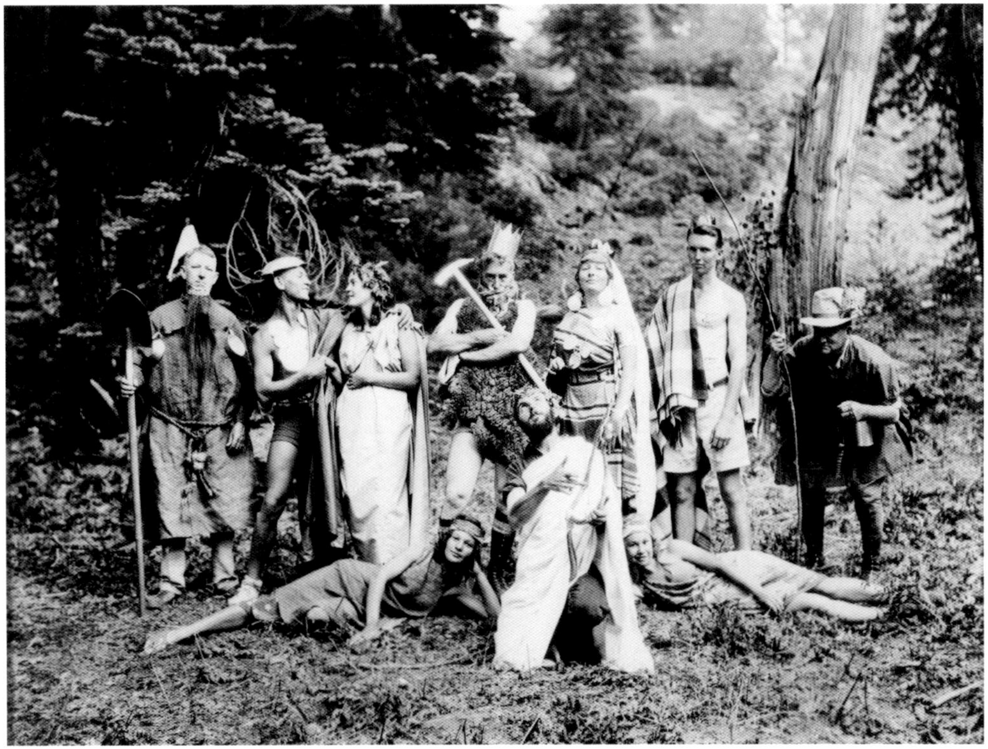

The Cast of *Exhaustos*, 1930. Ansel Adams in foreground as the Spirit of the Itinerary.

an uncommon blessing few have attained, and the resulting profound achievement of Adams in two distinct yet seminal areas of twentieth-century civilization was rare indeed.

Adams was blessed with great stamina, astonishing energy, and an intense commitment to hard work—characteristics that continued to the very end of a long life of protean activity. His productive, working years spanned every decade of the century, save the first and the last. His interests ranged from astrophysics and astronomy to vintage automobiles; from art to sensitometry; from classical piano to awful puns; from ecology to zoology. He made more than forty thousand photographs—some are among the visual icons of our time. He published several dozen books, which have sold more than four million copies. Trained as a concert pianist, he achieved an unrivaled mastery of the craft and technique of photography, in all its myriad aspects. His work as a consultant for Polaroid (he wrote more than three thousand technical memoranda in this capacity), and his multivolume, advanced photography manuals set standards for all who followed. He established a number of vital photographic teaching programs and workshops. He co-founded the first museum department of photography in the world, at the Museum of Modern Art in New York. He served for nearly four decades as an active, involved leader and director of the Sierra Club. He wrote and received (and saved!) perhaps one hundred thousand letters, cards, and missives on every subject.

The ebullience of Adams' personality, his intense joie de vivre, and his lifelong hyperactivity combined to give him an effectiveness that can only be described as Churchillian.

Much of what he accomplished was simply the result of working so long and trying so hard. His kindness and charisma were powerful allies, too. He *loved* people and, except for the long hours of enforced solitude in the darkroom, could not bear to be without a group of friends and colleagues. There were guests and students at cocktails *every* day—and more at dinner, night after night. Adams was an ardent believer in the facilitative properties of all manner of distilled spirits and vinous liquids! He was fortunate, too, in being blessed with a patient, devoted wife who shared his passion for art, environment—and entertainment. Appropriately, he met and wooed Virginia Best in Yosemite Valley.

Adams was much peeved by the tendency of many environmental activists to excessive self-seriousness and, often, sanctimonious self-righteousness. He sought to counter these traits with humor and gusto, often easing passions in heated board meetings and fostering agreement among a veritable pride of egos. He inculcated a broader sense of the important as well as the hilarious in life and culture. Typically, on a series of rainy days in the early 1930s, during the annual Sierra Club outings in the high country, he wrote and led performances of three marvelously mock Greek tragedies: *Exhaustos*, *The Trudgin' Women* and *The Oxides*. Alas, he was unable to finish the fourth play in the series, *The Mules* by Oresturphannies. Peopled by the likes of King Dehydros and his daughter, Clymenextra, the lord Rhykrispos, and a fisherman named Ogotellone, and backed by a Chorus of Weary Men and Sunburnt Women, these "literary" inspirations were characteristic of an approach to life that was deeply, avowedly affirmative.

Adams' philosophy of wilderness and the environment was both a product of his time and place and a prescient journey into the future. Rooted in the mythology of a nineteenth-century West hammered out of a wild and savage land, Adams' philosophical outlook anticipated a twenty-first-century vision of ecological unity and enlightened respect for the totality of natural resources. His early childhood coincided with the presidency of Theodore Roosevelt, unquestionably the most dynamic and articulate advocate of wilderness ever to occupy the White House. Roosevelt's enthusiasm for wilderness reflected his belief that it engendered values and virtues—courage, self-reliance, and physical toughness—that differentiated Americans from their more effete European ancestors. Adams' introduction to the idea of wilderness, Hutchings' *In the Heart of the Sierras*, was an apotheosis of this genre. It must be said, however, that the Rooseveltian view of wilderness as the quintessence of American virtue was relatively new in 1902. It had not always been thus.

Eighteenth- and nineteenth-century Americans feared and disliked wilderness and wildness because of the constant necessity of living in, with, and in a certain sense, against it. Virtually the entire continent had been wilderness in 1700. A century later the tide of westward movement and the rapid conquest of frontier and wilderness was about to burst into full flood. Indeed, between 1820 and 1850, a few important American writers and painters—John James Audubon, James Fenimore Cooper, William Cullen Bryant, Thomas Cole, Washington Irving, and Francis Parkman, Jr.-—were already lamenting the loss of a wilderness still seen as an object for subjugation by the many. Cole created a visual precedent for glorifying the natural beauty of this wild new continent. He and his colleagues of the Hudson River School, such as Asher B. Durand, Thomas Doughty, and Frederic E. Church, had considerable impact in a new nation with little tradition in the fine arts. Later in the century, Albert Bierstadt and Thomas Moran painted scenes of Yosemite and Yellowstone and the West that did much to foster a sense of the value of wilderness. Adams' father-in-law, Harry Cassie Best, was an adherent of the Rocky Mountain School and one of his Western landscapes hung in Theodore Roosevelt's White House.

Mourning the loss of pristine nature was one thing, but advocating its preservation and "reservation" (in the sense of nonconsumptive use) was something new and profound. George Catlin, the noted painter of Native Americans, proposed in 1832 the creation of "a nation's park" (including Native Americans). Thomas Cole followed, in the next decade, with renewed advocacy for the concept of wilderness preservation. By midcentury, Henry David Thoreau had begun to articulate a similar view—and to substantially and permanently expand the perception of wilderness in American life. He was perhaps the first to understand the importance of preserving wild places as more than mere curiosities, seeing their intrinsic aesthetic-spiritual-emotional value. Thoreau comprehended and articulated the connectedness between nature, men and women, and the millennia-long progress of civilization from forest to farm to factory. He argued that people, however civilized, *needed* wilderness and were profoundly better for experiencing it. He believed that some wilderness should be preserved "for modesty and reverence's sake, or if only to suggest that earth has higher uses than we put her to."[3]

Thoreau's philosophic perceptions of wilderness were to profoundly influence the subsequent thinking and writing of America's first full-time environmentalist, John Muir. In 1864 the federal government took a historic initiative by granting Yosemite Valley and the Mariposa Grove of giant sequoia to the state of California, to be protected in perpetuity for "public use, resort and recreation." Muir arrived in the Valley five years later, and like Adams' in 1916, his life was permanently altered. He explored Yosemite and the High Sierra with extraordinary intensity and enthusiasm. During those early Yosemite winters, Muir devoured Thoreau's writings. To Thoreau's philosophic framework, Muir added passion and exuberance, as well as the energy and the pen of a zealous publicist.

At the suggestion of Robert Underwood Johnson of *Century* magazine, Muir wrote several articles urging an expansion of the small Yosemite Valley state park into the vastly larger national park of today. With Johnson leading a skilled lobbying effort in Washington, Congress created the national park in 1890. Again at Johnson's suggestion, Muir and a small group of Bay Area colleagues founded the Sierra Club in 1892 to protect ("and explore, enjoy and render accessible") Yosemite and the Sierra. In the 1890s, Muir keenly advocated the establishment of the first national forests and emerged as the leader of the nascent preservationist movement at a time when it was beginning to grow to vitality. These historic events, coupled with the simultaneous demise of the frontier (pronounced in widely read articles by the noted historian Frederick Jackson Turner), opened the new century to a profoundly novel prospect for America.

If Henry David Thoreau was the philosopher of the wilderness movement and John Muir its popularizer, Ansel Adams was its artist. Adams differed from his spiritual godfathers in being less inclined to associate wilderness and nature with God. Adams' only religion was wilderness itself, without any reference to God, singular or plural. He would probably have denied as well a commitment to Thoreau's and Muir's fervent Transcendentalism, yet that sense of primacy of the spiritual and the nonmaterial over the empirical and material was at the very core of his reverential appreciation of nature.

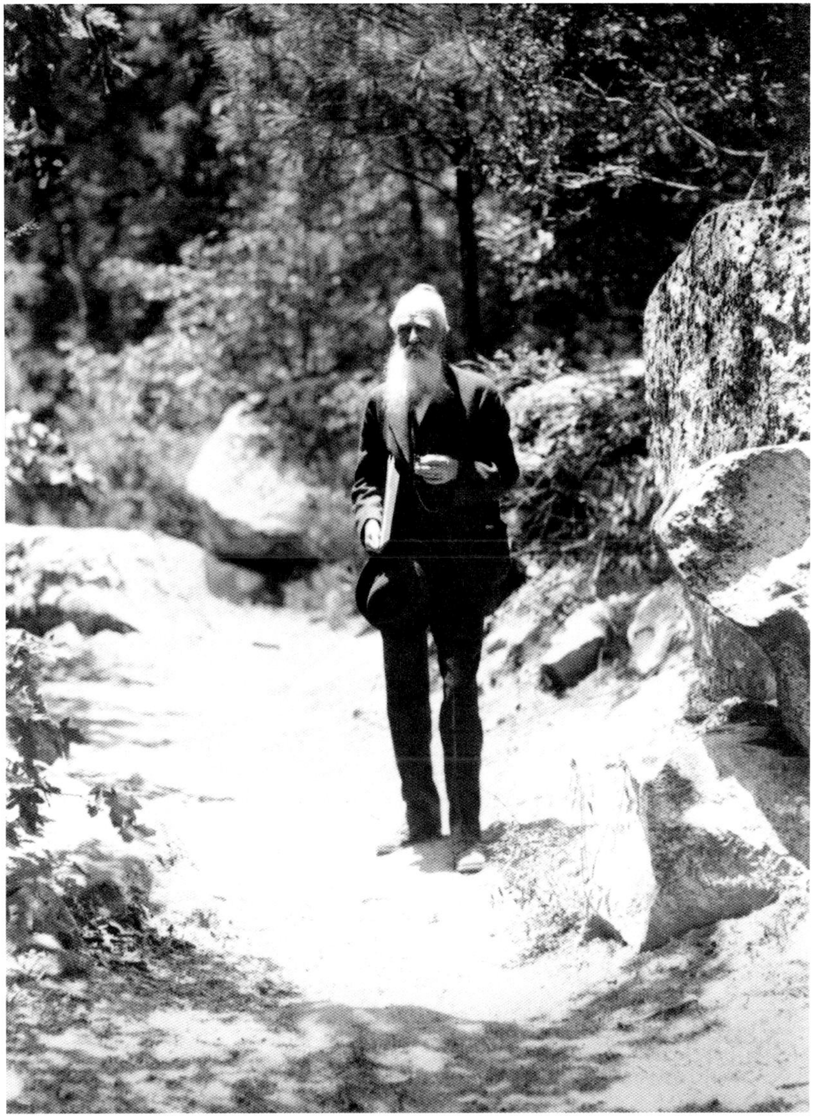

Thomas Moran at Cascade Fall, Yosemite National Park, California, 1925. By Ansel Adams

Interestingly, Adams was influenced more by the zeitgeist than by specific study and reading of Thoreau and Muir. But this context, in which Adams' lifelong and absolutely central relationship to wilderness and natural beauty evolved, was profoundly affected by his two remarkable precursors.

Just as the nineteenth century marked the modern apogee of rhetoric, our century ultimately has been characterized by the visual—with photography, film, video, and television the new language of civilization. In a similar sense, it can be said that what John Muir was to his century, Ansel Adams has been to ours...a kind of visual Muir, a symbol of conscience, of reverence, of caring for the land. Adams is almost certainly the best-known environmentalist—in terms of the American public—since Muir. Literally millions of Americans have seen the exhibitions of his photographs and portfolios and have read his books. His *identification* with wilderness is such that, not untypically, he received a letter in 1975 from a woman who began, "Dear Mr. Adams, In writing to you, I almost feel that I am writing to John Muir, or to Yosemite Valley itself."[4]

Adams, logically, extended the precepts of Thoreau and Muir into the twentieth-century milieu. An important element of this evolving philosophy was that of the existence of a *right* to wilderness. Adams asserted that "the concept that there are other (and equally important) values than those of obvious material and financial character is one that we must nourish and support to the utmost. Wilderness, to me at least, is a 'Mystique'; a valid, intangible, non-materialistic experience. The *right to experience* is a fundamental right, just as is the *right to possess*, the *right to believe* or the *right to work* and the *right to security*."[5] Adams dreamt of a new age of *philosophes*, inspired by the benevolent wilderness: "In contemplation of the eternal incarnations of the spirit which vibrate in every mountain, leaf, and particle of earth, in every cloud, stone, and flash of sunlight, we make new discoveries on the planes of ethical and humane discernments, approaching THE NEW SOCIETY AT LAST, PROPORTIONATE TO NATURE."[6] He argued for a total, ecological view of *all* natural resources (including the concept of the strategic value of sound resource protection): "We must take ALL resources under consideration: *all* resources, because they relate fatefully to our life on earth, reflect certain grandeurs, and deserve not only our attention, but our reverence. Hence, while it is as essential as ever to protect the National Parks and Wilderness Areas, it is also essential that we protect the forests, the crops, the minerals and oceans, and it is essential that we preserve the purity of the air we breathe and the water we drink."[7]

Adams' concern for the protection of wilderness and the wilderness experience ranged from the profound to the practical, and he fought myriad smaller battles and wrote more than a thousand letters regarding issues of basic park and wilderness management. His relationship with the National Park Service was nearly always cordial, though frequently uneasy and generally ambivalent. Adams never veered from a basically anthropocentric view of the purpose of wilderness preservation. He did not advocate preservation purely and simply as an act of reverence (though he would not have opposed a specific proposal in this regard), and he sought, consistently, to encourage people to *experience* wilderness. But his concept of "experiencing" was not preoccupied with *use* (as in hiking, backpacking, climbing, and the like). He saw *use* and *experience* as more intellectual and, particularly, emotional—again, more akin to Thoreau than to the "hiker-days and horsie-nights" approach that continues to characterize the Park Service and the Forest Service. He knew you had to walk to get there, and he surely knew how to walk, but that was simply a means to a more profound communion with nature and natural beauty. His criticism of the Park Service in this regard was unrelenting: "...a very two-dimensional idea when we consider mood and experience and emotional state-of-being. It never enters these people's (members of the Park Service's) minds at all. They just want everybody to see it: 'isn't it beautiful?'... something to be seen and not experienced."[8] In 1945 he wrote that "one weakness in our appreciation of nature is the emphasis placed upon *scenery*, which in its exploited aspect is merely a gargantuan curio. Things are appreciated for size, unusuality, and scarcity more than for their subtleties and emotional relationship to everyday life."[9]

Adams well understood the larger dilemma of use versus

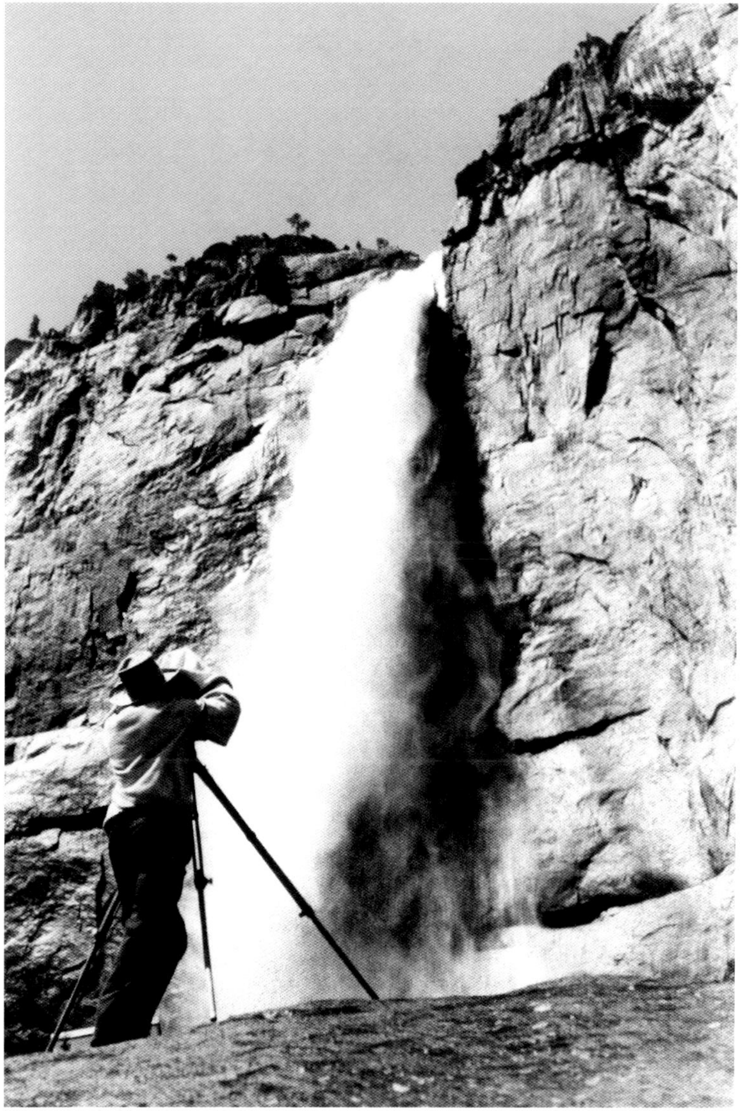

Ansel Adams photographing Upper Yosemite Fall, 1950. By George Waters, Jr.

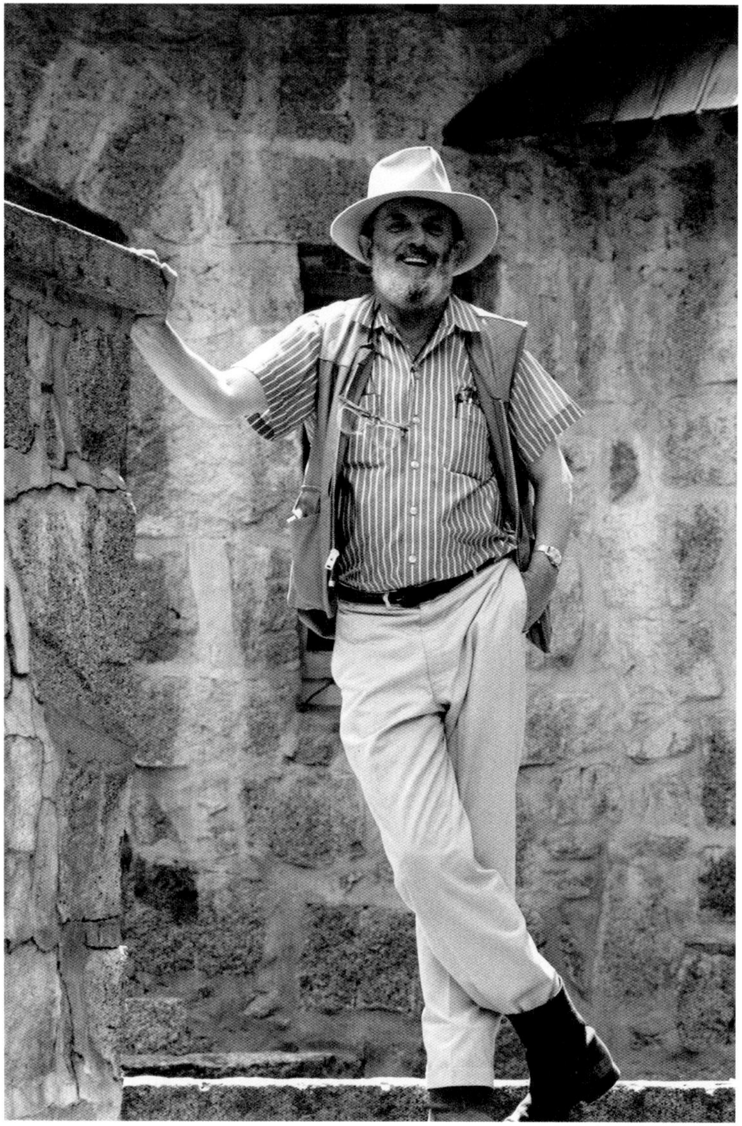

Ansel Adams at LeConte Lodge, Yosemite National Park, California, 1965. By Al Weber

preservation that developed as the parks began, after World War II, to attract large numbers of visitors. In 1979, he wrote that "the preservation and, at the same time, the human use of wild places present a mind- and spirit-wracking challenge for the future."[10] But whenever there was doubt about a choice between the two, he invariably opted for preservation and protection. Nature simply came first.

For nearly seven decades, Adams dedicated extraordinary energy to the preservation of wilderness, primarily through his seminal relationship with the Sierra Club. The mentors and colleagues who most influenced and abetted his environmentalism were old and young lions of the Club, from Muir's protégé, William E. Colby, and Joseph N. LeConte in his earlier days, to Richard M. Leonard and George Marshall in his maturity. The Sierra Club published several of the Adams books and portfolios that became such potent forces for wilderness. The Club and his colleagues provided Adams, neither a politician nor strategist himself, form and structure with which to focus and amplify his eloquent voice and vision.

Adams joined the Sierra Club, then a small, regional conservation and hiking club, in 1919, at the age of seventeen. That same summer, and for the succeeding four summers, he was employed by the Club as custodian of LeConte Lodge, its modest headquarters in Yosemite Valley. He led daily hikes, gave out maps and information, and assisted club members. In 1924 and 1925, Adams was invited to accompany Professor LeConte and his family on extended pack trips into the Kings Range of the High Sierra. It was on these trips that Adams became seriously committed to the work of conservation. In 1934, he was elected to the Sierra Club board of directors and served more than actively until his retirement in 1971. Although not of the "committee man" or club politician/officer sort, Adams was immensely influential in and through the Sierra Club. As Nancy Newhall wrote in *The Eloquent Light*: "He is instantly ready to act in any capacity where he may be useful—write a strong letter to a politician or a newspaper, give an eloquent address to a conference, dissolve an embattled meeting with a funny story, provide photographs for a campaign or map out a future project or program as though he were looking at it from the summit of Mt. Whitney. On anything to do with conservation . . . he is a fountainhead of ideas."[11]

Adams used his photographs as a proselytizing medium for nearly a half-century, from the early efforts to establish a Kings Canyon National Park in the Southern Sierra, to the great 1970s campaign to save wild Alaska, led by The Wilderness Society and the Sierra Club. As early as 1936, the Sierra Club dispatched him to Washington, D.C., armed with his photographs, to lobby Congress for Kings Canyon. In 1938, Adams published a magnificent, limited-edition book, *Sierra Nevada: The John Muir Trail*. He sent a copy to Interior Secretary Harold Ickes, who with considerable enthusiasm showed it to President Franklin D. Roosevelt. The President asked to keep the book for the White House and became an active supporter of the Kings Canyon cause. A year later, the President signed legislation establishing the park, marking a successful conclusion to the Sierra Club's most important campaign of the 1930s.

In 1954, with the collaboration of Nancy Newhall, the brilliant writer-curator who was Adams' closest artistic colleague, an exhibition of photographs (the majority by Adams) with some inspirational text (by Newhall) was presented at LeConte Lodge in Yosemite. Entitled "This Is the American Earth," the exhibition and ensuing book were to become landmarks in the evolution of a wider ecological conscience among Americans. The exhibition was circulated by the Smithsonian Institution, and in 1956, Adams suggested to David Brower, executive director of the Sierra Club, that a large-format, beautifully produced book be published by the Club. *This Is the American Earth* was the first of a series of "Exhibit Format Books" that were to alter the conservation movement and the Sierra Club in significant fashion. The era of "popular environmentalism" can be said to have begun in 1960, with the publication of the Adams-Newhall magnum opus. Adams described the exhibition and the book as "the first endeavor of its kind to relate to conservation at both the sociological and aesthetic level."[12]

Adams continued to be an ardent advocate of dramatic,

emotional use of all types of media. In the 1960s, during the Sierra Club campaign to prevent the damming of the Grand Canyon, Adams inspired the most famous of the Club's celebrated "battle ads," when he wrote Brower and George Marshall suggesting that the developer mentality would fill the Sistine Chapel with water so visitors could float around and see Michelangelo's frescoes more clearly![13]

Adams' impact on wilderness preservation was felt in many ways and at many levels—in the Sierra Club, in the conservation movement, among government officials, and by an increasingly attentive public. He was the only environmentalist likely to have personal access to the President. Despite the passion of his commitment, Adams invariably treated both friend and foe with dignity and courtesy. He was later to feel a trifle guilty about the strong language he used in one of his hottest fights, which he characterized in a contemporary (1959) letter to his good friend and fellow-photographer Dorothea Lange: "Am now in a really intense fight with the National Park Service over their desecration of Tenaya Lake by the construction of the new Tioga Road! Since you left I have had the privilege of sending the Secretaries of Interior and Commerce and the Director of the National Park Service telegrams in which I accused them of actions approaching Criminal Negligence in permitting the desecration of Tenaya Lake. THAT got them out of their foam-rubber swivel chairs and reactivated the old beans in the Conservation groups! For once, I have been truly useful!"[14]

In the last decade of his life, Adams' growing public renown as both artist and environmentalist made him a particularly effective and outspoken "elder statesman" of the movement. He vigorously lobbied senators, representatives, and presidents. In perhaps his most ardent and visible crusade, he teamed up with The Wilderness Society in leading a crusade against what he saw as the bizarre and retrograde vision of the arch-anti-environmentalist James Watt and his benighted President, Ronald Reagan.

The beauty and power of his art, the "eloquent light," was always Adams' most effective voice, and it gained steadily in impact in the years after 1971, as his fame and audience grew apace. He never made a particular photograph for a specific conservation purpose, and with important exceptions such as the use of his photographs to lobby for a Kings Canyon National Park, their impact was more at a broad level of consciousness-raising rather than as campaign illustrations. "I have been trained with the dominating thought of art as something almost religious in quality.... I existed only for the quality of art in relation to itself; the production of beauty without other motivation," he wrote in 1936.[15] Adams, perhaps more than any artist before, was able to send his art into battle, much as Churchill mobilized the English language.

Though he generally deprecated explicit documentary and socially motivated photography, unless done with rare vision and artistry (as by Dorothea Lange or Walker Evans), Adams increasingly felt that artists had a moral duty to contribute through their art: "The artist has an inescapable obligation... both the natural and human world are imperiled.... This peril lies in overpopulation, pollution, depletion of resources, and the destruction of natural and cultural beauty. The power of art to counteract this destruction, not merely to veil it, is—I am sure—tremendous. I believe photography has both a challenge and an obligation: to help us see more clearly and more deeply, and to reveal to others the grandeurs and potentials of the one and only world which we inhabit."[16]

Adams recognized the important roles played by the photographs of Carleton Watkins and William Henry Jackson in the preservation of, respectively, Yosemite and Yellowstone. John Szarkowski, the eminent critic and curator, remarked on the importance of Adams' role in taking up the traditions of the Hudson River and Rocky Mountain Schools of painting and that of the great nineteenth-century landscape photographers, defining and, in a sense, completing a profound tradition in American art and cultural history: "In these terms Adams' photographs are perhaps anachronisms. They are perhaps the last confident and deeply felt pictures of their tradition.... It does not seem likely that a photographer of the future will be able to bring to the heroic wild landscape the passion, trust and belief that Adams has brought to it."[17]

Adams' life spanned the most progressive and productive period of nature preservation in human history. Millions upon millions of acres of wilderness were protected. Thanks to President Jimmy Carter, more than one hundred million acres of wild Alaska were included in the national park, wildlife refuge, and wilderness preservation systems—the greatest single earth gesture any government has yet enacted. Adams lived through eras of conservation and preservation, emerging with a profoundly holistic view of wilderness and natural resources. In 1975 he declared, "I prefer the term 'environment,' not only because it is more specific but because it invites the element of *conscience*—your environment and my environment—a tangible situation which is easily comprehended by all."[18]

This comprehension of conscience, so rare among our public leaders; the sense that he was above the pursuit of power for ego's sake; the remarkable harmony of his vision; and his anticipation of the fundamental tenor of his times gave Adams a moral authority deeply respected by Presidents and politicians and made him a living symbol of wilderness. His great Californian friend, the political leader he most admired, Senator Alan Cranston, assured a lasting home for Adams in his beloved High Sierra, sponsoring the legislation establishing the 220,000-acre Ansel Adams Wilderness, immediately south of Yosemite National Park and north of the John Muir Wilderness. In an unusual act of bipartisanship, former President Gerald Ford asked President Carter to confer upon Adams the nation's highest award, the Presidential Medal of Freedom, which Adams received in 1980.

Yet Adams never lost the sense of humor and humility that helped him win so many conservation adherents. The Wilderness Society, in 1980, created the Ansel Adams Award for lifetime service to conservation—The Society's highest honor. Appropriately, Adams was the first recipient of the award. Nearing the end of a life marked by innumerable honors, and having been Lincolnesque in build most of his years, he had recently grown quite stout. The original manuscript of his acceptance speech has, scrawled in his nigh-inscrutable handwriting, a characteristic observation: "My doctor says there's only one more Award I can receive: if I am more careful with my diet, I might get the No-belly Prize!"[19]

Nor did he ever lose that deeply humanistic sense of caring—and of being willing to take the time, at the age of seventy-seven and in the midst of a still hyperactive schedule, to write a young protégé who had recently become president of The Wilderness Society:

> Dear Bill,
> Exploring my past a bit I came across a bit of poetry which seems to relate to what The Wilderness Society may be all about:
>
> . . . I love all waste
> And solitary places; where we taste
> The pleasure of believing what we see
> Is boundless, as we wish our souls to be. . . .
>
> —"Julian and Maddalo,"
> Percy Bysshe Shelley, 1819[20]

Perhaps, though, his best epitaph is that great wilderness, high in the Sierra Nevada . . . or the shimmering luminescence of his timeless photograph of the aspen trees in northern New Mexico.

NOTES

1. Ansel Adams, *Ansel Adams: An Autobiography* (Boston: New York Graphic Society, 1985), 50.

2. Ibid., 67.

3. Henry David Thoreau, *The Journals of Henry David Thoreau*, eds. B. Torry and F. H. Allen, vol. 14 (Boston: Houghton Mifflin, 1906), 305.

4. Archives of Ansel Adams, Center for Creative Photography, University of Arizona, Tucson, 1975.

5. Ansel Adams, Lecture, Yale School of Forestry and Environmental Studies, 1970.

6. Ansel Adams, *My Camera in the National Parks* (Boston: Houghton Mifflin Company, Yosemite National Park, Virginia Adams, 1950).

7. Ansel Adams, Commencement Address, Occidental College, 1967.

8. Ansel Adams, Taped interview with Robert Turnage, 1976.

9. Ansel Adams, "Problems of Interpretation of the Natural Scene." *Sierra Club Bulletin* vol. 30, no. 6 (December 1945), 47.

10. Ansel Adams, *Yosemite and the Range of Light* (Boston: New York Graphic Society, 1979), 11.

11. Nancy Newhall, *The Eloquent Light* (San Francisco: Sierra Club, 1963), 114.

12. Ansel Adams, Taped interview with Robert Turnage, 1976.

13. As related by Michael P. Cohen in *The History of the Sierra Club* (San Francisco: Sierra Club, 1988), 363.

14. Ansel Adams to Dorothea Lange, February 22, 1959, Archives of Ansel Adams, Center for Creative Photography, University of Arizona, Tucson.

15. Ansel Adams to Willard van Dyke, 1936, as quoted in Newhall, *Eloquent Light*, 126.

16. Ansel Adams, "A Photographer Talks about His Art," Address, Occidental College, 1969.

17. John Szarkowski, Introduction to *The Portfolios of Ansel Adams* (Boston: New York Graphic Society, 1977), xii.

18. Ansel Adams, Albright Lecture, 1975.

19. Ansel Adams, Address to The Wilderness Society, 1980.

20. Ansel Adams to W. A. Turnage, 1979.

TITLE INDEX

(Page numbers in *italic* refer to illustrations.)

SUBJECT INDEX

(Page numbers in *italic* refer to illustrations.)

ACKNOWLEDGMENTS

Many people were instrumental in the publication of *Ansel Adams in the National Parks*. I would like to begin by thanking the team of extraordinary people who made this book possible. First and foremost, Ansel's editor Michael Sand has been patient, creative, and supportive—the dream editor if ever there was one. Lance Hidy returns as our brilliant designer, who willingly altered layouts over and over without complaint. Thomas Palmer made the scans, and he continues to raise digital scanning to an art form. Sandra Klimt ably shepherded the book through production, as she has done over the past few years. Tish Rosales at The Ansel Adams Trust has been an indefatigable colleague, working on text editing and illustrations. Last, but never least, I thank Bill Turnage, whose knowledge, wisdom, and hard work make it possible for me to do what I love best: share Ansel's myriad gifts with the world.

I would also like to thank Leslie Calmes and Sarah Newby at the Center for Creative Photography, University of Arizona, who assisted in ways too numerous to list; David Arrington and Anne Pyne, who allowed us to scan their unique vintage photographs; John Sexton and Alan Ross, whose technical expertise I was fortunate to be able to call upon; Evelyne Thomas for southwestern hospitality; Christopher Gray for his editor's eye; and Ansel's son, Michael Adams, and daughter, Anne Adams Helms, who enthusiastically helped me with valuable information and anecdotes. The Ansel Adams Trust extends its gratitude to Page Stegner.

Lastly, special thanks to David Young and Jean Griffin, our ever-supportive publishers.

—AGS

COLOPHON

Design by Lance Hidy
Duotone separations by Thomas Palmer
Production supervision by Sandra Klimt
The text typeface is Magma, designed by Sumner Stone for the Stone Type Foundry. The titles are composed in Penumbra Flare Serif, designed by Lance Hidy for Adobe Systems.
The paper stock is 150 gsm Galaxi Keramic demi-matte.
Ansel Adams in the National Parks was printed and bound by Mondadori in Verona, Italy.